Problem Solving, Abstraction, and Design Using C++

FRANK L. FRIEDMAN
ELLIOT B. KOFFMAN

Temple University

ADDISON-WESLEY PUBLISHING COMPANY

Reading, Massachusetts ▪ Menlo Park, California
New York ▪ Don Mills, Ontario ▪ Wokingham, England
Amsterdam ▪ Bonn ▪ Sydney ▪ Singapore ▪ Tokyo
Madrid ▪ San Juan ▪ Milan ▪ Paris

Sponsoring Editor	Lynne Doran Cote
Associate Editor	Katherine Harutunian
Production Supervisor	Juliet Silveri
Editorial Production Services	Barbara Pendergast
Text Designer	Joyce Weston
Cover Design Supervisor	Peter Blaiwas / Eileen Hoff
Manufacturing Manager	Roy Logan

Library of Congress Cataloging-in-Publication Data

Friedman, Frank L.
    Problem solving, abstraction, and design using C++ /
    Frank L. Friedman, Elliot B. Koffman.
        p. cm.
    Includes index.
    ISBN 0-201-52649-2
    1. C++ (Computer program language) I. Koffman, Elliot B.
II. Title.
QA76.73.C153F75 1994
005.13'3—dc20   93-14288
                                              CIP

Reprinted with corrections June, 1994

2   3   4   5   6   7   8   9   10-CRW-9897969594

Preface

This is a textbook for a first course in problem-solving and program design. It is suitable for use by students with no programming background as well as those who may have had the equivalent of up to a one-semester course in another programming language. Students' backgrounds will determine the time required to cover the earlier chapters of the text and the extent of coverage possible for later chapters.

The book represents the culmination of a five-year effort, partially sponsored by the National Science Foundation,[1] to define an introductory-level course combining a presentation of rudimentary principles of software engineering with an introduction to an increasingly popular programming language, C++. Our primary goal has been to motivate and introduce sound principles of program engineering in a first course. Topics such as program style, documentation, algorithm and data structuring, procedure- and data-oriented modularization, component reuse, abstraction, and program verification are introduced early. From the beginning, the focus is on the problem-solving/software construction process, from problem analysis to program and component design and coding.

Object-oriented concepts are introduced midway through the text and further developed in succeeding chapters. Many fundamental software engineering and object-oriented concepts are illustrated: minimal component interfaces, high-level component cohesion, information hiding, separation of concerns, modeling problem domain entities and their relationships, user-defined types and type hierarchies, parameterized components, and, at the very end (in an appendix), inheritance. Abstraction is stressed throughout. Numerous complete case examples are provided consistent with the notion that there is much to be learned by studying such examples, from the analysis of the specification of a problem to a first stage of design to the final coding.

This is not a text on the engineering of large-scale, complex software systems, nor is it an introductory text on object-oriented programming. Rather it is an introductory text concerned with the development of relatively small-size programs to solve well-constrained problems. Some of the concepts presented may not be fully appreciated at the introductory level; they will bear repeating and elaboration in subsequent courses in computing science and in the workplace. Our goal is to start students on a reasonable course of practice in the use of C++.

---

[1]NSF Instrumentation and Laboratory Improvement (ILI) Grant Number USE-9250254 and NSF Undergraduate Curriculum Course Development (UCCD) Grant Number USE-9156079

The Choice of Language

There are a number of texts already on the market that were driven by the issues just described. Our goal is to provide more emphasis on program engineering and to do so through the use of a language almost certain to be encountered by students entering the job market in computing and information sciences. In our view, C++ satisfies both criteria as the rapidly increasing favorite for a wide variety of software systems implementation projects.

This is not meant to imply that C++ and the first course in programming are a perfect match. There are many traps and pitfalls awaiting unsuspecting C++ users. It is a complex language and it is not yet standardized (as of this printing). Perhaps more to the point for the introductory user, compiler and run-time diagnostics are often hard to understand and often not particularly helpful. Nonetheless, we believe that C++ can be a very effective vehicle for teaching problem-solving and software engineering concepts in the first programming course.

We have endeavored to emphasize the use of the language to illustrate some fundamental aspects of software engineering and the object-oriented paradigm. The use of pointers has been delayed deliberately until needed, and features such as call-by-reference arguments, stream input and output, and type and type hierarchy definition are introduced as early as possible. Thus, both from a pedagogic and practical viewpoint, we believe that C++ is a reasonable choice for the first course in programming.

Outline of Contents

It is important to emphasize that this is not simply a book on C++; many fine C++ texts already exist. C++ is merely the vehicle for our exposition—a practical, widely used language that we believe can serve effectively to explain the concepts being introduced, and to allow students to apply these ideas in solving simple programming problems. Clearly, there is much C++ to be learned—and quite a lot not to be learned, at least not in the early going.

Conceptually, the text may be partitioned into three sections. Chapters 1–9 provide introductory material that is rather typical of that found in first-course texts on other languages: an introduction to computers, programming, and problem-solving in the language to be studied; introductory material on functions and top-down design; detailed coverage of selection and repetition structures and program design strategies for using these structures; and coverage of simple data types, input and output, and structured data types (arrays and structs). The second section includes Chapters 10–13 which cover intermediate-level concepts. The final section, Chapters 14–16, contains more advanced material.

The connection between good problem-solving skills and effective software development is established early in the first three chapters. Included in the first two chapters are sections on the art and science of problem-solving and an introduction to software development methodologies based on a systematic approach to problem-solving. The method outlined in Chapter 2 is also used there to solve the first case study and is applied consistently to all case studies in the text. In Chapter 3, we continue the emphasis on basic problem-solving skills with a discussion of top-down design, divide and conquer, solution by analogy, and solution by generalization.

Top-down, procedural decomposition is further illustrated throughout Chapters 4–9. Decision structures are introduced in Chapter 4, and repetition structures are presented in Chapter 5. In Chapter 6, we revisit the C++ function, introducing functions with output arguments and providing three complete case studies illustrating much of what has been learned to this point. Chapter 7 contains a more detailed discussion of simple data types, including an introduction to the notion of data abstraction as well as a description of the internal and external distinctions among the simple types. In Chapter 9, the structured types (arrays and structs) are presented and an introduction to fixed-length character string representation and manipulation is provided.

Chapter 8 provides an introduction to external file input/output. Although studying external files may seem premature at this point, we believe it is nonetheless appropriate. Programs do not exist in a vacuum; they manipulate data that often come from external sources and produce results that may subsequently be manipulated by other programs. It is therefore important for students to gain a relatively early exposure to some fundamental concepts related to file input and output, so long as this exposure does not disrupt the presentation of other essential ideas. Of course, by the time Chapter 8 is reached, students will have already been introduced to the basics of stream input and output, including a minimal use of input/output manipulators, beginning in Chapter 4.

For students with the equivalent of a one-semester programming course in another language, Chapters 1–9 can be covered fairly quickly, perhaps in as little as 5 or 6 weeks. For students with little or no background, this coverage may take 10 to 12 weeks.

Chapters 10–13 cover intermediate-level concepts. Chapter 10 includes a discussion of program verification (focused on assertions and loop invariants) and an introduction to algorithm analysis and big-O notation. This chapter also provides an introduction to some basic terminology and concepts of software engineering and includes an introductory discussion of abstract data types and objects. This sets the stage for the introductory material in Chapters 11 and 12 on the definition and use of classes and objects of the types defined by these classes. The definition and use of template classes and functions is illustrated in Chapter 12. Chapter 13 provides expanded coverage of fixed length strings (using the `string.h` library) beyond the brief introduction provided in Chapter 9. The processing of variable length strings, using a home-grown variable length string class, is provided at the end of the chapter. Coverage of all four of these chapters should be possible in the first course. For students having little or no programming background, much of Chapter 12 may have to be skipped or covered lightly, and the discussion of variable length strings might be delayed to a second semester.

Chapters 14–16 contain more advanced material on data abstraction and the use of C++ classes and templates (Chapter 14), recursion (Chapter 15), linked lists, and stacks and queues (Chapter 16). It is expected that this material will be covered only by advanced students, those with at least a one-semester background in programming.

Coverage of Pointers

We have introduced the notion of pointers little by little, only as required, until finally they are treated in more detail where they really belong—in the discussion of dynamic data structures (Chapter 16). The pointer is one of the more dangerous, relatively unprotected aspects of the C++ language and need not be an essential part of an introductory text. Pointers must be introduced in Chapter 6 (on reference arguments), and further discussed in Chapters 12 and 14, where the dynamic creation of arrays is illustrated, and in Chapter 13, where strings and string functions are introduced. Nonetheless, we have been careful to limit our discussion and illustrations to what is needed to paint the larger picture and no more. An added advantage of this approach is that the pointer concept should be familiar by the time we enter into a more complete discussion of the topic toward the end of the text.

Software Engineering and Object-Oriented Concepts

Several aspects of software engineering and object-oriented programming are introduced in the text. Issues of program style are presented throughout in special displays. The concept of a program as a sequence of control structures is introduced in Chapter 3 and discussed in more detail in Chapters 4 and 5. The text embodies many of our choices for software-engineering concepts to be introduced in a first course. We have introduced functions and classes as early as we believed possible at the introductory level—functions in Chapters 3 and 6, and classes in Chapters 10–12.

Procedural abstraction is introduced early in Chapter 3 and illustrated first using functions with no arguments or return values. Then, functions with return values and input arguments are introduced. In Chapter 6, functions having output and input-output arguments are illustrated. The ideas of component reuse, information hiding, and separation of concerns are introduced in Chapter 3, and further developed, step-by-step, in Chapter 6 and later chapters.

There is a wealth of program library resources available in C++. Students need to begin to use these resources as soon as possible. They should become well accustomed to the idea of reusing software components and incorporating them into their program designs from the very start. An integral part of practicing sound principles of program design involves an awareness of components already written, how to access them, and how to read and understand their interfaces. Of course, it is also important for students to practice designing their own reusable components, and this too must be stressed in a first course. Designing and implementing general, highly cohesive, program components with a minimal interface to other parts of a program is stressed from the beginning.

Abstract data types, classes, and objects are introduced in Chapters 10 and 11, with slightly more advanced material presented in Chapter 12. The benefits of being able to define new data types as models of problem domain entities and to write programs in terms of objects of these types is discussed and illustrated. The importance of encapsulation (of data stores and operations) in limiting the scope of access to information, and in the separation of implementation details based upon the properties of and required operations on problem domain entities is explained and illustrated. The use of classes, and class and function templates is illustrated further in Chapters 12, 14, and 16. The concept of inheritance is discussed, and an illustration of the C++ inheritance and virtual function mechanisms is provided in Appendix E. Except for this appendix, these are topics for second-semester coverage.

Appendixes and Special Supplementary Material

Separate appendixes are provided summarizing information about character sets, C++ reserved words, C++ operators, and function libraries (with descriptions and first-page references). The last appendix contains an introductory example illustrating inheritance and virtual functions.

Several pedagogical features also have been included to enhance the usefulness of the text as an instructional tool. These include

- consistent use of analysis and design aids such as data requirements tables and program structure charts;
- end-of-section and end-of-chapter self-check and programming exercises (answers to the odd-number self-check exercises are included in the text);
- end-of-chapter programming projects;
- case studies and numerous examples carried through from analysis and design to implementation;

- syntax displays containing the syntax and semantics of each new C++ feature introduced;
- program style and design guideline displays;
- syntax and run-time error discussions at the end of each chapter;
- chapter reviews and review questions.

Materials to aid the instructor include

- an instructor's/solutions manual with

  - a statement of objectives for each chapter and a section-by-section guide for coverage of material based on student backgrounds and needs;
  - answers to even-numbered self-check exercises;
  - answers to review questions;
  - commentary on the analysis and design of selected programming projects;
  - test questions.

- on-line or diskette files containing

  - program source code (functions and classes) included in the text;
  - answers to all end-of-section programming exercises;
  - the implementation of selected programming projects;
  - a number of supplementary examples illustrating slightly more advanced concepts that could not be included in the text.

An on-line version of the instructor's manual, solutions manual, and source code is available for this edition. For additional information, send electronic mail messages to friedC++@aw.com. To obtain an information file, type information on the subject line and send information in the body of the text.

Acknowledgments

Many people helped with the development of this text. Rajiv Tewari of Temple University assisted in the development of the original proposals to the National Science Foundation and was a principal co-investigator in both. Professors Paul A. T. Wolfgang and Paul LaFollette (both at Temple University) wrote preliminary versions of three chapters and provided valuable comments on several others. Wolfgang also designed and implemented several of the classes used in the text. Donna Chrupcala, a Temple graduate student, also contributed significantly to the development of several chapters and proofread many versions of other chapters. Her thoroughness and painstaking attention to detail were an indispensable and significant part of the preparation of this book.

Judith Wilson (Susquehanna University) provided painstakingly detailed comments on all sixteen chapters; her pedagogic wisdom played a major role in shaping the text. Bruce Weiner (Temple graduate student) did a little of everything, but mostly a huge amount of programming, testing, and reprogramming (and retesting) of all examples, code segments, and case studies provided in the text, as well as some additional supplementary material not found in the book.

Steve Vinoski provided detailed comments concerning the C++ material in many of the later chapters of the text. Steve's knowledge of the language and its intent were instrumental in improving the accuracy of the descriptions and discussions of the C++ constructs presented in the text as well as the code written for the text.

The principal reviewers and class testers were enormously helpful in suggesting improvements and finding errors. They include Allen Alexander (Delaware Technical and Community College), Richard Reid (Michigan State University), Larry K. Cottrell (University of Central Florida), H. E. Dunsmore and Russell W. Quong (Purdue University), Donna Krabbe (College of Mount St. Joseph), Sally Kyvernitis (Neumann College), Xiaoping Jia (DePaul University), Xiannong Meng and Rick Zaccone (Bucknell University), Jeff Buckwalter and Kim Summerhays (University of San Francisco), and Jo Ellen Perry (University of North Carolina).

Valuable proofreading and editing assistance was provided by Sally Kyvernitis, Donna Skalski, a Temple graduate student, and Frank Friedman's daughters Dara and Shelley and Dara's friend Larry Snyder.

Frank Friedman is particularly indebted to several members of the staff at the Software Engineering Institute (Pittsburgh), particularly Mary Shaw, Norm Gibbs, and Gary Ford, for their support during the year in which the seeds that led to this book were sown. Dr. Friedman also extends his thanks to Dean Carolyn Adams and the staff of the Temple College of Arts and Sciences, and to the faculty and staff of the Temple Computer and Information Sciences Department, who so often picked up the missing pieces of his other work. Thanks, too, are due to the members of the ACM Computing Science Conference Steering Committee and the ACM staff who took charge without ever being asked.

As always, it has been a pleasure working with the people of Addison-Wesley throughout this endeavor. Lynne Doran Cote, Acquisitions Editor, and Katherine Harutunian, Associate Editor, were closely involved in all phases of the development of the manuscript, and provided friendship, guidance, and encouragement. Maite Suarez-Rivas (Editorial Assistant) and Juliet Silveri (Production Supervisor) provided timely assistance at a moment's notice. Barbara Pendergast coordinated the conversion of the manuscript to a finished book, and Mike Wile handled the composition and illustration of the book.

Philadelphia, PA   F. L. F.
                                                                      E. B. K.

To my wife, Martha
my children, Dara and Shelley
and my parents, George and Sylvia
you've made this, and everything else, possible.

FLF

To my wife, Caryn
my children, Richard, Deborah, and Robin
and my father, Edward
with much thanks for your love and support.

EBK

Contents

1 ———— **INTRODUCTION TO COMPUTERS AND PROGRAMMING   1**

1.1   Electronic Computers: Then and Now   2
1.2   Components of a Computer   7
1.3   Problem-Solving, Abstraction, and Program Engineering   12
1.4   Programming Languages   14
1.5   Processing a High-Level Language Program   18
1.6   Using the Computer   20
      Chapter Review   26

2 ———— **PROGRAM DESIGN   29**

2.1   The Software Development Method   30
      CASE STUDY: Converting Units of Measurement   34
2.2   Overview of C++   37
2.3   Declarations of Variables and Constants   41
2.4   Executable Statements   44
2.5   Recapitulation: The General Form of a C++ Program   52
2.6   Abstraction: Data Types and Expressions   56
      CASE STUDY: Finding the Value of a Coin Collection   59
2.7   Interactive Mode, Batch Mode, and Data Files   71
2.8   Common Programming Errors   74
      Chapter Review   80

3 ———— **TOP-DOWN DESIGN   85**

3.1   Problem-Solving and Program Development   86
      CASE STUDY: Finding the Area and Circumference of a Circle   89
3.2   Subproblems and Independent Modules   93
      CASE STUDY: Drawing Simple Figures   93
3.3   Functions without Arguments   96
3.4   Functions with Input Arguments and Return Values   108
3.5   How We Use Functions   111
3.6   Functions as Program Building Blocks; C++ Libraries   124
3.7   Some Comments on the Software Engineering Process   132
3.8   Common Programming Errors   132
      Chapter Review   136

4 ——— SELECTION STRUCTURES: if AND switch STATEMENTS   141

4.1   Control Structures   142
4.2   Logical Expressions   143
4.3   Introduction to the if Control Statement   151
4.4   if Statements with Compound Alternatives   155
4.5   Decision Steps in Algorithms   158
       CASE STUDY: Payroll Problem   158
4.6   Formatted Output: Introduction to Manipulators and Flags   165
4.7   Checking Correctness of an Algorithm   169
       CASE STUDY: Finding the Alphabetically First Letter   169
4.8   More Problem-Solving Strategies   173
       CASE STUDY: Computing Overtime Pay   174
       CASE STUDY: Computing Insurance Dividends   177
4.9   Nested if Statements and Multiple-Alternative Decisions   182
4.10   The switch Control Statement   189
4.11   Common Programming Errors   194
       Chapter Review   195

5 ——— REPETITION: while, for, AND do-while STATEMENTS   203

5.1   Repetition in Programs: The while Statement   204
5.2   Accumulating a Sum or Product in a Loop   209
5.3   Counting Loops and Conditional Loops   215
5.4   Loop Design   218
5.5   The for Statement   227
5.6   More for Statement Examples   233
5.7   The do-while Statement   237
5.8   Review of while, for, and do-while Loops   240
5.9   Nested Loops   242
5.10   Debugging and Testing Programs   246
5.11   Common Programming Errors   249
       Chapter Review   251

6 ——— PROGRAM DESIGN AND FUNCTIONS REVISITED   259

6.1   Functions in the Design Process   260
6.2   Using Function Return Values for Decision and Loop Control   265
6.3   Output Arguments   269
       CASE STUDY: Sorting Three Numbers   277

6.4   Syntax Rules for Functions with Argument Lists   283
6.5   Stepwise Design with Functions   287
       CASE STUDY: General Sum and Average Problem   287
6.6   Solving a More Complex Problem   302
       CASE STUDY: Checking Account Balance Problem   303
6.7   More Aspects of Software Engineering   316
6.8   Debugging and Testing a Program System   318
6.9   Common Programming Errors   320
       Chapter Review   321

7 _____ SIMPLE DATA TYPES   329

7.1   Constants Revisited   330
7.2   Internal Representations of Integer, Floating-Point, and Character
       Data Types   332
7.3   Logical Expressions   346
7.4   Character Variables and Functions   348
7.5   Enumeration Types   353
7.6   Common Programming Errors   362
       Chapter Review   365

8 _____ FORMATTING AND FILES   371

8.1   The Standard Input/Output Streams   372
8.2   Streams and External Files   381
8.3   Accessing and Using External Files   382
8.4   Using External File Functions: An Example   391
       CASE STUDY: Preparing a Payroll File   391
8.5   Putting It All Together   398
       CASE STUDY: Preparing Semester Grade Reports   398
8.6   Stream I/O Manipulator Functions and Flags   422
8.7   Common Programming Errors   424
       Chapter Review   426

9 _____ ARRAYS AND STRUCTURES   433

9.1   The Array Data Type   434
9.2   Selecting Array Elements for Processing   439
9.3   Arrays as Arguments   444
9.4   Reading Part of an Array   452
9.5   Searching and Sorting Arrays   456
9.6   Character Strings   463
9.7   The struct Data Type   473
9.8   Structs as Operands and Arguments   476

9.9   Hierarchical Structs   480
9.10   Unions (Optional)   483
9.11   Common Programming Errors   487
        Chapter Review   489

10 —— INTRODUCTION TO SOFTWARE ENGINEERING   497

10.1   The Software Challenge   498
10.2   The Software Life Cycle   500
        CASE STUDY: Telephone Directory Program   504
10.3   Procedural Abstraction Revisited   507
10.4   Data Abstraction and Abstract Data Types: Program Objects   511
10.5   Analysis of Algorithm Efficiency: Big-O Notation   516
10.6   Software Testing   519
10.7   Formal Methods of Program Verification   522
10.8   Professional Ethics and Responsibilities   530
        Chapter Review   531

11 —— DATA ABSTRACTION IN C++: THE C++ CLASS   537

11.1   The C++ Class   538
11.2   Classes versus Structs   547
11.3   The Abstract Data Type day   548
11.4   Automatic Initialization: Class Constructors   553
11.5   Problem Analysis and Design Using Classes   555
        CASE STUDY: Areas and Perimeters of Different Figures Revisited   555
11.6   A Complex Number Class (Optional)   566
11.7   Defining and Using Functions and Classes: Summary of Rules and Restrictions   573
11.8   Common Programming Errors   576
        Chapter Review   578

12 —— SOFTWARE ENGINEERING: BUILDING ABSTRACT DATA TYPES   585

12.1   The Indexed Collection as an Abstract Data Type   587
12.2   Class Extensions: An Introduction to Inheritance   596
        CASE STUDY: Home Budget Problem   596
12.3   Extending Reuse: An Introduction to Templates   611

12.4   Using Old Components to Solve New Problems   618
        CASE STUDY: Cryptogram Generator Problem   625
12.5   Common Programming Errors   637
        Chapter Review   640

13 _____ THE STRING DATA TYPE   649

13.1   String Functions in the string.h Library   650
13.2   An Illustration of Character String Processing   663
        CASE STUDY: Printing a Form Letter   663
13.3   Variable-Length Strings (Optional)   676
13.4   Common Programming Errors   685
        Chapter Review   688

14 _____ ARRAYS WITH STRUCTURED ELEMENTS   697

14.1   Arrays of Arrays: Multidimensional Arrays   698
14.2   Creating Arrays of Arrays   700
14.3   Arrays of Structs   703
14.4   Arrays of Class Elements   706
14.5   Abstraction and Generalization: Triangle and Polygon Classes   708
14.6   Modeling the Triangle: Illustrating Alternative Approaches   709
14.7   Design and Use of Abstract Data Types   727
        CASE STUDY: Assigning Final Grades for a Semester   727
14.8   Common Programming Errors   746
        Chapter Review   747

15 _____ RECURSION   755

15.1   The Nature of Recursion   756
15.2   Tracing Recursive Functions   761
15.3   Recursive Mathematical Functions   767
15.4   Recursive Functions with Array Arguments   773
        CASE STUDY: Recursive Selection Sort   773
15.5   Problem-Solving with Recursion   776
        CASE STUDY: Towers of Hanoi Problem   776
15.6   Picture-Processing with Recursion   780
        CASE STUDY: Counting Cells in a Blob   780
15.7   Common Programming Errors   784
        Chapter Review   785

16 ____ DYNAMIC DATA STRUCTURES   791

16.1   Review of Pointers and the new Operator   792
16.2   Manipulating the Heap   799
16.3   Linked Lists   801
16.4   The Stack as an Abstract Data Type   809
        CASE STUDY: Evaluating Postfix Expressions   813
16.5   Implementing a Stack Using an Array   820
16.6   Linked-List Representation of a Stack   824
16.7   The Queue Abstract Data Type   830
16.8   Queue Application   833
        CASE STUDY: Maintaining a Queue of Passengers   833
16.9   Implementing a Queue Using an Array   841
16.10   Linked-List Representation of a Queue   846
16.11   Common Programming Errors   850
        Chapter Review   852

APPENDIXES

A   Character Sets   861
B   Reserved Words and Special Characters   863
C   Selected C++ Library Facilities   864
D   Operators   869
E   A Brief Introduction to Inheritance and Polymorphism   871

ANSWERS   A-1

INDEX   I-1

1

Introduction to Computers and Programming

1.1   Electronic Computers: Then and Now
1.2   Components of a Computer
1.3   Problem Solving, Abstraction, and Program Engineering
1.4   Programming Languages
1.5   Processing a High-Level Language Program
1.6   Using the Computer
        Chapter Review

From the 1940s to the present—a period of only 50 years—the development of the computer has spurred the growth of technology into realms only dreamed of at the turn of the century. Computers have changed the way we live and how we do business. Today we depend on computers to process our paychecks, send rockets into space, build cars and machines of all types, and help us do our shopping and banking. The computer program's role in this technology is essential. Without a list of instructions to carry out, the computer is virtually useless. Programming languages allow us to write those instructions and thus to communicate with computers.

You are about to begin the study of computer science using one of the most versatile programming languages available today: the C++ language. This chapter introduces you to the computer and its components and to the major categories of programming languages.

1.1 ——— ELECTRONIC COMPUTERS: THEN AND NOW

It is difficult to live in today's society without having some contact with computers. Computers are used to provide instructional material in schools, to find library books, to send out bills, to reserve airline and concert tickets, to play games, to send and receive electronic mail, and to help authors write books. Several kinds of computers cooperate in dispensing cash from an automatic teller machine. Embedded or hidden computers help control the ignition, fuel, and transmission systems of modern automobiles. At the supermarket, computer devices scan the bar codes on the packages you buy, total your purchases, and help manage the store's inventory. Even a microwave oven has a special-purpose computer built into it.

Computers were not always so pervasive in our society. Just a short time ago, computers were fairly mysterious devices, which were familiar to only a small percentage of the population. Computer know-how spread when advances in solid-state electronics led to cuts in the size and cost of electronic computers. In the mid-1970s, a computer with the computational power of one of today's personal computers would have filled a 9-by-12-foot room and cost $100,000. Today, an equivalent personal computer sits on a desktop and costs less than $2000 (see Fig. 1.1, left). Furthermore, even smaller computers providing comparable computing capability may be carried in a briefcase and conveniently used in your lap (Fig. 1.1, right). These computers come with their own battery and may be operated for several hours in places such as airplanes or trains where other sources of power are not readily available.

If we take the literal definition for a *computer* as "a device for counting or computing," then we could consider the abacus to have been the first computer. The first electronic digital computer was designed in the late 1930s by

Figure 1.1   IBM Personal Computer with mouse (left); Apple Powerbook laptop computer (right). Right photo courtesy Martha Friedman.

Dr. John Atanasoff at Iowa State University. Atanasoff designed his computer to perform mathematical computations for graduate students.

The first large-scale, general-purpose electronic digital computer, called the ENIAC, was built in 1946 at the University of Pennsylvania. Its design was funded by the U. S. Army, and it was used to compute ballistics tables, predict the weather, and make atomic energy calculations.   The ENIAC weighed 30 tons and occupied 30×50 feet (see Fig. 1.2).

Although we are often led to believe otherwise, computers cannot reason as we do. Basically, computers are devices that perform computations at incredible speeds (more than one million operations per second) and with great accuracy. However, to accomplish anything useful, a computer must be given a sequence of explicit instructions, a *program*, to perform. The job of the *computer programmer* is to devise programs to carry out required tasks.

To program the ENIAC, engineers had to connect hundreds of wires and arrange thousands of switches in a certain way. In 1946, Dr. John von Neumann of Princeton University proposed the concept of a *stored-program computer*—a computer whose program was stored in computer memory rather than being set by wires and switches. Von Neumann knew that the data stored in computer memory could easily be changed by a program. He reasoned that programs, too, could be stored in memory and changed as required far more easily than connecting wires and setting switches. Von Neumann designed a computer based on this idea. His design was a success and greatly simplified the task of programming a computer. The *von Neumann design* is the basis of most of the digital computers we use today.

Figure 1.2   The ENIAC computer (Photo courtesy of Unisys Corporation)

Brief History of Computing

Table 1.1 lists some of the milestones along the path from the abacus to modern-day computers and programming languages. The entries before 1890 illustrate some of the earlier attempts to develop mechanical computing devices. In 1890, the first special-purpose computer that used electronic sensors was designed; this invention eventually led to the formation of the computer industry giant called International Business Machines Corporation (IBM).

As we look at the table from 1939 on, we see a variety of new computers introduced. The computers prior to 1975 were all very large, general-purpose computers called *mainframes*. The computers listed in the table after 1975 are all smaller computers. A number of important events in the development of programming languages and environments are also listed in the table, including FORTRAN (1957), CTSS (1965), C (1972), VisiCalc (1978), C++ (1983), and Windows (1989).

Table 1.1   Milestones in Computer Development

DATE	EVENT
2000 B.C.	The abacus is first used for computations.
1642 A.D.	Blaise Pascal creates a mechanical adding machine for tax computations. It is unreliable.
1670	Gottfried von Liebniz creates a more reliable adding machine that adds, subtracts, multiplies, divides, and calculates square roots.
1842	Charles Babbage designs an analytical engine to perform general calculations automatically. Ada Augusta (a. k. a. Lady Lovelace) is a programmer for this machine.
1890	Herman Hollerith designs a system to record census data. The information is stored as holes in cards, which are interpreted by machines with electrical sensors. Hollerith starts a company that will eventually become IBM.
1939	John Atanasoff, with graduate student Clifford Berry, designs and builds the first electronic digital computer. His project was funded by a grant for $650.
1946	J. Presper Eckert and John Mauchly design and build the ENIAC computer. It used 18,000 vacuum tubes and cost $500,000 to build.
1946	John von Neumann proposes that a program be stored in a computer in the same way that data are stored. His proposal, called the "von Neumann architecture," is the basis for modern computers.
1951	Eckert and Mauchly build the first general-purpose commercial computer, the UNIVAC.
1957	An IBM team, led by John Backus, designs the first successful high-level programming language, FORTRAN, for solving engineering and science problems.
1958	The first computer to use the transistor as a switching device, the IBM 7090, is introduced.
1964	The first computer to use integrated circuits, the IBM 360, is announced.
1965	The CTSS (Compatible Time-Sharing System) operating system is introduced. It allows several users simultaneously to use, or share, a single computer.
1970	A first version of the UNIX operating system is running on the DEC PDP-7.
1971	Nicklaus Wirth designs the Pascal programming language as a language for teaching structured programming concepts.
1972	Dennis Ritchie of Bell Laboratories in New Jersey develops the language C.
1973	Part of the UNIX operating system is implemented in C.
1975	The first microcomputer, the Altair, is introduced.
1975	The first supercomputer, the Cray-1, is announced.
1976	Digital Equipment Corporation introduces its popular minicomputer, the DEC VAX 11/780.

(continued)

Table 1.1   (Continued)

DATE	EVENT
1977	Steve Wozniak and Steve Jobs found Apple Computer.
1978	Dan Bricklin and Bob Frankston develop the first electronic spreadsheet, called VisiCalc, for the Apple computer.
1979–82	Bjarne Stroustrup of Bell Laboratories in New Jersey introduces "C with Classes."
1981	IBM introduces the IBM PC.
1983–85	C with Classes is redesigned and reimplemented as C++.
1984	Apple introduces the Macintosh, the first widely available computer with a "user-friendly" graphical interface using icons, windows, and a mouse device.
1988	Work on standardization of C++ begins.
1989	Microsoft Corporation introduces Windows for IBM computers.
1989	The American National Standards Institute (ANSI) publishes the first standard for the C programming language.

Categories of Computers

Modern computers are classified according to size and performance. The three major categories of computers are microcomputers, minicomputers, and mainframes.

Many of you have seen or used *microcomputers* such as the IBM PC (see Fig. 1.1, left). Microcomputers are also called *personal computers* (PCs) or *desktop computers* because they are used by one person at a time and are small enough to fit on a desk. *Notebook* or *laptop* computers are among the smallest microcomputers. The largest microcomputers, called *workstations*, are commonly used by engineers to produce engineering drawings and to assist in the design and development of new products (see Fig. 1.3).

Minicomputers are larger than microcomputers; they generally operate at faster speeds and can store larger quantities of information. Minicomputers can serve several different users simultaneously. A small- or medium-sized company might use a minicomputer to perform payroll computations and to keep track of its inventory. Engineers might use minicomputers to control a chemical plant or a production process.

The largest computers are called *mainframes*. A large company might have one or more mainframes at its central computing facility for performing business-related computations. These machines provide for the storage and manipulation of large data bases of information. Mainframes are also used as "number crunchers" to generate solutions to systems of equations that characterize an engineering or scientific problem. In a few seconds, a mainframe can solve equations that might take hours to solve on a minicomputer or even

Figure 1.3 Sun Microsystems SPARCstation 370 (Photo courtesy of Sun Microsystems, Inc.)

days on a microcomputer. The largest mainframes, called *supercomputers,* are used to solve the most complex systems of equations.

In the late 1950s, mainframe computers could perform only 50 instructions per second. Now, we commonly see much smaller workstations that can perform well over 20 million instructions per second. It is obvious that, in a relatively short time, there have been tremendous changes in the speed and size of computers.

Any of the above computers might be available to you in this course. It is quite likely, however, that you will be using a larger microcomputer, either *stand-alone* (operating by itself) or as part of a *network* of computers linked together through a common computer called a *server.* The availability of the network will enable you to share information with other students and your instructor and, perhaps, even to communicate with each other using *electronic mail.*

1.2 ——— COMPONENTS OF A COMPUTER

Despite large variations in cost, size, and capabilities, modern computers are remarkably similar to each other in a number of ways. Basically, a computer consists of the components shown in Fig. 1.4. The arrows connecting the com-

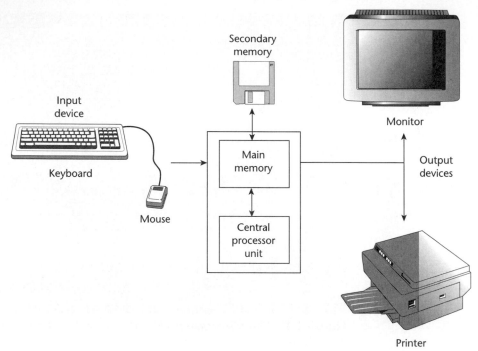

Figure 1.4   Components of a computer

puter components show the direction of information flow. These computer components are called the *hardware.*

All information that is to be processed by a computer must first be entered into the computer's *main memory* via an *input device.* The information in main memory is manipulated by the *central processor unit* (CPU), and the results of this manipulation are stored back in main memory. Information in main memory can be displayed through an *output device. Secondary memory* is often used for storing large quantities of information in a semipermanent form.

The Main Memory of a Computer

A computer's main memory stores information of all types: instructions, numbers, names, lists, and pictures. Think of a computer's memory as an ordered sequence of storage locations called *memory cells.* To be able to store and then retrieve or access information, we must have some way to identify the individual memory cells. Each memory cell has a unique *address* associated with it. The address indicates the cell's relative position in memory. The sample computer memory in Fig. 1.5 consists of 1000 memory cells, with addresses 0

Memory

Address	Contents
0	−27.2
1	354
2	0.005
3	−26
4	H
⋮	⋮
998	X
999	75.62

Figure 1.5 Computer memory with 1000 cells

through 999 (most computers have memories that consist of millions of individual cells).

The information stored in a memory cell is called its *contents*. Every memory cell always contains some information, although we may have no idea what that information is. Whenever new information is placed in a memory cell, any information already there is destroyed and cannot be retrieved. In Fig. 1.5, the contents of memory cell 3 is the number −26, and the contents of memory cell 4 is the letter H.

The memory cells shown in Fig. 1.5 are actually collections of smaller units called *bytes*. (The number of bytes in a memory cell is *machine dependent*; that is, it varies from computer to computer.) A byte is the amount of storage required to store a single character and is composed of a sequence of even smaller units of storage called *bits*, which are single binary digits (0 or 1). Generally, there are eight bits to a byte (see Fig. 1.6).

A number or a character is represented by a particular pattern of zeros and ones. The size of the pattern (the number of bits) depends on the nature of the

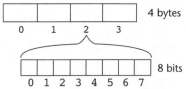

Figure 1.6 A computer memory cell with four bytes

value. A character requires 8 bits (1 byte); an integer, such as 30225, might require 16 or 32 bits (2 or 4 bytes, respectively). To store a value, the computer sets each bit of a selected memory cell to 0 or 1, thereby destroying what was previously in that bit. To retrieve and manipulate a value from a memory cell, the computer copies the pattern of zeros and ones stored in that cell to a storage area, the *memory buffer register* in the central processor unit, where the bit pattern can be processed. The copy operation does not destroy the bit pattern currently in the memory cell. This process is the same regardless of the kind of information—character, number, or program instruction—stored in a memory cell.

Central Processor Unit (CPU)

The CPU performs the actual processing or manipulation of information stored in memory; it also retrieves information from memory. This information can be data or instructions for manipulating data. The CPU can also store the results of those manipulations in memory for later use.

The *control unit* in the CPU coordinates all activities of the computer by determining which operations to perform and in what order to perform them. It then transmits coordinating control signals to the computer components.

Also found within the CPU are the *arithmetic-logic unit* (ALU) and special storage locations called *registers*. The ALU consists of electronic circuitry to perform arithmetic operations (addition, subtraction, multiplication, and division) and to make comparisons. The control unit copies the next program instruction from memory into the *instruction register* in the CPU. The ALU then performs the operation specified by the next instruction on data that are copied from memory into registers, and the results are copied to memory. The ALU can perform each arithmetic operation in less than a millionth of a second. It can also compare data stored in its registers to determine if the values are equal or, if not, which one is larger or smaller; the operations that are performed next depend on the results of the comparison.

Input and Output Devices

Input/output (I/O) devices enable us to communicate with the computer. Specifically, these devices provide us with the means to enter data for a computation and to observe the results of a computation.

A common I/O device used with large computers is the *computer terminal*, which is both an input and an output device. A terminal consists of a *keyboard* (used for entering information) and a *monitor* (used for displaying information). Frequently, microcomputers are connected to larger computers and are used as terminals.

A computer keyboard is similar to a typewriter keyboard except that it has some extra keys for performing special functions. On the IBM keyboard shown in Fig. 1.7, the 12 keys labeled F1 through F12 in the top row are *func-*

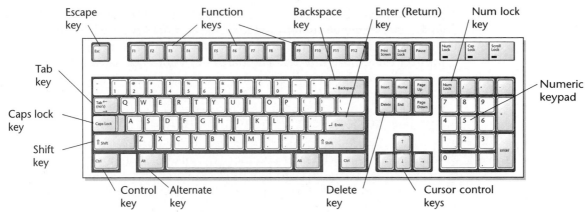

Figure 1.7   IBM keyboard

tion keys. The function performed by pressing one of these keys depends on the program that is executing.

Most PCs are equipped with graphics capability that enables the output to be displayed as a graph or picture (see Fig. 1.3). With some graphics systems, the user can communicate with the computer by using a mouse, which is an input device that moves an electronic pointer.

The only problem with using a monitor as an output device is that it leaves no written record of the computation. If you want *hard-copy output*, you have to send your computational results to an output device such as a *printer*.

Secondary Storage

Because computers have only a limited amount of main memory, *secondary storage* provides additional data-storage capability on most computer systems. For example, a *disk drive*, which stores data on a disk, is a common secondary storage device for today's PCs (Fig. 1.3).

There are two kinds of disks: *hard disks* and *floppy disks* (often referred to as diskettes), and a computer may have one or more drives of each kind. A hard disk normally cannot be removed from its drive; therefore, the storage area on a hard disk is often shared by all the users of a computer. However, each computer user may have his or her own floppy disk that can be inserted into a *floppy disk drive* as needed. Hard disks can store much more data and can operate much more quickly than floppy disks, but they are also much more expensive.

Information stored on a disk is organized into collections called *files*. The data for a program can be stored in an *input file* in advance rather than being entered at the keyboard while the program is executing. Results generated by the computer can be saved as an *output file* on a disk. Most of the programs that you write will be saved as *program files* on a disk.

The names of all the files stored on a disk are listed in the disk's *directory*. This directory may be subdivided into one or more levels called *subdirectories*. The details of how files are named and grouped in directories vary from one computer system to another. The names of your files must follow the conventions that apply on your system.

Main Memory versus Secondary Memory

Main memory is much faster and more expensive than the secondary memory provided by secondary storage devices. You must transfer data from secondary memory to main memory before they can be processed. Data in main memory are *volatile* because they disappear when you switch off the computer. Data in secondary memory are more *permanent* because they do not disappear when the computer is switched off. However, we should warn you that the permanency of information in secondary memory is subject to human error, device failure, *computer viruses*, and power outages. You are strongly encouraged to use both hard and floppy disk storage devices periodically to back up valuable information in order to protect against these problems. This textbook was stored on both floppy and hard disks.

Computer Networks

Often, several microcomputers in a laboratory are interconnected in what is called a *local area network* (LAN) so that they can share the use of a large hard disk and high-quality printers. The microcomputers in the network can also access common programs and data stored on the disk.

EXERCISES FOR SECTION 1.2

Self-Check
1. What are the contents of memory cells 0 and 999 in Fig. 1.5? Which memory cells contain the letter X and the fraction 0.005?
2. Explain the purpose of memory, the central processor unit, and the disk drive and disk. What input and output devices do you use with your computer?

1.3 _____ PROBLEM-SOLVING, ABSTRACTION, AND PROGRAM ENGINEERING

We mentioned earlier that a computer cannot think; therefore, to get it to do any useful work, it must be provided with a program, that is, a list of instructions. Programming a computer is a lot more involved than simply writing a list of instructions. Problem-solving is a crucial component of programming. Before we can write a program to solve a particular problem, we must consider carefully all aspects of the problem and then develop and organize its solution.

The Art and Science of Problem-Solving

You must be able to solve problems in order to succeed in academics or on the job. *Problem-solving ability* is a combination of art and science. The art of problem-solving is the transformation of an English description of a problem into a form that permits a mechanical solution. One relatively straightforward example of this process is transforming an algebra word problem into a set of algebraic equations, which can then be solved for one or more unknowns.

In practice, this process is more difficult because problem descriptions are often incomplete, imprecise, or ambiguous. The successful problem solver begins by carefully analyzing the statement of the problem in order to identify what is given (problem input) and what is required (problem output). During this *problem-analysis process*, the problem solver must be able to ask the right questions in order to clarify the problem and obtain any information missing from the problem statement. The process of extracting the essential information about a problem, often referred to as *abstraction*, is a key aspect of writing programs. We will illustrate and use abstraction throughout this text.

The problem solver must also be able to determine whether there are any constraints or simplifying assumptions that can be applied to facilitate the problem solution. Often, we cannot solve the most general case of a problem but must make some realistic assumptions that limit or constrain the problem so that it can be solved.

The science part of problem-solving involves knowledge of the problem environment, knowledge of the formulas or equations that characterize the environment, and the ability to apply and manipulate these formulas. Using this knowledge, the problem solver develops a series of steps whose successful completion will lead to the problem solution. Once the solution is obtained, the problem solver must verify its accuracy by comparing the computed results with observed results.

As is the case with most programming students, initially you will probably spend a great deal of time in the computer laboratory entering your programs. Later, you will spend more time removing the errors that inevitably will be present in your programs. One of our goals in this text is the development of tools and techniques to assist you in reducing the number of errors you make and, therefore, the amount of time spent finding and correcting your errors. In the next chapter, we will study one such approach to reducing the number of errors, which will be emphasized throughout the remainder of the text.

1.4 _____ PROGRAMMING LANGUAGES

High-Level Languages

Programming languages fall into three broad categories: machine, assembly, and high-level languages. *High-level languages* are more popular with programmers than machine and assembly languages because they are much easier to use. In addition, a high-level language program is *portable*, meaning that it can be used with minimal or no modification on many different types of computers. An assembly language or machine language program, on the other hand, can be used on only one type of computer.

Some common high-level languages are Ada, BASIC, C, COBOL, FORTRAN, Lisp, Pascal, and C++. Each language was designed with a specific purpose in mind. The development of Ada was driven largely by the U. S. Department of Defense, which sought a single high-level language to be used in the specialized program applications area known as *real-time, distributed systems*. BASIC (Beginners All-purpose Symbolic Instructional Code) was designed to be easily learned and used by students. C combines the power of an assembly language with the ease of use and portability of a high-level language; it is a highly versatile language that has been used in a wide variety of applications, from operating systems implementation (such as UNIX) to data base and large-scale, numeric-processing applications. COBOL (COmmon Business Oriented Language) is used primarily for business data-processing operations. FORTRAN is an acronym for FORmula TRANslation; its principal users are engineers and scientists. Lisp is a language used primarily in artificial intelligence applications. Pascal was developed primarily for teaching introductory programming by following a particular approach often referred to as structured programming.

C++ is a general-purpose programming language that is rapidly gaining wide acceptance in the computing field. (A general-purpose programming language is one that can be put to many different applications.) C++ is based on the C language, which was developed by Dennis Ritchie of AT&T Bell Laboratories. Currently, C++ is becoming increasingly popular for teaching programming concepts partly because it provides powerful features useful for practicing modern approaches to software development. Another reason for the popularity of C++ is that efficient C++ compilers are available for most computers.

C++ facilitates writing structured programs — programs that are relatively easy to write and understand. The technique of *structured programming* has been widely accepted as standard programming practice for well over a decade. C++ can be used for "high-level" purposes such as writing word processors, data management systems, and mathematical packages. It also has "low-level" capabilites that make it suitable for writing *operating systems* (see Section 1.6). For these reasons, there is an increasing demand for C++ and the language is becoming more widely used. Thus it is a practical language to be equipped with once outside the classroom.

The C programming language, which forms the basis for C++, has a standard recently (November, 1990) approved by the American National Standards Institute (ANSI). C++ has a proposed standard now undergoing the ANSI review and approval process. These standards help ensure a high degree of *portability* for programs that *conform* to the standard. That is, the standard ensures that programs written according to the syntax rules of the standard may be compiled and executed on a variety of computers with little or no change.

In this text we present many of the fundamental features of the C++ language. This is by no means a full compendium of all there is to know about C++. Rather, we have provided an introduction to those features required to achieve our goal of producing an introductory text emphasizing sound principles of program engineering.

Except for C++, each of the high-level languages just described has a *language standard* that describes the *syntax*, or grammatical form, of the language. Every high-level language instruction must conform to the syntax rules specified in the language standard. These rules are very precise — no allowances are made for instructions that are almost correct. The standard prescribes the same set of syntax rules for a given language regardless of the computer you are using. This is a major contributing factor to the portability of the standardized languages just described.

C++ also has a set of precise syntax rules that must be followed. However, at the time this book was written, the C++ standardization effort, under way since 1988, had not yet been completed. This lack of standardization leaves open the possibility of some variation in the syntax rules for versions of C++ produced by different companies. However, the language is close enough to standardization at this point that you will rarely notice these differences even if you move C++ programs from one computer to another.

An important feature of high-level languages is that they allow us to write program instructions (often referred to as *program statements* or *code*) that resemble English. In this code, we can reference data stored in memory using descriptive names like `price` and `tax` rather than the numeric memory-cell addresses discussed in Section 1.2. We can also use familiar symbols to describe operations that we want performed. For example, in several high-level languages, the statement

```
cost = price + tax;
```

means add `tax` to `price` and store the result in `cost`. `tax`, `price`, and `cost` are called *variables*. An example of numbers stored in these variables before and after the execution of this instruction is shown next.

Before			*After*		
price	tax	cost	price	tax	cost
7.00	0.50	?	7.00	0.50	7.50

Machine and Assembly Language

Machine language is the native tongue of the computer. It is the only programming language that the computer understands. Unfortunately, it is a language of numbers. If we wish to communicate directly with the computer (by writing a program and having it executed), we must do it in machine language. To do so, we must provide the computer with a numeric *encoding* of each instruction that it is to carry out. The operation to be performed must have a numeric encoding, and the information to be manipulated must have a numeric representation, which is usually the address of the memory cell containing the information. The exact form of these numeric encodings will differ from computer to computer.

It is rather cumbersome to write a program in machine language since the programmer must remember the numeric code for each instruction and the address in memory of each data item. If for some reason it becomes necessary to move a data item, all instructions that manipulate it must be changed to reflect the new address of the memory cell containing this data item. Consequently, it is difficult to make even minor modifications to machine-language programs.

To alleviate this difficulty somewhat, *assembly language* may be used to write programs. The use of assembly language allows a programmer to refer to each data item by a descriptive name (such as GROSS or TAX rather than by a numeric address. Furthermore, a descriptive mnemonic code is used instead of the numeric operation code.

As an example of the differences between machine and assembly language, we have shown, in Fig. 1.8, both versions of a program written for the Digital Equipment Corporation PDP-11 computer. These programs form the sum of two numbers stored in memory and save the result in a third memory cell. We do not expect you to understand these programs; they are provided solely as an illustration. However, we hope you will agree that the assembly-language program appears more readable.

Machine-Language Version			*Assembly-Language Version*			
013737	000016	000022	GO:	MOV	NMBR1,	SUM
063737	000020	000022		ADD	NMBR2,	SUM
000000				HALT		
000100			NMBR1:	.WORD	100	
000150			NMBR2:	.WORD	150	
000000			SUM:	.WORD	0	
				.END	GO	

Figure 1.8   Machine- and assembly-language versions of PDP-11 addition program

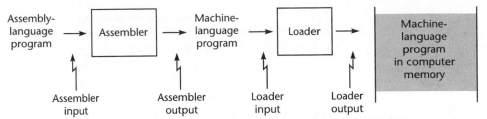

Figure 1.9   Preparing an assembly-language program for execution

Unfortunately, the computer cannot understand assembly language. Therefore, before an assembly-language program can be executed, it must first be *translated* into machine language by a special program called an *assembler*. The assembler processes (as its input) the assembly-language program and generates (as its output) the equivalent machine-language program ready for loading, as shown in Fig. 1.9.

This process is relatively straightforward since each assembly-language instruction is translated into one machine-language instruction. Programming in assembly language is considerably more convenient because the programmer does not have to keep track of as many details as with machine language. Instead, these details are handled by the assembler when the program is translated, and this makes program construction and subsequent modification easier.

However, there remain many problems associated with the use of assembly language. Assembly language is not very much closer to our natural language than is machine language. In addition, each assembly language is unique to a particular family of computers, so that assembly-language programs written for one computer are not likely to be executable on another. It is for these reasons that higher-level languages were developed.

EXERCISES FOR SECTION 1.4

Self-Check   1. What do you think the following high-level language statements mean?

```
x = a + b + c;
x = y / z;
d = c - b + a;
x = x + 1;
kelvin = celsius + 273.15;
```

2. Which high-level language was designed to teach programming? Which combines the features of both assembly language and a high-level language? Which was designed for business applications? Which was designed for translating scientific formulas?

3. Which type of language has instructions such as ADD X? Which type has instructions that are binary numbers?

4. Explain in your own words, perhaps based upon experiences in other courses you have taken, why it might be important to develop and use a consistent approach to problem-solving using the computer.

1.5 ———— PROCESSING A HIGH-LEVEL LANGUAGE PROGRAM

The steps involved in processing a program written in a high-level language such as C++ are shown in Fig. 1.10. Before the computer can process the program, it must be typed in (entered) using the keyboard at a computer terminal, personal computer, or workstation. The program is then stored on a disk *program file* or *source file*. The programmer uses an *editor* program to enter a program and to save it as a source file.

Once the source file is saved, it can be translated into machine language. The machine-language version is also stored on a disk as an *object file*. A *compiler program* processes the source file and attempts to translate each statement into machine language. One or more lines of code in the source file may contain a *syntax error*, meaning that the code does not correspond exactly to the syntax of the high-level language. In this case, the compiler displays an error message on the monitor screen and does not create a machine-language version of the program.

At this point, you can make changes to your source file and have the compiler translate the file again. If there are no more errors, the compiler creates the object file. This file and any additional object files—for example, programs for input and output operations—that may be needed are combined by the *linker program* into a *load file*. Finally, the *loader program* places the load file into memory, ready for execution. The editor, compiler, linker, and loader programs are part of a computer system. The entire process of preparing a program for execution is shown in Fig. 1.10.

Executing a Program

To execute a program, the CPU must examine each program instruction in memory and send out the command signals required to carry out the instruction. Normally, the instructions are executed in sequence; however, as we will discuss later, it is possible to have the CPU skip over some instructions or to have it execute some instructions more than once.

During execution, data can be entered into memory and manipulated in some specified way. Program instructions are used to copy a program's data (input data) into memory. After the input data are processed, instructions for

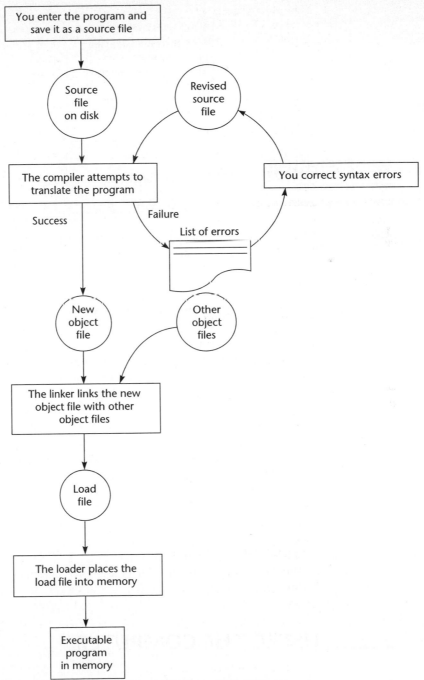

Figure 1.10 Preparing a program for execution

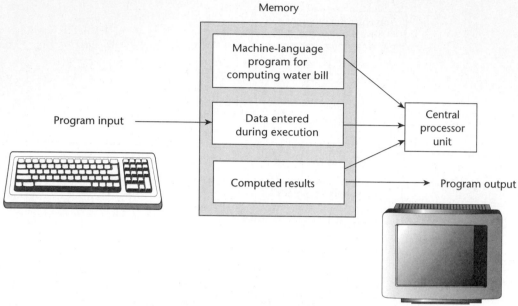

Figure 1.11   Flow of information during program execution

displaying or printing values in memory can be executed to display the program results. The lines displayed by a program are called the *program output.*

We will use the situation illustrated in Fig. 1.11—executing a water bill program stored in memory—as an example. In the first step, the program copies into memory data that describe the amount of water used and the water rate. In step 2, the program manipulates the data and stores the results of the computations in memory. In the final step, the computational results are displayed as a water bill.

EXERCISES FOR SECTION 1.5

Self-Check   1. What is a source file? An object file? A load file? Which do you create and which does the compiler create? Which does the linker create and which is processed by the loader? What do the compiler, linker, and loader programs do?
2. What is a syntax error? In which file (source, object, or load) would a syntax error be found?

1.6 ——— USING THE COMPUTER

The mechanics of entering a program as a source file and of translating and executing a machine-language program differ from system to system. We will not give specific details for a particular computer system, but instead will describe the general process involved for several different kinds of common *computer system environments*, including a single-user (or stand-alone) personal computer or workstation, a timeshared system, and a network of personal computers or workstations. At home you may use a stand-alone computer that is not connected in any way to other computing facilities. However, laboratories of such unconnected, single-user computers in colleges and universities and in the workplace are rapidly being replaced by networked systems. Even home computer users are usually linked by telephone to a networked computing facility. The information on the use of computer networks, therefore, may be most relevant for you.

Operating Systems

Regardless of the computing system that you use, you will need to interact with a supervisory program called the *operating system*. The main task of an operating system is the allocation and control of your computing system's resources, including the central processor, computer memory, and all of the input and output devices connected to the computer. This task is more complex for timeshared and networked systems than it is for single-user computers. MS-DOS, MS-DOS with Microsoft Windows, Solaris, and UNIX are all examples of computer operating systems.

Some tasks performed by an operating system include the following:

- validating user identification and account number;
- allocating memory and processor time;
- ensuring the security of each user's files and program execution;
- making the editor, compiler, linker, and loader programs as well as entire libraries of other programs available to users;
- providing input and output facilities;
- retrieving needed files;
- saving new files.

In general, performance of the first three of these tasks is not required of the operating system for a stand-alone computer.

Many of you will be using a personal computer, a small desktop computer used by one individual at a time. This is the simplest of the three computing environments just described. In general, except for the sharing of a hard disk (used for secondary storage), the operating system for such a computer need not be concerned about the sharing, allocation, or protection of other resources such as main memory, CPU, or input/output devices among multiple users.

Some of you will be using a *timeshared computer*. In a timeshared environment, many users are connected by terminals to one central computer, and all users share the central facilities, including secondary and main memory, the

CPU, and the input/output devices. In a timeshared environment, users need an account number and password to be able to access the system. The operating system controls the allocation of resources to all of the users, determining such things as how much memory each user gets and who controls the CPU at any given time. With a timeshared system, all files are stored on central secondary storage devices and all programs execute on the same shared CPU. Timeshared system users also have the capability to communicate with one another using electronic mail.

From the point of view of the user, a networked system of personal computers or workstations looks much like a timeshared system. Users need special account numbers and passwords to be able to use the system. They also may communicate with each other, and share a central secondary memory device (such as a large, hard disk drive) often referred to as a *network server*. Here, the similarity ends, however, as the computers attached to the network usually have the full capability of a personal computer or workstation—their own *local memory* (secondary and main memory), their own CPU, and perhaps even their own input/output devices (in addition to a keyboard and a screen). Users sometimes may be able to store some of their own files locally and *download* other files from the server for local use or execution. In some cases, network users also may be able to *upload* local files for saving on the central server.

Each of the computing environments just discussed has its own special *control language* for communicating with its operating system. We will not discuss the specifics of these languages here; your instructor will provide the specific *control language commands* for your system. Instead, we will provide an introductory discussion intended to give you a general idea of how to access each of the three computing environments just described.

Booting a Single-User Personal Computer or Workstation

Before you can use a single-user personal computer or workstation, you first need to *boot* the computer. Booting involves switching on the computer, which causes the operating system to be loaded into main memory (usually from a hard disk drive). Once booted, the operating system displays a prompt (for example, C:\>) to indicate that it is ready to accept commands. One command is usually sufficient to put you in a windowing environment, such as the X Window System (typically used with UNIX) or Microsoft Windows (used with MS-DOS). Once in such an environment, virtually all activity, such as typing in your program, compiling and correcting it, and finally executing it, is controlled by moving a mouse pointer (on your screen) to point to small symbols (*icons*) or *bars* in *pull down menus*. Aside from typing in your program and test data, very little typing is needed to tell the computer what to do next. Your instructor should be able to provide you with specific steps for using the windows system available on your computer.

Using a Timeshared System

Before you can use a timeshared computer, you must *log on*, or connect, to the computer. To log on, enter your account name and password (given to you by your instructor). For security reasons, your password is not displayed. Figure 1.12 illustrates this process for a Digital Equipment Corporation VAX computer. The computer user enters the characters that are in boldface type; the other characters are those that the operating system displays. The timeshared operating system shown, Ultrix-32 Version 3.1, displays the symbol > as a prompt.

Using a Network of Computers

To access a networked system of computers, you must first gain access to the network and to the server disk. This is usually accomplished by booting your personal computer or workstation and then entering a few special network commands. Next, you need to log on to the network using the unique user identification and password given to you by your instructor. Once you have logged on, all of the software that you are allowed to use should be accessible from the server in much the same way as if you were operating from a stand-alone computer.

Creating a Program File

Once you have booted your personal computer or workstation or logged on to a timeshared or networked system, you can begin to create your C++ pro-

```
Ultrix 32 V3.1 (rev. 9)  (cis.temple.edu)
login: stafford
Password: idunno

Last login: Sat Apr 25 09:57:55 from
peapod.astro.temple.edu
Ultrix 32 V3.0 (rev. 9)  System #4: Tue Apr 28
14:18:36 EDT 1993

Fri May 1 20:39:13 EDT 1993
>
```

Figure 1.12   Logging on to a timeshared computer

gram. In most cases, you will use a special program called an *editor* for this purpose. After accessing the editor, you can start typing in your C++ instructions. If you want a record of the program once it is entered, you must save it as a permanent file on disk; otherwise, your program disappears when your session with the editor is over. Listed next are the general steps to be followed to create and save a program file.

1. Access the editor program on your system, and indicate that you are creating a new file. (You may be able to specify the file name at this point.)
2. Enter each line of the program file.
3. Name your program file (if not named in step 1), and save it as a permanent file in secondary memory.
4. Exit from the editor or word processor.

After you have created your program and are satisfied that each line is typed correctly, you can attempt to compile, link, and execute the program. On some systems, you must give at least two separate commands (such as COMPILE and RUN) to accomplish these tasks; on other systems, one command, such as RUN or the name of the load file, initiates this sequence of operations.

If your program will not compile because it contains syntax errors, you must correct and recompile it following these general steps:

1. Again access the editor program, and have it display your program file for editing.
2. Correct the statements containing syntax errors.
3. Save your edited program file.
4. Compile, link, and execute the new program file.

Many modern computer systems provide special C++ *integrated environments* that make it easier to perform all of these tasks. Once you enter such an environment, switching from one task to another (for example, from edit to compile or compile to run) is accomplished simply by moving a mouse pointer to a particular icon or menu bar and clicking a button on the mouse. A programmer can switch from one window to another to view all that needs to be seen concerning the current activity in the computer. The screen shown in Fig. 1.13 provides a sample illustration of such an environment (the Borland C++, Version 3.1 environment) with the bottom window active. The upper window shows a very small program (with a syntax error) that has just been compiled. The error (just detected by the compiler) is shown in the window at the bottom of the screen.

In the programming environment illustrated, the lines in the program are not numbered. We identify the C++ statement causing a particular error message by moving the mouse pointer to the message shown in the error message window. Clicking the mouse button highlights the error message. At the same time, in the program window, the statement containing the error is high-

```
≡File  Edit  Search  Run  Compile  Debug  Project  Options  Window  Help
━━━━━━━━━━━━━━━━━━━━━━━━ HELLO.CPP ━━━━━━━━━━━━━━━━1━━
// FILE: Hello.cpp
// DISPLAYS A USER'S NICKNAME

#include <iostream.h>

void main ()
{
    // Local data ...
    char letter1, letter2, letter3;    // input: three letters to display

    // Enter letters and print message.
    cout << "Enter a three letter nickname and press return: ;
    cin >> letter1 >> letter2 >> letter3;
    cout << "Hello " << letter1 << letter2 << letter 3 << ".  ";
━━ 12.7 ━━━━━━━━━━━━━━━━━━━━━━━━━━━━━━━━━━━━━━━━━

━[■]━━━━━━━━━━━━━━━━━━━━ Message ━━━━━━━━━━━━━━━2━[↑]━
Compiling C:\HELLO.CPP:
Error C:\HELLO.CPP 12: Unterminated string or character constant in function
Error C:\HELLO.CPP 13: Expression syntax in function main()


F1 Help   Space   View source   ↵   F10 Menu
```

Figure 1.13   Program and error message windows in the Borland C++ (Ver. 3.1) programming environment

lighted, thereby assisting in locating the cause of the error (in this case, a missing right-hand double quote, ", just before the semicolon in the first line beginning with cout). We can now move the mouse pointer back to the program window, click the button, correct the program, and try again (see Self-Check Exercise 2 at the end of this section). All work—editing, compiling, error correction, etc.—is done by pulling down menus and moving the mouse pointer to one of the windows displayed. Once the program compiles correctly, we can execute it by pulling down the RUN menu and clicking on the RUN bar. The output from the program may be viewed in the output window, as shown in Fig. 1.14.

EXERCISES FOR SECTION 1.6

Self-Check   1. Explain one or two distinguishing factors among a stand-alone, a timesharing, and a networked system. Which are you using for this course?
2. Try following the steps outlined in this section for entering, compiling, and correcting (and recompiling) the program shown on the screen in Fig. 1.13. (Be sure you have a detailed list of the specific steps required for your computer system

```
≡ File   Edit   Search   Run   Compile   Debug   Project   Options   Window   Help
 [■]======================= HELLO.CPP ===================1=[↑]
  // FILE: Hello.cpp
  // DISPLAYS A USER'S NICKNAME

  #include <iostream.h>

  void main ()
  {
     // Local data ...
     char letter1, letter2, letter3;    // input: three letters to display

     // Enter letters and print message.
     cout << "Enter a three letter nickname and press return: ";
     cin >> letter1 >> letter2 >> letter3;
     cout << "Hello " << letter1 << letter2 << letter 3 << ". ";
     cout << "We hope you enjoy studying C++!" << endl;



 === 1.1 ==[■]█████████████████████████████████████████████▶[↲]
 ┌──────────────────────────── Output ───────────────────── 2 ──
  Enter a three letter nickname and press return: Bob
  Hello Bob. We hope you enjoy studying C++!



 F1 Help   F2 Save   F3 Open   Alt-F9 Compile   F9 Make   F10 Menu
```

Figure 1.14 **Program and output windows in the Borland C++ (Ver. 3.1) programming environment**

before attempting this.) If you can get your program to compile with no errors, try to execute it. The program should pause after the "three letter" prompt. At this point, type in three letters and press the RETURN key. Write down a description of what happened next.

CHAPTER REVIEW

In this chapter, we described the basic components of a computer: main and secondary memory, the CPU, and I/O devices. Remember these important facts about computers:

1. A memory cell is never empty, although its initial contents may be meaningless to your program.
2. The current contents of a memory cell are destroyed whenever new information is placed in that cell.

3. Programs must first be placed in the memory of the computer before they can be executed.

4. Data cannot be manipulated by the computer without first being copied into memory.

5. A computer cannot think for itself; you must use a programming language to instruct a computer to perform a task in a precise and unambiguous manner.

6. Programming a computer can be fun—if you are patient, organized, and careful.

We briefly reviewed the history of computing from both a hardware and a software view. The different categories of computers—microcomputers, minicomputers, and mainframes—were described, noting that a computer's size and performance capability determine its category.

Also discussed was problem solving and its importance in programming.

The three different categories of programming languages (machine, assembly, and high-level language) were described, and some differences among these categories were illustrated. We investigated how a high-level language source program is translated into a machine-language object file by a compiler, linked with other object files by a linker, and finally loaded into memory by a loader. We discussed how to use a computer and its operating system to accomplish the tasks of entering a new program and running it on a computer.

✔ QUICK-CHECK EXERCISES

1. The _____ translates a(n) _____ language program into _____ .

2. After a C++ program is executed, all program results are automatically displayed. True or false?

3. Specify the correct order for these four operations: execution, linking, translation, loading.

4. A high-level language program is saved on disk as a(n) _____ file or a(n) _____ file.

5. The _____ finds syntax errors in the _____ file.

6. A machine-language program is saved on disk as a(n) _____ file.

7. A(n) _____ program is used to create and save the source file.

8. The _____ creates the load file.

9. The _____ program is used to place the _____ file into memory.

10. Computers are becoming (more / less) expensive and (bigger / smaller) in size.

11. The first large-scale, general-purpose electronic computer was called the _____ . It (was / was not) a stored-program computer.

12. A list of the names of all the files stored on a disk is found in the _____ .

Answers to Quick-Check Exercises

1. compiler, high-level, machine language
2. false

3. translation, linking, loading, execution
4. source, program
5. compiler, source
6. object
7. word processor or editor
8. linker
9. loader, load
10. less, smaller
11. ENIAC, was not
12. directory

REVIEW QUESTIONS

1. List at least three kinds of information stored in a computer.
2. List two functions of the CPU.
3. List two input devices, two output devices, and two secondary storage devices.
4. A computer can think. True or false?
5. List the three categories of programming languages.
6. Give three advantages of programming in a high-level language such as C++.
7. What processes are needed to transform a C++ program into a machine-language program that is ready for execution?
8. What are three characteristics of a structured program?

2

Program Design

2.1   The Software Development Method
       CASE STUDY: Converting Units
       of Measurement
2.2   Overview of C++
2.3   Declarations of Variables and Constants
2.4   Executable Statements
2.5   Recapitulation: The General Form of a
       C++ Program
2.6   Abstraction: Data Types and Expressions
       CASE STUDY: Finding the Value of a
       Coin Collection
2.7   Interactive Mode, Batch Mode, and
       Data Files
2.8   Common Programming Errors
       Chapter Review

Programming is a problem-solving activity. So, if you are a good problem-solver, you are likely to become a good programmer. One important goal of this book is to help you improve your problem-solving ability. We believe it is beneficial to approach each programming problem in a systematic and consistent way. Therefore, in this text we focus on the description and illustration of a number of techniques that should prove useful in developing solutions to programming problems. In this chapter, we begin the discussion of these techniques.

This chapter also introduces the high-level language C++. Our focus will be on the C++ features for entering data, performing simple computations, and displaying results. In addition, we describe how to run C++ programs interactively and in batch mode. In interactive programming, the program user enters data during program execution; in batch mode, the program user must prepare a data file before program execution begins.

2.1 —— THE SOFTWARE DEVELOPMENT METHOD

A Problem-Solving and Programming Strategy

You may be tempted to rush to the computer laboratory and start entering your program as soon as you have some idea of how to write it. Please, try to resist this temptation. Instead, think carefully about the problem and its solution before you write any program instructions. When you have a potential solution in mind, plan it out beforehand, using either paper and pencil or a word processor, and modify the solution if necessary.

The process of planning and organizing your solution to a problem is similar to that of writing a term paper. In the case of a term paper, larger papers require much more planning to help obtain an organized outline before any substantial writing is done. The same is true in programming. As problems increase in size and complexity, considerable planning and organizing of the solution is required. Program engineering involves the consistent application of an organized and well thought out approach. The approach begins with a thorough analysis of the problem to be solved. An outline or high-level design of the solution to the problem is worked out next. Then, additional details are added to this outline, providing a clearer, lower-level view of the problem solution. Once sufficient detail has been provided, the outline may be used to write the desired program. Finally, the program is tested to verify that it behaves as intended.

These steps are illustrated in Fig. 2.1 and described in more detail in the next section.

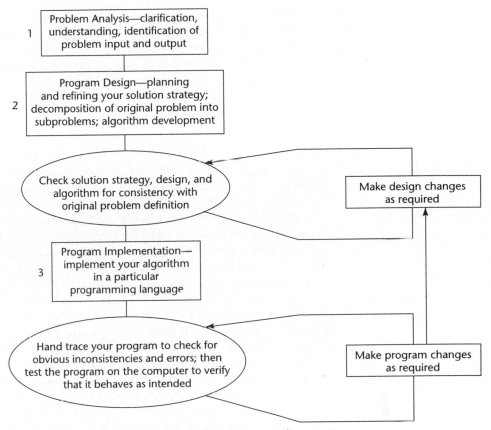

Figure 2.1 A problem-solving and programming strategy

Software Development Stages

Students in many subject areas receive instruction in specific problem-solving methods. For example, business students are encouraged to follow a *systems approach* to problem solving; engineering and science students are encouraged to follow the *engineering and scientific method*. Although these problem-solving methods are associated with very different fields of study, their essential ingredients are quite similar.

A *software engineer* is someone involved in the design and implementation of reliable software systems. As this title implies, programmers, like engineers, are concerned with developing practical, reliable solutions to problems. However, the product produced by a programmer is a software system rather than a physical system. Unfortunately, software systems create a collection of problems that are different from those found in working with physical systems. Software developers try to use a reasonably consistent problem solving approach or *software development method* for effectively resolving these problems. We have just outlined one such approach to computer program construction. We now begin to explore the primary stages of this approach in more detail. This exploration will continue throughout the text as we examine larger and more complicated problems.

1. **Problem Analysis:** The first step in solving a problem is to gain a clear understanding of the problem statement: what is given and what is required. Although this step sounds easy, it can be the most critical part of problem-solving. You must study the problem carefully; then eliminate aspects that are unimportant and focus on the essential aspects of the problem. If the problem is not clearly and completely defined, you should request more information from the person posing the problem.

   During the analysis process, you should work to identify the problem's input, desired output, and any additional data, formulas, requirements, or constraints on the solution. Identify what information is to be supplied as the problem's data and what results should be computed and displayed. Determine the required form and units in which the results should be displayed (for example, as a table with specific column headings).

2. **Program Design:** The first steps of the program design process involve the decomposition of the original problem into smaller subproblems. The main motivation behind this break down is the production and organization of smaller, relatively independent subproblems each of which is considerably easier to solve than the original. In this way, we are better able to *manage the complexity* of a problem, separately solving each subproblem and progressively adding more details to these smaller pieces.

   Once a sufficient amount of design detail has been added, we develop a list of steps called an *algorithm* to solve each subproblem, and verify that the algorithm solves the problem as intended.

3. **Program Implementation:** Implement the algorithm as a program. Knowledge of a particular programming language is required because each algorithm step must be converted to statements in that language.

These three steps in the software development method are critical; if they are not carried out properly, you will either solve the wrong problem or produce an awkward, inefficient solution. To perform these steps successfully, you must read the problem statement carefully before you attempt to solve the problem. You may need to read each problem statement two or three times. The first time you should get a general idea of what is being asked. The second time, you should try to answer the following questions:

- What information should the solution provide?
- What data do I have to work with?

The answer to the first question will tell you what the desired results, or *problem output,* are for the program. The answer to the second question will tell you the data provided, or *problem input.* It may help you to underline or highlight the phrases in the problem statement that identify the problem input and output.

The design stage is often the most difficult part of the problem-solving process. At this stage, you should first list the major steps, the *subproblems,* required for the solution of the given problem. Do not try to list every step imaginable, and try not to worry about the details of each step. Instead, concentrate on and outline an overall strategy. Once you have the list of subproblems, you can attack each one individually, in much the same way, thereby adding detail to or *refining* the problem. The process of solving a problem by breaking it up into its smaller subproblems, called *divide and conquer,* is a basic strategy for all kinds of problem-solving activities.

The software development method described in this section can be used with any programming language. Indeed, only the implementation phase requires knowledge of a language or a particular computer. In industry, testing is often carried out by individuals who specialize in developing good strategies for testing programs.

Check Your Programs Carefully

As Fig. 2.1 indicates, it is important to check your work at each step to ensure that your design and your program are indeed solving the given problem. As errors are found at any stage, it is necessary to locate and correct the cause and then recheck the corrected solution. Thus the software development process is repetitive in nature, and the distinction between the steps often can become blurred. There is no hard and fast rule as to where one stage stops and the other begins. Nonetheless, the stages just outlined provide a useful context for the problem-solving process. It is important to keep them in mind throughout the process and not to skip or short circuit any of the steps listed. We will have more to say about this as we progress through the text.

Checking your problem solution is particularly important once you have written the program. At this point, you should *hand trace* your solution by carefully performing each instruction much as the computer would. To hand trace a program, simulate the result of each program instruction using sample data that are easy to manipulate (for example, small whole numbers). Compare these results with the expected results, and make any necessary corrections to your program. Only then should you go to the computer laboratory and enter your program. Consistent practice in following this process usually can save hours of frustration later.

We walk you through a sample case study next. In this example, we provide a running commentary on the problem-solving and programming process being followed so that you will be able to apply it to other situations.

CASE STUDY: CONVERTING UNITS OF MEASUREMENT

Problem Statement

Imagine you work in a store that imports fabric. Most of the fabric you receive is measured in square meters; however, the store's customers want to know the equivalent amount in square yards. You need to write a program that performs this conversion.

Problem Analysis

The first step in understanding this problem is to determine what you are being asked to do. It should be clear that you must convert from one system of measurement to another, but are you supposed to convert from square meters to square yards, or vice versa? The problem states that you receive fabric measured in square meters, so the problem input is fabric size in square meters. Your customers want to know the equivalent amount in square yards, which must be your problem output. To write the program, an additional piece of information is needed, specifically, the *constant* 1.196, which we use to express the relationship between square meters and square yards; that is, 1 square meter equals 1.196 square yards. We will name this constant `meters_to_yards`. C++ associates our name with 1.196, and this name may be used in place of an actual constant value anywhere in the program.

We summarize the data requirements and relevant formulas below. We will use the identifier `size_in_sqmeters` to represent the locations in computer memory that will contain the problem input, and the name `size_in_sqyards` to represent the location that will contain the program result or the problem output. These names, `size_in_sqmeters` and `size_in_sqyards`, are called *variables*. We will use variable names from now on to represent memory locations containing information. Our goal is to become accustomed to thinking in terms of these problem-oriented descriptive names, rather than the *machine-oriented* memory locations they represent.

DATA REQUIREMENTS

> **Problem Constant**
>
> meters_to_yards = 1.196   — conversion constant
>
> **Problem Input**
>
> size_in_sqmeters   — the fabric size in square meters
>
> **Problem Output**
>
> size_in_sqyards   — the fabric size in square yards

FORMULAS

1 square meter equals 1.196 square yards

Program Design

Next, we try to formulate the algorithm that we must follow to solve the problem. We begin by listing the three major steps, or subproblems, of the original problem.

INITIAL ALGORITHM

1. Read the fabric size in square meters.
2. Convert the fabric size to square yards.
3. Display the fabric size in square yards.

We now must decide whether any steps of the algorithm need further *refinement* (additional details) or whether they are perfectly clear as stated. Step 1 (reading data) and step 3 (displaying a value) are basic steps and require no further refinement. Step 2 is fairly straightforward, but it might help to add some detail. The refinement of step 2 follows.

Step 2 Refinement

2.1. The fabric size in square yards is 1.196 times the fabric size in square meters.

The complete algorithm with refinements is listed below to show you how it all fits together. It resembles an outline for a paper. The refinement of step 2 is numbered as step 2.1 and is indented under step 2.

REFINED ALGORITHM

1. Read the fabric size in square meters.
2. Convert the fabric size to square yards.
    2.1. The fabric size in square yards is 1.196 times the fabric size in square meters.
3. Display the fabric size in square yards.

Program Implementation

To implement the solution, we must convert the algorithm to a C++ program. To do this, we must first tell the C++ compiler about the variables and constants to be used to specify the problem input and output. (See the three lines following `// Local Data ...` in Fig. 2.2.) Next, we convert each algorithm step into one or more C++ statements. If an algorithm step needs refinement,

Figure 2.2   Metric Conversion Program

```
// FILE: Metric.cpp
// CONVERTS FABRIC MEASURES IN SQUARE METERS TO SQUARE YARDS

#include <iostream.h>

void main ()
{
   // Local data ...
   const float meters_to_yards = 1.196; // conversion constant
   float size_in_sqmeters; // input: fabric size in square meters
   float size_in_sqyards;  // output: fabric size in square yards

   // Read the fabric size in square meters.
   cout << "Enter the fabric size in square meters: ";
   cin  >> size_in_sqmeters;

   // Convert the fabric size to square yards.
   size_in_sqyards = meters_to_yards * size_in_sqmeters;

   // Display fabric size in square yards.
   cout << "The fabric size in square yards is "
        << size_in_sqyards << endl;
   return;
}
```

———————— Program Output ————————

```
Enter the fabric size in square meters: 2.0
The fabric size in square yards is 2.392
```

we convert the refinements into C++ statements (for example, step 2.1). You will be able to do this yourself as you learn more about C++.

Figure 2.2 shows the C++ program along with a sample execution (the last two lines of the figure). Don't worry about understanding the details of this program yet. We will give an overview of the main points of the program here and go into more detail in the next section.

Program Testing

The last two lines of Fig. 2.2 show one sample run of this program. But how do we know that the program result is correct? You should always examine program results carefully to be sure they make sense. In this run, a fabric size of 2.0 square meters is converted to 2.392 square yards as it should be. To verify that the program works properly, we should enter a few more test values of square meters. We really don't need to try more than a few test cases to verify that a simple program like this is correct.

EXERCISES FOR SECTION 2.1

Self-Check
1. List the steps of the software development method.
2. What would the data requirements and formulas look like for a computer program that converts a weight in pounds to a weight in kilograms?
3. What is the difference between the design and implementation stages of the software development method?
4. At which stage of the software development method is the algorithm for a solution developed?
5. What is an algorithm? How does it differ from a program?

2.2 ——— OVERVIEW OF C++

In the remainder of this chapter, we provide a description of some basic features of the C++ programming language. We begin with a discussion of the program just shown in Fig. 2.2, then we proceed to another short example.

One thing you might notice in the Metric Conversion Program is a number of lines that begin with a double slash, such as

```
// CONVERTS FABRIC MEASURES IN SQUARE METERS TO SQUARE YARDS.
```

In C++, a double slash denotes a program *comment*. A program comment is like a parenthetical remark in a sentence; its purpose is to provide supplementary information to the person reading the program. Program comments are ignored by the C++ compiler and are not translated into machine language. A comment may also be placed at the end of a program line. For example, in the line

```
float size_in_sqmeters; // input: fabric size in square meters
```

the part beginning with // is a comment.

The line beginning with #include represents a different kind of C++ statement called a *compiler directive*. A compiler directive is a statement that is processed at compilation time, when the program is translated to machine language (as opposed to execution time, when the translated program statements are executed by the CPU). The #include directive instructs the compiler to insert the indicated C++ instructions into your program in place of the directive. In this case, iostream.h is the name of a C++ library *header file* whose contents are inserted in place of the #include line during compilation. The iostream.h file is one of the many *library files* that are included with the C++ programming system. This type of file name should be enclosed by the symbol pair < >. The use of libraries can help us to *reuse* C++ code that has already been written and tested. This saves us from having to type many extra, complex lines of code. There may be many #include, and possibly other, compiler directives in each program that you write.

The next word, `main`, is the name of the *function* that designates the start of the program. It must be typed in lowercase letters and followed by a pair of parentheses. All C++ programs consist of one or more functions with the requirement that exactly one be called `main`. A function contains a collection of related statements under one name. Anything typed within the braces { } is part of the function *body*.

The main function body consists of two kinds of statements: *declaration statements* and *executable statements*. Although not required in C++, we will adopt the convention of writing declaration statements in a separate section appearing before the executable statements. The declaration statements tell the compiler what constants and variables are needed in the program. These statements are based on the problem data requirements identified earlier during the problem analysis. In our program, the conversion constant `meters_to_yards` (value is 1.196) and the variables `size_in_sqmeters` and `size_in_sqyards` are declared.

The executable statements cause some kind of action to take place when a program is executed. When an executable statement begins with the word `cout` (pronounced c - out), it causes output to be displayed to the standard output device (generally, your monitor or screen). The first such line

```
cout << "Enter the fabric size in square meters: ";
```

displays the first output line in the sample execution. This *program prompt* tells the user to type in a fabric size value in square meters. The next line

```
cin >> size_in_sqmeters;
```

causes the data value (2.0), typed by the program user from the standard input device (usually the keyboard), to be read into the variable `size_in_sqmeters`. (`cin` is pronounced c - in.) The statement

```
size_in_sqyards = meters_to_yards * size_in_sqmeters;
```

computes the equivalent fabric size in square yards by multiplying the size in square meters by 1.196; the product is stored in memory cell `size_in_sqyards`.

Finally, the statement

```
cout << "The fabric size in square yards is "
     << size_in_sqyards << endl;
```

displays the *character string* (the text enclosed in double quotes) together with the value contained in `size_in_sqyards`. The value of `size_in_sqyards` is displayed as a floating-point number, that is, a number with a decimal point and a fractional part. `endl` stands for "endline" and causes a display or printer to advance to the beginning of a new line of output. The reserved word `return` shifts control from your running program back to the operating system. The last line of the program in Fig. 2.2 is a right brace, }, denoting the end of the main function.

Some punctuation marks, or *punctuators*, for short, appear in Fig. 2.2: Double slashes begin several lines; a semicolon appears at the end of each C++ statement, sets of parentheses and braces are present; and many *pairs of special characters* such as the less-than or greater-than symbol are interspersed. As we progress through this chapter, we will provide descriptions for the use of these symbols.

Example 2.1   Figure 2.3 contains a C++ program and a sample execution of that program (the last two lines of the figure). The program displays a personalized message to the program user.

The line starting with `char` is followed by three variable names (`letter1`, `letter2`, `letter3`) used to store each letter of the nickname. The instruction

```
cin >> letter1 >> letter2 >> letter3;
```

reads the three letters `Bob` (typed by the program user) into the three variables listed with one letter per variable name. The next line

```
cout << "Hello " << letter1 << letter2 << letter3 << ".  ";
```

displays `Bob` after the message string `"Hello "`. The string ". " causes a period and two blank spaces to be printed after the third letter. Finally the last `cout` line displays the rest of the second line shown in the sample execution.

Figure 2.3   Printing a welcoming message

```
// FILE: Hello.cpp
// DISPLAYS A USER'S NICKNAME

#include <iostream.h>

void main ()
{
   // Local data ...
   char letter1, letter2, letter3;   // input: letters to display

   // Enter letters and print message.
   cout << "Enter a three letter nickname and press return: ";
   cin >> letter1 >> letter2 >> letter3;
   cout << "Hello " << letter1 << letter2 << letter3 << ".  ";
   cout << "We hope you enjoy studying C++!" << endl;
   return;
}
```
                    ———— Program Output ————
```
Enter a three letter nickname and press return: Bob
Hello Bob. We hope you enjoy studying C++!
```

■

At this point, you probably can read and understand the two sample programs, even though you do not know how to write your own programs. A property of a high-level language, such as C++, is that it tries to mimic the English language, but it also relies heavily on punctuation that must be understood and used according to the rules of the language. In the following sections, you'll learn more details about the C++ programs we've looked at so far.

Reserved Words, Identifiers, and Special Symbols

Each line of the previous programs satisfies the rules of grammar (*syntax rules*) for the C++ language. Each line contains a number of different *syntactic elements,* such as reserved words, special character symbols, and identifiers used as names for variables and constants.

The *reserved words* have a specific meaning unique to C++. They cannot be used for other purposes. The reserved words that appear in Figs. 2.2 and 2.3 are

```
const, float, char, return
```

Some symbols and symbol pairs (e.g., =, *, ;, ", { }, ( ), //, <<, >>) have a special meaning in C++, and there are specific rules governing their use. As we proceed through the text, we will encounter many more reserved words and special character symbols, and we will learn the rules for using them. Appendix B contains a complete list of reserved words.

The identifiers that appear in Figs. 2.2 and 2.3, (for example, `meters_to_yards`, `size_in_sqyards`, and `letter1`) are used as constant and variable names and are described in more detail in the next section.

PROGRAM STYLE

Use of Uppercase and Lowercase in C++ Programs

Throughout the text, issues of good *programming style* will be discussed in displays such as this one. Programming style displays will provide guidelines for improving the appearance and readability of programs. Most programs that you write will be examined or studied by someone else. A program that follows some consistent style conventions will be easier to read and understand than one that is sloppy or inconsistent. Although these conventions make it easier for humans to understand programs, they have no effect whatsoever on the computer.

C++ is a case-sensitive language; the compiler differentiates between uppercase and lowercase letters. This means that you cannot write `const` as `CONST` or `cin` as `CIN`.

Identifiers representing constant or variable names can be any mixture of uppercase and lowercase, such as `SizeInSqMeters`. In this text we use all lowercase letters with an underline symbol "_" between multiple words (e.g., `size_in_sqmeters`). Your instructor may have a different preference that will work just as well. Whatever convention you adopt you should use it consistently. Remember that C++ considers `Size_in_sqmeters` and `size_in_sqmeters` to be different identifiers, so a lack of consistency in choosing identifier names can be quite harmful. ∎

EXERCISES FOR SECTION 2.2

Self-Check
1. What is the purpose of the special character pair of symbols // ?
2. What is the purpose of a program comment?
3. What is the purpose of the #include?
4. Can reserved words be used as names of variables or constants?
5. Why is it important to use consistent programming style?

2.3 ——— DECLARATIONS OF VARIABLES AND CONSTANTS

C++ requires that we tell the compiler what variables will be used in our programs and what kind of information will be stored in these variables. This can be done using the C++ *variable declaration*. In addition, it is often convenient to associate meaningful names with special program constants, such as 1.196 in the Metric Conversion Program. This association may be done using a *constant declaration*. Both variable and constant names are considered *user-defined identifiers*, that is, names that are given by the programmer. We explain variable and constant declarations next.

A memory cell used for storing program input data or computational results is called a *variable* because the value stored in it may change (and usually does) as the program executes. The *variable declarations*

```
float size_in_sqmeters;      // input: fabric size in meters
float size_in_sqyards;       // output: fabric size in yards
```

in Fig. 2.2 give the names of two variables used to store floating-point numbers (for example, 30.0, 562.57). The variable declaration

```
char letter1, letter2, letter3;
```

in Fig. 2.3 gives the names of three variables used for storing individual characters.

The *constant declaration*

```
const float meters_to_yards = 1.196;
```

specifies that the identifier `meters_to_yards` will be associated with the program constant 1.196; the identifier `meters_to_yards` is called a *constant* and should be used in the program in place of the value 1.196. Only data values that never change (e.g., the number of square yards in a square meter is always 1.196) should be associated with an identifier that is a constant. Instructions that attempt to change the value of a constant are not legal in a C++ program.

In a variable declaration, the reserved word (for example, `float` or `char`) appearing to the left of the identifier tells the C++ compiler the *data type* of the information stored in a particular variable. For example, `float` specifies that a floating-point value (a number written with a decimal point) is to be stored in the indicated variable. The reserved word `int` declares a variable that is used for storing an integer value (a number without a decimal point). The reserved word `char` specifies a single character data type. Data types will be discussed in more detail in Section 2.7.

In a constant declaration, the reserved words `float`, `int`, and `char` indicate the type of the constant to be associated with the indicated identifier. By convention, we will put constant declarations before variable declarations.

You have quite a bit of freedom in selecting constant or variable identifiers to be used in a program. The syntactic rules are as follows:

1. An identifier should always begin with a letter.
2. An identifier must consist of letters, digits, or underscores only.
3. You cannot use a C++ reserved word as an identifier.

Some valid and invalid identifiers are listed below.

- *valid identifiers*

```
letter1, Letter1, letter2, inches, cent, CentPerInch,
cent_per_inch, hello
```

- *invalid identifiers*

```
1Letter, const, two*four, two-dimensional, Joe's, float
```

Table 2.1 summarizes the two categories of names that we have discussed thus far.

Table 2.1   Reserved Words and Identifiers Illustrated to This Point

RESERVED WORDS	CONSTANT OR VARIABLE IDENTIFIERS
const	meters_to_yards
float	size_in_sqmeters
char	size_in_sqyards
int	letter1
return	letter2
	letter3

Syntax Displays for Declarations

We are now ready to provide a more formal and precise description of the compiler directive #include and the constant and variable declarations presented so far. We do this through the use of a syntax display summarizing the form of a C++ feature. Each display also provides an example and a narrative (called an interpretation). We will continue to use syntax displays for this purpose throughout the text.

C++
SYNTAX

Compiler Directive #include

Form: #include *<filename>*

Example: #include <iostream.h>

Interpretation: This line is a compiler directive that is replaced during translation by the named C++ library header file. The library iostream.h is required in order to be able to use the special stream input/output facilities provided by cin, cout, and endl. It is stylistically preferred that compiler directives, such as #include, be listed first, but they will work as long as they appear before they are used.

Note: A compiler directive should not end with a semicolon.   ∎

C++
SYNTAX

Constant Declaration

Form: const *type constant-identifier = value;*

Example: const float pi = 3.14159;

Interpretation: The specified *value* is associated with the *constant identifier*. This *value* cannot be changed at any time by the program. More than one constant declaration may be listed. A semicolon appears at the end of each such declaration.

Note: By convention, we place constant declarations after the compiler directives and before any variable declarations in a C++ program.   ∎

C++
SYNTAX

Variable Declaration

Form: *type variable-identifier-list;*

Example: float x, y;
            int me, you;

Interpretation: One or more bytes of computer memory are allocated for each identifier in the *variable-identifier-list*. The *type* of data (float, int, etc.) to be stored in each variable is specified. Commas are used to separate the identifiers in the *variable list*. More than one list of variables may be declared; each must be terminated by a semicolon. The actual number of bytes allocated depends on the indicated type and your C++ language system. This issue will be addressed in more detail in Chapter 7. ■

PROGRAM STYLE

Choosing Identifier Names

It is very important to pick meaningful names for identifiers; meaningful identifiers make it easier to understand their purpose. For example, the identifier `salary` would be a good name for a variable used to store a person's salary; the identifiers `s` and `bagel` would be bad choices.

Identifiers may be up to 127 characters long. It is difficult to form meaningful names using fewer than three letters, but, on the other hand, excessively long identifiers are more prone to typing errors. As a reasonable rule of thumb, use names that are readable and sufficiently unique.

If you mistype an identifier, the compiler will usually detect this as a syntax error and display an *undefined identifier* error message during program translation. Sometimes, mistyped identifiers resemble other identifiers, so it is best to avoid picking names that are very similar to each other. Try not to choose two names that are identical except for their use of case because, although the compiler will be able to distinguish between them, you might inadvertently get them mixed up and attempt to use them interchangeably. ■

EXERCISES FOR SECTION 2.3

Self-Check

1. Why should the value of `pi` (3.14159) be stored in a constant?
2. Which should normally come first, the constant or variable declarations?
3. Indicate which of the identifiers below are C++ reserved words, valid constant or variable identifiers, or invalid identifiers.

main	cin	Bill	Sue's	rate	start
const	xyz123	123xyz	'MaxScores'	int	return
y=z	Prog#2	ThisIsALongOne	so_is_this_one	two-way	go

Programming

1. Write the constant and variable declarations for a program that has variables `radius`, `area`, and `circum` (all type `float`) and a constant `pi` (3.14159).

2.4 ___ EXECUTABLE STATEMENTS

A common use for a computer is to perform arithmetic computations and display the results. These operations are specified by the *executable statements* of a C++ program. Executable statements cause some kind of action to occur when a program is run. Each executable statement is translated by the C++

compiler into one or more machine language instructions, which are copied to the object file and later executed.

Programs in Memory

Before examining each kind of executable statement in Figs. 2.2 and 2.3 in detail, let's see what computer memory looks like after a program is loaded into memory (but before it executes), and then again after that program executes. Figure 2.4a shows the Metric Conversion Program and the space allocated for its variables in memory before execution. The question marks in memory cells `size_in_sqmeters` and `size_in_sqyards` indicate that these variables are undefined (value unknown) before program execution begins. During execution, the data value 2.0 is read into variable `size_in_sqyards`. After the assignment statement

```
size_in_sqyards = meters_to_yards * size_in_sqmeters;
```

executes, the variables are defined as shown in Fig. 2.4b. We will study assignment statements next.

Assignment Statements

The *assignment statement* is used in C++ to specify computations and to indicate where the results of these computations are to be stored. The assignment statement

```
size_in_sqyards = meters_to_yards * size_in_sqmeters;
```

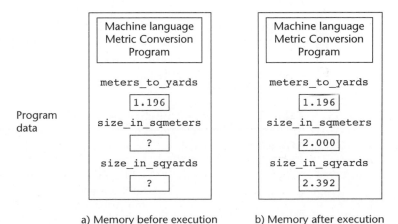

a) Memory before execution   b) Memory after execution

Figure 2.4   Memory before and after execution of a program

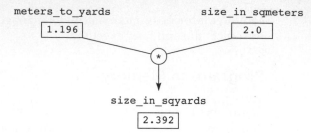

Figure 2.5   **Effect of** `size_in_sqyards = meters_to_yards *`
`size_in_sqmeters;`

in Fig. 2.2 assigns a value to the variable `size_in_sqyards`. In this case, `size_in_sqyards` is assigned the result of the multiplication (* means multiply) of the constant `meters_to_yards` by the variable `size_in_sqmeters`. This computation will produce a meaningful result only if meaningful information has been stored in both `meters_to_yards` and `size_in_sqmeters` before the assignment statement is executed. As shown in Fig. 2.5, only the variable on the left, `size_in_sqyards`, is affected by the assignment statement; the variables on the right side, `meters_to_yards` and `size_in_sqmeters`, retain their original values.

The symbol = is the *assignment operator* in C++ and should be pronounced "becomes" or "gets" or "takes the value of" rather than "equals." The general form of the assignment statement is shown in the next display.

C++
SYNTAX

Assignment Statement (arithmetic)

Form: *result = expression* ;

Example: `x = y + z + 2.0;`

Interpretation: The variable specified by *result* is assigned the value of *expression*. The previous value of *result* is destroyed. The *expression* can be a single variable, a single constant, or involve variables, constants, and the arithmetic operators listed in Table 2.2.   ■

Table 2.2   **Some Arithmetic Operators**

ARITHMETIC OPERATOR	MEANING
+	addition
−	subtraction
*	multiplication
/	division
%	modulus

Example 2.2   In C++, you can write assignment statements of the form

```
sum = sum + item;
```

where the variable sum is used on both sides of the assignment operator. This is obviously not an algebraic equation, but it illustrates a common programming practice. This statement instructs the computer to add the value of `item` to the current value of the variable `sum` and store the result back into `sum`. The previous value of `sum` is destroyed in the process, as illustrated in Fig. 2.6; however, the value of `item` is unchanged.

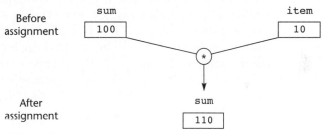

Figure 2.6   Effect of `sum = sum + item;`   ∎

Input/Output Operations

Data can be stored in memory in two different ways: through assignment to a variable or through an input statement. We have already discussed the first method. The second method, using an input statement to read data into a variable, is necessary if you want the program to manipulate different data each time it executes. Reading data into memory is called an *input operation*.

As it executes, a program performs computations and assigns new values to variables. These program results can be displayed to the program user by an *output operation*.

Among other things, the C++ libraries provide instructions for performing input and output. In this section, we will discuss how to use the input/output operations associated with the C++ identifiers `cin` and `cout` defined in the `iostream.h` library.

Program Input

The input line

```
cin >> size_in_sqmeters;
```

in Fig. 2.2 indicates that the next data value entered by the program user is received by `cin` and *directed to* the input variable `size_in_sqmeters`. The *input operator* `>>` directs the input to be placed into `size_in_sqmeters`. Where do the data come from that are stored in `size_in_sqmeters`? They are read from the *standard input device* (usually the keyboard). Consequently, the computer attempts to store in `size_in_sqmeters` whatever information is typed at the keyboard by the program user. Because `size_in_sqmeters` is declared as type `float`, the input operation will proceed correctly only if the program user types in a number. The number should contain a decimal point, but the operation will work if integer values, such as 16.0, are entered without the decimal point (as 16, for example). The program user should press the key labeled RETURN[1] after typing the number. The effect of the `cin` line is shown in Fig. 2.7. It is important to note that any blanks preceding the number entered (2.0) will be ignored during the input operation. This is true for the input of both type `int` and type `float` values.

The program in Fig. 2.3 reads a person's nickname. Each person using the program may have a different nickname; therefore, the input statement

```
cin >> letter1 >> letter2 >> letter3;
```

causes data to be directed from `cin` to each of the three variables listed. Because these variables are declared as type `char`, one character will be directed to each. Note that case is important for character data; the letters `B` and `b` are not the same. Again, the program user should press the RETURN key after typing in three characters. Figure 2.8 shows the effect of this statement when the letters `Bob` are entered.

The number of characters read by `cin` depends on the type of the variable in which the data will be stored. Only one character is read for a type `char` variable. For a type `float` variable, the program continues to read characters until it reaches a character that cannot be part of the number (usually indicated by entering a blank character or pressing the RETURN key).

How do we know when to enter the input data and what data to enter? Your program should print a *prompting message* as a signal that informs the program user what data to enter and when. (Prompting messages are dis-

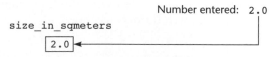

Figure 2.7   Effect of `cin >> size_in_sqmeters;`

---

[1] Many keyboards have a key marked ENTER in place of the RETURN key. On these keyboards, the names are interchangeable and have the same function.

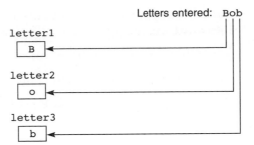

Figure 2.8   Effect of `cin >> letter1 >> letter2 >> letter3;`

cussed in more detail in the next section.) Each character entered is *echoed* on the screen and is also processed by `cin`.

<table>
<tr><td>C++
SYNTAX</td><td>

The Input Operator >>

Form: `cin` *input-list*;

Example: `cin >> age >> first_initial;`

Interpretation: The input operator >> causes data typed at the keyboard to be read into the indicated variable(s) during program execution. The *input-list* is a list of variable identifiers to which input is directed as it is entered. The program must read one data item for each variable specified in the *input-list*. The input operator symbol, represented by the *special-character-pair* >>, precedes each variable name in the *input-list*.

The order of the data must correspond to the order of the variables in the *input-list*. You must insert one or more blank characters between numeric data items, and you may insert blanks between consecutive character data items. The input operator >> skips any blanks that precede the data value to be read. Press the RETURN key after entering all data items. Note that the >> operator must appear with no blanks (or other characters) in between.   ∎

</td></tr>
</table>

Program Output

In order to see the results of a program execution we must have some way of specifying what variable values should be displayed. In Fig. 2.2, the line

```
cout << "The fabric size in square yards is " << size_in_sqyards
     << endl;
```

displays a line of program output containing two items: the character string `"The fabric ... is: "` and the value of `size_in_sqyards`. A *string* is a sequence of characters enclosed in double quotes; the characters inside the quotes are printed, but the quotes are not. The data on the right are directed into `cout` via the operator `<<`. This causes the line

```
The fabric size in square yards is 2.392
```

to be displayed. In Fig. 2.3, the line

```
cout << "Hello " << letter1 << letter2 << letter3 << ".  ";
```

displays

```
Hello Bob.
```

In this case, three variable values are printed between the strings `"Hello "` and `".   "`.

Finally, the lines

```
cout << "Enter the fabric size in square meters: ";
cout << "Enter a three letter nickname and press return: ";
```

in Figs. 2.2 and 2.3, respectively, display prompts or *prompting messages*. You should always display a prompting message just before a `cin` line to remind the program user to enter data. The prompt should always provide a description of the data to be entered, for example, `fabric size in square meters`, `account balance in dollars and cents`, or `three letter nickname`. Failure to precede each `cin` line with a prompt will leave the program user with no idea that the program is waiting for data or what data to enter when the `cin` line is executed.

The *cursor* is a moving place marker that indicates the next position on the screen where information will be displayed. Normally, the cursor moves from one position to the next along the same line as information is displayed. This is often desirable after a prompt so that the response will appear immediately following. It is also sometimes desirable, when we use more than one `cout` line, to display a single line (as in the Hello Program). But there are many times when we would like the cursor to be advanced to the start of the next line on the screen. This is accomplished by inserting `<<  endl` at the end of a `cout` line.

Example 2.3   **Inserting Blank Lines**

The lines

```
cout << "The fabric size in square yards is " << size_in_sqyards
     << endl << endl;
cout << "Metric conversion completed." << endl;
```

display

```
The fabric size in square yards is 2.392

Metric conversion completed.
```

A blank line occurred because of the two `endl`s in succession. Typing `endl` always causes the cursor to be advanced to the next line. If there is nothing between the two `endl`s, a blank line appears in the program output. It is wise to get in the habit of inserting `endl` after your last `cout` statement to ensure that anything displayed or typed to the screen immediately following your program run will appear beginning at the left margin on the next line. ∎

C++
SYNTAX

The Output Operator <<

Form: cout *output-list;*

Example: cout << "My height in inches is " << height << endl;

Interpretation: The *output-list* is a list of variables, constants, or strings, each of which must be preceded by the output operator. The output operator displays the value of the item that follows it. Each value is displayed in the order in which it appears in *output-list*. An `endl` at the end of the *output-list* advances the cursor to the next line. A string is printed without the quotes.

If no `endl` appears, the cursor does not advance to the next line, even after completing the requested display. It will remain at the position just after the last character that was output. This is desirable only if a short reply is expected after a prompting message. ∎

The two `cout` lines

```
cout << "The fabric size in square yards is ";
cout << size_in_sqyards << endl;
```

display the same output as the single `cout` line

```
cout << "The fabric size in square yards is "
     << size_in_sqyards << endl;
```

It is generally more convenient to use the latter form.

EXERCISES FOR SECTION 2.4

Self-Check

1. Show the output displayed by the program lines below when the data entered are 5.0 and 7.0.

```
cout << "Enter two numbers: ";
cin >> a >> b;
a = a + 5.0;
b = 3.0 * b;
cout << "a = " << a << endl;
cout << "b = " << b << endl;
```

2. Show the contents of memory before and after the execution of the program lines shown in Self-Check Exercise 1.

3. Show the output displayed by the lines below.

```
cout << "My name is: ";
cout << "Doe, Jane" << endl;
cout << "I live in ";
cout << "Ann Arbor, MI ";
cout << "and my zip code is " << 48109;
```

Programming
1. Write the C++ instructions that first ask a user to type three numbers then read the three user responses into the variables `first`, `second`, and `third`.
2. Write a C++ statement that displays the value of x as indicated in the line below.

The value of x is _____

3. Write a program that will ask the user to enter the radius of a circle and will compute and display the circle's area and circumference. Use the formulas

$$area = \pi r^2$$
$$circumference = 2\pi r$$

where r is radius and π is the constant `pi`: 3.14159.

2.5 ——— RECAPITULATION: THE GENERAL FORM OF A C++ PROGRAM

The programs shown so far have the general form described in Fig. 2.9. Each begins with optional comments that identify the name of the file in which the program is stored along with a brief program description.

The identifier `main` is required; it signifies the start of a program. The symbol { separates the line `main ()` from the rest of the main function body.

Figure 2.9   General form of a C++ program

```
// FILE: filename
// PROGRAM DESCRIPTION

#include directives

main ()
{
    constant declarations
    variable declarations

    executable statements
}
```

Every constant or variable identifier used in a program must be declared exactly once in the declaration section. All constant and variable declarations must appear before they are used. More than one constant may be declared, and there may be more than one variable list. The comma separates identifiers in a variable list. A semicolon is used to terminate a C++ statement. The executable statement section contains the statements that are translated into machine language and eventually executed. The executable statements we have looked at so far consist of statements that perform computations and input/output operations. The last line of the main function must be a closing brace, }.

A C++ statement can extend over more than one line. For example, the constant and variable declarations can start on one line and finish on the next. A statement that extends over more than one line should not be split in the middle of an identifier, a reserved word, a number, or a string.

PROGRAM
STYLE

Use of Blank Space

The consistent and careful use of blank spaces can significantly enhance the style of a program. A blank space is required between words in a program line (for instance, between `const`, `float`, and `meters_to_yards` in Fig. 2.3).

The compiler ignores extra blanks between words and symbols. You may insert space to improve the style and appearance of a program. As illustrated in Figs. 2.2 and 2.3, you should always leave a blank space after a comma and before and after operators such as `*`, `-`, `=`, and `<<` or `>>`. Remember to indent each line of the program except for the braces that mark the beginning and end of `main`. All lines between the `{ }` are indented three or more spaces. Finally, use blank lines between sections of the program.

We take all of these measures for the sole purpose of improving the style—and hence the clarity—of our programs. Stylistic issues have no effect whatsoever on the meaning of the program as far as the computer is concerned; however, they can make it easier for people to read and understand the program.

Be careful not to insert blank spaces where they do not belong. For example, there cannot be a space between the characters `<` and `<` when they form the output operator `<<`. Also, the identifier `start_salary` cannot be written as `start salary`. ∎

PROGRAM
STYLE

Comments in Programs

The programs in Figs. 2.2 and 2.3 contain some English phrases that are preceded by a double slash. These phrases are *program comments*; they are intended to make the program easier to understand by describing the purpose of the program (see the second comment line in Figs. 2.2 and 2.3). Comments are also used to describe the use of identifiers (see the comments in the variable declarations section) and the purpose of each program step (see the comments in the executable section). As shown in Fig. 2.2, a comment can appear by itself on a program line or at the end of a line after a statement. Comments are an important part of the *documentation* of a program because they help others read and understand the program. The compiler, however, ignores comments; they are not translated into machine language.

The double slash // can be used only when a comment fits on a single line or when the remainder of a line is a comment. The double slash marks the beginning of a comment that is then assumed to terminate at the end of the line. Another form of comment, the slash-asterisk combination /*   */, can stand alone or can be embedded in the middle of a statement. The slash-asterisk combination encloses a comment, marking both the beginning and the end as shown in Fig. 2.10. A comment that begins with /* may extend over any number of lines until it closes with */. The /* and */ are additional examples of special character pairs; no character, not even a blank, can come between the * and /. The two next displays describe the use and syntax of comments.

Figure 2.10   Two multiline comments using both styles

```
// FILE: MyProg1.cpp
// THIS PROGRAM DOES LOTS OF THINGS AND NEEDS SEVERAL LINES OF
//     EXPLANATION

/* Here are the
      several lines
         of explanation

   Written by Dara and Shelley Friedman
   June 1, 1993
*/
```

C++ SYNTAX

Comment

Form: // *comment*   or   /* *comment* */

Example: // This is a comment
           /* and so is this */

Interpretation: A double slash indicates the start of a comment. Alternatively, the symbol pair /* may be used to mark the beginning of a comment that is terminated by the symbol pair */. Comments are listed with the program but are otherwise ignored by the C++ compiler.

PROGRAM STYLE

Using Comments

Comments make a program more readable by describing the purpose of the program and by describing the use of each identifier. For example, the comment shown in the declaration

```
float size_in_sqmeters;      // input: fabric size in square meters
```

describes the use of variable `size_in_sqmeters`.

Also, you should place comments within the executable section to describe the purpose of each major algorithm step. Such comments should describe what the step does rather than simply restate the step in English. For example, the comment

```
// Converts fabric measures in square meters to square yards.
size_in_sqyards = meters_to_yards * size_in_sqmeters;
```

is more descriptive and hence preferable to

```
// Multiply meters_to_yards by size_in_sqmeters and save the
//     result in size_in_sqyards.

size_in_sqyards = meters_to_yards * size_in_sqmeters;
```

The C++ code for each step in the initial algorithm should be preceded by a comment that summarizes the purpose of the algorithm step. Carefully chosen identifier names should provide sufficient information about the individual statements, thereby eliminating the need to comment every line.

Each program you write should begin with a header section that consists of a series of comments specifying

- the name of the file in which the program is saved,
- a brief description of what the program does,
- the programmer's name,
- the date of the current version.

If you write the program for a class assignment, you should also list the class identification and your instructor's name.

```
/*
   FILE: assignmt.cpp
   This program reads a value in square meters and converts it to
   square yards.

   Programmer:  Donna Chrupcala    Date completed: May 15, 1993
   Instructor:  Dr. Elliot Koffman  Class: CIS61
*/
```

EXERCISES FOR SECTION 2.5

Self-Check   1. Explain what is wrong with the comments below.

```
// This is a comment? */

/* How about this one /* it seems like a comment */ doesn't it? */
```

2. Why are comments important in a computer program? When should they be used?
3. Correct the syntax errors in the program below, and rewrite it so that it follows our style conventions. What does each statement of your corrected program do? What values are printed?

```
include iostream.h FLOAT x, y, z:
MAIN() {   y = 15.0,
z= y + 3.5;   y + z = x;
cout >> x; y; z; }
```

2.6 ——— ABSTRACTION: DATA TYPES AND EXPRESSIONS

An *abstraction* is a model or simplification of a physical object or concept. We frequently use abstractions in problem-solving and programming. For example, in problem-solving, we sometimes make simplifying assumptions that enable us to solve a limited version of a more general problem.

Abstraction is an important concept in programming. The programs that we write present an abstract view of real world entities, their properties or *attributes*, and a collection of meaningful operations that can be performed on them. These programs also describe any relationships among these entities that might be relevant to the problem we are trying to solve. In fact, relevance is the key here, for the software development method described earlier is a step-by-step process of focusing on what we need to know, ignoring irrelevant details. At each *level of refinement*, we continue to add detail until we finally reach a level with which we are sufficiently comfortable to write our program. Thus, programming is a process of building multiple levels of abstraction; we begin with abstractions related to *problem domain* entities and end with those related to programming language entities.

We use abstraction in problem-solving throughout this text, introducing, in virtually every chapter, features of C++ that are useful in the abstraction process. C++ has a wealth of such features. In the following material, we introduce some of the most elementary *data abstractions*, the *basic* or predefined C++ data types.

float Data Type

A *data type* is a set of values and a set of operations on those values. A *basic data type* in C++ is a data type that is predefined (for example, float, int, char). In C++, we use the basic data type float as an abstraction for the real numbers (in the mathematical sense), or numbers that contain a decimal point. The data type float is an abstraction because it does not include all the real numbers. Some real numbers are too large or too small, and some cannot be represented precisely because of the finite size of a memory cell (more on this in Chapter 7). However, we can certainly represent enough of the real numbers in C++ to carry out most of the computations we wish to perform with sufficient accuracy.

The arithmetic operators (+, −, *, /) that you are accustomed to using as well as the assignment operator (=) can be performed on type float data in C++. We can also use cin and cout with type float data.

A type float constant is a number that contains a decimal point (such as 0.112, 456.0, 123.456). A type *float* constant may include a *scale factor*, the letter e (or E) followed by an optional sign and an integer (e.g., 0.112e3, 456.0e−2). The scale factor may also follow a string of digits without a decimal point (for example, 123e6 and 123.0e6 are equivalent floating-point numbers). A scale factor is interpreted to mean multiply the number before the letter e by 10 raised to the power appearing after the letter e (for example, 0.112e3 is 112.0; 456.0e−2 is 4.56; in general, $XXXeYY$ is $XXX \times 10^{YY}$). A float constant may be preceded by a + or − sign when it appears in a program. Table 2.3 shows examples of valid and invalid float constants.

The last valid constant in the table, 1.15e−3, has the same value as 1.15×10^{-3} in normal scientific notation, where the exponent −3 causes the decimal point to be moved left three digits. A positive exponent causes the decimal point to be moved to the right; the + sign may be omitted when the exponent is positive.

Table 2.3   Valid and Invalid Type float **Constants**

VALID float CONSTANTS		INVALID float CONSTANTS
3.14159		150 (no decimal point)
.005		245e (no exponent)
12345.		−15e−0.3 (0.3 is invalid exponent)
15.0e−04	(0.0015)	12.5e.3 (.3 is invalid exponent)
2.345e2	(234.5)	
12E+6	(12000000)	
1.15e−3	(0.00115)	

int Data Type

Another standard data type (or data abstraction) in C++ is type int, which is used to represent the integer numbers (for example, –77, 0, 999, +999). Because of the finite size of a memory cell, not all integers can be represented. The size varies from system to system, but a range of –32768 or –(2^{16}) to 32767 or (2^{16}) – 1 is fairly typical.

float and int data types differ in one basic way: Type float data represent values with a decimal point and a fractional part, whereas type int data represent integral values only. For this reason, type int data are more restricted in their use. We often use them to represent a count of items (for example, the number of children in a family) because a count must always be an integer.

We can use four of the arithmetic operators listed in Table 2.2 (+, –, *, /) and the assignment, input, and output operators with type int data as well as with data of type float. The *modulus* operator, %, may be used only with type int operands. Because these operands have no fractional part, some care must be exercised in the use of the division and modulus operators. For now, you need simply remember the descriptions of these operators given in the next display.

Division and Modulus Operators with Integer Operands

1. When used with two integer operands, the division operator always yields the *integral part* of the result of dividing its first operand by its second, and truncates the fractional part. If either or both of the operands are negative, the sign of the remainder is implementation-dependent. As can be expected, division by zero is undefined.

   $$15 / 3 = 5 \qquad\qquad 15 / 0 \text{ is undefined}$$
   $$15 / 2 = 7 \qquad\qquad -19 / 5 = -3 \text{ or } -4$$
   $$0 / 15 = 0$$

2. The modulus operator must be used only with integer operands and always yields the *integer remainder* of the result of dividing its first operand by its second. If either one of the operands is negative, the sign of the result is machine-dependent. As with /, the result is undefined when the second operand of % is zero. For example,

   $$7 \% 2 = 1 \qquad\qquad -5 \% 4 = +1 \text{ or } -1$$
   $$299 \% 100 = 99 \qquad 15 \% -7 = +1 \text{ or } -1$$
   $$49 \% 5 = 4 \qquad\qquad 15 \% 0 \text{ is undefined}$$

The magnitude of $m \% n$ must always be less than the divisor n; for example, if m is positive, the value of $m \% 100$ must be between 0 and 99. The formula

$$m = (m / n) * n + (m \% n)$$

defines the relationship between the operators / and % for a dividend of m and a divisor of n (not equal to zero). We can see that this formula holds for two of the examples discussed earlier by substituting values for m, n, m / $n,$ and m % n. In the first line below, m is 7 and n is 2; in the second line below, m is 299 and n is 100.

```
7 = (7 / 2) * 2 + (7 % 2) = 3 * 2 + 1 = 7
299 = (299 / 100) * 100 + (299 % 100) = 2 * 100 + 99 = 299
```

Example 2.4 The following examples illustrate some of the computations shown in the previous display, using long division. The top row shows that the remainder (1, 2, and −2) is lost when the / operator is used; the bottom row shows that the quotient (3, 2, and 9) is lost when the % operator is used.

Using Integer Data

The next case study provides an example of manipulating type `int` data in C++.

CASE STUDY: FINDING THE VALUE OF A COIN COLLECTION

Problem Statement

Your little sister has been saving nickels and pennies for quite a while. Because she is getting tired of lugging her piggy bank with her whenever she goes to the store, she would like to trade in her collection for dollar bills and some change. In order to do this, she would like to know the value of her coin collection in dollars and cents.

Program Analysis

In order to solve this problem, we must be given the count of nickels and the count of pennies in the collection. The first step is to determine the total value of the collection in cents. Once we have this figure, we can do integer division using 100 as the divisor to get the dollar value; the remainder of this division will be the loose change that she should receive. In the data requirements below, we list the total value in cents (`total_cents`) as a *program variable* because it is needed as part of the computation process but is not a required problem output.

DATA REQUIREMENTS

Problem Input

nickels (int)   — the count of nickels
pennies (int)   — the count of pennies

Problem Output

dollars (int)   — the number of dollars she should receive
change (int)   — the loose change she should receive

Additional Program Variable

total_cents (int)   — the total number of cents

FORMULAS

one dollar equals 100 pennies
one nickel equals 5 pennies

Program Design

The algorithm is straightforward and is presented next.

INITIAL ALGORITHM

1. Read in the count of nickels and pennies.
2. Compute the total value in cents.
3. Find the value in dollars and loose change.
4. Display the value in dollars and loose change.

Steps 2 and 3 require further refinement.

Step 2 Refinement

2.1. total_cents is 5 times nickels plus pennies.

Step 3 Refinement

3.1. dollars is the integer quotient of total_cents and 100.
3.2. change is the integer remainder of total_cents and 100.

Program Implementation

The program is shown in Fig. 2.11. The statement

```
total_cents = 5 * nickels + pennies;
```

implements algorithm step 2.1. The statements

```
dollars = total_cents / 100;
change = total_cents % 100;
```

use the / and % operators to implement algorithm steps 3.1 and 3.2, respectively.

Figure 2.11   Value of a coin collection

```
// FILE: Coins.cpp
// DETERMINES THE VALUE OF A COIN COLLECTION

#include <iostream.h>

void main ()
{
    // Local data ...
    int pennies;           // input: count of pennies
    int nickels;           // input: count of nickels
    int dollars;           // output: value of coins in dollars
    int change;            // output: value of coins in cents
    int total_cents;       // total cents represented

    // Read in the count of nickels and pennies.
    cout << "Enter the number of nickels and press return: ";
    cin >> nickels;
    cout << "Enter the number of pennies and press return: ";
    cin >> pennies;

    // Compute the total value in cents.
    total_cents = 5 * nickels + pennies;

    // Find the value in dollars and change.
    dollars = total_cents / 100;
    change = total_cents % 100;

    // Display the value in dollars and change.
    cout << "Your collection is worth " << dollars << " dollars and "
         << change << " cents." << endl;
    return;
}
```
─────────── Program Output ───────────
```
Enter the number of nickels and press return: 30
Enter the number of pennies and press return: 77

Your collection is worth 2 dollars and 27 cents.
```

Program Testing

To test this program, try running it with a combination of nickels and pennies that yields an exact dollar amount with no change left over. For example, 35 nickels and 25 pennies should yield a value of 2 dollars and no cents. Then increase and decrease the amount of pennies by 1 (26 and 24 pennies) to make sure that these cases are also handled properly.

Type of an Expression Involving Integer and Float Data

The data type of each variable must be specified in its declaration, but how does C++ determine the type of an expression? The data type of an expression depends on the type of its operands. For example, the expression

```
ace + bandage
```

is type `int` if both `ace` and `bandage` are type `int`; otherwise, it is type `float`. A C++ expression is type `int` only if all its operands are type `int`, and a C++ expression is type `float` if any of its operands is type `float`. For example, `5 / 2` is type `int`, but `5 / 2.0` is type `float`. This latter expression, containing an integer and a floating-point operand, is called a *mixed-type expression*. The type of a mixed-type expression involving integer and floating-point data must be `float`.

Expressions with Multiple Operators

In our programs so far, most expressions have involved a single operator; however, expressions with multiple operators are common in C++. To understand and write expressions with multiple operators, we must know the C++ rules for evaluating expressions. For example, in the expression `x + y / z`, is + performed before /, or vice versa? Is the expression `x / y * z` evaluated as `(x / y) * z` or `x / (y * z)`? Verify for yourself that the order of evaluation does make a difference by substituting some simple values for `x, y`, and `z`. In both these expressions, the / operator is evaluated first; the reasons for this are explained in the C++ rules for expression evaluation, which follow. These rules are based on standard algebraic rules that you have used for years.

Knowledge of these rules will help you understand how C++ evaluates expressions. Use parentheses as needed to specify the order of evaluation. Often, it is a good idea to use extra parentheses to document clearly the order of operator evaluation in complicated expressions. For example, the expression

```
x * y * z + a / b - c * d
```

> **Rules for Expression Evaluation**
>
> a) All parenthesized subexpressions must be evaluated separately. Nested parenthesized subexpressions must be evaluated inside out, with the innermost subexpression evaluated first.
>
> b) *The operator precedence rule:* Operators in the same subexpression are evaluated in the following order:
>
> | | |
> |---|---|
> | *, /, % | first |
> | +, − | last |
>
> c) *The left associative rule:* Operators in the same subexpression and at the same precedence level (such as + and −) are evaluated left to right.
>
> d) *Remember:* In an assignment statement, the entire expression to the right of the assignment operator is evaluated first before being assigned to the variable on the left.

can be written in a more readable form using parentheses:

```
(x * y * z) + (a / b) − (c * d)
```

Example 2.5   The formula for the area of a circle

$$a = \pi r^2$$

may be written in C++ as

```
area =  pi * radius * radius;
```

where `pi` is the constant 3.14159. Figure 2.12 shows the *evaluation tree* for this formula. In this tree, the lines connect each operand with its operator. The order of operator evaluation is shown by the number to the left of each operator; the rules that apply are shown to the right.

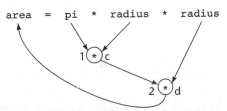

Figure 2.12   Evaluation tree for `area = pi * radius * radius;`   ■

Example 2.6   The formula for the average velocity, *v*, of a particle traveling on a line between points p_1 and p_2 in time t_1 to t_2 is

$$v = \frac{p_2 - p_1}{t_2 - t_1} \; .$$

This formula can be written and evaluated in C++ as shown in Fig. 2.13.

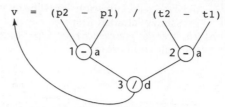

Figure 2.13   Evaluation tree for `v = (p2 - p1) / (t2 - t1);` ∎

Example 2.7   Consider the expression

```
z - (a + b / 2) + w * y
```

containing integer variables only. The parenthesized subexpression `(a + b / 2)` is evaluated first (Rule a) beginning with `b / 2` (Rule b). Once the value of `b / 2` is determined, it can be added to `a` to obtain the value of `(a + b / 2)`. Next, the multiplication operation is performed (Rule b) and the value for `w * y` is determined. Then, the value of `(a + b / 2)` is subtracted from `z` (Rule c). Finally, this result is added to `w * y` (see Fig. 2.14).

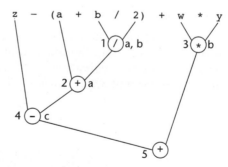

Figure 2.14   Evaluation tree for `z - (a + b / 2) + w * y;` ∎

Mixed-Type Assignment Statement

When an assignment statement is executed, the expression is first evaluated, and then the result is assigned to the variable listed to the left of the assignment operator (=). C++ allows any mixture of type `float` or `int` in such an assignment expression. This kind of flexibility can be very useful, but it is also quite error-prone. Be careful that you say what you mean. All assignment statements below are valid, assuming a, b, and x to be of type `float` and m and n to be of type `int`.

```
a = 10;     // the constant 10 (int) is converted to 10.0 (float)
            //     and then assigned to a
b = 5;      // 5 is converted to 5.0 and then assigned to b
m = 3.0;    // 3.0 is converted to 3 and then assigned to m
n = 2.5;    // 2.5 is converted to 2 and then assigned to n
x = m / n;  // the division result of 1 (type int) is converted
            //     to 1.0 and assigned to x
```

In the next to last statement above, the decimal portion of 2.5 is lost when it is assigned to the integer variable n. This may not always be desirable, and care must be taken because, according to C++, this is not an error. In the last statement, the expression m / n evaluates to the integer 1 because both operands, m = 3 and n = 2 are of type int. This value is converted to type `float` (1.0) before it is stored in x.

Example 2.8   The evaluation of multiple operator expressions containing both type `int` and `float` values can be quite tricky to follow, even though the principle of evaluation is quite simple—the final result is determined by examining the *intermediate results* of each operand-operator-operand subexpression as shown in Fig. 2.15, with x = 5.5 (type `float`), k = 5 (type `int`), and m (type `int`).

   The *operand-operator-operand triple* k / 2 is evaluated first (Rule b). Because both k and 2 are of type int, the result is of type int as well (k / 2 = 2).

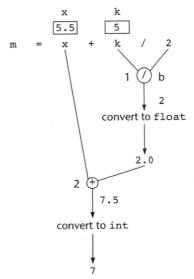

Figure 2.15   Evaluation tree for m = x + k / 2;

Next, the triple x + 2 is evaluated. Because x is type float, 2 is first converted to 2.0 so that the triple 5.5 + 2.0 is evaluated. The result 7.5 is then truncated to 7 before it is assigned to type *int* variable m.

There are several ways to avoid having to deal with complicated expressions, but perhaps the easiest is to split such computations into simpler ones. Thus if j were another type int variable we might replace the statement just illustrated with two statements:

```
j = k / 2;
m = x + j;
```

We will see others ways to help us cope with complicated expressions in Chapter 7.

Writing Mathematical Formulas in C++

There are two problem areas in writing a mathematical formula in C++: One concerns multiplication, and the other concerns division. Multiplication can often be implied in a mathematical formula by writing the two items to be multiplied next to each other; for example, $a = bc$. In C++, however, you must always use the * operator to indicate multiplication, as in

```
a = b * c
```

The other difficulty arises in formulas involving division. We normally write the numerator and denominator on separate lines:

$$m = \frac{y - b}{x - a}$$

In C++, all assignment statements must be written in a linear form. Consequently, parentheses are often needed to separate the numerator from the denominator and to clearly indicate the order of evaluation of the operators in the expression. The formula above would be written in C++ as

```
m = (y - b) / (x - a);
```

Example 2.9   This example illustrates how several mathematical formulas can be written in C++.

Mathematical Formula	C++ Expression
1. $b^2 - 4ac$	b * b - 4 * a * c
2. $a + b - c$	a + b - c
3. $\dfrac{a + b}{c + d}$	(a + b) / (c + d)

4. $\dfrac{1}{1+y^2}$ `1 / (1 + y * y)`

5. $ax-(b+c)$ `a * (-(b + c))`   ∎

The points illustrated are summarized as follows:

- Always specify multiplication explicitly by using the operator * where needed (1, 4).
- Use parentheses when required to control the order of operator evaluation (3, 4).
- Never write two arithmetic operators in succession; they must be separated by an operand or an open parenthesis (5).

Unary Minus

Formula 5 in Example 2.9 uses a unary minus to negate the value of (b + c) before performing the multiplication. The *unary minus* has a higher precedence than the subtraction operator. It has only one operand.

char Data Type

Another standard data type in C++ is type `char`. Type `char` variables can be used to store any single character value. A type `char` *constant* must be enclosed in single quotes (for example, `'A'`); however, you don't use quotes when you type character data at a keyboard. When `cin` reads character data into a type `char` variable, the next nonblank character you enter at the keyboard is stored in that variable. Any blanks that you enter (by pressing the space bar) preceding this nonblank will be ignored. This is consistent with mechanics for reading numeric values, when leading blanks (those that precede the number) are ignored.

Example 2.10   The program in Fig. 2.16 first reads and echoes three characters entered at the keyboard. Next, it prints them in reverse order enclosed in asterisks. Each character is stored in a variable of type `char`; the character value `'*'` is associated with the character constant `border`.

The line

```
cout << border << third << second << first << border << endl;
```

displays the three characters in reverse order. As shown in the program output, each character value takes up a single print position. Blanks between the letters are ignored (see Program Output #2).

Figure 2.16   Program for Example 2.10

```
// FILE: Mirror.cpp
// READS 3 CHARACTERS AND DISPLAYS THEM IN REVERSE ORDER

#include <iostream.h>

void main ()
{
   // Local data ...
   const char border = '*';         // encloses 3 characters
   char first, second, third;       // input/output: 3 characters

   cout << "Enter 3 characters: ";
   cin  >> first >> second >> third;
   cout << border << third << second << first << border << endl;
   return;
}
```

———————   Program Output #1   ———————

```
Enter 3 characters: EBK
*KBE*
```

———————   Program Output #2   ———————

```
Enter 3 characters: D G   F
*FGD*
```

In Fig. 2.16, the string "Enter 3 characters: " is displayed as a prompt. In this example and in other earlier examples, we have used strings enclosed in double quotes, " ", as prompts and to clarify program output. Only single characters (enclosed in single quotes), not strings, can be stored in type char variables; we will see how to process strings later in the text.

In addition to the characters that we are accustomed to seeing on the screen and keyboard, there are additional characters in the C++ character set. These characters, three of which are shown in Table 2.4, are represented using the *escape symbol* '\', the backslash character.

As shown in Table 2.4, the backslash, followed immediately by a particular letter, represents a single, nonprintable character. When written in a program

Table 2.4   Some Escape Sequences

CHARACTER	MEANING
\a	alert (bell)
\n	newline
\t	horizontal tab

output line, these characters cause a specific action to occur. Example 2.11 demonstrates the use of these characters in a slightly revised version of the Hello Program, which appeared in its original form in Fig. 2.3.   ∎

Example 2.11   The Hello Program, Slightly Revised

The only change in this version of the program, shown in Fig. 2.17, from the original is in the line

```
cout << "\tHello " << letter1 << letter2 << letter3 << ".\n\a\a";
```

This line now causes the following things to happen:

- the character \t causes a tab to be placed in the output line before the string "Hello ";
- the three letters just entered, Bob, followed by a period, are displayed;
- the character \n causes the display cursor to be placed at the beginning of the next line;
- the two consecutive occurrences of \a cause two beeps to be heard.

Figure 2.17   Printing a welcoming message (revised)

```
// FILE: HelloSpc.cpp
// DISPLAYS THE USER'S NICKNAME

#include <iostream.h>

void main ()
{
   // LOCAL DATA ...
   char letter1, letter2, letter3; // input: letters to display

   // Enter letters and print message.
   cout << "Enter a three letter nickname and press return: ";
   cin >> letter1 >> letter2 >> letter3;
   cout << "\tHello " << letter1 << letter2 << letter3
        << ".\n\a\a";
   cout << "We hope you enjoy studying C++!\n";
   return;
}
```
——————— Program Output ———————
```
Enter a three letter nickname and press return: Bob
   Hello Bob.
We hope you enjoy studying C++!
```

∎

Ordinal Types

The data types `int` and `char` have one property in common that is not shared by the data type `float`. We can list all of the values of these types that can be represented in a particular version of C++. However, we cannot list all of the values of type `float` that may be represented. For example, if we attempt to list all the floating-point numbers and we have 3.14 and 3.15 in our list, then someone could say that we omitted 3.141, 3.142, and so on. If we include these numbers, then someone could say that we left out 3.1411, 3.1412, and so on. A data type whose values can be listed is called an *ordinal type*. We will examine another kind of ordinal type called an enumeration in Chapter 7.

EXERCISES FOR SECTION 2.6

Self-Check

1. Indicate which of these constants are legal in C++ and which are not. Identify the data type of each valid value.

```
15    'XYZ'    '*'    $    25.123    15.    -999    .123    'x'
"x"    '9'    '-5'    'x"   $4.79    6.3E-2          .0986E3.0
```

2. Evaluate the following expressions with 7 and 22 as operands:

   a. 22 / 7   7 / 22   22 % 7   7 % 22

   Repeat this exercise for the pairs of integers:

   b. 15, 16   c. 3, 23   d. -4, 16

3. Show that the formula $m = (m / n) * n + (m \% n)$ holds when $m = 45$ and $n = 5$ (both of type int).
4. Draw the evaluation trees for the expressions below.

```
1.8 * celsius + 32.0
(salary - 5000.00) * 0.20 + 1425.00
```

5. Given the declarations

```
const float pi = 3.14159;
const int max_i = 1000;
float x, y;
int a, b, i;
```

indicate which C++ statements below are valid and find the value of each valid statement. Also, indicate which are invalid and why. Assume that a is 3, b is 4, and y is -1.0.

```
a. i = a % b;              b. i = (max_i - 990) / a;
c. i = a % y;              d. i = (990 - max_i) / a;
e. i = pi * a;             f. x = pi * y;
g. x = pi / y;             h. i = (max_i - 990) % a;
i. x = a % (a / b);        j. i = a % 0;
k. i = b / 0;              l. i = a % (max_i - 990);
```

    m. x = a / y;   n. i = a % (990 - max_i);
    o. x = a / b;

6. What values are assigned by the legal statements in Exercise 5 above, assuming a is 5, b is 2, and y is 2.0?

7. Assume that you have the following variable declarations:

   ```
   int color, lime, straw, yellow, red, orange;
   float black, white, green, blue, purple, crayon;
   ```

   Evaluate each of the statements below given the values: color is 2, black is 2.5, crayon is –1.3, straw is 1, red is 3, and purple is 0.3e+1.

   a. white = color * 2.5 / purple;
   b. green = color / purple;
   c. orange = color / red;
   d. blue = (color + straw) / (crayon + 0.3);
   e. lime = red / color + red % color;
   f. purple = straw / red * color;

8. Let a, b, c, and x be the names of four type float variables, and let i, j, and k be the names of three type int variables. Each of the statements below contains a violation of the rules for forming arithmetic expressions. Rewrite each statement so that it is consistent with these rules.

   a. x = 4.0 a * c;   b. a = ac;
   c. i = 2 * -j;   d. k = 3(i + j);
   e. x = 5a / bc;   f. i = 5j3;

Programming 1. Write an assignment statement that might be used to implement the equation below in C++.

$$q = \frac{ka(t_1 - t_2)}{b}.$$

2. Write a program that stores the values 'x', '0', and 1.345e10 in separate variables. Your program should input the three values as data items.

3. Extend the program in Fig. 2.11 to handle dimes and quarters as well as nickels and pennies. ∎

2.7 ____ INTERACTIVE MODE, BATCH MODE, AND DATA FILES

There are two basic modes of computer operation: batch and interactive. The programs that we have written so far are intended to be run in *interactive mode*. In this mode, the program user can interact with the program and enter data while the program is executing. In batch mode, all data must be supplied beforehand as the program user cannot interact with the program while it is executing. Batch mode is an option on most computers. If you use batch mode, then you must prepare a batch data file before executing your program. On a timeshared or personal computer, a batch data file is created and saved in the same way as a program or source file.

Input Redirection

Figure 2.18 shows the Metric Conversion Program rewritten as a batch program. We assume that the input is associated with a batch data file instead of the keyboard. In most systems this can be done relatively easily through *input/output redirection* using operating system commands. For example, in the

Figure 2.18   Batch version of Metric Conversion Program

```
// FILE: Metbatch.cpp
// CONVERTS FABRIC MEASURES IN SQUARE METERS TO SQUARE YARDS

#include <iostream.h>

void main ()
{
   // Local data ...
   const float meters_to_yards = 1.196; // conversion constant
   float size_in_sqmeters; // input: fabric size in square meters
   float size_in_sqyards;  // output: fabric size in square yards

   // Read in fabric size in square meters.
   cin >> size_in_sqmeters;
   cout << "The fabric size in square meters is "
        << size_in_sqmeters << endl;

   // Convert the fabric size to square yards.
   size_in_sqyards = meters_to_yards * size_in_sqmeters;

   // Display the fabric size in square yards.
   cout << "The fabric size in square yards is "
        << size_in_sqyards << endl;
   return;
}
```
───────── Program Output ─────────
```
The fabric size in square meters is 2
The fabric size in square yards is 2.392
```

UNIX and MS-DOS operating systems, you can instruct your program to take its input from file `mydata` instead of the keyboard, by placing the symbols

```
< mydata
```

at the end of the command line that causes your compiled and linked program to execute. If you normally used the UNIX or MS-DOS command line

```
metric
```

to execute this program, your new command line would be
```
metric < mydata
```

PROGRAM STYLE

Echo Prints versus Prompts

In Fig. 2.18, the statement

```
cin >> size_in_sqmeters;
```

reads the value of `size_in_sqmeters` from the first (and only) line of the data file. Because the program input comes from a data file, there is no need to precede this statement with a prompting message. Instead we follow `cin` with the statement

```
cout << "The fabric size in square meters is " << size_in_sqmeters
     << endl;
```

which *echo prints* or displays the value just read into `size_in_sqmeters`. This statement provides a record of the data manipulated by the program. Without it, we would have no easy way of knowing what value was read. Whenever you convert an interactive program to a batch program, make sure you replace each prompt with an echo print that follows the `cin` statement. ∎

Output Redirection

You can also redirect program output to a disk file instead of the screen. Then, you could send the output file to the printer (using an operating system command) to obtain a hard copy (printed version) of the program output. Some systems allow you to redirect your output directly to the printer. At the command line in UNIX or MS-DOS, type the symbol ">", followed by a new filename, such as

```
> myoutput
```

to redirect output from the screen to file `myoutput`. The command

```
metric > myoutput
```

executes the compiled and linked code for the Metric Conversion Program, reading program input from the keyboard and writing program output to the file myoutput. However, it would be difficult to interact with the running program because all program output, including any prompting messages, are sent to the output file. It would be better to use the command

```
metric < mydata > myoutput
```

which reads program input from the data file mydata and sends program output to the output file myoutput.

EXERCISES FOR SECTION 2.7

Self-Check   1. Explain the difference in placement of cout statements used to display prompts and cout statements used to echo data. Which are used in interactive programs and which are used in batch programs?
2. How are input data provided to an interactive program? How are input data provided to a batch program?

Programming   1. Rewrite the program in Fig. 2.11 as a batch program. Assume data are read from the file mydata.

2.8 _____ COMMON PROGRAMMING ERRORS

One of the first things you will discover in writing programs is that a program very rarely compiles, links and executes correctly on the first try. Murphy's law, "If something can go wrong, it will," seems to be written with the computer programmer or programming student in mind. In fact, errors are so common that they have their own special name, *bugs*, and the process of correcting them is called *debugging a program*. To alert you to potential problems, we will provide a section on common errors at the end of each chapter.

When the compiler detects an error, it will display an *error message* indicating you have made a mistake and informing you what the cause of the error might be. Unfortunately, error messages are often difficult to interpret and are sometimes misleading. They also vary from compiler to compiler. However, as you gain some experience, you will become more proficient at understanding them. Our goal in the Common Programming Errors section of each chapter is to describe the most common kinds of errors that can occur and to suggest appropriate corrections for these errors.

Two basic categories of errors can occur: those that are detected before the program can be executed and those that occur while the program is executing. There are also two basic types of errors in each category. We will describe all four next.

Syntax Errors

Syntax errors, or *compilation errors,* are detected and displayed by the compiler as it attempts to translate your program. If a statement has a syntax error, then it cannot be completely translated, and your program will not execute. Figure 2.19 shows a listing of the Metric Conversion Program printed by the compiler during program translation. The listing shows each line of the source program (preceded by a line number) and also displays any syntax errors detected by the compiler. *Note:* The following error messages were generated

Figure 2.19   Compiler listing of a program with syntax errors

```
1 // FILE: Metric.cpp
2
3 // CONVERTS FABRIC MEASURES IN SQUARE METERS TO SQUARE YARDS
4
5 #include <iostream.h>           // necessary for cout and cin
6
7 main ();
8 {
9     // Local data ...
10    const float meters_to_yards = 1.196;  // conversion constant
11    float size_in_sqmeters   input: fabric size in square meters
12
13    Read in fabric size in square meters.
14    cout << "Enter the fabric size in square meters: ;
15    cin  >> size_in_sqmeters;
16
17    // Convert the fabric size to square yards.
18    meters_to_yards * size_in_sqmeters = size_in_sqyards;
19
20    // Display the fabric size in square yards.
21    cout << "The fabric size in square yards is "
22         << size_in_sqyards << endl;
23 }
```

```
 8: Declaration was expected
12: , expected
12: Declaration missing ;
13: Expression syntax
13: Undefined symbol 'Read', Undefined symbol 'in', etc.
14: Unterminated string or character constant
14, 15, 18, 21: Type name expected
15: Expression syntax
18: Lvalue required
18, 22: Undefined symbol 'size_in_sqyards"
```

separately, one for each error, but are grouped together in one listing for illustration purposes. The errors are summarized at the bottom of the compiler listing. The program contains the following syntax errors:

- semicolon not expected after the main header (line 7)
- missing semicolon after the variable declaration (line 11)
- missing double slash preceding a comment (lines 11 and 13)
- missing double quote at the end of a string (line 14)
- missing declaration for variable `size_in_sqyards` (lines 18 and 22)
- assignment statement with transposed variable and expression part (line 18)

The actual format of the listing and error messages produced by your compiler may differ from Fig. 2.19. In some systems, whenever an error is detected the compiler displays a list of errors in a separate message window or box (see Chapter 1, Fig. 1.13). Each line of this display contains the program file name and line number where it detected a mistake, and a brief error message. Some systems also have a help feature that further explains the short message in greater detail. As you highlight a particular line in the message box, the corresponding line containing the error is highlighted simultaneously in your code. At times, a separate block cursor also is placed on the character where the compiler first detects the error.

As an example of how this works, we examine the first error in the program, which was detected when the opening brace { in line 8 was processed by the compiler. At this point, the compiler recognized that a semicolon was inserted (after the main header) and indicated this by printing the error message

```
Declaration was expected
```

In this case, the position of the cursor was misleading as the compiler could not detect the error until it started to process the next line. At this point, because of the extraneous semicolon, the compiler expected to find a declaration rather than a brace as it indicated with the error message.

There is also a missing semicolon after the declaration in line 11; however, this time the compiler prints several error messages

```
, expected
Declaration missing ;
Expression syntax
Undefined symbol
```

Since line 11 was not properly terminated, the compiler continues to look for another `float` type variable after `size_in_sqmeters`. Because it does not expect or recognize any of the symbols that follow on this line or the next one, it continues to display additional error messages. At least some of these messages could have been eliminated had the comment symbol // been used as required in lines 11 and 13.

The transposed assignment statement in line 18 causes the error

```
Lvalue required
```

to be displayed; the compiler is looking for only one variable on the left side of the assignment operator and detects an error when it reaches the asterisk.

An undefined symbol error occurs if the compiler cannot find the declaration for an identifier referenced in the program body. This can happen because the programmer forgot the declaration or misspelled the name of the identifier. In Fig. 2.19, omitting the declaration for variable `size_in_sqyards` in line 12 causes the display of the error message

```
Undefined symbol
```

in lines 18 and 22.

One syntax error often leads to the generation of multiple error messages. For example, forgetting to declare variable `size_in_sqyards` will cause an error message to be printed each time `size_in_sqyards` is used in the program. Then again, some C++ compilers will display the error only once and state that such errors will not be repeated. For this reason, it is often a good idea initially to concentrate on correcting the errors in the declaration part of a program and then recompile, rather than attempt to fix all the errors at once. Many later errors will disappear once the earlier ones are corrected.

Syntax errors are often caused by the improper use of double quote marks with strings, or the accidental use of single quotes rather than double quotes. Make sure that you always use double quotes to begin and end a string; single quotes are used only in writing single-character constants (such as `'c'` or `'\n'`); they cannot be used with strings. A string should begin and end on the same line.

Another common syntax error involves the omission of one of the double quote marks when writing a string of characters. If the quote mark at the end is missing, such as in line 14 (Fig. 2.19), the compiler will assume that whatever follows is part of the character string, rather than part of your executable statements. It will continue with this assumption until another double quote is found or the end of your program is encountered.

When using comments, if the opening `/*` is missing or you forget to precede a comment with `//`, the compiler will not recognize the beginning of the comment and will attempt to process the comment as a C++ statement (for example, line 13, Fig. 2.19). This should cause a syntax error (or a number of syntax errors). If the closing `*/` in a `/* ... */` style comment is missing, the comment will simply be extended to include the program statements that follow it. If the comment is not terminated, the rest of the program will be considered a comment, and a syntax error, such as

```
Unexpected end of file in Comment
Compound statement missing }
```

will be printed.

Link Errors

After your program has successfully been compiled, your C++ system will try to link your source code with any of the C++ libraries that you have included. Because you didn't provide any information for `cin` and `cout`, for instance, the compiler assumes these are defined elsewhere. If you forget to put

```
#include <iostream.h>
```

in your file, you will get a *link error*. As we progress, there may be many `.h` files that you will need to include. Always carefully check that any identifier used is accounted for, either in your main file or in another file that is being linked to your main file.

Run-Time Errors

There are two types of *run-time errors*: those that are detected by the C++ *run-time system* and those that allow your program to run to completion but give incorrect results.

A run-time error can occur as a result of the user directing the computer to perform an illegal operation, such as dividing a number by zero or trying to access an illegal address. When this type of run-time error occurs, the computer will stop executing your program and a diagnostic message, such as

```
Divide error, line number nnn
```

may be printed.

If you attempt to manipulate undefined or invalid data, your output may contain strange results. *Arithmetic overflow* can occur without warning. This happens when a program attempts to store a number that is larger than the maximum size that can be accommodated by your computer.

Figure 2.20 shows an example of a run-time error. The program compiles successfully but contains no statement assigning a value to variable x before the assignment statement

```
z = x + y;
```

is executed. Some compilers may give you a warning message but will still compile your program and allow you to run it. However, the program will produce incorrect results. In this case, because we did not assign a specific number to x, it will contain an unpredictable value. Many compilers initialize variables to zero automatically, making it more difficult to detect the omission when your program is transferred to another compiler that doesn't. Therefore, it is essential that you hand-check your results to make sure that your program does what you intend.

Figure 2.20   A program with a run-time error

```
1  // FILE: Test.cpp
2  // PROGRAM TO TEST RUN-TIME ERRORS
3
4  #include <iostream.h>
5
6  main ()
7  {
8     // Local data ...
9     float x, y, z;
10
11    y = 5.0;
12    z = x + y;
13    cout << "x = " << x << endl << "y = " << y << endl
14          << "z = " << z << endl;
15 }
```

——————— Program Output ———————

```
x = 6.111804e-09
y = 5.0
z = 5.0
```

Logic Errors

Logic errors are the most difficult to notice because the program appears to run without mishap. The statement

```
size_in_sqmeters = meters_to_yards * size_in_sqyards;
```

is a perfectly legal C++ statement, but it does not perform the computation specified by the Metric Conversion Problem. The compiler cannot know what you really meant to compute. It simply translates what you give it.

As we indicated earlier, debugging a program can be very time-consuming. You may find it to be particularly frustrating as you begin learning to use C++. Providing meaningful compiler diagnostics for any programming language is a challenge. But for a powerful and somewhat complicated language, such as C++, this is even more so the case. Sometimes, even the simplest of errors will produce a number of seemingly incomprehensible diagnostics, some containing terminology beyond the scope of this text.

As you gain more familiarity with the language and the C++ diagnostics, you will notice considerable improvement in your ability to understand what you may have done to cause these messages. In the meanwhile, the best approach is to plan each program carefully and hand trace through it to eliminate bugs before running the program. If you are not sure of the syntax for a particular statement, look it up in the text. If you follow this approach, you will save yourself much time and trouble. And always remember, if all else fails, ask someone for help. The computer is a wonderful tool for many things.

However, when you need help, there is no substitute for knowing the people who can assist you. Get to know the right people, and learn to ask questions.

CHAPTER REVIEW

In this chapter, we introduced some short, sample C++ programs and discussed in detail each C++ feature used in these programs. We illustrated how to use the C++ programming language to instruct the computer to perform some very fundamental operations: to read information into memory, to perform some simple computations, and to print the results of the computation. All of this was done using symbols (punctuators, variable names, and operators, such as +, −, *, and /) that are familiar, easy to remember, and easy to use.

The concept of abstraction and its importance in programming was presented. The predefined types char, int, and float were introduced, and the use of the arithmetic operators on int and float data was described. You do not have to know very much about your computer in order to understand and use C++.

In the remainder of this text, you will learn more about abstraction and programming and about many more features of the C++ language along with rules for using these features. You must remember throughout that, unlike the rules of English, the rules of C++ are precise and allow no exceptions. The compiler will be unable to translate C++ instructions that violate these rules. Remember to declare every identifier used as a constant or variable and to terminate program statements with semicolons.

New C++ Constructs   Table 2.5 describes the new C++ constructs introduced in this chapter.

Table 2.5   **Summary of New C++ Constructs**

CONSTRUCT	EFFECT
Compiler Directive `#include <iostream.h>`	A compiler directive that causes the contents of file `iostream.h` to be placed in the program where the directive appears.

Constant Declaration
`const float tax = 25.00;`
`const char star = '*';`
	Associates the constant identifier `tax` with the floating-point constant `25.00` and the constant identifier `star` with the character constant `'*'`.

(Continued)

Table 2.5 (Continued)

CONSTRUCT	EFFECT

Variable Declaration
`float x, y, z;`
`int me, it;`
	Allocates memory cells named **x**, **y**, and **z** for storage of floating-point numbers and cells named me and **it** for storage of integers.

Assignment Statement `distance = speed * time;`	Assigns the product of `speed` and `time` as the value of `distance`.
cin Statement `cin >> hours >> rate;`	Enters data into the variables `hours` and `rate`.
cout Statement `cout << "Net = " << net << endl;`	Displays the string "Net = " followed by the value of `net`. `endl` advances the output to the left margin of a new line after this information is displayed.
`return` *Statement*	Returns control from program to operating system

✔ # QUICK-CHECK EXERCISES

1. What value is assigned to x by the following statement?

   ```
   x = 25.0 * 3.0 / 2.5;
   ```

2. What value is assigned to x by the statement below assuming x is 10.0?

   ```
   x = x - 20.0;
   ```

3. Show the form of the output line displayed by the following cout lines when total is 352.74.

   ```
   cout << "The final total is: " << endl << total;
   cout << "$" << total << endl;
   ```

4. Show the form of the output line displayed by the following cout line when total is 352.74.

   ```
   cout << "The final total is $" << total << endl;
   ```

5. What data type would you use to represent the following items: number of children at school; a letter grade on an exam; the average numeric score of all students who took the last computer science exam?

6. In which step of the software development method are the problem input and output data identified?

7. If cin is reading two integers, what character should be typed following the first value? What should be typed after the second number?
8. If cin is reading two characters, what character is typed after the first character? What is typed after the second character?
9. How does the compiler determine how many data values are to be entered when a cin operation is performed?
10. How does the program user determine how many data values to enter when a cin operation is performed?
11. The compiler listing shows what kind of errors (syntax or run-time)?

Answers to Quick-Check Exercises

1. 30.0
2. −10.0
3. ```
The final total is:
$352.74
```
4. `The final total is $352.74`
5. int, char, float
6. problem analysis
7. a blank, RETURN key
8. the second character (or a blank), RETURN key
9. The number of values to be entered depends on the number of variables in the input list.
10. from reading the prompt displayed by the program
11. syntax errors

# REVIEW QUESTIONS

1. What type of information should be specified in the program header section comments?
2. Check the variables below that are syntactically correct.

| income | ____ | two fold | ____ |
| 1time | ____ | C3PO | ____ |
| const | ____ | income#1 | ____ |
| Tom's | ____ | item | ____ |

3. What is wrong with the declarations and assignment statement below?

```
const float pi = 3.14159;
float c, r;

pi = c / (2 * r * r);
```

4. What does the next statement do?

```
float cell;
```
```

5. Write the data requirements, necessary formulas, and algorithm for Programming Project 6.
6. If the average size of a family is 2.8 and this value is stored in the variable `family_size`, provide the C++ statement to display this fact in a readable way (leave the cursor on the same line).
7. List three basic data types of C++.
8. Convert the program statements below to read and echo data in batch mode.

```
cout << "Enter three numbers separated by spaces: " << endl;
cin >> x >> y >> z;
cout << "Enter two characters: ";
cin >> ch1 >> ch2;
```

9. Write an algorithm that allows for the input of an integer value, doubles it, subtracts 10, and displays the result.

PROGRAMMING PROJECTS

1. Write a program to convert a temperature in degrees Fahrenheit to degrees Celsius.

   DATA REQUIREMENTS

   Problem Input

   fahrenheit (int)   —temperature in degrees Fahrenheit

   Problem Output

   celsius (float)   —temperature in degrees Celsius

   FORMULA

   celsius = (5/9) * (fahrenheit − 32)

2. Write a program to read two data items and print their sum, difference, product, and quotient.

   DATA REQUIREMENTS

   Problem Input

   x, y (int)   — two items

   Problem Output

   sum (int)   — sum of x and y
   difference (int)   — difference of x and y
   product (int)   — product of x and y
   quotient (float)   — quotient of x divided by y

3. Write a program to read in the weight (in pounds) of an object, and compute and print its weight in kilograms and grams. (*Hint:* One pound is equal to 0.453592 kilograms or 453.59237 grams.)

4. Write a program that prints your first initial as a block letter. (*Hint:* Use a 6 × 6 grid for the letter and print six strings. Each string should consist of asterisks (*) interspersed with blanks.)

5. Write a program that reads in the length and width of a rectangular yard and the length and width of a rectangular house situated in the yard. Your program should compute the time required to cut the grass at the rate of 2 square meters per second.

6. Write a program that reads in the numerators and denominators of two fractions. The program should print the product of the two fractions as a fraction and as a percent.

7. Redo Programming Project 6, only this time, compute the sum of the two fractions.

8. The Pythagorean theorem states that the sum of the squares of the sides of a right triangle is equal to the square of the hypotenuse. For example, if two sides of a right triangle have lengths 3 and 4, then the hypotenuse must have a length of 5. The integers 3, 4, and 5 together form a Pythagorean triple. There is an infinite number of such triples. Given two positive integers, m and n, where $m > n$, a Pythagorean triple can be generated by the following formulas:

$$\text{side1} = m^2 - n^2$$
$$\text{side2} = 2mn$$
$$\text{hypotenuse} = \sqrt{m^2 + n^2}$$

Write a program that reads in values for m and n and prints the values of the Pythagorean triple generated by the formulas above.

3

Top-Down Design

3.1 Problem-Solving and Program Development
CASE STUDY: Finding the Area and Circumference of a Circle
3.2 Subproblems and Independent Modules
CASE STUDY: Drawing Simple Figures
3.3 Functions without Arguments
3.4 Functions with Input Arguments and Return Values
3.5 How We Use Functions
3.6 Functions as Program Building Blocks: C++ Libraries
3.7 Some Comments on the Software Engineering Process
3.8 Common Programming Errors
Chapter Review

In this chapter, we continue our discussion of problem-solving. We will introduce the idea of top-down design and show how to write a program once an appropriate design has been produced and documented. We will also illustrate how to solve a new problem by extending the solution to a problem that has already been solved.

Next, we show how to represent the relationship between a problem and its subproblems using a structure chart, a graphical, two-dimensional, program design tool. We will introduce an important programming language feature, the function, which will be used to implement the solution to each subproblem as a separate program entity.

The notion of abstraction is discussed and expanded upon further. We will illustrate the use of procedural abstraction (using the structure chart) as we design problem solutions, and we will describe how to use functions to implement such abstractions. The concept of code reuse is introduced, and we will begin to learn how to build more reusable code modules that have already been tested and debugged. We also introduce some C++ library functions and show how to use them to perform mathematical computations.

3.1 ___ PROBLEM-SOLVING AND PROGRAM DEVELOPMENT

In Chapter 2, we introduced the three primary stages of the program development process:

1. Problem analysis
2. Program design
3. Program implementation

In each of the problem-solving examples illustrated thus far, we have progressed step by step through each of these stages. We began with the problem statement and carefully analyzed this statement to be sure we understood the problem to be solved, the input data given, and the required output. We then outlined an algorithm for solving the problem and, finally, transformed this algorithm into a C++ implementation that could be compiled and executed on the computer. Finally we discussed the testing of the program and the importance of choosing an appropriate set of test data.

The focus on data identification and description (in the problem analysis stage) is easily overlooked when you are first learning the basics of programming with the principles of a new language. Yet, even at this early stage, it is important to understand and document exactly how each variable will be used in our programs and to choose carefully the types of these variables. Therefore, even as we focus on issues of algorithmic design in the early part of this text, we will continue to stress issues of data analysis—the identification of information needed to solve a problem and the proper representation and clear definition of use of that information in our programs.

The approach to algorithm development followed in the design stage is called *top-down design*. In practicing top-down design, we start with the most abstract formulation of a problem and work down to more detailed subproblems. In this chapter, we will illustrate tools and techniques useful in practicing the top-down approach to problem-solving. We begin by showing one way to move more efficiently from the analysis and design phases to implementation.

Developing a Program from Its Initial Documentation

If we follow the software development method introduced earlier, we will generate important *program documentation* even before we begin to write the program. This documentation describes the purpose of a program and its data. It should provide a summary of our intentions and thought processes as we develop the data requirements and algorithm.

We also provide some documentation inside the program itself in the form of comments. We use comments to describe the purpose of each program variable and constant, and we precede each major algorithm step in the executable statements with a comment that describes the purpose of that step. These comments are important: If carefully worded, they can be helpful in relating parts of the program to the original problem definition. They can serve to clarify the relationship between program constants or variables and the problem data entities they represent. In addition, comments can be used to identify the purpose of each logical group of executable statements in a program, making it easier for us to connect each such group to our initial program outline.

If you use your system editor to type in your program documentation, this information eventually can serve as a good starting point for writing your program. For example, you can begin writing your program declarations by adapting the problem data requirements (part of the analysis stage) as shown in Fig. 3.1. Edit these lines to conform to the C++ syntax for constant and variable declarations, thereby completing the declaration statements of the program (see Fig. 3.2).

To develop the executable statements, use the initial algorithm edited to appear as a list of comments for a framework. Then, place each algorithm refinement under the algorithm step that it refines, as shown in Fig. 3.3. After the refinements are in place, you can begin to write actual C++ statements. Place the C++ code for a step that is not refined directly under that step. For a step that is refined, either edit the refinement to change it from English to C++, or replace it with C++ code (see Fig. 3.4). We illustrate this process next.

Figure 3.1 Metric Conversion Program data requirements

Problem Constant

meters_to_yards = 1.196   — conversion constant

Problem Input

size_in_sqmeters (float)   — fabric size in square meters

Problem Output

size_in_sqyards (float)   — fabric size in square yards

Figure 3.2 Declarations after editing

```
// FILE: Metric.cpp
// CONVERTS FABRIC MEASURES IN SQUARE METERS TO SQUARE YARDS

main()
{
   // Local data ...
   const float meters_to_yards = 1.196;      // conversion constant

   float size_in_sqmeters; // input: fabric size in square meters
   float size_in_sqyards;  // output: fabric size in square yards
}
```

Figure 3.3 Using refined algorithm as program framework

```
// FILE: Metric.cpp
// CONVERTS FABRIC MEASURES IN SQUARE METERS TO SQUARE YARDS.
//      ANALYSIS STAGE ...

main()
{
   // Local data ...
   const float meters_to_yards = 1.196; // conversion constant

   float size_in_sqmeters; // input: fabric size in square meters
   float size_in_sqyards;  // output: fabric size in square yards

   // 1. Read the fabric size in square meters.
   // 2. Convert the fabric size to square yards.
   //    2.1   The fabric size in square yards is 1.196 times the
   //          fabric size in square meters.
   // 3. Display the fabric size in square yards.
}
```

Figure 3.4 **Final edited program**

```
// FILE: Metric.cpp
// CONVERTS FABRIC MEASURES IN SQUARE METERS TO SQUARE YARDS

#include <iostream.h>

void main ()
{
   // Local data ...
   const float meters_to_yards = 1.196; // conversion constant

   float size_in_sqmeters; // input: fabric size in square meters
   float size_in_sqyards;  // output: fabric size in square yards

   // Read the fabric size in square meters.
   cout << "Enter the fabric size in square meters: ";
   cin  >> size_in_sqmeters;

   // Convert the fabric size to square yards.
   size_in_sqyards = meters_to_yards * size_in_sqmeters;

   // Display the fabric size in square yards.
   cout << "The fabric size in square yards is "
        << size_in_sqyards << endl;
   return;
}
```

CASE STUDY: FINDING THE AREA AND CIRCUMFERENCE OF A CIRCLE

Problem Statement

Given the radius of a circle, compute and print its area and its circumference.

Problem Analysis

The problem input is the circle radius. Two output values are requested: the circle's area and circumference. These data should be represented as type float because each element may contain a fractional part.

From our knowledge of geometry, we know the relationship between a circle's radius and its area and circumference; these formulas are listed next along with the data requirements.

DATA REQUIREMENTS

> ### Problem Constant
>
> pi = 3.14159
>
> ### Problem Input
>
> radius (float)   — radius of a circle
>
> ### Problem Output
>
> area (float)   — area of a circle
> circum (float)   — circumference of a circle

FORMULAS

area of a circle = π * radius^2
circumference of a circle = 2π * radius

Program Design

Once you know the problem input and output, you should list the steps necessary to solve the problem. It is very important that you pay close attention to the order of the steps. The initial algorithm follows.

INITIAL ALGORITHM

1. Read radius of circle.
2. Compute area of circle.
3. Compute circumference of circle.
4. Display area and circumference.

ALGORITHM REFINEMENTS

Next, we should refine any steps that do not have an obvious solution (for instance, steps 2 and 3).

> ### Step 2 Refinement
>
> 2.1. Assign pi * radius * radius to area.
>
> ### Step 3 Refinement
>
> 3.1. Assign 2 * pi * radius to circum.

Program Implementation

Figure 3.5 shows the C++ program so far. Function `main` consists of the initial algorithm with its refinements.

Figure 3.5   Outline of Area and Circumference Program

```
// FILE: Circle.cpp
// COMPUTES AND PRINTS THE AREA AND CIRCUMFERENCE OF A CIRCLE
//     ANALYSIS STAGE ...

void main ()
{
   // Local data ...
   const float pi = 3.14159;

   float radius;          // input: radius of circle
   float area;            // output: area of circle
   float circum;          // output: circumference of circle

   // 1. Read radius of circle.
   // 2. Compute area of circle.
   //    2.1 Assign pi * radius * radius to area.
   // 3. Compute circumference of circle.
   //    3.1 Assign 2 * pi * radius to circum.
   // 4. Display area and circumference.
}
```

To write the final program, we must convert the refinements (steps 2.1 and 3.1) to C++, write C++ code for the unrefined steps (steps 1 and 4), and delete the step numbers from the comments. Figure 3.6 shows the final program.

Program Testing

The sample output shown in Fig. 3.6 provides a good test of the solution because it is relatively easy to compute the area and circumference by hand

Figure 3.6   Finding the area and circumference of a circle

```
// FILE: Circle.cpp
// COMPUTES AND PRINTS THE AREA AND CIRCUMFERENCE OF A CIRCLE

#include <iostream.h>

void main ()
{
   // Local data ...
   const float pi = 3.14159;

   float radius;              // input: radius of circle
   float area;                // output: area of circle
   float circum;              // output: circumference of circle
```

(Continued)

Figure 3.6   (Continued)

```
// Read radius of circle.
cout << "Enter the circle radius: ";
cin >> radius;

// Compute area of circle.
area = pi * radius * radius;

// Compute circumference of circle.
circum = 2 * pi * radius;

// Display area and circumference.
cout << "The area of the circle is " << area << endl;
cout << "The circumference of the circle is " << circum
    << endl;
return;
}
```

────────── Program Output ──────────

```
Enter the circle radius: 5.0
The area of the circle is 78.539749
The circumference of the circle is 31.415901
```

for a radius value of 5.0. The radius squared is 25.0, so the value of the area is correct. The circumference should be ten times π, which is also an easy number to compute by hand.

EXERCISES FOR SECTION 3.1

Self-Check   Introduction to a Simple Payroll Problem:
1. Describe the problem input and output and algorithm for computing an employee's gross salary given the hours worked and hourly rate.
2. Write a program outline from the algorithm you developed in Exercise 1. Use Fig. 3.5 as a model for your outline.

Programming   1. Add refinements to the program outline shown next and write the final C++ program.

```
// COMPUTES AND PRINTS THE SUM AND AVERAGE OF TWO NUMBERS
//     ANALYSIS STAGE ...
void main()
{
    // Local data ...
    // Any local constants and variables you need will go here.

    // 1. Read two numbers.
    // 2. Compute the sum of the two numbers.
    // 3. Compute the average of the two numbers.
    // 4. Display sum and average.
}
```

2. (More on the Simple Payroll Problem) Write a complete C++ program for Self-Check Exercise 1.

3.2 — SUBPROBLEMS AND INDEPENDENT MODULES

The Structure Chart

As we mentioned earlier, one of the most fundamental ideas in problem-solving involves dividing a problem into subproblems and solving each sub-problem independently of the others. In attempting to solve a subproblem at one level, we often introduce a new subproblem at a lower level. The splitting of a problem into related subproblems is analogous to the process of refining an algorithm. Each time we refine an algorithm step (a problem), we generate new refinements (subproblems) at a lower level. For the problems we have analyzed thus far, this was not a difficult task. Only one subproblem required refinement, and it was not complicated. In many situations, one or more sub-problems may require significant refinement. A *structure chart* is a documen-tation tool that can be used to enable you to keep track of the relationships among subproblems as this refinement process is practiced. We illustrate the use of this tool in the following case study.

CASE STUDY: DRAWING SIMPLE FIGURES

Problem Statement

Write a program to draw the picture of the house and the stick figure of a young girl (both shown in Fig. 3.7) on your terminal or workstation monitor.

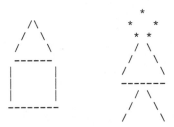

Figure 3.7 A house diagram and stick figure

(Do not attempt to draw the pictures side-by-side; the house should be drawn first; then, leave three spaces and draw the figure of the little girl.)

Problem Analysis

The figure shown on the left of Fig. 3.7 consists of a triangle, without its base, on top of a rectangle. The figure on the right consists of a shape that resembles a circle, on top of a triangle which is in turn on top of a triangle without its base. We should be able to draw both figures using the four basic graphic components described next.

- a circle
- a base line
- parallel lines
- intersecting lines

Program Design

Let's focus on the stick figure of the girl. We can divide the problem of drawing this figure into three subproblems as shown in the structure chart in Fig. 3.8. From this structure chart we can write the initial algorithm and, for this simple problem, the refinements for step 2.

INITIAL ALGORITHM

1. Draw a circle.
2. Draw a triangle.
3. Draw intersecting lines.

ALGORITHM REFINEMENTS

Since a triangle is not one of our basic components, we must refine step 2.

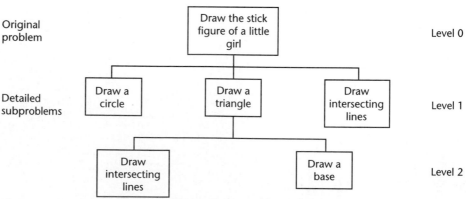

Figure 3.8   Structure chart for drawing a stick figure

Step 2 Refinement

2.1. Draw intersecting lines.
2.2. Draw a base.

We use the structure chart to illustrate the structural, hierarchical relationship between the original problem and its subproblems. As we scan down the chart shown in Fig. 3.8, we go from an abstract problem to a more detailed subproblem. The original problem is shown at the top, or level 0, of the structure chart. Each of the major subproblems appears at level 1. The different subproblems resulting from the refinement of each level 1 step are shown at level 2, and are connected to their respective level 1 subproblems. The structure chart shows that the subproblem "Draw a triangle" (level 1) is dependent on the solutions to the subproblems "Draw intersecting lines" and "Draw a base" (level 2). Since the subproblem "Draw a circle" is not refined further, no level 2 subproblems are connected to it. Although the boxes appearing at a particular level of a structure chart often show the ordering of a group of steps, it is the algorithm (not the structure chart) that is intended to show the order in which we must carry out each step to solve the problem.

EXERCISES FOR SECTION 3.2

Self-Check
1. Draw the structure chart for the subproblem of drawing the house (see Fig. 3.7) in the Simple Figures Problem.
2. Draw the structure chart for the complete Simple Figures Problem. You need not redraw any parts of the chart that have already been completed.
3. Draw the structure chart for the problem of drawing a triangle and a rectangle with a circle in between.
4. Draw the structure chart for the problem of drawing the rocket ship shown next.

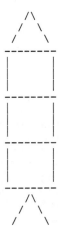

3.3 _____ FUNCTIONS WITHOUT ARGUMENTS

The structure chart proceeds from the original problem (at the top level) down to its detailed subproblems (at the bottom level). We would like to follow this *top-down* description when we write a program. The C++ function construct enables us to do this.

A C++ function is a grouping of statements into a single unit. We may think of a function as a "black box" that performs a task whenever it is called upon to do so. We can call, or *activate,* a function through the execution of a *function call.* Figure 3.9 shows the code for the original top-level problem, "Draw a figure" (assuming the solution to each subproblem at level 2 in Fig. 3.8 is implemented as a separate function). Note that main itself is just a function, but it is called by the operating system rather than your program. Thus, we can view each C++ program that we write as made up of a collection of one or more functions. Exactly one of these functions, the one corresponding to the top-level block in a structure chart, must be named main.

Figure 3.9   main **function for drawing a stick figure**

```
// FILE: StkFigMn.cpp
// DRAW A STICK FIGURE (Main function only)

#include <iostream.h>

void main ()
{
    // Functions used ...
    // DRAWS A CIRCLE
    void draw_circle ();

    // DRAWS A TRIANGLE
    void draw_triangle ();

    // DRAWS INTERSECTING LINES
    void draw_intersect ();


    // Draw the figure.
    // Draw a circle.
    draw_circle ();
    // Draw a triangle.
    draw_triangle ();
    // Draw intersecting lines.
    draw_intersect ();
    return;
}
```

As shown in Fig. 3.9, the `main` function implements our top-level or original algorithm. This implementation consists of three function calls, one for each of the three primary tasks described in the structure chart and algorithm presented in the previous section. Because of its position relative to the called functions in the structure chart, we sometimes refer to the calling function as the *parent* of those that it calls. In the remainder of this section, we discuss those aspects of the code in Fig. 3.9 that relate to the use of functions: the declaration, the call, and the definition of each function to be used.

Function Declarations

Every function called from a parent function must be declared in or before the parent. The lines

```
// Functions used ...
// DRAWS A CIRCLE
void draw_circle ();

// DRAWS A TRIANGLE
void draw_triangle ();

// DRAWS INTERSECTING LINES
void draw_intersect ();
```

provide the declarations of the three functions called by the parent function `main`. The lines beginning with the reserved word **void** are C++ *function prototypes*.

C++ SYNTAX

Function Prototype (declaration of a function)

Form: *type fname* ( );

Example: // SKIPS THREE LINES
        void skip_three ();

Interpretation: A function prototype begins with the *type specification, type* (for example, `int`, `char`, or `float`) associated with the function. (The meaning of this type association will be discussed later in this chapter.) If no type is associated with the function, the reserved word **void** is used as the type specification. The identifier *fname* is declared as the name of a function. The prototype provides all of the information that the C++ compiler needs to know to translate references to the function correctly.

Although not required by C++, we will adopt the convention of placing prototypes inside, rather than before, the calling function. And, we will place them before any of the other local declarations in the calling function. This placement also is not required in C++. A descriptive comment, indicating in

English what the function does, should precede each prototype declaration. C++ requires the use of a prototype for each function referenced in a parent function. In the case of multiple prototypes, it makes no difference which function is declared first; their order of execution is determined by the order of the function calls in the function body.   ∎

Function Calls

The function `main`, shown in Fig. 3.9, contains three function calls. The rules for writing function calls are given next.

C++
SYNTAX

Function Call

Form: *fname* ( );

Example: `draw_circle ();`

Interpretation: The function call initiates the execution of function *fname*. After *fname* has finished executing, the next statement in the parent function will be executed.   ∎

Defining Functions

We have now examined the two aspects of function use, the declaration and call. We now turn our attention to the third aspect, the description or *definition* of what each function is to do. In C++, these descriptions must be provided separately for each function; they cannot be incorporated within another function.

Figure 3.10 shows the original `main` function from Fig. 3.9, together with the declarations (prototypes) and the definitions for all functions used in `main`,

Figure 3.10   Function `main` **and all lower-level functions**

```
// FILE: StickFig.cpp
// DRAWS A STICK FIGURE OF A GIRL

#include <iostream.h>

void main ()
{
    // Functions used ...
    // DRAWS A CIRCLE
    void draw_circle ();
```

(Continued)

Figure 3.10 (Continued)

```cpp
    // DRAWS A TRIANGLE
    void draw_triangle ();

    // DRAWS INTERSECTING LINES
    void draw_intersect ();


    // Draw a circle.
    draw_circle ();
    // Draw a triangle.
    draw_triangle ();
    // Draw intersecting lines.
    draw_intersect ();
    cout << endl << endl << endl;
    return;
}   //


// DRAWS A CIRCLE
void draw_circle ()
{
    cout << "    *   " << endl;
    cout << " *    *" << endl;
    cout << "    * *  " << endl;
    return;
}   // end draw_circle


// DRAWS A TRIANGLE
void draw_triangle ()
{
    // Functions used ...
    void draw_intersect();
    void draw_base ();

    // Draw a triangle.
    draw_intersect ();
    draw_base ();
    return;
}   // end draw_triangle


// DRAWS AN INVERTED V
void draw_intersect ()
{
    cout << "   / \\   " << endl;
    cout << "  /   \\  " << endl;
    cout << " /     \\" << endl;
    return;
```

(Continued)

Figure 3.10 (Continued)

```
}  // end draw_intersect


// DRAWS A HORIZONTAL LINE
void draw_base ()
{
   cout << " -------" << endl;
   return;
}  // end draw_base
```

and for function `draw_base` (called by `draw_triangle`). A *function definition* describes the sequence of steps to be carried out by a function. The details of what must be included in a function definition are summarized in the following display.

**C++
SYNTAX**

Function Definition

Form: *type fname* ( )   — function header
```
            {
                local-declarations      } — function body
                executable-statements   
            }
```

Example:
```
// DRAWS A TRIANGLE
void draw_triangle ()
{
    // Functions used ...
    void draw_intersect ();
    void draw_base ();

    // Draw a triangle.
    draw_intersect ();
    draw_base ();
}  // end draw_triangle
```

Interpretation: A function consists of two parts, a *function header* and a *function body*. A function body consists of *local-declarations* (optional) and *executable-statements*. The form of the function header is very similar to that of the function prototype described earlier. The one notable exception is that a prototype must be terminated by a semicolon, just as any other declaration in a C++ program.

A *function header* begins with a *type specification* (such as int, float, char, or void) followed by the function name, *fname*, a user-defined identifier, and left and right parentheses. The function name is subject to the same rules of formation as the constant and variable identifiers described in Chapter 2. The *function header* is followed by the *function body*. The *function body* always starts with a left brace and ends with a right brace. We will adopt the convention of starting every function definition with a comment describing the purpose of the function, although this is not required by C++.

Any identifiers (constants, variables, or function prototypes) declared in the *local-declarations* are defined only during the execution of the function and can be referenced only within the function. In fact, these identifiers have no meaning outside the function in which they are declared.

The *executable-statements* describe the data manipulation to be performed by the function.   ∎

In Fig. 3.10, the body of function `draw_circle` contains three lines beginning with `cout`. These lines cause the computer to draw a shape that resembles a circle. The function call

```
draw_circle ();
```

in `main` causes the `cout` statements to execute. When the `return` statement is executed, execution resumes with the calling function (`main`, in this case).

If you look closely in Fig. 3.10, you will notice several occurrences of the pair of characters \\. We must always remember that the backslash character '\' is used as an *escape character* in C++. That is, it is used to indicate special characters, such as the *newline* character '\n', that have no single character representation. Because of this special use of '\', if we wish to use this character in a character string (see function `draw_intersect`), it is necessary to indicate this using the pair of characters \\.

Use of Comments in Function Declarations and Definitions

The functions in Fig. 3.10 include several comments. Each function (and its prototype) begins with a comment (which we have capitalized) that describes its purpose. For clarity, the right brace at the end of each function is followed by a comment, such as

```
// end fname
```

identifying which function is being terminated. We will adopt this style of commenting functions throughout this text, even though it is not required in C++.   ∎

Order of Execution of Functions

In the Stick Figure subproblem, we wrote the `main` function as a sequence of calls to other functions before we specified the details of these functions. For each function called in `main`, we needed only to specify the prototype of the function and a comment (to indicate its purpose). The details of implementation of each of these functions (the function definitions) were handled separately.

Once we have completed the implementation details, we can compile all of the functions that we have written. The compiler translates a function call as a *transfer of control* to the called function. When the compiler translates a `return` statement in this function, it inserts a *transfer of control* back from this function to the calling function.

Figure 3.11 illustrates how this works using functions `main` and `draw_circle` from the Stick Figure Program. The code for these functions is assumed to be in separate areas of memory. The arrows illustrate the *flow of control* from the function `main` to `draw_circle` and back. The actual mechanisms by which this transfer takes place are handled by the compiler when it translates these functions.

When execution of function `main` begins, the first statement executed is the call to `draw_circle`. When the computer carries out this function call, it transfers control to the referenced function (indicated by the top arrow in Fig. 3.11). The computer then executes the statements in the function body. After the `return` statement in the function body is executed, control is returned to `main` (indicated by the bottom arrow in Fig. 3.11). Upon return to `main`, the next statement will be executed (the call to `draw_triangle` in Fig. 3.11).

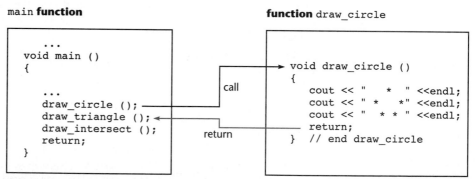

Figure 3.11   Flow of control between functions

Procedural Abstraction

The C++ function is an important feature of the language because it makes it possible for us to solve a problem in terms of simpler, lower-level subproblems. Through use of the function feature of C++, we are able to delay the detailed implementation of a complicated subproblem until a later stage and to focus entirely on the solution to the problem at hand. As discussed earlier in this chapter, we begin this top-down problem-solving process with the development of a structure chart defining the *decomposition* of a problem into its subproblems. We then devise an algorithm for solving the original problem in terms of these subproblems. The use of functions allows us to complete this process by writing the C++ instructions to implement the algorithm using calls to functions that correspond to the subproblems. We do not need to worry about the details of these lower-level functions until later.

For example, consider the structure chart shown earlier (Fig. 3.8) for the Stick Figure subproblem. In developing the problem solution, we were able to focus initially on solving the original problem in terms of abstract descriptions (without detail) of lower-level subproblems. Then, because these details were provided separately in the functions corresponding to these subproblems, and not in function `main`, we were able to write `main` using these functions as soon as we had specified the top-level algorithm. All we needed to tell the compiler about the functions to be called by `main` was how to call them. This was specified in the function prototypes at the very beginning of `main`. The subproblem functions could be written later, once we had refined the solutions to these problems.

Each of the function definitions that you write is treated as a separate unit (each unknown to the other) by the compiler. They are connected only through the name by which one function references another during execution. Yet, when it translates a calling function, it is important for the compiler to know about this connection so that it can verify that each reference is consistent. The information required for the compiler to perform this *consistency check* is provided through the use of function prototypes.

This top-down approach to program design involves *procedural abstraction*. It enables us to associate meaningful names with more complicated algorithm steps, reference these steps by name, and defer their implementation details until later. We then can write our programs using logically independent sections in the same way that we develop the solution algorithm. Use of these logically independent program sections enables us to hide the details of subproblem implementations from one another. This feature of *information hiding* is important in all stages of the program development process.

Another advantage of using functions is that a function may be executed more than once. For example, function `draw_intersect` is called twice in Fig. 3.10. Each time `draw_intersect` is called, a list of output statements is executed and intersecting lines are drawn. If we were not using functions, these three output statements would each have to be listed twice in function `main`, thereby increasing its length and the chance of error (see the programming exercises at the end of this section).

Finally, once you have written and tested a function, you may use it in other programs. For example, the functions we created for the Stick Figure

Program could easily be used to write programs that draw other figures. We will discuss this reuse of code in Section 3.6.

Example 3.1   Many figures contain triangles and rectangles. We have seen how to use the functions `draw_intersect` and `draw_base` to define a new function, `draw_triangle`. Similarly, we can use two functions `draw_parallel` and `draw_base` to define the new function `draw_rectangle` as shown in Fig. 3.12.

Figure 3.12   Function `draw_rectangle`

```
// FILE: DrawRect.cpp
// FUNCTION TO DRAW RECTANGLE

// DRAWS A RECTANGLE
void draw_rectangle ()
{
   // Functions used ...
   // DRAWS A HORIZONTAL LINE
   void draw_base ();

  // DRAWS TWO VERTICAL LINES
   void draw_parallel ();

   // Draw the rectangle.
   draw_base ();
   draw_parallel ();
   draw_base ();
   return;
}   // end draw_rectangle
```

∎

The prototypes written in the new function in Fig. 3.12 remind us that we must provide the definitions of the functions that they call.

Local Declarations in Functions

Identifiers declared within a function are called *local identifiers* because they can be referenced only within the function. Figure 3.13 shows another version of the function `draw_circle` with a local symbol named `print_symbol`. The output statements in the function body display `print_symbol` at various locations in order to draw a shape that resembles a circle. The advantage of using this local constant is that we can easily change the appearance of the circle being displayed just by changing the line that defines the value of

Figure 3.13   Function to draw a circle

```
// FILE: DrawCirc.cpp
// DRAWS A CIRCLE USING A CONSTANT CHARACTER SYMBOL

void draw_circle ()
{
   // Local data ...
   const char print_symbol = '@';

   // Draw the circle.
   cout << "     " << print_symbol << endl;
   cout << "  " << print_symbol << "     " << print_symbol << endl;
   cout << "     " << print_symbol << " " << print_symbol << endl;
   return;
}  // end draw_circle
```

`print_symbol`. The circle displayed by the version of the function shown in Fig. 3.13 is shown next.

```
   @
@     @
  @ @
```

Note that the detail of what symbol is displayed for the circle is hidden from the view of any parent functions that might use `draw_circle`. Among other things, using a local constant here would enable us to change this symbol without worrying about the effect of the change on any of the other functions in our program.

Displaying User Instructions

Functions, as we have described them to this point, have very limited utility because we do not yet know how to transmit, or *pass*, information into or out of a function that we write. Until we have this capability, we will use functions only to display information or instructions to a program user, as shown in the next example.

Example 3.2   The function in Fig. 3.14 displays instructions to a user of the Area and Circumference Program (see Fig. 3.6). If the prototype for this function

```
void instruct_user ();
```

is placed in the declaration part of the original `main` function, then the `main` function body can begin with the call statement

```
instruct_user ();
```

The rest of the `main` function body will consist of the executable statements shown in Fig. 3.6. Figure 3.15 shows the output displayed by calling function `instruct_user`. The rest of the program output will be the same as the output shown earlier.

Figure 3.14   Function `instruct_user`

```
// FILE: DispInst.cpp
// DISPLAYS INSTRUCTIONS TO THE USER OF AREA/CIRCUMFERENCE
// PROGRAM

void instruct_user ()
{
    cout << "This program computes the area and " << endl;
    cout << "circumference of a circle. " << endl << endl;
    cout << "To use this program, enter the radius of the "
        << endl;
    cout << "circle after the prompt" << endl;
    cout << " Enter radius: " << endl << endl;
    cout << "The circumference will be computed in the same "
        << endl;
    cout << "units of measurement as the radius. The area "
        << endl;
    cout << "will be computed in the same units squared." << endl
        << endl;
    return;
}  // end instruct_user
```

Figure 3.15   Output lines displayed by function `instruct_user`

——————— Program Output ———————

```
This program computes the area and
circumference of a circle.

To use this program, enter the radius of the
circle after the prompt

Enter radius:

The circumference will be computed in the same
units of measurement as the radius. The area
will be computed in the same units squared.
```

EXERCISES FOR SECTION 3.3

Self-Check

1. Assume that you have functions `print_h`, `print_i`, `print_m`, and `print_o` that print 5 × 5 letters, such as the M shown below:

```
M           M
M   M   M   M
M       M   M
M           M
M           M
```

What is the effect of executing the `main` function body below?

```
{
    print_o();
    cout << endl;
    print_h();
    skip_three (); // see Programming Exercise Number 2

    print_h();
    cout << endl;
    print_i();
    cout << endl;
    print_m();
}
```

2. Why is it better to place the user instructions in a separate function rather than to insert the necessary statements in the `main` function body itself?

Programming

1. Write the function `draw_parallel` to draw two horizontal, parallel lines, each 5 spaces in length and 3 lines apart.
2. The line

   ```
   cout << endl << endl << endl;
   ```

   may be used to cause three blank lines to be inserted into your printed output. Write a function `skip_three` that uses this line to insert three blank lines into your output. Write `draw_parallel` using `skip_three`.
3. Write a program to print "HI HO" in block letters. First, provide a structure chart for this problem.
4. Provide functions `print_h`, `print_i`, `print_m`, and `print_o` for the "OH HIM" Self-Check Exercise (number 1 above).
5. Show the revised `main` function for the Area and Circumference Problem (see Fig. 3.6) with the `instruct_user` prototype and the call to `instruct_user`.
6. Rewrite the Metric Conversion Program shown in Fig. 3.4 so that it includes a function that displays instructions to its user. Write the function, the prototype, and the call for `instruct_user`.

3.4 —— FUNCTIONS WITH INPUT ARGUMENTS AND RETURN VALUES

Programmers use functions like building blocks to construct large programs. We can make an analogy between a carefully designed program that uses functions and a stereo system. Each stereo component is an independent device that performs a specific function. The tuner and amplifier may contain similar electronic parts, but each component uses its own internal circuitry to perform its required function.

Information in the form of electronic signals is passed back and forth between these components over wires. If you look at the rear of a stereo amplifier, you will find that some plugs are marked input and others are marked output. The wires attached to the plugs marked input carry electronic signals to the amplifier, where they are processed. (These signals may come from a cassette deck, tuner, or compact disc player.) New electronic signals are generated. These signals come out of the amplifier from the plugs marked output and go to the speakers or to the back of the tape deck for recording. Thus, the wires are used for the transmission of information (electronic signals) between components of your stereo system.

Currently, we know a little about how to design the separate components (functions) of a programming system, but we don't know how to pass data between the `main` function and the other functions that we write. In this section, we will learn how to use function return values and argument lists to provide communication paths between two functions. We begin with an illustration of function return values.

Example 3.3   *Squaring the Integer 6.*   The function `square_six,` shown at the top of Fig. 3.16, computes the square of the integer 6. This function differs from the others that we have written thus far in that it returns a value, namely the square of 6, to the calling function. This value can then be used in a C++ arithmetic expression as part of another computation, as illustrated in the C++ code at the bottom of Fig. 3.16.

Figure 3.16   Definition and use of the function `square_six`

definition of the function square_six

```
// FILE: SqreSix.cpp
// COMPUTES AND RETURNS THE SQUARE OF 6

int square_six ()
{
    // Local data ...
    int value; // used to store computation result to be returned
```

(Continued)

Figure 3.16   (Continued)

```
    // Compute and return the square of 6.
    value = 6 * 6;
    return value;
}   // end square_six
```

use of the function square_six — compute the volume of a cube

```
// Functions used ...
int square_six ();        // COMPUTE AND RETURN THE SQUARE OF 6

// Local data ...
int volume;               // contains the volume of the cube

// Compute the volume of a cube having edges of length 6.
volume = 6 * square_six ();
...
```

In the statement

```
volume = 6 * square_six ();
```

the reference to the function name `square_six` causes this function to be executed even before the multiplication is carried out. In the execution of this function, the value 6 * 6 is computed and then returned by `square_six` to the calling function. This value is then used in the computation specified in the calling function as though it were substituted for the reference

```
square_six ()
```

The *type specifier* `int` that appears before `square_six ()` in the function prototype and definition tells the compiler what type of *return value* to expect.

As a result, the value 6 * 36 = 216 is stored in the variable named `volume` in the calling function. The local variable `value` declared in `square_six` is used to store temporarily the result of the multiplication 6 * 6 before this result is returned. In fact, this variable is really not required. We could have written

```
return 6 * 6;
```

in place of the two executable statements in the function `square_six`. ∎

Although the function `square_six` returns a value to the calling function, it still has a very limited use, because it can square only the integer 6. If we want a function to square any other integer, we must write a new one. Thus, `square_six` is limited because it carries out a very specific task; the user has no mechanism for even squaring the integer 7 with this function. The next example illustrates how to use *input arguments* to solve this problem, enabling us to *generalize* functions and make them far more useful.

Example 3.4   *Squaring the Integer* k.   The function `square_int`, shown at the top of Fig. 3.17, computes the square of any integer we provide it. This function has a single type `int` input argument through which the user can indicate which integer is to be squared each time the function is called. The last line in function `square_int` returns the square of the integer, represented by k, to the calling function. This value can then be used in a C++ arithmetic expression as part of another computation, as shown at the bottom of Fig. 3.17.

Figure 3.17   **Definition and use of the function** `square_int`

definition of the function square_int

```
// COMPUTE THE SQUARE OF AN INTEGER
int square_int
   (int k)                 // IN: represents the integer to be squared
{
   // Compute and return square of the integer represented by k
   return k * k;
}   // end square_int
```

use of the function square_int — compute the volume of a cube

```
...
// Functions used ...
// COMPUTE THE SQUARE OF AN INTEGER
int square_int
   (int);                  // IN: represents the integer to be squared
...

// Local data ...
int edge_length;       // input: contains the length of edge of cube
int volume;            // contains the volume of the cube
...

// Compute the cube volume.
volume = edge_length * square_int (edge_length);
...
```

The reference to `square_int` in the statement

```
volume = edge_length * square_int (edge_length);
```

causes this function to be executed. As part of this execution, the *actual argument* `edge_length` is substituted for the *formal argument* k (both arguments are of type `int`). In this illustration, the integer input argument is indicated by the *formal argument specification*

```
int k
```

in the header line of the function definition and by the specification

```
int
```

in the function prototype. These specifications are required by C++, and they should be the same, although no identifier name (such as k) is required in the prototype. We will be addressing these and other issues concerning argument specifications in more detail in the next few sections of this chapter.

The function square_int computes the square of the input argument and returns the result to the calling function. This value is then used in the calling function computation as though it were substituted for the reference

```
square_int (edge_length)
```

Thus, if edge_length had a value of 9 prior to the computation of the volume, the value 81 would be returned by square_int, and 729 would be computed as the volume of the cube. If edge_length had the value 4, the computed cube volume would be 64.   ∎

EXERCISES FOR SECTION 3.4

Self-Check
1. What is the purpose of function arguments?
2. Consider the function cube shown below:

```
void cube
   (int k)
{
    cout << "k cubed is ";
    cout << k * k * k << endl;
    return;
}  // end cube
```

a. What is displayed when the function call cube(3) executes?
b. If m is 5, what happens when the function call cube(m) executes?
c. What is the value of the actual argument m after the function cube executes?
d. Where should m be declared and what should its data type be?

Programming
1. Write a function square_neg_7 that computes and returns the square of the integer –7. Note carefully any differences

a. between this function and square_six;
b. between this function and square_int.

2. Write the function square_float. Note any differences between this function and the function square_int implemented in Example 3.4.

3.5 _____ HOW WE USE FUNCTIONS

Most of the algorithms we will develop involve three kinds of steps:

- data entry
- one or more computation steps
- display of results

For the time being, we can use cin and cout for data entry and display. The real creative aspect of our work comes in finding ways to instruct the computer to perform the computation steps required. In the remainder of this chapter, we will stress the use of functions for this purpose. We will illustrate how to write new functions to perform computations. We will also discuss how to save and later reuse the functions we write and how to take advantage of functions written by others (principally those functions stored in libraries accessible to the C++ language system you are using).

We begin by revisiting the Area and Circumference case study from Section 3.1. For convenience, we restate the algorithm for this problem:

1. Read radius of circle.
2. Compute area of circle.
3. Compute circumference of circle.
4. Display area and circumference.

Step 1 performs the data entry, steps 2 and 3 perform the computation, and step 4 displays the results. We will now provide another implementation of this algorithm, using functions compute_area and compute_circum to carry out steps 2 and 3, respectively. The main function is shown in Fig. 3.18;

Figure 3.18 Revised main function for Area and Circumference Problem

```
// FILE: AreaMain.cpp
// FINDS AND PRINTS THE AREA AND CIRCUMFERENCE OF A CIRCLE
//      USING FUNCTIONS

#include <iostream.h>

#include "AreaCirc.cpp"      // compute_area(), compute_circum()

void main ()
{
   // Functions used ...
   // COMPUTES THE AREA OF A CIRCLE
   float compute_area
      (float);                // IN: radius of the circle

   // COMPUTES THE CIRCUMFERENCE OF A CIRCLE
   float compute_circum
      (float);                // IN: radius of the circle

   // Local data ...
   float radius;             // input: radius of circle
   float area;               // output: area of circle
   float circum;             // output: circumference of circle
```

(Continued)

Figure 3.18   (Continued)

```
    // Read radius of circle.
    cout << "Enter the circle radius: ";
    cin  >> radius;

    // Compute area of circle.
    area = compute_area (radius);

    // Compute circumference of circle.
    circum = compute_circum (radius);

    // Display area and circumference.
    cout << "The area of the circle is " << area << endl;
    cout << "The circumference of the circle is " << circum
         << endl;
    return;
}
```

we will show how to write the `compute_area` and `compute_circum` functions after discussing this function.

The `main` function begins with a declaration of the prototypes for the functions `compute_area` and `compute_circum`. These prototypes define the type of the returned result and the order and type of the *input arguments* for each of the functions referenced in `main`. The purpose of each function and the meaning of the arguments is also described (using comments). In addition to this documentation, the prototypes also provide information to the compiler, enabling it to verify that each call to these functions in `main` is consistent with the intent of the function. We will return to this later in this section.

The prototype declarations are followed by three variable declarations (for `radius`, `area`, and `circum`). These are the same as in the original version of the program (see Fig. 3.6). Note, however, that because the constant `pi` is no longer referenced in the `main` function, it is no longer declared here. This constant is, instead, declared where it is needed: in the functions that perform the required computations.

The assignment statements

```
area = compute_area (radius);
circum = compute_circum (radius);
```

call the functions that perform the computation steps. The variable `radius` is the *actual argument* in each function call. The first statement calls the function `compute_area` and stores the returned result from this function in the `main` function variable `area`; the second statement calls `compute_circum` and stores its result in the `main` function variable `circum`.

The file `AreaMain.cpp`, shown in Fig. 3.18, does not include the definition of either of the lower-level functions. Rather than place these functions directly in the main function file, we have chosen instead to put them in a separate file, `AreaCirc.cpp`. The line

```
#include "AreaCirc.cpp"
```

is a compiler directive requesting that the compiler *include* the file `AreaCirc.cpp` (and therefore the two lower-level functions) in the main function file at compile time. This include directive is required any time we save functions that we have written in a file separate from the one being compiled. References to such user-created files in a `#include` line should be enclosed in double quotes, ", rather than the < and > symbols used when including C++ library files such as `iostream.h`. Note that prototypes for library functions that are provided by your C++ language system are not required, because the compiler already knows about the return and argument types for these functions. We will have more to say about these topics in Chapter 6.

Of course, in using the `#include` line in `AreaMain`, we are assuming that the functions `compute_area` and `compute_circum` were written earlier and saved in the file `AreaCirc.cpp`. We have yet to carry out this task, so we must now turn our attention to writing the definitions of the functions `compute_area` and `compute_circum` (see Fig. 3.19). These functions are very similar; they both begin with a function header line of the form

```
// COMPUTES THE ___ OF A CIRCLE
float fname
    (float r)              // IN: radius of the circle
```

The function name is represented by *fname*; the type specifier `float` that precedes this name indicates the type of the value to be returned by the function. The *formal argument list* indicates that each function has one floating-point formal argument, `r`. Note that with respect to the function name, return value type, and formal argument types, the function definition headers are completely consistent with the function prototype used in the calling program. As we will explain shortly, this consistency is extremely important.

Figure 3.19   Functions `compute_area` and `compute_circum`

```
// FILE: AreaCirc.cpp
// FUNCTIONS TO COMPUTE THE AREA AND CIRCUMFERENCE OF A CIRCLE

#include "SqrFloat.cpp"      // the square_float(float) function

// COMPUTES THE AREA OF A CIRCLE
float compute_area
    (float r)                  // IN: radius of the circle
{
    // Functions used ...
    // COMPUTES THE SQUARE OF A FLOATING-POINT NUMBER
    float square_float
        (float);               // IN: number to be squared
```

(Continued)

Figure 3.19   (Continued)

```
    // Local data ...
    const float pi = 3.14159;

    // Compute and return the area.
    return pi * square_float (r);
}   // end compute_area


// COMPUTES THE CIRCUMFERENCE OF A CIRCLE
float compute_circum
    (float r)                    // IN: radius of the circle
{
    // Local data ...
    const float pi = 3.14159;

    // Compute and return the circumference.
    return 2.0 * pi * r;
}   // end compute_circum
```

Each function contains the declaration of the floating-point constant `pi` (representing the mathematical symbol π), which is required to compute both the area and circumference of a circle. Such duplication of the definition of universal constants is prone to error and defeats the purpose of the use of the constant. We can avoid this duplication by placing the declaration in front of the functions that reference the constant, for example, just following the `#include` in Fig. 3.19. Such a constant is said to be `global` to the functions that follow its declaration. The constant duplication also may be avoided by moving the declaration to the parent function (in this case, function `main` in Fig. 3.18) and passing the constant to those functions that need to use it. This change is left as an exercise (Programming Exercise 2 at the end of this section).

The declaration part of `compute_area` also contains the prototype for the function `square_float`, which is similar to the `square_int` function described in Example 3.4. Writing the `square_float` function definition is an exercise at the end of Section 3.4 (Programming Exercise 2).

The executable part of each function consists of a single statement that computes and returns a value to the calling program. In `compute_area`, the statement

```
return pi * square_float (r);
```

references the constant `pi`, the formal argument `r`, and the function `square_float`. When the function `compute_area` begins executing, this statement causes the following actions:

1. The function `square_float` is called with `r` as the actual argument.

2. `square_float` computes and returns the square of the floating-point value associated with `r`.
3. In `compute_area`, the value returned from `square_float` is multiplied by `pi`.
4. This product (`pi` multiplied by the value returned from `square_float`) is returned from `compute_area` to the calling function.

This sequence is illustrated in the diagram in Fig. 3.20. We will assume that the value `5.0` is read as the value of `radius`.

As shown in Fig. 3.20, the following sequence of events occurs when the statement

```
area = compute_area (radius);
```

is executed (with `radius` assumed to be equal to `5.0`).

1. The value (`5.0`) of the radius (the actual argument) is passed to `compute_area` in correspondence with the formal argument, `r`.
2. The function `compute_area` executes; the statement

```
return pi * square_float (r);
```

causes the following sequence of events to occur:

a) The function `square_float` is called, and the actual argument, `r`, which now has the value 5.0, is placed in correspondence with the formal argument in `square_float`.

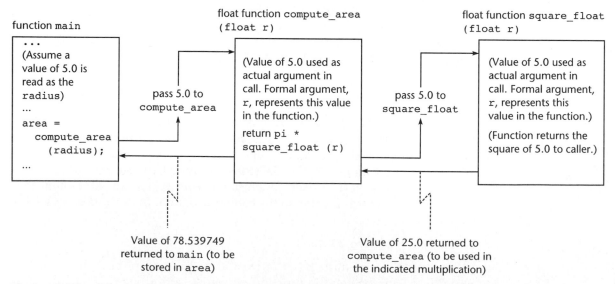

Figure 3.20   **Argument and result passing between** main, compute_area, **and** square_float

    b) `square_float` is executed and returns a value of 25.0 to `compute_area`.

    c) In `compute_area`, the value of the constant `pi` is multiplied by the returned value, 25.0.

    d) The value of this product (78.539749) is returned to the `main` function.

3. The value returned by `compute_area` is assigned to the variable area.

Use of Formal Arguments

Formal argument `r` is used in the functions `compute_area` and `compute_circum` to describe the computations to be performed by these functions. We say that `r` *represents* the actual value passed to these functions each time they are called. For example, the function call

```
compute_area (radius);
```

defines a correspondence between the calling function variable `radius` (the actual argument) and the formal argument `r` listed in the header for the function `compute_area`. The value of `radius` is *passed to* the function and used as the value of formal argument `r` wherever this argument appears in the function body. This is summarized in the following two displays.

C++
SYNTAX

Function Definition (with arguments)

Form: *type fname* (*formal-argument-list*)
```
{
    local-declarations
    executable-statements  } — function body
}
```

Example:
```
// COMPUTES THE INVERSE OF THE SUM OF TWO
// FLOATING-POINT VALUES
float inverse_sum
    (float x,        // IN: first value to be added
     float y)        // IN: second value to be added
{
    return 1.0 / (x + y);
}   // end inverse_sum
```

Interpretation: The function *fname* is defined. The rules for specifying a function with arguments are the same as for functions without arguments except for the addition of the *formal argument list.* This list is enclosed in parentheses and consists of a sequence of one or more formal argument specifications of the form

type user-defined-identifier

Multiple argument specifications are separated from each other by commas. The parentheses are required even if there are no formal arguments. A formal argument cannot be declared as a local identifier. There is no semicolon following the right parenthesis enclosing the formal argument list.

The *executable-statements* describe the data manipulation to be performed by the function using the formal argument names in the description. When a formal argument is referenced during function execution, the value of the corresponding actual argument is manipulated.

Unless *type* is `void`, function *fname* returns a single result of the indicated *type*. This is accomplished through the use of the C++ `return` statement

`return` *expression*`;`

If *type* is `void`, the `return` statement must not have an *expression* part.   ∎

C++
SYNTAX

Function Prototype (declaration of a function with arguments)

Form: *type fname* (*formal-argument-type-list*)`;`

Example:
```
// COMPUTES THE INVERSE OF THE SUM OF TWO
// FLOATING-POINT VALUES
float inverse_sum
    (float,          // IN: first value to be added
     float);         // IN: second value to be added
```

Interpretation: The identifier *fname* is declared as the name of a function returning the indicated *type*. This declaration provides all the information that the C++ compiler needs to know to translate correctly all references to the function. The *formal-argument-type-list* is a list of one or more type specifiers separated by commas.

Note: C++ permits the specification of formal argument names in function prototypes, as in

```
// COMPUTES THE INVERSE OF THE SUM OF TWO FLOATING-POINT VALUES
float inverse_sum
   (float x,      // IN: first value to be added
    float y);     // IN: second value to be added
```

We have chosen not to use names in prototypes, however, because there is no connection between these names and those used as the formal arguments in the function definition or the actual arguments in a function call.   ∎

C++
SYNTAX

Function Call (with arguments)

Form: *fname* (*actual-argument-list*);

Example: `inverse_sum (3.0, z);`

Interpretation: The *actual-argument-list* is enclosed in parentheses (the parentheses are required even if there are no actual arguments). An actual argument may be a constant, variable, or an expression; multiple arguments are separated by commas. When function *fname* is called into execution, the first actual argument is placed in correspondence with the first formal argument, the second actual argument with the second formal argument, and so on. The type of each actual argument must be consistent with the corresponding formal argument type. If the use of a function requires that a value be returned, then the function must be written so as to return a value of the expected type. Following the execution of the function, the returned result replaces the reference to the function. Note that a function defined with a *type* of `void` cannot return a value.   ■

PROGRAM
STYLE

Writing Formal Argument Lists

The formal argument list

```
(float,        // IN: first value to be added
 float);       // IN: second value to be added
```

for function `inverse_sum` is written on two lines to improve readability. In addition, this allows us room to provide a descriptive comment next to the specification of each formal argument. (This comment is not required by C++, but it can provide useful information about the use of each function argument.) The order of the actual arguments in the function call must correspond to the order of the formal arguments in the function prototype (and in the function definition). We will continue with the convention of writing formal argument descriptions on separate lines throughout the remainder of the text.   ■

More on Function Arguments

`compute_area`, `compute_circum`, and the other functions that we have seen so far (except for `inverse_sum`) all have a single argument. However, as indicated in the `inverse_sum` example in the previous displays, a function can have more than one argument. Figure 3.21 provides a diagrammatic view of a function having more than one argument. As shown in this figure, we have now extended the concept of a function from our original view of a

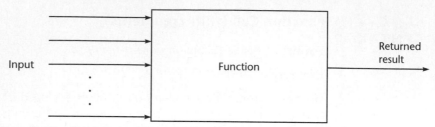

Figure 3.21   Function with multiple input and a single return value

"black box" with no information connectors to a "black box" that may have a number of input connectors (arguments) and one output connector (the return value). The input arguments of a function are used to receive information passed in from a calling function. The return statement is used to return a value from the called function to the caller.

A call to a function establishes a pair-wise correspondence between actual and formal arguments. The function call

```
inverse_sum (3.0, z);
```

establishes the correspondence between actual and formal arguments shown below:

ARGUMENT CORRESPONDENCE FOR `inverse_sum (3.0, z)`

Actual Argument	Formal Argument
3.0	x
z	y

The function call

```
inverse_sum (x + 2.0, y);
```

establishes a different correspondence:

ARGUMENT CORRESPONDENCE FOR `inverse_sum (x + 2.0, y)`

Actual Argument	Formal Argument
x + 2.0	x
y	y

This correspondence is perfectly fine, as long as x + 2.0 and y are type float in the calling function. Note that it is possible for an actual argument to be an expression (such as x + 2.0), although a formal argument must always be an identifier.

Finally, the function call

```
inverse_sum (y, x);
```

establishes the following correspondence:

ARGUMENT CORRESPONDENCE FOR `inverse_sum (y, x)`

Actual Argument	Formal Argument
y	x
x	y

This, too, is okay according to C++ rules, as long as the calling function declares x and y to be type `float`. However, for obvious reasons, we discourage this type of argument correspondence; it is very prone to mistakes.

Prototypes Revisited: Functional Independence and Scope

The last correspondence just illustrated may seem confusing at first, but it actually causes no problems whatsoever for the compiler. To understand why this is so, all you need remember is that the compiler separately translates each function that we provide it. This means that the identifiers used in one function have no connection to those used in another except through the positional correspondence defined between actual and formal arguments when one function calls another. This applies to all identifiers in a function definition—including formal arguments, local constants, variables, and function prototypes occurring within the *scope of definition* of the function, that is, between the function header and the outermost right brace, }. Because the only connection between any two functions is through argument correspondence and return values, it is extremely important that these corresponding values be *type consistent*. This is explained in the next display.

Type Consistency Between Functions

- The type of a value returned by a called function must be consistent with the type expected by the caller as indicated in the prototype of the called function.
- The type of a value (actual argument) used as input to a called function must be consistent with the type expected by that function as indicated by the corresponding formal argument in the function prototype.

Argument substitution is a key concept that must be mastered if functions are to be used effectively. Numerous examples illustrating how this substitution works will be provided in the remainder of this chapter and again in

Chapter 6. In studying these examples, you should keep the following in mind:

1. The substitution of the value of an actual argument in a function call for its corresponding formal argument is strictly positional. That is, the value of the first actual argument is substituted for the first formal argument; the value of the second actual argument is substituted for the second formal argument, and so on.
2. The names of these corresponding pairs of arguments are of no consequence in the substitution process—the names may be different, or they may be the same.
3. The substituted value is used in place of the formal argument at each point where that argument appears in the called function.

Type inconsistencies between actual and formal arguments and function return values are among the most common programming errors. If not detected by your compiler, they can be very difficult to find during program testing. The function prototype can help in this respect, for it provides all of the information that the compiler needs to check the consistency of the input arguments and of the returned type for our functions. It is still important for you to double check the consistency of arguments, but understand that the compiler also performs this check.

You may have noticed, by this time, that we have not exactly defined what we mean by "type consistent." For now, we will adopt a very rigid view of type consistency, insisting that there be an identical *type match* between an actual argument in a function call and the corresponding formal argument in the function prototype. In fact, C++ is more tolerant than this, allowing considerable room for differences in these corresponding types. In most instances, when these differences occur, C++ converts the actual argument type to that of the formal argument. If the standard conversion rules used by C++ are not clearly understood, the results produced can be very confusing. So for now, we urge you to ensure that there is always a perfect type match in corresponding argument types in a function call and its prototype. If necessary, to ensure this perfect match, there is a way to do your own explicit conversions using C++ *casting operators* to create a copy of a value of the correct type.

Casting Operators for Type Conversion

Example 3.5   *Casting Operations.*   If x is a floating-point variable, the expression

```
int (x)
```

can be used to create a copy of x of type integer. The reserved word `int` used in this manner is called a casting operator. We will see more about casting operators and type conversions in Chapter 7. For now, however, all you need to know is that int may be used as a casting operator to create an integer copy of a floating-point value; float may be used to create a floating-point copy of an integer value. The use of the casting operator will not destroy the original value. Rather, a copy is made and saved. Note that in converting a floating-point value to an integer, the fractional part (the part following the decimal point) is truncated (chopped off) and lost. You need to be careful when performing such conversions to ensure you are getting the desired result. ∎

Problem-Solving Revisited

All of the points just raised regarding the use of functions, prototypes, and arguments fit well with our earlier discussion regarding the separation of concerns and information hiding in designing and implementing computer programs. For example, the top-down problem-solving strategy illustrated in both the Area and Circumference and the Simple Figures problems involved a decomposition of problems into subproblems, and a further decomposition of some of these subproblems into still smaller problems. As we indicated at the start of this section, the C++ function enables us to carry this strategy through to the coding stage of the program development process. We can completely implement functions to solve higher-level problems in terms of lower-level functions. To do so, we follow the steps shown in the following box.

The Problem-Solving Process

1. Read the problem carefully and be certain that all aspects are clearly understood.
2. Describe all problem input and output data, the type of the data, and their relevance to the problem.
3. Break the problem into subproblems and begin constructing the program structure chart showing the relationships between the top-level problem and the subproblems at the next level.
4. Be sure you have a clear definition of each subproblem and then develop a top-level algorithm for the main function. Identify any additional information (type and description) required by your algorithm. The algorithm should be written in terms of lower-level functions that will eventually be designed to implement each of the subproblems. Note that to reference a lower-level function, we need to know only what this function is to do and what input arguments and return value are required (if any).
5. Once this information has been determined and your algorithm has been formulated and refined as necessary, the main function may be written (including the prototypes for each lower-level function-to-be). We do not need to write the lower-level functions yet.

---

6. For each subproblem, you now repeat steps 2 through 5, further developing the structure chart as necessary and designing and coding your algorithms. This process will continue until each of the subproblems is sufficiently straightforward as to not require further development.

EXERCISES FOR SECTION 3.5

Self-Check

1. Discuss the importance of the C++ function prototype declaration

   a. with respect to the top-down design process;
   b. with respect to compile-time type consistency checks on return values and input arguments.

2. In the Area and Circumference program shown in Fig. 3.18, assume that a value of 2.0 is entered in response to the radius prompt. Using the step-by-step analysis illustrated in this section (see Fig. 3.20 and the related discussion), trace

   a. the computation of the area of the circle;
   b. the computation of the circumference.

   Indicate what values would be printed during the execution of the `main` function.

3. Provide a complete structure chart for the revisited version of the Area and Circumference Problem.

Programming

1. Write a function `cube_int` to compute the cube, k^3, of an integer, k. Then write a function `main` that calls `cube_int` to compute the volume of a sphere with radius r. Test your program for $r = 2$. The formula for computing the volume of a sphere of radius r is

   $$volume = (4/3)\pi r^3$$

   where π is the constant 3.14159.

2. Rewrite functions `main`, `compute_area`, and `compute_circum` in the Area and Circumference Problem with the following changes:

   - Remove the declarations of the constant `pi` from both `compute_area` and `compute_circum` and, instead, declare `pi` in function `main`; and
   - pass `pi` to `compute_area` and `compute_circum` as the second actual argument.

3.6 — FUNCTIONS AS PROGRAM BUILDING BLOCKS: C++ LIBRARIES

Among other things, C++ functions allow us to write independent program components that can be reused as is or with minor changes. For example, we have written functions `square_int` and `square_float`, which can now be reused over and over again in programs that you write.

To reuse functions that you write, or those that your instructor writes, we need a mechanism for saving and later retrieving these functions. The mechanisms for doing this will vary according to the computer that you are using, but every computer provides such a mechanism as a standard part of its operating system. Your instructor can provide you with the special *operating system commands* that you need to use to save and, as needed, retrieve your collection of functions. In fact, by now you may already be familiar with these commands and many, many more.

One of the nice things about C++ and, for that matter, most other higher-level languages, is that they provide access to a large collection of previously written and tested functions and other program components, ready to be used and reused in our work. In your C++ language system, these components are organized in *libraries*, a few of which are described in Table 3.1. In this section, we will introduce some of the functions in the `math.h` library. As we progress through the text, we will introduce functions in the other libraries listed in this table. You are encouraged to make frequent use of the material in

Table 3.1 Summary of Libraries Accessible in Your C++ System

LIBRARY NAME	DESCRIPTION
`assert.h`	Provides facilities for adding assertions about the expected behavior of a program and for generating diagnostics if these assertions fail.
`ctype.h`	Contains functions for case conversion and for testing characters (for example, checking for uppercase or lowercase letters or for special characters or blanks).
`float.h`	Contains definitions of various type `float` and `double` limits for your computer system (for example, the maximum integer n such that 10^n is representable in your computer).
`iostream.h`	The library containing operations (such as << and >>) for performing stream input/output.
`limits.h`	Contains definitions of various type integer and character limits for your computer system (for example, the largest and smallest integers that can be stored and manipulated).
`math.h`	Contains mathematical functions such as square root, trigonometric, logarithmic, and exponentiation functions.
`stdlib.h`	Contains functions for number conversion (such as `atoi`), memory allocation (`free`), sorting (`qsort`), searching (`bsearch`), random-number generation (`rand`, `srand`), and program termination (`exit`).
`string.h`	Contains the string manipulation functions. Included are functions for comparing, concatenating, and copying strings, and for testing strings for the presence of specific characters or substrings.
`time.h`	Contains functions for manipulating date and time.

Appendix C, which contains a more complete description of these libraries and the functions that are in them. You are also urged to examine other reference material for the version of C++ that you are using.

Mathematical Functions

C++ provides access to a number of functions in library `math.h`, which perform useful mathematical computations. For example, function `sqrt` is a function that performs the square root computation. If x is 16.0 (`sqrt` takes a type `float` argument), the assignment statement

```
y = sqrt (x);
```

is evaluated as follows:

1. Function `sqrt` computes the square root of x as 4.0;
2. The function result 4.0 is assigned to y.

If w = 9.0, the assignment statement

```
z = 5.7 + sqrt (w);
```

is evaluated in the following sequence:

1. Function `sqrt` computes and returns the value 3.0;
2. the values 5.7 and 3.0 are added together;
3. the sum, 8.7, is stored in z.

The two calls to function `sqrt` just illustrated have different actual arguments, x and w. Further illustration of the capabilities of this function is provided in the next example.

Example 3.6 The C++ program in Fig. 3.22 displays the square root of two numbers that are provided as input data (`first` and `second`) and also displays the square root of their sum. Finally, the program displays the square root of the sum of the squares of `first` and `second`. The function `sqrt` is called four times, each time with different actual arguments:

```
answer = sqrt (first);
answer = sqrt (second);
answer = sqrt (first + second);
answer = sqrt (square_float (first) + square_float (second));
```

All arguments must be nonnegative or the function will not work correctly (see Programming Exercise 1 at the end of this section).

For the first two calls, the function arguments are variables. The third call shows an expression (`first + second`) used as a function argument. The fourth call illustrates that the actual argument of a function may be an expression that itself contains function calls. For all four calls, the result returned by function `sqrt` is assigned to the variable `answer`. The `main` function begins with a call to the function `instruct_user`, which displays some user instructions. The `main` function is written using the library function `sqrt` and two of our own functions, one (`square_float`) that returns a value and another (`instruct_user`) that does not. We have included the code for `instruct_user`, but we used the compiler directive

```
#include "SqrFloat.cpp"
```

to request the inclusion of the `square_float` function from the file `SqrFloat.cpp`. This, of course, assumes that we have written and tested this function sometime earlier and saved it in the file `SqrFloat.cpp` (see Programming Exercise 2, Section 3.4).

Figure 3.22   Illustration of the use of the C++ `sqrt` function

```
// FILE: SqreRoot.cpp
// PERFORMS FOUR SQUARE ROOT COMPUTATIONS

#include <iostream.h>          // i/o functions
#include <math.h>              // sqrt function

#include "SqrFloat.cpp"        // square_float function

void main ()
{
   // Functions used ...
   // DISPLAYS USER INSTRUCTIONS
   void instruct_user ();

   // COMPUTES SQUARE OF FLOATING POINT NUMBER
   float square_float
      (float);                 // IN: number to be squared

   // Local data ...
   float first;                // input:  one of two data values
   float second;               // input:  second of two data values
   float answer;               // output: a square root value

   // Display instructions.
   instruct_user ();

   // Get first number and display its square root.
   cout << "Enter the first number: ";
   cin >> first;
   answer = sqrt (first);
   cout << "The square root of the first number is " << answer
        << endl;
```

(Continued)

Figure 3.22   (Continued)

```
    // Get second number and display its square root.
    cout << "Enter the second number: ";
    cin  >> second;
    answer = sqrt (second);
    cout << "The square root of the second number is " << answer
         << endl;

    // Display the square root of the sum of first and second.
    answer = sqrt (first + second);
    cout << "The square root of the sum of both numbers is "
         << answer << endl;

    // Display the square root of the sum of the squares of first
    //    and second.
    answer = sqrt (square_float (first) + square_float (second));
    cout << "The square root of the sum of the squares of both"
         << endl;
    cout << "    numbers is " << answer << endl;
    return;
}



// DISPLAYS USER INSTRUCTIONS
void instruct_user ()
{
    cout << "This program demonstrates the use of the function"
         << endl;
    cout << "sqrt (square root).  You will be asked to enter two"
         << endl;
    cout << "numbers, and the program will display the square root"
         << endl;
    cout << "of each number, the square root of their sum, and"
         << endl;
    cout << "the square root of the sum of the squares." << endl
         << endl;
    return;
}   // end instruct_user
```

——————— Program Output ———————

```
This program demonstrates the use of the function
sqrt (square root). You will be asked to enter two
numbers, and the program will display the square root
of each number, the square root of their sum, and
the square root of the sum of the squares.

Enter the first number: 9
The square root of the first number is 3
Enter the second number: 16
```

(Continued)

Figure 3.22   (Continued)

```
The square root of the second number is 4
The square root of the sum of both numbers is 5
The square root of the sum of the squares of both
    numbers is 18.35756
```

■

Predefined Functions and Reusability

The function `sqrt` and a number of other mathematical functions are described in Table 3.2. In Table 3.2, except where noted, both `x` and `y` are of floating-point type and all functions return a value of this same type. It is important to note that the arguments for the square root and logarithmic functions must be positive. In addition, the arguments for the `cos`, `sin`, and `tan` functions must be expressed in radians as opposed to degrees. The functions `acos`, `asin`, and `atan` return a value expressed in radians.

Table 3.2   Some Mathematical Functions in the `math.h` Library

FUNCTION	PURPOSE
`acos (x)`	Inverse cosine—returns the angle y in radians satisfying $x = \cos(y)$. $-1 \leq x \leq 1$; $0 \leq y \leq \pi$
`asin (x)`	Inverse sine—returns the angle y in radians satisfying $x = \sin(y)$. $-1 \leq x \leq 1$; $-\pi/2 \leq y \leq \pi/2$
`atan (x)`	Inverse tangent—returns the angle y in radians satisfying $x = \tan(y)$. $-\pi/2 \leq y \leq \pi/2$
`ceil (x)`	Smallest integer not less than x.
`cos (x)` `sin (x)` `tan (x)`	Cosine, sine, and tangent of x, respectively. Result is returned in radians.
`exp (x)`	e^x, where $e = 2.71823$
`fabs (x)`	Absolute value, $\lvert x \rvert$
`floor (x)`	Largest integer not greater than x.
`log (x)`	$\ln(x)$—the natural log of x (base e) for $x > 0$.
`log10 (x)`	$\log_{10}(x)$—base 10 log of x for $x > 0$.
`pow (x, y)`	x^y. An error will occur if $x = 0$ and $y \leq 0$, or $x < 0$ and y is not an integer.
`sqrt (x)`	The positive square root of x, $\sqrt{x}$. $x \geq 0$.

The computations carried out by the functions shown in Table 3.2 are quite complicated. The ease with which we may reuse these functions in our own programs offers a sizable advantage in that it frees us from concern with the considerable detail involved in these calculations. This reuse will be emphasized throughout the remainder of the text because it is one of the key aspects of managing and reducing the complexity of writing programs.

Example 3.7   *Roots of Quadratic Equations.*   We can use the C++ function `sqrt` and our own function `square_float` to compute the roots of a quadratic equation in x of the form

$$ax^2 + bx + c = 0.$$

These two roots are defined as

$$\text{root}_1 = \frac{-b + \sqrt{b^2 - 4ac}}{2a}, \qquad \text{root}_2 = \frac{-b - \sqrt{b^2 - 4ac}}{2a},$$

whenever the *discriminant* $(b^2 - 4ac)$ is greater than zero. Assuming that this is the case, we can use the assignment statements below to assign values to the variables `root1` and `root2`.

```
// Compute two roots, root1 & root2, for discriminant values > 0.
disc = square_float (b) - 4.0 * a * c;
root1 = (-b + sqrt (disc)) / (2.0 * a);
root2 = (-b - sqrt (disc)) / (2.0 * a);
```
■

Example 3.8   *The Length of the Third Side of a Triangle.*   If we know the length of two sides, b and c, of a triangle (see Fig. 3.23) and the angle, *alpha*, between them (in degrees), we can compute the length of the third side, a, using the formula

$$a^2 = b^2 + c^2 - 2bc(\cos(alpha)).$$

To use the C++ cosine function, however, we must express its argument (`alpha`) in radians instead of degrees. To convert an angle from degrees to radians, we multiply the angle by $\pi/180$. Assuming `pi` represents the constant π, the C++ assignment statement below computes the unknown side length. The function `convert_to_radians` performs the conversion from units in degrees to units in radians (see Programming Exercise 1 at the end of this section).

```
a = sqrt (square_float (b) + square_float (c)
    - 2.0 * b * c * cos (convert_to_radians (alpha)));
```

You may assume that all computations are of type floating point. Write a short test program and test your function using several different pairs of points to be sure the function works. The test program should read in the coordinates before the call to the function and display the distance returned after the call.

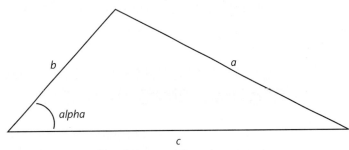

Figure 3.23   Triangle with unknown side *a*

EXERCISES FOR SECTION 3.6

Self-Check

1. Rewrite the following mathematical expressions using C++ functions.

   a. $\sqrt{u + vw^2}$
   b. $\log_{10}(x^y)$
   c. $\sqrt{(x - y)^2}$
   d. $|xy - w/z|$

2. Evaluate the following function calls.

   a. `sqrt (fabs (-15.8))`
   b. `square_float (3.0)`
   c. `ceil (3.5)`
   d. `floor (3.5)`
   e. `pow (2.5, 3.0)`

3. Let a = 3.0, b = 25.0, and c = 1.0. Evaluate the following pairs of expressions. If the results of the evaluation are different for each expression in the pair, explain why.

   a. `disc = square_float (b) - 4.0 * a * c;`
      `disc = square_float (b) - (4.0 * a) * c;`
   b. `x1 = (-b + sqrt (disc)) / (2.0 * a);`
      `x1 = (-b + sqrt (disc)) / 2.0 * a;`
   c. `x2 = (-b - sqrt (disc)) / (2.0 * a);`
      `x2 = -b - sqrt (disc) / (2.0 * a);`

Programming

1. Write the function `convert_to_radians` used in Example 3.7. Note that if `alpha` represents an angle measured in degrees, then the equivalent angle given in radians is computed as

   `alpha * pi / 180.0`

2. Modify the `main` function in Fig. 3.22 to ensure that nonnegative values for `first` and `second` are entered by the user before the square root calculation is performed.

3. Write a C++ function `compute_distance` with four formal arguments representing the Cartesian coordinates of two points (x_1, y_1) and (x_2, y_2). Your function should compute the distance between these points using the formula

$$distance = \sqrt{(x_1 - x_2)^2 + (y_1 - y_2)^2} .$$

3.7   SOME COMMENTS ON THE SOFTWARE ENGINEERING PROCESS

In this text, most of the problems we examine are comparatively simple and their solutions relatively short and uncomplicated. In reality, things are quite different. Problems are often exceedingly complex and difficult to describe in a complete and unambiguous fashion (you may even find this to be the case with some of the simpler problems encountered in this text). Solutions can require hundreds of *person-years of effort* and result in millions of *lines of code*.

Procedural and data abstraction are two important tools that can help in decomposing such large, complex problems into small and manageable components. Such decomposition is important in allocating programming effort among members of a team of programmers. It is also helpful to individuals working on a relatively small programming task. Decomposition of even small problems enables us to focus on one aspect of a problem solution at a time, and get it right before moving on to the next subproblem. There is considerable evidence that this focus on one small piece of a problem at a time is of significant benefit to the entire *software engineering process*. Issues related to this process will be revisited again later in this text, especially in Chapters 6, 10, and 11. We have barely scratched the surface in this chapter.

3.8   COMMON PROGRAMMING ERRORS

■ *Semicolons in a Function Header and Prototype:* A missing semicolon at the end of a function prototype may cause a "Statement missing ;" or "Declaration terminated incorrectly" diagnostic (a prototype is a declaration and must be terminated with a semicolon). However, the accidental inclusion of a semicolon separating a function header from its definition will cause numerous compiler errors following the header.

■ *Inconsistencies in the Number of Formal and Actual Arguments:* Although we have used arguments only sparingly thus far, experienced programmers know that the omission or incorrect ordering of function arguments is a common programming error. As your programs increase in size and complexity, you will find yourself writing many calls to functions. It is important that you carefully check the number of actual arguments used in each call to ensure that this number is the same as the number of formal arguments in the prototype. If the number of arguments in a function call is not the same as the number in the prototype, error messages such as

```
"Too few arguments in call to int_power(int, int)."
"Too many arguments in call to int_power(int, int)."
"Incorrect number of arguments in call to int_power(int, int)."
"Extra argument in call to int_power (int, int)."
```

will be generated by your compiler. As shown, in most cases the function prototype, `int_power(int, int)` in this case, is listed in the error message as an aid to determining the exact nature of the error.

  ▪ *Argument Mismatches:* It is also important to verify that each actual argument in a function call is in the correct position relative to its corresponding formal argument. This check may be done most easily by comparing each actual argument to the type and description of its corresponding formal argument in the function prototype. Remember, the actual argument name is not what is important. Rather, it is the positional correspondence that is critical.

  Argument list errors often result in type mismatches between actual and formal argument lists. However, this is not always the case. For example, consider the function

```
// RAISE FIRST ARGUMENT TO POWER OF SECOND
int int_power
   (int,       // IN: argument to be raised to specified power
    int);      // IN: power (greater than or equal to 0)
```

The call

```
result = int_power (5, 2);
```

would produce the result 25. The call

```
result = int_power (2, 5);
```

would yield the result 32. Clearly, the order of the arguments makes a difference. Yet both are integers, so an accidental reversal of the arguments will not even result in a type mismatch. We simply get the wrong answer.

  Usually, however, argument list errors will result in type mismatches, such as a character actual argument corresponding to a floating-point formal argument. Most mismatches that you are likely to create at this point in your programming work are perfectly permissible in C++ and usually will not even produce a warning message from the compiler. Instead, the compiler will perform a *standard conversion* on the actual argument (see Section 3.5), converting it to the type specified by the formal argument. In most cases, these conversions will produce incorrect results, which in turn will cause other errors during the execution of your program. The same often is true for mismatches in function return value types. These errors can be extremely difficult to locate during debugging or the testing of your program. The only reasonably certain way to avoid them is carefully to check your arguments first, thus minimizing the potential for such mistakes. If actual argument conversions are required to ensure exact argument matching, use the casting functions introduced in Section 3.5 for explicit conversion.

There are two situations in which some compilers may provide help. One occurs when floating-point actual arguments are used where character formal arguments are expected. The other occurs when a floating-point value is returned where a character is expected. Even these mismatches are legal, but the results of the standard conversion are so likely to produce an execution error that most compilers will give you a warning diagnostic such as

```
"Float or double assigned to integer or character data type."
```

■ *Function Prototype and Definition Mismatches:* Once a prototype has been specified in a calling function, it can be duplicated, comments and all, in building the header for the function definition. All that remains to be done with the copied header is to provide an identifier for each function argument and to be sure to remove the semicolon at the end of the prototype. Conversely, if a function written by you or someone else is to be called, the prototype may be easily extracted from the header of the existing function. Just remove the argument identifiers and put a semicolon at the end.

Type mismatches between a function prototype and its definition will not be detected by the compiler. In all likelihood, these mismatches will be detected by the linker program for your C++ system, but the error message may be hard to interpret, indicating something such as

```
"Undefined symbol int_power (int, int) in module square."
```

The cause of such a message is usually either a missing function definition (such as for function `int_power`) or the use of a function prototype that does not match the function definition (possibly because one or more of the arguments is of a different type, such as `float` instead of `char`). If the arguments in a function prototype don't match those in the definition, the linker assumes that the prototype refers to a different function, one for which there is no definition.

■ *Return Statement Errors:* All functions that you write should terminate execution with a `return` statement. Except in type `void` functions, the `return` statement should include the specification of a constant, variable, or expression indicating the value to be returned. Type mismatch errors in return values were discussed earlier in this section. Care should be taken to ensure that the expression (or even worse, the entire return statement) is not omitted. If no return value is specified when one is expected, a message to this effect will be generated:

`"Return value expected."`

or

`"Function should return a value..."`

If a return value is specified for a `void` function, a message such as the one shown below will be produced, indicating that the `void` function does not take a return value:

`"Function cannot return a value..."`
`"Warning: return with a value in function returning void."`

Although the `return` statement is not required for `void` functions, we recommend that you use it anyway, even though there will be no expression part associated with the `return` statement.

■ *Logic Errors in Your Program — Testing a Program and Checking Your Results:* Argument mismatches are not the only errors that may go undetected by the compiler. Numerous other errors, such as the incorrect specification of computations (writing mathematical formulas) may also go undetected by the compiler, yet produce incorrect results. For example, if you are given the formula

$$y = 3k^2 - 9k + 7$$

to program, and you write the C++ code

`y = 9 * int_power (k, 2) - 3 * k + 7`

(accidentally reversing the coefficients 9 and 3), no error will be detected by the compiler. As far as the compiler is concerned, no mistake has been made— the expression is perfectly legal C++ code, assuming `int_power` is properly defined and that k is an integer.

There is usually just one way to find these errors, and that is by testing your program using carefully chosen *test data samples* and verifying, for each sample, that your answer is correct. Such testing is a critical part of the programming process and cannot be omitted. As we proceed through the text, we will have more to say about testing strategies. One example of such a strategy was introduced in this chapter. It involved the decomposition of a problem into subproblems, writing the solutions to the subproblems using separate functions, and then separately testing these functions. This strategy can help simplify the testing process and make it easier for you to perform a more thorough test of your entire program.

CHAPTER REVIEW

In the first part of this chapter, we outlined an approach for solving problems on the computer. This approach stressed the following points:

- Be sure that you have a clear and complete statement of the problem to be solved. If you feel you don't have such a statement, ask questions of the problem presenter to improve your understanding of what is required.
- Identify the input and output data for the problem as well as other relevant data.
- Decompose the problem into more manageable subproblems. This decomposition may need to be repeated until each of the lowest-level subproblems is easily solvable.
- Develop a list of steps (an algorithm) for solving the initial problem.
- Refine the algorithm—develop algorithms for the subproblems.
- Implement the algorithm and its refinements in C++, taking advantage of the C++ function construct as needed.

The important concept of procedural abstraction was introduced. We showed how to divide a problem into subproblems and how to use a structure chart to indicate the relationship between subproblems. We introduced the function as a means of implementing subproblems as separate program units, and indicated that a C++ program is simply a collection of one or more functions, each representing the boxes in a structure chart.

Initially, functions with no connections (no arguments or return values) were presented. The limitations of such functions were discussed, and the idea of providing input arguments and return value connections was introduced. It was shown how we could use each of these features of C++ to call functions and have them manipulate different data each time, thereby increasing the generality and reusability of the function.

The importance of ensuring the proper one-to-one correspondence between associated pairs of actual and formal arguments of a function was stressed, as was the compatibility of expected and actual return values. The prototype declaration was introduced as a C++ feature that was used by the compiler to check for this compatibility.

We listed a number of the C++ function libraries, and we provided some examples of the use of functions in one of these libraries, math.h. We indicated that prototypes for the library functions were not needed because the compiler already knew about the types of return values and arguments for these functions. We emphasized the reuse of our own functions, as well as the C++ library functions, as one of the primary means of reducing problem complexity to manageable proportions. We also promised to continue this thrust throughout the remainder of the text.

Comments play an important role in program documentation, especially pertaining to functions. We have consistently used comments to describe the purpose of each function that we have written. We have also used them to provide a description of the use of the input arguments and local variables of a function, and the purpose of each logical section of code within a function. By now, you should have absorbed several guidelines for using program comments.

New C++ Constructs   The new C++ constructs introduced in this chapter are described in Table 3.3.

Table 3.3   Summary of New C++ Constructs

CONSTRUCT	EFFECT
Function Prototype (with comments)	
`// DISPLAYS A DIAMOND OF STARS` `void display ();`	Prototype for a function that has no arguments and returns no result.

`// COMPUTES AVERAGE OF TWO INTEGERS`
`float average`
`  (int, int); // IN: the input args`
	Prototype for a function with two integer input arguments and a type `float` result.

Function Call	
`display ();`	Calls function `display` and causes it to begin execution. When execution is complete, control returns to the statement in the calling function that immediately follows the call.
`ave = average (k1, k2);`	Calls function `average`. Returned value replaces the call and becomes part of the assignment statement (and is assigned to `ave`).
Function Definition (with comments)	

`// DISPLAYS A DIAMOND OF STARS`
`void display ()`
`{`
	Definition of a function that has no arguments and returns no result.

```
    cout << "          *          ";
    cout << "        *   *        ";
    cout << "      *       *      ";
    cout << "    *           *    ";
    cout << "      *       *      ";
    cout << "        *   *        ";
    cout << "          *          ";
    return;
}   // end display
```

Return with no expression part (function returns no value).

(Continued)

Table 3.3   (Continued)

CONSTRUCT	EFFECT
```// COMPUTES AVERAGE OF TWO INTEGERS``` ```float average``` ``` (int m1, int m2) // IN: integer values```	Definition of a function with two integer input arguments and a floating-point result.
```{``` ``` return float (m1 + m2) / 2.0;```	Returns a floating-point result.
```}```	

✔ QUICK-CHECK EXERCISES

1. Each function is executed in the order in which it is declared in the main program. True or false?
2. Describe the ordering of declarations as shown in this text.
3. What is a local declaration?
4. What is a structure chart?
5. Explain how a structure chart differs from an algorithm.
6. What does the function below do?

```
void nonsense ()
{
    cout << "*****";
    cout << "*    *";
    cout << "*****";
    return;
}  // end nonsense
```

7. Given the function nonsense from Exercise 6, describe the output that is produced when the following lines are executed.

```
{
    nonsense;
    nonsense;
    nonsense;
}
```

Answers to Quick-Check Exercises

1. False
2. We have placed function declarations first, followed by constant and then variable declarations.
3. The declaration of a symbol inside the scope of a function and hence accessible only to that function.
4. A structure chart is a diagram used to show an algorithm's subproblems and their interdependence.

5. A structure chart shows the hierarchical relationship between subproblems; an algorithm lists the sequence in which subproblems are performed.
6. It would display a rectangle whenever it was called.
7. It displays three rectangles on top of each other.

REVIEW QUESTIONS

1. Discuss the strategy of divide and conquer.
2. Provide guidelines for the use of comments.
3. Briefly describe the steps you would take to derive an algorithm for a given problem.
4. The diagram that shows the algorithm steps and their interdependencies is called a _____ .
5. What are three advantages of using functions?
6. A C++ program is a collection of one or more _____ , one of which must be named _____ .
7. When is a function executed? Can function definitions be nested?
8. Is the use of functions a more efficient use of the programmer's time or the computer's time? Explain your answer.
9. Write a program that draws a rectangle made up of asterisks. Draw a structure chart for the problem. Use two functions: `draw_sides` and `draw_line`. Discuss the reusability of your functions for drawing rectangles of different sizes.

PROGRAMMING PROJECTS

1. Add one or more of your own unique functions to the Stick Figure Program presented in Section 3.2. Create several more pictures combining the `draw_circle`, `draw_intersect`, `draw_base`, and `draw_parallel` functions with your own. Make any modifications to these functions that you need in order to make the picture components fit nicely.
2. Write functions that display each of your initials in block letter form. Use these functions to display your initials.
3. Write a function that displays a triangle. Use this function to display six triangles on top of each other.
4. Four track stars entered the mile race at the Penn Relays. Write a program that will read in the race time in minutes and seconds for one runner and compute and print their speed in feet per second and in meters per second. (*Hints:* There are 5280 feet in one mile, and one kilometer equals 3281 feet (one meter is equal to 3.281 feet). Test your program on each of the times below.

Minutes	Seconds
3	52.83
3	59.83
4	00.03
4	16.22

Write and call a function that displays instructions to the program user. Write two other functions, one to compute the speed in meters per second and the other to compute the speed in feet per second.

5. A cyclist coasting on a level road slows from a speed of 10 miles/hr to 2.5 miles/hr in one minute. Write a computer program that calculates the cyclist's constant rate of deceleration and determines how long it will take the cyclist to come to rest, given an initial speed of 10 miles/hr. (*Hint:* Use the equation

$$a = (v_f - v_i) / t,$$

where a is acceleration, t is time interval, v_i is initial velocity, and v_f is the final velocity.) Write and call a function that displays instructions to the program user and another function that computes and returns the deceleration given v_f, v_i, and t.

6. In shopping for a new house, you must consider several factors. In this problem the initial cost of the house, estimated annual fuel costs, and annual tax rate are available. Write a program that will determine the total cost after a five-year period for each set of house data below. You should be able to inspect your program output to determine the "best buy."

Initial house cost	Annual fuel cost	Tax rate
$67,000	$2300	0.025
$62,000	$2500	0.025
$75,000	$1850	0.020

To calculate the house cost, add the fuel cost for five years to the initial cost, then add the taxes for five years. Taxes for one year are computed by multiplying the tax rate by the initial cost. Write and call a function that displays instructions to the program user and another function that computes and returns the house cost given the initial cost, the annual fuel cost, and the tax rate.

4

Selection Structures: if and switch Statements

4.1   Control Structures
4.2   Logical Expressions
4.3   Introduction to the if Control Statement
4.4   if Statements with Compound Alternatives
4.5   Decision Steps in Algorithms
       CASE STUDY: Payroll Problem
4.6   Formatted Output: Introduction to Manipulators and Flags
4.7   Checking Correctness of an Algorithm
       CASE STUDY: Finding the Alphabetically First Letter
4.8   More Problem-Solving Strategies
       CASE STUDY: Computing Overtime Pay
       CASE STUDY: Computing Insurance Dividends
4.9   Nested if Statements and Multiple-Alternative Decisions
4.10   The switch Control Statement
4.11   Common Programming Errors
       Chapter Review

In this text we teach programming as a disciplined technique that results in programs that are easy to read and less likely to contain errors. The emphasis in this approach is on crafting programs in a consistent, clear, and concise fashion, building larger programs from smaller components and reusing existing and tested components whenever possible.

In the next two chapters we continue to show how to construct these smaller components. Our approach, often referred to as *structured programming*, involves the use of a small number of easy-to-understand *control structures* to describe the steps required to solve a problem. To this point, we have used just one of these control mechanisms, the sequencing of steps in order of execution. In Chapters 4 and 5 we introduce the other two important control structures, *selection structures*, which enable us to choose from among several alternatives to be carried out, and *iteration structures*, which enable us to specify repeated execution of steps to be carried out.

As in the previous chapters, our focus will be on consistency and clarity of expression. We will emphasize commonly accepted guidelines (such as using meaningful names for identifiers) to write code that is adequately documented with comments and is clear and readable. Government organizations and industry are strong advocates of this structured programming approach because structured programs are much more cost effective in the long term.

4.1 ——— CONTROL STRUCTURES

The control structures of a programming language enable us to extend the top-down program development process to the level of specifying the *algorithm steps* or logic of each function that we write. We begin by expressing the algorithm in terms of the basic control steps required. Then we can write the more detailed steps necessary to implement each of these control steps. The completed program component will still retain its higher-level structure as a sequence of control structures with one entry point and one exit point (see Fig. 4.1).

There are three categories of control structures: *sequence, selection,* and *iteration.* So far, we have illustrated sequential control using *compound statements* or blocks in C++. A compound statement is a group of statements bracketed by { and }.

```
{
    statement₁;
    statement₂;
    .
    .
    .
    statementₙ;
}
```

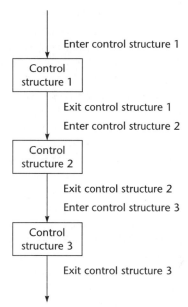

Enter control structure 1

Control structure 1

Exit control structure 1

Enter control structure 2

Control structure 2

Exit control structure 2

Enter control structure 3

Control structure 3

Exit control structure 3

Figure 4.1   A program as a sequence of three control structures

Control flows from $statement_1$ to $statement_2$, and so on. In C++, local declarations may be specified at the beginning of a compound statement. However, we will not use this feature when writing function definitions.

In this chapter we show how to write algorithms and programs with steps that select from several alternative courses of action. We will see two ways to do this in C++. The first technique is to use a C++ `if` control statement with a logical expression; the second approach is to use the `switch` control statement. This chapter provides many examples of the use of `if` and `switch` statements.

We continue our study of problem-solving and introduce one more problem-solving strategy: *solution by analogy*. We describe how to use data flow information in structure charts to provide additional program documentation. We also show how to hand trace the execution of a program containing selection structures to ensure that it does what we expect.

4.2 ⎯⎯⎯ LOGICAL EXPRESSIONS

In all the algorithms illustrated, we executed each algorithm step exactly once in the order in which it appeared. Often we are faced with situations in which we must provide alternative steps that may or may not be executed, depending on the input data. For example, the percentage tax rate assessed by the

Internal Revenue Service (IRS) depends on an individual's salary. Single persons who earn less than \$18,550 pay a tax rate of 15%, whereas those who earn between \$18,550 and \$44,900 pay a tax rate of 15% on the first \$18,550 and a tax rate of 28% on the rest. Consequently, an accountant's income tax program must be able to select the correct tax rate to use in a tax computation.

To accomplish this goal, a program must be able to determine whether the correct answer to the question, "Is annual income less than \$18,550?" is yes or no. In C++, this is accomplished by evaluating a *logical expression* or *condition*. Assuming that the taxable income is stored in the type `float` variable `income`, the logical expression corresponding to the above question is

```
income < 18500.00
```

There are only two possible values for a logical expression: 1, which represents true, or 0, which represents false. If `income` is less than 18500.00, the value of the logical expression above is 1 (true); if income is not less than 18500.00, the value of the expression is 0 (false).

Logical expressions may be formed by using combinations of three kinds of operators: *relational, equality,* and *logical* (see Table 4.1). In the following sections we describe the permissible forms of C++ expressions that use these operators.

Table 4.1   C++ Operators Used in Logical Expressions

RELATIONAL	EQUALITY	LOGICAL
< less than	== equal to	&& and
<= less than or equal to	!= not equal to	|| or
> greater than		! not
>= greater than or equal to		

Logical Expressions Involving Relational Operators

Most logical expressions that we use will have one of the forms

variable	*operator*	*variable*
constant	*operator*	*variable*
variable	*operator*	*constant*

(Other forms involving more general expressions on the left or the right are permissible but less often used.) The *relational operators* are familiar symbols. (Do not confuse them with the unrelated character pairs >> or << used for input and output operations.) Both operands of the relational operator must be the same data type (`char`, `int`, or `float`), or one may be type `float` and the other type `int`. A *constant* may be an actual value (for example, 3, 4.5, 'x') or a constant identifier.

Be careful not to confuse the assignment operator = with the equality operator ==. The not symbol ! may be used alone as a logical operator or as part of the symbol pair !=, meaning the opposite of ==. As with all C++ symbol pairs, they must appear together with no space between them.

Example 4.1 Table 4.2 shows the relational and equality operators with some sample conditions. Each condition is evaluated assuming the variable values below.

x	power	max_power	y	item	min_item	mom_or_dad	num	sentinel
−5	1024	1024	7	1.5	−999.0	'm'	999	999

Table 4.2   Use of C++ Relational and Equality Operators

OPERATOR	SAMPLE CONDITION	ENGLISH MEANING	LOGICAL VALUE
<=	x <= 0	x less than or equal to 0	1 (true)
<	power < max_power	power less than max_power	0 (false)
>=	x >= y	x greater than or equal to y	0 (false)
>	item > min_item	item greater than min_item	1 (true)
==	mom_or_dad == 'm'	mom_or_dad equal to 'm'	1 (true)
!=	num != sentinel	num not equal to sentinel	0 (false)

Logical Expressions Involving Logical Operators

We also can use *logical operators* to form more complicated logical expressions. There are two logical binary operators: && (and) and || (or). These operators each require two logical expressions as operands. There is also one unary operator, ! (not), which operates on a single logical operand and reverses its condition. Some logical expressions formed with the binary operators are:

```
(salary < min_salary) || (number_dependents > 5)
(temperature > 90.0) && (humidity > 0.90)
```

The first logical expression determines whether an employee is eligible for special scholarship funds. The expression is true if either condition in parentheses is true. The second logical expression describes an unbearable summer day, with temperature and humidity both in the nineties. The expression is true only when both conditions are true.

Simple expressions such as

```
x == y;
x < y;
```

can be negated by applying the unary ! operator to the entire expression.

```
!(x == y);
!(x < y);
```

However, using the *logical complement* of the relational operator often works just as well in these situations:

```
x != y;
x >= y;
```

The best time to use the ! operator is when you want to reverse the truth value of a long or complicated expression that involves many operators. For example, expressions such as:

```
(salary < min_salary) || (number_dependents > 5)
```

are most easily negated by enclosing the entire expression in parentheses and preceding it by the ! operator.

```
!((salary < min_salary) || (number_dependents > 5))
```

Remember, logical operators can be used only with logical expressions. The three types are described next in Tables 4.3, 4.4, and 4.5.

Table 4.3 shows that the && operator yields a 1 (true result) only when both of its operands are true; Table 4.4 shows that the || operator yields a 0 (false

Table 4.3   && **Operator**

OPERAND1	OPERAND2	OPERAND1 && OPERAND2
1 (true)	1 (true)	1 (true)
1 (true)	0 (false)	0 (false)
0 (false)	1 (true)	0 (false)
0 (false)	0 (false)	0 (false)

Table 4.4 || **Operator**

OPERAND1	OPERAND2	OPERAND1 || OPERAND2
1 (true)	1 (true)	1 (true)
1 (true)	0 (false)	1 (true)
0 (false)	1 (true)	1 (true)
0 (false)	0 (false)	0 (false)

Table 4.5   ! Operator

OPERAND1	!OPERAND1
1 (true)	0 (false)
0 (false)	1 (true)

result) only when both of its operands are false. The ! operator has a single operand; Table 4.5 shows that the ! operator yields the logical complement, or negation, of its operand.

Operator Precedence

The *precedence* of an operator determines its order of evaluation in an expression. Table 4.6 shows the precedence of all the operators we have learned thus far in C++.

As you can see, the ! operator has the highest precedence, followed by the arithmetic, relational, equality, then logical operators. Expressions involving operators having different precedence levels should generally be written with parentheses to prevent syntax errors.

Table 4.6   Operator Precedence

OPERATOR	DESCRIPTION
highest (evaluated first)	
!, +, -	logical not, unary plus, unary minus
*, /, %	multiplication, division, modulus
+, -	addition, subtraction
<, <=, >=, >	relational inequality
==, !=	equal, not equal
&&	logical and
||	logical or
=	assignment
lowest (evaluated last)	

Example 4.2   The expression

```
x < min + max
```

involving the float variables x, min, and max is interpreted correctly in C++ as

```
x < (min + max)
```

because + has higher precedence than <. The expression

```
min <= x && x <= max
```

is also correct, but providing the extra parentheses makes the intent much clearer:

```
(min <= x) && (x <= max)
```

■

Testing for a Range of Values

Expressions similar to the second one just shown are quite common in programming. If min represents the lower bound of a range of values and max represents the upper bound (min is less than max), this expression tests whether x lies within the range min through max inclusive. In Fig. 4.2, this range of values is shaded. The expression is true if x lies within this range and is false if x is outside this range.

Figure 4.2   Range of true values for (min <= x) && (x <= max)

More Logical Expressions

Example 4.3   The following are all legal logical expressions if x, y, and z are type float. The value of each expression, shown in brackets, assumes that x is 3.0, y is 4.0, and z is 2.0. Note that not all of the parentheses used in these examples are necessary. Rather, they are included here for clarity.

1. `(x > z) && (y > z)`   1 (true)
2. `(x + y / z) <= 3.5`   0 (false)
3. `(z > x) || (z > y)`   0 (false)
4. `!(y == z)`   1 (true)
5. `(x == 1.0) || (x == 3.0)`   1 (true)
6. `(z < x) && (x < y)`   1 (true)
7. `(x <= z) || (x >= y)`   0 (false)
8. `!(x > y) || ((y + z) >= (x - z))`   1 (true)
9. `!((x > y) || ((y + z) >= (x - z)))`   0 (false)

Expression 1 gives the C++ form of the relationship "x and y are greater than z." It is often tempting to write this as

```
x && y > z
```

Although such an expression is syntactically correct in C++, it may not produce the desired result because the left operand x is not a logical expression. Similarly, expression 5 shows the correct way to express the relationship "x is equal to 1.0 or to 3.0."

Expression 6 is the C++ form of the relationship $z < x < y$ (i.e., "x is in the range 2.0 to 4.0)." The boundary values, 2.0 and 4.0, are excluded from the range of x values that yield a true result.

Expression 7 is true if the value of x lies outside the range bounded by z and y. In Fig. 4.3, the shaded areas represent the values of x that yield a true result. Both y and z are included in the set of values that yield a true result.

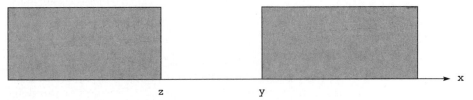

Figure 4.3   Range of true values for `(x <= z) || (x >= y)`

Finally, expression 8 is evaluated in Fig. 4.4; the values given at the beginning of Example 4.3 are shown above the expression.

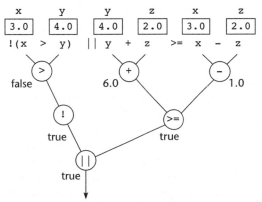

Figure 4.4   Evaluation tree for `!(x > y) || y + z >= x - z`

The expression in Fig. 4.4 is rewritten below with parentheses to show the order of evaluation. Although these parentheses are not required, they do clarify the meaning of the expression and we recommend their use.

```
(!(x > y)) || ((y + z) >= (x - z))
```

Besides comparing numbers, it is also possible to compare characters using the relational and equality operators. Several examples of such comparisons are shown in Table 4.7.

Table 4.7   Examples of Comparisons

EXPRESSION	VALUE
`'a' < 'c'`	1 (true)
`'X' <= 'A'`	0 (false)
`'3' > '4'`	0 (false)
`('A' <= ch) && (ch <= 'Z')`	1 (true) if ch contains an uppercase letter; otherwise 0 (false)

In writing such comparisons it is safe to assume for any C++ system that the uppercase letters appear in dictionary order. Lowercase letters also appear in dictionary order, and the *digit characters* are ordered as expected: '0' < '1' < '2' < ... < '9'. However, the relationships among other characters (such as '+', '<', '!', etc.) or between two characters not in the same group (for example, 'a' and 'A', or 'B' and 'b', or 'c' and 'A') are less certain and must be carefully checked for the computer you are using (see, for example, Appendix A). On some computers, the expression (`'A' <= ch`) && (`ch <= 'Z'`) is true even for some characters that are not uppercase letters. We will have more to say about this in Chapter 7.

Example 4.4   Consider the expression

```
even = (n % 2 == 0)
```

If n is an even number, the expression

```
(n % 2 == 0)
```

is true because all even numbers are divisible by 2; otherwise, the expression is false. Therefore, if the remainder of the modulus operation is zero, the variable **even** will be assigned the integer value 1. If the remainder of the modulus operation is not zero, (`n % 2 == 0`) will evaluate to false, and **even** will be assigned the integer value 0.   ■

EXERCISES FOR SECTION 4.2

Self-Check   1. Assuming x is 15.0 and y is 25.0, what are the values of the following conditions?

x != y   x < x   x >= (y - x)   x == (y + x - y)

2. Evaluate each expression below if a is 5, b is 10, c is 15, and d is 0.

```
a. (c == (a + b)) || (c == d)
b. (a != 7) && (c >= 6) || ((a + c) <= 20)
c. !(b <= 12) && (a % 2 == 0)
d. !((a > 5) || (c < (a + b)))
```

3. Draw the evaluation tree for expression 9 of Example 4.3.

Programming   1. Write a logical expression that is true for each of the following conditions.

a. x is in the range −1.5 to 3.2.
b. a is in the range 17 to 23, inclusive.
c. y is greater than x and less than z.
d. w is equal to 6 or not greater than 3.

2. Write the logical expression for each of the following conditions.

a. n is in the range −k and +k inclusive.
b. ch is an uppercase letter.
c. m is a divisor of n.

4.3 —— INTRODUCTION TO THE if CONTROL STATEMENT

A C++ programmer can use the if control statement to select from several alternatives of executable statements. An if statement always contains a logical expression. For example, the if statement

```
if (gross > 100.00)
    net = gross - tax;
else
    net = gross;
```

selects one of the two assignment statements listed. It selects the statement immediately following the condition (gross > 100.00) if the logical expression is true (i.e., gross is greater than 100.00); it selects the statement following the reserved word else if the logical expression is false (i.e., gross is not greater than 100.00). It is never possible for both statements to execute after testing a particular condition. A semicolon does not follow the condition in parentheses, only the statements that follow.

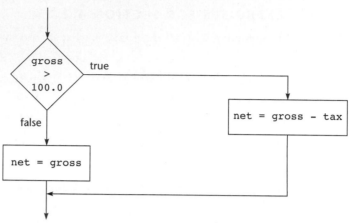

Figure 4.5   Flowchart of `if` control statement with two alternatives

Figure 4.5 provides a graphical description, called a *flowchart*, of the *flow of execution control* for the `if` control statement above. Figure 4.5 shows that the condition (`gross > 100.00`) enclosed in the diamond-shaped box is evaluated first. If the condition is true, the arrow labeled true is followed, and the assignment statement in the rectangle on the right is executed. If the condition is false, the arrow labeled false is followed, and the assignment statement in the rectangle on the left is executed.

More if Statement Examples

The `if` control statement above has two alternatives, but only one will be executed for a given value of `gross`. Example 4.5 illustrates that an `if` statement can also have a single alternative that is executed only when the condition is true.

Example 4.5   The `if` statement below has one alternative that is executed only when `x` is not equal to zero. It causes `product` to be multiplied by `x`; the new value is saved in `product`, replacing the old value. If `x` is equal to zero, the multiplication is not performed. Figure 4.6 is a flowchart of this `if` statement.

```
// Multiply product by a non zero x only.
if (x != 0)
    product = product * x;
```

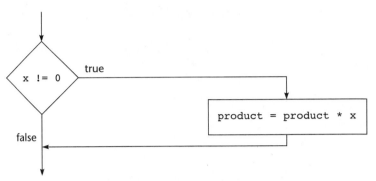

Figure 4.6   Flowchart of `if` with one alternative   ∎

Example 4.6   The `if` statement below has two alternatives. It displays either `"Hi Mom"` or `"Hi Dad"` depending on the character stored in variable `mom_or_dad` (type `char`).

```
if (mom_or_dad == 'm')
    cout << "Hi Mom" << endl;
else
    cout << "Hi Dad" << endl;
```
∎

Example 4.7   The `if` control statement below has one alternative; it displays the message `"Hi Mom"` only when `mom_or_dad` has the value `'m'`. Regardless of whether or not `"Hi Mom"` is displayed, the message `"Hi Dad"` is always displayed.

```
if (mom_or_dad == 'm')
    cout << "Hi Mom" << endl;
cout << "Hi Dad" << endl;
```
∎

In all examples shown thus far, the true and false alternatives of an `if` control structure consist of a single C++ statement. In the next section, we will see how to write true and false alternatives consisting of more than one statement.

PROGRAM STYLE

Format of the if Control Statement

In all the `if` statement examples, *statement*$_T$ and *statement*$_F$ are indented. If you use the word `else`, enter it on a separate line, aligned with the word `if`. The format of the `if` statement makes its meaning apparent. Again, we do this solely to improve program readability; the format used makes no difference to the compiler.   ∎

C++ Syntax for if Control Statement

The following display summarizes the forms of the if control statement we have used so far.

C++
SYNTAX

if Control Statement (one alternative)

Form: if (*condition*)
              statement$_T$

Example: if (x > 0.0)
             positive_product = positive_product * x;

Interpretation: If the *condition* evaluates to true, then *statement$_T$* is executed; otherwise, it is skipped.

C++
SYNTAX

if Control Statement (two alternatives)

Form: if (*condition*)
              statement$_T$
         else
              statement$_F$

Example: if (x >= 0.0)
             cout << "Positive" << endl;
         else
             cout << "Negative" << endl;

Interpretation: If the *condition* evaluates to true, then *statement$_T$* is executed and *statement$_F$* is skipped; otherwise, *statement$_T$* is skipped and *statement$_F$* is executed.   ■

EXERCISES FOR SECTION 4.3

Self-Check   1. What do the following statements display?

```
a. if (12 < 12)
       cout << "Never" << endl;
   else
       cout << "Always"  << endl;
b. var1 = 15.0;
   var2 = 25.12;
   if (2 * var1 >= var2)
       cout << "O.K." << endl;
   else
       cout << "Not O.K." << endl;
```

2. What value is assigned to x for each segment below when y is 15.0?

    a. `x = 25.0;`
      ```
      if (y != (x - 10.0))
          x = x - 10.0;
      else
          x = x / 2.0;
      ```
    b.
      ```
      if (y < 15.0 && y >= 0.0)
          x = 5 * y;
      else
          x = 2 * y;
      ```

Programming   1. Write C++ statements to carry out the steps below.

   a. Store the absolute difference of x and y in z, where the absolute difference is (x - y) or (y - x), whichever is positive. Do not use the abs or fabs function in your solution.
   b. If x is zero, add 1 to zero_count. If x is negative, add x to minus_sum. If x is greater than zero, add x to plus_sum.

4.4 _____ if STATEMENTS WITH COMPOUND ALTERNATIVES

The *statement* following the condition to be tested or the word else may be a single executable statement or a compound statement. Assignment statements, function call statements, or even other if statements may be used in writing these alternatives. Note that in C++, a compound statement is syntactically equivalent to a single statement. Thus, compound statements may be used anywhere the element *statement* appears in our earlier syntax displays. We provide some illustrations of this next.

Example 4.8   In later chapters we will see that it is useful to be able to order a pair of data values in memory so that the smaller value is stored in one variable (say x) and the larger value in another (y). The if statement in Fig. 4.7 rearranges any two values stored in x and y so that the smaller number will always be in x and the larger number will always be in y. If the two numbers are already in the proper order, the compound statement will not be executed.

The variables x, y, and temp should all be the same data type. Although the values of x and y are being switched, an additional variable, temp, is needed for storage of a copy of one of these values.

Table 4.8 provides a step-by-step simulation of the execution of the if control statement when x is 12.5 and y is 5.0. We will *hand trace* through each statement much like the computer would do. The table shows that temp is ini-

Figure 4.7   if control statement to order x and y

```
if (x > y)
{                       // exchange values in x and y
    temp = x;           // store original value of x in temp
    x = y;              // store original value of y in x
    y = temp;           // store original value of x (from temp) in y
}   // end if
```

tially undefined (indicated by ?). Each line of the table shows the part of the if statement that is being executed, followed by its effect. If any variable gets a new value, its new value is shown on that line. The last value stored in x is 5.0, and the last value stored in y is 12.5 as desired.

Table 4.8   Step-by-Step Hand Trace of if Control Statement

STATEMENT PART	x	y	temp	EFFECT
	12.5	5.0	?	
if (x > y)				12.5 > 5.0 is true
{				
temp = x;			12.5	Store x in temp
x = y;	5.0			Store original y in x
y = temp;		12.5		Store original x in y
}				

■

Example 4.9   As manager of the clothing boutique, you may want to keep records of your checking transactions. In the if statement below, the true task processes a transaction (transaction_amount) that represents a check you wrote as payment for goods received (in which case, transaction_type is 'c'); the false task processes a deposit made into your checking account. In either case, an appropriate message is printed and the account balance (balance) is updated. Both the true and false statements are compound statements.

```
if (transaction_type == 'c')
{   // process check
    cout << "Check for $" << transaction_amount << endl;
    balance = balance - transaction_amount;
}
else
{   // process deposit
    cout << "Deposit of $" << transaction_amount << endl;
    balance = balance + transaction_amount;
}   // end if
```

■

PROGRAM STYLE

Writing if Statements with Compound True or False Statements

Each `if` statement in this section contains at least one compound statement bracketed by { }. The placement of the braces is a stylistic preference. Your instructor may want the opening { at the end of the same line as the condition. The closing } of a compound `if` may also appear on the same line as the `else`:

```
} else {
```

We chose to use the readable style shown in Example 4.9 above; your instructor may prefer another style. Whatever style you follow, do so with consistency. ∎

EXERCISES FOR SECTION 4.4

Self-Check

1. Insert the semicolons where needed below to avoid syntax errors. Indent as needed to improve readability.

```
if (x > y)
{
x = x + 10.0
cout << "x bigger" << endl;
}
else
cout << "x smaller" << endl

cout << "y is " << y << endl;
```

2. What would be the effect of removing the braces { } in Self-Check Exercise 1 above?
3. What would be the effect of placing braces around the last two lines above?
4. Correct the following `if` statement.

```
if (num1 < 0)
    product = num1 * num2 * num3;
    cout << "Product is " << product << endl;
}
else
{
    sum = num1 + num2 + num3;
    cout << "Sum is " << sum << endl;
}
```

Programming

1. Write an `if` statement that might be used to compute the average of a set of n numbers whose sum is `total` when n is greater than 0 and prints an error message when n is not greater than 0. The average should be computed by dividing `total` by n.
2. Write an interactive program that contains a compound `if` statement and may be used to compute the area of a square (area = side^2) or triangle (area = 1/2 × base × height) after prompting the user to type the first character of the figure name (`t` or `s`).

4.5 _____ DECISION STEPS IN ALGORITHMS

In the problem that follows, we will see how to write a payroll program that can be used to compute an employee's gross pay and net pay after deductions.

CASE STUDY: PAYROLL PROBLEM

Problem Statement

Write a payroll program that computes an employee's gross pay. The program should also compute net pay using the following criterion to determine the amount to be deducted from the employee's gross salary for social security tax: If an employee earns more than $100.00 in a week, deduct a tax of $25.00; otherwise, deduct no tax. We will approach the solution to this problem in a top-down fashion.

Problem Analysis

To compute gross pay, we must know the hours worked and the hourly rate (the problem input). Be sure to prompt the user properly for correct entry. After reading these data, we will need to determine the gross and net pay. For now, we will not concern ourselves with how to arrive at the gross and net pay figures; we need know only that they must be computed. With this information we can construct the main function, which will include calls to two unwritten functions: one to compute gross pay, the other to compute net pay. The details for these computations will be hidden in the lower-level functions. The data requirements for the main function follow.

DATA REQUIREMENTS

> *Problem Constants*
>
> tax_bracket = 100.00   — maximum salary without a tax deduction
> tax = 25.00   — amount of tax withheld
>
> *Problem Input*
>
> hours (float)   — hours worked
> rate (float)   — hourly rate
>
> *Problem Output*
>
> gross (float)   — gross pay
> net (float)   — net pay

Program Design

The structure chart is shown in Fig. 4.8. It shows the decomposition of the original problem into five subproblems. We have added to the structure chart *data flow* information that shows the input and output of each program step. For each subproblem that can be solved using a separate function, the function name appears underneath its box. The structure chart shows that the step "enter data" provides values for `hours` and `rate` as its output (data flow arrow points up). Similarly, the step "compute gross pay" uses `hours` and `rate` as input to the function (data flow arrow points down) and provides `gross` as the function output. We will discuss the relevance of the data flow information after we complete the problem solution.

We can now write the initial algorithm to show the order in which these subproblems are solved.

INITIAL ALGORITHM

1. Display user instructions (function `instruct_user`).
2. Enter hours worked and hourly rate.
3. Compute gross pay (function `compute_gross`).
4. Compute net pay (function `compute_net`).
5. Print gross pay and net pay.

Analysis for instruct_user (step 1)

The two constant identifiers, `tax_bracket` and `tax`, are treated as input arguments so that their values may be referenced directly in the function. This practice is preferable to just including the constant values inside the function. If values associated with these constants should change in the future, only the `main` function would have to be modified.

Both steps 3 and 4 need more details. We will solve them one step at a time.

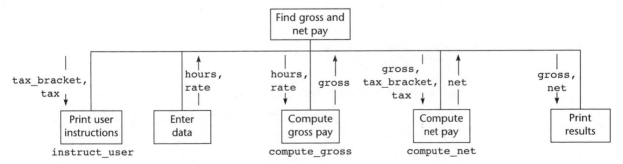

Figure 4.8   Structure chart for Payroll Problem

Analysis for compute_gross (step 3)

Before we can write the code we must determine what data elements function `compute_gross` will need.

DATA REQUIREMENTS FOR compute_gross

Input Arguments

hours (float)	— hours worked
rate (float)	— hourly rate

Function Return Value

gross pay (float)

FORMULA

gross pay = hourly rate × hours worked

Design for compute_gross

Because the formula for computing gross pay is relatively simple, we don't need any local variables within the function. The result of *hours × rate* is returned to the main function, where that value is then assigned to the variable `gross`. We therefore may readily write

Algorithm for compute_gross

1. Return hours times rate.

We can now progress directly to writing the function code.

Implementation of compute_gross

```
// FIND THE GROSS SALARY
float compute_gross
   (float hours,        // IN: number of hours worked
    float rate)         // IN: hourly payrate
{
   // Compute gross pay.
   return hours * rate;
} // end compute_gross
```

Analysis for compute_net (step 4)

Once we have the information provided by `compute_gross`, we are ready to refine step 4 and compute the net pay.

DATA REQUIREMENTS FOR compute_net

Input Arguments

gross (float)   — gross pay

tax_bracket (const float)   — maximum salary without a tax deduction
tax (const float)   — amount of tax withheld

Function Return Value

net pay (float)

FORMULA

net pay = gross pay – deductions

We will now write the refinement of algorithm step 4 as a *decision step*.

Algorithm for compute_net

4.1. If the gross pay is larger than $100.00 (tax_bracket)
　　　　4.1.1. deduct a tax of $25 (tax) and return result.
　　　else
　　　　4.1.2. deduct no tax—return gross pay.

The decision step above is expressed in *pseudocode,* which is a mixture of English and C++ reserve words that is used to describe algorithm steps. In the pseudocode for a decision step, we use indentation and the reserved words `if` and `else` to show the flow of control where alternative algorithm steps are involved.

Implementation of compute_net

We are now ready to write the code for step 4 as a function.

```
// FIND THE NET SALARY
float compute_net
  (float gross,         // IN: gross salary
   float tax_bracket,   // IN: maximum salary for no deduction
   float tax)           // IN: tax amount
{
   // Compute net salary.
   if (gross > tax_bracket)
      return gross - tax;     // deduct a tax amount
   else
      return gross;           // deduct no tax
} // end compute_net
```

Implementation of main Function

The complete program for the Payroll Problem is shown in Fig. 4.9. It begins with a multiple-line comment explaining the program purpose.

　　The program begins by calling function `instruct_user` to display the user instructions (the first six lines of program output). After the input data are read, function `compute_gross` is called. The result of this computation is passed on to the next function, `compute_net`, after which all results can now be displayed. This provides a good illustration of how functions and

Figure 4.9   Program and sample output for Payroll Problem

```cpp
// FILE: Payroll.cpp
// COMPUTES AND PRINTS GROSS PAY AND NET PAY GIVEN AN HOURLY
//    RATE AND NUMBER OF HOURS WORKED.  DEDUCTS A TAX OF $25 IF
//    GROSS SALARY EXCEEDS $100; OTHERWISE, DEDUCTS NO TAX.


#include <iostream.h>               // needed for cin and cout

void main ()
{
   // Functions used ...
   // DISPLAYS USER INSTRUCTIONS
   void instruct_user
     (const float,                  // IN: max salary for no deductions
      const float);                 // IN: tax amount

   // FIND THE GROSS SALARY
   float compute_gross
     (float,                        // IN: number of hours worked
      float);                       // IN: hourly payrate

   // FIND THE NET SALARY
   float compute_net
     (float,                        // IN: gross salary
      const float,                  // IN: max salary for no deductions
      const float);                 // IN: tax amount

   // Local data ...
   const float tax_bracket = 100.00;   // maximum salary for no
                                       //     deductions
   const float tax = 25.00;            // tax amount

   float hours;                     // input: hours worked
   float rate;                      // input: hourly payrate
   float gross;                     // output: gross pay
   float net;                       // output: net pay

   // Display user instructions.
   instruct_user (tax_bracket, tax);

   // Enter hours and rate.
   cout << "Hours worked: ";
   cin  >> hours;
   cout << "Hourly rate: ";
   cin  >> rate;

   // Compute gross salary.
   gross = compute_gross (hours, rate);
```

(Continued)

Figure 4.9   (Continued)

```
    // Compute net salary.
    net = compute_net (gross, tax_bracket, tax);

    // Print gross and net.
    cout << "Gross salary is $" << gross << endl;
    cout << "Net salary is $" << net << endl;
    return;
}


// DISPLAYS USER INSTRUCTIONS
void instruct_user
  (const float tax_bracket,       // maximum salary for no deduction
   const float tax)               // tax amount
{
   cout << "This program computes gross and net salary." << endl;
   cout << "A tax amount of $" << tax << " is deducted for"
        << endl;
   cout << "an employee who earns more than $" << tax_bracket
        << endl << endl;
   cout << "Enter hours worked and hourly rate" << endl;
   cout << "on separate lines after the prompts." << endl;
   cout << "Press <return> after typing each number." << endl
        << endl;
   return;
}  // end instruct_user


// FIND THE GROSS SALARY
float compute_gross
  (float hours,                   // IN: number of hours worked
   float rate)                    // IN: hourly payrate
{
   // Compute gross pay.
   return hours * rate;
}  // end compute_gross


// FIND THE NET SALARY
float compute_net
  (float gross,                   // IN: gross salary
   const float tax_bracket,       // IN: max salary for no deduction
   const float tax)               // IN: tax amount
{

   // Compute net salary.
   if (gross > tax_bracket)
```

(Continued)

Figure 4.9   (Continued)

```
        return gross - tax;              // deduct a tax amount
    else
        return gross;                    // deduct no tax
}   // end compute_net
```

———— Program Output ————

```
This program computes gross and net salary.
A tax amount of $25 is deducted for
an employee who earns more than $100.

Enter hours worked and hourly rate
on separate lines after the prompts.
Press <return> after typing each number.

Hours worked: 40
Hourly rate: 5
Gross salary is $200
Net salary is $175
```

functional decomposition can be used to localize data and hide the details of specific computations.

Program Testing

To test this program, we need to be sure all possible alternatives work properly. Therefore we need three sets of data, one for the if (gross salary greater than $100), one for the else (gross salary less than $100), and one for the pivotal point (gross salary exactly $100).

Adding Data Flow Information to Structure Charts

In Fig. 4.8, we added data flow information to the structure chart showing the input and output of each of the top-level problem solution steps. The data flow information is an important part of the program documentation. It shows what program variables are processed by each step and the manner in which these variables are processed. If a step gives a new value to a variable, then the variable is considered an *output of the step.* If a step displays a variable's value or uses it in a computation without changing its value, the variable is considered an *input to the step.* For example, the step "compute net pay" consists of a function that processes variables gross and net. This step uses the value of the variable gross, as well as the constants tax_bracket and tax (its input) to compute net (its output).

Figure 4.8 also shows that a variable may have different roles for different subproblems in the structure chart. When considered in the context of the original problem statement, hours and rate are problem input (data supplied by the program user). However, when considered in the context of the subproblem "enter data," the subproblem's task is to deliver values for hours and rate to the main function, so they are considered output from this step. When considered in the context of the subproblem "compute gross pay," the subproblem's task is to use hours and rate to compute a value of gross, so they are considered input to this step. In the same way, the role of the variables gross and net changes as we go from step to step in the structure chart.

PROGRAM STYLE

Using Constants to Enhance Readability and Maintenance

The constants tax_bracket and tax appear in function compute_net in Fig. 4.9. We could just as easily have placed the constant values (100.00 and 25.00) directly in the if statement. The result would be

```
if (gross > 100.00)
    net = gross - 25.00;       // deduct a tax amount
else
    net = gross;               // deduct no tax
```

However, use of constant identifiers rather than constant values provides two advantages. First, the original if statement is easier to understand because it uses the descriptive names tax_bracket and tax rather than numbers, which have no intrinsic meaning. Second, a program written with constants is much easier to maintain than one written with constant values. For example, if we want to use different constant values in the Payroll Program in Fig. 4.9, we need to change only the constant declaration in the main function. However, if we had inserted constant values directly in the if statement, we would have to change the if statement and any other statements that manipulate or display the constant values. ∎

4.6 ___ FORMATTED OUTPUT: INTRODUCTION TO MANIPULATORS AND FLAGS

In our programming so far, we have exercised very little control over the appearance of an output line. For example, in the Payroll Problem just illustrated, cout displayed our gross and net salary to the precision of however many decimal places it required. If you had worked 35.5 hours at an hourly rate of 4.75, the program would have printed gross and net salaries of 168.625 and 143.625, respectively. This, of course, is not how we expect a dollar value to be written. To force our output to show the exact number of decimal places that we intend, and to exercise control over the total width of the data to be displayed, we use C++ *input/output manipulators*.

We have already seen one example of an I/O manipulator, `endl`, which was used to indicate the end of a line of displayed output. In this section, we introduce three more manipulators, `setprecision`, `setw`, and `setios-flags`. These can be used to control the total number of characters to be used for each item displayed, as well as (for floating-point values) the exact number of digits to appear to the right of the decimal point.

Example 4.10   *Specifying Number of Decimal Places in Output.*   The following C++ instructions can be used to display the gross and net salaries in the Payroll Problem accurate to exactly two decimal places.

```
cout << setiosflags (ios::showpoint | ios::fixed);
cout << "Gross salary is $" << setprecision (2) << gross << endl;
cout << "Net salary is $" << net << endl;
```

The I/O manipulator `setprecision` is used to indicate that the values to be printed (`gross` and `net` in this case) are to be displayed accurate to two decimal places. The `setiosflags` manipulator, shown here with the two *format flags* `showpoint` and `fixed`, is required to ensure that for floating-point values

1. a decimal point and two decimal places are always displayed even if one or both of the decimal places are zero;
2. all values are displayed in *fixed* notation rather than in *scientific* notation.

If the `showpoint` format flag is not turned on, trailing zeros to the right of the decimal point will not be displayed. Thus, for dollars and cents values such as thirteen dollars or thirteen dollars and fifty cents, our output would appear as 13 and 13.5, respectively. This is not wrong, but it can be disconcerting in programs involving dollars and cents values where we might normally expect to see a decimal point and two digits to the right of the decimal point.

Setting the C++ format flag `fixed` ensures that all dollars and cents values printed by our program, even larger values such as 1738964.75, appear in the fixed format we are accustomed to seeing. If this flag is not set, some of these larger numbers would be displayed in scientific notation, such as 1.738964e+06. Setting the format flag to `scientific` (by specifying `ios::scientific` in the call to `setiosflags`) ensures that all floating-point values are displayed in scientific notation.

Example 4.11   *Specifying Width of Output.*   The `setw` manipulator can be used to set the width of the field in which a data item is to be displayed. Unless otherwise indicated, numeric values displayed in such a *fixed width field* are shown *right adjusted* with *blank fill* on the left if needed.

The `setw` manipulator can be especially handy in displaying information in columns. If we wished to display the values of two points $(x_1, y_1) = (3, -12.6)$

and $(x_2, y_2) = (-102.4, 0)$ in a neat, aligned fashion, we might use the following instructions:

```
cout << setiosflags (ios::showpoint | ios::fixed);
cout << setprecision (1);
cout << '(' << setw (7) << x1 << ',' << setw (7) << y1 << ')';
cout << '(' << setw (7) << x2 << ',' << setw (7) << y2 << ')';
```

These instructions would produce the output

```
(    3.0,  -12.6)
( -102.4,    0.0)
```

   The flags and manipulators just discussed are summarized in Table 4.9. The use of these flags and manipulators requires that the header file iomanip.h be included in your program in the same manner as iostream.h. We will discuss I/O flags and manipulators in far greater detail in Chapter 8.

Table 4.9 An introduction to I/O Manipulators and Format Flags

MANIPULATORS	USE AND COMMENTS

setiosflags
   (ios::a | ios::b | ios::c)
	▪ For setting and resetting values of C++ I/O flags a, b, c
	▪ Flags remain set until explicitly reset
	▪ Flags to be set are specified in parentheses in the form
	       ios::*flagname*
	▪ If more than one flag is listed, each is separated from the others by a composition operator (|)

setprecision (i)	▪ Used to specify the number of decimal places (i) of accuracy to be used in the display of floating-point values ▪ i must be positive ▪ Accuracy remains in effect until explicitly reset
setw (i)	▪ Used to specify the field width to be used for the next item printed ▪ i must be positive ▪ Item appears right adjusted in the field ▪ The field width remains in effect only for the next data item displayed
endl	▪ Indicates the beginning of a new line of output

(Continued)

Table 4.9   (Continued)

FLAGS	USE AND COMMENTS
fixed	• Ensures floating-point output is in fixed format (no scientific notation)
scientific	• Ensures that floating-point output is in scientific notation
showpoint	• Ensures that decimal point and trailing zeros are displayed

EXERCISES FOR SECTION 4.6

Self-Check

1. Assuming the line

   ```
   cout << setiosflags (ios::showpoint | ios::fixed);
   ```

   has already been executed, what exactly will the output look like? (Show all blanks precisely.)

   a. if radius = 4.5:

   ```
   cout << "The value of pi is " << setprecision (6) << pi
        << endl;
   cout << "The value of radius is " << radius << endl;
   ```

   b. (assume setprecision (6) is not in effect) x = 4, x_square = 16, y = 10, y_square = 100:

   ```
   cout << setw (3) << x << x_square;
   cout << setw (3) << y << y_square;
   ```

2. a. Write an output statement to display a floating-point value of width six, accurate to three decimal places.
   b. Write an output statement to display an integer of width 10 followed by a floating-point value of width 10, accurate to one decimal place, and in scientific notation.

Programming

1. Modify the Payroll Problem main function so that steps 2 and 5 are implemented as calls to the functions get_hours, get_rate, and display. Make all necessary changes to the Payroll Program structure chart (Fig. 4.8) before making any changes to the program code. Write the definitions for these three functions.
2. In the original Payroll Problem, no attempt was made to verify that the input values make sense, e.g., that hours are within the range ($0 \le$ hours ≤ 24). Include some error checking (using if statements) with your input statements. If you have done Programming Exercise 1 (above), put the error checking in the functions get_hours and get_rate.
3. Rewrite the cout statements in Example 4.9 (from Section 4.4) using I/O manipulators.
4. Write a void function set_output that sets the ios flags showpoint and fixed and sets output precision to k, where k is the single input argument for the function. How could you have used this function in the Payroll program?

4.7 ____ CHECKING CORRECTNESS OF AN ALGORITHM

CASE STUDY: FINDING THE ALPHABETICALLY FIRST LETTER

Problem Statement

Read three letters and find and display the one that comes first in the alphabet.

Problem Analysis

Recall from Section 4.2 that we can use the relational operator < (less than) to determine whether one letter precedes another in the alphabet. For example, the condition `'A' < 'F'` is true because A precedes F in the alphabet. Because we have no direct way to compare three items, our strategy will be to do a sequence of pair-wise comparisons. We will start by comparing the first two letters to find the smaller of that pair. Next, we can compare this result to the third letter and find the smaller of that pair. The result of the second comparison will be the smallest of all three letters.

DATA REQUIREMENTS

> *Problem Input*
>
> ch1, ch2, ch3 (char)   — the three letters to be processed
>
> *Problem Output*
>
> alpha_first (char)   — the alphabetically first letter

Program Design

The structure chart in Fig. 4.10 shows the decomposition of the original problem into three subproblems. The algorithm following the structure chart shows the order in which these subproblems must be solved. The second subproblem requires further refinement.

INITIAL ALGORITHM

1. Read three letters into ch1, ch2, and ch3.
2. Put the alphabetically first of ch1, ch2, and ch3 in alpha_first.
3. Display the alphabetically first letter (alpha_first).

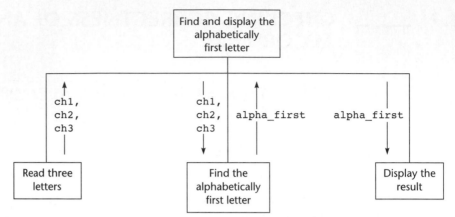

Figure 4.10   Structure chart for Alphabetically First Letter Problem

ALGORITHM REFINEMENTS

Because we need to do two pair-wise comparisons, we can construct a function (`get_first`) that will return the lesser of any two characters. This way, if we decide to expand the program to compare more characters, we would just call our function a few more times.

The first call to `get_first` returns the smaller of `ch1` and `ch2`, which is then saved in `alpha_first`. The second call to `get_first` returns the smaller of `ch3` and the current value of `alpha_first`, which is again saved in `alpha_first`. After both statements execute, `alpha_first` contains the smallest of all three letters as required.

Step 2 Refinement

2.1. Save the alphabetically first of ch1 and ch2 in alpha_first. (Call function get_first with ch1 and ch2 as input and save returned result in alpha_first.)
2.2. Save the alphabetically first of ch3 and alpha_first in alpha_first. (Call function get_first with ch3 and alpha_first as input.)

Program Implementation

The program that finds the alphabetically first letter is shown in Fig. 4.11.

Figure 4.11   Program for finding the Alphabetically First Letter

```
// FILE: FirstLet.cpp
// FINDS AND DISPLAYS THE ALPHABETICALLY FIRST LETTER

#include <iostream.h>        // needed for cin and cout
```

(Continued)

Figure 4.11   (Continued)

```
void main ()
{
   // Functions used ...
   // FINDS THE ALPHABETICALLY FIRST LETTER OF PAIR
   char get_first
     (char,                    // IN: first letter
      char);                   // IN: second letter

   // Local data ...
   char ch1;                   // input: three letters to be processed
   char ch2;
   char ch3;
   char alpha_first;           // output: alphabetically first letter

   // Read three letters.
   cout << "Enter any three letters: ";
   cin >> ch1 >> ch2 >> ch3;

   // Save the alphabetically first of ch1 and ch2 in alpha_first.
   alpha_first = get_first (ch1, ch2);

   // Save the alphabetically first of ch3 and alpha_first.
   alpha_first = get_first (ch3, alpha_first);

   // Display result.
   cout << alpha_first << " is the first letter alphabetically."
        << endl;
}

// FINDS THE ALPHABETICALLY FIRST LETTER OF PAIR
char get_first
   (char letter1,              // IN: first letter
    char letter2)              // IN: second letter
{
   if (letter1 < letter2)
      return letter1;          // letter1 comes before letter2
   else
      return letter2;          // letter2 comes before letter1
}
```

——————— Program Output ———————

```
Enter any three letters: EBK
B is the first letter alphabetically.
```

Program Testing

To test this program, you should make sure that it works when the smallest letter is in any of the three positions. The next section describes the four cases that should be tested. You should also see what happens when one of the letters is repeated and when one or more of the letters is in lowercase.

TRACING AN ALGORITHM

In Section 4.4, we simulated the execution of an if statement that switches the values of two variables. Next, we will simulate the execution of the refined algorithm for the smallest-letter problem.

REFINED ALGORITHM

1. Read three letters into ch1, ch2, and ch3.
2. Put the alphabetically first of ch1, ch2, and ch3 in alpha_first.
     2.1. Save the alphabetically first of ch1 and ch2 in alpha_first.
          2.1.1. If ch1 precedes ch2
               2.1.2. alpha_first is assigned ch1.
          else
               2.1.3. alpha_first is assigned ch2.
     2.2. Save the alphabetically first of ch3 and alpha_first in alpha_first.
          2.2.1. If ch3 precedes alpha_first
               2.2.2. alpha_first is assigned ch3.
          else
               2.2.3. alpha_first remains in alpha_first.
3. Display the alphabetically first letter.

Table 4.10 shows a trace of the algorithm for the three characters t, h, and e. Each step is listed at the left in order of its execution. If a program step changes the value of a variable, then the table shows the new value. The effect of each step is described at the far right. For example, the table shows that the effect of executing the line

```
cin >> ch1 >> ch2 >> ch3;
```

stores the letters t, h, and e in the variables ch1, ch2, and ch3.

Table 4.10   Trace of program in Fig. 4.12

ALGORITHM STEP	ch1	ch2	ch3	alpha_first	EFFECT
	?	?	?	?	
1. Read three letters		t	h	e	Reads the data
2.1.1. if ch1 precedes ch2					Is 't' < 'h'? expression is false
2.1.3. alpha_first is assigned ch2				h	'h' is first so far
2.2.1. if ch3 precedes alpha_first					Is 'e' < 'h'? expression is true
2.2.2. alpha_first is assigned ch3				e	'e' is first
3. Display alpha_first					Prints e as the first letter

The trace in Table 4.10 clearly shows that the alphabetically first letter, e, of the input string is stored in `alpha_first` and then is printed. In order to verify that the algorithm is correct, you would need to select other data that cause the two conditions to evaluate to different combinations of their values. Because there are two conditions and each has two possible outcomes (true or false), there are 2×2, or 4, different combinations that should be tried. (What are they?) An exhaustive hand trace of the algorithm would show that it works for all of these combinations.

Besides the four cases discussed above, you should verify that the algorithm works correctly for unusual data. For example, what would happen if all three letters or a pair of letters were the same? Would the algorithm still provide the correct result? To complete the hand trace, you would need to show that the algorithm does indeed handle these special situations properly.

In testing each case, you must be very careful to hand trace the algorithm exactly as the computer would execute it. Often, programmers assume that a particular step will be executed without explicitly testing each condition and tracing each step; however, a trace performed in this way is of little value.

EXERCISES FOR SECTION 4.7

Self-Check
1. Provide sample data and traces for the remaining three cases of the Alphabetically First Letter Problem.

   a. Case 1, both conditions are true.
   b. Case 2, first condition is true, second is false.
   c. Case 3, both conditions are false.

2. Consider two special cases of the Alphabetically First Letter Problem. Determine the value returned by each of the two calls to `get-first` when:

   a. two of the three letters are the same.
   b. all three letters are the same.

3. Trace the Payroll Program in Fig. 4.9 when:

   a. hours is 30.0 and rate is 5.00.
   b. hours is 20.0 and rate is 4.00.

Programming
1. Modify the structure chart and program for the Alphabetically First Letter Problem to find the first of four letters.
2. Write a structure chart and program to find the alphabetically last of three letters.

4.8 ____ MORE PROBLEM-SOLVING STRATEGIES

It often happens that what appears to be a new problem will turn out to be a variation of one that you have already solved. Consequently, an important skill in problem-solving is the ability to recognize that a problem is similar to one solved earlier. The solution to such a problem may well involve the reuse of previously written components or adaptations of these components. It may also involve the reuse of *structural forms* or *patterns of solutions* that you have worked out before. As you progress through this course, you will start to build up a small repertoire of problem-solving approaches and solution patterns, as well as your own collection or *library* of functions. You will also learn a lot more about the standard C++ function libraries. Whenever possible, you should try to adapt or reuse parts of successful programs, or at least patterns of program or algorithm structures, that you have tested and applied before.

Modifying a Problem Solution

An experienced programmer usually writes programs that can be easily changed or modified to fit other situations. One reason is that programmers (and program users) often wish to make slight improvements to a program after having used it. If the original program is designed carefully from the beginning, the programmer will be able to accommodate changing specifications with a minimum of effort. As you will find by working through the next problem, it may be possible to modify a function by changing one or two control statements rather than having to rewrite the entire program. We will also see that if programs are properly modularized (using functions), then changes can be localized within one or a few functions, thereby limiting potential side effects with respect to the rest of a program.

CASE STUDY: COMPUTING OVERTIME PAY

Problem Statement

We need to modify the Payroll Program in Fig. 4.9 so that employees who work more than 40 hours a week are paid double for all overtime hours worked. Since this affects only the gross pay computation, we can focus on the effect of this change to function `compute_gross` and not concern ourselves with the other components of the program.

Analysis for compute_gross

Employees who work more than 40 hours are to be paid one rate for the first 40 hours and a higher rate for the extra hours over 40. Employees who work 40 hours or less are to be paid the same rate for all hours worked. In order to perform the required computations, we need to know the total number of hours worked, the maximum number of regular hours (40), and the overtime rate (2.0).

DATA REQUIREMENTS FOR compute_gross

Problem Constants

max_hours = 40.0   — maximum hours without overtime pay
overtime_rate = 2.0   — double pay for overtime

Input Arguments

hours (float)   — hours worked
rate (float)   — hourly rate

Function Return Value

gross pay (float), including overtime pay, if any

FORMULAS

regular pay = hourly rate × hours worked
overtime pay = hours over max_hours × overtime_rate × hourly rate

Design for compute_gross

We can revise the compute_gross function by replacing the code in compute_gross with a decision step that selects either a straight pay computation or a computation with overtime pay.

ALGORITHM REFINEMENTS FOR compute_gross

1. If no overtime hours were worked
    1.1. Return hours × rate.
  else
    1.2. Compute the gross pay for regular hours.
    1.3. Add the pay for overtime hours to gross pay and return result.

Implementation of compute_gross

To rewrite the function compute_gross, we can add the two new constants max_hours and overtime_rate by declaring them locally within this function. We can then replace the computation in the return statement in Fig. 4.9 that computes gross pay:

```
// Compute gross pay.
return hours * rate;
```

with the if statement

```
// Compute gross pay including any overtime pay.
if (hours <= max_hours)
    return hours * rate;
```

```
else
{   // compute overtime
    gross = max_hours * rate;
    return gross + (hours - max_hours) * overtime_rate * rate;
}   // end if
```

If the condition (`hours <= max_hours`) is true, there is no overtime pay so the gross pay is computed as before; otherwise, `gross` is computed in two steps. The first step computes the pay for regular hours only; the second step adds the pay for any overtime hours (`hours - max_hours`) to the value just computed.

Figure 4.12 shows the complete revised function.

Commentary

This problem illustrates a very important benefit of problem decomposition and program modularization. Because the computation of the gross pay was separated from the rest of the program and implemented as a function, we were able to restrict all modification concerns to this function, without regard for other program components. We will have more to say about other benefits of this separation in later chapters.

Figure 4.12   Revised function `compute_gross`

```
// FILE: CompGros.cpp

// FIND THE GROSS SALARY
float compute_gross
    (float hours,               // IN: number of hours worked
     float rate)                // IN: hourly payrate
{
    // Local data ...
    const max_hours = 40.0;     // maximum hours without overtime
                                //    pay
    const overtime_rate = 2.0;  // double pay for overtime
    float gross;                // temporary storage for
                                //    intermediate calculations

    // Compute gross pay including any overtime pay.
    if (hours <= max_hours)
        return hours * rate;
    else
    {   // compute overtime
        gross = max_hours * rate;
        return gross + (hours - max_hours) * overtime_rate * rate;
    }   // end overtime
}       // end compute_gross
```

More Problem-Solving: Solution by Analogy

Sometimes a new problem is simply an old one presented in a new guise. Each time you face a problem, you should try to determine whether you have solved a similar one before and, if so, adapt the earlier solution. To accomplish this, you must carefully read the problem statement in order to detect requirements similar to those of earlier problems that may be worded differently.

CASE STUDY: COMPUTING INSURANCE DIVIDENDS

Problem Statement

Each year an insurance company sends out dividend checks to its policy-holders. The basic dividend rate is a fixed percentage (4.5%) of the policy-holders' paid premium. If the policyholder has made no claims, the dividend rate for that policy is increased by a bonus rate (0.5%). Write a program to compute the dividends for a particular policyholder given his or her premium and number of claims.

Problem Analysis

This problem is quite similar to the modified Payroll Problem discussed earlier. Just as there was a bonus pay rate for workers with overtime hours, we now have a bonus dividend for policyholders with no claims. We must first provide instructions for the program user, and then read the input data (number of claims and premium). Using the number of claims and the premium, we can compute and display the correct dividend. The data required to solve this problem are listed below.

DATA REQUIREMENTS

Problem Constants

basic_rate = 0.045   — the basic dividend rate of 4.5%
bonus_rate = 0.005   — the bonus dividend rate of 0.5%

Problem Input

premium (float)   — premium amount
number_claims (int)   — number of claims

Problem Output

dividend (float)   — dividend amount

Program Design

The structure chart (Fig. 4.13) illustrates the steps required to solve the problem. The algorithm below can be derived directly from the structure chart.

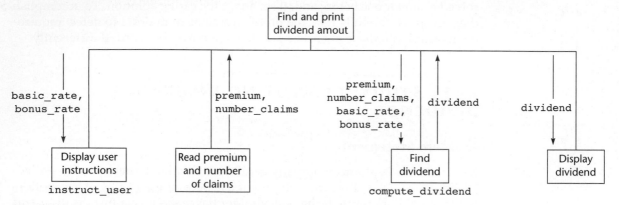

Figure 4.13   Structure chart for Insurance Dividend Problem

ALGORITHM

1. Display user instructions (function `instruct_user`).
2. Read premium amount and number of claims.
3. Compute dividend including a bonus dividend when earned (function `compute_dividend`).
4. Print total dividend.

The analysis, design, and implementation of the main function and function `instruct_user` is left to the reader (see Self-Check Exercise 2 at the end of this section). We will continue our discussion with the solution to step 3.

Analysis for compute_dividend (step 3)

In order to figure out the correct dividend, we need to know the basic rate as well as the bonus rate. These values are passed in from the main function. In function `compute_dividend` we introduce a temporary variable, which we chose to name `dividend`. Because it is declared within function `compute_dividend`, the local variable `dividend` is in no way connected to the variable `dividend` declared in the main function. We could have given it any name, but we preferred to keep it relevant to the formula at hand.

DATA REQUIREMENTS FOR compute_dividend

Input Arguments

premium (float)   — premium amount
number_claims (int)   — number of claims

basic_rate (const float)   — basic premium rate
bonus_rate (const float)   — bonus rate

Function Return Value

total dividend (float), including any bonuses applicable

FORMULAS

dividend = (premium × basic_rate)

or, if there is a bonus:

dividend = (premium × basic_rate) + (premium × bonus_rate)

Design for compute_dividend

After computing the basic dividend, we use a decision step with one alternative to determine whether a bonus dividend computation is required. We assign the first computation to the temporary variable `dividend` for the sake of clarity. It is much easier to understand exactly what is going on in the formula when the two parts are separated. The refinement of step 3 in this problem has the same pattern as the refinement of step 3 (`compute_gross`) in the modified Payroll Problem.

ALGORITHM FOR compute_dividend

3.1. Compute premium times basic rate.
3.2. If qualified for a bonus
      3.2.1. add bonus to basic dividend.
3.3. Return dividend (with possible bonus).

Implementation of compute_dividend

The complete program is shown in Fig. 4.14. The basic dividend rate, 4.5%, is written as the decimal fraction 0.045, and the bonus rate, 0.5%, is written as the decimal fraction 0.005. The `if` statement at the end of the program displays an extra message to policyholders who receive a bonus dividend.

Figure 4.14   Insurance Company Dividend program and sample output

```
// FILE: CompDiv.cpp
// FINDS AND PRINTS THE INSURANCE DIVIDEND

#include <iostream.h>              // needed for cin and cout
#include <iomanip.h>               // needed for setprecision

void main ()
```

(Continued)

Figure 4.14   (Continued)

```
{
    // Functions used ...
    // DISPLAYS USER INSTRUCTIONS
    void instruct_user
        (float,                         // IN: basic dividend rate
         float);                        // IN: bonus dividend rate

    // COMPUTE DIVIDEND USING BONUS RATE WHEN EARNED.
    float compute_dividend
        (float,                         // IN: premium amount
         int,                           // IN: number of claims
         float,                         // IN: basic dividend rate
         float);                        // IN: bonus dividend rate

    // Local data ...
    const float basic_rate = 0.045;     // basic dividend rate 4.5%
    const float bonus_rate = 0.005;     // bonus dividend rate 0.5%

    float premium;                      // input: premium amount
    int number_claims;                  // input: number of claims
    float dividend;                     // output: dividend amount

    // Display user instructions.
    instruct_user (basic_rate, bonus_rate);

    // Enter premium and number of claims.
    cout << "Premium amount: $";
    cin >> premium;
    cout << "Number of claims: ";
    cin >> number_claims;

    // Compute the dividend.
    dividend = compute_dividend (premium, number_claims, basic_rate,
                                 bonus_rate);

    // Print total dividend.
    cout << "Total dividend is $" << setprecision(2) <<
    setiosflags(ios::showpoint | ios::fixed) << dividend
        << endl;
    if (number_claims == 0)
        cout << "This includes a bonus dividend for zero claims!"
            << endl;
    return;
}

// Displays user instructions.
void instruct_user
    (float basic_rate,                  // IN: basic dividend rate
     float bonus_rate)                  // IN: bonus dividend rate
```

(Continued)

Figure 4.14   (Continued)

```
{
    cout << "This program displays an insurance policy dividend."
        << endl;
    cout << "The basic dividend is " << basic_rate
        << " times the premium." << endl;
    cout << "A bonus dividend of " << bonus_rate
        << " times the premium is paid" << endl;
    cout << "for policies with no claims against them." << endl
        << endl;
    return;
} // end instruct_user

// COMPUTE DIVIDEND USING BONUS RATE WHEN EARNED.
float compute_dividend
    (float premium,            // IN: premium amount
     int number_claims,        // IN: number of claims
     float basic_rate,         // IN: basic dividend rate
     float bonus_rate)         // IN: bonus dividend rate
{
    // Local data ...
    float dividend;

    dividend = premium * basic_rate;  // basic dividend
    if (number_claims == 0)
        dividend = dividend + premium * bonus_rate;   // plus bonus
    return dividend;
} // end compute_dividend
```

————— Program Output —————

```
This program displays an insurance policy dividend.
The basic dividend is 0.045 times the premium.
A bonus dividend of 0.005 times the premium is paid
for policies with no claims against them.

Premium amount: $1200
Number of claims: 0
Total dividend is $60.00
This includes a bonus dividend for zero claims!
```

EXERCISES FOR SECTION 4.8

Self-Check
1. Draw a structure chart for Programming Exercise 2 below; include data flow information.
2. Complete the analysis and design of the main function and `instruct_user` function for the Computing Insurance Dividend Case Study found in this section.

Programming
1. Provide the complete program for the Overtime Pay Problem.
2. Rewrite the function `compute_gross` (Fig. 4.1) so that it allows the user to enter the overtime rate (rather than treating this rate as a constant).

4.9 _____ NESTED if STATEMENTS AND MULTIPLE-ALTERNATIVE DECISIONS

Until now, we used if statements to implement decisions involving up to two alternatives. In this section, we will see how the if statement can be used to implement decisions involving several alternatives.

A nested if statement occurs when the true or false statement of an if statement is itself an if statement. A nested if statement can be used to implement decisions with several alternatives as shown in the next examples.

Example 4.12   The nested if statement below has three alternatives. It causes one of three variables (pos_count, neg_count, or zero_count) to be increased by one depending on whether x is greater than zero, less than zero, or equal to zero, respectively.

```
// Increment pos_count, neg_count, or zero_count
//     depending on the value of x.
if (x > 0)
   pos_count = pos_count + 1;
else
   if (x < 0)
      neg_count = neg_count + 1;
   else  // x == 0
      zero_count = zero_count + 1;
```

The execution of this if statement proceeds as follows: the first condition (x > 0) is tested; if it is true, pos_count is incremented and the rest of the if statement is skipped. If the first condition is false, the second condition (x < 0) is tested; if it is true, neg_count is incremented; otherwise, zero_count is incremented. It is important to realize that the second condition is tested only when the first condition is false.

Table 4.11 traces the execution of this statement when x is –7. Figure 4.15 contains a flowchart that shows the execution of the nested statement. This diagram shows that one and only one of the statement sequences in a rectangular box will be executed.

Table 4.11   Trace of if Statement in Example 4.12 for x = –7

STATEMENT PART	EFFECT
if (x > 0)	–7 > 0 is false

else
    if (x < 0)
      neg_count = neg_count + 1;
	–7 < 0 is true
	add 1 to neg_count

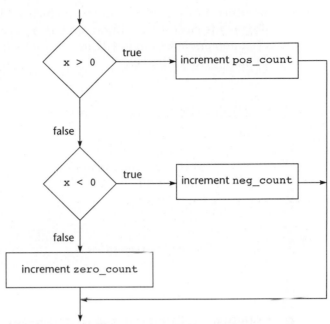

Figure 4.15   Flowchart of nested if statement in Example 4.12 ■

PROGRAM STYLE

Nested if Statements versus a Sequence of if Statements

Beginning programmers sometimes prefer to use a sequence of if statements rather than a single nested if statement. For example, the previous if statement is rewritten below as a sequence of if statements.

```
if (x > 0)
    pos_count = pos_count + 1;
if (x < 0)
    neg_count = neg_count + 1;
if (x == 0)
    zero_count = zero_count + 1;
```

Although the above sequence is logically equivalent to the original, it is not as readable or as efficient. Unlike the nested if, the sequence does not show clearly that exactly one of the three assignment statements is executed for a particular value of x. With respect to efficiency, all three of the conditions are always tested. In the nested if statement, only the first condition is tested when x is positive. ■

Writing a Nested if as a Multiple-Alternative Decision

Nested if statements may become difficult to read and write. If there are more than three alternatives and indentation is not done consistently, it may be difficult to determine the if to which a given else belongs. (In C++, this is always the closest if without an else.) We find it easier to write the nested if statement in Example 4.12 in a *multiple-alternative decision* form described in the next syntax display.

C++
SYNTAX

Multiple-Alternative Decision Form

Form:
```
if (condition₁)
    statement₁
else if (condition₂)
    statement₂
    .
    .
    .
else if (conditionₙ)
    statementₙ
else
    statementₑ
```

Example:
```
// Figuring final grade for lab homework.
if (days_late < 0)
    grade = grade + bonus_points;
else if (days_late > 0)
    grade = grade - late_points;
else   // day_late == 0
    cout << "Lab submitted on time, full credit"
        << endl;
```

Interpretation: The conditions in a multiple-alternative decision are evaluated in sequence until a true condition is reached. If a condition is true, the statement following it is executed and the rest of the multiple-alternative decision is skipped. If a condition is false, the statement following it is skipped and the next condition is tested. If all conditions are false, then *statementₑ* following the last else is executed. ∎

PROGRAM
STYLE

Writing a Multiple-Alternative Decision

In a multiple-alternative decision, the word else and the next condition appear on the same line. All the words else align, and each *dependent statement* is indented under the condition that controls its execution.

Keep in mind that the multiple-alternative decision form is not a new type of C++ if statement but is simply another way to write nested if statements.

Order of Conditions

Very often the conditions in a multiple-alternative decision are not *mutually exclusive;* in other words, more than one condition may be true for a given data value. If this is the case, then the order of the conditions becomes very important because only the statement following the first true condition is executed.

Example 4.13   Suppose you want to match exam scores to letter grades for a large class of students. The table below describes the assignment of grades based on each exam score.

EXAM SCORE	GRADE ASSIGNED
90 and above	A
80 to 89	B
70 to 79	C
60 to 69	D
below 60	F

The multiple-alternative decision below prints the letter grade assigned according to this table. If you had an exam score of 85, the last three conditions would be true; however, a grade of B would be assigned because the first true condition is (score >= 80).

```
// correct grade assignment
if (score >= 90)
   cout << 'A';
else if (score >= 80)
   cout << 'B';
else if (score >= 70)
   cout << 'C';
else if (score >= 60)
   cout << 'D';
else
   cout << 'F';
```

The order of conditions can also have an effect on program efficiency. If we know that low exam scores are much more likely than high scores, it would be more efficient to test first for scores below 60, next for scores between 60 and 69, and so on (see Programming Exercise 1 at the end of this section).   ■

Some caution is advised in using multiple-alternative decision structures. For example, it would be incorrect to write the previous decision structure as shown below. All passing exam scores (60 or above) would be incorrectly categorized as a grade of D because the first condition would be true and the rest would be skipped.

```
// incorrect grade assignment
if (score >= 60)
    cout << 'D';
else if (score >= 70)
    cout << 'C';
else if (score >= 80)
    cout << 'B';
else if (score >= 90)
    cout << 'A';
else
    cout << 'F';
```

Example 4.14   You could use a multiple-alternative if statement to implement a *decision table* that describes several alternatives. For instance, let's say you are an accountant setting up a payroll system for a small firm. Each line of Table 4.12 indicates an employee's salary range and a corresponding base tax amount and tax percentage. Given a salary, you can calculate the tax by adding the base tax for that salary range to the product of the percentage of excess and the amount of salary over the minimum salary for that range.

Table 4.12   Decision Table for Example 4.14

RANGE	SALARY	BASE TAX	PERCENTAGE OF EXCESS
1	0.00 to 1499.99	0.00	15%
2	1500.00 to 2999.99	225.00	16%
3	3000.00 to 4999.99	465.00	18%
4	5000.00 to 7999.99	825.00	20%
5	8000.00 to 15,000.00	1425.00	25%

For example, the second line of the table specifies that the tax due on a salary of $2000.00 is $225.00 plus 16% of the excess salary over $1500.00 (i.e., 16% of $500.00, or $80.00). Therefore, the total tax due is $225.00 plus $80.00, or $305.00.

The if statement in Fig. 4.16 implements the tax table. If the value of salary is within the table range (0.00 to 15,000.00), exactly one of the statements assigning a value to tax will be executed. A hand trace of the if statement for salary = $2000.00 is shown in Table 4.13. You can see that the value assigned to tax, $305.00, is correct.

Remember not to include symbols such as the dollar sign or commas in a C++ condition. A valid float may contain digits and a decimal point only (e.g., 1500.00, not $15,000.00).

Figure 4.16   if statement for Table 4.12

```
if (salary < 0.00)
    cout << "Error!  Negative salary $" << salary << endl;
else if (salary < 1500.00)           // first range
    tax = 0.15 * salary;
else if (salary < 3000.00)           // second range
    tax = (salary - 1500.00) * 0.16 + 225.00;
else if (salary < 5000.00)           // third range
    tax = (salary - 3000.00) * 0.18 + 465.00;
else if (salary < 8000.00)           // fourth range
    tax = (salary - 5000.00) * 0.20 + 825.00;
else if (salary <= 15000.00)         // fifth range
    tax = (salary - 8000.00) * 0.25 + 1425.00;
else
    cout << "Error!  Salary outside table range $" << salary
         << endl;
```

Table 4.13 Trace of if Statement in Fig. 4.16 for salary equals $2000.00

STATEMENT PART	salary	tax	EFFECT
	2000.00	?	
if (salary < 0.00)			2000.00 < 0.00 is false
else if (salary < 1500.00)			2000.00 < 1500.00 is false
else if (salary < 3000.00)			2000.00 < 3000.00 is true
tax = (salary - 1500.00)			Evaluates to 500.00
* 0.16			Evaluates to 80.00
+ 225.00	305.00		Evaluates to 305.00

■

PROGRAM STYLE

Validating the Value of Variables

It is important to validate the value of a variable before performing computations using invalid or meaningless data. Instead of computing an incorrect tax amount, the if statement in Fig. 4.16 prints an error message if the value of salary is outside the range covered by the table (0.0 to 15,000.00). The first condition detects negative salaries; an error message is printed if salary is less than zero. Such a condition test is often called a *structure entry guard*, since it guards the entry to a structure and prevents its execution on meaningless data.

Within the structure, all conditions evaluate to false if salary is greater than 15,000.00 and the alternative following else displays an error message. The use of structure entry guards and the else alternative in a multiple-alternative decision is a good habit to get into.   ■

Short-Circuit Evaluation of Logical Expressions

When evaluating logical expressions, we often employ a technique called *short-circuit evaluation*. This means that we can stop evaluating a logical expression as soon as its value can be determined. For example, if the value of (`single == 'y'`) is false, then the logical expression

```
(single == 'y') && (gender == 'm') && (age >= 18) && (age <= 26)
```

must be false regardless of the value of the other conditions (i.e., false && (...) must always be false). Consequently, there is no need for us to continue to evaluate the other conditions when (`single == 'y'`) evaluates to false.

Your C++ compiler also uses short-circuit evaluation. This means, for example, that evaluation of a logical expression of the form s_1 && s_2 will stop if the subexpression s_1 on the left evaluates to false.

Example 4.15   If x is zero, the `if` condition

```
if ((x != 0.0) && (y / x > 5.0))
```

is false because (`x != 0.0`) is false, and false && (...) must always be false. Thus, there is no need to evaluate the subexpression (`y / x > 5.0`) when x is zero. In this case, the first condition *guards* the second and prevents the second from being evaluated when x is equal to 0. However, if the conditions were reversed, the expression

```
if ((y / x > 5.0) && (x != 0.0))
```

would cause a "division by zero" run-time error when the divisor x is zero. Therefore, the order of conditions listed in this situation is critical.   ■

EXERCISES FOR SECTION 4.9

Self-Check
1. Trace the execution of the nested `if` statements in Fig. 4.16 for `salary` = 13500.00.
2. What would be the effect of reversing the order of the first two `if` statements of Fig. 4.16?
3. Evaluate the expressions below, with and without short-circuit evaluation, if x is equal to 6 and y equals 7.

   a. `((x > 10) && (y / x <= 10))`
   b. `((x <= 10) || (x / (y - 7) > 3))`

Programming
1. Implement the decision table below using a nested `if` statement. Assume that the grade-point average is within the range 0.0 through 4.0.

GRADE-POINT AVERAGE	TRANSCRIPT MESSAGE
0.0 to 0.99	Failed semester—registration suspended
1.0 to 1.99	On probation for next semester
2.0 to 2.99	(no message)
3.0 to 3.49	Dean's list for semester
3.5 to 4.0	Highest honors for semester

2. Implement the decision table from Programming Exercise 1 without using a nested if statement.

4.10 ——— THE switch CONTROL STATEMENT

The switch control statement also may be used in C++ to select one of several alternatives. It is especially useful when the selection is based on the value of a single variable or a simple expression (called the switch *selector*). The switch selector may be an integer or character variable or expression.

Example 4.16 The switch statement

```
switch (mom_or_dad)
{
   case 'M': case 'm':
      cout << "Hello Mom - Happy Mother's Day" << endl;
      break;
   case 'D': case 'd':
      cout << "Hello Dad - Happy Father's Day" << endl;
      break;
}  // end switch
```

behaves the same way as the if statement below when the character stored in mom_or_dad is one of the four letters listed (M, m, D, or d).

```
if ((mom_or_dad == 'M') || (mom_or_dad == 'm'))
   cout << "Hello Mom - Happy Mother's Day" << endl;
else if ((mom_or_dad == 'D') || (mom_or_dad == 'd'))
   cout << "Hello Dad - Happy Father's Day" << endl;
```

The message displayed by the switch statement depends on the value of the switch selector mom_or_dad (type char). If the switch selector value is 'M' or 'm', the first message is displayed. If the switch selector value is 'D' or 'd', the second message is displayed. The character constants 'M', 'm' and 'D', 'd' are called case *labels*.

Once a particular case label statement has been executed, the reserved word break causes control to be passed to the first statement following the switch control statement. ∎

Example 4.17 The switch statement that follows finds the average life expectancy of a standard light bulb based on the bulb's wattage. Since the value of the variable watts controls the execution of the switch statement, watts must have a value before the statement executes.

```
// Determine average life expectancy of a standard light bulb.
switch (watts)
{
```

```
            case 25:
               life = 2500;
               break;
            case 40:
            case 60:
               life = 1000;
               break;
            case 75:
            case 100:
               life = 750;
               break;
            default:
               life = 0;
         } // end switch
         cout << "Life expectancy of " << watts << "-watt bulb: "
              << watts << endl;
```

C++
SYNTAX

switch Statement

Form: switch (*selector*)
{
    case *label$_1$* : *statements$_1$*;
           break;
    case *label$_2$* : *statements$_2$*;
           break;
       .
       .
       .
    case *label$_n$*:   *statements$_n$*;
           break;
    default: *statements$_d$*; (optional)
}

Example:
```
// Determine ship class.
switch (class)
{
   case 'B': case 'b':
      cout << "Battleship" << endl;
      break;
   case 'C': case 'c':
      cout << "Cruiser" << endl;
      break;
   case 'D': case 'd':
      cout << "Destroyer" << endl;
      break;
   case 'F': case 'f':
      cout << "Frigate" << endl;
      break;
   default:
      cout << "Unknown ship class " << class << endl;
} // end switch
```

Interpretation: The *selector* expression is evaluated and compared to each of the `case` labels. Each *label*$_i$ is a single, constant value, and each label must have a different value from the others. If the value of the selector expression is equal to one of the `case` labels, for example, *label*$_i$, then execution will begin with the first statement of the sequence *statements*$_i$ and continue until a `break` statement is encountered (or until the end of the `switch` control statement is encountered). [Expressions are also allowed as labels, but only if each operand in the expression is itself a constant—e.g., 5 + 7 or x * 13 (the latter is allowed only if x was previously defined as a named constant).] The type of each label should be the same as that of the selector expression.

If the value of the selector is not listed in any `case` label, none of the options will execute unless a default action is specified. Omission of a default label may create a logic error that is difficult to pinpoint. Although the `default` label is optional, we recommend its use unless you are absolutely positive that all possible selector values are covered in a `case` label. It is not necessary to enclose multiple statements for individual cases in braces; C++ treats the `switch` statement as one compound statement.   ∎

Proper Use of break

The placement of the reserved word `break` in a switch statement is very important. If the `break` is omitted following a statement sequence, *statements*$_i$, for example, then when the last statement in *statements*$_i$ is executed, execution will continue, or *fall through*, to *statements*$_{i+1}$. There are very few cases in which such a fall-through is desirable. Thus, although the `break` is not syntactically required in a `switch` statement, it is almost always necessary to ensure that only one statement sequence is executed. We can selectively leave out a `break` if multiple cases share the same outcome, e.g., `case 40` and `case 60` in Example 4.17.

Example 4.18   The next `switch` statement uses a character selector (`musical_note`).

```
switch (musical_note)
{
   case 'c':
      cout << "do";
      break;
   case 'd':
      cout << "re";
      break;
   case 'e':
      cout << "mi";
      break;
   case 'f':
      cout << "fa";
      break;
   case 'g':
```

```
            cout << "sol";
            break;
        case 'a':
            cout << "la";
            break;
        case 'b':
            cout << "ti";
            break;
        default:
            cout << "An invalid note was read." << endl;
    }  // end switch
```
■

Comparison of Nested if Statements and the switch Statement

You can use nested if control statements, a more general control form than the switch statement, to implement any multiple-alternative decision. The switch statement, however, is more readable and should be used whenever practical. Remember that case labels that contain type float values or strings are not permitted.

You will probably find it convenient to use the switch statement when you need to test a series of like types, for instance, a collection of individual integer values. You may want to use nested if statements when there are a large number of situations that require no action to be taken. Also, if the actions to be taken are dependent on the values of more than one variable, then an if statement is more flexible in its ability to combine logical expressions.

PROGRAM STYLE

Positioning of the Case Labels in a switch Statement

When more than one case label applies to the same statement, the case labels can be written on separate lines, as in Example 4.17, or we can place several labels on the same line, as in Example 4.16. C++ doesn't distinguish between the two styles, as long as the punctuation is correct. However, the more case labels you put on one line, the less readable the switch statement becomes, so use good judgment when arranging your alternatives.

The break after the last case label is structurally unnecessary, but we recommend its inclusion when you don't have a default statement. If you decide to add more labels later, there's a good chance you'll forget to add a break at that time. We prefer to practice error prevention whenever possible. ■

Using a switch Statement for Function Calls

As your programs become more complex, you may find your code for some switch alternatives also becoming more complex and lengthy. In such cases, you will usually find it helpful to place this code in a separate function. This leads us to a very common use for the switch statement: selecting a particular function from a group of possible choices, depending on perhaps an interactive question to the user.

Example 4.19   The char variable transaction contains a data value that indicates the kind of banking transaction you wish to take place.

```
switch (transaction)
{
    case 'B': case 'b':
        check_balance ();
        break;
    case 'D': case 'd':
        deposit_money ();
        break;
    case 'W': case 'w':
        withdraw_money ();
        break;
    case 'T': case 't':
        transfer_funds ();
        break;
    case 'P': case 'p':
        make_payment ();
        break;
    default:
        cout << "An invalid code was entered." << endl;
} // end switch
```

With this structure, we can place all processing code for each transaction type in a separate function. These functions might prompt the user for specific information, such as the account number and the amount of money to be processed, and perform all necessary computations on this input (possibly by calling other functions).

Program decomposition into separate components is the key here. The details of how our money is processed can be written and modified without affecting the simple *control code* we have written. In Chapter 5 we will learn how to write menus to make selections for our switch statement.   ∎

EXERCISES FOR SECTION 4.10

Self-Check   1. What will be printed by this carelessly constructed switch statement if the value of color is 'R'?

```
switch (color)
{
    case 'R': case 'r':
        cout << "red" << endl;
    case 'B': case 'b':
        cout << "blue" << endl;
```

```
        case 'Y': case 'y':
            cout << "yellow" << endl;
    }
```

2. Write an if statement that corresponds to the switch statement below.

```
switch (x > y)
{
    case 1 :
        cout << "x greater" << endl;
        break;
    case 0 :
        cout << "y greater or equal" << endl;
        break;
}
```

3. Why can't we rewrite our nested if statement examples from Section 4.9 using switch statements?
4. Why is it preferable to include a default label in a switch statement?

Programming

1. Write a switch statement that prints a message indicating whether next_ch (type char) is an operator symbol (+, -, *, /, %), a punctuation symbol (comma, semicolon, parenthesis, brace, bracket), or a digit. Your statement should print the category selected.
2. Write a nested if statement equivalent to the switch statement described in Programming Exercise 1.
3. Guard the switch statement described in Programming Exercise 1 by a default label.

4.11 — COMMON PROGRAMMING ERRORS

• *Parentheses:* For the most part, the defined precedence levels of C++ will prevent you from making a syntax error. But they will also allow you to do things you may not intend. The rule of thumb is, when in doubt, use parentheses.

• *Operators:* You can use the logical operators, &&, | |, and !, only with logical expressions. Remember that the C++ operator for equality is the double symbol ==. Do not mistakenly use the assignment operator (single =) in its place. Your expression will probably compile, but the logic will undoubtedly be incorrect.

• *Compound Statements:* Don't forget to bracket a compound statement used as a true or false task in an if control statement with braces. If the { } bracket is missing, only the first statement will be considered part of the task. This can lead to a syntax error or, worse, a logic error that could be very difficult to find. In the example below, the { } bracket around the true task is missing. The compiler assumes that only the statement

```
sum = sum + x;
```

is part of the true task of the `if` control statement. This creates a "misplaced else" syntax error. Of course, the correct thing to do is to enclose the compound statement in braces.

```
if (x > 0)                          // missing { }
    sum = sum + x;
    cout << "Greater than zero" << endl;
else
    cout << "Less than zero" << endl;
```

■ *Nested if's:* When writing a nested `if` statement, try to select the conditions so that the multiple-alternative form shown in Section 4.9 can be used. If the conditions are not mutually exclusive (i.e., more than one condition may be true), the most restrictive condition should come first.

■ *switch Statements:* When using a `switch` statement, make sure the `switch` *selector* and `case` *labels* are of the same type (`int` or `char` but not `float`). If the selector evaluates to a value not listed in any of the `case` labels, the `switch` statement will fall through without any action being taken. For this reason it is often wise to guard the `switch` with a `default` label. This way you can ensure that the `switch` executes properly in all situations. Be very careful in your placement of the `break` statements. Missing `break` statements will allow control to drop through to the next case label. Don't forget to terminate a `switch` statement with a closing brace `}`.

CHAPTER REVIEW

In this chapter, we discussed how to represent decision steps in an algorithm (using *pseudocode*) and how to implement them in C++ using the `if` and `switch` control statements. We also introduced the logical operators (`&&`, `||`, `!`) and showed how to use them to form logical expressions.

We continued our discussion of problem-solving and showed how to solve a new problem by making an analogy to an earlier problem. We also showed how to add data flow information to structure charts to improve system documentation. We saw that a variable processed by a subproblem is classified as input or output based on how it is used by that subproblem. The same variable may be input to one subproblem and output from another, again based on usage.

You also saw how to use a *hand trace* to verify that an algorithm or program is correct. You can discover errors in logic by carefully tracing an algorithm or program before entering the program in the computer. The extra measure will save you time in the long run.

We showed how to use the `if` statement to implement decisions with one and two alternatives. By nesting `if` statements, you can implement decisions with several alternatives. We also introduced a second selection structure, the `switch` statement, as a convenient means of implementing decisions with several alternatives. We saw how to use the `switch` statement to implement decisions that are based on the value of a variable or simple expression (the `switch` selector).

New C++ Constructs   The new C++ constructs introduced in this chapter are described in Table 4.14.

Table 4.14   Summary of New C++ Constructs

CONSTRUCT	EFFECT
if Control Statement	
One Alternative	
`if (y != 0)` `    result = x / y;`	Divides x by y only if y is non-zero.
Two Alternatives	

`if (x >= 0)`
`    cout << x << " is positive" << endl;`
`else`
`    cout << x << " is negative" << endl;`
	If x is greater than or equal to 0, display " is positive"; otherwise, display the message " is negative".

Several Alternatives	

`if (x < 0)`
`{`
`    cout << "Negative" << endl;`
`    abs_x = -x;`
`}`
`else if (x == 0)`
`{`
`    cout << "Zero" << endl;`
`    abs_x = 0;`
`}`
	One of three messages is printed depending on whether x is negative, positive, or zero. abs_x is set to represent the absolute value or magnitude of x.

(Continued)

Table 4.14   (Continued)

CONSTRUCT	EFFECT

```
else
{
    cout << "Positive" << endl;
    abs_x = x;
}
```

switch Statement

```
switch (next_ch)
{
    case 'A': case 'a':
        cout << "Excellent" << endl;
        break;
    case 'B': case 'b':
        cout << "Good" << endl;
        break;
    case 'C': case 'c':
        cout << "Fair" << endl;
        break;
    case 'D': case 'd':
    case 'F': case 'f':
        cout << "Poor, student is"
             << " on probation" << endl;
        break;
    default :
        cout << "Invalid grade entered."
             << endl;
} // end switch
```

Prints one of five messages based on the value of next_ch (type char). If next_ch is 'D', 'd' or 'F', 'f', the student is put on probation.

✔ QUICK-CHECK EXERCISES

1. An if statement implements _____ execution.
2. What is a compound statement?
3. A switch statement is often used instead of _____ .
4. What values can a logical expression have?
5. The operator != means _____ .
6. A hand trace is used to verify that a(n) _____ is correct.
7. Correct the syntax errors below.

```
if x > 25.0
    y = x
```

```
else
    y = z;
```

8. What value is assigned to fee by the if statement below when speed is 75?

```
if (speed > 35)
    fee = 20.00;
else if (speed > 50)
    fee = 40.00;
else if (speed > 75)
    fee = 60.00;
```

9. Answer Question 8 for the if statement below. Which if statement is correct?

```
if (speed > 75)
    fee = 60.00;
else if (speed > 50)
    fee = 40.00;
else if (speed > 35)
    fee = 20.00;
```

10. What output line(s) are displayed by the statements below when grade is 'I'? When grade is 'B'? When grade is 'b'?

```
switch (grade)
{
    case 'A':
        points = 4;
        break;
    case 'B':
        points = 3;
        break;
    case 'C':
        points = 2;
        break;
    case 'D':
        points = 1;
        break;
    case 'F':
    case 'I':
    case 'W':
        points = 0;
        break;
}  // end switch

if (('A' <= grade) && (grade <= 'D'))
    cout << "Passed, points earned = " << points << "."
        << endl;
else
    cout << "Failed, no points earned." << endl;
```

11. Explain the difference between the statements on the left and the statements on the right below. For each of them, what is the final value of x if the initial value of x is 0?

```
if (x >= 0)            if (x >= 0)
   x = x + 1;             x = x + 1;
else if (x >= 1)       if (x >= 1)
   x = x + 2;             x = x + 2;
```

Answers to Quick-Check Exercises

1. conditional
2. a block that combines one or more statements into a single statement
3. nested `if` statements or a multiple-alternative `if` statement
4. 1 (true) or 0 (false)
5. not equal
6. algorithm
7. Add parentheses around test condition and insert a semicolon before `else`.
8. 20.00, first condition is met
9. 40.00; the one in Exercise 9
10. when `grade` is `'I'`: `Failed, no points earned.`
    when `grade` is `'B'`: `Passed, points earned = 3.`
    when `grade` is `'b'`: `Failed, no points earned.`
11. A nested `if` statement is on the left; a sequence of `if` statements is on the right. x becomes 1 on the left; x becomes 3 on the right.

REVIEW QUESTIONS

1. A decision in C++ is actually an evaluation of a(n) _____ expression.
2. How does a relational operator differ from a logical operator?
3. What is short-circuit logical evaluation? What are its benefits?
4. Trace the following program fragment and indicate which function will be called if a data value of 27.34 is entered.

```
cout << "Enter a temperature: ";
cin >> temp;
if (temp > 32.0)
   not_freezing ();
else
   ice_forming ();
```

5. Write a nested `if` statement to display a message indicating the educational level of a student based on his or her number of years of schooling. (0, none; 1 through 6, elementary school; 7 through 8, middle school; 9 through 12, high school; >12, college). Print a message to indicate bad data as well.

6. Write a `switch` statement to select an operation based on the value of `inventory`. Increment `total_paper` by `paper_order` if inventory is `'b'` or `'c'`; increment `total_ribbon` by 1 if inventory is `'e'`, `'f'`, or `'d'`; increment `total_label` by `label_order` if inventory is `'a'` or `'x'`. Do nothing if inventory is `'m'`.

PROGRAMMING PROJECTS

1. Write a program that displays a "message" consisting of three block letters where each letter is an X or an O. The program user's data determines whether a particular letter will be an X or O. For example, if the user enters the three letters XOX, the block letters X, O, and X will be displayed.
2. Write a program to simulate a state police radar gun. The program should read an automobile speed and print the message "speeding" if the speed exceeds 55 mph.
3. While spending the summer as a surveyor's assistant, you decide to write a program that transforms compass headings in degrees (0 to 360) to compass bearings. A compass bearing consists of three items: the direction you face (north or south), an angle between 0 and 90 degrees, and the direction you turn before walking (east or west). For example, to get the bearing for a compass heading of 110.0 degrees, you would first face due south (180 degrees) and then turn 70.0 degrees east (180.0 − 110.0). Be sure to check the input for invalid compass headings.
5. Write a program that will determine the additional state tax owed by an employee. If the state charges a 4% tax on net income, determine net income by subtracting a $500 allowance for each dependent from gross income. Your program will read gross income, number of dependents, and tax amount already deducted. It will then compute the actual tax owed and print the difference between tax owed and tax deducted followed by the message "SEND CHECK" or "REFUND" depending on whether this difference is positive or negative.
6. The New Telephone Company has the following rate structure for long-distance calls:

   - Any call started at or after 6:00 P.M. (1800 hours) but before 8:00 A.M. (0800 hours) is discounted 50%.
   - Any call started at or after 8:00 A.M. (0800 hours) but before 6:00 P.M. (1800 hours) is charged full price.
   - All calls are subject to a 4% federal tax.
   - The regular rate for a call is $0.40 per minute.
   - Any call longer than 60 minutes receives a 15% discount on its cost (after any other discount is subtracted before tax is added).

   Write a program that reads the start time for a call based on a 24-hour clock and the length of the call. The gross cost (before any discounts or tax) should be printed followed by the net cost (after discounts are deducted and tax is added). Use separate functions to print instructions to the program user and to compute the net cost.
7. Write a program that will calculate and print out bills for the city water company. The water rates vary depending on whether the bill is for home use, commercial use,

or industrial use. A code of h means home use, a code of c means commercial use, and a code of i means industrial use. Any other code should be treated as an error. The water rates are computed as follows:

code h: $5.00 plus $0.0005 per gallon used

code c: $1000.00 for the first 4 million gallons used and $0.00025 for each additional gallon

code i: $1000.00 if usage does not exceed 4 million gallons; $2000.00 if usage is more than 4 million gallons but does not exceed 10 million gallons; and $3000.00 if usage exceeds 10 million gallons

Your program should prompt the user to enter an account number (type int), the code (type char), and the gallons of water used (type float). Your program should echo the input data and print the amount due from the user.

5

Repetition: while, for, and do-while Statements

5.1   Repetition in Programs: The while
       Statement
5.2   Accumulating a Sum or Product in a Loop
5.3   Counting Loops and Conditional Loops
5.4   Loop Design
5.5   The for Statement
5.6   More for Statement Examples
5.7   The do-while Statement
5.8   Review of while, for, and do-while Loops
5.9   Nested Loops
5.10   Debugging and Testing Programs
5.11   Common Programming Errors
       Chapter Review

So far we have covered C++ control structures for sequence and selection. In this chapter, we discuss the C++ control structures for repetition. We show how to specify the repetition of a group of program statements (called a *loop*) using the `while`, `for`, and `do-while` statements.

We discuss the relative advantages of each of the three loop forms and determine when it is best to use each one. We also reexamine nested control structures, illustrate nested loops, and see how to use them.

5.1 _____ REPETITION IN PROGRAMS: THE while STATEMENT

Just as the ability to make decisions is a very important programming tool, so is the ability to specify the repetition of a group of operations. For example, in doing a payroll for a company with seven employees, we will want to perform the same gross pay and net pay computations for each of the employees. Rather than duplicate these steps seven times in a program, we can write them once and tell the computer to repeat them.

The repetition of steps in a program is called a *loop*. The *loop body* contains the steps to be repeated. C++ provides three control statements for specifying repetition, the `while`, `for`, and `do-while` loop statements. We will first concentrate on the `while` statement.

The while Statement

The program segment shown in Fig. 5.1 computes and displays the weekly pay for each of seven employees (assuming no overtime pay). The loop body (steps that are repeated) starts on the line beginning with `while`. Inside the loop body, an employee's payroll data are read and the employee's gross pay is computed and displayed. After the loop body has been executed seven times and seven weekly pay amounts are displayed, the last statement displays the message "All employees processed."

There are three lines that control the looping process. The first statement

```
employee_count = 0;      // no employees processed yet
```

stores an initial value of 0 in the variable `employee_count`, which represents the count of employees processed so far. The next line evaluates the logical expression (`employee_count < 7`). If it is true, the loop body is executed, causing a new pair of data values to be read and a new pay to be computed and displayed. The last statement in the loop body,

```
employee_count++;        // increment count of employees
```

Figure 5.1   **Loop to process seven employees**

```
cout << setiosflags (ios::showpoint | ios::fixed);
cout << setprecision (2);
employee_count = 0;        // no employees processed yet
while (employee_count < 7)
{                          // test value of the employee count
   cout << "Hours: ";
   cin >> hours;
   cout << "Rate : $";
   cin >> rate;
   pay = hours * rate;
   cout << "Weekly pay is $" << pay << endl;
   employee_count++;       // increment count of employees
} // end while

cout << "All employees processed" << endl;
```

is a feature of C++ that is widely used in counter-controlled loops. This is
shorthand for and identical to the familiar longer statement

```
employee_count = employee_count + 1;
```

which increments the value of `employee_count` by one. After executing
the last step in the loop body, control returns to the line beginning with
`while`, and the logical expression is reevaluated for the next value of
`employee_count`.

The loop body will be executed once for each value of `employee_count`
from 0 to 6. Eventually `employee_count` will become 7, and the logical
expression will evaluate to false. When this happens the loop body is not
executed, and control passes to the display statement that follows the loop
body.

The logical expression following the reserved word `while` is called the
loop repetition condition. The loop is repeated when this condition is true. We
say that the loop is exited when this condition is false.

The flowchart of the `while` loop in Fig. 5.2 summarizes what we have
learned about `while` loops. It shows that the expression in the diamond-
shaped box is evaluated first. If it is true, the loop body is executed, and the
process is repeated. The `while` loop is exited when the expression becomes
false.

Make sure you understand the difference between the `while` statement in
Fig. 5.1 and the following `if` statement.

```
if (employee_count < 7)
{
   ...
}  // end if
```

The compound statement of an `if` statement executes at most one time. In a `while` statement, the compound statement (loop body) may execute more than one time.

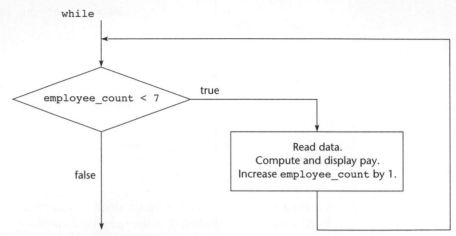

Figure 5.2   Flowchart of `while` loop

Syntax of while Statement

In Fig. 5.1, variable `employee_count` is called the *loop control variable* (*lcv*) because its value determines whether or not the loop body is repeated. There are three critical steps in loop control involving the lcv `employee_count`.

1. **Initialize:** `employee_count` is set to a starting value of 0 before the `while` statement is reached.
2. **Test:** the value of `employee_count` is tested before the start of each loop repetition (called an *iteration* or a *pass*).
3. **Update:** `employee_count` is updated (its value increases by 1) during each iteration.

Steps similar to these must be performed for every `while` loop. If the first step is missing, the initial test of `employee_count` will be meaningless. If the test step is missing we will have no way of stopping the loop repetition; thus an *infinite loop* will be created. The last step ensures that we make progress toward the final goal (`employee_count >= 7`) during each repetition of the loop. If this update is missing, the value of `employee_count` cannot change, so the loop will execute "forever," again creating an *infinite loop*. The syntax display for the `while` statement follows.

C++
SYNTAX

while Statement

Form: while (*logical expression*)
            statement

Example: // display n asterisks
```
        count_star = 0;
        while (count_star < n)
        {
            cout << "*";
            count_star++;
        } // end while
```

Interpretation: The *logical expression* (a condition to control the loop process) is tested; if it is true, the *statement* is executed and the *logical expression* is retested. The *statement* is repeated as long as (while) the *logical expression* is true. When the *logical expression* is tested and found to be false, the while loop is exited and the next program statement after the while statement is executed.

Notes: If the *logical expression* evaluates to false the first time it is tested, the *statement* will not be executed.

You must be careful with the placement of semicolons in a while statement. Make sure you do not place a semicolon after the *logical expression* on the first line of a while loop. If you make this error, the C++ compiler will assume that you have an *empty statement* for your loop body and execute this statement (which does nothing) forever or until your patience or time limit expires.   ■

PROGRAM
STYLE

Formatting the while Statement

For clarity, we will indent the body of a while loop. If the loop body is a compound statement enclosed in braces, we will terminate it with the comment // end while after the closing }.   ■

Increment and Decrement Operators

The *increment operator* ++ is used here for the first time in the text. It is discussed along with its companion *decrement operator* in the following display and example. As we will see throughout this chapter, these operators are especially useful when writing loop statements.

C++
SYNTAX

The Unary Operators Increment (++) and Decrement (--)

Form: These operators may be applied to any single integer-valued variable, simply by writing the operator as either a prefix or a postfix to the variable.

Example: ++i   i++   --i   i--

Interpretation: The first and third examples illustrate the *prefix* use of the increment and decrement operators. The second and fourth examples illustrate the *postfix* use of the operators. The differences between the prefix and postfix forms are illustrated in the next example. ∎

Example 5.1   *Prefix and Postfix Forms of ++ and --.*   If i is an integer variable containing the value 3, then

```
k = i++;               // assigns the value 3 to k
k = ++i;               // assigns the value 4 to k
k = i--;               // assigns the value 3 to k
k = --i;               // assigns the value 2 to k
```

These examples illustrate an important difference between the postfix and prefix forms of the increment and decrement operators:

- When the postfix versions of these operators are used, the increment (or decrement) takes place after the current value of the variable has been used;
- When the prefix versions of these operators are used, the increment (or decrement) takes place first and the new value of the variable is then used as prescribed.

Thus, if i contains 3,

```
cout << "Value of i is " << i;
cout << "Value of i++ is " << i++;   // displays 3, increments i
                                     //    to 4
cout << "Value of --i is " << --i;   // decrements i to 3,
                                     //    displays 3
```

The output produced would be

```
Value of i is 3
Value of i++ is 3
Value of --i is 3
```
∎

EXERCISES FOR SECTION 5.1

Self-Check   1. How many times is the loop body below repeated? What is printed during each repetition of the loop body?

```
x = 3;
count = 0;
while (count < 3)
```

```
    {
        x = x * x;
        cout << setw (5) << x;
        count++;
    } // end while
```

2. Answer Self-Check Exercise 1 if the last statement in the loop is

```
count = count + 2;
```

3. Answer Self-Check Exercise 1 if the last statement in the loop body is omitted.

Programming
1. Write a while loop that displays each integer from 1 to 5 together with its square. Have each pair print on a separate line.
2. Write a while loop that displays each integer from –2 to 3 on a separate line. Display the values in the sequence –2, –1, 0, and so on.

5.2 _____ ACCUMULATING A SUM OR PRODUCT IN A LOOP

We often use loops to accumulate a sum or a product by repeating an addition or multiplication operation. The next example uses a loop to accumulate a sum.

Example 5.2   The program in Fig. 5.3 has a while loop similar to the loop of Fig. 5.1. Besides displaying each employee's weekly pay, it accumulates the total payroll (total_pay) for a company. The assignment statement

```
total_pay += pay;                        // add next pay
```

is shorthand for

```
total_pay = total_pay + pay;
```

Figure 5.3   Computing Company Payroll Program

```
// FILE: CompPay.cpp
// COMPUTES THE PAYROLL FOR A COMPANY

#include <iostream.h>
#include <iomanip.h>

void main ()
{
    // Local data ...
    int number_employees;                    // number of employees
```

(Continued)

Figure 5.3   (Continued)

```
int employee_count;                 // current employee number
float hours;                        // hours worked
float rate;                         // hourly rate
float pay;                          // weekly pay
float total_pay;                    // company payroll

// Get number of employees from user.
cout << "Enter number of employees: ";
cin >> number_employees;

// Compute each employee's pay and add it to the payroll.
total_pay = 0.0;
employee_count = 0;
cout << setiosflags (ios::fixed | ios::showpoint)
     << setprecision (2);
while (employee_count < number_employees)
{
    cout << "Hours: ";
    cin >> hours;
    cout << "Rate : $";
    cin >> rate;
    pay = hours * rate;
    cout << "Pay is $"  << pay << endl << endl;
    total_pay += pay;          // accumulate total pay
    employee_count++;
}   // end while

cout << "All employees processed." << endl;
cout << "Total payroll is $" << total_pay << endl;
return;
}
```

——————— Program Output ———————

```
Enter number of employees: 3
Hours: 5
Rate : $4
Pay is $20.00

Hours: 6
Rate : $5
Pay is $30.00

Hours: 1.5
Rate : $10
Pay is $15.00

All employees processed.
Total payroll is $65.00
```

and adds the current value of pay to the sum being accumulated in total_pay. Figure 5.4 traces the effect of repeating this statement for the three values of pay shown in the sample run.

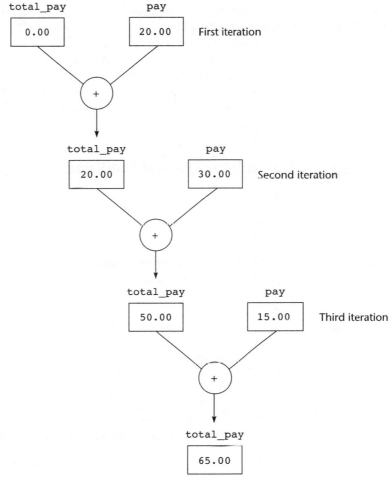

Figure 5.4   Accumulating partial sums

Prior to loop execution, the statement

```
total_pay = 0.0;
```

initializes the value of total_pay to zero. This step is critical; if it is omitted, the final sum will be off by whatever value happens to be stored in total_pay when the program begins execution.   ∎

Generalizing a Loop

The first loop shown in Fig. 5.1 has a limited utility: It can be used only when the number of employees is exactly 7. If we want to reuse this program for a different number of employees, we would first have to change the loop repetition test to reflect this number rather than 7. The program segment in Fig. 5.3 is much better because it can be reused without change for any number of employees. This program begins by reading the total number of employees into variable `number_employees`. Before each execution of the loop body, the loop repetition condition compares the number of employees processed so far (`employee_count`) to `number_employees`.

Accumulating Partial Products

In a similar way, we can use a loop to accumulate a product as shown in the next example.

Example 5.3   The loop below accumulates and displays the product of its data items as long as this product is less than 10,000.

```
// Display partial products less than 10000.
product = 1;
while (product < 10000)
{
    cout << product << endl;      // display partial product
    cout << "Enter data item: ";
    cin >> item;
    product *= item;              // compute next product
}   // end while
```

It computes each new partial product by repeated execution of the statement

```
product *= item;                 // compute next product
```

which is the shorthand version of the statement

```
product = product * item;
```

Figure 5.5 traces the change in the value of `product` with each execution of the above statement. If the data items are 10, 500, and 3, the partial products 1, 10, and 5000 are displayed.

Loop exit occurs when the value of `product` is greater than or equal to 10,000. Consequently, the last value assigned to `product` (15,000 in Fig. 5.5) is not displayed.

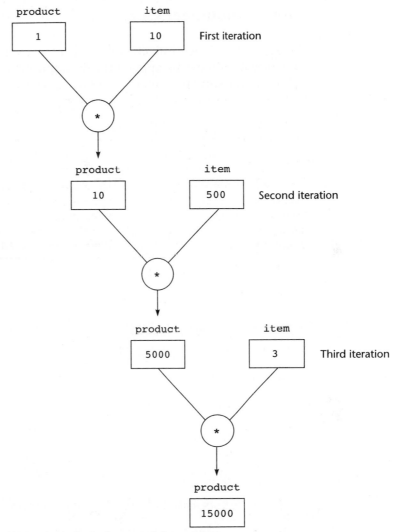

Figure 5.5   Accumulating partial products   ■

The loop in Fig. 5.5 differs from the other loops in this section. Its repetition condition involves a test of the variable `product`. Besides controlling loop repetition, the variable `product` also stores the result of the computation being performed in the loop. The other loops involve a test of a variable, `employee_count`, that represents the count of loop repetitions. `employee_count` is not directly involved in the computation being performed in the loop. We will discuss these differences further in the next section.

More Assignment Operators

In Example 5.2, we introduced the use of an *assignment operator*, +=. This shorthand form can be applied to any single binary arithmetic operator. They all work in a similar fashion, as shown in Table 5.1.

Table 5.1   Assignment Operators

SHORTHAND NOTATION	EQUIVALENT NOTATION
balance += deposit;	balance = balance + deposit;
balance -= withdrawal;	balance = balance - withdrawal;
rabbits *= 4;	rabbits = rabbits * 4;
total /= x + y * z;	total = total / (x + y * z);
hour %= 13;	hour = hour % 13;

EXERCISES FOR SECTION 5.2

Self-Check

1. What output values are displayed by the `while` loop below for a data value of 5?

```
cout << "Enter an integer: ";
cin >> x;
product = x;
count = 0;
while (count < 4)
{
    cout << product << endl;
    product *= x;
    count++;
}  // end while
```

2. What values are displayed if the `cout` line comes at the end of the loop instead of at the beginning?

3. In the C++ instruction shown below, insert the opening and closing braces where needed, add the proper indentation, and correct the errors. The corrected segment should read exactly five numbers and display their sum.

```
count = 0;
while (count <= 5)
cout << "Enter data item: ";
cin >> item;
item += sum;
count++;
cout << count << " data items were added;" << endl;
cout << "their sum is " << sum << endl;
```

4. How would the program in Fig. 5.3 need to be modified to display the average employee salary in addition to the total payroll amount?

Programming   1. Write a program segment that computes and displays $1 + 2 + 3 + \cdots + (n - 1) + n$, where n is a data value.

5.3 ⎯⎯ COUNTING LOOPS AND CONDITIONAL LOOPS

The `while` loop shown in Fig. 5.3 is called a *counter-controlled loop* (or *counting loop*) because its repetition is controlled by a loop control variable (the lcv) whose value represents a count. A counter-controlled loop follows the general form shown next.

Set lcv to an appropriate initial value (usually 0).
While lcv < final value
    Perform loop processing.
    Increase lcv (usually by 1).

We use a counter-controlled loop when we can determine prior to loop execution exactly how many loop repetitions will be needed to solve a problem. The lcv should be incremented as the final line of the `while` condition.

Conditional Loops

In many programming situations, we cannot determine the exact number of loop repetitions before loop execution begins. The number of repetitions may depend on some aspect of the data that is not known before the loop is entered but that usually can be stated by a condition. For example, we may want to continue writing checks as long as our bank balance is positive, as shown next.

While balance is still positive
    Read in next transaction.
    Update and print balance.

The actual number of loop repetitions performed depends on the type of each transaction (deposit or withdrawal) and its amount.

Example 5.4   The program in Fig. 5.6 traces the progress of a swimmer training for the Olympics as she approaches the opposite side of the pool. Each time she moves, the swimmer cuts the distance between her and the goal by two-thirds her own body length until she is close enough to touch the edge (and hopefully win a gold medal). A `while` loop is the correct looping structure to use because we have no idea beforehand how many moves are required for the swimmer to reach the other end of the pool.

Figure 5.6   Swimmer wins gold medal

```
// FILE: Swimmer.cpp
// PRINTS DISTANCES BETWEEN A SWIMMER AND THE FAR SIDE OF THE POOL
// The swimmer keeps cutting the distance by 2/3 her body length
//     on each stroke, until she is close enough to touch the edge
//     of the pool.

#include <iostream.h>
#include <iomanip.h>

void main ()
{
   // Local data ...
   const float body_length = 5.8;    // swimmer body length in feet

   float initial_distance;           // starting distance of swimmer
   float distance;          // distance between swimmer and other side

   cout << "Enter the initial distance of the swimmer from "
        << endl;
   cout << "the opposite side of the pool in feet: ";
   cin >> initial_distance;

   // Cut the distance between the swimmer and the opposite side
   //     by 2/3 the swimmer's body length until she is close
   //     enough to touch the edge.
   distance = initial_distance;
   while (distance >= body_length)
   {
      cout << "The distance is " << setprecision (2) << distance
           << endl;
      distance -= body_length / 1.5;     // reduce distance
   }  // end while

   // Print final distance before touching the opposite edge.
   cout << endl;
   cout << "The last distance before the swimmer touches the edge"
        << endl;
   cout << "on the opposite side of the pool is "
        << setprecision (1) << distance << endl;
   return;
}
```

——————— Program Output ———————

```
Enter the initial distance of the swimmer from
the opposite side of the pool in feet: 75
The distance is 75
The distance is 71.13
The distance is 67.27
The distance is 63.4
```

(Continued)

Figure 5.6   (Continued)

```
The distance is 59.53
The distance is 55.67
The distance is 51.8
The distance is 47.93
The distance is 44.07
The distance is 40.2
The distance is 36.33
The distance is 32.47
The distance is 28.6
The distance is 24.73
The distance is 20.87
The distance is 17
The distance is 13.13
The distance is 9.27

The last distance before the swimmer touches the edge
on the opposite side of the pool is 5.4
```

Let's take a close look at the `while` loop in Fig. 5.6. The assignment statement just before the loop initializes the variable `distance` to the starting distance (75), which was previously read into `initial_distance`. Next, the loop header is reached and the *loop repetition condition* (or `while` condition)

```
distance >= body_length
```

is evaluated. Because this condition is true, the loop body enclosed in braces is executed. The loop body displays the value of `distance`, and the statement

```
distance -= body_length / 1.5;        // reduce distance
```

reduces the value of `distance` by two-thirds of a body length, thereby bringing the swimmer closer to the opposite edge of the pool. The loop repetition condition is retested with the new value of `distance` (71.13); because 71.13 >= 5.8 is true, the loop body displays `distance` again, and `distance` becomes 67.27. The loop repetition condition is tested a third time; because 67.27 >= 5.8 is true, the loop body displays `distance` again, and `distance` becomes 63.4. The loop repetition condition continues to be tested again and again until we reach `distance  == 5.4`. Because 5.4 >= 5.8 is false, loop exit occurs, and the statements following the loop end are executed.

It is important to realize that the loop is not exited at the exact instant that `distance` becomes 5.4. If more statements appeared in the loop body after the assignment to `distance`, they would be executed. Loop exit does not occur until the loop repetition condition is retested at the top of the loop and found to be false.

Just as in the counting loop shown earlier, there are three major steps in Fig. 5.6 that involve the loop control variable `distance`.

1. **Initialize:** `distance` is initialized to `initial_distance` before the loop header is reached.
2. **Test:** `distance` is tested before each execution of the loop body.
3. **Update:** `distance` is updated (reduced by approximately 3.87) during each iteration.

Remember that steps similar to these must appear in every loop that you write.   ∎

EXERCISES FOR SECTION 5.3

Self-Check   1. What is the least number of times that the body of a `while` loop may be executed?
2. a. What is displayed by the segment below?

```
sum = 0;
while (sum < 100)
    sum += 5;
cout << sum << endl;
```

   b. Rewrite the loop so that it prints all multiples of 5 from 0 through 100, inclusive.

3. a. What values are displayed if the data value in the sample run of the program in Fig. 5.6 is 9.45?
   b. What values would be displayed by this program if the order of the statements in the loop body were reversed?

4. a. How would you modify the loop in Fig. 5.6 so that it also determines the number of strokes (`count_strokes`) made by the swimmer before arriving at the opposite side of the pool?
   b. In your modified loop, which is the loop control variable, `distance` or `count_strokes`?

Programming   1. There are 9870 people in a town whose population increases by 10% each year. Write a loop that determines how many years it takes for the population to go over 30,000.

5.4 ——— LOOP DESIGN

It is one thing to be able to analyze the operation of a loop (such as the loop in Fig. 5.6) and another to design our own loops. We will attack this problem in two ways. One approach is to analyze the requirements for a new loop to determine what initialization, test, and update of the loop control variable are needed. A second approach is to develop *structural patterns* for loops that frequently recur and to use this as the basis for the new loop. We will discuss structural loop patterns later in this section.

To gain some insight into the design of the loop needed for the Swimmer Problem, we should study the comment in Fig. 5.6 that summarizes the goal of this loop.

```
// Cut the distance between the swimmer and the opposite side by
//    2/3 the swimmer's body length until she is close enough to
//    touch the edge.
```

In order to accomplish this goal, we must concern ourselves with loop control and loop processing. Loop control involves making sure that loop exit occurs when it is supposed to; loop processing involves making sure the loop body performs the required operations.

To help us formulate the necessary loop control and loop processing steps, it is useful to list what we know about the loop. In this example, if `distance` is the distance of the swimmer from the edge of the pool, we can make the following observations:

a) `distance` must be equal to `initial_distance` just before the loop begins.
b) `distance` during pass `i` must be less than the value of `distance` during pass `i-1` by two-thirds the body length of the swimmer.
c) `distance` must be between 0 and the swimmer's body length just after loop exit.

Statement (a) simply indicates that `initial_distance` is the starting distance of the swimmer from the opposite side of the pool. Statement (b) says that the distance of the swimmer from the far edge must be cut by two-thirds of the swimmer's body length during each iteration. Statement (c) derives from the fact that the swimmer must be close enough to touch the edge on her next move right after loop exit. Therefore, after loop exit, the swimmer's distance from the edge must be less than her body length. Because the swimmer has not yet touched the edge, the distance cannot be negative.

Statement (a) by itself tells us what initialization must be performed. Statement (b) tells us how to process `distance` within the loop body (that is, subtract two-thirds the body length). Finally, statement (c) tells us when to exit the loop. Because `distance` is decreasing, loop exit should occur when `distance < body_length` is true. These considerations give us the outline below, which is the basis for the `while` loop shown in Fig. 5.6. The loop repetition condition, `distance >= body_length`, is the opposite of the exit condition, `distance < body_length`. The structural pattern for the `while` loop used in the Swimmer Problem is shown next.

1. Initialize `distance` to `initial_distance`.
2. While `distance` is greater than or equal to `body_length`
    2.1. Display `distance`.
    2.2. Reduce `distance` by 2/3 `body_length`.

while Loops with Zero Iterations

The body of a `while` loop is not executed if the loop repetition test fails (evaluates to false) when it is first reached. To verify that you have the initialization steps correct, you should make sure that a program still generates the correct results for zero iterations of the loop body. If `body_length` is greater than the value read into `initial_distance` (say, 3.4), the loop body in Fig. 5.6 would not execute and the lines below would be correctly displayed.

```
Enter the initial distance of the swimmer from
the opposite side of the pool in feet: 3.4

The last distance before the swimmer touches the edge
on the opposite side of the pool is 3.4
```

Displaying a Table of Values

The next example shows how to use a loop to display a table of values.

Example 5.5   Your physics professor wants you to write a program that displays the effect of gravity on a free-falling object. He would like a table that shows the height of an object dropped from a tower for every second that it is falling.

Assuming `t` is the time of free-fall, we can make the following observations about the height of an object dropped from a tower.

- At `t` equal to 0.0, the height of the object is the same as the height of the tower.
- While it is falling, the height of the object is the height of the tower minus the distance that it has traveled.
- Free-fall ends when the object height is ≤ 0.0.

These considerations form the basis for the `while` loop shown in Fig. 5.7. The height of the object (`object_height`) is initialized to the height of the tower (`tower_height`). The `while` condition

```
(object_height > 0.0)
```

ensures that loop exit occurs when the object hits the ground. Within the loop body the assignment statement

```
object_height = tower_height - 0.5 * g * pow (t,2);
```

computes the height of the object where the distance traveled is represented by the formula

$$distance = 1/2 \times gt^2$$

where g is the gravitational constant.

The number of lines in the table depends on the time interval between lines (`delta_t`) and the height of the tower (`tower_height`), both of which are data values. During each loop iteration, the current elapsed time (`t`) and the current height of the object (`object_height`) are displayed and new values are assigned to these variables. The message following the table is displayed when the object hits the ground.

Figure 5.7 *Dropping an object from a tower*

```
// FILE: FreeFall.cpp
// DISPLAY HEIGHT OF A DROPPED OBJECT AT EQUAL INTERVALS
// Displays the height of an object dropped from a tower
//    at user specified intervals, until it hits the ground.

#include <iostream.h>
#include <iomanip.h>
#include <math.h>

void main ()
{
   // Local data ...
   const float g = 9.80665;          // gravitational constant for
                                     //    metric units
   float object_height;              // height of object
   float tower_height;               // height of tower
   float t;                          // elapsed time
   float delta_t;                    // time interval

   // Enter tower height and time interval.
   cout << "Enter tower height in meters: ";
   cin >> tower_height;
   cout << "Enter time in seconds between table lines: ";
   cin >> delta_t;
   cout << endl;

   // Display object height until it hits the ground.
   cout << setw (10) << "Time" << setw (10) << "Height" << endl;
   t = 0.0;
   object_height = tower_height;

   cout << setprecision(2);
   while (object_height > 0.0)
   {
      cout << setw (9) << t << setw (10) << object_height << endl;
      t += delta_t;
      object_height = tower_height - 0.5 * g * pow (t, 2);
   }  // end while

   // Object hits the ground.
```

(Continued)

Figure 5.7 (Continued)

```
    cout << endl;
    cout << "SPLAT!!!" << endl << endl;
    return;
}
```

─────── Program Output ───────

```
Enter tower height in meters: 100
Enter time in seconds between table lines: 1

        Time    Height
          0     100.00
          1      95.10
          2      80.39
          3      55.87
          4      21.55

SPLAT!!!
```

                                                                    ■

Determining Loop Initialization

It is not always so easy to come up with the initialization steps for a loop. In some cases, we must work backward from the results that we know are required in the first pass to determine what initial values will produce these results.

Example 5.6   Your little cousin is learning the binary number system and has asked you to write a program that displays all powers of 2 that are less than a certain value (say, 10,000). Assuming that each power of 2 is stored in the variable `power`, we can make the following observations about the loop:

a) `power` during pass i is 2 times `power` at pass $i-1$ (for $i > 1$).
b) `power` must be between 10,000 and 20,000 just after loop exit.

Statement (a) follows from the fact that the powers of 2 are all multiples of 2; statement (b) follows from the stipulation that only powers less than 10,000 are to be displayed. From statement (a) we know that `power` must be multiplied by 2 in the loop body. From statement (b) we know that the loop exit condition is `power >= 10000`, so the loop repetition condition is `power < 10000`. These considerations lead us to the following loop outline.

1. Initialize `power` to ___ .
2. While `power` < 10000
        2.1. Display `power`.
        2.2. Multiply `power` by 2.

One way to complete step 1 is to ask what value should be displayed during the first loop repetition. The value of n raised to the power 0 is 1 for any number n. Therefore, if we initialize power to 1, the value displayed during the first loop repetition will be correct.

1. Initialize power to 1   ■

Sentinel-Controlled Loops

Frequently, you will not know exactly how many data items a loop will process before it begins execution. This may happen because there are too many data items to count beforehand or because the number of data items to be processed depends on how the computation proceeds.

One way to handle this situation is to instruct the user to enter a unique data value, called a *sentinel value*, as the last data item. The loop condition then tests each data item and terminates when the sentinel value is read. The sentinel value should be carefully chosen and must be a value that cannot possibly occur as data.

Example 5.7 The following statements (a and b) must be true for a sentinel-controlled loop that accumulates the sum of a collection of exam scores where each data item is read into the variable score. The sentinel value must not be included in the sum.

a) sum is the total of all scores read so far.
b) score contains the sentinel value just after loop exit.

From statement (a) we know that we must add each score to sum in the loop body, and that sum must initially be zero in order for its final value to be correct. From statement (b) we know that loop exit must occur after the sentinel value is read into score.

A solution is to read the first score as the initial value of score before the loop is reached, then perform the steps

■ add score to sum
■ read the next score

in the loop body. The algorithm outline for this solution is shown next.

1. Initialize sum to zero.
2. Read first score into score.
3. While score is not the sentinel
    3.1. Add score to sum.
    3.2. Read next score into score.

Step 2 reads in the first score and step 3.1 adds this score to zero (initial value of sum). Step 3.2 reads all remaining scores, including the sentinel. Step 3.1 adds all scores except the sentinel to sum.

The read before the loop (step 2) is often called the *initial read* because it is required prior to entry into the loop. If this read is omitted or misplaced, your loop may not work correctly. The C++ implementation shown in Fig. 5.8 uses −1 as the sentinel because all exam scores should be nonnegative. A sentinel value is best declared as a constant, because its value must not change for the duration of the loop.

You might initially think you can reverse the order of steps 3.1 and 3.2 in an attempt to avoid the need for step 2, which at first might seem like an unnec-

Figure 5.8   **A sentinel-controlled loop**

```
// FILE: SumScore.cpp
// ACCUMULATES THE SUM OF EXAM SCORES

#include <iostream.h>

void main ()
{
   // Local data ...
   const int sentinel = -1;        // sentinel value
   int score;                      // each exam score
   int sum;                        // sum of scores

   sum = 0;
   cout << "Enter scores one at a time as requested." << endl;
   cout << "When done, enter " << sentinel << " to stop." << endl;
   cout << "Enter the first score: ";
   cin >> score;
   while (score != sentinel)
   {
      sum += score;
      cout << "Enter the next score : ";
      cin >> score;
   }  // end while

   cout << endl << endl;
   cout << "Sum of exam scores is " << sum << endl;
   return;
}
```

───────── Program Output ─────────

```
Enter scores one at a time as requested.
When done, enter -1 to stop.
Enter the first score: 55
Enter the next score : 33
Enter the next score : 77
Enter the next score : -1

Sum of exam scores is 165
```

essary duplication. Be assured that in doing so, the sentinel will be added to the sum and sum will be incorrect.   ■

It is usually instructive (and often necessary) to question what happens when there are no data items to process. To test this idea, the sentinel value should be entered as the "first score." Loop exit would occur right after the first and only test of the loop repetition condition, so the loop body would not be executed (that is, it is a loop with zero iterations). sum would correctly retain its initial value of zero.

Sentinel-controlled loops have the general form shown next.

General Structural Pattern for a Sentinel- Controlled Loop

1. Read the first value of input variable.
2. While input variable is not equal to the sentinel
    2.1 Process value just read.
    2.2 Read the next value of input variable.

Loops Controlled by Flags

Integer variables are often used as *status flags* controlling the execution of a loop. The value of the flag is initialized (usually to 0 (false)) prior to loop entry and is redefined (usually to 1 (true)) when a particular event occurs inside the loop. A *flag-controlled loop* executes until the anticipated event occurs and the flag value is changed.

For example, let's assume we are reading various data characters entered at the keyboard and are waiting for the first digit character that is entered. The variable digit_read could be used as a flag to indicate whether a digit character has been entered.

> *Program Variable*
>
> digit_read (int)   status flag—value is 1 (true) after a digit charac-
>   ter has been read; otherwise, value is 0 (false).

Because no characters have been read before the data entry loop executes, we should initialize digit_read to 0. The while loop must continue to execute as long as digit_read is 0 because this means that the event "digit character entered as data" has not yet occurred. Therefore, the loop repetition condition should be (!digit_read), i.e., not zero, because this condition is true when digit_read is 0. Within the loop body we will read each data item and set the value of digit_read to 1 if that data item is a digit charac-ter. The while loop follows.

```
digit_read = 0;   // false: assume no digit character has been
                  //    read
```

```
while (!digit_read)
{
    cout << "Enter another data character: ";
    cin >> next_char;
    digit_read = (('0' <= next_char) && (next_char <= '9'));
    // Process digit_read.
    ...
}  // end while
```

The assignment statement

```
digit_read = (('0' <= next_char) && (next_char <= '9'));
```

assigns a value of 1 (true) to `digit_read` if `next_char` is a digit character (within the range `'0'` through `'9'`); otherwise, `digit_read` remains 0 (false). If `digit_read` becomes nonzero, loop exit occurs; if `digit_read` remains 0, the loop continues to execute until a digit character is finally read.

We will examine better ways of testing for "digit characters" as well as for other categories of characters (lowercase letters, etc.) in later chapters of the text.

The general form of a flag-controlled loop is shown next.

General Structural Pattern for a Flag-Controlled Loop

1. Initialize flag to 0 (false).
2. While flag is still 0
   2.1 Perform loop processing.
   2.2 Reset flag to 1 (true) if event occurs.

The last step in the loop body updates the flag value, setting it to 1 after the first occurrence of the event.

EXERCISES FOR SECTION 5.4

Self-Check

1. Why would it be incorrect to move the assignment statement in the sentinel-controlled loop of Fig. 5.8 to the end of the loop body?

Programming

1. Modify the counter-controlled loop in Fig. 5.3 so that it is a sentinel-controlled loop. Use a negative value of `hours` as the sentinel.
2. Write a program segment that allows the user to enter values and prints out the number of positive and negative values entered. Use 0 as the sentinel value.
3. Write a `while` loop that displays all powers of an integer, n, less than a specified value, `max_power`. On each line of a table, show the power (0, 1, 2, ...) and the value of the integer n raised to that power.
4. Write a loop that prints a table of angle measures along with their sine and cosine values. Assume that the initial and final angle measures (in degrees) are available in `initial_degree` and `final_degree` (type `float`), respectively, and that the change in angle measure between table entries is given by `step_degree`. (Remember that C++ trigonometric functions perform their computations in radians, so you will have some conversion to do from degrees to radians and vice versa.)

5. Write a flag-controlled loop that continues to read pairs of integers until it reads a pair with the property that the first integer in the pair is evenly divisible by the second.

5.5 _____ THE for STATEMENT

An Introduction to the for Statement

So far we have used the `while` statement to implement repetition in programs. C++ provides another loop form, the `for` statement, that is more convenient for implementing loops, especially those involving *counter-controlled repetition*. For example, we can write the `while` loop form of the counter-controlled loops illustrated in Section 5.2 as follows:

Set *lcv* to *initial value*.
While (*lcv* < *final value*)
     Perform loop processing.
     Update *lcv* to *next value*.

The `for` statement having the same behavior as this `while` statement is shown next.

for (set *lcv* to *initial value*; *lcv* < *final value*; update *lcv* to *next value*)
     Perform loop processing.

An important feature of the `for` loop is that all loop control operations are specified in the `for` *statement header*. These three operations are:

1. Set the *lcv* to *initial value*.
2. Test *lcv* against *final value* (the *repetition condition test*).
3. Update *lcv* to *next value* before next test.

It is important to understand the order of execution in a `for` loop with executable statements in its body. The lcv initialization is done first and only once. The repetition condition test is performed next. If the condition is false, nothing further in the loop is executed. If the condition is true, the statements in the loop body are executed next. Finally, the lcv is updated, but only if the repetition condition was true and only after the execution of the loop body completes.

Example 5.8   The statements below behave in the same way.

```
// print n blank lines          // print n blank lines
line = 0;                       for (line = 0; line < n; line++)
while (line < n)                    cout << endl;
```

```
{
    cout << endl;
    line++;
}  // end while
```

If `line` is declared as an integer variable, the `for` statement on the right causes the `cout` operation to be performed n times. The `while` loop implementation shown on the left is longer because the assignment statements

```
line = 0;
line++;
```

which are needed to initialize and update the loop control variable, appear on their own separate lines.   ■

Example 5.9   The `for` statement in Fig. 5.9 reads payroll data for seven employees and computes and displays each employee's weekly pay. Compare it with the `while` statement shown in Fig. 5.1.

Figure 5.9   `for` loop for seven employees

```
for (employee_count = 0; employee_count < 7; employee_count++)
{
    cout << "Hours: ";
    cin >> hours;
    cout << "Rate : $";
    cin >> rate;
    pay = hours * rate;
    cout << "Weekly pay is $" << setprecision (2) << pay << endl;
}  // end for

cout << "All employees processed" << endl;
```

The first line of Fig. 5.9 can be interpreted as follows:

a) Initialize loop control variable `employee_count` to 0.
b) Test the repetition condition (`employee_count` is < 7).
c) Update value of `employee_count` (increment by 1).   ■

Example 5.10   Figure 5.10 shows a function `print_I` that displays the capital letter I in block form. The `for` loop prints five lines that contain asterisks in columns 4 and 5. A blank line is printed just before the return from the function.

Figure 5.10   Function `print_I`

```
// PRINTS THE BLOCK LETTER I
void print_I ()
```

(Continued)

Figure 5.10   (Continued)

```
{
    // Local data ...
    int next_line;               // loop control variable

    cout << "********" << endl;
    for (next_line = 0; next_line < 5; next_line++)
        cout << "    **" << endl;
    cout << "********" << endl << endl;
    return;
}
```

The `for` statement in Fig. 5.10 specifies that the loop control variable `next_line` should take on each of the values in the range 0 to 4 during successive loop repetitions. This means that the value of `next_line` is 0 during the first loop repetition, 1 during the second loop repetition, and 4 during the last loop repetition. ■

PROGRAM STYLE

Loop Control Variables as Local Variables

In Fig. 5.10, the loop control variable `next_line` is declared as a local variable in function `print_I`. All loop control variables should be declared as local variables in any function in which they are used. ■

All of the `for` loops illustrated thus far have been similar in the following way:

- The *initial value* has been 0;
- The *increment* step has been of the form `counter++`, where `counter` is the loop control variable;
- The *final value* is actually the number of repetitions for the loop, that is, the number of times the loop body is to be repeated.

This is one of the simplest versions of the general C++ `for` loop. However, it is easy to understand and is by far the most often used. As we will see in many of the remaining examples in this chapter, we are not restricted to this `for` loop form.

The following example illustrates a `for` statement in which the loop control variable is referenced in the loop body.

Example 5.11   The program in Fig. 5.11 uses a `for` loop to print a list of integer values, their squares, and their square roots. During each repetition of the loop body, the statement

```
square = pow (i, 2);
```

calls function pow to compute the square of the loop control variable i. pow takes two arguments, x and y, and returns x^y. Since we want i^2, we pass in the variable i for x, and the number 2 for y. A good idea would be to declare the 2 as a constant and use it as pow's second argument.

The statement

```
root = sqrt (i);
```

calls function sqrt to compute the square root of i. Both of these functions require the inclusion of the math header file math.h. In the last steps of the loop, the values of i, i squared, and the square root of i are displayed. Table 5.2 traces the execution of the for loop.

Figure 5.11   Table of integers, squares, and square roots

```
// FILE: Squares.cpp
// DISPLAYS A TABLE OF INTEGERS AND THEIR SQUARES

#include <iostream.h>
#include <iomanip.h>           // needed for setw and setprecision
#include <math.h>              // needed for pow() and sqrt()
void main ()
{
    // Local data ...
    const int max_i = 4;       // largest integer in table

    int i;                     // loop control variable
    int square;                // output: square of i
    float root;                // output: square root of i

    // Prints a list of integers, their squares, and square roots.
    cout << setw (5) << "i" << setw (10) << "square" << setw (14)
         << "square root" << endl;
    for (i = 1; i <= max_i; i++)
    {
        square = pow (i, 2);
        root = sqrt (i);
        cout << setw (5) << i;
        cout << setw (8) << square;
        cout << setw (11) << setprecision (1) << root << endl;
    }   // end for
    return;
}
```

——————— Program Output ———————

i	square	square root
1	1	1.0
2	4	1.4
3	9	1.7
4	16	2.0

Table 5.2 Trace of Program in Fig. 5.11

STATEMENT	i	square	root	EFFECT
	?	?	?	
for (i = 1; i <= max_i; i++)	1			Initialize i to 1
square = pow (i, 2);		1		Assign 1 to square
root = sqrt (i);			1.0	Assign 1.0 to root
cout << ...				Print 1, 1, 1.0
Increment and Test i	2			2 ≤ 4 is true
square = pow (i, 2);		4		Assign 4 to square
root = sqrt (i);			1.4	Assign 1.4 to root
cout << ...				Print 2, 4, 1.4
Increment and Test i	3			3 ≤ 4 is true
square = pow (i, 2);		9		Assign 9 to square
root = sqrt (i);			1.7	Assign 1.7 to root
cout << ...				Print 3, 9, 1.7
Increment and Test i	4			4 < 4 is true
square = pow (i, 2);		16		Assign 16 to square
root = sqrt (i);			2.0	Assign 2.0 to root
cout << ...				Print 4, 16, 2.0
Increment and Test i	5			5 ≤ 4 is false
				Exit loop

The hand trace in Table 5.2 shows that the loop control variable i is initialized to 1 when the for loop is reached. Although most loops generally start with 0, it is not required by C++. In this particular case, starting our loop with 1 has more relevance. After each loop repetition, i is incremented by one and tested to see whether its value is still less than max_i (4). If the test result is true, the loop body is executed again, and the next values of i, square, and root are printed. If the test result is false, the loop is exited.

The last loop repetition occurs when i is equal to max_i. After this repetition, the value of i becomes one greater than max_i, and the loop is exited. You can reference the last value of the variable i anytime after leaving the loop. ∎

Example 5.12 The counting loop shown in Fig. 5.12 computes the sum of all integers from 1 to n.

Figure 5.12 Program for sum of integers from 1 to n

```
// FILE: Sum_Int.cpp
// FINDS AND PRINTS THE SUM OF ALL INTEGERS FROM 1 TO n
```

(Continued)

Figure 5.12 (Continued)

```cpp
#include <iostream.h>

void main ()
{
    // Local data ...
    int n;                      // last integer to be added to sum
    int sum;                    // sum of all integers from 1 to n
    int i;                      // lcv

    // Read the last integer.
    cout << "Enter the last integer in the sum: ";
    cin >> n;

    // Find the sum of all the integers from 1 to n inclusive.
    sum = 0;
    for (i = 1; i <= n; i++)
        sum += i;

    // Print the sum.
    cout << "The sum is " << sum << "." << endl;
    return;
}
```

The `for` loop causes the assignment statement

```cpp
sum += i;
```

to be repeated n times. Each time, the current value of i is added to the sum being accumulated and the result is saved back in sum. This is illustrated in Fig. 5.13 for n equal to 3.

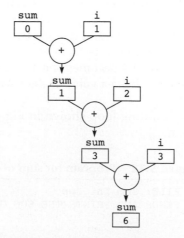

Figure 5.13   Effect of loop repetitions for n equal to 3

EXERCISES FOR SECTION 5.5

Self-Check   1. What is the result of execution of the program shown in Fig. 5.12 for n = 5? What is the value of sum, as computed by the formula

$$sum = \frac{n(n + 1)}{2}$$

Do you think you would get the same result if n = 50? Which approach to computing sum do you think is more efficient? Explain your answer.

Programming   1. Modify the program in Fig. 5.12 so the main function calls a separate function to implement the initialization and loop that computes the sum.

5.6 ——— MORE for STATEMENT EXAMPLES

So far, we have used the for loop to implement counting loops, or loops that are executed once for each integer value between an initial and a specified final value. In these examples, the loop control was a special variable whose value was increased by 1 each time the loop is repeated. In fact, as shown in the next examples, the for loop may be used in more general ways.

Example 5.13   It is actually possible to specify any positive or negative change to the value of a for loop control variable in the loop header. Thus, the value of the for loop control variable may increase or decrease by any specified amount after each loop repetition. The following for loop computes the sum of all odd integers from 1 to n.

```
// Add the odd integers between 1 and n.
sum = 0;
for (odd = 1; odd <= n; odd += 2)
   sum += odd;
```

The update expression

```
odd += 2
```

causes the value of the loop control variable odd to increase by 2 instead of 1. In the trace shown in Table 5.3, n is 5 so the values of odd that get summed are 1, 3, and 5. Note that loop exit occurs when the value of odd *passes* (becomes larger than) n, so the value of odd after loop exit is 7. If the value entered for n is 6 instead of 5, the final values of odd and sum would be the same (7 and 9, respectively).

Table 5.3 Trace of Loop for Computing the Sum of Odd Integers

STATEMENT	n	odd	sum	EFFECT
	5	?	?	
sum = 0;			0	Initializes sum to 0.
for (odd = 1;		1		Initializes odd to 1.
odd <= n;				$1 \leq 5$ is true
odd += 2)				(no action yet)
sum += odd;			1	adds odd to sum $(1 + 0)$
Increment odd		3		add 2 to odd $(2 + 1)$
Test odd <= n;				$3 \leq 5$ is true
sum += odd;			4	adds odd to sum $(3 + 1)$
Increment odd		5		add 2 to odd $(2 + 3)$
Test odd <= n;				$5 \leq 5$ is true
sum += odd;			9	adds odd to sum $(5 + 4)$
Increment odd		7		add 2 to odd $(2 + 5)$
Test odd <= n;				$7 \leq 5$ is false
				exit loop

∎

Decrementing the Loop Control Variable

The examples seen so far showed the for loop using an incrementing loop control variable in the iteration section to increase that variable's value. It is just as easy to use a decrementing counter. In the next example, we will demonstrate a loop using decrements of 5.

Example 5.14   The program in Fig. 5.14 prints a table for converting Celsius temperatures to Fahrenheit temperatures.

Figure 5.14   Converting Celsius to Fahrenheit

```
// FILE: Temperat.cpp
// CONVERSION OF CELSIUS TO FAHRENHEIT TEMPERATURE

#include <iostream.h>
#include <iomanip.h>

void main ()
{
   // Local data ...
   int celsius;
   float fahrenheit;
```

(Continued)

Figure 5.14   (Continued)

```
// Print the table heading.
cout << setw (10) << "Celsius" << setw (15) << "Fahrenheit"
    << endl;

// Set ios flags to show decimal point.
cout << setiosflags (ios::showpoint);

// Print the table.
for (celsius = 20; celsius >= -20; celsius -= 5)
{
    fahrenheit = 1.8 * celsius + 32;
    cout << setw (7) << celsius << setw (14) << setprecision (2)
        << fahrenheit << endl;
}  // end for
return;
}
```

───────── Program Output ─────────

```
Celsius    Fahrenheit
   20         68.00
   15         59.00
   10         50.00
    5         41.00
    0         32.00
   -5         23.00
  -10         14.00
  -15          5.00
  -20         -4.00
```

The for Statement Syntax

The syntax display for the general form of the for statement follows. Make sure that you place semicolons between the three parts of the for statement within the parentheses. You should not place a semicolon after the closing parenthesis or you will create a null loop. The for statement

```
for (i = -5; i <= 5; i++);     // empty statement after parenthesis
    cout << i << endl;
```

executes an empty statement 11 times then prints only the final value of i after loop exit, which will be 6. If the semicolon after the closing parenthesis were removed, the for statement would list the integers from –5 through 5.

**C++
SYNTAX**

for Statement

Form: for (*initialize expression; test expression; update expression*)
                statement

Examples:
```
for (time = start; time >= 1; time -= interval)
{
    ...
}

sum = 0.0;
for (i = 0; i < 5; i++)
{
    cin >> next_number;
    sum += next_number;
}
```

Interpretation: The loop control variable (*lcv*) is normally an integer variable, and the *initial expression* normally has an integer value (often a constant or variable). The *test expression* must have a true or false value and usually will consist of a comparison of two integer-valued expressions, one involving the *lcv*.

The *statement* is executed once for each value of the *lcv*, starting with the value indicated by the *initial expression*. Before each repetition of *statement* (including the first), the *test expression* is evaluated. If it is false, execution control passes to the first statement following *statement* (loop exit); otherwise, *statement* is executed. After *statement* is executed, the value of *lcv* is updated as specified in the *update* component, and the *test expression* is evaluated once again. ∎

As shown in this display, C++ allows considerable flexibility in the form of the *initialize, test,* and *update* expressions that can be used in a **for** loop header. In later chapters we will illustrate more of the versatility of this construct.

EXERCISES FOR SECTION 5.6

Self-Check   1. Trace the following program segment.

```
j = 10;
for (i = 0; i < 3; i++)
{
    cout << i << "   " << j << endl;
    j -= 2;
}  // end for
```

2. Write **for** loop headers that process all values of Celsius (type **int**) in the ranges indicated below.

   a. −10 through +10
   b. 100 through 1
   c. 15 through 50
   d. 50 through −75

Programming   1. a. Write a program to print a table for converting kilometers to miles (1 km = 0.6 mile). Test your `for` loop with several different start and end values.
   b. Reverse the direction of your loop in part (a) (increasing or decreasing).

5.7 ———— THE do-while STATEMENT

The `do-while` statement is used to specify a conditional loop that executes at least once. That is, the loop repetition test is specified at the bottom of the loop so that the test cannot be made until at least one execution of the statement has been completed.

Example 5.15   Both program segments in Fig. 5.15 print the powers of 2 whose values lie between 1 and 1000.

Figure 5.15   `while` (left) and `do-while` (right) statements

```
power = 1;                              power = 1;
while (power < 1000)                    do
{                                       {
    cout << power << endl;                  cout << power << endl;
    power *= 2;                             power *= 2;
}   // end while                        }   while (power < 1000);
```

The test used in the `do-while` loop (`power < 1000`) is the same test used in the `while` loop; it is just in a different place. The loop body is repeated as long as the value of `power` is less than 1000. Loop repetition stops when the condition becomes false. The major difference between the two forms is that the `do-while` loop test is at the bottom of the loop following the execution of the loop body. Thus, `do-while` loops are guaranteed to execute at least one time. ∎

The syntax display for the `do-while` statement follows. Note that, just as with the other loop statements, braces are needed around multistatement loop bodies.

C++
SYNTAX

do-while Statement

Form: do
               statement
        `while` *(expression)*

Example:
```
do
{
    cout << "Enter a digit: ";
    cin >> ch;
} while ((ch < '0') || ('9' < ch));
```

Interpretation: After each execution of the *statement*, the *expression* is evaluated. If the *expression* is false, loop exit occurs and the next program statement is executed. If the *expression* is true, the loop body is repeated. ∎

Example 5.16   A do-while statement is often used to control a *menu-driven program* that prints a list of choices from which the program user selects a program operation. For example, the menu displayed for a statistics program might look like this:

```
1. Compute an average.
2. Compute a standard deviation.
3. Find the median.
4. Find the smallest and largest value.
5. Plot the data.
6. Exit.
```

The main control routine for such a program would follow the pseudocode below where exit_choice represents the constant 6.

```
do
    Display the menu.
    Read the user's choice.
    Perform the user's choice.
while choice is not exit_choice
```

The program segment (Fig. 5.16) implements this loop in C++. For each iteration, function display_menu displays the menu and reads and performs the user's choice. Function do_choice is called with actual argument choice. do_choice could contain a series of alternatives in a switch structure, as suggested by Section 4.10. It is assumed that do_choice would carry out the action specified by the choice value (between 1 and 5). For any other value of choice, do_choice does nothing but return control to the loop. Note that the loop continues to repeat for all values of choice except exit_choice. Therefore, if the user enters in improper values (such as a negative value or a value larger than exit_choice), the loop provides another chance for entry of a correct value.

Figure 5.16   Main control loop for menu-driven program

```
do
{
    display_menu ();        // display the menu choices
```

(Continued)

Figure 5.16   (Continued)

```
    cout << "Enter a number between 1 and " << exit_choice << endl;
    cin >> choice;
    do_choice (choice);     // perform the user's choice
}   while (choice != exit_choice);
```

∎

Example 5.17   The program in Fig. 5.17 uses a `do-while` loop to find the largest value in a sequence of data items. The variable `item_value` is used to hold each data item, and the variable `largest_so_far` is used to save the largest data value encountered. Within the loop, the `if` statement

```
if (item_value > largest_so_far)
    largest_so_far = item_value;  // save the new largest number
```

redefines the value of `largest_so_far` if the current data item is larger than all previous data values. The loop continues to repeat as long as the `min_value` (a sentinel value in this case) is not read.

Figure 5.17   Finding the largest value

```
// FILE: Largest.cpp
// FINDS THE LARGEST NUMBER IN A SEQUENCE OF INTEGER VALUES

#include <iostream.h>          // needed for cin and cout
#include <limits.h>            // needed for INT_MIN

void main ()
{
    // Local data ...
    int item_value;            // each data value
    int largest_so_far;        // largest value so far
    int min_value;             // the smallest integer

    // Initialize largest_so_far to the smallest integer.
    min_value = INT_MIN;
    largest_so_far = min_value;

    // Save the largest number encountered so far.
    cout << "Finding the largest value in a sequence: " << endl;
    do
    {
        cout << "Enter an integer or " << min_value << " to stop: ";
        cin >> item_value;
        if (item_value > largest_so_far)
            largest_so_far = item_value;    // save new largest number
    }   while (item_value != min_value);
```

(Continued)

Figure 5.17   (Continued)

```
cout << "The largest value entered was " << largest_so_far
    << endl;
return;
}
```
——————— Program Output ———————
```
Finding the largest value in a sequence:
Enter an integer or -32768 to stop: -999
Enter an integer or -32768 to stop: 500
Enter an integer or -32768 to stop: 100
Enter an integer or -32768 to stop: -32768
The largest value entered was 500
```

The variable `min_value`, which represents the smallest integer value (see Section 3.7), serves two purposes in the program shown in Fig. 5.17. Note that you must include `limits.h`, which defines `INT_MIN` for your particular system. By initializing `largest_so_far` to `min_value` before loop entry, we ensure that the condition (`item-value > largest_so_far`) will be true during the first loop repetition. Thus, the first data item will be saved as the largest value so far. We are also using `min_value` as a sentinel because it is unlikely to be entered as a data item for a program that is finding the largest number in a sequence.   ∎

5.8 ——— REVIEW OF while, for, AND do-while LOOPS

C++ provides three loop control statements: `while`, `for`, and `do-while`. The `while` loop is repeated as long as its loop repetition condition is true; the `do-while` loop executes in a similar manner except its statement is always performed at least once. The `for` loop is normally used where counting is involved, either for loop control, where the number of iterations required can be determined at the beginning of loop execution, or simply when there is a need to track the number of times a particular event has taken place. In such cases, initialization and increment steps are required, and the `for` loop enables us to specify these steps together in one line at the top of the loop. Table 5.4 describes when to use each of these three loop forms. In C++, the `for` loop is the most frequently used of the three. The generality of the `for` loop significantly reduces the importance of the `while` loop in C++.

It is relatively easy to rewrite a `do-while` loop as a `while` loop by inserting an initial assignment of the conditional variable. However, not all `while` loops can be conveniently expressed as `do-while` loops because a `do-while` loop will always execute at least once, whereas a `while` loop body may be

Table 5.4 Three Loop Forms

while	Most commonly used when repetition is not counter controlled; condition test precedes each loop repetition; loop body may not be executed at all
for	Counting loop—when number of repetitions is known ahead of time and can be controlled by a counter; also convenient for loops involving non-counting loop control with simple initialization and update steps; condition test precedes the execution of the loop body
do-while	Convenient when at least one repetition of loop body must be ensured

skipped entirely. For this reason a while loop is preferred over a do-while loop unless you are certain that at least one loop iteration must always be performed.

As an illustration of the three loop forms, a simple counting loop is written in Fig. 5.18. (The dotted lines represent the loop body.) The for loop is the best to use in this situation. The do-while loop must be nested in an if statement to prevent it from being executed when start_value is greater than stop_value. For this reason, the do-while version of a counting loop is least desirable.

In Fig. 5.18, the assignment statement

```
count++;
```

Figure 5.18 Comparison of three loop forms

```
count = start_value;
while (count < stop_value)
{
    .....
    count++;
}   // end while
for (count = start_value; count < stop_value; count++)
{
    .....
}   // end for
count = start_value;
if (start_value < stop_value)
    do
    {
        .....
        count++;
    } while (count < stop_value);
```

is used in all three loops to update the loop control variable count. count will be equal to stop_value after the loops are executed; count will remain equal to start_value if these loops are skipped.

EXERCISES FOR SECTION 5.8

Self-Check

1. What does the while statement below display? Rewrite it as a for statement and as a do-while statement.

```
num = 10;
while (num <= 100)
{
    cout << num << endl;
    num += 10;
} // end while
```

2. What does the for statement below display? Rewrite it as a while statement and as a do-while statement.

```
for (n = 3; n > 0; n--)
    cout << n << " squared is " << pow (n, 2) << endl;
```

3. When would you make use of a do-while loop rather than a while loop in a program?

Programming

1. Write a program fragment that skips over a sequence of positive integer values read as data until it reaches a negative value. Write two versions: one using do-while and one using while.

2. Write a program fragment that could be used as the main control loop in a menu-driven program for updating an account balance (D = deposit, W = withdrawal, Q = quit). Assume that functions process_withdrawal and process_deposit already exist and are called with the actual argument balance. Prompt the user for a transaction code (D, W, or Q) and call the appropriate function.

5.9 _____ NESTED LOOPS

This section examines nested control structures. You have seen examples of nested if statements in earlier programs. It is also possible to nest loops. Nested loops consist of an outer loop with one or more inner loops. Each time the outer loop is repeated, the inner loops are reentered, their loop control components are reevaluated, and all required iterations are performed.

Example 5.18

Figure 5.19 shows a sample run of a program with two nested for loops. The outer loop is repeated four times (for i equals 0, 1, 2, 3). Each time the outer loop is repeated, the statement

```
cout << "Outer" << setw (7) << i << endl;
```

displays the string "Outer" and the value of i (the outer loop control variable). Next, the inner loop is entered, and its loop control variable, j, is reset to 0. The number of times the inner loop is repeated depends on the current value of i. Each time the inner loop is repeated, the statement

```
cout << "  Inner" << setw (10) << j << endl;
```

displays the string "Inner" and the value of j.

Figure 5.19 Nested for loop program

```
// FILE: NestLoop.cpp
// ILLUSTRATES A PAIR OF NESTED FOR LOOPS

#include <iostream.h>              // needed for cin and cout
#include <iomanip.h>               // needed for setw

void main ()
{
   // print heading
   cout << setw(12) << "i" << setw(6) << "j" << endl;

   for (int i = 0; i < 4; i++)
   {
      cout << "Outer" << setw (7) << i << endl;
      for (int j = 0; j < i; j++)
      cout << "  Inner" << setw (10) << j << endl;
   }  // end for - outer loop
   return;
}
```

——————— Program Output ———————

```
              i     j
Outer         0
Outer         1
   Inner             0
Outer         2
   Inner             0
   Inner             1
Outer         3
   Inner             0
   Inner             1
   Inner             2
```

A compound statement executes each time the outer for loop is repeated. This statement displays the value of the outer loop control variable and then executes the inner for loop. The body of the inner for loop is a single statement displaying the value of the inner loop control variable. This statement executes i times, where i is the outer loop control variable.

The outer loop control variable i determines the number of repetitions of the inner loop, which is perfectly valid. On the other hand, you should not use the same variable as the loop control variable of both an outer and inner for loop in the same nest.   ∎

In this example, we have declared and used each of the two loop control variables directly in their respective for loop headers. This is allowed by C++ and is a feature that we find quite convenient. When a loop control variable is declared in this manner, it may be referenced anywhere below the point of declaration in the current function. Only one such declaration may be placed in each function.

Example 5.19   Program Triangle in Fig. 5.20 prints an isosceles triangle. The program contains an outer loop (lcv row) and two inner loops. Each time the outer loop is repeated, two inner loops are executed. The first inner loop prints the leading blank spaces; the second inner loop prints one or more asterisks.

Figure 5.20   Isosceles Triangle Program

```
// FILE: Triangle.cpp
// DRAWS AN ISOSCELES TRIANGLE

#include <iostream.h>

void main ()
{
   // Local data ...
   const int number_lines = 5; // number of rows in triangle
   const char blank = ' ';      // output characters
   const char star = '*';       // display character

   // start on new line
   cout << endl;

   // draw each row - outer loop
   for (int row = 1; row <= number_lines; row++)
   {
      // print leading blanks - 1st inner loop
      for (int lead_blanks = number_lines - row; lead_blanks > 0;
             lead_blanks--)
        cout <<  blank;

      // print asterisks - 2nd inner loop
      for (int count_stars = 1; count_stars < 2 * row;
          count_stars++)
```

(Continued)

Figure 5.20 (Continued)

```
        cout << star;

    // terminate line
    cout << endl;
  }   // end for - outer loop
  return;
}
```

——————— Program Output ———————

```
    *
   ***
  *****
 *******
*********
```

The outer loop is repeated five times; the number of repetitions performed by the inner loops is based on the value of row. Table 5.5 lists the inner loop control expressions for each value of row. As shown in Table 5.5, four blanks and one asterisk are printed when row is 1, three blanks and three asterisks are printed when row is 2, etc. When row is 5, the first inner loop is skipped and nine ($2 \times 5 - 1$) asterisks are printed. ■

Table 5.5 Loop Control Variable Values

row	lead_blanks	count_stars	EFFECT
1	4 down to 1	1	Displays 4 blanks and 1 star
2	3 down to 1	1 up to 3	Displays 3 blanks and 3 stars
3	2 down to 1	1 up to 5	Displays 2 blanks and 5 stars
4	1	1 up to 7	Displays 1 blank and 7 stars
5	0	1 up to 9	Displays 0 blanks and 9 stars

EXERCISES FOR SECTION 5.9

Self-Check 1. What is displayed by the following program segments assuming m is 3 and n is 5?

```
a. for (int i = 0; i < n; i++)
   {
      for (int j = 0; j < i; j++)
         cout << "*";
      cout << endl;
   }  // end for i
b. for (int i = n; i > 0; i--)
   {
      for (int j = m; j > 0; j--)
```

```
            cout << "*";
        cout << endl;
    }  // end for i
```

2. Show the output printed by the nested loops below.

```
for (int i = 0; i < 2; i++)
{
    cout << "Outer" << setw (5) << i << endl;
    for (int j = 0; j < 3; j++)
        cout << "  Inner" << setw (3) << i << setw (3) << j
            << endl;
    for (int k = i; k >= 0; k--)
        cout << "  Inner" << setw (3) << i << setw (3) << k
            << endl;
}  // end for i
```

Programming   1. Write nested loops that cause the output below to be printed.

```
1
1 2
1 2 3
1 2 3 4
1 2 3
1 2
1
```

5.10 ━━━ DEBUGGING AND TESTING PROGRAMS

In Section 2.8, we described the general categories of errors that you are likely to encounter: syntax, link, run-time, and logic errors. As you may have already discovered, it is possible for a program to execute without generating any error messages but still produce incorrect results. Sometimes the origin of incorrect results is apparent, and the error can easily be fixed. However, very often the error is not obvious and may require considerable effort to locate.

The first step in attempting to find a hidden error is to examine the program output to determine which part of the program is generating incorrect results. Then you can focus on the statements in that section to determine which one(s) are at fault. You may want to insert extra cout statements to trace the values of certain critical variables during program execution. For example, if the loop in Fig. 5.8 is not computing the correct sum, you might want to insert an extra *diagnostic statement,* as shown in the second line of the loop below.

```
cin >> score;
while (score != sentinel)
{
```

```
        sum += score;
        cout << "***** score is " << score << " and sum is " << sum
             << endl;
        cout << "Enter the next score : ";
        cin >> score;
}  // end while
```

The diagnostic `cout` statement will display the current value of `score` and each partial sum that is accumulated. This `cout` statement displays a string of asterisks at the beginning of its output line. This makes it easier to identify diagnostic output in the debugging runs and makes it easier to locate the diagnostic `cout` statements in the source program.

Take care when inserting extra diagnostic `cout` statements. Sometimes it will be necessary to add an additional pair of braces if a single statement inside an `if` or `while` statement becomes a compound statement when a diagnostic `cout` is added.

Once it appears that you have located an error, you will want to take out the extra diagnostic statements. As a temporary measure, it is sometimes advisable to make these diagnostic statements comments by prefixing them with the double slash (//). If these errors crop up again in later testing, it is easier to remove the slashes than to retype the diagnostic statements. (Later you may become comfortable with using special debug flags or *conditional compilation* to control the execution of diagnostic statements. Your instructor can tell you more about these topics if it is desirable for you to use them.)

Off-by-One Errors

A fairly common error in programs with loops is a loop that executes one more time or one less time than it is supposed to. If a sentinel-controlled `while` loop performs an extra repetition, it may erroneously process the sentinel value along with the regular data.

If a `for` loop performs a counting operation, make sure that the initial and final values of the loop control variable are correct. For example, the loop body below executes n + 1 times instead of n times. In this particular case, the program will hang waiting for an extra entry, and the loop will not exit until you enter one too many items. If your intention is to execute the loop body n times, change the logical condition to (`count < n`).

```
sum = 0;
cout << "Enter " << n << " integers and press return:" << endl;
for(int count = 0; count <= n; count++)
{
   cin >> item;
   sum += item;
} // end for
```

A general rule of thumb for most C++ loops is to begin with a start value of 0. When the start value is 0, the test will normally involve the relational operator *less than:*

```
count = 0;
(count < n)
```

But if starting with 1 is more convenient for a problem (see Fig. 5.20), the test usually will involve the relational operator *less than or equal to:*

```
count = 1;
(count <= n)
```

You can get a good idea as to whether a loop is correct by checking what happens at the *loop boundaries,* that is, at the initial and final values of the loop control variable. For a `for` loop, you should carefully evaluate the *initial expression* and *final expression* to make sure that these values make sense. Then substitute these values everywhere the loop control variable appears in the loop body and verify that you get the expected result at the boundaries. As an example, in the `for` loop

```
sum = 0;
for (int i = k; i <= n - k; i++)
   sum += i * i;
```

check that the first value of the loop control variable i is supposed to be k and that the last value is supposed to be n − k. Next, check that the assignment statement

```
sum += i * i;
```

is correct at these boundaries. When i is k, sum gets the value of k squared. When i is n − k, the value of n − k squared is added to the previous sum. As a final check, pick some small values of n and k (say, 3 and 1) and trace the loop execution to see that it computes sum correctly for this case.

Using Debugger Programs

Most computer systems have *debugger programs* available to help you debug a C++ program. The debugger program lets you execute your program one statement at a time (*single-step execution*) so that you can see the effect of each statement. You can select several variables whose values will be automatically displayed after each statement executes. This allows you to trace the program's execution.

You can also separate your program into segments by setting *breakpoints* at selected statements. A breakpoint is like a fence between two segments of a program. You can request the debugger to execute all statements from the last breakpoint up to the next breakpoint. When the program stops at a breakpoint, you can select variables to examine. This would allow you to determine whether the program segment executed correctly. If there are no errors, you will want to execute through to the next breakpoint. Otherwise, you may want to set more breakpoints in that segment or perhaps perform single-step execution through that segment.

Testing

After all errors have been corrected and the program appears to execute as expected, the program should be tested thoroughly to make sure that it works in every given situation. In Chapter 4, we discussed tracing an algorithm and suggested that enough sets of test data be provided to ensure that all possible paths are traced. The same statement is true for the completed program. Make enough test runs to verify that the program works properly for representative samples of all possible data combinations.

EXERCISES FOR SECTION 5.10

Self-Check
1. For the `for` loop in the subsection entitled "Off-by-One Errors," add debugging statements to show the value of the loop control variable at the start of each repetition. Also, add debugging statements to show the value of `sum` at the end of each loop repetition.
2. Repeat Self-Check Exercise 1 for the second `for` loop in the same subsection.

5.11 —— COMMON PROGRAMMING ERRORS

- *Confusing the if and while Statements:* Beginners sometimes confuse `if` and `while` statements because both statements contain a condition. Make sure that you use an `if` statement to implement a decision step and a `while` statement to implement a conditional loop.

- *Writing Loop Exit Conditions:* Be very careful when using tests for inequality to control the repetition of a `while` loop. For instance, the loop below is intended to continue executing as long as the acceleration of a projectile is positive.

```
while (acceleration != 0.0)
{
    ...
}
```

If the acceleration rate goes from a positive to a negative amount without being exactly 0.0, the loop will not terminate; it will become an infinite loop. The loop below would be safer.

```
while (acceleration > 0.0)
{
   ...
}
```

- *Using a Sentinel Value:* You always should verify that the repetition condition for a `while` loop will eventually become false. If you use a sentinel-controlled loop, remember to provide a prompt that tells the program user what value to enter as the sentinel. Make sure that the sentinel value cannot be confused with a normal data item.

- *Writing Compound Loop Statements:* If the loop body contains more than one statement, remember to bracket it with a pair of braces { }. Otherwise, only the first statement will be repeated, and the remaining statements will be executed when and if the loop is exited. The loop below will not terminate (an infinite loop), because the step that updates the loop control variable is not considered part of the loop body. The program will continue to print the initial value of power until either it exceeds its time limit or you instruct the computer to terminate its execution.

```
while (power <= 10000)
   cout << "Next power of n is " << setw(6) << power << endl;
   power *= n;
```

To avoid the possibility of omitting required braces, some programmers always insert braces even with single-statement loops. You may elect to use this style if you think it will be a problem for you.

- *Initializing Variables:* Be sure to initialize to zero a variable used for accumulating a sum by repeated addition, and to initialize to one a variable used for accumulating a product by repeated multiplication. Omitting this step will lead to results that are inaccurate. An easy way to determine if a variable needs to be initialized is if the same variable appears on both sides of an assignment statement in a mathematical formula.

- *Writing Loop Entry Conditions:* The value of the loop control variable in a `for` statement either increases or decreases after each repetition. If m is greater than n (e.g., m is 10, n is 5), the `cout` statement below will not execute, because the initial value that would be assigned to i (10) is larger than the limiting value (5).

```
for (int i = m; i <= n; i++)
   cout << setw (4) << i << setw (4) << m << setw (4) << n
        << endl;
```

Similarly, the cout statement below will not execute because the initial value that would be assigned to i (5) is smaller than the limiting value (10).

```
for (int i = n; i >= m; i--)
   cout << setw (4) << i << setw (4) << m << setw (4) << n
        << endl;
```

• *Using the do-while Loop:* A do-while loop always executes at least once. Use a do-while statement only if you are certain that there is no possibility of zero loop iterations; otherwise, use a while loop instead.

• *Loop Control Variables:* Be sure to trace each nest of loops carefully, checking the inner loop and outer loop control variables. A loop control variable in a for statement can be altered inside the loop body if you are not careful. This could lead to undesirable results. It is also bad practice to use the same loop control variable for two for statements within the same nest.

CHAPTER REVIEW

In this chapter, we examined the while statement and used it to repeat steps in a program. We learned how to implement counter-controlled loops, or loops where the number of repetitions required can be determined before the loop is entered. The while statement was shown to be useful when we do not know the exact number of repetitions required before the loop begins.

In designing a while loop, we need to consider both the loop control and loop processing operations that must be performed. Separate C++ statements are needed for initializing and updating the loop control variable that is tested in the loop repetition condition.

We discovered a common technique for controlling the repetition of a while loop: using a special sentinel value to indicate that all required data have been processed. In this case, an input variable must appear in the loop repetition condition. This variable is initialized when the first data value is read (the initial read), and it is updated at the end of the loop when the next new data value is read. Loop repetition terminates when the sentinel value is read.

The for statement (for loop) and do-while statement (do-while loop) were introduced. The for statement was used to implement counting loops in which the exact number of loop iterations can be determined before loop repetition begins. The loop control variable may be increased or decreased by any value after each loop iteration. The for loop is also convenient in numerous other situations involving simple loop initialization and update steps. More of these examples are illustrated in later chapters.

The do-while statement was used to implement conditional loops. With the do-while statement, you can implement a loop that will always execute at least one time.

We also analyzed nested loops. Every inner loop of a nest is reentered and executed to completion each time an outer loop is repeated.

New C++ Constructs   The new C++ constructs introduced in this chapter are described in Table 5.6.

Table 5.6   Summary of New C++ Constructs

CONSTRUCT	EFFECT
while Statement	
```sum = 0;``` `while (sum <= max_sum)` `{` `    cout << "Next integer: ";` `    cin >> next_int;` `    sum += next_int;` `}   // end while`	A collection of input data items is read and their sum is accumulated in sum. The process stops when the accumulated sum exceeds max_sum.
for Statement	
```for (int current_month = 3;``` `     current_month <= 9;` `     current_month++)` `{` `    cin >> month_sales;` `    year_sales += month_sales;` `}   // end for`	The loop body is repeated for each value of current_month from 3 to 9, inclusive. For each month, the value of month_sales is read and added to year_sales.
do-while Statement	
```sum = 0;``` `do` `{` `    cout << "Next integer: ";` `    cin >> next_int;` `    sum += next_int;` `}   while (sum <= max_sum);`	Integer values are read and their sum is accumulated in sum. The process terminates when the accumulated sum exceeds max_sum.

✔ QUICK-CHECK EXERCISES

1. A while loop is called a _____ loop.
2. It is an error if a while loop body never executes. (True/False)

3. The sentinel value is always the last value added to a sum being accumulated in a sentinel-controlled loop. (True/False)
4. Which loop form (for, do-while, while)

   a. executes at least one time?
   b. is the most general?
   c. should be used to implement a counting loop?

5. What does the following segment display?

```
product = 1;
counter = 2;
while (counter < 6)
    product *= counter;
    counter++;
cout << product;
```

6. What does the segment of Exercise 6 display if the opening and closing braces are inserted where intended?
7. During the execution of the program segment below:

```
for (int i = 0; i < 10; i++)
{
    for (int j = 0; j <= i; j++)
        cout << setw (4) << (i * j);
    cout << endl;
}
```

   a. How many times does the first cout statement execute?
   b. How many times does the second cout statement execute?
   c. What is the last value displayed?

Answers to Quick-Check Exercises

1. conditional
2. False
3. False; the sentinel should not be processed.
4. a. do-while   b. while   c. for
5. Nothing; the loop executes "forever."
6. The value of $1 \times 2 \times 3 \times 4 \times 5$ (or 120).
7. a. $1 + 2 + 3 + \cdots + 9 + 10$ (or 55)   b. 10   c. 81

REVIEW QUESTIONS

1. How does a sentinel value differ from a program flag as a means of loop control?
2. For a sentinel value to be used properly when reading in data, where should the input statements appear?
3. Write a program to sum and print a collection of payroll amounts entered at the terminal until a sentinel value of –1 is entered.

4. Hand trace the program below given the following data:

4 2 8 4   1 4 2 1   9 3 3 1   -2 2 10 8 2   3 3 4 5

```cpp
// FILE: Slope.cpp
// CALCULATES SLOPE OF A LINE

#include <iostream.h>

void main ()
{
    // Local data ...
    const float sentinel = 0.0;

    float slope;
    float y2;
    float y1;
    float x2;
    float x1;

    cout << "Enter four numbers separated by spaces."
        << endl;
    cout << "The program terminates if the last two"
        << endl;
    cout << " numbers are the same."
        << endl;
    cout << "Numbers entered will be in the order:"
        << "y2, y1, x2, x1." << endl << endl;
    cout << "Enter four floating point numbers: ";
    cin >> y2 >> y1 >> x2 >> x1;

    while ((x2 - x1) != sentinel)
    {
        slope = (y2 - y1) / (x2 - x1);
        cout << "Slope is " << slope << endl;
        cout << "Enter four more floating point numbers: ";
        cin >> y2 >> y1 >> x2 >> x1;
    }  // end while
    return;

}
```

5. Rewrite the while loop appearing in the Slope Program as a

a. do-while loop.
b. flag-controlled loop.

6. Consider the program segment shown below.

```
count = 0;
for (i = 0; i < n; i++)
{
    cin >> x;
    if (x == i)
        count++;
}  // end for
```

   a. Write a while loop equivalent to the for loop.
   b. Write a do-while loop equivalent to the for loop.

7. Explain when it is appropriate to use semicolons with
   a. an if statement.
   b. a case statement.
   c. a while statement.
   d. a for statement.
   e. a do-while statement.

PROGRAMMING PROJECTS

1. Write a program that will find the product of a collection of data values. Your program should ignore any negative data and should terminate when a zero value is read.
2. Bunyan Lumber Co. needs to create a table of the engineering properties of its lumber. The dimensions of the wood are given as base and height in inches. Engineers need to know the following information about lumber:

   cross sectional area: (base × height)
   moment of inertia: (base × height³) / 12
   section modulus: (base × height²) / 6

   The owner, Paul, makes lumber with base sizes 2, 4, 6, 8, 10, and 12 inches. The height sizes are 2, 4, 6, 8, and 10 inches. Produce a table with appropriate headings to show these values and the computed engineering properties. Do not repeat your computations and display for boards having the same dimensions. For example, you may consider a 2-by-6 and a 6-by-2 board to be the same.
3. Write a program to read a collection of integer data items and find and print the index of the first occurrence and the last occurrence of the number 12. Your program should print index values of 0 if the number 12 is not found. The index is the sequence number of the data item 12. For example, if the eighth data item is the only 12, then the index value 8 should be printed for the first and last occurrence.
4. Write a program to find the largest, smallest, and average values in a collection of n numbers where the value of n will be the first data item read.

5. a. Write a program to read in a collection of exam scores ranging in value from 0 to 100. Your program should count and print the number of outstanding scores (90 to 100), the number of satisfactory scores (60 to 89), and the number of unsatisfactory scores (0 to 59). It should also display the category of each score as it is read in. Test your program on the following data:

```
63   75   72   72   78   67   80   63   0
90   89   43   59   99   82   12   100   75
```

b. Modify your program so that it also displays the average exam score (a real number) at the end of the run.

c. Modify your program to disallow out-of-range scores.

6. Write a program to process weekly employee time cards for all employees of an organization. Each employee will have three data items indicating an identification number, the hourly wage rate, and the number of hours worked during a given week. Each employee is to be paid time-and-a-half for all hours worked over 40. A tax amount of 3.625 percent of gross salary will be deducted. The program output should show the employee's number and net pay. Display the total payroll and average amount paid at the end of the run.

7. Write a menu-driven savings account transaction program that will process the following sets of data:

		Group 1
I	1234	1054.07
W		25.00
D		243.35
W		254.55
Z		

		Group2
I	5723	2008.24
W		15.55
Z		

		Group 3
I	2814	128.24
W		52.48
D		13.42
W		84.60
Z		

		Group 4
I	7234	7.77
Z		

		Group 5
I	9367	15.27
W		16.12
D		10.00
Z		

Group 6

```
I    1134    12900.00
D            9270.00
Z
```

The first record in each group contains the code (I) along with the account number and its initial balance. All subsequent transaction records show the amount of each withdrawal (W) and deposit (D) made for that account, followed by a sentinel value (Z). Display the account number and its balance after processing each record in the group. If a balance becomes negative, print an appropriate message and take whatever corrective steps you deem proper. If there are no transactions for an account, print a message so stating. A transaction code (Q) should be used to allow the user to quit program execution.

8. Suppose you own a soft drink distributorship that sells Coca-Cola (ID number 1), Pepsi (ID number 2), Canada Dry (ID number 3) and Hires (ID number 4) by the case. Write a program to

   a. read in the case inventory for each brand at the start of the week.
   b. process all weekly sales and purchase records for each brand.
   c. print out the final inventory.

   Each transaction will consist of two data items. The first item will be the brand identification number (an integer). The second will be the amount purchased (a positive integer value) or the amount sold (a negative integer value). The weekly inventory for each brand (for the start of the week) will also consist of two items: the identification and initial inventory for that brand. For now, you may assume that you always have sufficient foresight to prevent depletion of your inventory for any brand. (*Hint:* Your data entry should begin with eight values representing the case inventory. These should be followed by the transaction values.)

9. Revise Project 8 to make it a menu-driven program. The menu operations supported by the revised program should be (E)nter inventory, (P)urchase soda, (S)ell soda, (D)isplay inventory, and (Q)uit program. Negative quantities should no longer be used to represent goods sold.

6

Program Design and Functions Revisited

6.1   Functions in the Design Process
6.2   Using Function Return Values for
       Decision and Loop Control
6.3   Output Arguments
       CASE STUDY: Sorting Three Numbers
6.4   Syntax Rules for Functions with
       Argument Lists
6.5   Stepwise Design with Functions
       CASE STUDY: General Sum and Average
       Problem
6.6   Solving a More Complex Problem
       CASE STUDY: Checking Account Balance
       Problem
6.7   More Aspects of Software Engineering
6.8   Debugging and Testing a Program System
6.9   Common Programming Errors
       Chapter Review

In Chapter 3, we began the study of top-down programming. We introduced the idea of solving a problem through decomposition into smaller subproblems. This decomposition continued until the subproblems became sufficiently small and manageable to be implemented in C++. Structure charts provided documentation of the hierarchical relationships among these subproblems and the information to be communicated among them. We introduced the C++ function as an important tool in this top-down design process. We used functions to provide separate implementations of the subproblems; the only communication among these functions (if any) was through a single return value and one or more input arguments. We learned how to write and call our own user-defined functions, and how to use C++ standard library functions such as cos and sqrt.

In this chapter we more fully develop the C++ function feature. We begin with an examination of some fundamental issues related to the use of functions in the program design process. We discuss the importance of validating function input and writing "driver programs" to test our functions thoroughly before we integrate them into larger program systems. We also introduce the concept of preconditions and postconditions for a function. These describe, respectively, what conditions must be true before the function is called and what conditions must be true once the function has completed execution.

We then introduce functions with multiple output arguments—that is, functions that return more than one value to the caller. The concepts of value (input) and reference (output) arguments are introduced and illustrated.

Our goal will be to use functions as building blocks of larger systems. As you progress through the course, your programming skills and personal function library will grow. We will continue to emphasize the reuse of your own functions as well as C++ library functions in the development of solutions to new problems.

6.1 _____ FUNCTIONS IN THE DESIGN PROCESS

We begin our expanded discussion of functions with a simple example of a function having a single return value. We will use this function to illustrate several important points concerning function input and output. In particular, we need to ensure that function input argument values are defined and that they make sense in terms of the given problem, and that the function terminates properly and returns correct values.

Example 6.1   The function compute_tax shown in Fig. 6.1 computes the federal income tax for a couple filing a joint return whose income after deductions (adjusted gross income) is given by the input argument adj_income.

Figure 6.1   Function to compute tax amount

```
// FILE: CmpTaxAm.cpp
// COMPUTES TAX OWED ON ADJUSTED GROSS INCOME

float compute_tax
   (float adj_income)       // IN: adjusted gross income

// Pre:  adj_income must be assigned a nonnegative value.
// Post: Tax amount computed based on tax category rate and max.
// Returns: Tax owed if adj_income is nonnegative; otherwise -1.0.
{
   // Local data ...
   const float cat1_max = 34000.0;
   const float cat2_max = 82150.0;
   const float cat1_rate = 0.15;
   const float cat2_rate = 0.28;
   const float cat3_rate = 0.31;
   const float min_valid_amount = 0.0;
   const float invalid_input = -1.0;

   float tax_amount;       // computed tax amount to be returned

   // Compute and return tax.
   if (adj_income < min_valid_amount)
      return invalid_input;
   else if (adj_income > cat2_max)
      tax_amount = cat1_rate * cat1_max
         + cat2_rate * (cat2_max - cat1_max)
         + cat3_rate * (adj_income - cat2_max);
   else if (adj_income > cat1_max)
      tax_amount = cat1_rate * cat1_max
         + cat2_rate * (adj_income - cat1_max);
   else
      tax_amount = cat1_rate * adj_income;

   return tax_amount;
}  // end compute_tax
```

∎

Preconditions and Postconditions as Function Documentation

A function cannot execute properly and return correct results if it is not given correct input argument values. Furthermore, the parent function of several subordinates will not behave as desired if the subordinates do not return the correct output. It is important that the implementor of a function carefully consider and document the input argument values for which the function can be expected to behave correctly. It is equally as important that the values to be computed and returned by a function be clearly specified by the implementor. We use function preconditions and postconditions to record these input and output specifications. These informal English descriptions are intended as a reminder to both the function implementor and user of exactly what is required as function input and expected as output.

A *precondition* describes a condition that must be true before the function is called. The precondition for function `compute_tax` may be described by the following comment:

```
Pre: Adj_income must be assigned a nonnegative value.
```

A *postcondition* describes what must be true about those data items that have been altered by the time a function completes execution. The postcondition for `compute_tax` is described by the following comment:

```
Post: Tax amount computed based on tax category rate and max.
```

The explicit use of function precondition and postcondition documentation provides valuable information to a programmer who might want to use the function. For example, the preconditions provide the programmer with information about the required values of the function input arguments before the function is called. In this case, a nonnegative data value must be assigned or read into the actual function argument prior to calling `compute_tax`. The postconditions tell the programmer the effect of the function's execution on its output arguments. In this case, a nonnegative tax amount is computed and returned (unless the adjusted income is negative, in which case a value of −1.0 is returned). Occasionally, an argument may be used for both input and output purposes (an input/output, or *inout,* argument). The value of such an argument will normally be prescribed in both the precondition and postcondition for such a function.

You might say that the preconditions and postconditions serve as an informal contract between a given function and any other function that calls it. The preconditions indicate any expectations the function may have with respect to its arguments. The postconditions tell what the function does and what will happen to its arguments if the preconditions are met. All bets are off if the preconditions are not met; therefore, a calling function must check to ensure that all actual arguments satisfy the preconditions of a function before it calls that function.

We have added a third component, the "returns summary," to the information describing the contract between a function and its callers. This summary is intended solely to describe the value (if any) returned to the caller through the use of the function return statement. It should be kept separate from the postcondition documentation, which describes changes made to data items during the execution of the function.

Validating Input Arguments

The `if` statement in function `compute_tax` first tests for an invalid value of the input argument `adj_income` before performing the tax computation. For any function that you write, you should be sure to validate its input arguments in a similar fashion, thereby ensuring that its preconditions are met. There are no guarantees that the values passed into the function will be meaningful. If they are not meaningful (the preconditions are not met), it is likely that the postconditions will not be met either.

Writing Driver Functions

The main function body in Fig. 6.2 has been written for the purpose of testing the function `compute_tax`. Such a program is called a *driver program*. This driver program contains a `while` loop that allows the user to enter several different values for the input argument `my_income` in order to test `compute_tax` fully. The body of the loop accepts a value for `my_income`, calls `compute_tax` (with `my_income` as input), and then prints the computed tax (or a diagnostic if the income was negative). The values used in the test should be carefully chosen to ensure that all possible paths through `compute_tax` are tested (see Self-Check Exercise 4 at the end of Section 6.2).

Figure 6.2   Driver program for function `compute_tax`

```
// FILE: CmpTaxDr.cpp
// DRIVER PROGRAM FOR FUNCTION COMPUTE_TAX

#include <iostream.h>
#include <iomanip.h>

#include "CmpTaxAm.cpp"

void main ()
{
   // Functions used ...
   // COMPUTES TAX OWED ON ADJUSTED GROSS INCOME
   float compute_tax
      (float);              // IN: adjusted gross income

   // Local data ...
   const float sentinel = -1.0;
```

(Continued)

Figure 6.2   (Continued)

```
float my_income;        // input: adjusted gross income (taxable)
float my_tax;           // output: computed tax amount


// Output manipulator settings.
cout << setiosflags (ios::fixed | ios::showpoint)
     << setprecision (2);

// Test compute_tax function -- all possible paths.
cout << "Driver program for function compute_tax." << endl;
cout << "Enter income greater than zero (or -1 to stop test): ";
cin >> my_income;
while (my_income != sentinel)
{
   my_tax = compute_tax (my_income);
   if (my_tax >= 0.0)
   {
      cout << "The tax on $" << my_income;
      cout << " is $" << my_tax << endl;
   }  // end if
   else
   {
      cout << "Income $ " << my_income << " was negative. ";
      cout << "Try another value." << endl;
   }  // end else
   cout << endl << endl;
   cout << "Enter income greater than zero (or " << sentinel
        << " to stop test): ";
   cin >> my_income;
}  // end while

cout << "A " << sentinel << " was entered.   "
     << "Test execution terminated." << endl;
return;
}
```

Experienced programmers often use driver programs to pretest functions before integrating them into the program system under development. The importance of such a testing process will become clearer as your programs become larger and more complicated. Generally, the small investment in time and effort required to write a short driver program will result in a noticeable reduction in the total time spent debugging a large program system.

PROGRAM STYLE

Cohesive Functions

Function compute_tax is concerned only with the tax computation. It neither reads in a value for adj_income nor displays the computed result. The result is returned to the calling function, which may display it or pass it on to a function that prints results. Note that `compute_tax` does not display an error message in the event that the value passed to `adj_income` is out of range. It simply returns a special value (−1.0) to indicate this, and the calling function displays the error message.

Functions written for a single purpose are called *functionally cohesive*. It is good programming style to write such single-purpose, highly cohesive functions, as this helps to keep each function relatively compact and easy to read, write, and debug. One usually easy and useful test of whether a function is highly cohesive involves the comment describing what the function does. If the purpose of a function can be summarized with a short sentence or phrase with no connectives such as "and" or "or," then the function should be highly cohesive. If more than one or two connectives or separate sentences are needed to describe the purpose of a function, this may be a hint that the function is doing too many things and should be further decomposed into subfunctions. ∎

6.2 —— USING FUNCTION RETURN VALUES FOR DECISION AND LOOP CONTROL

It is often convenient to be able to use function return values as conditions in `if` statements or in `while` and `do-while` statement conditions.

Example 6.2   You have written an algorithm that contains the decision step shown below (ch is assumed to represent a variable containing character type data). For the purposes of this example, we have no interest in the details of the three functions called in the algorithm, but are just interested in making sure that the correct function is called.

if ch is a letter
   call function `process_letter`
else if ch is a digit character
   call function `process_digit`
else
   call function `process_special`

There are many ways to implement this decision. One would be to use a `switch` statement with separate `case` labels for letters, for digits, and for special characters. Another approach is to write the `if` statement below, which utilizes the user-defined functions `is_letter` and `is_digit` to determine whether the contents of the variable ch is a letter or a digit.

```
if (is_letter (ch))
   process_letter (ch);
else if (is_digit (ch))
   process_digit (ch);
else
   process_special (ch);
```

The function call is_letter (ch) is an integer expression that returns either of two values, 0 or 1 (false or true). It returns a value of 1 (true) if ch is a letter, and a value of 0 (false) if ch is not a letter. Similarly, the integer expression is_digit (ch) returns the value 1 if ch is a digit character; otherwise, it returns 0.

Figure 6.3 shows functions is_letter and is_digit. Both functions consist of a single statement that returns the type int value 0 or 1 (to be used as false or true, respectively) to the caller. For example, if is_digit returns a 1, then ch is a digit character (any of the characters '0', '1', '2', ...,'9'). Similarly, if is_letter returns a 0, then ch is neither an uppercase nor a lowercase letter. As currently written, both functions make certain assumptions about the ordering relationships among uppercase letters and lowercase letters.

Figure 6.3 Functions is_letter and is_digit

```
// FILE: IsLetDig.cpp

// TESTS IF CHARACTER ARGUMENT IS A LETTER
int is_letter
   (char ch)                      // IN: character to be tested

// Pre:  ch must be defined.
// Post: (none)
// Returns: 1 (true) if ch is a letter; otherwise 0 (false).
{
   return ((('A' <= ch) && (ch <= 'Z')) ||
           (('a' <= ch) && (ch <= 'z')));
}   // end is_letter



// TESTS IF CHARACTER ARGUMENT IS A DIGIT
int is_digit
   (char ch)                      // IN: character to be tested

// Pre:  ch must be defined.
// Post: (none)
// Returns: 1 (true) if ch is a digit; otherwise 0 (false).
{
   return (('0' <= ch) && (ch <= '9'));
}   // end is_digit
```

We will discuss the ordering issue in Chapter 7, and we will introduce C++ library functions that do not depend on assumptions about the ordering relationships between letters and digits.

Example 6.3   The function is_small_enough (see Fig. 6.4) may be used to verify that the absolute value of the difference of its first two arguments (x and a) is less than the value of the third argument (eps). If $|x - a| <$ eps, the function returns a value of 1 (true); otherwise, the function returns a value of 0 (false).

Figure 6.4   Function is_small_enough

```
// FILE: IsSmEngh.cpp
// TESTS IF ABSOLUTE VALUE OF DIFFERENCE OF FIRST TWO ARGUMENTS
//      IS LESS THAN VALUE OF THIRD ARGUMENT

#include <math.h>

int is_small_enough
   (float x,      // IN: first of two arguments used in computing
                  //      difference
    float a,      // IN: second of two arguments used in computing
                  //      difference
    float eps)    // IN: value of epsilon compared against
                  //      abs (x - a)

// Pre:  x, a, and eps must be defined.
// Post: (no changes)
// Returns: 1 or 0 depending on value of abs (x - a).
{
   if (fabs (x - a) < eps)
      return 1;   // true
   else
      return 0;   // false
}  // end is_small_enough
```

We can use such a function in a variety of ways. Programming Exercise 4 at the end of this section provides an illustration of one such use.

EXERCISES FOR SECTION 6.2

Self-Check   1. Trace the execution of the if statement currently used in function compute_tax (Fig. 6.1). Then trace the execution of the if statements shown below. Each trace should test a different branch of the decision structure involved. Are the same results produced? If not, why not?

```
//Compute and return tax.
if (adj_income < min_valid_amount)
   return invalid_input;
else if (adj_income <= cat1_max)
   tax_amount = cat1_rate * adj_income;
else if (adj_income <= cat2_max)
   tax_amount = cat1_rate * cat1_max
       + cat2_rate * (adj_income - cat1_max);
else
   tax_amount = cat1_rate * cat1_max
                + cat2_rate * (cat2_max - cat1_max)
                + cat3_rate * (adj_income - cat2_max);
```

2. What does the following function do?

```
float hypot
  (float x, float y)
{
   return sqrt (x * x + y * y);
}  // end hypot
```

Write a statement that calls this function with arguments a and b and stores the function result in c.

3. Write preconditions and postconditions and describe the return values for

a. function hypot shown in Self-Check Exercise 2;
b. the absolute difference function described in Programming Exercise 2 (below).

4. Provide an example of a list of values for taxable income that could be used in conjunction with the driver program for compute_tax to test all possible paths through compute_tax.

Programming   1. Write a driver function that tests function hypot (see Self-Check Exercise 3).

2. Write a function that computes the absolute difference of its two arguments, where the absolute difference of A and B is $A - B$ if A is greater than B and $B - A$ if B is greater than A. (Do not use the C++ library function here.)

3. Write a function that raises a floating-point number (X) to an integer power (N) by multiplying X by itself N times (use a for loop). Will your function work for negative values of X or N? *Hint:* To make your function work for negative values of N, use abs (N) as the final expression in the for loop. Then use the fact that

$$X^N = 1.0 / X^{-N}$$

to compute the correct result when N is negative. Do not use the C++ library function pow to write your function, but it would be useful to check your function's result against pow's.

4. Write a short program to compute and print successive powers of $1/2$—for example, $(1/2)^k$, for $k = 0, 1, 2, ...$ The repetition should continue until a value of k is found for which $(1/2)^k < 0.00001$. Use the function is_small_enough, shown in Fig. 6.4, to determine when the repetition is to be terminated. Use a while or do-while loop construct.

6.3 _____ OUTPUT ARGUMENTS

So far we know how to write functions that take several input values and return a single result. In this section, we will learn how to write functions that use *output arguments* to return more than one result.

Recall that when a function is called, space is allocated locally in the function data area for each of its formal input arguments. The value of each actual input argument is copied into the local memory cell allocated to its corresponding formal argument. The function body manipulates only this local copy; the original data cannot be altered. The function may return a single value to the calling function using a `return` statement. We now turn our attention to a discussion of how a function can return output to the function that called it through the use of output arguments.

Function `compute_sum_ave` in Fig. 6.5 has four arguments: two for input (`num1` and `num2`) and two for output (`sum` and `average`). The symbol `&` (ampersand) in the function header indicates that the arguments `sum` and `average` are output arguments. The function computes the sum and average of its input but does not display them. Instead, these values are assigned to formal arguments `sum` and `average` and returned as function results to the calling function.

To see how this works, assume that the calling function declares `x`, `y`, `sum`, and `mean` as type `float` variables. The function call

```
compute_sum_ave (x, y, sum, mean);
```

sets up the argument correspondence shown on the following page.

Figure 6.5   Function to compute sum and average

```
// FILE: CmpSumAv.cpp
// COMPUTES THE SUM AND AVERAGE OF NUM1 AND NUM2

void compute_sum_ave
   (float num1, num2,          // IN: values used in computation
    float& sum,                // OUT: sum of num1 and num2
    float& average)            // OUT: average of num1 and num2

// Pre:  num1 and num2 are assigned values.
// Post: The sum and average of num1 and num2 are computed
//       and returned as output arguments.
{
   sum = num1 + num2;
   average = sum / 2.0;
   return;
}  // end compute_sum_ave
```

ACTUAL ARGUMENT	FORMAL ARGUMENT
x	num1 (input)
y	num2 (input)
sum	sum (output)
mean	average (output)

The values of x and y are passed to the function when it is first called. These values are associated with formal input arguments num1 and num2. The statement

```
sum = num1 + num2;
```

stores the sum of the function input arguments in the calling function variable sum (the third actual argument). The statement

```
average = sum / 2.0;
```

divides the value stored in the function variable sum by 2.0 and stores the quotient in the calling function variable mean (the fourth actual argument). Figure 6.6 shows the data areas for compute_sum_ave and the calling function after the function call but before the execution of compute_sum_ave begins,

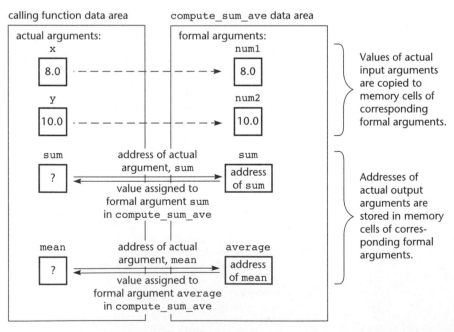

Figure 6.6   Data areas after call to compute_sum_ave **(but before execution)**

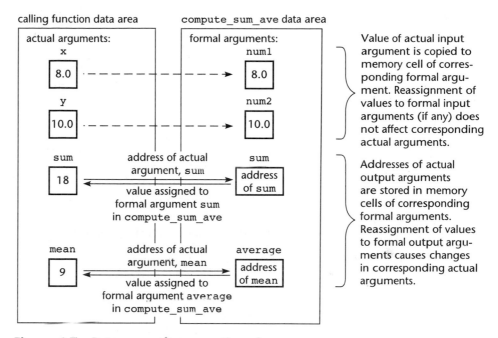

Figure 6.7   Data areas after execution of `compute_sum_ave`

and Fig. 6.7 shows these data areas just after `compute_sum_ave` finishes execution. The execution of `compute_sum_ave` sets the values of calling function variables `sum` and `mean` to 18.0 and 9.0, respectively. (We will provide an explanation of the phrases "address of sum" and "address of `mean`" in the following paragraphs.)

Call-by-Value and Call-by-Reference Arguments

As indicated earlier, the ampersand symbol, &, immediately following the type of a formal argument in the function header is used to distinguish between arguments that are used only for input and those that are used for returning a value to the calling function. Thus, in the function `compute_sum_ave` in Fig. 6.5, the formal arguments `num1` and `num2` are used only for input; the arguments `sum` and `average` are used for output (to return values to the caller).

This distinction provides important information for the compiler, enabling it to set up the correct *argument passing mechanism* for each function argument. For arguments used only as input, this mechanism is known as *call-by-value* because the value of the argument is copied to the called function's memory space (see Figs. 6.6 and 6.7 formal arguments num1 and num2). For output arguments and for arguments used as both input and output, the ampersand indicates that a *call-by-reference* mechanism is to be used. That is, the address of the actual argument is passed to the called function (see Figs. 6.6 and 6.7 sum and `average`). This address is then used for all references to the corresponding formal argument. If a value is assigned to this formal argument (as is the case for the formal arguments sum and `average`), the passed address is used to ensure that the new value is stored in the memory space of the calling function, that is, assigned to the actual argument.

Thus, the address passed is used by the called function to access the actual variable in the calling function and change its value, or use its value in a computation. In Figs. 6.6 and 6.7, this relationship is shown using double arrows to connect each reference argument with its corresponding actual argument. Note that the ampersand appears only in the formal argument list, not the actual argument list. It also must be used in the prototype for the function `compute_sum_ave` as shown below:

```
// COMPUTE SUM AND AVERAGE OF TWO TYPE FLOAT VALUES
void compute_sum_ave
    (float, float,      // IN: values used in computation
     float&,            // OUT: sum of the two input values
     float&);           // OUT: average of two input values
```

Protection Afforded by Value Arguments

Since the call-by-value argument passing mechanism passes a value (not an address) to the called function, there is no further connection between formal argument and its corresponding actual argument. The address of the actual argument is not available to the called function, so the argument cannot be referenced by this function (see the dashed lines in Figs. 6.6 and 6.7).

The advantage of the call-by-value argument passing mechanism is that there is no way that the passed value of the actual argument can be destroyed during the execution of the called function. Thus in `compute_sum_ave`, the values of formal arguments num1 and num2 could be used in computations or even changed by the function without affecting the corresponding actual arguments (x and y). For example, if we add the statement

```
num1 = -5.0;
```

to the end of function `compute_sum_ave`, the value of formal argument num1 will be changed to −5.0, but the value stored in the actual argument x will still be 8.0. Thus, by using the call-by-value mechanism, we protect x from being changed during the execution of the called function.

For call-by-reference arguments (indicated by using the ampersand), however, the local memory cell in the called function's data area is used to store the address (not the value) of the actual argument. We are no longer manipulating a copy of the actual argument in this case; rather, we are using the address to manipulate the actual argument itself. Thus any change to a formal argument will be reflected by a change in the value of the corresponding actual argument as well. Because of this, the statement

```
average = sum / 2.0;
```

will change the value of the corresponding actual argument (`mean`) in the calling program. This call-by-reference mechanism provides us with a way to return values computed by a function to its calling function, but we must remember that this will change the value of the actual argument. On the other hand, if we forget to declare a function output argument as a call-by-reference argument (using the ampersand), then its value (not its address) will be stored locally and any change to its value will not be returned to the caller. This is a very common source of error.

PROGRAM
STYLE

Writing Formal Argument Lists (revisited)

In Fig. 6.5, the formal argument list is written using the same style introduced in Chapter 3. That is, each argument (except for those used in a similar manner) is written on a separate line to improve readability:

```
(float num1, num2,      // IN: values used in computation
 float& sum,            // OUT: sum of num1 and num2
 float& average)        // OUT: average of num1 and num2
```

This line-by-line separation is even more important in documenting which arguments are call-by-value (input) and which are call-by-reference (output or input/output). The order of the actual arguments in the function call must correspond to the order of the formal arguments.   ∎

When to Use a Reference or a Value Argument

You may be wondering how to decide when to use a reference argument and when to use a value argument. Some rules of thumb follow:

- If information is to be passed into a function and does not have to be returned or passed back from the function, then the formal argument representing that information should be an input (call-by-value) argument (for example, `num1` and `num2` in Fig. 6.5).
- If information is to be returned to the calling function through an argument, then the corresponding formal argument must be a reference argu-

ment (`sum` and `average` in Fig. 6.5). An argument used in this way is called an output argument.

- If information is to be passed into a function, modified, and a new value returned through an argument, then the corresponding formal argument must be a reference argument. An argument used in this way is called an input/output argument.

Although we make a distinction between output arguments and input/output arguments, C++ treats them in the same way. Both must be specified as reference arguments (using the ampersand) so that the address (not the value) of the corresponding actual argument will be stored in the called function data area when the function is called. For an input/output argument as well as for an input argument, there must be some meaningful data stored in the corresponding actual argument before the function executes; for an output argument, this need not be the case.

Passing Expressions to Value Arguments

You can use an expression, variable, or a constant as an actual value (input) argument. For example, the function call

```
compute_sum_ave (x + y, 10, my_sum, my_ave)
```

calls `compute_sum_ave` to compute the `sum` (returned in `my_sum`) and the `average` (returned in `my_ave`) of the expression `x + y` and the integer 10. However, only variables can correspond to reference arguments, so `my_sum` and `my_ave` must be variables (declared as type `float`) in the calling function. This restriction is imposed because an actual argument corresponding to a formal reference argument may be modified when the called function executes; it is illogical to allow a function to change the value of either a constant or an expression.

Further Illustrations

In this section we will study two functions, each of which would generally be called more than once in a given application program, would process different input values, and would return different output values each time. Both of these functions illustrate the use of input, output, and input/output arguments.

Example 6.4   Function `make_change` (see Fig. 6.8) can be used to determine the quantity of a particular denomination of bills or coins to be given as change. The formal input argument `change_denom` specifies the value of each change unit (for example, 10.00 for ten-dollar bills, 0.10 for dimes). The formal input/output argument `change_needed` indicates the total amount of money for which change is to be made. The function determines how many units of the given change denomination should be dispensed and returns this value through the formal output argument `num_units`. The value returned through `change_needed` is the amount of change remaining after the calculated units of `change_denom` is dispensed. For example, if the value passed as `change_needed` is 20.45 and `change_denom` is 10.00, the value returned through `num_units` will be 2 (2 ten-dollar bills), and the value returned through `change_needed` will be the remaining change needed (0.45) after the 2 ten-dollar bills have been dispensed.

Figure 6.8   Function `make_change`

```
// FILE: MkChange.cpp
// DETERMINES THE NUMBER OF UNITS OF CHANGE OF A PARTICULAR
//    DENOMINATION TO DISPENSE WHEN MAKING CHANGE

void make_change
   (float change_denom,    // IN:    denomination in which change
                           //        is to be returned
    float& change_needed,  // INOUT: amount for which change needed
    int& num_units)        // OUT:   number of units of specified
                           //        denomination to be returned

// Pre:  Change_denom > 0.0 and change_needed >= 0.0.
// Post: num_units is the number of units of change to dispense
//       and change_needed is reduced by the change amount given.
{
   num_units = int (change_needed / change_denom);
   change_needed = change_needed - (num_units * change_denom);
   return;
}   // end make_change
```

If the calling function for `make_change` declares `change` as type `float` and `num_tens` as type `int`, the statements

```
change = 20.45;
make_change (10.00, change, num_tens);
cout << "The number of tens dispensed is " << num_tens << endl;
cout << "The change left to dispense is " << change << endl;
```

determine how many ten-dollar bills to dispense and the amount of change remaining after these bills have been given out. The `cout` statements display the function results

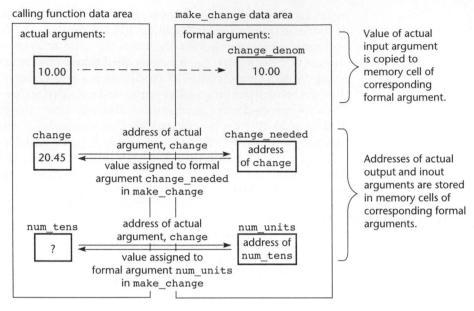

Figure 6.9   Data areas after call to make_change (but before execution)

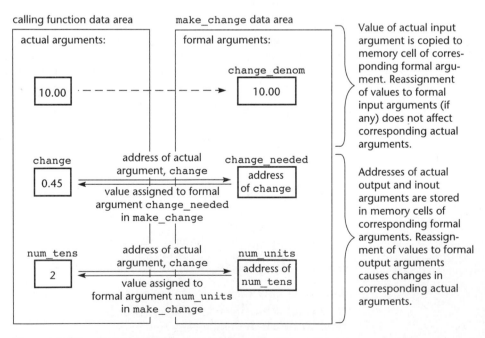

Figure 6.10   Data areas after execution of make_change

```
The number of tens dispensed is 2
The change left to dispense is 0.45
```

Figure 6.9 shows the calling and called function data areas just after the call to make_change; Fig. 6.10 shows these data areas just after the execution of function make_change. These figures show that the function execution updates the value of change (from 20.45 to 0.45) and defines the value of num_tens as 2.

If the calling function continues with the statements

```
make_change (0.10, change, num_dimes);
cout << "The number of dimes dispensed is " << num_dimes << endl;
cout << "The change left to dispense is " << change << endl;
```

where num_dimes is type int, the lines below would be displayed:

```
The number of dimes dispensed is 4
The change left to dispense is 0.05
```

CASE STUDY: SORTING THREE NUMBERS

Problem Statement

In many real-life and programming situations, we wish to arrange a set of data so that it follows some numerical or alphabetical sequence. In programming, this is called the sorting problem. We aren't able to solve this problem for large data sets yet; however, we can write a program that reads any three numbers into the variables num1, num2, num3 and rearranges the data so that the smallest number is stored in num1, the next smallest number in num2, and the largest number in num3. This exercise will provide some insights as to how to sort larger data sets, and also enables us to illustrate some important things about functions and their arguments.

Problem Analysis

This is a special case of a sorting problem—rearranging a collection of data items so that the values are in either increasing or decreasing order. Because we have only three items to be sorted, we will solve this special case now; the general sorting problem is a bit more complicated, so we will consider it in a later chapter. We will follow an approach similar to the one used to find the "smallest" (alphabetically first) of three letters (Section 4.7); that is, we will develop a sequence of pairwise comparisons of three numbers and reorder them as necessary so that the first number is the smallest of the three and the last is the largest.

DATA REQUIREMENTS

Problem Input

num1, num2, num3 (float)   — three numbers to be processed

Problem Output

the three numbers stored in increasing order in num1, num2, num3

Program Design

The structure chart for this problem is left as an exercise (see Self-Check Exercise 6 at the end of this section). The initial algorithm follows.

INITIAL ALGORITHM

1. Read the three numbers into num1, num2, and num3.
2. Sort the three numbers: place the smallest number in num1, the next smallest in num2, and the largest number in num3.
3. Print num1, num2, and num3.

ALGORITHM REFINEMENTS

We can think of the three variables num1, num2, num3 as representing a collection of adjacent storage locations. To perform step 2, we can compare pairs of numbers, always moving the smaller number in the pair closer to the front of the collection (num1) and the larger number closer to the end of the collection (num3). It should take three comparisons to sort the numbers in the list; one possible sequence of comparisons is shown here.

Step 2 Refinement

2.1. Compare num1 and num2, and store the smaller number in num1 and the larger number in num2.
2.2. Compare num1 and num3, and store the smaller number in num1 and the larger number in num3.
2.3. Compare num2 and num3, and store the smaller number in num2 and the larger number in num3.

Table 6.1 traces this refinement for the input sequence 8.0, 10.0, 6.0. The final order is correct.

The structure chart for step 2 of this algorithm is shown in Fig. 6.11. The data flow information for step 2.1 shows that num1 and num2 are used as both input and output. Because steps 2.1, 2.2, and 2.3 perform the same operation on different data, it would be a waste of time and effort to write a different function for each step. We will use one function, order, to order any pair of numbers.

Table 6.1   Trace of Step 2 Refinement for Data: 8.0, 10.0, 6.0

ALGORITHM STEP	num1	num2	num3	EFFECT
	8.0	10.0	6.0	
2.1	8.0	10.0		num1, num2 are in order
2.2	6.0		8.0	Switch num1 and num3
2.3		8.0	10.0	Switch num2 and num3

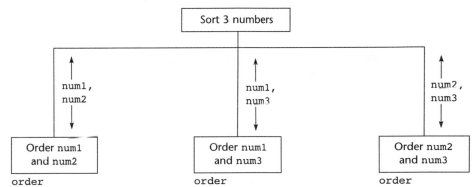

Figure 6.11   Structure chart for step 2 of Sorting Three Numbers Problem

Program Implementation

The function call

```
order (num1, num2);
```

can be used to perform step 2.1 of the algorithm—store the smaller number in num1 and the larger number in num2. Similar calls may be used to perform steps 2.2 and 2.3. The complete program (the order function and a driver) for sorting three numbers is shown in Fig. 6.12. The main function contains three statements that call function order:

```
order (num1, num2);    // order the data in num1 and num2
order (num1, num3);    // order the data in num1 and num3
order (num2, num3);    // order the data in num2 and num3
```

Because each of these statements contains a different actual argument list, a different pair of variables will be manipulated each time the function is called.

Figure 6.12   Function to order three numbers

```cpp
// FILE: Sort3Nmb.cpp
// READS THREE FLOATING POINT NUMBERS AND SORTS THEM IN ASCENDING
//     ORDER

#include <iostream.h>
#include <iomanip.h>

void main ()
{
   // Functions used ...
   // SORTS A PAIR OF FLOATING POINT NUMBERS
   void order
      (float&, float&);          // INOUT: numbers to be ordered

   // Local data ...
   float num1, num2, num3;    // input: holds numbers to be sorted

   // Read and sort numbers.
   cout << "Enter 3 numbers to be sorted separated by spaces:"
        << endl;
   cin >> num1 >> num2 >> num3;
   order (num1, num2);          // order the data in num1 and num2
   order (num1, num3);          // order the data in num1 and num3
   order (num2, num3);          // order the data in num2 and num3

   // Print results.
   cout << "The three numbers in order are:" << endl;
   cout << setw(6) << num1 << setw(6) << num2 << setw(6) << num3
        << endl;
   return;
}



// SORTS A PAIR OF NUMBERS REPRESENTED BY x AND y
void order
   (float& x, float& y)         // INOUT: numbers to be ordered

// Pre:  x and y are assigned values.
// Post: x is the smaller of the pair and y is the larger.
{
   // Local data ...
   float temp;                  // temp holding cell for number in x

   // Compare x and y and exchange values if not properly ordered.
   if (x > y)
   {                            // exchange the values in x and y
      temp = x;                 // store old x in temp
```

(Continued)

Figure 6.12   (Continued)

```
      x = y;             // store old y in x
      y = temp;          // store old x in y
   }  // end if
   return;
}  // end order
```

─────────── Program Output ───────────

```
Enter 3 numbers to be sorted separated by spaces:
8.0  10.0  6.0
The three numbers in order are:
    6    8    10
```

The executable part of the function `order` consists of the `if` statement shown below:

```
if (x > y)
{
   temp = x;
   x = y;
   y = temp;
}  // end if
```

The function heading contains the formal argument list

```
(float& x, float& y)        // INOUT: numbers to be ordered
```

which identifies x and y as the formal arguments. These arguments are classified as input/output because the function uses the current actual argument values as input and may return new values as output.

The sequence of the actual arguments is most important. The first actual argument is paired with the first formal argument, the second actual argument is paired with the second formal argument, and so on. If the first function call in Fig. 6.12 were written as

```
order (num2, num1);
```

the smaller number would be stored in num2 and the larger number in num1 instead of the other way around. ∎

EXERCISES FOR SECTION 6.3

Self-Check

1. Trace the execution of function make_change when change_needed is 5.56 and change_denom is 5.00.
2. Show the output displayed by the function show listed below in the form of a table of values for x, y, w, and z.

```
void show ()
{
```

```
    // Functions used ...
    // ???
    void sum_diff
      (int, int,                // IN: ...
        int&, int&);            // INOUT: ...

    // Local data...
    int w, x, y, z;

    // Perform ...
    x = 5;   y = 3;   z = 7;   w  = 9;
    cout << "   x    y    z    w " << endl;
    sum_diff (x, y, z, w);
    cout << setw (4) << x << setw (4) << y << setw (4) << z
          << setw (4) << w << endl;
    sum_diff (y, x, z, w);
    cout << setw (4) << x << setw (4) << y << setw (4) << z
          << setw (4) << w << endl;
    sum_diff (z, w, y, x);
    cout << setw (4) << x << setw (4) << y << setw (4) << z
          << setw (4) << w << endl;
}   // end show

// ???
void sum_diff
    (int num1, int num2,        // IN: ...
      int& num3, int& num4)     // INOUT: ...
{
    num3 = num1 + num2;
    num4 = num1 - num2;
}   // end sum_diff
```

a. Show the function output.
b. Briefly describe what function sum_diff computes. Include a description of how the input and input/output arguments to sum_diff are used.
c. Write the preconditions and postconditions for function sum_diff.

3. a. Trace the execution of the three function calls

```
    order (num3, num2);
    order (num3, num1);
    order (num2, num1);
```

   for the data sets: 8.0, 10.0, 6.0 and 10.0, 8.0, 60.0.
b. What is the effect of this sequence of calls?

4. A function has four formal arguments: w, x, y, and z (all type float). During its execution it stores the sum of w and x in y and the product of w and x in z. Which arguments are input and which are output?

5. a. What changes would you need to make in function order (Fig. 6.12) so that it can be reused to order two integer values rather than two floating-point values?

   b. Given the answers to part (a), what changes would have to be made to the main function for it to work with integers? Make sure you identify all changes required.

Programming

1. Write a main function that reads in an amount of change to make and calls function make_change (Fig. 6.8) with different arguments to determine the number of twenties, tens, fives, ones, quarters, dimes, nickels, and pennies to dispense as change. (Warning: For some change amounts, make_change will produce incorrect results. The problem can be corrected by rounding change_needed to the nearest two decimal places (see Fig. 7.4 in Section 7.2). But a more interesting question concerns why these errors occurred in the first place.

2. Write the function in Self-Check Exercise 4.

3. Write a function that displays a table showing all powers of its first argument (an integer) from zero through the power indicated by its second argument (a positive integer). The function should also return the sum of all power values displayed. For example, if the first argument is 10 and the second argument is 3, the function should display 1, 10, 100, and 1000 and return 1111 as its result.

6.4 ———— SYNTAX RULES FOR FUNCTIONS WITH ARGUMENT LISTS

The syntax rules for functions with value arguments are presented in Chapter 3; except for the required use of the ampersand, these rules remain the same for reference arguments. Remember that for a reference argument, the function manipulates the corresponding actual argument through a local memory cell. This cell is initialized to the address of the actual argument when the function is called. For a value argument, a local memory cell is initialized to the corresponding actual argument value, and the function manipulates a local copy without altering the actual argument.

Recall, also, that the formal argument list for a function determines the form of any actual argument list that may be used to call the function. An actual argument list and its corresponding formal argument list must agree in number, order, and type as described in the rules below.

Rules for Argument List Correspondence

1. Correspondence between actual and formal arguments is determined by position in their respective argument lists. These lists must be the same size.
2. Formal arguments and corresponding actual arguments should agree with respect to type. Recall from Chapter 3 that the standard conversions performed by C++ provide considerable flexibility in this regard (perhaps too much). We urge you not to leave argument conversion to the compiler. Do it yourself, using the casting operators.
3. For reference arguments, an actual argument must be a variable. For value arguments, an actual argument may be a variable, constant, or expression.

The compiler is first told about the order, type, and structure of the formal arguments for a function when it processes its prototype. Later, when it reaches a function call, the compiler checks the actual argument list for consistency with the formal argument list. We strongly encourage you to ensure that each actual argument used in a call to a given function exactly matches the type of the corresponding formal argument. However, as hinted in item 2 in the above list, some flexibility is allowed because the compiler will do some type conversion automatically. Some examples in which this is done are illustrated in the next example, but a more comprehensive discussion of this topic will be given in Chapter 7. In the meanwhile, we encourage you to do your own conversion explicitly, using type casting operators, such as int or float, as described in Chapter 3 (Section 3.6).

Example 6.5   Assume main is a function containing the following declarations:

```
void main ()
...
// Functions used ...
void test        // prototype argument names provided for
                 //    illustration ONLY
   (int a, int b,
    float& c, float& d,
    char& e);

// Local data ...
float x, y;
int m;
char next;
```

Function test has two value arguments (a and b) and three reference arguments (c, d, and e). Any of the function calls below would be syntactically correct in the main function.

```
test (m + 3, 10, x, y, next);
test (m, -63, y, x, next);
test (35, m * 10, y, x, next);
```

The correspondence specified by the first argument list above is shown in Table 6.2. The last column in Table 6.2 describes each formal argument. Table 6.2 shows that an expression (m + 3) or a constant (10) may be associated with a value argument. Table 6.3 illustrates and explains several syntactically illegal calls to test. The last function call in Table 6.3 points out an error that is often made in using functions. The actual argument names (c, d, e) are the same as their corresponding formal argument names. However, because these names are not declared in the main function, they cannot appear in an actual argument list used in this function. An easy way to avoid this error is to remember that the use of formal argument names in function prototypes is not required and, in fact, is very much discouraged. (In other words, don't do what we just did when you write function prototypes.)

Table 6.2   Argument Correspondence for test (m + 3, 10, x, y, next)

ACTUAL ARGUMENT	FORMAL ARGUMENT	DESCRIPTION
m + 3	a	int, value
10	b	int, value
x	c	float, reference
y	d	float, reference
next	e	char, reference

Table 6.3   Invalid Function Calls

FUNCTION CALL	ERROR
test (30, 10, m, 19, next)	Constants not allowed for reference arguments. Note that the integer m will automatically be converted to floating point by the compiler.
test (m, 19, x, y)	Not enough actual arguments.
test (m, 10, 35, y, 'E')	Constants 35 and 'E' cannot correspond to reference arguments.
test (m, 3.3, x, y, next)	THIS IS LEGAL! However, the type of 3.3 is not integer; the value will be truncated—the fractional part will be lost.
test (30, 10, x, x + y, next)	Expression x + y cannot correspond to a reference argument.
test (30, 10, c, d, e)	c, d, and e are not declared in the main function.

∎

When writing relatively long argument lists such as those above, you must be very careful not to transpose two actual arguments; this would cause a compilation (syntax) error if it results in the violation of the argument correspondence rule. If this rule is not violated, no compilation error will occur; but the execution will generate incorrect results, and the cause may be very difficult to find.

EXERCISES FOR SECTION 6.4

Self-Check

1. Provide a table similar to Table 6.2 for the other correct argument lists shown in Example 6.5.
2. Correct the syntax errors in the prototype argument lists below.

```
(int&, int&; float)
(value int, char x, y)
(float x + y, int account&)
```

3. Assuming the declarations

```
// Functions used ...
void massage
    (float&, float&,
     int);

// Local data ...
const int maxint = 32767;

float x, y, z;
int m, n;
```

determine which of the following function calls are invalid and indicate why. If any standard conversions are required, indicate which one(s) and specify the result of the conversion.

```
a. massage (x, y, z);
b. massage (x, y, 8);
c. massage (y, x, n);
d. massage (m, y, n);
e. massage (25.0, 15, x);
f. massage (x, y, m+n);
g. massage (a, b, x);
h  massage (y, z, m);
i. massage (y+z, y-z, m);
j. massage (z, y, x);
k. massage (x, y, m, 10);
l. massage (z, y, maxint);
```

6.5 _____ STEPWISE DESIGN WITH FUNCTIONS

Now that we have learned how to write decision and looping algorithms and pass data in and out of functions, we can begin to tackle more complicated problems and further develop the practice of stepwise function design. We will follow the same design process introduced in Chapter 3. Now, however, we will be able to illustrate this process more fully with somewhat more substantial case studies. We will develop one such case study in each of the next two sections of this chapter. The problem solutions illustrated should be analyzed carefully; one of the best ways to develop and polish your own design and implementation skills is through the study of complete examples done by others.

The problem that we will examine will be decomposed into small subproblems, and the relationships among these subproblems will be illustrated using a structure chart. If the solution to a subproblem cannot be written easily using just a few C++ statements, it will be implemented as a function. Once again, we will trace the development of a program from the first stage of the problem analysis through to the implementation of each subproblem that emerges through the design process.

CASE STUDY: GENERAL SUM AND AVERAGE PROBLEM

Problem Statement

In Chapter 3, we wrote C++ code fragments to compute the sum or product of a collection of data items. Accumulating a sum of data values is a problem that occurs again and again in programming. We would like to solve the general case of this problem by writing a function that finds and displays the sum and average of a collection of floating-point data values. In our approach, we will develop solution functions that can be reused when similar problems surface again.

Problem Analysis

In Chapter 5, we showed how to use a loop that computes the total payroll for a company. We can adapt this approach to compute the sum of a collection of data values. To compute an average, we simply divide this sum by the number of items considered. We must be careful not to perform this division if the number of items to be summed is zero.

Our approach to solving this problem involves four major steps: reading the number of items to be processed, computing the sum, computing the average, and then printing these two results. These four steps and the accompanying data are shown next.

DATA REQUIREMENTS

Problem Input

num_items (int)   — number of data items to be added
the data items to be read and summed

Problem Output

sum (float)   — accumulated sum of data items
average (float)   — average of all data items

FORMULA

average = sum of data / number of data items

Program Design

The structure chart for our solution is shown in Fig. 6.13. The data flow between subproblems is documented in this chart. We have chosen to implement each step as a separate function. A label under a step denotes the name of each such function. It should be noted at this point that there is no mention of the processing of the individual data items. In addition, the formula for computing the average of the data items has not yet entered into our discussion. The reason is that our concern at this point is not with the details of reading data and computing the sum and the average, but rather with decisions about the basic steps required to solve the problem. We listed the data items and the formula in the data requirements table only because they would occur to most of us as necessary elements of the solution to this problem. Yet if we had neglected to concern ourselves with these details at this point, it would not have mattered, for they will be dealt with at a later stage in the development of our problem solution.

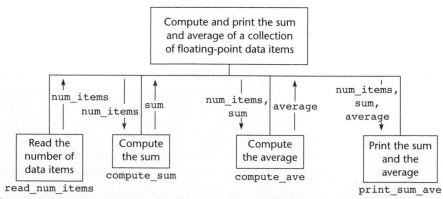

Figure 6.13   Structure chart with data flow information

Figure 6.13 shows the data flow between the main function (top, or level 0, function) and each level 1 function (shown at the next level down). Note that any actual argument whose value is determined by a function is considered to be an output of that function (indicated by an arrow pointing out of the function). All variables whose values are used in a computation but are not changed by a function are considered to be a function input (indicated by an arrow pointing into the function). Since the step "Read the number of data items" defines the value of the variable `num_items`, `num_items` is an output of this step. Function `compute_sum` needs this value in order to know how many data items to read and sum. Consequently, `num_items` must be an input to `compute_sum`.

With the information given in the structure chart, we can now write the initial algorithm as follows.

INITIAL ALGORITHM

1. Read the number of items to be processed (`read_num_items`).
2. Compute the sum by reading each data item and accumulating it in the sum (`compute_sum`).
3. Compute the average of the data items (`compute_ave`).
4. Print the sum and the average (`print_sum_ave`).

Program Implementation

Once the data flow information has been added to the structure chart, the main function can be written. We can follow the approach described in Chapter 3 to do this. We begin by converting the data requirements shown earlier into local function declarations. All the variables that appear in the structure chart should be declared in the main function because they are used to store data passed to a function or results returned from a function. We omit any declaration of a variable to contain the individual data items because we simply have no need for such a variable at this stage in the development of our solution. Rather, this variable will be declared and used later in function `compute_sum`. We will revisit this issue at the end of the case study.

Once the data requirements information has been converted to local declarations, we can move the initial algorithm into the main function body, writing each algorithm step as a comment (see Fig. 6.14).

Figure 6.14 Outline and declarations for General Sum and Average Problem

```
// COMPUTES AND PRINTS THE SUM AND AVERAGE OF A COLLECTION
//    OF DATA ITEMS
void main ()
{
   // Functions used ...
   //    (to be completed)
```

(Continued)

Figure 6.14   (Continued)

```
    // Local data ...
    int num_items;      // input: number of data items to be added
    float sum;          // output: accumulated sum of data items
    float average;      // output: average of all data items

    // Read the number of items to be processed.

    // Compute the sum by reading each data item and accumulating
    //    it in the sum.

    // Compute the average of the data items.

    // Print the sum and the average.
}
```

To complete the main function, we must implement each algorithm step indicated by the comments. We can do this either in-line (as part of the main function code) or as a call to a separate function. For this problem, each step will be implemented as a separate function even though some of them ("Compute the average of the data items" and "Print the sum and the average") are, in fact, simple enough to be written in-line. We use functions here for illustrative purposes.

To proceed, we must review the structure chart in Fig. 6.13. This chart shows all the functions that we need to implement the main function and indicates the flow of information between main and the level 1 functions beneath it. We now must decide exactly how we will design the *function interfaces*—in other words, how we will communicate the indicated information between functions (as arguments or as return values). Once these function interface decisions have been made, we can write the prototypes and calls for the lower-level functions.

We have already provided guidelines for distinguishing between function input and output. Usually, if there is only one output data item, its value can be returned to a calling function using a `return` statement. If there is more than one data item flowing out of a function, all but possibly one of these items must be returned to the caller through an output argument.

In many cases, it is important to know whether a called function has successfully completed its task. Such status information may be used by the caller to decide what to do next—continue executing normally (if the called function executed successfully) or print a diagnostic message and perhaps terminate execution (if the called function failed to complete its mission). This is the case with the function `read_num_items`. Should this function fail to execute properly and return a meaningful value, there would be no point in continuing with the execution of the rest of the function.

There are at least two ways to design the interface of `read_num_items` so that this success or failure information is appropriately communicated to a calling function. One convenient way is to return the value of the number of items to be processed (a positive value) through the `return` statement, using a negative or zero value to indicate the failure of the function—that is, to indicate that the function did not read a positive value. Another way to handle this is to have the function return the number of items through an output argument and use the `return` statement to pass back an explicit success/failure indication. For illustration purposes, we have chosen the second of these two approaches. We will have the function `read_num_items` return a value of 1 if it executes successfully and a value of 0 if it fails to execute properly. This change should be reflected in the structure chart for this problem and in the initial algorithm as well.

The revised structure chart is shown in Fig. 6.15. The diamond-shaped element is used to indicate that a decision must be made as to which of the indicated steps is to be executed next. In this case, if a status indicator value of 1 is returned by `read_num_items`, our program should continue normal execution, computing and printing the sum and the average of the data read. If a status indicator of 0 is returned, a diagnostic message is printed and program execution terminates. The initial algorithm shown earlier must be modified to reflect this change (see Self-Check Exercise 7 at the end of this section).

With this revised structure chart, we can complete the main function by adding the prototypes and calls shown in Fig. 6.16. As long as data flow information in a structure chart is complete, it provides us with all of the information we need to know about the return values and arguments involved in each function interface.

As shown in the structure chart (Fig. 6.13) and main function (Fig. 6.16) for this problem, functions `compute_sum` and `compute_ave` return exactly one value. In Fig. 6.16, the statements

```
sum = compute_sum (num_items);
average = compute_ave (num_items, sum);
```

assign these returned values to the main function variables `sum` and `average`, respectively.

If we modify `read_num_items` as described earlier, then it would return two values: the number of items read (returned through an output argument) and a status flag indicating whether the read was successful (a 1 is returned) or not (a 0 is returned). The status flag (an integer) is returned using the `return` statement. The status information returned by the function is used directly as the condition in the `if` statement of the main function. This is perfectly legal and reasonable because `read_num_items` returns either a 1 (true) or a 0 (false). On the other hand, `num_items` is treated as an actual output argument whose value is defined during the execution of `read_num_items`. This value is returned to the main function and then passed to each of the other functions. Function `print_sum_ave` displays the value of `num_items`.

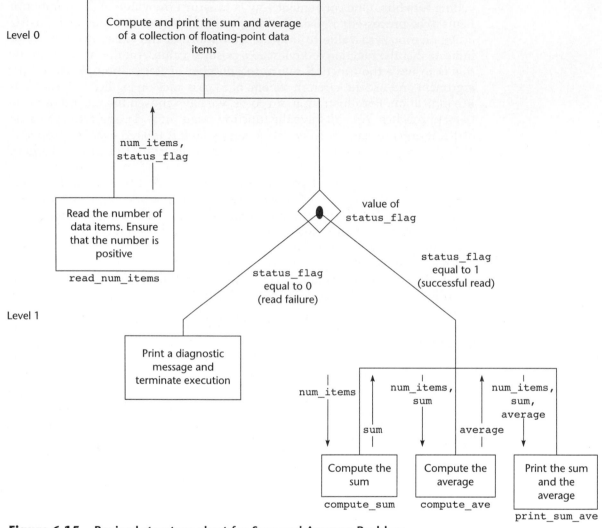

Figure 6.15   Revised structure chart for Sum and Average Problem

Figure 6.16   Main function for General Sum and Average Problem

```
// FILE: CmpSmAvN.cpp
// COMPUTES AND PRINTS THE SUM AND AVERAGE OF A COLLECTION OF DATA
//    ITEMS

#include <iostream.h>
#include <iomanip.h>
```

(Continued)

Figure 6.16 (Continued)

```cpp
#include "ReadFunc.cpp"
#include "SumNFunc.cpp"
#include "AveNFunc.cpp"
#include "PrntFunc.cpp"

void main ()
{
   // Functions used ...
   // READS NUMBER OF ITEMS TO BE PROCESSED
   int read_num_items
      (int&);                // OUT: number of items to be processed.

   // COMPUTES SUM OF DATA
   float compute_sum
      (int);                 // IN: number of data items

   // COMPUTES AVERAGE OF DATA
   float compute_ave
      (int,                  // IN: number of data items
       float);               // IN: sum of data items

   // PRINTS NUMBER OF ITEMS, SUM, AND AVERAGE
   void print_sum_ave
      (int,                  // IN: number of data items
       float,                // IN: sum of the data
       float);               // IN: average of the data

   // Local data ...
   int status_flag;     // indicates if read_num_items successful
   int num_items;       // input: number of items to be added
   float sum;           // output: accumulated sum of data
   float average;       // output: average of data being processed

   // Reads the number of items to be processed, ensures it is
   //    positive.
   status_flag = read_num_items (num_items);
   if (status_flag)
   {
      // Compute the sum of the data.
      sum = compute_sum (num_items);
      // Compute the average of the data.
      average = compute_ave (num_items, sum);

      // Print the sum and the average.
      print_sum_ave (num_items, sum, average);
   }
   else
   {
```

(Continued)

Figure 6.16 (Continued)

```
        cout << "Failure in read_num_items." << endl;
        cout << "Program execution terminated." << endl;
    }
    return;
}
```

Now that the main function is complete, we can concentrate in turn on each of the individual functions. We will begin with `read_num_items`. In specifying the data requirements for this function, we first list the function interface information.

Analysis for read_num_items

This is a relatively simple function. It simply reads and returns the number of items to be processed by the program. As long as this value is meaningful (greater than zero), the function returns a 1; otherwise, it returns a 0.

FUNCTION INTERFACE FOR read_num_items

> *Input Arguments*
>
> (none)
>
> *Output Arguments*
>
> num_items (int)   — number of items to be processed
>
> *Function Return Value*
>
> status indicator (set to 1 for success; 0 otherwise)

Design of read_num_items

This function prompts the user for a positive integer value. If a positive value is entered, the function returns a status value of 1 indicating success. If the user fails to enter a meaningful (positive) value, an error message is displayed, and the function returns with failure indication (value of 0).

INITIAL ALGORITHM FOR read_num_items

1. Read in number of items to be processed.
2. If number of items to be processed is positive
   - 2.1 Return with a value of 1 (indicating read successful).
   - else
   - 2.2 Display an error message.
   - 2.3 Return with a value of 0 (indicating a read failure).

We leave the implementation of this function as an exercise (see Programming Exercise 1 at the end of this section).

Analysis for compute_sum

In specifying the data requirements for `compute_sum`, we once again begin with the function interface information. This function is given the number of items to be processed as an input argument (`num_items`). It is responsible for reading and computing the sum of this number of values. This sum is then returned using the `return` statement.

FUNCTION INTERFACE FOR compute_sum

> ### Input Arguments
>
> num_items (int)   — number of items to be processed
>
> ### Output Arguments
>
> (none)
>
> ### Function Return Value
>
> the sum (float) of the data items processed

Design of compute_sum

The main computation for this function involves a loop in which each item is read and accumulated in a sum. The loop terminates when we have processed the specified number of data items. We need a counter to keep track of the number of items processed at any point during the execution of the program. Given this algorithm outline, we can now provide the local data for `compute_sum`.

> ### Local Data
>
> | | |
> |---|---|
> | item (float) | — contains each data item as it is read (read in) |
> | sum (float) | — used to accumulate the sum of each data item as it is read |
> | count (int) | — used to keep track of the count of the number of data items processed at any point |

We can now address the specifics of the initial algorithm. When we discussed the accumulation of a sum in Chapter 5, we emphasized the need to initialize the sum to zero prior to loop entry. The loop control steps must ensure that the correct number of data items is read and included in the sum being accumulated. Because we know the number of items to sum beforehand (`num_items`), we can use a counting loop. These considerations lead to the algorithm for `compute_sum` shown below. The implementation of `compute_sum` appears in Fig. 6.17. The validation check on the input argument `num_items` will be discussed in more detail at the end of this section.

INITIAL ALGORITHM FOR compute_sum

1. If num_items is not greater than zero, print a message and return immediately with a value of 0.
2. Initialize sum to zero.
3. For each value of count from 0, as long as count < num_items
    3.1. Read in a data item.
    3.2. Accumulate data item in sum.
4. Return sum.

Figure 6.17   Function `compute_sum`

```
// FILE: SumNFunc.cpp
// COMPUTES SUM OF DATA

float compute_sum
  (int num_items)     // IN: number of data items

// Pre:  num_items is assigned a value.
// Post: num_items data items read; their sum is stored in sum.
// Returns: Sum of all data items read if num_items >= 1;
//     otherwise 0.0.
{
   // Local data ...
   float item;        // input: contains current item being added
   float sum;         // output: used to accumulate sum of data
                      //            items read
   int count;         // count of items added so far

   // If num_items is valid, read each data item and accumulate it
   //    in sum.
   if (num_items < 1)
   {
      cout << "Invalid number of items = " << num_items << endl;
      cout << "Sum of items not computed." << endl;
      return 0.0;
   }  // end if

   sum = 0.0;
   for (count = 0; count < num_items; count++)
   {
      cout << "Enter a number to be added: ";
```

(Continued)

Figure 6.17 (Continued)

```
      cin >> item;
      sum += item;
   }  // end for
   return sum;
}  // end compute_sum
```

Analysis for compute_ave and print_sum_ave

Both `compute_ave` and `print_sum_ave` are relatively straightforward. We list their interface information and algorithms next. Neither function requires any local data, but both algorithms include a test of `num_items`. If `num_items` is not positive, it makes no sense to compute or display the average of the data items.

FUNCTION INTERFACE FOR compute_ave

Input Arguments

num_items (int)   — the number of data items to be processed
sum (float)   — the sum of all data processed

Output Arguments

(none)

Function Return Value

the average of all the data (float)

Design of compute_ave

INITIAL ALGORITHM

1. If num_items is positive
    1.1. Return the value of the sum divided by num_items.
   else
    1.2. Display "invalid number of items" message.
    1.3. Return a value of 0.

FUNCTION INTERFACE FOR print_sum_ave

Input Arguments

num_items (int)   — the number of data items to be processed

sum (float)	— the sum of all data processed
average (float)	— the average of all the data

Output Arguments

(none)

Design of print_sum_ave

INITIAL ALGORITHM

1. If the number of items is positive
    1.1. Display the number of items and the sum and average of the data.
  else
    1.2. Display "invalid number of items" message.
    1.3. Return a value of 0.

Implementation of compute_ave and print_sum_ave

The implementation of the compute_ave and print_sum_ave functions is shown in Figs. 6.18 and 6.19.

Figure 6.18   Function compute_ave

```
// FILE: AveNFunc.cpp
// COMPUTES AVERAGE OF DATA

float compute_ave
   (int num_items,        // IN: number of data items
    float sum)            // IN: sum of data

// Pre:  num_items and sum are defined; num_items must be
//       greater than 0.
// Post: If num_items is positive, the average is computed as
//       sum / num_items;
// Returns: The average if num_items is positive; otherwise, 0.
{
   // Compute the average of the data.
   if (num_items < 1)
   {
      cout << "Invalid value for num_items = " << num_items
           << endl;
      cout << "Average not computed." << endl;
      return 0.0;
   }  // end if
   return sum / float (num_items);      // recast operand num_items
}  // end compute_ave
```

Figure 6.19   Function `print_sum_ave`

```
// FILE: PrntFunc.cpp
// PRINTS NUMBER OF ITEMS, SUM, AND AVERAGE OF DATA


void print_sum_ave
    (int num_items,            // IN: number of data items
     float sum,                // IN: sum of the data
     float average)            // IN: average of the data

// Pre:  num_items, sum, and average are defined.
// Post: Displays num_items, sum and average if num_items > 0.
{
    // Display results if num_items is valid.
    if (num_items > 0)
    {
        cout << setprecision (2)
             << setiosflags (ios::showpoint | ios::fixed);
        cout << "The number of items is " << num_items << endl;
        cout << "The sum of the data is " << sum << endl;
        cout << "The average of the data is " << average << endl;
    }
    else
    {
        cout << "Invalid number of items = " << num_items << endl;
        cout << "Sum and average are not defined." << endl;
        cout << "No printing done.  Execution terminated." << endl;
    }  // end if
    return;
}   // end print_sum_ave
```

Program Testing

The program that solves the General Sum and Average Problem consists of four separate components, each implemented as a function. When building and testing such a *program system,* it is generally a good idea first to write the main function along with skeletons or *stubs* of the lower-level modules. (These stubs would each contain little more than the correct function headers and a print statement indicating that the function had been called. The details of implementation of the function would be deferred until later.) This as yet incomplete version of the program system could then be tested at least to verify that the basic flow of control through the main function is as intended.

Once the main function and lower-level function stub testing has been completed, some (or all) of these lower level modules can be completed and tested, either individually or in small groups of functions. For example, we might first code and test the `read_num_items` function and then move on to code and test the other three functions. Finally, some (or all, as is the case here) of these tested groups can be *integrated* to form a larger group or subsystem. This process repeats itself until, finally, the combination of tested subsystems forms the intended system, which then undergoes *final integration testing.*

In testing the fully integrated sum and average functions, you should make sure that `sum` and `average` are displayed correctly when `num_items` is positive and that a meaningful diagnostic is displayed when `num_items` is zero or negative. A sample run of the completed program system is shown next.

——————— Program Output ———————

```
Enter the number of items to be processed.
This value must be greater than 0: 3
Enter a number to be added: 5.0
Enter a number to be added: 6.0
Enter a number to be added: 17.0
The number of items is 3
The sum of the data is 28.00
The average of the data is 9.33
```

We will have more to say about program testing in Chapter 10, which is devoted to issues of software engineering. In the meanwhile, your instructor will probably encourage you to adopt his or her own preferred testing strategies. Although such strategies may seem a bit silly for such simple problems as this, we assure you that your programs will rapidly grow in complexity. Some practice in deciding which subsystems to test at each stage, in writing driver test programs, and in designing a good set of test data can never start too early. Now is certainly an important time to be sure to begin this practice if you have not done so already.

Commentary for the General Sum and Average Problem

The functions `compute_sum`, `compute_ave`, and `print_sum_ave` all check to ensure that `num_items` has a meaningful value before continuing with their work. These checks may seem unnecessary as long as we can guarantee that, in fact, none of these functions could be called if `num_items` were less than or equal to zero. For our relatively simple problem, it would seem as though function `read_num_items` provides this guarantee. However, when working with larger, more complex problems, such assurances are usually hard to come by. Furthermore, what might be assured at one point in the life of a function can easily change as modifications are made to the code of a system that uses the function.

It is therefore a good idea to perform such checks on input arguments, especially if one or more operations to be performed by a function would be rendered meaningless (or worse, cause the program to abort in the middle of execution) for certain values of these inputs. This is clearly the case for all three of the functions, compute_sum, compute_ave, and print_sum_ave. We have therefore chosen to use these functions to illustrate the validation of an input argument upon function entry.

Using Functions to Implement Individual Algorithm Steps

The structure chart for the General Sum and Average Problem shown in Fig. 6.13 contains four level-one steps, each of which is implemented as a separate function. Even though it was relatively easy to implement the step for computing the average, we used a function (compute_ave) for this step, too. Although a bit more writing, planning, and perhaps some execution inefficiency might result from this approach, we want to encourage the use of functions even for relatively simple-to-implement algorithm steps. Such separation of algorithm step implementations helps keep the details of these steps (no matter how minor) separate and hidden. This, in turn, can be expected to make debugging, testing, and later function modification easier to perform. From this point on, you can expect that the executable code of the higher-level functions in example programs will consist primarily of a sequence of function calls.

Multiple Declarations of Identifiers in a Program System

The identifier num_items is declared as a variable in the main function and as a formal argument in the three functions called by main. Each function call in the main function associates the main function variable num_items with formal argument num_items. You may be wondering if this violates any rules of C++. The answer is no, because the two uses of the identifier num_items are considered to be distinct from one another.

As we discussed in Chapter 3, when functions were first introduced, each function that you write is treated as a separate program component and is compiled separately. The only connection among these functions is the elements in the formal and actual argument lists.

EXERCISES FOR SECTION 6.5

Self-Check

1. Function compute_ave returns a single value using a return statement. Rewrite this function to return this result through an output argument (see Fig. 6.8 for an example).
2. Draw the before and after data areas for the main function and revised compute_ave (see Self-Check Exercise 1) assuming compute_ave is called with sum equal to 100.0 and num_items equal to 10.

3. Draw the main function and `print_sum_ave` data areas given the data value assumptions in Self-Check Exercise 2.

4. Rewrite function `compute_sum` to return the sum through an output argument rather than through the return statement.

5. Consider the three functions `compute_sum`, `compute_ave`, and `print_sum_ave` as though the code to validate the value of the argument `num_items` had been omitted. For each of these functions, describe what would happen now that the function would be allowed to proceed with its work even if `num_items` were zero or negative.

6. Draw the main function and revised `compute_sum` (see Self-Check Exercise 4) data areas assuming `compute_sum` is called with `num_items` defined to be 10.

7. Rewrite the initial algorithm for the General Sum and Average Problem to reflect the structure chart changes shown in Fig. 6.15. [In this implementation, the function `read_num_items` is expected to return the number of items read (as an output argument) and a status flag (using the `return` statement) indicating whether the input operation was successful.]

8. Rewrite the structure chart, problem analysis, and main function for the General Sum and Average Problem assuming that the structure chart functions "Compute the average" and "Print the sum and average" are written in-line rather than as separate functions.

9. a. Draw the structure chart corresponding to the algorithm for `read_num_items`. A diamond shape will be needed in this chart to indicate decision control.

   b. Draw the structure chart corresponding to the algorithm for `compute_sum`. A diamond shape (to indicate decision) and loop control are required in this chart.

10. If you were to design and test the General Sum and Average program as suggested in the previous material on Program Testing (test main program and stubs, then test `read_num_items`, and finally test the entire system), would you need to write any special driver programs? Why or why not? Defend your answer in a few sentences.

Programming

1. Using the algorithm given in this section, write the function `read_num_items`.

2. Design and implement an algorithm for `read_num_items` that uses a loop to ensure that the user enters a positive value. The loop should execute repeatedly, each time prompting the user for a positive value (the number of items to be processed) until a positive value for the number of items has been entered. Is the status flag still needed? Explain your answer. Don't forget to rewrite the function interface and interface documentation.

6.6 ——— SOLVING A MORE COMPLEX PROBLEM

In this section, we provide a demonstration of the top-down design process in solving a more complex problem. Again, the problem solution will be implemented in a stepwise manner starting at the top of the structure chart, or with the main function. The problem solution makes extensive use of functions with arguments.

CASE STUDY: CHECKING ACCOUNT BALANCE PROBLEM

Problem Statement

You have just purchased a new personal computer and would like to write a program to help balance your checking account each month. The program will process your transactions (check or deposit) one at a time, adjust your current balance accordingly, and keep track of the number of checks and deposits processed. A new balance should be printed after each transaction is processed, and a warning message should be displayed if the balance becomes negative. At the end of the session, the starting and final balances should be printed, along with a count of the number of checks and deposits processed.

Problem Analysis

The program will begin by printing a brief set of user instructions and then asking the user to enter the starting balance (the balance at the beginning of the month). The program should then process all transactions and finally print the starting and final balances and the counts of the number of checks and deposits.

The starting balance must be available at the end, so we will save it in variable `start_balance`. We will use a different variable, `current_balance`, to keep track of the current balance as each transaction is processed. In other words, `current_balance` will be used as an accumulator for keeping the account balance up to date during the processing of each transaction. In addition to this accumulator, we need two others for keeping count of the number of checks (`num_checks`) and number of deposits (`num_deps`). The final value of these counters and of the current balance are our problem output values.

DATA REQUIREMENTS

> **Problem Input**
>
> start_balance (float)   — starting checkbook balance
> the transaction data, consisting of a code (char) for the transaction type (deposit or check) and an amount (float)
>
> **Problem Output**
>
> current_balance (float)   — current balance after each transaction
> start_balance (float)   — starting checkbook balance

num_checks (int)   —number of checks at any point in processing

num_deps (int)   —number of deposits at any point in processing

Program Design

Figure 6.20 shows the structure chart for this algorithm. The level-one sub-problems will be implemented as separate functions instruct_user, initiate, process_transactions, and print_report, respectively. The data flow information shows that start_balance is read by initiate and passed to process_transactions. Function process_transactions defines the results (current_balance, num_checks, and num_deps); these results, together with the starting balance, are passed to print_report and printed.

As illustrated in the General Sum and Average Problem in the previous section, those variables that are passed between the main function and a level-one function (as shown in the structure chart) must be declared in main. You should verify that each variable appearing in your structure chart also is described in your data requirements table.

Given the information in the structure chart, we can now write the initial algorithm. Once again, we are not concerned about the details of these steps at this point, but only with identifying and properly ordering them. The initial algorithm follows.

INITIAL ALGORITHM

1. Display instructions (instruct_user).

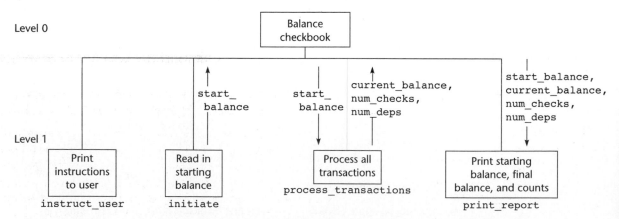

Figure 6.20   Structure chart (levels 0 and 1) for Checking Account Balance Problem

2. Read in the starting balance (`initiate`).
3. Process each transaction. If it is valid, update current balance and the counters; if not, ignore the transaction (`process_transactions`).
4. Print the starting and final balances and the number of checks and deposits processed (`print_report`).

Program Implementation

Now that we have completed the structure chart and data flow information (Fig. 6.20) and initial algorithm for the Checking Account Balance Problem, we can complete the implementation of the main program. The data flow information shown in Fig. 6.20 is used to specify the argument lists in the function prototypes and calls shown in this function (see Fig. 6.21).

Figure 6.21   Checking Account Balance Program (with stub for `process_transactions`)

```
// FILE: ChkBalSt.cpp
// CHECKING ACCOUNT BALANCE PROGRAM
//    (with stub for process_transactions)
//    Processes monthly checking account transactions.

#include <iostream.h>
#include <iomanip.h>

#include "PrcTrnSt.cpp" // process_transactions stub

void main ()
{
   // Functions used ...
   // PROVIDE USER INSTRUCTIONS
   void instruct_user ();

   // INITIATE PROCESSING
   void initiate
      (float&);             // OUT: account balance at start of period

   // PROCESS ALL TRANSACTIONS (stub)
   void process_transactions
      (float,               // IN: account balance at start of period
       float&,              // INOUT: current balance at any point
       int&,                // INOUT: number of checks at any point
       int&);               // INOUT: number of deposits at any point

   // PRINT REPORT
   void print_report
      (float,               // IN: account balance at start of period
       float,               // IN: current balance at any point
       int,                 // IN: number of checks at any point
```

(Continued)

Figure 6.21   (Continued)

```
        int);                    // IN: number of deposits at any point

    // Local data ...
    float start_balance;    // input: balance at start of period
    float current_balance;  // output: balance at end of period
    int num_checks;         // output: number of checks for period
    int num_deps;           // output: number of deposits for period

    // Output manipulator settings.
    cout << setiosflags (ios::fixed | ios::showpoint)
         << setprecision (2);

    instruct_user ();
    initiate (start_balance);
    process_transactions
        (start_balance, current_balance, num_checks, num_deps);
    print_report (start_balance, current_balance, num_checks,
                  num_deps);
    return;
}


// PROVIDE USER INSTRUCTIONS
void instruct_user ()
{
    // Prints user instructions.
    cout << "This is your Checkbook Balancing Program. It will"
         << endl;
    cout << "keep a record of all checks written and deposits"
         << " made." << endl;
    cout << "Please enter all information as prescribed." << endl
         << endl;
    return;
}


// INITIATE PROCESSING
void initiate
    (float& start_balance)   // OUT: account balance at the start of
                             //      the month

// Reads the starting balance.
// Pre:  (none)
// Post: Starting balance defined.
{
    // Local data ...
    char response;                   // user's response to input question
```

(Continued)

Figure 6.21   (Continued)

```
do
{
    cout << "Enter checkbook balance at start of current "
        << "period: $ ";
    cin >> start_balance;
    cout << "Is this starting balance of $ " << start_balance
        << " correct?" << endl;
    cout << "(Enter Y or N) => ";
    cin >> response;
} while (response != 'Y' && response != 'y');

    cout << " Thank you! Now we can begin processing your"
        << " transactions." << endl << endl;
    return;
} // end initiate


// PRINT REPORT
void print_report
    (float start_balance,      // IN: starting balance for the account
     float current_balance,    // IN: current balance at any point
     int num_checks,           // IN: number of checks at any point
     int num_deps)             // IN: number of deposits at any point

// Pre:  Starting balance and current balance have nonnegative
//       values. Number of checks and deposits are both
//       nonnegative.
// Post: All four input arguments have been printed.
{
    // Print starting and ending balances and transaction counts.
    cout << endl;
    cout << "Balance at start of period: $ " << start_balance
        << endl;
    cout << "Balance at end of period: $ " << current_balance
        << endl << endl;
    cout << "Number of deposits for this period: " << num_deps
        << endl;
    cout << "Number of checks for this period: " << num_checks
        << endl << endl;
    cout << "End of report." << endl;
    return;
} // end print_report
```

Because functions `instruct_user`, `initiate`, and `print_report` are relatively straightforward, consisting mostly of input/output statements, we have included the code for these functions along with the main function. The only bit of complexity is in `initiate`, where we have reused a form of a `do_while` loop convenient for ensuring that the user provides the correct value for the starting balance for the month. Because function `process_transactions` is more complicated and requires further refinement, we have included only the *function stub* for this component; the details are to be completed later.

The executable part of the main function body consists of calls to all four of the level-one functions. The stub for `process_transactions` is stored in the separate file `PrcTrnSt.cpp`, shown in Fig. 6.22.

Figure 6.22   Stub for function `process_transactions`

```
// FILE: PrcTrnSt.cpp
// PROCESS ALL TRANSACTIONS (stub)

void process_transactions
   (float start_balance,      // IN: starting balance for account
    float& current_balance,   // INOUT: current balance at any point
    int& num_checks,          // INOUT: nmbr of checks at any point
    int& num_deps)            // INOUT: nmbr of deposits at any point

// Pre:  Start_balance is assigned a value.
// Post: Current_balance is start_balance plus deposits minus
//       checks; number of checks is the count of checks;
//       number of deposits is the count of deposits.
// Uses: read_transaction, process_one_transaction, display_record
{
   cout << "Function process_transactions entered." << endl;
   current_balance = start_balance;
   num_checks = 0;
   num_deps = 0;
   return;
}  // end process_transactions
```

The statement

```
#include "PrcTrnSt.cpp"
```

appearing near the top of Fig. 6.21 will cause this file to be included during the compilation of the main function. A function stub can be viewed as a temporary substitute for the complete function. Stubs are used to facilitate the testing of a higher level function without having to worry about the details of all its called components. Further discussion of the form and purpose of stubs may be found in Section 6.8.

Analysis for process_transactions

Function `process_transactions` performs step 3 of the main algorithm, which we have rewritten below with a bit more detail:

> For each transaction: read the transaction code and amount.
>   If the code and amount are valid, update and print the current balance and increment the counts of checks or deposits; otherwise, print a diagnostic message and ignore the transaction.

The argument specifications are taken directly from the structure chart in Fig. 6.20. The starting balance must be provided as an input argument, and the current balance and counts of checks and deposits are to be computed and returned as output.

FUNCTION INTERFACE FOR process_transactions

Input Arguments

start_balance (float)   — starting checkbook balance

Output Arguments

current_balance (float)   — current balance after each transaction
num_checks (int)   — number of checks processed at any point
num_deps (int)   — number of deposits processed at any point

Design of process_transactions

The function must read both the type and amount of each transaction, so local input variables must be provided to store this information.

Local Data for process_transactions

Transaction data
    transaction_code (char)   — code for each transaction (read in)
    transaction_amount (float)   — amount of each transaction (read in)

This function is responsible for reading each transaction code and amount and carrying out the processing specified by the code. The decomposition of the function is shown in the structure chart in Fig. 6.23. The reading and valida- tion of the code and amount is the responsibility of a lower-level function, `read_transaction`. `read_transaction` returns both the code read and the transaction amount. A code of `'I'` is returned if the transaction code or amount is not valid.

If the code returned by `read_transaction` is `'C'` or `'D'`, then functions `process_one_transaction` and `display_record` are called to complete the processing of the current transaction. If a code of `'I'` is returned by

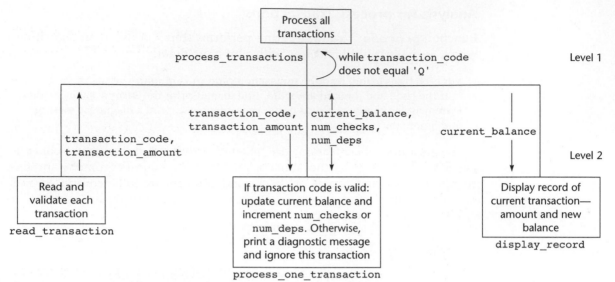

Figure 6.23   Structure chart for function `process_transactions`

`read_transaction`, indicating that either an invalid code or transaction was entered, the current transaction is ignored entirely.

The arc under the top box in the structure chart (Fig. 6.23) indicates that a loop is needed to control execution of these three subfunctions. Assuming that we do not know how many transactions will occur, we can use a sentinel-controlled `while` loop that compares the transaction code to a sentinel value (`'Q'`). This loop will continue to repeat as long as the quit code `'Q'` is not entered by the user. At the end of execution of this loop, the following must be true:

a) the current balance must be equal to the starting balance plus the sum of the amounts of all deposit transactions and minus the sum of the amounts of all check transactions;
b) `num_checks` must be equal to the number of checks processed;
c) `num_deps` must be equal to the number of deposits processed;
d) the transaction code must be equal to `'Q'`.

This suggests the following algorithm.

ALGORITHM FOR `process_transactions`

1. Initialize the current balance to the starting balance.
2. Initialize number of checks and number of deposits to zero.
3. Read the first transaction (`read_transaction`).

4. While the transaction code is not the sentinel
    4.1. If the current transaction code and amount are not valid (code is 'I')
        4.1.1. Print a diagnostic message and ignore the transaction.
    else
        4.1.2. Update the current balance and increment the number of checks or number of deposits (`process_one_transaction`).
        4.1.3. Display record of current transaction—transaction_amount and current_balance (`display_record`).
    4.2. Read the next transaction (`read_transaction`).

The implementation of function `process_transactions` is shown in the top section of Fig. 6.24 (shown following the design of `process_one_transaction`).

Analysis of read_transaction

The three functions subordinate to `process_transactions` are fairly easy to write. However, we need to be sure that `read_transaction` properly carries out its responsibilities, returning to `process_transactions` the correct transaction code (`'C'`, `'D'`, or `'Q'`, or the code `'I'` for an invalid transaction code or amount). The amount of the transaction also must be returned. The function interface for `read_transaction` follows.

FUNCTION INTERFACE FOR read_transaction

Input Arguments

(none)

Output Arguments

transaction_code (char)   — code for each transaction
transaction_amount (float)   — amount of each transaction

Design of read_transaction

This function is written in a rather unforgiving fashion. If the user enters an invalid transaction code (not `'C'`, `'D'`, or `'Q'`), a diagnostic message is printed and the current transaction is ignored (a code of `'I'` and a transaction amount of 0.0 are returned to `process_transactions`). If a valid code (a `'C'` or a `'D'`) is entered, then the transaction amount is read and validated. If the amount is less than or equal to zero, the transaction is ignored (again, a code of `'I'` and a transaction amount of 0.0 are returned to `process_transactions`). If the transaction code and amount are both valid, they are returned to `process_transactions`. The code `'Q'` indicates that there are no more transactions to process—the code `'Q'` and a transaction amount of 0.0 are returned to `process_transactions`. The main control structure for this algorithm is a `switch`.

ALGORITHM FOR read_transaction

1. Read a transaction code.
2. Switch (transaction_code)
    case 'C' or 'D':
        2.1. Enter the transaction amount.
        2.2. If the amount is less than or equal to zero, set the code to 'I' and the amount to 0.0 (to ignore the transaction).
    case 'Q':
        2.3. Set the transaction_amount to 0.0.
    default:
        2.4. Set the transaction code to 'I' and the amount to 0.0 (to ignore the transaction).

The algorithm implementation is left as an exercise (see Programming Exercise 1 at the end of this section).

Analysis for process_one_transaction

Function `process_one_transaction` uses the code and amount of a transaction to update the values of its three input/output arguments, `current_balance`, `num_checks`, and `num_deps`.

FUNCTION INTERFACE FOR process_one_transaction

Input Arguments

transaction_code (char)   — code for each transaction
transaction_amount (float)   — amount of transaction

Input/Output Arguments

current_balance (float)   — current balance after each transaction
num_checks (int)   — number of checks processed at any point
num_deps (int)   — number of deposits processed at any point

Design of process_one_transaction

The strategy for the current balance and counters update is outlined in the decision table shown in Table 6.4. This logic can be implemented using a `switch` statement (see Programming Exercise 1 at the end of this section).

Table 6.4   Decision Table for `process_one_transaction`

CONDITION	DESIRED ACTION
`transaction_code` = 'D'	Increment num_deps, add `transaction_amount` to current_balance
`transaction_code` = 'C'	Increment num_checks, subtract transaction_amount from current_balance
default	Print error message, set `transaction_code` to 'I' and `transaction_amount` to 0.0

Function `display_record` checks to see if an account has been over-drawn and prints an appropriate message in this case. We will not discuss `display_record` further; its implementation is relatively straightforward. Figure 6.24 shows only function `process_transactions`; the implementations of `read_transaction`, `process_one_transaction`, and `display_record` are left as exercises (see Programming Exercise 1 at the end of this section).

We have added the line

```
// USES: read_transaction, process_one_transaction, display_record
```

to the documentation section for `process_transactions`. This provides an easily located summary of the functions called by `process_transactions`. This is important information for anyone attempting to read and understand this function and the functions it calls.

Implementation of process_transactions

Figure 6.24   Function `process_transactions`

```
// FILE: PrcTrans.cpp
// PROCESS ALL TRANSACTIONS

#include "ReadTran.cpp"
#include "Prc1Tran.cpp"
#include "DisplRec.cpp"

void process_transactions
   (float start_balance,        // IN: starting balance for account
    float& current_balance,     // OUT: current balance at any point
    int& num_checks,            // OUT: number of checks at any point
    int& num_deps)              // OUT: number of deposits at any point
```

(Continued)

Figure 6.24   (Continued)

```
// Pre:  start_balance must be defined and must be nonnegative.
// Post: current_balance is start_balance plus deposits minus
//        checks; number of checks is the count of checks;
//        number of deposits is the count of deposits.
// Uses: read_transaction, process_one_transaction, display_record
{
   // Functions used ...
   // READ TRANSACTION CODE AND AMOUNT
   void read_transaction
      (char&,               // OUT: transaction code
       float&);             // OUT: transaction amount

   // PROCESS ONE TRANSACTION
   void process_one_transaction
      (char,                // IN: transaction code
       float,               // IN: transaction amount
       float&,              // INOUT: current balance at any point
       int&,                // INOUT: nmbr of checks at any point
       int&);               // INOUT: nmbr of deposits at any point

   // DISPLAY CURRENT TRANSACTION RECORD
   void display_record
      (char,                // IN: current transaction code
       float,               // IN: current transaction amount
       float);              // IN: current balance after transaction

   // Local data ...
   char transaction_code;          // type of each transaction
   float transaction_amount;       // amount of each transaction

   // Initialize accumulators.
   current_balance = start_balance;
   num_checks = 0;
   num_deps = 0;

   // Process each valid transaction.
   read_transaction (transaction_code, transaction_amount);
   while (transaction_code != 'Q')
   {
      if (transaction_code != 'I')
      {
         process_one_transaction (transaction_code,
            transaction_amount, current_balance, num_checks,
            num_deps);
         display_record (transaction_code, transaction_amount,
            current_balance);
      }  // end if
      else
```

(Continued)

Figure 6.24 (Continued)

```
        cout << "Invalid transaction posted.  Transaction "
           << "ignored." << endl;

     read_transaction (transaction_code, transaction_amount);
   }  // end while
   return;
}  // end process_transactions
```

Program Testing

At the very least, the main function for the Checking Account Balance Problem should be tested first with the function stub for `process_trans-actions` (see Fig. 6.21). In this way, not only can the flow of the main function be tested, but also the implemented lower-level functions `initiate` and `print_report` can be checked. Once these components have been checked, you can then proceed to code and test `process_transactions` and its subordinate functions.

If the completed version of `process_transactions` is stored in file `PrcTrans.cpp`, then the only change required to execute the completed Checking Account Balance Program is in the include statement at the top of Fig. 6.21. To test the completed program, the current `#include` line

```
#include "PrcTrnSt.cpp"
```

which included the stub for `process_transactions` must be changed to

```
#include "PrcTrans.cpp"
```

to include the completed version of the function.

Testing should always include the use of valid as well as invalid data. In this case, especially, try invalid as well as valid transaction codes.

EXERCISES FOR SECTION 6.6

Self-Check
1. Write the data requirements and algorithm for function `display_record`.
2. Write the algorithm for function `process_one_transaction`.

Programming
1. Write the C++ implementations of functions `read_transaction`, `process_one_transaction`, and `display_record`. Be sure that any information displayed would be understandable to the program user.
2. Draw the structure chart corresponding to the algorithm for `compute_sum` in the Sum and Average Problem (see Section 6.5). A decision control diamond and a loop control arc will be required in this chart.
3. Rewrite the `switch` statements in functions `process_one_transaction` and `display_record` as `if` statements.

4. Modify the Checking Account Balance Program so that a penalty amount of $15.00 is deducted for each overdrawn check, and a count of overdrawn checks is maintained and printed next to each overdrawn check. Reset the count of overdrafts to zero whenever the balance becomes positive. List the names of all functions that had to be modified to accommodate this change; list the names of those functions that did not need to be changed.

5. Provide a detailed description of each change to the Checking Account Balance Program that you would need to make if the problem definition were changed to include a third transaction type `'W'` (for withdrawal—for example, from an automated teller machine).

6.7 ───── MORE ASPECTS OF SOFTWARE ENGINEERING

Stepwise Design and Procedural Abstraction

The design process and resulting system for the Checking Account Balance Problem is a good illustration of stepwise design and the use of procedural abstraction in programming. At the highest level of consideration, we decomposed the solution to this problem into four subproblems. Each of these subproblems was described in relatively abstract terms, with as little discussion as possible of the details of implementation. Short, English descriptive phrases were used to specify each subproblem shown in the structure chart, and a function name, appropriate to the task described, was attached to each box in the chart (see Fig. 6.13). To complete this high-level decomposition, we have added to the structure chart information about the data that must be communicated among the functions. Each of the functions used to implement a subproblem was clear and concise and contained the C++ code required to implement the procedural abstraction represented by the corresponding box in the structure chart.

The main function at the top of Fig. 6.21 contained three function calls. The function call

```
process_transactions
    (start_balance, current_balance, num_checks, num_deps);
```

was used to process all transactions. This processing step is relatively complicated, involving a number of details that are not germane in the top-level solution. In keeping with the top-down approach, we delayed getting involved with the details of function `process_transactions` until we had completed the analysis, design, and implementation of the top-level function. Thus, function `process_transactions` was originally written as a stub—none of the variables or algorithm steps eventually needed to implement this function was considered at this point. Instead, these steps were left for later consideration so that we could keep our focus on the main function.

Once the analysis, design, implementation, and testing of the top-level functions of a system was complete, we focused our attention on the next level of detail, repeating the top-down process all over again. The structure chart for this level of the design stage was shown in Fig. 6.23. Three procedural abstractions and the data to be communicated among them are illustrated there, too. Function `process_transactions` was decomposed into subproblems named `read_transaction`, `process_one_transaction`, and `display_record`, which performed the read, update, and display operations, respectively, for each transaction that is processed. Once this decomposition was complete, function `process_transactions` could be implemented and tested. The implementation of `process_transactions` was shown in Fig. 6.24.

One of the important results of this top-down approach is that the implementation details for each of the functions in a structure chart are hidden from the other functions. Thus, for example, when we concentrate our efforts on the implementation details of the main function or any one of its subfunctions, the details of processing the transactions, including the read, update, and display operations, are of no concern.

At any point in the development process, the goal is to delay, insofar as possible, consideration of any nonessential details for later stages of program development. A variable should be declared in the highest-level function that uses it and no higher. The variable may be used by lower-level functions, but its declaration and manipulation are hidden from all higher-level functions and even from those functions on the same level in a structure chart. A function can grant a lower-level function access to a variable by passing that variable as an actual argument in a call to the lower-level function. Thus, for example, `process_transactions` granted access to `process_one_-transaction` for processing the variables `current_balance`, `num_checks`, and `num_deps`. However, these variables were accessible neither to the main function nor to function `initiate`, which was at the same level as `process_transactions`.

Thus, the top-town process also leads to the distribution of problem data only to those functions that require knowledge of those data. If we can consistently achieve a high degree of localization of problem information in our code, we can expect to find that all aspects of program development, from analysis and design to testing and modification, are easier to perform.

PROGRAM STYLE

Avoidance of Aliases

The functions written for the Checking Account Balance Program are a little different from others we have written in that there is little likelihood that they can be reused in other function systems. For this reason we have not attempted to use generic names to represent the formal arguments in these functions. In cases like this, we recommend that each function use the same formal argument name to represent a particular data item in each function, rather than choosing different names, or *aliases*, for that data item. The use of aliases makes it more difficult to read and understand a program system that contains multiple functions. ∎

6.8 DEBUGGING AND TESTING A PROGRAM SYSTEM

Top-Down and Bottom-Up Debugging and Testing

As the number of statements in a program system grows, the possibility of error also increases. If we restrict each function to a manageable size, the likelihood of error will increase more slowly. Each function also will be easier to read and test. Careful use of arguments, passing only those required for a function to do its work, can further minimize the chance of harmful side effects that are always difficult to locate.

In the last case study, we first used a stub for function `process_transactions` along with the main function. When a team of programmers is working on a problem, this is a common practice. Obviously, not all functions will be ready at the same time, so the use of stubs enables us to test and debug the main function and those functions that are available.

Each stub should display an identification message and assign values to its output arguments to prevent execution errors caused by undefined values (see Fig. 6.22). The message printed by each stub when it is called provides a trace of the call sequence and allows the programmer to determine whether the main function is executing the desired sequence of steps. The process of testing a main function in this way is called *top-down testing* or *stub testing*.

When a lower-level function is completed, it can be substituted for its stub in the main function. However, we often perform a preliminary test of a new function first because it is easier to locate and correct errors when dealing with a single function rather than a complete program system. We can test a new function by writing a short driver function similar to the driver function shown in Fig. 6.2, which is used to test function `compute_tax`.

Don't spend a lot of time creating an elegant driver function, because you will discard it as soon as the new function is tested. A driver function should contain only the declarations and executable statements necessary to perform a test of a single function. A driver function should begin by reading or assigning values to all input and input/output arguments of the function it tests. Next comes the call to the function being tested. After calling the function, the driver function should display the function results. Once we are confident that a function works properly, it can be substituted for its stub in our program system. The process of separately testing individual functions before inserting them in a program system is called *bottom-up testing*.

By following a combination of top-down and bottom-up testing, a programming team can be fairly confident that the complete function system will be relatively free of errors when it is finally put together. Consequently, the final debugging sessions should proceed quickly and smoothly. A list of suggestions for debugging a program system follows.

Debugging Tips for Program Systems

1. Carefully document each function argument and local identifier using comments as you write the code. Also describe the basic purpose of the function using comments.
2. Leave a trace of execution by printing the function name as you enter it.
3. Print the values of all input and input/output arguments upon entry to a function. Check that these values make sense.
4. Make sure that a function stub assigns a value to each of its output arguments.
5. Upon return from a function, print the values of all information returned to the caller (the return value and the values of the actual output and input/output arguments). Verify that these values are correct by hand computation. Make sure that all input/output and output arguments are declared as reference arguments.

It is a good idea to plan for debugging as you write each function rather than after the fact. Include any output statements that you might need to help determine that the function is working. When you are satisfied that the function works as desired, you can remove these *debugging statements*. One efficient way to remove them is to change them to comments by preceding them with the symbol //. If you have a problem later, you can remove this symbol, thereby changing the comments back to executable statements for further testing.

Another approach to turning debugging statements on and off is to use a special integer constant (say, `debug`). The declaration

```
const int debug = 1;          // turn debugging on
```

should be used during debugging runs, and the declaration

```
const int debug = 0;          // turn debugging off
```

should be used during production runs. Within a function, each diagnostic print statement should be part of an `if` statement with `debug` as its condition. If function `process` begins with the `if` statement below, the `cout` statements will execute only during debugging runs [`debug` is 1 (`true`)] as desired.

```
if (debug)
{
   cout << "Function process entered.";
   cout << "Input argument start_balance has value "
        << setprecision (2) << start_balance;
} // end if
```

Self-Check

1. Provide a set of test data to show that the program in Fig. 6.21 behaves as expected. Remember that only the stub for function `process_transactions` appears in this version of the Checking Account Balance Program, so little processing of data will be done.

2. Illustrate how we might have written the stubs for the three functions called by `process_transactions` had we chosen to delay the implementation of these functions to a later stage in the development of the Checking Account Balance Program. Once you have written these stubs, produce a set of test data for the program shown in Fig. 6.21 with the full code for `process_transactions` (shown in Fig. 6.24) and these three stubs.

3. Write a driver program to test function `process_transactions` and its three subordinate functions (as shown in Fig. 6.24). Produce a set of test data that could be used to test function `process_transactions` before it is integrated into the full system in place of its stub.

6.9 _____ COMMON PROGRAMMING ERRORS

We have already discussed many of the most common programming errors that arise when using functions in the Common Programming Errors section of Chapter 3. You are urged to review this material. One issue not discussed before, related to the handling of type inconsistencies in call-by-reference arguments, is discussed next.

■ *Argument Inconsistencies with Call-by-Reference Arguments:* In Chapter 3, where call-by-value argument passing was discussed, we indicated that argument inconsistencies involving character, integer, and floating-point data usually do not cause even a warning message from the compiler. However, such inconsistencies will cause a warning message if they occur when using call-by-reference arguments.

For example, for the function

```
void initiate (char &);
```

the call

```
initiate (sum);
```

where `sum` is type `float` will result in a compiler warning such as

```
"Temporary used for parameter 1 in call to 'initiate (char &)'"
```

In one sense, this message may be viewed as informational—a report on the usual action taken by the compiler when such an argument-passing inconsistency occurs. Remember that C++ allows some degree of type mixing when passing arguments, so the message may not be an indication of anything illegal. However, at this stage in your programming work, such a warning should also be considered an indication that you may have made a mistake that needs to be fixed. The indicated call should be carefully checked to ensure that you have written exactly what you wanted.

CHAPTER REVIEW

This chapter completes our presentation of the main concepts of procedural decomposition and abstraction. We began this discussion in Chapter 3, where we introduced the idea of top-down problem decomposition. Here, we first used functions to provide a means of separating and hiding the details for each component of a problem solution. The use of functions made it possible to carry this separation through from the early problem analysis and program design stages to the implementation of a program in C++.

In Chapter 3, our discussion of functions was limited to relatively simple problems and to functions that returned a single value. In this chapter, with additional, important material on decision and loop structures completed (Chapters 4 and 5), we were able to provide case studies involving slightly more complex problems requiring several levels of decomposition. We also introduced another mechanism, the reference argument, for transmitting information between two functions. The reference argument provides an additional means (beyond the use of the return statement) for transmitting information from a called function back to its caller.

The argument list provides a highly visible communication path between two functions. By using arguments, we can cause different data to be manipulated by a function each time we call it, making the function easier to reuse within the current program or in another program. These arguments are used in three different ways, depending on the direction of communication that is desired. Input arguments are used to enable a calling function to pass information to a function it is calling. Output arguments are used by a function to return information to a calling function, and input/output arguments are used when bidirectional communication is required.

C++ uses a call-by-value argument passing mechanism (introduced in Chapter 3) to transmit information as input to a called function. Actual arguments corresponding to a call-by-value formal argument cannot be altered by the called function and therefore cannot be used to return values to the caller. The call-by-reference argument passing mechanism, designated by an ampersand (&) in the specification of a formal argument, is used to return results to a calling function. Thus, formal arguments used to represent output only or input/output data transmission must always be specified as call-by-reference. The actual argument corresponding to a value argument may be an expression, a variable, or a constant; the actual argument corresponding to a reference argument must always be a variable.

The patient, step-by-step practice of procedural abstraction and decomposition is a very important part of the process of building good software. We will continue to emphasize this process throughout the remainder of the text. Later in the text (Chapter 11), we will augment this procedural approach with an even more powerful idea involving the use of data-oriented abstraction and decomposition.

New C++ Constructs   The new C++ constructs introduced in this chapter are described in Table 6.5.

Table 6.5   **Summary of New C++ Constructs (functions with output arguments)**

CONSTRUCT	EFFECT
Function Prototype	

```
void function do_it
  (float,
   char,
   float&,
   char&);
```

Prototype for a function having 2 input and 2 output arguments.

Function Definition

```
void function do_it
  (float x,
   char op,
   float& y,
   char& sign)
{
   switch (op)
   {
      case '+': y = x + x; break;
      case '*': y = x * x; break;
   }  // end switch

   if (x >= 0.0)
      sign = '+';
   else
      sign = '-';
}  // end do_it
```

x and op are input arguments that contain valid values passed in from the calling function. The memory calls corresponding to the output arguments y and sign are undefined upon entrance to function do_it, but contain valid values that are passed back to the calling function upon exit.

(Continued)

Table 6.5 (Continued)

CONSTRUCT	EFFECT
Function Call Statement `do_it (-5.0, '*', y, my_sign)`	Calls function `do_it`. −5.0 is passed into x and '*' is passed into op. 25.0 is returned to y, and '-' is returned to `my_sign`.

✔ QUICK-CHECK EXERCISES

1. Actual arguments appear in a function _____ ; formal arguments appear in a function _____ .
2. Constants and expressions may be used as actual arguments corresponding to formal _____ arguments.
3. In a function header, _____ arguments must be used for function output and are designated by using the special character _____ following the type specifier.
4. A _____ must be used as an actual argument corresponding to a call-by-reference formal argument.
5. For _____ arguments, the argument's address is stored in the called function data area for the corresponding formal argument. For _____ arguments, the argument's value is stored in the called function data area for the corresponding formal argument.
6. Which of the following is used to test a function: a driver or a stub?
7. Which of the following is used to allow an upper-level function to be tested before all lower-level functions are complete: a driver or a stub?
8. What are the values of main function variables x and y after the function below executes?

```
void main ()
{
   // Functions used ...
   void silly
     (float);

   // Local data ...
   float x;
   float y;

   // Do something silly.
   silly (x);
}


void silly
  (float x)
```

```
    {
        // Local data ...
        float y;

        // This is something silly.
        y = 25.0;
        x = y;
    } // end silly
```

9. Answer Exercise 8 if argument x of silly is a reference argument.
10. Answer Exercise 8 if argument x of silly is a reference argument and the function call is changed to

```
    silly (y);
```

11. In what ways can a function return values to its caller?

Answers to Quick-Check Exercises

1. call; definition
2. value (or call-by-value)
3. reference (or call-by-reference), &
4. variable
5. call-by-reference; call-by-value
6. driver
7. stub
8. both x and y are undefined
9. x is 25.0; y is undefined
10. x is undefined; y is 25.0
11. A function can return values by using a return statement or by assigning the values to be returned to reference arguments.

REVIEW QUESTIONS

1. Write the prototype for a function called script that has three input arguments. The first argument will be the number of spaces to print at the beginning of a line; the second argument will be the character to print after the spaces; and the third argument will be the number of times to print the second argument on the same line.
2. Write a function called letter_grade that has a single integer argument called score and that returns the appropriate letter grade using a straight scale (90 to 100 is an A; 80 to 89 is a B; 70 to 79 is a C; 60 to 69 is a D; and 0 to 59 is an F). Be sure to include a validity check for score and to specify some appropriate action if score is not between 0 and 100 inclusive.
3. Why you would choose to make a formal argument a value argument rather than a reference argument?
4. Explain the allocation of memory cells when a function is called. Illustrate using an example.

5. Write the prototype for a function named `pass` that has two integer arguments. The first argument should be a value argument and the second a reference argument.
6. Explain the use of a stub in the top-down program development process.

PROGRAMMING PROJECTS

1. Write a program that computes and prints the fractional powers of 2 (1/2, 1/4, 1/8, and so on). The function should also print the decimal value of each fraction as shown below.

Power	Fraction	Decimal Value
1	1/2	0.5
2	1/4	0.25
3	1/8	0.125

Print all values through power equal to 10.

2. The assessor in your town has estimated the market value of all of the properties in the town and would like you to write a program that determines the tax owed on each property and the total tax to be collected. The tax rate is 125 mils per dollar of assessed value (a mil is 0.1 of a penny). The assessed value of each property is 28% of its estimated market value. (This assessed value is the value to be used in computing the taxes owed for each property.)

Design and implement a program for the town assessor. First develop the structure chart indicating the functions you will need and the relationships among them. Carefully develop the data tables for these functions, and be sure to add the input and output argument information to the structure chart. Test your program on the following market values:

$50,000	$48,000	$45,500	$67,000	$37,600	$47,100
$65,000	$53,350	$28,000	$58,000	$52,250	
$56,500	$43,700				

Your program should continue to read and process market values until a zero value is read. A meaningful, readable table of output values should be produced by your program. The table should consist of four columns of information: the initials of the owner of each property (three characters), the market value of each property, the assessed value, and the taxes owed. At the end of the table, the total taxes and the count of the number of properties processed should be printed. Don't forget to print column headers for your column output. Also, be sure to include some other information at the top of the assessor's report, such as the assessor's name, the name of your township, and the date of the report. You should provide separate functions at least for the following subproblems (and maybe more):

- display instructions to the user of your program;
- display the informational heading (name, date, etc.) at the top of the report;
- process all market values (and print table);
- display final totals.

3. The trustees of a small college are considering voting a pay raise for the 12 faculty. They want to grant a 5.5% pay raise; however, before doing so, they want to know how much this will cost. Write a program that will print the pay raise for each faculty member and the total amount of the raises. Also, print the total faculty payroll before and after the raise. Test your function for the salaries:

$42,500	$34,029.50	$46,000	$53,250
$45,500	$32,800	$40,000.50	$38,900
$53,780	$57,300	$54,120.25	$34,100

4. Redo Programming Project 3 assuming that faculty earning less than $30,000 receive a 7% raise, faculty earning more than $40,000 receive a 4% raise, and all others receive a 5.5% raise. For each faculty member, print the raise percentage as well as the amount.

5. Patients required to take many kinds of medication often have difficulty in remembering when to take their medicine. Given the following set of medications, write a function that prints an hourly table indicating what medication to take at any given hour. Use a counter variable clock to go through a 24-hour day. Print the table based on the following prescriptions:

Medication	Frequency
Iron pill	0800, 1200, 1800
Antibiotic	Every 4 hours starting at 0400
Vitamin	0800, 2100
Calcium	1100, 2000

6. A monthly magazine wants a program that will print out renewal notices to its subscribers and cancellation notices when appropriate. Using functions when needed, write a program that first reads in the current month number (1 through 12) and year (00 through 99). For each subscription processed, read in four data items: the account number, the month and year the subscription started, and the number of years paid for the subscription.

Read in each set of subscription information and print a renewal notice if the current month is either the month prior to expiration or the month of expiration. A cancellation notice should be printed if the current month comes after the expiration month.

Sample input might be:

10, 93   for a current month of October 1993
1364, 4, 91, 3   for account 1364 whose 3-year subscription began in April, 1991

7. The square root of a number N can be approximated by repeated calculation using the formula

$$NG = 0.5 \, (CG + N \, / \, CG)$$

where NG stands for next guess and CG stands for current guess. Write a function that implements this computation. The first argument will be a positive real number, the second will be an initial guess of the square root of that number, and the third will be the computed result.

The initial guess will be the starting value of CG. The function will compute a value for NG using the formula above. To control the computation, we can use a while loop. Each time through the loop, the difference between NG and CG is checked to see whether these two guesses are almost identical. If so, the function returns *NG* as the square root; otherwise, the next guess (*NG*) becomes the current guess (*CG*) and the process is repeated (i.e., another value is computed for *NG*, the difference is checked, and so forth).

For this problem, the loop should be repeated until the magnitude of the difference between *CG* and *NG* is less than 0.005 (Delta). Use an initial guess of 1.0 and test the function for the numbers 4.0, 120.5, 88.0, 36.01, and 10,000.0.

8. It is a dark and stormy night. Our secret agent (007) is behind enemy lines at a fuel depot. He walks over to a cylindrical fuel tank that is 20 feet tall and 8 feet in diameter. He opens a 2-inch-diameter circular nozzle. He knows that the volume of the fuel leaving the tank is

volume lost = velocity × (area of the nozzle) × time

and that

velocity = 8.02 × (height of fluid in the tank) × 0.5.

How long will it take to empty the tank?

Hint: Although this is really a calculus problem, we can simulate it with the computer and get a close answer. We can calculate the volume lost over a short period of time, such as 60 seconds, and assume that the loss of fluid is constant. We can then subtract the volume from the tank and determine the new height of the fluid inside the tank at the end of the minute.

We can then calculate the loss for the next minute. This can be done over and over until the tank is dry. Print a table showing the elapsed time in seconds, the volume lost, and the height of the fluid. At the very end convert the total elapsed seconds to minutes. The fluid height can be negative on the last line of the table.

9. Write a program to simulate a hand-held electronic calculator. (In other words, write a program that will cause your computer to behave as though it were a hand-held calculator.) Your program should execute as follows.

- Step 1: Display a prompt and wait for the user to enter an instruction code (a single character):

  '+' for addition   '-' for subtraction
  '*' for multiplication   '/' for division
  'p' for power (exponentiation)   's' for square root
  'c' to clear the current accumulator
       value (set the value to 0.0)
  'q' for quit

- Step 2 (if needed): Display a prompt and wait for the user to enter a type `float` number (which we will call the *left-operand*).
- Step 3 (if needed): Display a prompt and wait for the user to enter a type `float` number (which we will call the *right-operand*).
- Step 4: Display the accumulated result at any point during processing and repeat steps 1 through 3 (unless, of course, the instruction code 'q' was entered).

Use a separate function, `enter_code`, to prompt the user for the instruction code and to ensure that a valid code is entered. Also use a separate function, `enter_operand`, for the entry of the left-operand and the right-operand. Finally, use another function, `compute`, to perform the indicated operation (unless 'q' was entered).

7

Simple Data Types

7.1   Constants Revisited
7.2   Internal Representations of Integer, Floating-Point, and Character Data Types
7.3   Logical Expressions
7.4   Character Variables and Functions
7.5   Enumeration Types
7.6   Common Programming Errors
        Chapter Review

So far in your programming experience, you have used three of the *fundamental data types* of C++: int, float, and char. In this chapter we take a closer look at these data types and introduce several variants of the integer type, such as long and short integers. The forms in which these data types are stored in computer memory (their internal representations) will be examined and related to the forms that we commonly use (the external representations). Some new operators that can be applied to these types will be introduced. We will also introduce a new data type, the enumeration type. All of these data types (int, the variants on int, float, and char, and enumeration types) are characterized by the fact that only a single value can be stored in a variable of the type. Such types are often referred to as *simple* or *scalar* data types.

7.1 ___ CONSTANTS REVISITED

Additional Representations of Integers

We begin by re-examining the concept of constants in C++. Constant definitions have the form

const type *identifier* = *constant*;

where *constant* is normally of the same type as specified for the *identifier*.

There are three reasons for using constant identifiers. First, if we are careful in our choice of the identifier we use for a constant, it should be more recognizable than the constant itself. The identifier speed_of_light has more meaning than the value 2.998E+5. Second, declaring a constant identifier tells the compiler not to allow any changes in the value associated with the identifier.

A third benefit relates to the concern for writing good programs. It may be reasonable to expect that the constant associated with the speed of light will never change (unless the units of measurement or the precision change). However, other constants (such as city wage tax or federal tax bracket maximum and minimum values) may remain fixed for a long period of time but are subject to change when new legislation is passed. Once we associate a constant with an identifier (give the constant a name), we can subsequently refer to that constant by its identifier name, rather than its value. Any change in the specification of the value of the constant can be handled in the program by changing just one statement—the declaration of the constant. We would not be forced to search through the entire program looking for other uses of the constant value, an exercise that at best can be very time consuming and, at worst, quite prone to mistakes.

Example 7.1   Several sample constant declarations are illustrated below.

```
a) const int max = 100;
   const float speed_of_light = 2.998E+5;
   const char initial = 'A';
b) const short int age = 32;
   const long int mask = 8476376;
```

We have seen examples of the declarations shown in (a) in our earlier work; (b) illustrates two integer type declarations to be discussed further in the next section.   ∎

The #define Line

Another feature of C++ is useful in defining important constants in one place in a program. The #define line is a compiler directive that can be used to associate an identifier with a particular sequence of characters, called the *replacement-text*. The general form of the #define line follows:

```
#define identifier replacement-text
```

Once this line has appeared in a program, any occurrence of *identifier* (not enclosed in quotes and not part of another name) will be replaced by the associated *replacement-text* during compilation. The *identifier* has the same form as any C++ identifier. The *replacement-text* can be any sequence of characters. It is not a character string and is therefore not enclosed in quotes.

The #define is the second example of a compiler directive that we have seen so far; #include was the first compiler directive we introduced.

Example 7.2   In the Area and Circumference Problem (Section 3.1), we could replace the constant declaration

```
const float pi = 3.14159;
```

with the #define line

```
#define pi 3.14159
```

The remainder of the program would not change; all references to the identifier pi would be textually replaced by the floating-point constant 3.14159 during the compilation process. Note that pi is simply an identifier; it is not treated as a variable and has no storage associated with it. During compilation, the replacement text is substituted for the identifier wherever the identifier appears. A define line must begin with the symbol # and has no equal sign or ending semicolon.   ∎

The #define line was the only vehicle available for naming constants in earlier versions of the C language. However, with the addition of the constant declaration and enumerated types in C++, this device is needed only occasionally.

EXERCISES FOR SECTION 7.1

Self-Check

1. Which of the constants declared below are valid and which are invalid? Explain your answers briefly.

```
const int maxint = 32767;
const int minint = -maxint;
const char last_letter = 'Z';

const int max_size = 50;
const int min_size = max_size - 10;
const int id = 4FD6;

const int koffman_age = 47;
const int friedman_age = z59;

const float price = $3,335.50;
const float price = 3335.50;
const float price = "3335.50";
```

2. Why would you declare an identifier as a constant rather than as a variable?
3. Explain the difference between the #define line and the constant declaration.

7.2 —— INTERNAL REPRESENTATIONS OF INTEGER, FLOATING-POINT, AND CHARACTER DATA TYPES

In this section, we take a closer look at the different data types seen thus far and discuss the differences in their external and internal representations and their uses in programming.

Differences between Numeric Types

The data types int and float are used to represent numeric information. We have used integer variables as loop counters and to represent data, such as exam scores, that did not have fractional parts. In most other instances we used type float numeric data.

You may be wondering why it is necessary to have two numeric types. Can the data type `float` be used for all numbers? The answer is yes, but on many computers, operations involving integers are faster than those involving type `float` numbers and less storage space may be needed to store integers. Also, operations with integers are always precise, whereas there may be some loss of accuracy when dealing with type `float` numbers.

These differences result from the way in which type `float` numbers and integers are represented internally in your computer's memory. All data are represented in memory as strings of *binary digits* or *bits* (0s and 1s). However, the binary string stored for the integer 13 is not the same as the binary string stored for the type `float` number 13.0. The actual internal representation is computer-dependent, but the general forms are consistent in all computers. Compare the sample integer and floating-point formats shown in Fig. 7.1.

type int format	
sign	binary number

type float format		
sign	characteristic	mantissa

Figure 7.1   Internal forms of representation of type `int` and type `float` data

As shown in Fig. 7.1, integers are represented by a sign and a binary number. The sign is a single binary digit, either a 0 (for a nonnegative integer) or a 1 (for a negative integer).

The internal representation of floating-point data is analogous to scientific notation. Recall that in scientific notation, 3.57×10^3 referred to the same number as 3570. Similarly, 3.57×10^{-4} referred to 0.000357.

The storage area occupied by a floating-point number is divided into three sections: the sign (a single bit), the *characteristic,* and the *mantissa.* The mantissa is a binary fraction between 0.5 and 1.0 for positive numbers (between −0.5 and −1.0 for negative numbers). The characteristic is a power of 2. The mantissa and characteristic are chosen to satisfy the formula

$$type\text{-}float\text{-}number = 2^{characteristic} \times mantissa$$

Because the size of a memory cell is finite, not all floating-point numbers (in the mathematical sense) can be represented precisely in the range of type `float` numbers provided on your computer system. We will talk more about this later.

In addition to the capability of storing fractions, the range of numbers that may be represented in type `float` form is considerably larger than for the integer form. For example, positive type `float` numbers might be expected to range between 10^{-37} (a very small fraction) and 10^{+37} (a rather large number), whereas positive type `int` values might range from 1 to +32767 (2^{15}). The actual ranges are dependent on the particular C++ compiler and the computer you are using. Specifically, they depend on the number of binary digits that the compiler uses to store these different data types. This variation is caused by the fact that C++ does not specify the number of bits (length) for type `int` or `float` data. These lengths are *implementation-dependent;* that is, it is left to the discretion of the company that writes the particular compiler you are using.

Variations of Integer Types

C++ provides three sizes of integers, `short int`, `int`, and `long int`. The actual lengths corresponding to the sizes are implementation-defined. C++ does, however, place some restrictions on the lengths of *short integers* (minimum of 16 bits) and *long integers* (minimum of 32 bits). It also requires that the following must be true:

- short integers may be no longer than type `int` values;
- type `int` values may be no longer than long integers.

On most computers, short integers are 16 bits long and long integers are 32 bits long.

If you are writing a program for which correct execution depends on the number of bits used to store your integer data, use of the type modifiers `long` or `short` provides a greater assurance of consistency across compilers and can help make your program more portable. That is, it can help increase the likelihood that your program, written for one computer using one compiler, will compile and execute correctly on another computer. There are no iron-clad guarantees, however.

Both long and short integers are examples of *integral data types* in C++, that is, types that, like type `int`, have integer values. The use of short integers can save considerable space in programs with large volumes of integer data. However, as we have noted, the largest positive integer that may be stored in a short integer on most computers is $2^{15}-1$, or 32767. (Remember, one bit is used for the sign of the integer, leaving 15 bits to store the magnitude of the integer. See the Self-Check Exercises at the end of this section for more detail.) This may not always be sufficient for storing and manipulating your data.

Variations on Floating-Point Types

C++ provides three sizes of floating-point types: `float`, `double`, and `long double`. As with integers, these are implementation-defined, but with the following restrictions: `double` is no less precise than `float`, and `long double` provides no less precision than `double`. Some C++ compilers provide a `double` with approximately twice the precision as `float`, and a `long double` with twice the precision as `double`. Others are not so generous.

Types of Numeric Constants

The data type of a numeric constant is determined in the following way. If the constant has a decimal point, then it is considered to be of type `float`. For example, in the constant `2.998E+5` (read as 2.998×10^5), the scale factor is 10^5 or 100,000. A constant written with a decimal *scale factor* is also considered to be a floating-point type constant whether or not it has a decimal point. For example, the value `5E2` is considered type `float` (value is 500.0) because it has a scale factor. Every floating-point constant is considered to be of type `double` unless the suffix `1` or `L` is provided, in which case it is `long double`. For example, the constant `2.0L` is `long double`.

Value Ranges for Integer and Floating-Point Types

C++ provides names for the ranges of integer and floating-point types. Some of these names, their interpretations, and the values they represent are shown in Table 7.1. These definitions are included along with many others in the C++ `limits.h` and `float.h` libraries. It is important to note that the values shown in this table are acceptable minimum (or maximum) values for these constant identifiers. The actual values on your computer may be larger (or smaller). You should try to print the values associated with some of the names in this table to learn their values in your computing environment. This will help you determine the sizes used for the various integer and floating-point types just discussed.

Table 7.1   Special C++ Constants

	FROM `limits.h`	

Name	Value	Interpretation
CHAR_BIT	8	number of bits in a character type item
INT_MAX	+32767	maximum value of int (16 bits)
INT_MIN	−32767	minimum value of int (16 bits)
LONG_MAX	+2127483647L	maximum value of long integer (32 bits)
LONG_MIN	−2127483647L	minimum value of long integer (32 bits)
SHRT_MAX	+32767	maximum value of short integer (16 bits)
SHRT_MIN	−32767	minimum value of short integer (16 bits)

(Continued)

Table 7.1   (Continued)

FROM `limits.h`

Name	Value	Interpretation
FLT_DIG	6	number of decimal digits of precision (32-bit float type)
FLT_MAX	1E+37	maximum floating-point number
FLT_MIN	1E-37	minimum floating-point number
FLT_EPSILON	1E-5	minimum positive number x such that $1.0 + x$ does not equal 1.0
DBL_DIG	10	decimal digits of precision for `double`
DBL_EPSILON	1E-9	minimum positive number x such that $1.0 + x$ does not equal 1.0
LDBL_DIG	10	decimal digits of precision for `long double`

Review of Integer Division

In Section 2.6, we discussed the computation of integer quotients and remainders using the C++ divide (`/`) and modulus (`%`) operators with integer operands only. The division operator `/` yields the integer quotient of its first operand divided by its second; the modulus operator `%` yields the integer remainder of its first operand divided by its second (for example, 7 / 2 is 3, and 7 % 2 is 1). The next example illustrates the use of these operators.

Example 7.3   Function `print_digits_reversed` in Fig. 7.2 prints the individual decimal digits of its argument `number` in reverse order (e.g., if `number` is 738, the digits printed are 8, 3, 7). This is accomplished by printing successive remainders of `number` divided by 10. To preserve the original value of `number`, a local variable, `temp_number`, is used in the computation of these successive remainders. In each loop iteration, the integer quotient of `temp_number` divided by 10 becomes the new value of `temp_number` to be used in the next iteration. The function `abs` computes the absolute value of its integer operand; this function may be found in the libraries `math. h` and `stdlib.h`.

Figure 7.2   Printing decimal digits in reverse order

```
// FILE: DgtsRvrs.cpp

#include <math.h>          // for function abs()
#include <iostream.h>
```

(Continued)

Figure 7.2 (Continued)

```
// PRINTS THE DIGITS IN AN INTEGER IN REVERSE ORDER
void print_digits_reversed
   (int number)            // IN:  number to be printed digit by digit

// Pre : number is nonzero.
// Post: Each digit of number is displayed, starting with the
//       least significant one.
{
   // Local data ...
   const int base = 10;       // number system base

   int temp_number;           // local store for value of number / 10
   int digit;                 // contains each digit as computed

   // Determine and print each digit beginning with the least
   //    significant one.
   temp_number = abs(number);
   while (temp_number != 0)
   {
      digit = temp_number % base;   // get next digit
      cout << digit;
      // Get quotient for next iteration.
      temp_number /= base;
   }  // end while
   cout << endl;
   return;
}  // end print_digits_reversed
```

The local variable `temp_number` is used as the loop control variable. Within the `while` loop, the modulus operator `%` is used to determine the right-most digit of the number stored in `temp_number`. The division operator is used to compute the rest of the number (with the right-most digit "tossed away") to be used in the next iteration. The loop is exited when this number (in `temp_number`) becomes 0.

Table 7.2 shows a trace of the execution of `print_digits_reversed` for an actual parameter of 3704. The digits 4, 0, 7, and 3 are displayed in that order.

Table 7.2 Trace of Execution of `print_digits_reversed`: Initial Value of Number = 3704

temp_number	digit	STATEMENT	EFFECT
3704	?	temp_number = abs(number); while (temp_number != 0)	3704 != 0 is true

(Continued)

Table 7.2   (Continued)

temp_number	digit	STATEMENT	EFFECT
	4	`digit = temp_number % base;`	
		`cout << digit;`	print 4
370		`temp_number /= base;`	
		`while (temp_number != 0)`	370 != 0 is true
	0	`digit = temp_number % base;`	
		`cout << digit;`	print 0
37		`temp_number /= base;`	
		`while (temp_number != 0)`	37 != 0 is true
	7	`digit = temp_number % base;`	
		`cout << digit;`	print 7
3		`temp_number /= base;`	
		`while (temp_number != 0)`	3 != 0 is true
	3	`digit = temp_number % base;`	
		`cout << digit;`	print 3
0		`temp_number /= base;`	
		`while (temp_number != 0)`	0 != 0 is false
			exit loop

■

Numerical Inaccuracies

One of the problems in processing floating-point numbers is that sometimes an error occurs in representing floating-point data. Just as certain numbers cannot be represented exactly in the decimal number system (e.g., the fraction 1/3 is 0.333333...), so some numbers cannot be represented exactly in floating-point form in the computer. The *representational error* will depend on the number of binary digits (bits) used in the mantissa: The more bits, the smaller the error.

The number 0.1 is an example of a number that has such a representational error. The effect of a small error is often magnified through repeated computations. Therefore, the result of adding 0.1 ten times is not exactly 1.0. As a result, some loops, such as the one shown next, may fail to terminate on some computers.

```
trial = 0.0;
while (trial != 1.0)                 for(int trial = 0.0, trial != 1.0;
{                                              trial += 0.1)
    ...                                   {
                        or                     ...
    trial += 0.1;                         }  // end for
}  // end while
```

If the loop repetition test is changed to `trial < 1.0`, the loop may execute 10 times on one computer and 11 times on another. This is yet another reason why it is best to use integer variables whenever possible in loop repetition tests.

Other problems occur when manipulating very large or very small real numbers. In adding a large number and a small number, the larger number may "cancel out" the smaller number (resulting in a *cancellation error*). If X is much larger than Y, then X + Y may have the same value as X (e.g., 1000.0 + 0.0001234 is equal to 1000.0 on some computers).

If two very small numbers are multiplied, the result may be too small to be represented accurately, so it will be represented as zero. This phenomenon is called *arithmetic underflow.* Similarly, if two very large numbers are multiplied, the result may be too large to be represented. This phenomenon, called *arithmetic overflow,* is handled in different ways by C++ compilers. Arithmetic overflow can occur when processing very large integer values as well.

Example 7.4   The program in Fig. 7.3 draws a sine curve. It uses the C++ function `sin` (library `math.h`), which returns the trigonometric sine of its argument, an angle expressed in radians. As an illustration of the numerical inaccuracy that may result in performing real computations, examine the sine value displayed for angles of 180 and 360 degrees. The actual sine should be zero; the sine value computed is quite small (approximately 10^{-6}) in both cases—but it is not zero. Because the value of the constant `pi` is imprecise, the result of any computation involving `pi` will have a small numerical error.

The `while` loop in Fig. 7.3 executes for values of `theta` equal to 0, 18, 36, ... , 360 degrees. For each `theta`, the first assignment statement below

```
radians = theta * rad_per_degree;
indent = 4 + round (scale * (1.0 + sin (radians)), 0);
```

computes the number of radians corresponding to `theta`. Then the variable `indent` is assigned a value based on `sin(radians)`. This value increases from 4 (when `sin(radians)` is −1.0) to 44.0 (= 4 + `scale` × 2.0 when `sin(radians)` is 1.0). Finally the statement

```
cout << setw (indent + |) << star; // plot * in column indent
```

plots an asterisk somewhere in columns 4 through 44 as determined by the value of `indent`. `indent` is computed by applying the function `round` (see Fig. 7.4) to the scaled value to be plotted. Function `round` takes two input arguments, a floating-point value `x` and an integer `n`, and returns the value of `x` rounded to the nearest `n` decimal places.

The use of the casting operators `int` and `float` is discussed later in this section.

Figure 7.3   Plotting a sine curve

```cpp
// FILE: PlotSine.cpp
// PLOTS A SINE CURVE

#include <math.h>
#include <iostream.h>
#include <iomanip.h>

#include "round.cpp"

void main ()
{
   // Local data ...
   const float pi = 3.14159;
   const char blank = ' ';           // symbol for blank character
   const char star = '*';            // symbol used to mark plot
   const int scale = 20;             // scale factor for plot
   const int min_angle = 0;          // smallest angle
   const int max_angle = 360;        // largest angle
   const int step_angle = 18;        // increment in degrees

   int i;                            // loop control variable
   int theta;                        // angle in degrees
   int indent;                       // positions each column of *
   float radians;                    // angle in radians
   const float rad_per_degree = pi / 180.0; // radians per degree

   // Functions used ...
   // ROUND FLOATING POINT VALUE TO N PLACES
   float round
     (float,          // IN: value to be rounded
      int);           // IN: number of decimal places to be rounded

   // Plot sine curve.
   cout << "Theta" << setw (36) << "Sine Curve Plot " << endl
        << endl;
   theta = min_angle;                           // initial value of theta
   while (theta <= max_angle)
   {
      radians = theta * rad_per_degree;
      indent = 4 + round (scale * (1.0 + sin (radians)), 0);
      cout << setw (4) << theta << '|';
      cout << setw (indent + 1) << star; // plot * in column indent
      cout << setiosflags (ios::scientific | ios::showpoint)
           << setprecision (6)
           << setw (20) << sin (radians) << endl;
      theta += step_angle;                      // get next angle
   }
   cout << "-----------------------------------------------------";
   cout << "--" << endl;
```

(Continued)

Figure 7.3   (Continued)

```
    return;
}   // end main
```
──────── Program Output ────────

```
Theta                    Sine Curve Plot

    0|                        *            0.000000e+00
   18|                          *            3.090168e-01
   36|                            *            5.877849e-01
   54|                             *            8.090166e-01
   72|                              *            9.510562e-01
   90|                               *            1.000000e+00
  108|                              *            9.510569e-01
  126|                             *            8.090180e-01
  144|                           *            5.877867e-01
  162|                         *            3.090191e-01
  180|                       *            2.296763e-06
  198|                     *            -3.090145e-01
  216|                 *            -5.877830e-01
  234|             *            -8.090152e-01
  252|           *            -9.510554e-01
  270|          *            -1.000000e+00
  288|           *            -9.510577e-01
  306|             *            -8.090194e-01
  324|                 *            -5.877888e-01
  342|                     *            -3.090215e-01
  360|                       *            -4.593526e-06
     ----------------------------------------------------------
```

Figure 7.4   Function round

```cpp
// FILE: Round.cpp
// ROUNDS TYPE FLOAT NUMBER X TO NEAREST N PLACES (N >=0)

float round
   (float x,        // input: type float value to be rounded
    int n)          // input: number of decimal places (nonnegative)
{
   // Local data ...
   float half;              // holds -0.5 or +0.5
   float ten_to_n;          // pow (10.0, n)

   // Compute x to nearest n places.
   if (x < 0 )
      half = -0.5;
```

(Continued)

Figure 7.4 (Continued)

```
else
   half = 0.5;
ten_to_n = pow (10.0, n);

return float (int (x * ten_to_n + half)) / ten_to_n;
} // end round
```

■

PROGRAM STYLE

Checking Boundary Values

The discussion for Example 7.4 states that the value of `indent` ranges from 4 to 44 as the sine value goes from −1 to 1. It is always a good idea to check the accuracy of these assumptions; you can usually do so by checking the boundaries of the range, as shown below.

■ For `sin(radians)` equal to −1.0:

```
indent = 4 + round (scale * (1.0 + (-1.0)), 0)
       = 4 + round (20 * 0.0, 0)
       = 4
```

■ For `sin(radians)` equal to +1.0:

```
indent = 4 + round (20 * (1.0 + 1.0), 0)
       = 4 + round (20 * 2.0, 0)
       = 44
```

■

The Internal Representation of Character Values

The number of bits required to store a character value must be sufficient to store any member of the character set being used by your C++ language system. Three such character sets are illustrated in Appendix A. One of these, the ASCII (American Standard Code for Information Interchange) character set, is most often used in C++ systems. The discussion that follows assumes the use of this character set.

In C++, the value of a character is equivalent to the *numeric (integer) code* that represents the character. (These codes are shown for each character of each of the three sets in Appendix A.) Thus, the `char` data type is another example of an integral data type in C++.

We will assume a one-byte (8-bit) representation for character values. For our purposes, only the right-most seven bits (values 0 to 127) will be considered, and each of the characters—letters, digits, punctuation characters, and special characters (designated using the escape character \)—will have a value within this range.

Mixing Types: Integral Promotions, Numeric Conversions, and Type Casting

You have now been introduced to a variety of different fundamental types in the C++ language, including characters, several different types of integers, and the types `float` and `double`. You may have wondered what happens if these types are mixed when used in expressions or assignments. In Chapter 2 (Section 2.6), we first introduced the notion of mixed-type expressions and assignments as they related to type `int` and `float` data. In Chapter 3, we discussed the mixing of formal and actual argument types. We suggested that care should be taken to ensure that the types of all actual arguments in a function call exactly match those of the corresponding formal arguments.

C++ allows many uses of mixed types: in expressions, in assignment, and in argument passing. When data values of mixed type are used in expressions, the compiler examines the operands involved with each operation and *converts* (or *promotes*) mixed operands to make them all the same. For example, short integers and characters would be promoted to type `int`, type `int` to type `float`, and type `float` to `double`. The result of the operation is always the same as the type of the operands involved following promotion.

For example, in the expression

```
3 + x/2
```

where x is type `float`, the constant 2 is promoted to `float` before the division is performed. Because the result of the division is type `float`, the constant 3 would be promoted to `float` before the addition is performed.

All such conversions are intended to be *value-preserving*. For the most part, whatever integral conversions are performed (`char` to `int`, `short int` to `int`) will not alter the value of the data. This is also true when integers are converted to floating point, except that some loss of accuracy can occur because not all type `float` values can be precisely represented in the computer.

Conversions similar to those just described for expressions are performed whenever mixed assignments are specified. Again the conversions are intended to preserve value. Some examples of value-preserving assignment conversion are shown next. The variable x is assumed to be type `float`, i of type `int`, and ch as type `char`.

```
x = 3;          // The integer 3 is converted to 3.0.
x = 'A';        // x is assigned the ASCII value of character 'A':
```

```
                        //    'A' is converted to floating-point type;
                        //    x is equal to 65.0.
ch = 35;                // ch is assigned the character ('#') having the
                        //    ASCII value of 35.
print_int ('A'); // print_int has the prototype
                        //    void print_int (int);
                        //    The integer value 35 is printed.
```

Value preservation is often not the case with either assignment or argument passing when the type conversion is in the "other direction." In these cases, actual changes in value are likely to occur. For example, the assignment of a type float value to an integer variable will result in the *truncation* (chopping off) of the fractional part of the floating-point value (the assignment of the value 13.78 to the integer variable m stores the integer 13 in m). A few other examples are shown next.

```
i = 3.89;               // Floating-point value 3.89 is truncated.
                        //    The value stored in i is 3.
ch = 64.97;             // The floating-point value 64.97 is truncated.
                        // The character with ASCII value 64 (a '@') is
                        //    stored in ch.
print_int (27.7);  // The value 27 is printed.
```

Especially in the early stages of learning to program, we believe it is important for you to avoid mixing data types in expressions, assignments, and argument passing. Casting operators, such as int and float, can be used to ensure the use of matching data types in such cases. For example, to compute the floating-point average (average) of the sum of n floating-point values (where n is an integer), the following assignment might be written:

```
average = sum / float (n);
```

The *cast operator*, float, is applied to n using a functional notation to create a floating-point copy of n for use in the division operation. The floating-point result is then assigned to average. The value of n is not altered by the casting change.

Casting operators can be extremely useful in their own right, as illustrated in the next example.

Example 7.5   *Rounding to the Nearest n Decimal Places.*   As illustrated in Example 7.4, it is sometimes useful to be able to compute the value of a number rounded to the nearest n decimal places. In function round in Fig. 7.4, the expression

```
float (int ( x * ten_to_n + half)) / ten_to_n
```

uses the casting operators int and float to force *explicit type conversion*. For example, if x = 7.0862 and n = 2, the evaluation of this expression would proceed as shown in Fig. 7.5.

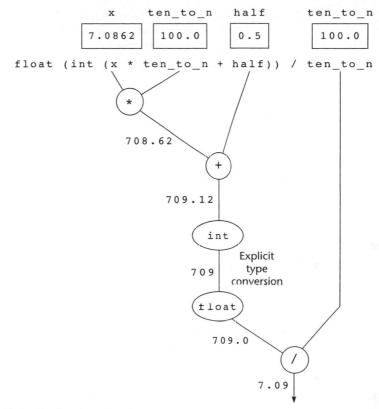

Figure 7.5 Evaluation tree for
`float (int (x *ten_to_n + half))/ten_to_n`

EXERCISES FOR SECTION 7.2

Self-Check   1. (Relating integer values to the number of bits used to store an integer) Consider a hypothetical C++ compiler that uses 8 bits to store all `int` data. What is the largest positive integer that may be stored (with sign) in a type `int` variable of size 2 bytes (16 bits)?
2. How does cancellation error differ from representational error?
3. Assume that the program shown in Fig. 7.3 has been modified to plot the C++ function `log` found in library `math.h`. Determine the largest and smallest values for `indent` using the assignment statement below as x goes from 0.1 to 5.0.

```
indent = 4 + round (scale * (1.0 + log (x)), 0)
```

Programming   1. Write a C++ program to print the largest integer and largest floating-point values that can be used on your computer system.

2. (Machine dependence and the importance of scratching below the surface—at least a little) Write a short program to print the value of FLT_DIG (see Table 7.1) and then enter a loop to do the following:

- prompt the user for a floating-point number x and an integer n (greater than or equal to zero)
- round the floating-point number x to the nearest n digits.

You might terminate the execution of your loop whenever a negative value of n is read.

Test your program by rounding several floating-point numbers, some to n_1 digits of accuracy (for any integer n_1 less than or equal to FLT_DIG) and some to n_2 digits (where n_2 is any integer value greater than FLT_DIG). Describe in English what happens and try to explain why. For example, if FLT_DIG is 6 for your computer, try rounding some values of a floating-point number to $n_1 \leq 6$ digits; try rounding some other floating-point numbers to $n_2 > 6$ digits.

7.3 ———— LOGICAL EXPRESSIONS

We first introduced logical expressions in Chapter 4 as conditions in if and while statements. In this section, we discuss how to *complement* a logical expression.

The logical operator ! (not) is used to form the complement or opposite of a condition. If a logical expression is nonzero (true), then its complement is zero (false) and vice versa.

Some facility in determining the complements of conditions may come in handy when you write if and while statements in C++. For example, certain expressions involving the use of the ! operator are more difficult to read and think about than an equivalent, *complement expression* written without the ! operator. We can complement a simple condition just by changing the relational operator as shown below.

Operator	Operator Used in Complement
<	>=
<=	>
>	<=
>=	<
==	!=
!=	==

For example, the complement of x <= y is x > y. Thus, if a simple expression such as !(x <= y) is used in a condition, its equivalent condition may be obtained by removing the ! operator and complementing the relational operator. In this example, this process would yield the simpler but equivalent condition x > y.

DeMorgan's theorem explains how to complement a compound logical expression:

1. write the complement of each simple logical expression;
2. change each && (and) to || (or) and each || to &&, respectively.

DeMorgan's Theorem (viewed in C++)

!($expression_1$ && $expression_2$)   !($expression_1$ || $expression_2$)
    is the same as   is the same as
!$expression_1$ || !$expression_2$!$expression_1$ && !$expression_2$

Another way to complement a logical expression is to precede the entire expression with the not operator. Table 7.3 shows the complements of some more complicated logical expressions as determined by applying DeMorgan's theorem.

Table 7.3   Complements of Logical Expressions

EXPRESSION	COMPLEMENT
x >= 1 && x <= 5	x < 1 || x > 5
!flag || x <= y	flag && x > y
flag && !swap	!flag || swap
n % m == 0 && flag	n % m != 0 || !flag
next == 'A' || next == 'a'	next != 'A' && next != 'a'
next == 'A' || next == 'a'	!(next == 'A' || next == 'a')

In Table 7.3, flag and swap are integer variables; next is type char; and x, y, m, and n are type int. In the complement of the expression on the first line, the relational operators are reversed (e.g., >= changed to <) and the operator && (and) is changed to || (or). The last two lines show two complements of the same expression. In the last line, the expression is complemented by simply inserting the logical operator ! (not) in front of the entire condition. Any logical expression can be complemented in this way.

EXERCISES FOR SECTION 7.3

Self-Check   1. Write the complements of the conditions below (assume the variables are all of type int).

a. x <= y && x != 15

b. x <= y && x != 15 || z == 7
c. x != 15 || z == 7 && x <= y
d. flag || !(x != 15)
e. !flag && x <= 8

Programming   1. Write a function that has two integer input arguments m and n and returns an integer value of 1 (true) when the value of m is a divisor of n and 0 (false) otherwise.

7.4 —— CHARACTER VARIABLES AND FUNCTIONS

C++ provides a character data type for storing and manipulating individual characters such as those that comprise a person's name, address, and other personal data. Character variables are declared using the type specifier char. A type char constant consists of a single character (a letter, digit, punctuation mark, or the like) enclosed in single quotes. A character value may be associated with a constant identifier or assigned to a character variable as shown next.

```
const char star = '*';
char next_letter;
next_letter = 'A';
```

The character variable next_letter is assigned the character value 'A' by the assignment statement (third line above). A single character variable or value may appear on the right-hand side of a character assignment statement. Character values may also be compared, read, and printed, as illustrated next.

Using Relational Operators with Characters

Assuming next and first are type char, the logical expressions

```
next == first
next != first
```

determine whether two character variables have the same or different values. Order comparisons can also be performed on character variables using the relational operators <, <=, >, >=.

To understand the result of an order comparison, you must know something about the way your computer represents characters internally. As discussed earlier in this chapter, each character has its own unique numeric code representing the value of the character. It is the binary form of this code that is stored in a character memory location.

If you examine the three tables of common character codes shown in Appendix A, you will see that the digit characters are an increasing sequence of characters in all three codes. For example, in ASCII, this sequence is consecutive—the digit characters '0' through '9' have code values of 48 through 57 (decimal). In all three cases, the order relationship shown below holds for the digit characters:

'0'<'1'<'2'<'3'<'4'<'5'<'6'<'7'<'8'<'9'.

The uppercase letters are also an increasing sequence of characters, but they are not necessarily consecutive. In ASCII, the uppercase letters have the decimal code values 65 through 90. The order relationship below holds for uppercase letters:

'A'<'B'<'C'<...<'X'<'Y'<'Z'.

If the lowercase letters are included in the character set, they are also an increasing, but not necessarily consecutive, sequence of characters. In ASCII, the lowercase letters have the decimal code values 97 through 122, and the order relationship below holds:

'a'<'b'<'c'<...<'x'<'y'<'z'.

In our examples and programs we will assume that the lowercase letters are included in the character set used in your C++ system. We will also assume that the digit characters are consecutive and that the upper- and lowercase sequences of letters are consecutive. You should check with your instructor or your user manual to verify that this is the case for your C++ system.

In ASCII, the *printable characters* have codes from 32 (the code for a blank or space) to 126 (the code for the symbol ~). The other codes represent nonprintable *control characters*. Sending a control character to an output device causes the device to perform a special operation, such as returning the cursor to column one, advancing the cursor to the next line, or sounding a beep.

Some Useful Character Functions

The C++ standard library ctype.h provides a number of useful character functions. These functions are explained in Table 7.4. The first two of these functions may be used to convert uppercase characters to lowercase (and vice versa). The remaining functions are used for testing characters. All of the test functions have a single character input argument, and all return an integer value (either nonzero (true) or zero (false)). The conversion functions (tolower and toupper) also have a single character input argument, but they return

Table 7.4   Some Character Functions from the Library `ctype.h`

FUNCTION	PURPOSE
`tolower (c)`	If `c` is uppercase, this function returns the corresponding lower-case letter. Otherwise, it returns `c`.
`toupper (c)`	If `c` is lowercase, this function returns the corresponding upper-case letter. Otherwise, it returns `c`.
`isalnum (c)`	Returns nonzero (true) if either `isalpha (c)` or `isdigit (c)` is nonzero. Otherwise, returns zero (false).
`isalpha (c)`	Returns nonzero if either `isupper (c)` or `islower (c)` is nonzero. Otherwise, returns zero.
`iscntrl (c)`	Returns nonzero if `c` is a control character. Otherwise, returns zero.
`isdigit (c)`	Returns nonzero if `c` is a digit character (`'0'`, `'1'`, `'2'`, ..., `'9'`). Otherwise, returns zero.
`isgraph (c)`	Returns nonzero if `c` is a printing character (other than a space). Otherwise, returns zero.[*]
`islower (c)`	Returns nonzero if `c` is a lowercase letter. Otherwise, returns zero.
`isprint (c)`	Returns nonzero if `c` is a printing character (including the space). Otherwise, returns zero.
`ispunct (c)`	Returns nonzero if `c` is a printing character other than a space, letter, or digit. Otherwise, returns zero.
`isspace (c)`	Returns nonzero if `c` is a space, newline, formfeed, carriage return, tab, or vertical tab. Otherwise, returns zero.
`isupper (c)`	Returns nonzero if `c` is an uppercase letter. Otherwise, returns zero.

[*] A printing character is any character in the ASCII table (Appendix A) between the space (ASCII value 32) and the tilde (~, ASCII value 126).

a character rather than an integer value. The use of some of these functions is illustrated in the examples that follow.

In most cases, the function `isdigit` described in this table produces the same result as the function `is_digit` defined in Section 6.2. However, as we mentioned in Section 6.2, `is_digit` will not return the correct result if the digit characters are not adjacent and arranged in sequence in the character set used in your C++ implementation.

Similarly, if `ch` is a character, then `isalpha(c)` produces the same result as `is_letter(c)` as long as the in-sequence assumption holds for the upper-case and for the lowercase letter. If this assumption does not hold for the character set in your implementation, then `is_letter` will not produce the desired result.

The following examples illustrate the use of a few of the functions in Table 7.4, as well as the definitions of new functions that return character and integer values. Several of the functions defined in these examples will be used later in solving larger problems.

Example 7.6   The integer function to_digit in Fig. 7.6 returns a 1 (true) if the input argument ch is a digit character (i.e., is one of the characters '0', '1', ..., '9'); otherwise, to_digit returns a 0 (false). The output argument, i, for this function will be used to return the equivalent integer form of ch, if this character is a digit. Otherwise, i will be assigned a value of −1.

Figure 7.6   Function to_digit

```
// FILE: ToDigit.cpp

#include <ctype.h>              // for isdigit ()

// DETERMINES THE EQUIVALENT INTEGER FORM OF ITS CHARACTER INPUT
int to_digit
   (char ch,                    // IN: the character to be converted
    int& i)                     // OUT: the integer form of ch (or -1)

// Pre : ch must be a digit character.
// Post: converts ch to a decimal digit.
// Returns: 1 (true) if ch is a digit character and 0 (false)
//          otherwise.  Also returns through the output argument
//          i the integer form of the character input argument
//          (or -1 if this character is not a digit).
{
   // Determine if ch is a digit character.
   if (isdigit (ch))
   {
      i = int (ch) - int ('0');
      return 1;
   }
   else
   {
      i = -1;
      return 0;
   }
}  // end to_digit
```

The type cast operator int is used in the first assignment statement to show explicitly that integer values are involved in the indicated subtraction operation. Although this particular use of the cast operator has no effect on the internal value of its character operand, it provides for program clarity and complete type consistency in the specified data manipulation. This clarity and consistency is an important aspect of programming in C++, and we will continue to follow this convention in the remainder of the text. We strongly urge you to do the same, even when not required by C++.

The subtraction indicated in the expression

```
int (ch) - int ('0')
```

is required to ensure that the correct integer form of ch is returned through the output argument i. The desired result would not be returned simply by assigning int (ch) to i. For example, if the ch were the digit character '7', the value of int (ch) would be 55 (the ASCII value of the character '7' is 55). On the other hand, the value of the expression int (ch) - int ('0') would be 55 − 48 = 7, which is the desired result.   ∎

Example 7.7   A *collating sequence* for characters is the ordering of characters according to their numeric codes. The program in Fig. 7.7 prints part of the C++ collating sequence for the ASCII character set. It lists the characters with numeric codes 32 through 126, inclusive. The first character printed is a blank (numeric code 32); the last one printed is the tilde (numeric code 126). These are precisely the C++ printing characters discussed in Table 7.4.

Figure 7.7   ASCII collating sequence illustration

```
// FILE: CollSeq.cpp
// PRINTS PART OF THE CHARACTER COLLATING SEQUENCE

#include <iostream.h>

void main ()
{
   // Local data ...
   const int min = 32;    // smallest numeric code
   const int max = 126;   // largest numeric code

   char next_char;        // character form of next_code (to be
                          //    printed)

   // Print sequence of characters.
   cout << "Program output ..." << endl;
   for (int next_code =  min; next_code <= max; next_code++)
   {
      next_char = char (next_code);
      cout << next_char;
      if (next_char == 'Z')
         cout << endl;
   }  // end for
   return;
}
```

∎

EXERCISES FOR SECTION 7.4

Self-Check   1. Evaluate the following C++ expressions using the ASCII character set.

```
a. int ('D') - int ('A')
b. char ((int ('M') - int ('A')) + int ('a'))
c. int ('m') - int ('a')
d. int ('5') - int ('0')
```

2. What is the purpose of the type cast operators `int` and `char` used in Self-Check Exercise 1?
3. What is the result of each of the following function references? (First indicate the type of the result, and then the actual value of the result.) Briefly explain your answers.

```
a. isdigit ('8');
b. isdigit ('A');
c. isdigit (7);
d. toupper ('#');
e. tolower ('Q');
f. to_digit ('6', i);   (indicate also what value is returned in i)
```

Programming   1. Write a short segment of C++ code that prompts the user to type a single-digit integer and repeats this prompt as necessary until the user enters a digit. Your code segment should read the user input as a character and call the function `to_digit` (from Fig. 7.5) to verify that a digit character was indeed typed, and to return its equivalent integer representation.

7.5 ———— ENUMERATION TYPES

In many programming situations, the `int`, `char`, and `float` data types are inadequate to provide the desired degree of program readability and understandability. In this section, we introduce a new data type, called an *enumeration type,* which can be used to improve program readability and understandability.

Example 7.8   In many of the programs presented thus far, we have used the integer constants 0 and 1 to represent the logical concepts false and true, respectively. For readability, we have often provided comments as reminders that 0 is being used to represent false and 1 to represent true. We can use enumeration types to make this association explicit. The declaration

```
enum logical {false, true};
```

creates a new data type `logical` that defines a positional association of the enumerators (listed in braces) with the integers 0 and 1 (`false` is associated with 0, and `true` is associated with 1). Once this association has been defined in a function, we can declare a variable of our new data type and write statements such as

```
flag = true;
```

or

```
status = false;
```

to assign meaningful values to integer variables being used as status flags. Although the actual values being assigned are still integers, the intent of the use of these integers as status flags is now clearer. Because `logical` is a new data type that can be defined by the programmer, it is sometimes referred to as a *user-defined data type*. ∎

Example 7.9 The enumeration type `day` declared below has the values `sunday`, `monday`, and so on.

```
enum day {sunday, monday, tuesday, wednesday,
          thursday, friday, saturday};  // days of the week
```

The first identifier in the *enumerator list* has the value 0; the second, the value 1; the third, the value 2, and so on. ∎

We can alter this *default association* by explicitly specifying a different association for some or all of the identifiers in an enumeration type, as shown in the following example.

Example 7.10 The 12 identifiers in the enumeration type `months` are associated with the constant integer values 1, 2, 3, ..., 12. When an associated value for an identifier in an enumeration type is specified, any unspecified values continue the progression from the last specified value.

```
enum months {jan = 1, feb, mar, apr, may, jun, jul, aug, sep, oct,
             nov, dec};
```
∎

Example 7.11 The 12 identifiers in the enumeration type `month_length` have the constant integer values specified. The identifiers `may_len`, `jul_len`, `oct_len`, and `dec_len` all have the value 31. The specification of the value for `sep_len` shows that expressions may be used as values, provided all elements of the expression are constants.

```
enum month_length {jan_len = 31, feb_len = 28, mar_len = 31,
                   apr_len = 30, may_len, jun_len = 30, jul_len,
                   aug_len = 31, sep_len = feb_len + 2, oct_len,
                   nov_len = 30, dec_len};
```

As this example shows, *enumerator values* used within the same enumeration need not be unique. However, identifiers within the same enumeration must be different, and no identifier may be used more than once in any enumeration within the same scope of definition. Thus, given the declaration for `months` just shown, the declaration

```
enum cold_months {nov, dec, jan, feb, mar};
```

appearing within the same scope as the declaration of `months` would cause a compiler error.   ∎

The points just illustrated are summarized in the next display.

C++
SYNTAX

Enumeration Type Declarations

Form: enum *enumeration-type* = {*enumerator-list*};

Example: enum class_id = {freshman, sophomore, junior,
                            senior};

Interpretation: A new, distinct integral data type (an *enumeration-type*) is declared. The values associated with this type are specified in the *enumerator-list*. The enumerators in the list may be either identifiers or of the form

identifier = constant-expression

Each enumerator is a constant, type `int` identifier defined within the scope containing the type declaration statement. (Normally, for our purposes in this text, this scope will be the function containing the declaration.) Unless explicitly indicated otherwise (using the *identifier = constant-expression* form), these values start at 0 and increase in steps of one. If not all values are specified, unspecified values continue in steps of one from the last specified value. Values in the same enumeration need not be distinct, but a particular identifier can appear in only one enumerator list within its scope of definition and must be distinct from any variable or constant name within that scope.   ∎

Example 7.12   In a budget program you might want to distinguish among several categories of expenditures: entertainment, rent, utilities, food, clothing, automobile, insurance, miscellaneous. Although you could create an arbitrary code that associates entertainment with a character value of `'e'`, rent with a character value of `'r'`, and so on, the use of enumeration types is clearly a preferred way of writing readable code. The declaration shown next defines a new type, `expenses`, as an enumeration type with eight enumerators . The variable, `expense_category`, is of type `expenses` and therefore can contain any of these eight enumerators.

```
enum expenses {entertainment, rent, utilities, food, clothing,
               automobile, insurance, other};
```

```
expenses expense_category;
```

These declarations can also be combined as shown below:

```
enum expenses {entertainment, rent, utilities, food, clothing,
               automobile, insurance, other} expense_category;
```

In either case, the following `if` statement can be used to test the value stored in `expense_category`.

```
if (expense_category == entertainment)
   cout << "Postpone until after your payday.";
else if (expense_category == rent)
   cout << "Pay before the first of the month!";
...
else if (expense_category == other)
   cout << "Do you really think you needed that?";          ■
```

Characters as Enumerator Values

Because characters also have integer values, character constants may also be used to specify the value of an enumerator. In this case, the value of the identifier in the enumerator is the value of the character's numeric code.

Example 7.13   Although it is fairly easy to remember the character descriptions of many of the special characters that we commonly use, we could define an enumeration type to associate names with each of these special characters, as shown next.

```
enum escape_chars {backspace = '\b', bell = '\a', newline = '\n',
                   return = '\r',    tab = '\t',  vtab = '\v'};     ■
```

The identifiers in an enumerator list have integer values and are considered by C++ as names for type `int` constants. Thus, each enumeration type declaration you use in a function defines another C++ integral type, in addition to the integer and character data types we have already seen. As with integers and characters, variables of an enumeration type may also be assigned type `int` values. However, usually only a small subset of these values are meaningful for a given enumeration type. For example, only the integer values 0 through 7 are meaningful for type `expenses`; 1 through 12 are meaningful for type `months`, and 0 through 6 are meaningful for type `day`. Attempts to assign values outside the meaningful range to an enumeration variable (such as assigning 10 to a variable of type `day`) can produce unpredictable results and should be discouraged. Some compilers may produce a warning message when such an assignment is attempted. However, this is not required.

Enumeration types behave like integers and thus may be used in C++ in much the same way as variables of the other integral types. For example, they may be used in `switch` and `for` statements.

Example 7.14   The `switch` statement shown next provides a clear and convenient way to represent the multiple decision shown in Example 7.12.

```
switch (expense_category)
{
case entertainment:
   cout << "Postpone until after your payday.";
   break;
case rent:
   cout << "Pay before the first of the month!";
   break;
...
case other:
   cout << "Do you really think you needed that?";
   break;
}
```

■

Example 7.15   The following `switch` statement can be used to execute different processing code for vowels versus consonants.

```
switch (ch)
{
   case 'b': case 'c': case 'd': case 'f': case 'g': case 'h':
   case 'j': case 'k': case 'l': case 'm': case 'n': case 'p':
   case 'q': case 'r': case 's': case 't': case 'v': case 'w':
   case 'x': case 'z':
      // Process a consonant.
      break;
   case 'a': case 'e': case 'i': case 'o': case 'u':
      // Process a vowel.
      break;
   case 'y':
      // Process however you want.
      break;
}
```

■

Example 7.16   We can use enumeration type variables as loop control variables in `for` statements. The `for` loop in Fig. 7.8 reads hours worked during each weekday for an employee and accumulates the sum of the hours worked in `weekly_hours_sum`. Assuming that the loop control variable `today` is of the enumeration type `day`, the loop executes for values of `today` equal to `monday` through `friday`.

Figure 7.8   Accumulating hours worked for one week

```
cout << "At prompt, enter hours for one day of the week ";
     << "(MO, TU, ... SU)." << endl;
cout << "After each entry, press RETURN." << endl;
```

(Continued)

Figure 7.8 (Continued)

```
weekly_hours_sum = 0.0;
for (today = monday; today <= friday; today++)
{
    cout << "Enter hours: ";
    cin >> hours;
    weekly_hours_sum += hours;
}  // end for

cout << "Total weekly hours: " << weekly_hours_sum << endl;
```

∎

Comparisons Involving Enumeration Types

The order relationship among the identifiers of an enumeration type is fixed when the enumeration type is declared. For example, for types **day** and **expense**, the following ordering relationships are all true:

```
sunday < monday
wednesday != tuesday
wednesday == wednesday
wednesday >= tuesday
entertainment < rent
other >= automobile
utilities != food
jan_len == mar_len
```

Distinctions among Integral Types

When using enumeration types, it is important to remember that each declaration of an integral type is different from all the others (and therefore also different from the **int** type). These different types cannot be mixed in an expression. Thus the expression

```
entertainment + wednesday
```

and the order relation

```
entertainment < wednesday
```

each would cause a syntax error because the values shown are associated with two different enumeration types. Note, however, that the expression

```
int (entertainment) + int (wednesday)
```

and the order relation

```
int (entertainment) < int (wednesday)
```

are legal, because both involve the use of type int operands. (From a problem point of view, however, it might be difficult to make any sense of either.)

Reading and Writing Enumeration Type Values

Enumeration types are defined by the programmer; thus, their values are not known in advance, and the C++ input/output systems cannot read or write these values. However, you can write your own functions for this purpose. The next example illustrates one approach to displaying the value of an enumeration variable in a readable form.

Example 7.17 Function write_color in Fig. 7.9 prints a character string that represents a value of type color. If the value of eyes is defined, the statement

```
write_color (eyes);
```

displays the value of eyes as a string. This function returns the status back to the calling function, informing the caller of its success or failure in attempting to print the correct string. Make sure you understand the difference between the string "blue" and the constant identifier blue.

Figure 7.9 **Function to print a value of type** color

```
// FILE: DispEnum.cpp

#include <iostream.h>

enum color {red, green, blue, yellow};

// DISPLAYS THE VALUE OF this_color
int write_color
  (color this_color)        // IN: color to be printed as string

// Pre : this_color is assigned a value.
// Post: The value of this_color is displayed as a string.
// Returns: Status flag indicating if execution successful.
{
   // Local data ...
   int status;       // indicates if function executes successfully

   // Print correct color as string literal.
   status = 1;  // true
```

(Continued)

Figure 7.9   (Continued)

```
switch (this_color)
{
   case red:
      cout << "red";
      break;
   case green:
      cout << "green";
      break;
   case blue:
      cout << "blue";
      break;
   case yellow:
      cout << "yellow";
      break;
   default:
      status = 0;        // false
      cerr << "*** ERROR: Invalid color for value." << endl;
} // end switch
return status;
} // end write_color
```

With the case statement shown in Fig. 7.9 (having enumerated constants as case labels), we take this opportunity to remind you not to give in to the temptation to use a character string (such as "green") as a case label. Enumerators are allowed as case labels; character strings are not.

Motivation for Using Enumeration Types

At this point you may have a legitimate concern as to whether it is worth using enumeration types. The fact is that the use of enumeration types in a program can make that program considerably easier to read and understand.

Example 7.18   The switch statement

```
switch (day_num)
{
   case 6:
      pay_factor = 1.5;   // time and a half for Saturday
      break;
   case 7:
      pay_factor = 2.0;   // double pay for Sunday
      break;
   default:
      pay_factor = 1.0;   // regular pay
}
```

might appear in a payroll program without enumeration types if `saturday` and `sunday` are "encoded" as the integers 6 and 7, respectively. If we use the enumeration type `day` and variable `today` (type `day`), we can write this statement as

```
switch (today)
{
   case saturday:
      pay_factor = 1.5;
      break;
   case sunday:
      pay_factor = 2.0;
      break;
   default:
      pay_factor = 1.0;    // regular pay
}
```

The second form is obviously more readable because, instead of an obscure code, it uses enumerators (`saturday` and `sunday`) that are meaningful to the problem. Consequently, the comments on the right in the first version of the `switch` are not needed. ∎

EXERCISES FOR SECTION 7.5

Self-Check

1. Given the enumeration type `expenses` as defined in Example 7.12, for which integer values of the type `int` variable `i` will the expression

   `expense_category (i)`

   produce a meaningful result?

2. Evaluate each of the following, assuming before each operation that `today` (type `day`) is `thursday`.

   a. `int (monday)` b. `int (today)`
   c. `today < tuesday` d. `day (int (wednesday) + 1)`
   e. `wednesday + monday` f. `int (today) + 1`
   g. `today >= thursday` h. `wednesday + thursday`

3. Indicate whether each sequence of type declarations below (a., b., c., or d.) is valid or invalid. Explain what is wrong with each invalid sequence.

   a. `enum logical {true, false};`
   b. `enum letters {A, B, C};`
      `enum two_letters {A, B};`
   c. `enum day {sun, mon, tue, wed, thu, fri, sat};`
      `enum week_day {mon, tue, wed, thu, fri};`
      `enum week_end {sat, sun};`
   d. `enum traffic_light {red, yellow, green};`
      `int green;`

Programming

1. Given the enumeration type `months`, rewrite the `if` statement below assuming that `current_month` is type `months` instead of type `int`. Also, write the equivalent `switch` statement.

```
if (current_month == 1)
    cout << "Happy new year." << endl;
else if (current_month == 6)
    cout << "Summer begins." << endl;
else if (current_month == 9)
    cout << "Back to school." << endl;
else if (current_month == 12)
    cout << "Happy holidays." << endl;
```

2. Write function write_day for enumeration type day.

7.6 ____ COMMON PROGRAMMING ERRORS

- *Unbalanced or Missing Parentheses:* Considerable care is required when writing complicated expressions, especially those involving the use of parentheses. Two kinds of errors are most prevalent: omitting pairs of parentheses and unbalanced parentheses.

  - *Omitting pairs of parentheses:* This error will often go undetected by the compiler because the resulting expression may well be syntactically legal even though it is logically incorrect. For example, the statement

    $$m = y_2 - y_1 / x_2 - x_1$$

    might be intended to compute the slope of a line through two points, (x_1, y_1) and (x_2, y_2), in the xy-plane. Yet because of the missing parentheses, the expression will actually compute m as

    $$y_2 - (y_1 / x_2) - x_1$$

    rather than

    $$\frac{y_2 - y_1}{x_2 - x_1}$$

  - *Unbalanced parentheses:* The omission of a single left or right parenthesis is also quite common in programming. This error will be detected by the compiler, causing a message such as "parse error before)" or "parse error before ?". The first error usually indicates a missing left parenthesis; the second usually indicates a missing right parenthesis. The part of your program appearing in place of the ? represents the point in your program code at which the missing right parenthesis was finally detected.

    To help prevent such errors in the use of parentheses, it is important to study the C++ operator precedence rules summarized in Appendix D.

In addition, it sometimes helps to break a complicated expression into subexpressions that are separately assigned to *temporary variables*, and then to manipulate these temporary variables. For example, it may be easier to write correctly the three assignment statements

```
temp1 = sqrt (x + y);
temp2 = 1 + temp1;
z = temp1 / temp2;
```

than the single assignment statement

```
z = sqrt (x + y) / (1 + sqrt (x + y));
```

which has the same effect. Using three assignment statements is also more efficient because the square root operation is performed only once; it is performed twice in the single assignment statement above.

- *Missing Operators:* When writing mathematical expressions such as

$$y = mx + b$$

or

$$d = b^2 - 4ac$$

in C++, it is easy to forget the multiplication that is implied. C++ assignments such as

```
y = mx + b;
```

or

```
d = b * b - 4.0ac;
```

are incorrect representations of the original formulas. The second of these assignments will cause at least one `"missing operator"` error message from the compiler. The first assignment may or may not cause an error. If there happens to be a variable `mx` already declared in the function containing this assignment, no error will be generated because the appearance of `mx` in the expression would be a legal reference to this variable. If no such variable `mx` has been declared in the function, an `"undeclared or undefined variable"` message would be produced.

- *Mixing Operators and Operands of Different Types:* It is easy to make mistakes when writing expressions using mixed data types. To make matters worse, most errors of this nature are not detected by the compiler. Thus, for example, the expressions `'3' + '4'` and `gross_pay != '3'` (`gross_pay` of type `float`) are syntactically correct but will likely yield an unexpected and undesirable result at execution time.

The best advice we can give for avoiding these problems is not to mix data types in the first place. Instead, use the casting operators discussed earlier in this chapter to ensure that you have explicitly specified all conversions desired.

■ *Operator Precedence Errors:* Because of the operator precedence hierarchy in C++, very little use of parentheses is normally required when writing expressions involving relational and equality operators. The one major exception lies in the use of the not operator, !, which has a higher precedence than most of the other operators used to this point. Care must be taken to ensure that the scope of application of this operator is as desired for your problem. For example, if x is nonzero (true) and y is 0 (false), then !x && y is false, but !(x && y) is true.

The precedence of all operators used in this text is summarized in Appendix D. Note that the unary operators have a higher precedence than the others [except the parentheses ( )] and that they associate right to left. Expressions such as

```
-5.0 <= x && x <= 5.0
```

may be written correctly without parentheses. You may, however, find such expressions easier to read when parentheses are used:

```
(-5.0 <= x) && (x <= 5.0)
```

■ *Using Enumeration Types:* When declaring enumeration types, remember that only identifiers can appear in the list of values for an enumeration type. Strings, characters, and numbers are not allowed. Make sure that the same constant identifier does not appear in more than one enumeration-type declaration in a given declaration scope. Remember that there are no standard functions available to read or write the values of an enumeration type. You will need to write your own when printing such values is required.

C++ treats enumeration and `char` data as integral data types (having integer values). Therefore, it is permissible to perform the standard arithmetic and relational operations on values of these data types. You must be careful, however; neither the compiler nor the run-time system will attempt to verify that the results of the arithmetic operations fall within the range of meaningful values for these types. Remember, each enumeration type you define, as well as the `char` type, are considered to be different integral types. Thus elements of different enumeration types or of `char` should not be mixed in the same arithmetic or relational expression.

Note that you cannot assign a type `int` value to an enumeration type without first applying the appropriate type casting operator. Thus for the variable `today` of type `day`, the statement

```
today = i;
```

(for an i of type `int`) must be written as

```
today = day (i);
```

where i is first recast to type `day` before the assignment takes place.

CHAPTER REVIEW

In this chapter, we reviewed the manipulation of simple data types, including the standard types—short int, int, long int, float, double, and char—and user-defined enumeration types. We discussed the internal representation of these simple types as well as the differences between the numeric types, int and float, and the enumeration types and char.

The finite capacity of computer memory introduces representational inaccuracies and limitations. Floating-point arithmetic is inherently less precise because not all type float numbers can be represented precisely. Other sources of numerical errors, such as cancellation error and arithmetic overflow and underflow, can occur due to the finite nature of computer memory.

More topics related to the character data type were presented, and the character function library ctype.h was introduced. The use of the relational and equality operators (<=, >=, <, >, ==, !=) and the logical operators (&&, ||, !) were elaborated further. DeMorgan's theorem, which describes how to form the complement of a logical expression, was presented. A number of examples illustrating the declaration and use of enumeration types to make programs more readable and understandable were presented.

New C++ Constructs The new C++ constructs introduced in this chapter are described in Table 7.5.

Table 7.5 Summary of New C++ Constructs

CONSTRUCT	EFFECT
Integer Variants	
const long int big = 123456789L;	a long integer constant
const short int small = 32;	a short integer constant
Floating-Point Variants	
double x;	provides additional accuracy over float
Enumeration Types	
enum coins {penny, nickel, dime, quarter, half_dollar};	

✔ QUICK-CHECK EXERCISES

1. a. Evaluate the logical expression

    1 && ((30 % 10) == 0)

b. Is the outer pair of parentheses required?

c. What about the inner pair?

d. Write the complement of this expression.

2. a. Evaluate the following assignment for k = 13 (an integer) and an integer m.

```
m = 2.5 + k / 2
```

b. Reevaluate this assignment assuming m is type `float`.

3. What is the value of each of the following in ASCII?

a. `char (int ('a'))`   b. `char (int ('a') + 3)`

c. `char (int ('z') - 20)`   d. `char (int ('z') - 40)`

e. `int ('z') - 40`   f. `ch - '0'` (where ch is any digit character)

4. What is the value of `'9' - '0'`? Is this answer the same for all C++ compilers? What about `'z' - 'a'`?

5. Can an enumerator of the enumeration type `day` be assigned to a variable of another enumeration type? (In other words, is the assignment `today = entertainment` valid if `today` is a variable of type `day` and `entertainment` is an enumerator of type `expense`?)

6. If two variables are not of the same integral type (`int`, `long int`, `char`, enumeration, and so on),

a. can they be mixed in the same arithmetic expression?

b. can one be assigned to the other?

7. Under what condition can a type `int` variable or value be assigned to a variable of an enumeration type?

8. What is wrong with the following enumeration type declaration?

```
enum prime {2, 3, 5, 7, 11, 13};
```

Answers to Quick-Check Exercises

1. a. true   b. outer not needed   c. inner not needed
   d. `false || !((30 % 10) == 0)`

2. a. 8; 13/2 is an integer 6; the 6 is converted to `float` and added to 2.5, yielding 8.5; when 8.5 is stored in the integer m, the fractional part is lost

   b. 8.5; 13 /2 is still an integer 6; the 6 is converted to float and added to 2.5, yielding 8.5; since m is type `float`, the entire number, 8.5 is stored in m

3. a. `'a'` b. `'d'` c. `'f'` d. 'R'
   e. 82   f. the result is the integer form of the character—e.g., 7 if ch = `'7'`

4. 9; no—the subtraction assumes the digit characters are in sequence in the implementation character set; 25 on ASCII and CDC character sets but not on EBCDIC.

5. no

6. a. Yes, but carefully. Remember that these data are each considered to be different C++ types and are subject to the C++ conversion/promotion given earlier in the chapter.

   b. The same applies to assignment except that integer type values may not be assigned to variables of enumeration types.

7. only if the enumerated variable's type cast is applied to the type int variable or value (e.g., today = day (i);)
8. Integers are not allowed as enumerators in enumeration types.

REVIEW QUESTIONS

1. What are the advantages of data type int over data type float?
2. List and explain three computational errors that may occur in type float expressions.
3. a. Write an enumeration type declaration for fiscal as the months from July through June.
   b. Write an enumeration type declaration for winter as December through February.
4. Write functions for writing values for variables of type season:

   enum season {winter, spring, summer, fall};

5. Write a for loop that runs from 'Z' to 'A' and prints only the consonants. Include 'Y' in this collection.
6. Write a switch statement that tests to see if the type day variable today is a working day. Print the message "Workday" or "Weekend".
7. Write an if statement that will write out true or false according to the following conditions: either flag is 1 or color is red, or both money is plenty and time is up.
8. Write the statement to assign a true value to the integer variable over_time only if a worker's weekly hours are greater than 40.
9. a. Write the C++ instructions to determine whether the value for 'a' is greater than the value for 'z'.
   b. What is the value of this expression?
10. Write the C++ statements necessary to enter an integer between 0 and 9, inclusive, and convert it to an equivalent character value (e.g., 0 to '0', 1 to '1') to be stored in a character variable dig_char.

PROGRAMMING PROJECTS

1. An integer n is divisible by 9 if the sum of its digits is divisible by 9. Recall that we used the modulus operator % in function print_digits_reversed (Fig. 7.2) to print the digits in a number one at a time in reverse order. Develop a program to determine whether or not the following numbers are divisible by 9:

   $n = 154368$
   $n = 621594$
   $n = 123456$

2. Redo Programming Project 1 by reading each digit of the number to be tested into the type char variable digit. Form the sum of the numeric values of the digits. *Hint:* The numeric value of digit is (int) digit - (int) '0'.

3. If a human heart beats on an average of once a second (60 beats per minute), how many times does the heart beat in a lifetime of 78 years? (Use 365.25 for the number of days in a year.) Rerun your program for a heart rate of 75 beats per minute. Implement the program first using beats per minute and years as integers and total beats and all constants as type `double`. Then try changing all type `double` data to type `float` and see what happens. Can you explain the difference (if any) in the execution output of the two versions?

4. A number is said to be *perfect* if the sum of its divisors (except for itself) is equal to itself. For example, 6 is a perfect number because the sum of its divisors (1 + 2 + 3) is 6. The number 8 is said to be *deficient* because the sum of its divisors (1 + 2 + 4) is only 7. The number 12 is said to be *abundant* because the sum of its divisors (1 + 2 + 3 + 4 + 6) is 16. Write a program that lists the factors of the numbers between 1 and 100 and classifies each number as perfect, deficient, or abundant.

5. Find out how to access the printer from a C++ program running on your computer system. Write a program for generating a bar graph on the printer summarizing the rainfall in Bedrock for one year. Include the average monthly rainfall and the maximum monthly rainfall during the year as part of the program output.

Prompt the user for the amount of rainfall for a particular month and instruct the computer to send an appropriate output line to the printer. Assume that no one month will have more than 14 inches of rainfall. Your graph should resemble Fig. 7.10.

```
January     |* * * * * * * * * * * * * * * * *
            |
February    |* * * * * * * * * * * *
            |
March       |
            |
December    |* * * * * * * * * * * * * * * * * * * * * * * * * * * * * * * * * *
            | -----1-----2-----3-----4-----5-----6-----7-----8-----9...

                        Inches of Rainfall
```

Figure 7.10   Bar graph for inches of rainfall

Write functions corresponding to prototypes shown below as part of your solution.

```
// WRITE THE MONTH VALUE AS A STRING
void write_month
    (int);              // IN: month to be written as a string


// GET RAINFALL FOR MONTH; UPDATE TOTALS
void get_monthly_total
    (int                // IN: current month
     float&,            // OUT: inches of rain for month
     float&,            // INOUT: max inches of rain
     float&);           // INOUT: total inches of rain

// User is prompted for inches of rainfall during a month.
```

```
// Max inches and total inches are updated so that they contain
//     the maximum and the total inches of rainfall input so far.


// DRAW BAR OF LENGTH GIVEN BY INCHES
void draw_bar
  (int,          // IN: the month to be written as a string
   float);       // IN: the inches of rain for the month
// Draw a bar whose length is computed from inches with label
//     determined by the value of month.


// DRAW SCALE AND LABEL AT BOTTOM OF GRAPH
void draw_scale_line ();
```

6. The interest paid on a savings account is compounded daily. This means that if you start with `startbal` dollars in the bank, at the end of the first day you will have a balance of

   `startbal` $* (1 + \text{rate}/365)$

   dollars, where `rate` is the annual interest rate (0.10 if the annual rate is 10 percent). At the end of the second day, you will have

   `startbal` $* (1 + \text{rate}/365) * (1 + \text{rate}/365)$

   dollars, and at the end of n days you will have

   `startbal` $* (1 + \text{rate}/365)^n$

   dollars. Write a program that processes a set of data records, each of which contains values for `rate`, `startbal`, and n and computes the final account balance.

7. Experiments that are either too expensive or too dangerous to perform are often simulated on a computer when the computer is able to provide a good representation of the experiment. Find out how to call the random-number generator (usually a function returning a floating-point value in the range 0 to 1) for your C++ system (look up the functions `rand` and `srand` in the library `stdlib.h`). Write a program that uses the random-number generator to simulate the dropping of glass rods that break into three pieces. The purpose of the experiment is to estimate the probability that the lengths of the three pieces are such that they might form the sides of a triangle.

   For the purposes of this experiment, you may assume that the glass rod always breaks into three pieces. If you use the line segment 0 to 1 (on the real number line) as a mathematical model of the glass rod, a random-number generator (function) can be used to generate two numbers between 0 and 1 representing the coordinates of the breaks. The triangle inequality (the sum of the lengths of two sides of a triangle are always greater than the length of the third side) may be used to test the length of each piece against the lengths of the other two pieces.

   To estimate the probability that the pieces of the rod form a triangle, you will need to repeat the experiment many times and count the number of times a triangle can be formed from the pieces. The probability estimate is the number of successes divided by the total number of rods dropped. Your program should prompt the user for the number of rods to drop and allow the experiment to be repeated. Use a sentinel value of −1 to halt execution of the program.

8

Formatting and Files

8.1   The Standard Input/Output Streams

8.2   Streams and External Files

8.3   Accessing and Using External Files

8.4   Using External File Functions: An
       Example
       CASE STUDY: Preparing a Payroll File

8.5   Putting It All Together
       CASE STUDY: Preparing Semester Grade
       Reports

8.6   Stream I/O Manipulator Functions and
       Flags

8.7   Common Programming Errors
       Chapter Review

This chapter is devoted to a discussion of the concepts of files and streams in C++. The features presented are part of the input and output facilities provided by the C++ libraries that support stream input and output (for example, `iostream.h` and `iomanip.h`). We will focus on four main issues:

- files, streams, and the connection between them;
- stream output;
- stream input;
- formatting.

We begin with a discussion of files and streams.

8.1 —— THE STANDARD INPUT/OUTPUT STREAMS

A *stream* is a sequence of characters. To this point in the text, all input and output has been implemented using the *standard output stream* (named `cout`) and the *standard input stream* (named `cin`). Every C++ program has these streams available automatically (as long as you include the `iostream.h` header). As you have probably guessed by now, the stream `cin` is normally connected to your keyboard and `cout` is usually connected to your display. Reading characters from the standard input stream `cin` is equivalent to reading from the keyboard; writing characters to the standard output stream `cout` is equivalent to displaying these characters on your screen.

All stream input/output facilities are concerned with converting typed data (`float`, `int`, etc.) to a stream of characters (for output) and converting streams of characters to typed data (for input). This conversion is illustrated in Fig. 8.1 for the streams `cin` and `cout`.

As shown in Fig. 8.1, all typed data specified in an output instruction is converted to characters and "inserted into" the output stream (`cout`). Conversely, an input instruction specifies that we "extract from" the keyboard all data (a stream of characters) entered and convert and store these data in the specified typed storage locations. The output operator `<<` is intended to suggest that information is being "inserted into a stream"; the input operator `>>` suggests "extracting information from a stream."

Any character, whether printable or not, may be read from or written to a stream. Thus the nonprintable characters, such as `'\a'` and `'\n'` may also be read from or written to streams. As their name suggests, these characters are not printed. Rather, on many computers, they cause special actions to occur, such as sounding a beep (`'\a'`) or moving the cursor to the beginning of the next line on your screen (`'\n'`). In this chapter, we will need to represent only the newline character (`'\n'`) in a stream. We will use the symbol `<nwln>` for this purpose, as shown in the next example.

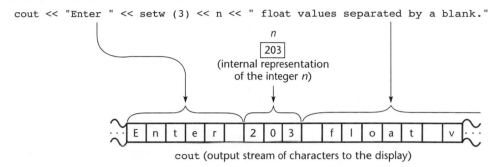

Output conversion (from internal representation to characters)

cout << "Enter " << setw (3) << n << " float values separated by a blank."

cout (output stream of characters to the display)

Input conversion

cin >> month >> day >> year;

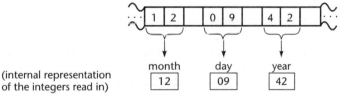

cin (stream of characters entered at the keyboard)

Figure 8.1   **Conversion of data to and from streams**

Example 8.1   *Streams as a Sequence of Lines.*   The newline character partitions a stream into a sequence of lines. For example, the following represents a stream of two lines of data consisting of letters, blank characters, ' . ' (a period), and ' ! ' (an exclamation point).

This is a stream!<nwln>It would be displayed as two lines.<nwln>

The <nwln> character separates one line of data in the stream from the next. The letter I following the first <nwln> is the first character of the second line. If we were to display this stream, each <nwln> character would cause a *line feed* and a *carriage return*, ensuring that everything that follows it would appear at the beginning of a new line. The displayed stream would appear as follows:

This is a stream!
It would be displayed as two lines.   ■

A stream has no fixed size. As we write (insert) information to a stream, we are simply adding characters to the end of the stream (increasing its size). We use the C++ stream output library functions to keep track of the size of the stream. As we read (extract) information from a stream, the C++ stream input library functions keep track of the last character read using an *input stream buffer pointer*. Each new attempt to get information from an input stream begins at the current position of this pointer.

Example 8.2   *Reading Using cin.*   When reading a character data element using `cin`, any leading *white space* (blanks, tab, and newline characters, for example) is skipped until the first nonwhite space character is found. This first character is then read and stored in the designated character variable. The input stream buffer pointer is advanced past all characters processed (all preceding white space and the single nonwhite-space character) and positioned at the next character. For example, given the input stream

□□□□□CIS 642 ...

the line

```
cin >> ch;   // read one character into the character variable ch
```

causes the five blanks (indicated using the symbols □□□□□) at the start of the stream to be skipped and then reads the character c into the variable ch. The stream buffer pointer would be positioned at the character I.

When reading a numeric value, `cin` skips over any leading white-space characters until a nonwhite-space character is encountered. Next, all characters that are part of the numeric value (a sign, digits, etc.) are processed until a character that is not legally part of a number in C++ is read. At this point, the number processed is returned to the program. If no digits are read before an illegal numeric character is encountered, the result returned is undefined.

For example, when processing the stream

```
347an old man
```

the line

```
cin >> my_age;   // my_age is an integer variable
```

will read the characters 347 and stop as soon as the character a is encountered. The integer value 347 would be stored in `my_age`. However, if the line to be read is

```
an old man
```

reading will stop as soon as the a is encountered, and the result stored in `my_age` would be undefined.

As another example, consider the input stream consisting of exam score *records* (initials and a score) for each of five students, where each record is entered as a single line, with the return key pressed after each score is typed:

```
f l f 78<nwln>e b k 89<nwln>j a s 95<nwln>p a c 66<nwln>
```

Assuming that the variable `score` is type int, and `fst_init`, `mdl_init`, and `lst_init` are type char, the C++ instructions

```
for (i = 0; i < nmbr_students; i++)
{
    cin >> fst_init >> mdl_init >> lst_init >> score;
    // Process the information just read.
    ...
}
```

may be used to read in this information. If `numbr_students` is 4, this loop will read the stream just shown, four data elements (three characters and an integer) at a time, processing the four elements after they have been read, until all four student records have been read. In each `for` loop iteration, the next student's initials would be read into the character variables, `fst_init`, `mdl_init`, `lst_init`, and the integer that follows them would be read and stored in `score`.

The newline character in the stream has no special impact on the processing of the data just shown. Leading white space, including blanks and the newline character, is always skipped when the reading of a data element using `cin` is initiated. After the score for the first student has been read, the input stream buffer pointer is positioned past all characters just processed, at the character that stopped the processing (in this case, the white space character `<nwln>`):

```
f l f 78<nwln>e b k 89<nwln>j a s 95 p a c 66<nwln>
      ↑
```

When reading for the second student is begun, the white space (`<nwln>`) that precedes this student's first initial is skipped. If we replaced each newline with a blank, as shown in Fig. 8.2, the processing would be the same. In fact, if there were no white-space characters anywhere in the line, the processing of the line would not change. This point is illustrated next.

Figure 8.2   **An input stream without the newline character**

```
f l f 78 e b k 89 j a s 95 p a c 66 d m s 97
```

Example 8.3   The processing of the stream shown in Fig. 8.2 would be the same even if all of the blanks were eliminated from the stream. In this case, the C++ instructions

```
for (i = 0; i < nmbr_students; i++)
{
    cin >> fst_init >> mdl_init >> lst_init >> score;
    // Process the information just read.
    ...
}
```

would process the line

```
flf78ebk89jas95pac66<nwln>
```

as follows:

a) in the first repetition of the loop,

- the characters `flf` are read and stored in `fst_init`, `mdl_init`, and `lst_init`, respectively;
- the integer `78` is read; reading is stopped when the letter `e` is encountered and the value `78` is stored in `score`; the stream buffer pointer is moved to point to the `e`;

b) in the second repetition of the loop,

- the characters `ebk` are read and stored in `fst_init`, `mdl_init`, and `lst_init`, respectively;
- the integer `89` is read; reading is stopped when the letter `j` is encountered and the value `89` is stored in `score`; the stream buffer pointer is moved to point to the `j`;

c) repetition continues in this fashion until finally,

- the characters `pac` are read and stored in `fst_init`, `mdl_init`, and `lst_init`, respectively;
- the integer `66` is read; reading is stopped when the `<nwln>` is encountered and the value `66` is stored in `score`; the stream buffer pointer is moved to point to the `<nwln>`.

Reading One Character at a Time

There are numerous situations in which it is convenient to read data from a stream one character at a time with white space treated the same way as any other character. The following examples illustrate how this might be done using the stream input and output functions `get` and `put`, which are part of the C++ `iostream` library. Function `put` is the output analog of `get`; `get` is used to read one character at a time; `put` is used to display one character at a time, and is included in this example for illustrative purposes.

Example 8.4   The program in Fig. 8.3 counts and displays the number of blanks in a stream of information. It also counts and displays the number of lines in the stream. The inner loop terminates each time the `<nwln>` character is detected, marking the beginning of a new line. The detection of the beginning of a new line is required to count the number of lines appearing in the stream. The `put` function is used to display each character in the stream as it is processed.

Figure 8.3   Counting blanks in an input stream

```cpp
// File: CntBlPer.cpp
// COUNTS THE NUMBER OF BLANKS IN EACH LINE OF A FILE

#include <iostream.h>

void main ()
{
   // Local data ...
   const char blank = ' '; // character being counted
   const char nwln = '\n'; // newline character

   char next;              // next character in current line
   int blank_count;        // number of blanks in current line
   int line_count;         // keeps track of number of lines in file

   line_count = 0;
   cin.get (next);         // get first char of new line
   while (!cin.eof ())
   {
      blank_count = 0;     // initialize blank count for new line
      while ((next != nwln) && !cin.eof ())
      {
         cout.put (next);
         if (next == blank)
            blank_count++; // increment blank count.
         cin.get (next);   // get next character.
      }  // end inner while
      cout.put (nwln);     // marks end of current display line
      line_count++;
      cout << "The number of blanks is " << blank_count << "."
           << endl;
      cin.get (next);      // get next character.
   }  // end outer while

   cout << "The number of lines processed is " << line_count
        << "." << endl;
   return;
}
```

The inner loop condition (`next != nwln`) `&&` `!cin.eof` is true as long as the newline character has not been read and we have not run out of characters. Therefore, this inner loop processes all of the characters in the current data line, including the blanks. When the newline character is read by the inner call to `get`, the inner `while` loop expression evaluates to false, and loop exit occurs. At this point, the newline is displayed (marking the end of the current line of output), the line count is incremented, and the number of blanks in the line is printed. This sequence of steps is repeated as long as the outer loop condition is true.

This example illustrates the use of a third `iostream` function, `eof`, which is used to detect the end of the stream of characters entered at the keyboard. This function returns a value of 0 (false) as long as there are more characters to be read in a stream. When the end of the stream has been reached, a nonzero (true) value is returned. From the keyboard, the end of a file may be indicated by typing a special character. Exactly which character depends on the computer you are using. For MS-DOS, the character CTRL-Z (typed by pressing the CONTROL and Z keys simultaneously) is used to enter an end of file. On UNIX computers the character CTRL-D is used. Your instructor can tell you which character to use on your computer system to indicate the end of a file.

You may find the "dot notation" used in the references to `get`, `put`, and `eof` a bit disconcerting at first. In the next section of this chapter, we will see that these functions may be used with different streams (having different names). The dot notation is used to indicate which stream is involved in the designated operation (`get`, `put`, `eof`). We simply precede the function name with the name of the stream to which it is to be applied, followed by a dot:

```
cin.get(next);
```

We will see numerous additional examples of the use of this notation throughout this chapter. By the time we have completed Chapter 11 of this text, you will have a better understanding as to why the dot notation is used in this manner.

If you are wondering why two tests for end-of-file are required, remove either test and trace the execution of CntBlPer for a short sample of data (see Self-Check Exercise 5 at the end of this section).   ∎

Converting a Sequence of Input Characters to an Integer

The following example illustrates several of the new features just introduced. It also shows how a sequence of *decimal digit characters* (the characters `'0'`, `'1'`, ...,`'9'`) might be converted to an internal integer representation as shown in Chapter 7.

Example 8.5   It is sometimes desirable to read a number as a string of characters. This enables the program to detect and ignore possible data entry errors. Function `read_int` in Fig 8.4 reads in a string of characters ending with `'\n'` and ignores any character that is not a digit. It also computes and returns the value of the number (an integer) formed by the digits only. For example, if the characters $15,43AB2% were entered, the value returned through `integer_value` would be 15432.

Figure 8.4   Reading a number as a string of characters

```
// FILE: ReadInt.cpp
// READS CONSECUTIVE CHARACTERS AND CONVERTS TO INTEGER

#include <iostream.h>
#include <ctype.h>

void read_int
    (int& integer_value)          // OUT: converted integer_value

// Reads consecutive characters ending with "\n". Computes the
//    integer value of the digit characters, ignoring non digits.
// Pre:  Numbers to be evaluated must be between 0 and 9 (base
//       10).
// Post: Returns in integer_value the numeric value of the digit
//       characters read. Advances to the next line.
{
    // Local data ...
    const int base = 10;        // the number system base
    const char nwln = '\n';     // newline character

    char next;                  // each character read
    int  digit;                 // the value of each numeric character

    // Instruct user to enter one line of characters followed by
    //     <CR>
    cout << "Enter one line of characters,"
         << " followed by a carrage return." << endl;

    // Accumulate the numeric value of the digits in integer_value.
    integer_value = 0;          // initial value is zero
    cin.get (next);             // initial character read
    while (next != nwln)
    {
        if (isdigit (next))
        {
            digit = int (next) - int ('0');   // get digit value
            integer_value = base * integer_value + digit;
        } // end if
        cin.get (next);
    } // end while
    return;
} // end read_int
```

In Fig. 8.4, the statements

```
digit = int (next) - int ('0');                // get digit value
integer_value = base * integer_value + digit;  // add digit value
```

assign to `digit` an integer value between 0 (for character value `'0'`) and 9 (for character value `'9'`). The number being accumulated in `integer_value` is multiplied by the base, 10, and the value of `digit` is added to it. Table 8.1 traces the function's execution for the character input stream

3N5<nwln>

The `get` function will read each character, but the program will ignore any character that is not a decimal digit character.

Table 8.1　Trace of Execution of Function `read_int` for 3N5<nwln>

STATEMENT	next	integer_digit	value	EFFECT
integer_value = 0;	?	?	0	Initialize `integer_value`.
(the leading blanks are read one at a time and ignored by the program)				
cin.get(next);	'3'	?	0	Get initial character.
next != nwln	'3'	?	0	next is '3'; therefore evaluation is nonzero.
if (isdigit (next))				
digit = int (next) - int ('0');	'3'	?	0	'3' is a digit.
integer_value =	'3'	3	0	digit value is 3.
base * integer_value + digit;				
cin.get (next);	'3'	3	3	`integer_value` becomes 3.
	'N'	3	3	Get next character.
next != nwln	'N'	3	3	next is 'N'; therefore evaluation is nonzero.
if (isdigit (next))				
cin.get(next);	'N'	3	3	'N' is not a digit.
	'5'	3	3	Display 'N' and get next character.
next != nwln	'5'	3	3	next is '5'; therefore evaluation is nonzero.
if (isdigit (next))				
digit = int (next) - int ('0');	'5'	3	3	'5' is a digit.
integer_value =	'5'	5	3	digit value is 5.
base * integer_value + digit;				
cin.get (next);	'5'	5	35	`integer_value` becomes 35.
	'\n'	5	35	Get next character.
next != nwln	'\n'	5	35	next is <nwln>; therefore evaluation is zero.
return;	?	?	35	Return from function.

EXERCISES FOR SECTION 8.1

Self-Check
1. Provide a careful and detailed explanation of what would happen in Example 8.5 if the `cin.get` line were replaced by the use of `cin <<`.
2. Let `x` be type `float`, `n` type `int`, and `c` type `char`. Indicate the contents of each variable after each read operation is performed assuming that the input stream consists of the following lines:

   ```
   123 3,145 XYZ<nwln>
   35 Z <nwln>
   ```

   a. `cin >> n >> x; cin >> c;`
   b. `cin >> n; cin.get (c);`
   c. `cin >> x; cin.get (c); cin >> n;`
   d. `cin >> c >> n >> x; cin >> c;`
   e. `cin >> c >> c >> c >> x >> n;`

3. What would happen to the displayed output if the line `cout.put (nwln);` were omitted from the program in Fig. 8.3?
4. Describe the behavior of the program in Fig. 8.3 if the statement containing the innermost `cin.get` had been omitted.
5. Describe the behavior of the program in Fig. 8.3 if the input stream being processed were empty (contained no data at all).
6. Describe the problems that would occur (a) if the inner end-of-file test were omitted from the function in Fig. 8.3; (b) if the outer end-of-file test were omitted in Fig. 8.3.
7. Describe what would happen if the end-of-file test were omitted from the loop in the function in Fig. 8.4.

Programming
1. Write a function that reads a `float` constant (*not* in scientific notation) typed from the keyboard one character at a time and returns the number of digits to the left of the decimal point and the number digits to the right of the decimal point. This function should call another that ensures that each character read meets the criteria for a type `float` constant and that asks for another character any time this validation test fails. We will assume that at most one sign is present in a legal `float` numeric value and that it must appear in front of the value. In addition, if no period is encountered in the line, then the number of digits appearing to the right of this nonexistent point would be zero.

8.2 ——— STREAMS AND EXTERNAL FILES

Interactive versus Batch Processing

In all of the example C++ code segments, programs, and case studies presented so far, we have used interactive input. Interactive programs read their input data from the `cin` stream associated with the keyboard and display their output to the `cout` stream associated with your display. This mode of operation is fine for small programs. However, as you begin to write larger programs, you will see that there are many advantages to using external data files. These files are stored on a secondary storage device, normally a disk. Except under extreme circumstances, external files are permanent—you can create and save them one day and return to your computer some later day and find them still stored on your disk.

You can create an external data file using a text editor in the same way that you create a program file. Once the data file is entered in computer memory, you can carefully check and edit each line and then save the final data file as a permanent disk file. When you enter data interactively, you do not always have the opportunity to examine and edit the data. Also, the data are processed as they are entered—they are not saved permanently.

After the data file is saved on disk, you can instruct your program to read from the data file rather than from the keyboard. This mode of execution is called *batch processing*. Because the program data are supplied before execution begins, prompting messages are not required for batch programs. Instead, batch programs should contain display statements that print back, or *echo print*, those data values read by the program that are important to its successful execution. This provides a record of the values read and processed in a particular program run, which can be useful, especially for debugging and testing.

In addition to giving you the opportunity to check for errors in your data, using data files provides another advantage. A data file can be read many times. Therefore, during debugging you can rerun the program as often as you need to without reentering the test data each time.

You can also instruct your program to write its output to a disk file rather than display it on the screen. When output is written to the screen, it disappears when it scrolls off the screen and cannot be retrieved. However, if program output is written to a disk file, you have a permanent copy of it. You can get a *hard copy* (on paper) of the file by sending it to your printer, or you can use an operating system command such as

```
type filename
```

to list file `filename` on the screen.

Finally, you can use the output generated by one program as a data file for another program. For example, a payroll program may compute employee salaries and write each employee's name and salary to an output file. A second program, which prints employee checks, could then be run, using the output from the payroll program as its input data file.

8.3 ———— ACCESSING AND USING EXTERNAL FILES

Directory Names for Files

To access a file in a program, you must know both the name of the file and the *disk directory* in which the file resides. A disk directory lists the names of all files stored on the disk. We need to communicate both pieces of information to the operating system so it can locate the files for processing by the program. The details as to how you provide directory names and information will vary according to the system you are using. Your instructor can give you the proper steps to follow for your particular computer system.

File names also must follow whatever conventions apply on your particular computer system. As an example, some systems limit you to a file name that consists of eight characters, a period, and a three-letter *extension*. Many programmers use the extensions .cpp and .dat to designate C++ program and data files, respectively.

In the discussion that follows, we will not concern ourselves with the details of locating the directory of a file you wish to read or write. We will assume that you already know how to do this or that, for the time being, you do not even need to know in order to proceed. We will therefore confine our attention to the issue of how we tell a C++ program the names of the external files it is to process.

As we mentioned earlier, the iostreams that we have been using are automatically attached to the keyboard and display, respectively, by the C++ language system. To read from or write to any external data file, however, we must first *attach* a C++ iostream to that file. We will now see how this is done.

Attaching Streams to External Files

Writing programs that manipulate external disk files is complicated by the fact that two different names are involved: the *external file name*, which appears in your directory and is the name by which the operating system knows the file, and the *stream name*, which is the *internal name* by which your program accesses the file. In C++, the connection between these two names is accomplished through the use of a special function, called the open function. The open function is illustrated in the following example, together with a number of other iostream functions.

Example 8.6   For security reasons, it is a good idea to have a backup or duplicate copy of a file in case the original is lost. Even though most operating systems provide a single command for copying a file, we will write our own C++ program to do this. Program CopyFile.cpp in Fig. 8.5 copies each character in file in_data.dat to file out_data.dat.

Figure 8.5   Copying a file

```
// FILE: CopyFile.cpp
// COPIES FILE IN_DATA.DAT TO FILE OUT_DATA.DAT
```

(Continued)

Figure 8.5   (Continued)

```
#include <stdlib.h>          // for the definition of EXIT_FAILURE
#include <fstream.h>         // required for external file streams

// ASSOCIATE PROGRAM IDENTIFIERS WITH EXTERNAL FILE NAMES
#define in_file "in_data.dat"
#define out_file "out_data.dat"

int main()
{
   // Functions used ...
   // COPIES ONE LINE OF TEXT
   void copy_line
      (ifstream&,            // IN: infile stream
       ofstream&);           // OUT: outfile stream

   // Local data ...
   int line_count;           // output: number of lines processed

   ifstream ins;             // associates ins as an input stream
   ofstream outs;            // associates outs as an output stream

   // Open input and output file, exit on any error.
   ins.open (in_file);       // ins connects to file in_file
   if (ins.fail ())
   {
      cerr << "*** ERROR: Cannot open " << in_file
           << " for input." << endl;
      return EXIT_FAILURE;
   }  // end if

   outs.open (out_file);     // outs connects to file out_file
   if (outs.fail ())
   {
      cerr << "*** ERROR: Cannot open " << out_file
           << " for output." << endl;
      return EXIT_FAILURE;
   }  // end if

   // Copy each character from in_data to out_data.
   line_count = 0;
   copy_line (ins, outs);    // initialize line_count to zero (0)
   line_count++;
   while (!ins.eof ())
   {
      copy_line (ins, outs);
      line_count++;
   }  // end while

   // Display a message on the screen.
```

(Continued)

Figure 8.5 (Continued)

```
    cout << "Input file copied to output file." << endl;
    cout << line_count << " lines copied." << endl;

    ins.close();                    // close input file stream
    outs.close();                   // close output file stream
    return 0;
}


// COPY ONE LINE OF TEXT FROM ONE FILE TO ANOTHER
void copy_line
    (ifstream& ins,                 // IN: ins stream
     ofstream& outs)                // OUT: outs stream

// Pre:  ins is opened for input and outs for output.
// Post: Next line of ins is written to outs.
//       The last character processed from ins is <nwln>;
//       the last character written to outs is <nwln>.
{
    // Local data ...
    const char nwln = '\n';         // newline character

    char next_ch;                   // inout: character buffer

    // Copy all data characters from ins file stream to outs file
    //     stream.
    ins.get (next_ch);
    while ((next_ch != nwln) && !ins.eof())
    {
        outs.put (next_ch);
        ins.get (next_ch);
    }  // end while

    // If last character read was nwln write it to out_data.
    if (!ins.eof ())
        outs.put(nwln);
    return;
}  // end copy_line
```
——————— Program Output ———————

```
Input file copied to output file
37 lines copied
```

Before we can read or write an external file in a program, we must first declare an iostream variable for each of the streams to be processed by our program. As shown in Fig. 8.5, the required declarations

```
ifstream ins;
ofstream outs;
```

have the same form as those we have been using, but they involve two new data types, `ifstream` (input file stream) and `ofstream` (output file stream). These two types are defined in the C++ library header `fstream.h`. Once the stream variables have been declared, the files may be opened using the library function `open`:

```
ins.open(in_file);
outs.open(out_file);
```

This function performs some communication with the operating system we are using (which need not concern us here) and attaches the declared stream (`ins`, for example) to the external file. The dot notation used in calling the open function is the same as that introduced earlier in this chapter.

The use of the `#define` compiler directive enables us to associate the name of a file used by the program (for example, `in_file`) with the actual external name of a file (such as `in_data.dat`). The advantage of this association lies in the ease that we can reuse this program with different input and output files. All we would need to change is the two `#define` lines in the program, and the program would be ready to run with different files.

The connection established by the `open` statement between the file name and associated stream is depicted in Fig. 8.6.

Immediately following the call to the `open` function is an `if` statement used to determine whether or not the requested open operation was successful. The success or failure of the open operation can be checked via a call to the function `fail`. It is a good idea always to test whether an open operation is successful and terminate execution of the program if the value returned by `fail` is nonzero (true). A return with the integer value `EXIT_FAILURE` (defined in the library `stdlib.h`) may be used to report unsuccessful termination to the C++ system. A return with `EXIT_SUCCESS` may be used when a

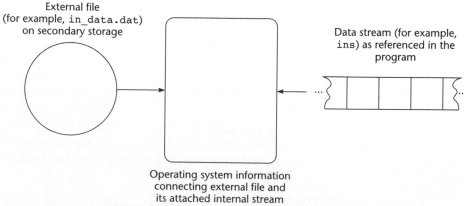

Figure 8.6   Connection between an external file and a stream

program terminates successfully. Note that the function `main` header line starts with `int` to reflect the fact that `main` returns an integer.   ■

In addition to the `open` function, the program in Fig. 8.6 illustrates five other iostream functions in the C++ `fstream.h` library: `eof`, `get`, `put`, `fail`, and `close`. These functions are explained in the next display, and their use in the copy file program is discussed following the display. Functions `get` and `put` are essentially the same as shown in the previous section, except that these versions are applied to external files rather than to the keyboard and display. (Similarly, `eof` and `fail`, as discussed in the display, apply to external file input rather than to a stream of characters entered at the keyboard.)

C++
SYNTAX

The File Manipulation Member Functions: open, get, put, eof, fail, close

Requires: fstream.h

Forms:
```
fs.open ( fname );
fs.get (ch);
fs.put (ch);
fs.eof ();
fs.fail ();
fs.close ();
```

Examples:
```
ifs.open (in_file);
fs.fail ();
if (ifs.eof ()) {... }
ifs.close ();
```

Interpretation: For each of these functions, the variable name before the period, `ifs`, designates the input/output stream (`ifs` in this case) to be manipulated by the designated operation. For `open`, the argument is a character string that represents the name of the external file to be opened. The `open` function connects the iostream (for example, `ifs`) to the external file designated by the first argument, *fname*. Function `get` *extracts* (reads) the next character from the iostream and places it in the character variable (for example, `ch`) designated by the argument. Function `put` *inserts* (writes or displays) character `ch` into the iostream. The `close` function disconnects the stream and its associated file, and `eof` tests for the end-of-file condition. The `eof` function returns nonzero (true) when the end is reached. Function `fail` may be used to check if an isostream operation such as `open` failed to execute properly. This function also returns a nonzero value (true) if the operation failed.

The name of the iostream associated with each of these operations is specified using the dot notation, for example, `ins.get (ch)`.   ■

In the main function in Fig. 8.5, the loop that does the actual copying follows the `open` instructions. This loop calls the function `copy_line` to copy one line of information at a time from the input file to the output file and keep a count of the number of lines copied. Copying continues as long as the end of the input file has not been reached. Once the end of this file is encountered, loop execution terminates, a message indicating the number of lines just copied is displayed on the screen, and both files are closed.

Function `copy_line` copies a single line of the input file to the output file each time it is called. The `while` loop

```
// Copy all data characters from in_data to out_data.
ins.get (next_ch);
while ((next_ch != nwln) && !ins.eof ())
{
    outs.put (next_ch);
    ins.get (next_ch);
}  // end while
```

performs this copy one character at a time as long as neither a newline character nor the end of the input file has been encountered. When either of these events occurs, the character copy loop terminates. In case this termination is caused by the occurrence of the newline character, this character is copied to the output file before `copy_line` returns to the calling program:

```
// If last character read was nwln write it to out_data.
if (!ins.eof ())
    outs.put (nwln);
```

The Standard Iostream, cerr

In addition to the standard iostreams `cin` and `cout`, there is another standard stream, `cerr`, the *standard error stream*, which is also usually connected to your terminal or workstation. As shown in Fig. 8.5, this stream is used to provide an alert to an error or exception condition that might occur during the execution of a C++ program.

The standard error stream is used throughout this chapter to provide an alert related to stream input or output exceptions such as invalid data, premature end of file, or failure during an attempt to open a file. However, it can also be used to provide an alert for other exceptions such as divide by zero:

```
if (a == 0.0)
{   cerr << "+++ Error: attempt to divide by zero.";
    return;
}
x = discr/2.0 * a;
```

Using the for Loop with Input-Controlled Repetition

In Chapter 5 (Section 5.6) we introduced a general form of the `for` loop construct

for (*initialization-expression*; *test-expression*; *update-expression*)

We indicated that there was considerable flexibility in the form of the three *loop parameter* expressions, but we restricted our examples to counting loops with parameter expressions such as

```
i = 0; i < n; i++
```

Figure 8.7 illustrates the use of the `for` loop in specifying program repetition controlled file input expressions, in this case using the functions `get` and `eof`. In this loop, the `for` loop parameter expressions are as follows:

`ins.get (next_ch)`	— used as both the initialization and update expressions
`(next.ch != nwln) && !ins.eof ()`	— used as the loop repetition test expression

The loop works in exactly the same way as the `while` loop shown in Fig. 8.5. The initialization step, `ins.get (next ch)`, is executed prior to the start of loop repetition. The loop repetition test is carried out at the top of the loop (just prior to the start of the next loop iteration), and the update step is performed at the end of each iteration of the loop.

This use of the `for` loop enables us to keep the initialization, test, and update steps together in a single place—the `for` loop header—and yet maintain the same functionality as provided by the `while` loop. For this reason, we will continue to use the `for` loop to specify program repetition controlled by file input as well as for counter-controlled repetition.

Figure 8.7   The `while` loop from `copy_line` rewritten as a `for` loop

```
for (ins.get (next_ch); (next_ch != nwln) && (!ins.eof ());
     ins.get (next_ch))
   outs.put (next_ch);
```

Processing the newline Character

The processing of newline characters in `copy_file` should be clearly understood. Consider the input file shown next:

```
This is a text file!<nwln>It has two lines.<nwln><eof>
```

When the first `<nwln>` is read during the execution of the `while` loop, the input and output files (and their respective stream buffer pointers) would appear as follows:

```
This is a text file!<nwln>It has two lines.<nwln><eof>        (input file)
                    ↑
This is a text file!                                          (output file)
                    ↑
```

If the lines

```
// If last character read was nwln write it to out_data.
if (!ins.eof ())
   outs.put(nwln);
```

were omitted from `copy_line`, the `<nwln>` character just read from the input file would not be written to the output file. As this continued throughout the program, the output file `out_data.dat` would contain all the characters in `in_data.dat`, but the line separators would have been lost:

```
This is a text file!It has two lines.
```

The call to function `put` following the `while` loop in function `copy_line` ensures that a newline character is written to the output file at the end of each complete line. Once the `<nwln>` has been copied to the output file, control is returned to the calling program. When `copy_line` is called the next time, the input and output files would appear as shown below:

```
This is a text file!<nwln>It has two lines.<nwln><eof>        (input file)
                             ↑
This is a text file!<nwln>                                     (output file)
                          ↑
```

The first call to function `get` (just prior to the `while` loop in `copy_line`) causes the next character (the `I` in `It`) to be read. This loop continues copying characters from input to output until the second newline is encountered. This newline then is copied to the output file, and control is returned to the calling function. What happens upon the next call to `copy_line` is left as an exercise at the end of this section (see Self-Check Exercise 1).

Note that reading from and writing to a file stream modifies the file position pointer associated with the stream. For this reason, we must pass all file stream arguments by reference. The streams are otherwise used just like `cin` and `cout`.

EXERCISES FOR SECTION 8.3

Self-Check

1. Consider the following input file (with the file position pointer shown below the information in the file):

```
This is a text file!<nwln>It has two lines.<nwln><eof>
                             ↑
```

   Examine the file copy program shown in Fig. 8.5 and provide a complete, step-by-step description of the completion of the processing of this line.
2. What is the purpose of the `open` function?
3. What are some of the advantages to having external (permanent) storage files in which to store program input and output?

Programming

1. Rewrite the program shown in Fig. 8.3 (counting the number of blanks per line in a stream) to read from an external file named `my_txt.dat` (rather than from the keyboard).
2. Rewrite the copy program shown in Fig. 8.5 as a reusable function component with two arguments, specifically, the input and output file streams. The function should return an integer indicating the number of lines copied (0, if the input file is empty).

8.4 _____ USING EXTERNAL FILE FUNCTIONS: AN EXAMPLE

If one program writes its output to a disk file rather than to the screen, a second program may use this output file as its own data input file. In this way, the two programs communicate with each other through the disk file. In this section we provide an example to show how this is done. The program illustrates the use of all of the external file functions introduced in the previous section. It is a relatively complex program and will provide still further illustration of the program design techniques we have stressed so far.

CASE STUDY: PREPARING A PAYROLL FILE

Problem Statement

Your company accountant wants you to write two programs for processing the company payroll. The first program reads a data file consisting of employee salary data. The data for each employee is stored on two consecutive lines: The first line is the employee's name, and the second line contains that employee's hours worked and hourly rate. A sample data file follows:

```
Kirby Puckett<nwln>
40.0  500.00<nwln>
Jim McMahon<nwln>
20.0  10.00<nwln><eof>
```

The first program reads each employee's name and copies it to an output file. The program then reads the hours worked and hourly rate for this employee, computes the gross salary, writes this value to the output file, and accumulates the value in the total payroll for the company. When the processing of all employees has been completed, the total payroll amount is displayed. The second line of the output for each employee contains the product of the two values read from the second line of the data file. A sample output file, corresponding to the previous input file, is shown next.

```
Kirby Puckett<nwln>
20000.00<nwln>
Jim McMahon<nwln>
200.00<nwln><eof>
```

The second program reads the file created by the first program and prints payroll checks based on the contents of this file. For example, the first check issued should be a check for $20,000.00 made out to Kirby Puckett.

Problem Analysis

We will write the first program now and leave the second one as a Programming Project (see Programming Project 1 at the end of this chapter).

As already explained, our program must copy each employee's name to the output file. It must also compute each employee's salary, write it to the output file, and add it to the payroll total.

DATA REQUIREMENTS

Streams Used

eds (ifstream) — employee data information
pds (ofstream) — payroll data information

Problem Input (from stream eds)

next_char (char) — used to store the letters in each employee's name

each employee's hours worked
each employee's hourly rate

Problem Output (to stream pds)

each employee's name
each employee's salary

Problem Output (to cout stream)

payroll (float) — the payroll total

Program Design

The main function will prepare the streams and associated files for input and output and call function process_emp to process all employees and determine the total payroll amount. After process_emp is finished, the main function will display the final payroll total. Figure 8.8 shows the structure chart for this problem. The main algorithm is shown below.

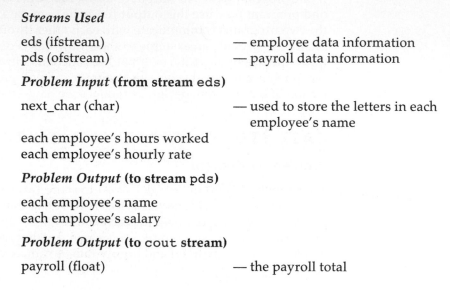

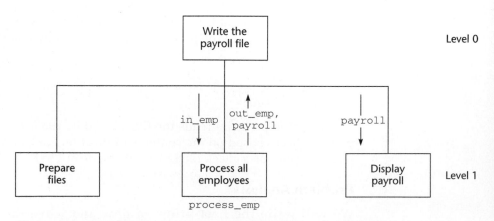

Figure 8.8   Top levels of structure chart for Payroll Problem

ALGORITHM FOR FUNCTION main

1. Prepare streams and associated files for processing.
2. Process all employees and compute payroll total.
3. Display the payroll total.

Program Implementation

The C++ code for function main is shown in Fig. 8.9. Only the three streams cout, eds (employee data stream), and pds (payroll data stream) and the total payroll variable need to be visible in this function. The hours worked and hourly rate will be used exclusively in process_emp and therefore are not declared until needed.

Figure 8.9   Writing a payroll file (main function)

```
// FILE: Payroll.cpp
// WRITES EACH EMPLOYEE NAME AND GROSS SALARY TO AN
//     OUTPUT FILE AND COMPUTES TOTAL PAYROLL AMOUNT

#include <fstream.h>        // required for file streams
#include <stdlib.h>         // for definition of EXIT_FAILURE

#include "PrcsEmpl.cpp"     // process one employee

// ASSOCIATE PROGRAM IDENTIFIERS WITH EXTERNAL FILE NAMES
#define in_file "Emp_File.dat" // employee file
#define out_file "Salary.dat"  // payroll file

int main()
{
  // Functions used ...
  // PROCESS ALL EMPLOYEES AND COMPUTE TOTAL
  void process_emp
    (ifstream&,             // IN: employee data stream
     ofstream&,             // OUT: payroll data stream
     float&);               // OUT: total company payroll

  // Local data ...
  ifstream eds;             // input: employee data stream
  ofstream pds;             // output: payroll data stream
  float total_payroll;      // output: total payroll

  // Prepare files.
  eds.open (in_file);
  if (eds.fail())
  {
    cerr << "*** ERROR: Cannot open " << in_file
         << " for input." << endl;
    return EXIT_FAILURE;
  }
```

(Continued)

Figure 8.9   (Continued)

```
pds.open(out_file);
if (pds.fail())
{
    cerr << "*** ERROR: Cannot open " << out_file
        << " for output." << endl;
    eds.close ();
    return EXIT_FAILURE;
}

// Set precision and flags for floating point output.
cout.precision (2);
cout.setf (ios::fixed | ios::showpoint);

// Process all employees and compute total payroll.
process_emp (eds, pds, total_payroll);

// Display result.
cout << "Total payroll is $" << total_payroll << endl;

// Close files.
eds.close ();
pds.close ();
return 0;
}
// end main
```

———————— Program Output ————————

```
Total payroll is $20200.00
```

Design of process_emp

The function `process_emp` performs the tasks required for building the output file and determining the total payroll amount. The structure chart outlining the required steps is shown in Fig. 8.10; the algorithm is shown at the top of the next page.

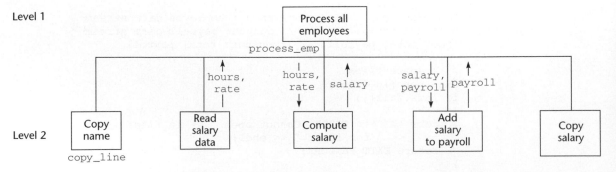

Figure 8.10   Structure chart for `process_emp`

ALGORITHM FOR process_emp

1. Initialize payroll total to 0.0.
2. While there are more employees
    2.1. Read next employee's name from eds and write it to pds.
    2.2. Read next employee's salary data.
    2.3. Compute next employee's salary.
    2.4. Write next employee's salary to pds and add it to payroll total.

Implementation for process_emp

Figure 8.11 shows the function process_emp. We declare variables hours, rate, and salary to be local variables in process_emp because they are referenced only in this component and are not needed anywhere else.

Figure 8.11   Implementation of process_emp and subordinate functions

```
// FILE: PrcsEmpl.cpp
// PROCESS ALL EMPLOYEES AND COMPUTE TOTAL PAYROLL AMOUNT

#include "CopyLine.cpp"
#include "SkipNwln.cpp"

void process_emp
   (ifstream& eds,              // IN: employee file stream
    ofstream& pds,              // OUT: payroll file stream
    float& payroll)             // OUT: total company payroll

// Pre:  eds and pds are prepared for input/output.
// Post: All employee data are copied from eds to pds and
//       the sum of their salaries is returned through payroll.
// Uses: copy_line(); skip_new_line;
{
   // Functions used ...
   // COPY ONE LINE OF TEXT
   int copy_line
      (ifstream&,               // IN: employee file stream
       ofstream&);              // OUT: payroll file stream

   // SKIP NEW LINE
   void skip_newline
      (ifstream&);              // IN: stream to file involved

   // Local data ...
   float hours;                 // input: hours worked.
   float rate;                  // input: hourly rate.
   float salary;                // output: gross salary.
```

(Continued)

Figure 8.11   (Continued)

```
    // set for floating point output
    pds.precision (2);
    pds.setf (ios::fixed | ios::showpoint);

    payroll = 0.0;
    while (!eds.eof ())
    {
        // Copy employee name.
        copy_line (eds, pds);
        if (eds.eof ())
            break;
        // Get salary data.
        eds >> hours >> rate;
        if (eds.eof ())
            break;
        skip_newline (eds);
        salary = hours * rate;
        pds << salary << endl;
        payroll += salary;
    }  // end while
    return;
}  // end process_emp
```

The `while` loop in `process_emp` tests whether the end of the input file has been encountered. If not, `copy_line` copies an employee's name from the input stream (designated by `eds`) to the output stream (`pds`); then it copies the newline character from `eds` to `pds`. The statement

```
eds >> hours >> rate;  // get salary data.
```

reads the current employee's salary data from `eds` and advances the file position pointer to the first character beyond the last legal floating-point character in `rate`. The statement

```
pds << salary << endl;
```

writes the salary for the current employee to stream `pds`. After the current employee's salary is added to the payroll total, the data for the next employee is processed. It is at this point that problems can occur if we are not careful in processing our input. Although we have discussed these problems earlier in this chapter and illustrated them with numerous examples, we will use this case study to provide an additional illustration.

The function calls `pds.precision` and `pds.setf` represent alternative ways of referencing the `precision` and `setiosflags` manipulators. We will have more to say about this in Section 8.6.

The Importance of Advancing Past the Newline Character

The newline problem in the Payroll Program arises because the statement

```
eds >> hours >> rate;  // get salary data.
```

advances the input stream buffer pointer for stream `eds` to just beyond the last legal floating-point character in the `rate` value. In our problem, this character is likely to be a blank or the newline character, as shown below.

```
40.0  500.00<nwln>
        ↑
```

If we were to leave the input stream buffer pointer here, the next call to `copy_line` (to copy the second employee's name) would cause the `while` loop exit to occur immediately without reading the name. In this case, the first character encountered by `copy_line` would be `<nwln>`; `copy_line` would process `<nwln>` and return control to the main function.

At this point, the next character in the file would be the first letter of an employee's name. However, the next input statement to execute is

```
inp >> hours >> rate;
```

This statement expects numeric information consisting of perhaps a sign, decimal digits, and perhaps a decimal point. When a letter (part of an employee's name) or any other "nonnumeric" character is encountered while reading a numeric value, the read terminates and control is returned to the calling function. If this "nonnumeric" character is the first character in the number to be read, unpredictable results will be returned. If the nonnumeric character appears in the middle of the read operation, the value returned will be computed based only on the preceding numeric characters. Thus an attempt the read the characters 2Q8.5 into the floating-point variable `hours` would result in the return of the value 2; the returned result from an attempt to read `"ebk"` into a numeric variable is unpredictable. Note that the lines

```
inp >> hours >> rate;
```

and

```
outs << salary << endl;
```

are written in exactly the same form that we have been using since Chapter 2 for doing stream I/O with the streams `cout` and `cin`. All that we have changed is the names of the streams involved (`inp` and `outs`).

To minimize the impact of this newline problem in our case study solution, we have provided the function `skip_newline`. This function, which has been left as an exercise (see Programming Exercise 2 at the end of this section) will read from the specified stream (`eds` in our case) and skip all characters in the file up to and including the first newline encountered, at which point it stops. In the above example, only one character, the newline, would be read and skipped, leaving the file pointer at the first character just beyond the newline. This is precisely what we need for the Payroll Program to execute correctly.

EXERCISES FOR SECTION 8.4

Self-Check

1. a. What would be the effect, if any, of trailing blanks at the end of data lines in the input stream for the Payroll Program?
   b. What would be the effect of blank lines?

2. In the discussion of the Payroll Program we wrote the name and salary data on separate lines. Rewrite this program so that it writes this data on the same line. Which is easier, the single-line or the two-line version? Explain.

Programming

1. Write a program that reads from file SALARY.DAT produced by the Payroll Program and displays a count of the number of employees processed by the Payroll Program and their average salary.

2. Write a function skip_newline that, regardless of the current position of a stream buffer pointer, will read one at a time all characters in the designated stream up to and including the next newline (if any), and then leave the pointer at the next character in the stream. Function skip_newline should require only one input argument, specifically, the stream for which the skip operation is to be carried out.

8.5 ____ PUTTING IT ALL TOGETHER

The next case study illustrates many of the C++ input/output features introduced in this chapter. The problem to be addressed, however, is somewhat different from the earlier examples we have studied. Rather than emphasize computations, our focus in this problem will be on transforming data from one form to another and presenting the customer (the user of the program) with information in a concise and readable form. As part of the problem analysis, we will design the layout of the required program output and the format of each line of the input data file. This is the first time that we have been concerned with such issues. Our goal in this study is to illustrate the importance of a careful analysis of the type and structure of all problem data, especially input and output data, and the impact of our decisions concerning this data on the overall design of a program system. The code that is finally generated is almost of secondary importance.

CASE STUDY: PREPARING SEMESTER GRADE REPORTS

Problem Statement

The registrar of your school needs a program that can be used to prepare grade reports for students at the end of each semester. For each student, the program should display a table showing each course taken during the semester and the grade and credits for that course. The program should also compute the student's semester grade point average (GPA) and write it on the grade report along with the number of credits earned toward graduation.

Problem Analysis

This problem is different from the others we have studied, because its main purpose is to produce a report (a student grade report) rather than compute numeric results. There is little computation involved (aside from computing a few totals and the GPA for each student).

We will assume that we have a great deal of freedom in designing the format of the program input and output. We can decide to have each student's data typed at the keyboard during program execution or stored in a previously prepared data file. To enable some editing beforehand, it would make more sense to prepare a data file rather than to have to enter the data interactively. It would also be beneficial to write the program output to a file rather than display it on the screen. Once we have written the output file, we can *route* the file to a printer to print the grade reports (perhaps on special university grade report forms) for mailing to each student.

The first step is to determine the format of the grade report we would like to have prepared for each student. Figure 8.12 shows the report form we will use. The grade report displays the student's name and his or her performance in each course. At the bottom of the report, some totals and the semester grade point average are printed. In the example illustrated, the grade point average, 1.8, was computed by accumulating the total number of points earned in courses that received a grade of A through F (4×3 or 12 for CIS101, 0 for CIS210, 2×3 or 6 for HIS356) and dividing by the total number of credits for those courses (10).

Next, we must decide the contents of the input data file and its organization. We can place the data for each student on a separate line in the sample form shown on the next page (for four students).

Figure 8.12   Grade report format—an example

```
Fall Semester 1999
Grade Report for: Carolyn Adams

Course          Grade       Credits     Points
CIS101            A            3           12
CIS210            F            4            0
HIS356            C            3            6
PHI210            P            3            0

Total credits earned:     13
Total credits earned toward GPA:     10
Total points earned toward GPA:     18
Semester grade point average: 1.80
```

```
Carolyn Adams/CIS101A3 CIS210F4  HIS356C3 PHI210P3
Linda Berg/PHI025B4    HIS120C3  MAT255
Elton Kahn/CIS310A3  CIS499B4 MUS356A3 PHI210P3
Bonnie Straight/PHY005C4 SOC341B3  MUS101A3
```

Each student's name comes first followed by a slash and a list of course data. The course data consists of a six-character course identification code, a grade, and the number of credit hours. One or more blanks may appear between courses. The first line shows that Carolyn Adams took four courses and received a grade of A for CIS101, a three-credit course. She received a grade of F in CIS210 (four credits), a C in HIS356 (three credits), and P in PHI210 (three credits). A newline character is assumed at the end of each of these input lines, even though it is not shown.

If we examine the grade report shown in Fig. 8.12, we see that each input data line generates a multiline table in the output file. Some of the information on the data line simply will be echoed (the student's name, each course ID), and some will be used in the computations (course grade and credits).

In the problem data requirements shown next, only minimal information is provided. All other problem input and output will be declared as local variables in those functions in which they are needed. We have been careful to declare each data element only where it is required for program computation and not in higher-level program components in which the data are not used. Access to these variables is therefore kept as restricted as possible.

DATA REQUIREMENTS

Streams Used

sts (ifstream)	— student grades stream
grs (ofstream)	— grade report stream

Problem Input

student data (read from sts)

semester (int)	— semester for this grade report :
	(value between 1 and 4)
	1 indicates Fall semester
	2 indicates Spring semester
	3 indicates first Summer session
	4 indicates second Summer session
year (int)	— last two digits of the year of the report

Problem Output

grade report (written to grs)	
student_count (int)	— count of students

Program Design (top level)

In this section, we discuss the top-level design of the required program system and outline the algorithm for the main function. The main function must first prepare the streams and files for input and output and then prompt the user to enter the semester and the year for the current grade reports. Once the correct semester and year have been entered, the main part of the processing may be performed: for each student, the entire grade record for the semester must be processed and a grade report printed. When all student records have been processed, a count of the number of students involved must be printed. Figure 8.13 shows a structure chart for the top levels of the program system. Separate functions (enter_semester_data and process_one_student) will be used respectively to read the semester and year involved and to process the input data line for one student. The other steps are sufficiently straightforward to be implemented in line, without the use of separate functions.

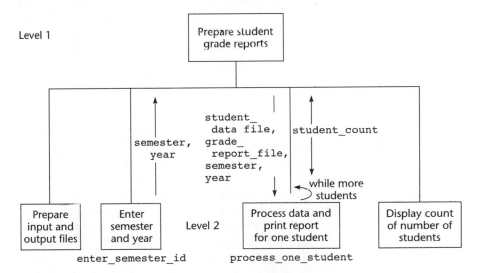

Figure 8.13   **Structure chart for Grade Report Program**

The algorithm for function main is shown next.

ALGORITHM FOR main FUNCTION

1. Prepare student data stream and file for input and grade report stream and file for output.
2. Ask user to enter semester and year (enter_semester_id).
3. Initialize the student count to zero.

4. While more students
  4.1. Process data for one student and increment student count
       (`process_one_student`).
5. Display the count of students processed.

Program Implementation

Now that we have completed the data requirements, structure chart, and algorithm for the main function, we can provide its implementation. Figure 8.14 shows the function `main` for the Grade Report Problem. The included file `GrdRprt5.cpp` is not provided in the text. The two functions to be included in this file are left as Programming Exercises 1 and 2 at the end of this section. The declaration section contains all of the information in the data requirements table as well as the prototypes for functions `enter_semester_id` and `process_one_student` shown in the structure chart in Fig. 8.13. The variable `io_flag` (of type `io_status`) is used to communicate success or failure information among all of the functions in the programming system. Any error that occurs when opening a file or reading from the student data file will be reflected in this variable, which can then be tested as necessary in other parts of the program. For example, if the end-of-file is reached in trying to process a student, `io_flag` will be set to `file_end`. Thus, the loop repetition condition

```
(io_flag != file_end)
```

will remain `true` as long as there are students left to process. The type `io_status` will be declared and referenced in a number of the lower-level functions for the Grade Report Problem. It is common practice when programming in C++ to define an include file (usually using the file name extension h) to contain this definition. This file is shown in Fig. 8.15. Note that the file stream header `fstream.h` must be included when file input/output is required. This header will automatically include `iostream.h` if it has not already been included elsewhere.

Figure 8.14   Implementation of `main` function for Grade Report Problem

```
// FILE: GrdRptMn.cpp
// GRADE REPORT MAIN PROGRAM
// WRITES A SEMESTER GRADE REPORT FOR EACH STUDENT

#include <fstream.h>   // file stream input/output

#include "IoStat.h"
#include "Prc1Stdt.cpp"

#include "GrdRprt5.cpp"
```

(Continued)

Figure 8.14   (Continued)

```
// *** NOT IN TEXT *** see Programming Exercises 1 and 2
// for enter_semester_id, find_average

#define in_file "STURCRDS.dat" // student data file
#define out_file "GRDRPRT.dat" // grade report file

int main()
{
   // Functions used ...
   // Prototypes for enter_semester_id and process_one_student
   #include "GrdRptP1.h"

   // Local data ...
   const int file_err = 1; // file access error value

   ifstream sts;           // input: file of student grades
   ofstream grs;           // output: creates output file stream

   int semester;           // inout: semester for report
   int year;               // inout: year for report
   int student_count;      // output: count of students processed
   io_status io_flag;      // status flag returned by
                           //    process_one_student;

   // Prepare student data file for input and grade report file
   //    for output.
   sts.open (in_file);     // sts connects to file in_file
   if (sts.fail ())
   {
      cerr << "*** ERROR: Cannot open " << in_file
           << " for input." << endl;
      return file_err;
   }

   grs.open (out_file);    // grs connects to file out_file
   if (grs.fail ())
   {
      cerr << "*** ERROR: Cannot open" << out_file
           << "for output." << endl;
      return file_err;
   }

   // Enter semester and year for report.
   enter_semester_id (semester, year);

   // Process all students until done.
   student_count = 0;
   io_flag = process_one_student (sts, grs, semester, year,
                                  student_count);
   while (io_flag != file_end)
```

(Continued)

Figure 8.14   (Continued)

```
{
    io_flag = process_one_student (sts, grs, semester, year,
                                    student_count);
}   // end while

// Display number of students processed and close files.
cout << endl << endl;
if (student_count <= 0)
    cout << "No students were processed!" << endl;
else
    cout << student_count << " students were processed."
        << endl;

sts.close ();              // close the sts stream
grs.close ();              // close the grs stream

return io_flag;
}
```

Figure 8.15   Include file to define `io_status`

```
// FILE: IoStat.h
// INCLUDE FILE TO DEFINE THE TYPE io_status
// TO BE USED BY THE PROGRAMS THAT GENERATE THE GRADE REPORT

#ifndef IOSTAT_H_
#define IOSTAT_H_

enum io_status
{ // identifies possible results in i/o processing
    success,              // successful processing
    file_end,             // end of file encountered
    record_end,           // end of student record (end of line)
    data_error,           // invalid (out of range) data entered
    file_error            // system file processing error
};

#endif // IOSTAT_H_
```

The lines

```
#ifndef IOSTAT_H_
#define IOSTAT_H_
```

in `IoStat.h` are compiler directives (similar to `#include`). The purpose of these directives is to prevent duplicate definitions of the symbols, such as `io_status`, `success`, `file_end`, and so on, defined in `IoStat.h`. Such duplication can occur if IoStat.h is included in more than one of the function components of the grade report program. This frequently happens when functions are tested separately and later integrated into a complete system. The #ifndef line is a conditional directive that tells the compiler to skip all lines down to the matching #endif if the symbol IOSTAT_H_ has already been defined. Once all functions have been integrated, the IOSTAT_H_ symbol will be defined during compilation at the first occurrence of an include for IoStat.h. For any subsequent includes of IoStat.h, all C++ lines between the #ifndef IOSTAT_H_ and its matching #endif will be skipped. The choice of the symbol used to control the conditional compilation directive is based on a C++ convention and is otherwise arbitrary.

The prototypes for functions enter_semester_id and process_one_student are shown next (file GrdRptP1.h).

```
// File: GrdRptP1.h
// INCLUDE FILE FOR enter_semester_id AND process_one_student.
//     USED IN GrdRptMn.cpp

// ENTER SEMESTER AND YEAR
void enter_semester_id
   (int&,                    // OUT: semester of report
    int&);                   // OUT: year of report

// PROCESS ONE STUDENT RECORD
io_status process_one_student
   (ifstream&,               // IN: student data file stream
    ofstream&,               // OUT: grade report file stream
    int,                     // IN: semester for report
    int,                     // IN: year for report
    int&);                   // INOUT: student count
```

The detailed design for function enter_semester_id is left as Programming Exercise 1 at the end of this section. We next turn our attention to the design and implementation of function process_one_student.

Analysis for process_one_student

The processing of the data for one student is done by function process_one_student. This function writes the report header, including the name of the student and the header for the course information table. It then processes the grade and credit information for each course taken by the student, producing a line of report output for each course and accumulating student credit and point totals. Once all courses for the student have been processed, the credit and point totals are printed and the GPA is computed and printed. The input, output, and local variables for process_one_student are shown next.

DATA REQUIREMENTS FOR `process_one_student`

Input Arguments

sts (ifstream)   — student data file stream
semester (int)   — semester for report
year (int)   — year for report
student_count (int)   — count of students

Output Arguments

grs (ofstream)   — grade report data file stream
student_count (int)   — count of students

Local Variables

total_credits (int)   — total credits earned (all courses)
total_gpa_credits (int)   — total credits earned toward GPA
total_gpa_points (int)   — total points earned toward GPA
gpa (float)   — grade point average
io_flag (io_status)   — input/output status flag
course_error (int)   — indicates if unexpected data input error
                                occurred in middle of processing data for
                                one course

FORMULAS

gpa = (total points earned toward GPA) / (total credits earned toward GPA)

Design of process_one_student

The structure chart for `process_one_student` is shown in Fig. 8.16, and the algorithm is given next.

ALGORITHM FOR process_one_student

1. Initialize total credits, total gpa credits, and total gpa points to zero.
2. Write the grade report heading (`write_gr_heading`).
3. If there are still more courses and no errors
   3.1. Write student grade table heading.
   3.2. Increment student count.
   3.3. While there are more courses and no errors
      3.3.1. Read and process the data for the next course (`process_one_course`). (Update total credits, total gpa credits, and total gpa points and write course data. If an error occurs, update error flag.)
   3.4. If course error, file error, or data error
      3.4.1. Display appropriate error message.
      else (if file end or record end and no course error)
      3.4.2. Compute GPA (`compute_average`).

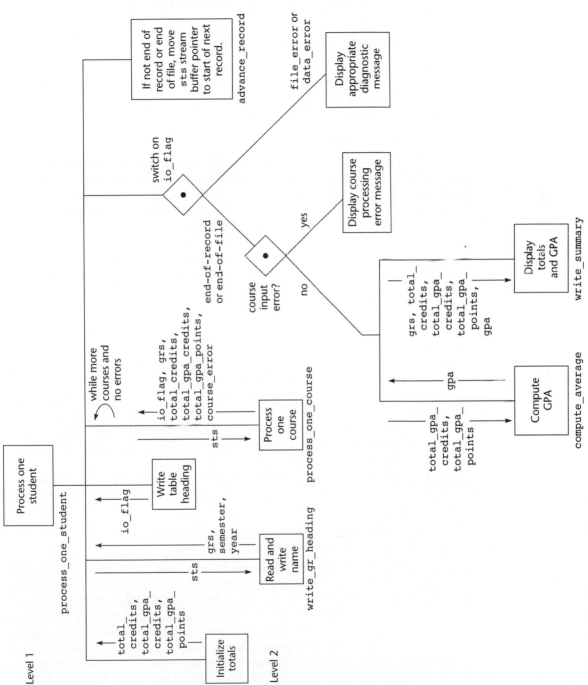

Figure 8.16 Structure chart for process_one_student

3.4.3. Write all totals (`write_summary`).
3.5. Advance to top of next report page.
4. Ensure input stream positioned at start of next line (`advance_record`).

Implementation of process_one_student

The implementation of function `process_one_student` is shown in Fig. 8.17. Again, `io_flag` is used to indicate the resulting status from any attempt to process information (name or a course data) in a student record. The `while` condition

```
(io_flag == success)
```

is true as long as the end of the student record (a newline) has not been reached and no errors have been detected in processing the information for a given student. Errors detected include system file errors, a premature end-of-file, or invalid data. When an error is detected, the program status is reset to allow for the termination of the processing for the current student and the start of the processing for the next student. The function `advance_record` (not shown in Fig. 8.17) is used to move the input stream buffer pointer to the start of the next student's data record and to reset `io_flag`. The statement

```
grs.put ('\f');
```

causes each student's grade report to start on a new page when the grade report file is sent to the printer. When written to a stream to be displayed or printed, the character `'\f'` causes a "form feed" operation to be performed.

Figure 8.18 shows the implementation of the subordinate modules `write_gr_heading`, `write_summary`, and `advance_record` for `process_one_student`. Of the remaining two subordinate modules, `process_one_course` will be discussed later; `compute_average` will be implemented through the reuse of the function described in Chapter 6 (see Programming Exercise 2 at the end of this section).

The function `write_gr_heading` reads the name of the student from the student data file, one character at a time, and writes this name as part of the report header. The `while` condition

```
(!sts.bad () && (name_char != name_sentinel) &&
(name_char != nwln) && (!sts.eof ()))
```

is true as long as no system file error has occurred in reading the student name and as long as the sentinel character (`'/'`), newline, or end-of-file has not been read. The iostream function `bad` can be used to detect the occurrence of a system file error. This function returns a nonzero (true) value if a system file error is detected. The end-of-line test was included to detect a missing sentinel character. The end-of-file test was included to test for a premature end-of-file (perhaps caused by a bad record or by an empty file). The `if` statement

Figure 8.17   Implementation of `process_one_student`

```
// FILE: Prc1Stdt.cpp
// PROCESS ONE STUDENT GRADE RECORD

#include "IoStat.h"
#include "GenGrprt.cpp"    // write_gr_heading, write_summary,
                           //    advance_record
#include "Prc1Crse.cpp"    // process_one_course
#include "GrdRprt5.cpp"    // find_average


// PROCESS ONE STUDENT GRADE RECORD
io_status process_one_student
  (ifstream& sts,          // IN: student data file stream
   ofstream& grs,          // OUT: grade report file stream
   int semester,           // IN: semester for report
   int year,               // IN: year for report
   int& student_count)     // INOUT: student count

// Pre:     student_count is the sequence number of the student
//          being processed. The file position pointer for the
//          student_data file (sts) is at the start of the next
//          student input record. Semester must be defined
//          (between 1 and 4) and year must be defined (between 0
//          and 99).
// Post:    A grade report for one student is written to the
//          output file.  student_count is incremented by one. The
//          file position pointer for the student_data file has
//          been advanced to the start of the next student input
//          record. If an error occurs, the grade report is
//          terminated and an error message is written to the
//          screen.
// Returns: a flag indicating if processing was successful.
// Uses:    write_gr_heading(), process_one_course(),
//          compute_average(), write_summary(), and
//          advance_record.
{
   // Functions used ...
   // Protypes for the functions in the uses list (above).
   #include "GrdRptP2.h"

   // Local data ...
   int total_credits;        // total graduation credits earned
   int total_gpa_credits;    // total credits toward GPA
   int total_gpa_points;     // total points toward GPA
   float gpa;                // grade point average (GPA)
   io_status io_flag;        // input status flag
                             //    set by process_name or by
                             //    process_one_student
   int course_error;         // flag to indicate error in course
                             //    information
```

(Continued)

Figure 8.17 (Continued)

```cpp
// Perform initialization.
total_credits = 0;
total_gpa_credits = 0;
total_gpa_points = 0;

// Write grade report heading with student name.
io_flag = write_gr_heading (sts, grs, semester, year);

// Process all course data for a student.
if (io_flag == success)
{
   // Write table header.
   grs << endl << endl;
   grs << "Course        Grade    Credits   Points" << endl;

   student_count++;
   io_flag = process_one_course (sts, grs, total_credits,
            total_gpa_credits, total_gpa_points,
            course_error);

   while (io_flag == success)
      io_flag = process_one_course (sts, grs, total_credits,
               total_gpa_credits, total_gpa_points,
               course_error);

   // Act based on results of course data processing.
   switch (io_flag)
   {
      case file_end :
      case record_end : // display totals; compute and print GPA
         if (course_error)
         {
            cerr << "*** ERROR: Unexpected error "
                 << "in processing course data for student "
                 << student_count << "." << endl;
            cerr << "Program will attempt to"
                 << " continue with next student." << endl;
         }
         else
         {
            gpa = compute_average (total_gpa_credits,
                  total_gpa_points);
            write_summary (grs, total_credits,
                  total_gpa_credits, total_gpa_points,gpa);
         }
         break;
      case file_error :      // display file error message
         cerr << "*** ERROR: File error reading student "
              << student_count << "." << endl;
```

(Continued)

Figure 8.17 (Continued)

```
                cerr << "Program will attempt to recover and continue"
                    << " with next student." << endl;
                break;
            case data_error :     // display data error message
                cerr << "*** ERROR: Invalid data for student "
                    << student_count << "." << endl;
                cerr << "Program will attempt to recover and continue"
                    << " with next student." << endl;
                break;
            default:                  // catch unexpected i/o conditions
                cerr << "*** ERROR: Unexpected condition in"
                    << " processing student " << student_count << "."
                    << endl;
                cerr << "Program will attempt to recover and continue"
                    << " with next student." << endl;
        }   // end switch
        // Advance to top of next report page and to next input line
        grs.put ('\f');
    }   // end if
    if ((io_flag != file_end) && (io_flag != record_end))
        io_flag = advance_record (sts);

    return io_flag;
}   // end process_one_student
```

Figure 8.18 Functions write_gr_summary, write_summary, **and** advance_record

```
// FILE: GenGRprt.cpp
// GENERATE GRADE REPORT

#include <iomanip.h>

#include "IoStat.h"

// WRITE GRADE REPORT HEADING INCLUDING STUDENT NAME
io_status write_gr_heading
  (ifstream& sts,                 // IN: student data file stream
   ofstream& grs,                 // OUT: grade report file stream
   int semester,                  // IN: the semseter
   int year)                      // IN: the year
// Pre :    The pointer for the student data file is at the start
//          of the next student record.
// Post:    The pointer for the student data file is just past the
//          sentinel character.  Each data character read is
//          written to the grade_report file except for the
//          sentinel.
```

(Continued)

Figure 8.18   (Continued)

```
// Returns: A flag indicating if processing was successful.
{
    // Local data ...
    const char nwln = '\n';           // newline character
    const char name_sentinel = '/';   // end of name sentinel

    char name_char;                   // contains each character as read

    // Write grade report header for this student.
    switch (semester)
    {
        case 1: grs << endl << "Fall "; break;
        case 2: grs << endl << "Spring "; break;
        case 3: grs << endl << "Summer I "; break;
        case 4: grs << endl << "Summer II ";
    } // end switch
    grs << "Semester 19" << year << endl << "Grade Report for: ";

    // Read and write student name.
    sts.get(name_char);
    if (!sts.eof ())
    {
        while (!sts.bad () && (name_char != name_sentinel) &&
               (name_char != nwln) && (!sts.eof ()))
        {
            grs.put (name_char);
            sts.get (name_char);
        } // end while
    } // end if

    // Update state of processing input
    if (name_char == name_sentinel)
        return success;
    else if (name_char == nwln)
        return data_error;
    else if (!sts.eof ())
        return file_end;
    else
        return file_error;
} // end write_gr_heading

// WRITE STUDENT SUMMARY DATA
void write_summary
    (ofstream& grs,            // OUT: grade report file stream
     int total_credits,        // IN: total credits earned
     int total_gpa_credits,    // IN: total credits earned toward GPA
     int total_gpa_points,     // IN: total points earned toward GPA
     float gpa)                // IN: student grade point average

// Pre : All totals must be defined upon entry.
```

(Continued)

Figure 8.18 (Continued)

```
// Post: GPA defined equal to total_gpa_points / total_gpa_credits
{
    // Write grade report summary.
    grs << endl;
    grs << "Total credits earned: " << total_credits << endl;
    grs << "Total credits earned toward GPA: " << total_gpa_credits
        << endl;
    grs << "Total points earned toward GPA: " << total_gpa_points
        << endl;
    grs << setprecision (2)
        << setiosflags (ios::showpoint | ios::fixed);
    grs << "Semester grade point average: " << gpa << endl;
    return;
}   // end write_summary



// ADVANCE TO NEXT STUDENT RECORD ON ERROR
io_status advance_record
    (ifstream& sts)                 // IN: student data file stream

// Pre:     (none)
// Post:    Student grades file pointer points to start of new
//          record or eof encountered.
// Returns: a flag indicating if processing was successful.
{
    // Local data ...
    const char nwln = '\n';     // newline character
    char record_char;           // contains each character as read

    // Read characters until newline encountered.
    // (Illustrates a for loop with an empty loop body. All
    //    activity described in header.)
    for (sts.get (record_char);
        !sts.bad () && (record_char != nwln) && !sts.eof ();
        sts.get (record_char));

    // Update state of processing input.
    if (record_char == nwln)
        return success;
    else if (sts.eof ())
        return file_end;
    else
        return file_error;
}   // end advance_record
```

following the while loop sets io_flag according to the kind of condition that caused the loop to terminate.

Function write_summary writes the credit and point total information to the grade report file. It then computes the GPA and writes it to the file.

Function `advance_record` is used to ensure that regardless of whether the processing of one student is satisfactorily completed or not, the student data file position pointer will always be pointing to the beginning of the next student record (or to the end-of-file).

Analysis for process_one_course and Its Subordinate Modules

Function `process_one_course` must read and process the data for a single course. These data consist of a six-character course ID, a letter grade, and a digit character representing the number of credits awarded for the course. The data requirements and algorithm for `process_one_course` follow.

DATA REQUIREMENTS FOR process_one_course

Input Arguments

sts (istream)	— student data file stream
total_credits (int)	— total credits earned (all courses)
total_gpa_credits (int)	— total credits earned toward GPA
total_gpa_points (int)	— total points earned toward GPA

Output Arguments

grs (ostream)	— grade report file stream
total_credits (int)	— total credits earned (all courses)
total_gpa_credits (int)	— total credits earned toward GPA
total_gpa_points (int)	— total points earned toward GPA
course_error (int)	— indicates kind of error that occurred

Local Variables

grade (char)	— the letter grade for course (A to D, F, P)
points (int)	— point value of letter grade (A = 4, B = 3, C = 2, D = 1, F = 0)
credit_char (char)	— the number of credits (as a character)
credits (int)	— the number of credits (as an integer)
io_flag (io_status)	— input/output status flag

Design of process_one_course

The structure chart for `process_one_course` and its subordinate modules is shown in Fig. 8.19. The top-level algorithm is shown below.

ALGORITHM FOR process_one_course

1. Read and write the course ID, grade, and credits (`course_io`).
2. If successful, process grade and credit data: read
    2.1. Convert letter grade to points.
    2.2. Convert credits read to an integer.

2.3. Validate credits read and print total points (credits × points) for course.

2.4. Update total credits earned, total credits toward GPA, and total points toward GPA, based on the course grade and credits.

else

2.5. Print appropriate diagnostic messages and return appropriate error indicator.

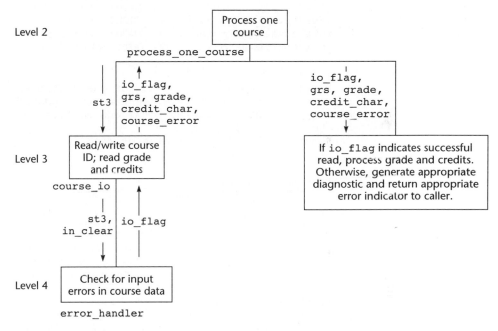

Figure 8.19 Structure chart for `process_one_course`

We will use the level-three function `course_io` to implement step 1 of the algorithm. Function `course_io` will read and write the six characters of a course ID, the single character `grade`, and the character `credit_char`, ignoring any blanks at the start of the course ID. `course_io` itself will have a level-four subordinate function, `error_handler`, to test for any input errors. The implementation of function `process_one_course` is shown in Fig. 8.20.

Figure 8.20 Function `process_one_course`

```
// FILE: Prc1Crse.cpp
// PROCESS A SINGLE COURSE

#include <iomanip.h>
```

(Continued)

Figure 8.20   (Continued)

```
#include "iostat.h"
#include "P1CrsSub.cpp"      // course_io

// PROCESS A SINGLE COURSE
io_status process_one_course
  (ifstream& sts,            // IN: student data file ptr
   ofstream& grs,            // OUT: grade report file ptr
   int& total_credits,       // INOUT: total credits earned
   int& total_gpa_credits,   // INOUT: total credits toward GPA
   int& total_gpa_points,    // INOUT: total points toward GPA
   int& course_error)        // OUT: course error flag

// Pre :    None.
// Post:    Reads all the data for one course and writes it to
//          the output file. Returns the updated values of
//          total_credits, total_gpa_credits, and
//          total_gpa_points.
// Returns: the updated status of file input/output.
// Uses:    course_io
{
    // Functions used ...
    // READS AND WRITES COURSE ID TO OUTPUT
    io_status course_io
      (ifstream&,            // IN: student data file
       ofstream&,            // OUT: grade report file
       char&,               // OUT: letter grade earned
       char&,               // OUT: credits for course
       int&);               // OUT: course error flag

    // Local data ...
    const int max_credits = 5; // max credits for one course

    char grade;               // letter grade earned for course
    int points;               // point value of grade
    char credit_char;         // number of credits for course (char)
    int credits;              // number of credits for course
    io_status io_flag;        // input/output status flag

    // Read and print course ID, letter grade, and course credits.
    io_flag = course_io (sts, grs, grade, credit_char,
                         course_error);
    if (io_flag == success)
    {
        // Convert grade to points.
        switch (grade)
        {
            case 'A':
            case 'B':
            case 'C':
            case 'D': points = int ('A') - int (grade) + 4; break;
```

(Continued)

Figure 8.20   (Continued)

```
            case 'F': points = 0; break;
            case 'P': points = 0; break;
            default:
                cerr << "Illegal grade entered for this course."
                    << endl;
                cerr << "Remaining input for this student ignored."
                    << endl;
                return data_error;
        }   end switch
        // Convert the character in credit_char to an integer.
        credits = int (credit_char) - int ('0');
        // Validate credit hours read; print total course points.
        if ((credits < 0) || (credits > max_credits))
        {
            cout << "Illegal credits amount for course." << endl;
            cout << "Remaining input for this student ignored."
                << endl;
            return data_error;
        }
        else
            grs << setw (10) << credits * points << endl;

        // Update totals.
        total_credits += credits;
        if (grade != 'P')
        {
            total_gpa_credits  += credits;
            total_gpa_points += credits * points;
        }  // end if (grade != 'P')
    }
    else if (course_error)   // if io.flag is not equal to success
    {
        // Error in inital read.
        cerr << "Error in reading data for one course." << endl;
    }  // end if (course_error)
    return io_flag;
}  // end process_course
```

Steps 2.1 and 2.2 of the algorithm (converting the course grade and credits) deserve some explanation. The conversion of the letter grade (`grade`) to an appropriate integer value (`points`) is accomplished by applying the cast operator `int` to the grade character, which produces the ASCII value of the grade (an integer). We then take advantage of the fact that the letters are arranged in sequence, beginning with `'A'` (see discussion in Chapter 7), so that subtracting the ASCII value of the grade from the ASCII value of `'A'` and adding 4 gives us the result needed to compute accurately the point total for grades `'A'` through `'D'`. Specifically, the assignment statement

```
points = int ('A') - int (grade) + 4;
```

produces the results shown in Table 8.2. For a grade of F, the points tallied will be set to 0; for a grade of P (for pass—as in Pass/Fail), the credits do not figure in the computation of the GPA.

Table 8.2   Results of computation `int ('A') - int (grade) + 4`

GRADE	CORRESPONDING POINTS
A	4
B	3
C	2
D	1

Similarly, the conversion of the character `credit_char`, representing the number of credits associated with a course, may be implemented using the statement

```
credits = int (credit_char) - int ('0');
```

Here we are taking advantage of the fact that the characters `'0'`, `'1'`, ..., `'9'` are in sequence in the ASCII character set (see Chapter 7 for details).

Figure 8.21 shows the subordinate module `course_io` for function `process_one_course`. Function `course_io` begins by skipping over any blanks that might precede the start of a six-character course ID. This is accomplished using the input stream functions `peek` and `get`. The `while` loop

```
while ((in_char = sts.peek()) == ' ')
   sts.get (in_char);
```

skips all blanks (if any) preceding the course ID. The `peek` function behaves exactly as `get` except that it does not advance the input stream buffer pointer. `peek` looks ahead in the input stream at the next character to be read and returns this character (or eof if there is no character to return). In `course_io`, if this character is a blank, `get` is called to read it. This loop continues executing until a nonblank has been encountered.

After processing the course ID, `course_io` reads and writes the letter grade and credits for the course. If any errors are detected during the reading of any of these characters, processing stops and an appropriate error flag is returned to `process_one_course`. The `error_handler` function, also shown in Fig. 8.21, handles the checking for errors.

Figure 8.21   Subordinate functions for function `process_one_course`

```
// FILE: P1CrsSub.cpp
// READS AND WRITES COURSE INFORMATION TO OUTPUT FILE

#include "IoStat.h"
```

(Continued)

Figure 8.21   (Continued)

```
io_status course_io
  (ifstream& sts,        // IN: student data file stream
   ofstream& grs,        // OUT: grade report file stream
   char& grade,          // OUT: letter grade earned
   char& credit_char,    // OUT: credits for course (char)
   int& error)           // OUT: error flag

// Pre :    Student data file position pointer is past the name
//          sentinel (the slash).
// Post:    Writes the next six nonblank characters to the output
//          file. Then writes the grade and finally the credits to
//          the output file. Returns grade and credits if no
//          errors.
// Returns: flag indicating if processing was successful.
// Uses:    error_handler
{
  // Functions used ...
  // CHECKS FOR INPUT FILE ERRORS
  io_status error_handler
    (ifstream&,          // IN: student data file ptr
     char);              // IN: last character read

  // Local data ...
  const int id_size = 6; // length of course code

  io_status io_flag;     // input/output status flag
  int i;                 // counter of characters read
  char in_char;          // contains last character read for
                         // course ID

  // Initialize grade and credit_char to blanks, error to false.
  grade = ' ';
  credit_char = ' ';
  error = 0;

  // Perform initial read, skipping blanks if any.
  while ((in_char = sts.peek ()) == ' ')
    sts.get (in_char);

  if (sts.eof ())
    return file_end;

  in_char = ' ';         // initialize in case of file error
  // Read and write course ID.
  for (i = 1; i <= id_size; i++)
  {
    sts.get (in_char);
```

(Continued)

Figure 8.21 (Continued)

```
        if ((error = (io_flag = error_handler (sts, in_char))) !=
            success)
        {
            error = (i != 1) || ((io_flag != record_end) &&
                    (io_flag != file_end));
            return io_flag;
        }  // end if
        grs.put(in_char);
    }  // end for

    // Read and write course grade.
    sts.get(grade);
    if ((error = (io_flag = error_handler (sts, grade))) !=
        success)
        return io_flag;
    grs.width(11);
    grs << grade;

    // Read and write course credits.
    sts.get (credit_char);
    if ((io_flag = error_handler (sts, credit_char)) != success)
        return io_flag;
    grs.width (11);
    grs << credit_char;

    return io_flag;
}  // end course_io



// UPDATE GRADUATION STATISTICS BASED ON GRADE AND CREDITS
io_status error_handler
    (ifstream& sts,         // IN: student data file ptr
     char in_char)          // IN: last character read

// Pre :    in_char is defined
// Post:    (none)
// Returns: flag indicating success or failure of operation.
{
    const char nwln = '\n';

    // Check file status and return correct result.
    if (sts.bad ())
        return file_error;
    else if (sts.eof ())
        return file_end;
    else if (in_char == nwln)
        return record_end;
```

(Continued)

Figure 8.21 (Continued)

```
    else
        return success;
}   // end error_handler
```

Testing the Grade Report Program

When you run the grade report program with some sample student data, you should generate grade reports in the form shown earlier. Verify that the error tests included in the program work and that an error in one student's data does not propagate, preventing you from processing another student's data. Test for the effect of a missing sentinel character after a student name, missing blanks between course data, an incorrect grade, or an invalid number of credits; test for a premature newline character (in the middle of a student data record) and a premature end-of-file. Also, make sure that the grade point average computed and the graduation credits earned are accurate for a variety of different grades.

Commentary: Handling Data Input Errors

As we indicated in the development of the Grade Report Program, we made an important decision concerning the handling of errors in the student course list information. Rather than permit these errors to terminate the processing of a student data record prematurely, we chose instead to record the occurrence of an error using the flag `course_error`. We generated an error message when a course error occurred, but the processing of the student record containing the error continued so that subsequent course information could be processed.

Among other things, the Grade Report Program provides an illustration of the design and coding complications that can arise in attempting to handle errors in program input. Had we been assured that no such errors existed in the student input data, the program would have been considerably shorter and easier to write. However, errorless input data are clearly the exception in programming, and decisions as to how to treat each possible error can be a problem of substantial complexity. Wrong decisions can make software users extremely unhappy. Perhaps as a user of computer software yourself, you have already suffered from this problem. Substantial strides in *error detection and recovery* by computer programs have been made in the past decade, but there is always room for improvement.

EXERCISES FOR SECTION 8.5

Self-Check   1. In the Grade Report Program, there are several program checks for invalid data. In each case, we designed the program to recover from such errors without skipping any additional data (except perhaps for the current student).

a. Locate each such invalid data check made by the program and describe the particular error being checked. Also describe the steps taken in the program to ensure no loss of data beyond, perhaps, data for the current student.

b. Can you think of any invalid data checks that could have been made but weren't? Describe one such additional check and indicate how you would have the program recover from any error that might be detected.

2. Would it be easy to modify the Grade Report Program so that bad input data would be written to a separate report file? Why or why not?

3. Write the function prototypes header file (GrdRptP2.h) for functions write_gr_heading, process_one_course, compute_average, write_summary, and advance_record (see Fig. 8.17).

Programming

1. Write the function enter_semester_id. This function should prompt the user for two integers: first, a single-digit integer between 1 and 4 representing the semester for which student grades are to be processed; then, a two-digit integer representing the year. In each case, the function should continue looping, asking for a valid prompt, until such a prompt is entered by the user.

2. Figure 6.16 (Chapter 6) contains a function compute_average, which computes the average of a collection of floating-point data items given the number of items in the collection and their sum. What changes, if any, are needed in this function for it to be reused in the Grade Report Problem?

3. Write a function skip_blanks that skips over any blanks in an input file. Do *not* use the stream function peek. Your function should return the first nonblank read from a data file (its first argument) The function should be of type io_status returning an indicator as to the status of the function processing.

8.6   ——   STREAM I/O MANIPULATOR FUNCTIONS AND FLAGS

The Manipulators

You have already been introduced to the setprecision, setw, and setiosflags manipulators in Chapter 4, Section 4.6. An expanded set of manipulators is defined in the following display. Thus far, we have used these manipulators by inserting references to them directly in iostream statements wherever they were required and including the iomanip.h header file in our programs. However, these manipulators may also be referenced as functions in the iostream.h library, as illustrated in Table 8.3. As is the case with the other functions in the iostream library (eof, close, get, etc.), these functions may be used with streams of type ifstream or ofstream.

Table 8.3   I/O Manipulators Referenced as Functions

MANIPULATOR/ FUNCTION NAME	ARGUMENT/ RETURN VALUE	EFFECT	FUNCTION EXAMPLE
setiosflags/ setf	list of flags to be set/ long	Turns on the flag bits corresponding to those in the argument list.	cout.setf (ios::left, ios::adjustfield);
unsetiosflags/ unsetf	list of flags to be unset/ long	Turns off the flag bits corresponding to those in the argument list.	cout.unsetf (ios::show point);
setprecision/ precision	int/ int	Sets the precision to the argument. The default is 6. Returns the previous precision setting.	n = sts.precision (10); sts.precision (10);
setw/ width	int/ int	Sets the width to the argument. Affects only the next output value, after which the width returns to the default of 0. Returns the previous width setting.	k = grs.width (6); grs.width (6);

The Flags

The manipulator `setiosflags` (function `setf`) controls the formatting of output by setting various *format state flags* associated with stream input and output. The flags are elements of an enumeration type defined for all iostreams. The notation `ios::flag_name` is used to reference these flags. As is the case with the dot notation used to reference the iostream functions, the reason for the colon notation will become apparent by the end of Chapter 11. Some of the flags that must be directly manipulated by `setiosflags` (`setf`) are listed in Table 8.4.

Table 8.4   Format State Flags

FLAG NAME	MEANING IF SET	DEFAULT VALUE
skipws	Skip white space on input	On

(Continued)

Table 8.4   (Continued)

FLAG NAME	MEANING IF SET	DEFAULT VALUE
left	Left-adjust output in field (turns off right-adjust flag if on)	Off
right	Right-adjust output in field (turns off left-adjust flag if on)	Off
showpoint	Force decimal point and trailing zeros (floating output)	Off
scientific	Use 1.2345E2 floating notation (turns off fixed flag if on)	Off
fixed	Use 123.45 floating notation (turns off scientific flag if on)	Off

8.7 —— COMMON PROGRAMMING ERRORS

• *Connecting Streams and External Files:* In any programming language, the processing of external (permanent) files tends to be difficult to master; C++ is no exception. To use an external file in your program, you first must declare a stream variable and establish a connection between the name of the file as it is known to the operating system and the name of the stream variable known to your program. In C++, this connection is established using the file open function, open. Once this connection has been established, you must use the stream name (for example, ins, outs) in all subsequent references to the file in your program. Normally, you will not receive a compiler or an execution-time diagnostic if a call to the open function fails to open a file successfully. For this reason, you are urged always to check to ensure all files have been successfully opened (see, for example, the program shown in Fig. 8.5).

• *Preparing Files for Input and Output:* The C++ cin and get can be used only after a file has been prepared for input. Similarly, cout and put can be used only after a file has been prepared for output. The omission of an open statement will not be detected by the compiler, and the failure of an open to execute properly may not be detected at run time. In either case, your program will simply not execute correctly. For example, if your program contains a while loop with an end-of-file termination condition, the loop could execute without termination as it repeatedly looks for a nonexistent end-of-file. No data will be read and no useful processing will take place, but the program will not terminate.

Always be careful to prefix each call to a file processing function with the correct stream name. For example, accidental use of an output stream name with a file input operation such as `get` will cause a compiler error message such as `"Get is not a member of ofstream"`. This message indicates that the `get` function, which you have tried to use with an output file stream, can be used only with input file streams.

■ *Reading Past the End of a File:* An execution time error such as "`attempt to read beyond end of file`" will occur if a read operation is performed after all data in a file have been processed. The most likely cause for such an error is a loop that has executed once too often.

■ *Matching Data in an Input Stream to Input Variables Listed in a `cin` Line:* It is completely up to you, the programmer, to ensure that the order and type of the variables in your `cin` lines are listed consistently with the data in the stream to be read. In general, no execution-time diagnostics will be issued as a direct result of data inconsistencies. Instead, incorrect and sometimes undefined information will be stored in your input variables. It is imperative that you always check to ensure that the input to your programs is correct. Input failures will guarantee wrong answers; one of the first tasks you should perform in debugging and testing a program is to ensure that your test data are being read correctly.

Remember that any character (not just white space) detected during numeric input that is not a valid numeric character will terminate the reading of the current numeric input value and return the value read to that point (or an undefined value if no digits have been read).

■ *White Space and Input:* Always remember that, for all input using `cin`, leading white space (blanks, tabs, newlines, for example) is ignored—even when reading a single character! If your program requires that all white space be considered as any other character, use the function `get` to read a single character at a time.

■ *Proper Handling of the Newline Character During Input:* When using `get`, remember to skip over the newline character after you reach the end of a data line. Note that if you press the RETURN key an extra time when you are finished creating a data file, you may place an extra empty line at the end of the file. The file below contains one number per line and an empty line at the end.

```
500<nwln>
37<nwln>
<nwln> <eof>
```

Although the empty line seems perfectly harmless, if we use the `while` condition

```
while (!ins.eof ()) do
```

to control a loop that reads and processes one number at a time, the empty line will cause the loop to execute one extra time. Because there are no data to be read in this empty line, an error will occur.

• *Input/Output Argument and Flag Settings:* Once set, most input/output settings and flags remain in effect until reset. Remember, however, that the field width setting always reverts back to your system default value if it is not set again prior to the input or output of the next data element.

CHAPTER REVIEW

In this chapter, we learned more about the input and output features supported by the C++ input/output libraries. We began with the use of functions get and put to extract characters from the keyboard and insert characters into the display. We briefly discussed the differences in the use of these functions and the iostream operators << and >>.

Considerable attention was devoted to the use of *external (permanent) data files.* Two new C++ data types, ifstream and ofstream, were introduced as part of this discussion. A number of examples and two case studies illustrated how to declare variables (data streams) of these types and how to use the library functions associated with these variables.

We explained that your operating system keeps a *directory* of all external files associated with your computer and that all of these files are known to the system by an *external file name.* We showed how to use the C++ iostream library function open to *establish a connection* between this external file name and the name of the stream of characters by which the file will be known to your program.

The newline character breaks a stream into a sequence of lines. We showed how to test for the presence of a newline character in a file and how to skip past this character, leaving the *input stream buffer pointer* at the beginning of the next line. Finally, we showed how to reference the manipulators introduced in Chapter 4 using stream functions, and we discussed a number of the format flags that must be set using the setiosflags manipulator or setf function.

New C++ Constructs Stream manipulator functions and related flags are summarized in Tables 8.3 and 8.4 in Section 8.6. The other new C++ constructs introduced in this chapter are described in Table 8.5.

Table 8.5 Summary of New C++ Constructs

CONSTRUCT	EFFECT
Stream Declarations	
ifstream ins; ofstream outs;	Declares ins and outs as stream variables.

(Continued)

Table 8.5   (Continued)

CONSTRUCT	EFFECT

Open and Close Operations on Data File Streams

```
ins.open (in_data);
```
Establishes the connection between the external file named in_data and the stream ins.

Input and Output Operations for External Data File Streams

```
sts.get (ch);
```
Gets the next character from the stream sts.

```
sts >> i;
```
The next integer is read from file sts as a string of characters then converted to an integer.

```
grs.put (ch);
grs << i;
```
Puts the character in ch to the stream grs, followed by the integer value of i (output is a stream of characters).

```
ch = sts.peek ();
```
Examines the next character in the stream sts and stores it in ch. The stream input buffer pointer is not moved by this operation.

End-of-File Function

```
ins.get (ch);
while (!ins.eof ())
{
   outs.put (ch);
   ins.get (ch);
}
```
A character is read from stream ins and written to the stream outs as long as there are more characters to be processed. (Can also be written as a for loop.)

The Newline Character

(reads characters from a line, one character at a time; can also be written as a for loop)

```
ins.get(next_char);
```
Read first character from stream.

```
while (next_char != nwln)
```
If character read is not newline, write character to file outs.

```
{
   outs.put (next_char);
   ins.get (next_char);
```
Read next character from file ins.

```
}
ins.get (next_char);
```
Read past newline character to start of next line.

```
         or
for (ins.get (next_char); next_char != nwln;
     ins.get (next_char))
   outs.put (next_char);
```

✔ **QUICK-CHECK EXERCISES**

1. The _____ operation prepares a file for input or output by connecting the _____ name of the file to a _____ name.
2. The _____ character separates a stream into lines, and a _____ appears at the end of a stream data file.
3. What data types can be read or written to a stream?

4. Where are external files stored?
5. Correct the C++ program segment shown below.

```
while (!ins.eof())
{
    ins.get (...);
    outs.put (...);
}
```

Answers to Quick-Check Exercises

1. open; external, stream
2. <nwln>, <eof>
3. any data type can be read or written
4. secondary storage or disk
5.
```
ins.get (...);
while (!ins.eof())
{
    outs.put (...);
    ins.get (...);
}
```

REVIEW QUESTIONS

1. List three advantages to using files for input and output as opposed to the standard input and output you have used thus far in this course.
2. Explain how `get` and `cin` differ in reading data items from a stream.

3. a. Explain why there are usually two distinct names associated with a file.
   b. What conventions are followed for choosing each name?
   c. What does the name appearing in a program represent?
   d. Which name appears in the stream variable declaration?
   e. Which one of the names is known to the operating system?

4. Let `x` be type `float`, `n` and `m` type `int`, and `ch` type `char`. Indicate the contents of each variable after each input operation is performed, assuming the file consists of the lines below. Discuss any errors that might arise and indicate what causes them.

```
23 53.2 ABC<nwln>
145 Z<nwln>
```

```
a. cin >> n >> x >> ch;
   cin >> m;
b. cin >> ch >> n >> x >> ch1 >> ch2 >> ch3;
   cin >> m >> ch5;
c. cin >> n >> ch;
```

5. Write a loop that reads up to 10 integer values from a data file and displays them on the screen. If there are not 10 integers in the file, the message `"That's all, folks"` should be displayed after the last number.

6. Write a function that copies several data lines typed at the keyboard to an external file. The copy process should be terminated when the user enters a null line (indicated by two consecutive newlines).

PROGRAMMING PROJECTS

1. Write a program system that prints payroll checks using the file produced by the Payroll Program described in Section 8.4. The format of the checks should be similar to the one shown in Fig. 8.22.

```
Temple University                    Check No. 12372
Philadelphia, PA                     Date: 03-17-92


Pay to the
Order of:   William Cosby         $   20000.00

                                  Jane Smith
```

Figure 8.22   Format of check for Programming Project 1

2. Each year the state legislature rates the productivity of the faculty of each of the state-supported colleges and universities. The rating is based on reports submitted by the faculty members indicating the average number of hours worked per week during the school year. Each faculty member is rated, and the university receives an overall rating.

The faculty productivity ratings are computed as follows:

a. Highly productive means over 55 hours per week reported.
b. Satisfactory means reported hours per week are between 35 and 55.
c. Overpaid means reported hours per week are less than 35.

Read the following data from a data file (assuming all names are padded with blanks to 10 characters):

Name	Hours
Herm	63
Flo	37
Jake	20
Maureen	55
Saul	72
Tony	40
Al	12

Your program should include functions corresponding to the function prototypes shown below as part of your solution: You need not check for input errors to the extent done in the Grading Problem (Section 8.5).

```
// DISPLAYS TABLE HEADING
void print_header ();

// DISPLAYS PRODUCTIVITY RANKING GIVEN HOURS WORKED
void display_productivity
    (float);                    // IN: hours worked per week

// READS AND DISPLAYS ONE FACULTY NAME FROM A DATA STREAM FILE
void process_name
    (ifstream&);                // IN: stream of names and hours worked

// READS DATA LINES FROM FILE FAC_HOURS AND DISPLAYS BODY OF
//     TABLE. RETURNS NUMBER OF FACULTY AND SUM OF HOURS WORKED.
void process_data
    (ifstream&,                 // IN: stream containing names and hours
     int&,                      // INOUT: count of number of faculty
     float&);                   // INOUT: sum of hours worked by faculty
// Uses: process_name and display_productivity.
```

3. Write a program system that reads several lines of information from a data file and prints each word of the file on a separate line of an output file followed by the number of letters in that word. Also print a count of words in the file on the screen when done. Assume that words are separated by one or more blanks. Reuse as many functions introduced in the text or in the C++ library as possible.

4. Compute the monthly payment and the total payment for a bank loan, given:

   a. the amount of the loan;
   b. the duration of the loan in months;
   c. the interest rate for the loan.

   Your program should read in one loan at a time, perform the required computation, and print the values of the monthly payment and the total payment.

   Test your program with at least the following data (and more if you want).

Loan	Months	Rate
16000	300	12.50
24000	360	10.50
30000	300	9.50
42000	360	9.50
22000	300	8.25
100000	360	9.125

   Hints:

   a. The formula for computing monthly payment is

   $$\texttt{monthly\_pay} = \frac{\texttt{ratem} \times \texttt{expm}^{\,\texttt{months}} \times \texttt{loan}}{\texttt{expm}^{\,\texttt{months}} - 1.0},$$

   where

   ```
   ratem = rate / 1200.0,
   expm = (1.0 + ratem).
   ```

   You will need a loop to multiply expm by itself months times.

b. The formula for computing the total payment is

`total = monthpay × months`.

5. Use your solution to Programming Project 4 as the basis for writing a program that will write a data file containing a table of the following form:

```
Loan Amount: $1000
INTEREST   DURATION    MONTHLY      TOTAL
  RATE     (YEARS)     PAYMENT     PAYMENT
  10.00       20       _____     _____
  10.00       25       _____     _____
  10.00       30       _____     _____
  10.25       20       _____     _____
```

The output file produced by your program should contain payment information on a $1000 loan for interest rates from 10% to 14% with increments of 0.25%. The loan durations should be 20, 25, and 30 years.

6. Whatsamata U. offers a service to its faculty in computing grades at the end of each semester. A program will process three weighted test scores and will calculate a student's average and letter grade (A is 90 to 100, a B is 80 to 89, etc.). Read the student data from a file and write each student's name, test score, average, and grade to an output file.

Write a program system to provide this valuable service. The data will consist of the three test weights followed by three test scores and a student ID number (four digits) for each student. Calculate the weighted average for each student and the corresponding grade. This information should be printed along with the initial three test scores. The weighted average for each student is equal to

weight1 × score1 + weight2 × score2 + weight3 × score3

For summary statistics, print the "highest weighted average," "lowest weighted average," "average of the weighted averages," and "total number of students processed." Sample data:

```
0.35   0.25   0.40      (test weights)
100    76     88   1014 (test scores and ID)
```

7. Write a program to read in a string of characters that represent a Roman numeral and then convert it to Arabic form (an integer). The character values for Roman numerals are as follows:

```
M     1000
D      500
C      100
L       50
X       10
V        5
I        1
```

Test your program with the following data: LXXXVII (87), CCXIX (219), MCCCLIV (1354), MMDCLXXIII (2673), MCDLXXVI (1476).

9

Arrays and Structures

9.1   The Array Data Type
9.2   Selecting Array Elements for Processing
9.3   Arrays as Arguments
9.4   Reading Part of an Array
9.5   Searching and Sorting Arrays
9.6   Character Strings
9.7   The struct Data Type
9.8   Structs as Operands and Arguments
9.9   Hierarchical Structs
9.10   Unions (Optional)
9.11   Common Programming Errors
        Chapter Review

In the programs written through Chapter 8, each variable was associated with a single memory location. We call these *simple variables;* their types, *simple data types.* In this chapter we introduce two C++ language features that enable us to build new data types consisting of *aggregates,* or groupings, of related elements. We call variables of these user-defined data types *structured variables.*

C++ provides two types of structured variables, the array (an aggregate in which each element must be of the same type) and the structure (or `struct`), which allows the grouping of elements having different types. These structured variables are the subject of this chapter.

9.1 ———— THE ARRAY DATA TYPE

An *array* is a collection of variables having the same data type; for example, all the exam scores (type `int`) for a class of students. Using an array, we can associate a single name such as `scores` with the entire collection of data. Each individual element in the array is accessed by its position in the array. To refer to any one of these elements, we need to specify both the array name and the position of the element to be selected. Thus, for example, in C++, the first element in the array named `scores` is referred to as `scores[0]`, the second element as `scores[1]`, and the tenth element (if it exists) as `scores[9]`. In general, the kth element in the array is referred to as `scores[k-1]`.

As indicated earlier in the text, there are certain kinds of problems for which it may be highly desirable or even necessary to store an entire collection of data values in memory at the same time. Because each value is saved in a separate location in main memory, we can process these values more than once and in any order we wish. In previous programs we would have reused the same location to store each value. Consequently, we could no longer access the third element once the fourth one had been read.

Mathematical applications such as those involving the manipulation of vectors or matrices provide just one example of a situation in which arrays can be useful. Problems that require sorting (arranging in order) a data collection are another such case.

Array Type Declaration

Arrays in C++ are specified using *array declarations* that specify the type, name, and size of the array:

```
float x[8];
```

C++ associates eight memory cells with the name `x`. Each element of array `x` may contain a single floating-point value. Therefore, a total of eight floating-point values may be stored and referenced using the array name `x`.

x[0]	x[1]	x[2]	x[3]	x[4]	x[5]	x[6]	x[7]
16.0	12.0	6.0	8.0	2.5	12.0	14.0	−54.5

| first element | second element | third element | . . . | | | | eighth element |

Figure 9.1   The eight elements of the array x

To process the data stored in an array, we must be able to reference each individual element. The *array subscript* is used to differentiate among elements of the same array. For example, if x is the array with eight elements declared above, then we may refer to the elements of array x as shown in Fig. 9.1. The *subscripted variable* x[0] (read as "x sub 0") references the first element of the array x, x[1] the second element, and x[7] the eighth element. The number enclosed in brackets is the array subscript. Later, we will see that the subscript can be an expression of any integral type (int, long, short, char, or any enumeration type).

Example 9.1   Let x be the array shown in Fig. 9.1. Some example statements manipulating the elements of this array are shown in Table 9.1. The contents of array x after execution of the statements in Table 9.1 are shown in Fig. 9.2. Note that only x[2] and x[3] are changed.

Table 9.1   Statements that manipulate elements of array x

STATEMENT	EXPLANATION
cout << x[0];	Displays the value of x[0], or 16.0.
x[3] = 25.0;	Stores the value 25.0 in x[3].
sum = x[0] + x[1];	Stores the sum of x[0] and x[1], or 28.0, in the variable sum.
sum += x[2];	Adds x[2] to sum. The new sum is 34.0.
x[3] += 1.0;	Adds 1.0 to x[3]. The new x[3] is 26.0.
x[2] = x[0] + x[1];	Stores the sum of x[0] and x[1] in x[2]. The new x[2] is 28.0.

x[0]	x[1]	x[2]	x[3]	x[4]	x[5]	x[6]	x[7]
16.0	12.0	28.0	26.0	2.5	12.0	14.0	−54.5

| first element | second element | third element | . . . | | | | eighth element |

Figure 9.2   The contents of array x after execution of statements in Table 9.1 ■

Example 9.2   The declaration section for a plant operations program is shown below. Two arrays, `vacation` and `plant_hours`, are declared as local data.

```
// Local data ...
const int num_employees = 10; // number of employees

enum day {sunday, monday, tuesday, wednesday, thursday,
          friday, saturday};
enum logical {false, true};

logical vacation[num_employees];
float plant_hours[saturday + 1];
```

The array `vacation` has 10 elements with subscripts 0 through num_employees−1. Each element of array `vacation` can store a `logical` value. The contents of this array could indicate which employees were on vacation (`vacation[i-1]` is `true` if employee i is on vacation). If employees 1, 3, 5, 7, and 9 were on vacation, the array would have the values shown in Fig. 9.3.

vacation[0]	true
vacation[1]	false
vacation[2]	true
vacation[3]	false
vacation[4]	true
vacation[5]	false
vacation[6]	true
vacation[7]	false
vacation[8]	true
vacation[9]	false

Figure 9.3   Array `vacation`

The array `plant_hours` has seven elements (subscripts `sunday` through `saturday`). The array element `plant_hours[sunday]` could indicate how many hours the plant was operating during Sunday of the past week. The array shown in Fig. 9.4 indicates that the plant was closed on the weekend, operating single shifts on Monday and Thursday, double shifts on Tuesday and Friday, and a triple shift on Wednesday.

plant_hours[sunday]	.0.0
plant_hours[monday]	8.0
plant_hours[tuesday]	16.0
plant_hours[wednesday]	24.0
plant_hours[thursday]	8.0
plant_hours[friday]	16.0
plant_hours[saturday]	0.0

Figure 9.4   Array plant_hours   ∎

C++
SYNTAX

Array Declaration

Form: *element-type array-name* [*dimension*]

Example: char my_name[5]

Interpretation: The identifier *array-name* describes a collection of array elements, each of which may be used to store data values of type *element-type*. The *dimension*, enclosed in brackets, [ ], specifies the number of elements contained in the array. The dimension value must be a constant expression; that is, it must consist solely of constant values and constant identifiers. This value must be an integer and must be greater than or equal to 1. There is one array element for each value between 0 and the value *dimension* −1. All elements of an array must be the same type, *element-type*, which may be one of the fundamental C++ types or an enumeration type.   ∎

Example 9.3   The following illustrate some legal and illegal array declarations. Several of the legal arrays are also shown.

```
a) const int buf_size = 256;
   const int max_dice = 12;
   char buffer[buf_size];       // constant integer dimension
   int dice_freq[max_dice-1];   // constant integer expression
                                //     used as dimension
```

Array dice_freq

 [0] [1] [2] [3] [4] [5] [6] [7] [8] [9] [10]

```
b) int roll_value;             // variable integer
   float payroll[roll_value];  // not valid; roll_value not
                               //     constant
```

c)
```
const int size = 7;
int scores[size] = {100, 73, 88, 84, 40, 97};
char grades[] =  {'A', 'C', 'B', 'B', 'F', 'A'};
char my_name[size] = {'F', 'R', 'A', 'N', 'K'};
```

Array scores (size 7)

100	73	88	84	40	97	0
[0]	[1]	[2]	[3]	[4]	[5]	[6]

Array grades (size 6)

'A'	'C'	'B'	'B'	'F'	'A'
[0]	[1]	[2]	[3]	[4]	[5]

d)
```
enum day {sun, mon, tue, wed, thu, fri, sat};
int worker_count[sat] = {0, 5, 9, 9, 9, 6}; // six elements
```

Array worker_count (size 6)

0	5	9	9	9	6
[sun]	[mon]	[tue]	[wed]	[thu]	[fri]

In part a, both dimensions are integer-valued constant expressions greater than or equal to 1. In part b, `roll_value` is an integer variable, not a constant, and is therefore not legal in the specification of an array dimension.

Part c illustrates how arrays may be initialized as part of their declaration. The length of the list of initial values (enclosed in braces) must not exceed the size of the array if this size is specified in the declaration. If it does exceed the array size, the compiler will generate an error message. If the size of the array is not specified, indicated by an empty pair of brackets [ ], the compiler will determine the size as equal to the number of elements in the initial value list. If the list contains fewer elements than the array dimension allows, then the array elements not explicitly initialized will be assigned a value of 0. As illustrated in part d, enumerators (such as mon or `sat`) may be used as array dimensions because each is associated with an integer value (`sat` is associated with 6). ∎

EXERCISES FOR SECTION 9.1

Self-Check 1. What is the difference between the expressions x3 and x[3]?

2. For the following declarations, how many memory cells are reserved for data and what type of data can be stored there?

   a. `int scores[10];`
   b. `char grades[100];`
   c. `logical left_diag[8];`

3. Write array declarations for each of the following:

   a. subscript type `int`, element type `complex` (assuming `complex` to be a user-defined type), size 100.
   b. subscript type `day` (enumeration type), element type `float`, size 7

4. Which of the following array declarations are legal? Defend your answer and describe the result of each legal declaration. Assume `day` and `size` are defined as in Example 9.3.

   a. `float payroll[fri];`
   b. `int workers[3] = {6, 8, 8, 0};`
   c. `char vowels[] = {'a', 'e', 'i', 'o', 'u'};`
   d. `int freq[12] = {0, 0, 3, 7, 10, 16, 28, 31,`
      `                30, 19, 13, 5, 2};`
   e. `day today[] = {mon, tue, wed, thu, fri};`

9.2 ___ SELECTING ARRAY ELEMENTS FOR PROCESSING

Using Subscripts

Each array reference includes the array name and a subscript enclosed in brackets; the subscript determines which array element is processed. The subscript (sometimes called an *index*) used in an array reference must be an expression with an integral value between 0 and the dimension of the array minus 1. For the array x declared in Example 9.1, the allowable subscript values are the integers 0 through 7.

Example 9.4 Table 9.2 shows some simple statements involving the array x shown in Fig. 9.1. In these statements, i is assumed to be an integer variable with value 5. Make sure you understand the effect of each statement.

In Table 9.2 you can see two attempts to display element x[10], which is not in the array. These attempts will result in the display of an unpredictable value. C++ does not provide any run-time checking that an array reference does not exist.

Table 9.2   Some Simple Statements Referencing Array x in Fig. 9.1

STATEMENT	EFFECT
cout << 3 << ' ' << x[3];	Displays 3 and 8.0 (value of x[3]).
cout << i << ' ' << x[i];	Displays 5 and 12.0 (value of x[5]).
cout << x[i] + 1;	Displays 13.0 (value of 12.0 + 1).
cout << x[i] + i;	Displays 17.0 (value of 12.0 + 5).
cout << x[i+1];	Displays 14.0 (value of x[6]).
cout << x[i+i];	Value in x[10] is undefined.
cout << x[2*i];	Value in x[10] is undefined.
cout << x[2*i-3];	Displays −54.5 (value of x[7]).
cout << x[floor(x[4])];	Displays 6.0 (value of x[2]).
x[i] = x[i+1];	Assigns 14.0 (value of x[6]) to x[5].
x[i-1] = x[i];	Assigns 14.0 (new value of x[5]) to x[4].
x[i] - 1 = x[i-1];	Illegal assignment statement. Left side of an assignment operator must be an addressable expression.

C++
SYNTAX

Array Reference

Form: *name* [*subscript*]

Example: x[3*i-2]

Interpretation: The *subscript* must be an expression with an integral value. If the expression value is not in range between 0 and one less than the array size (inclusive), a memory location outside the array will be referenced. If this reference occurs, for example, on the right side of an assignment statement, the accessed element value is unpredictable. If the reference occurs on the left side of an assignment, a memory location that is not part of the array may be modified unexpectedly.

The last cout line in Table 9.2 uses floor(x[4]) as a subscript expression. Because this evaluates to 2, the value of x[2] is displayed. If the value of floor(x[4]) were outside the range 0 through 7, an unpredictable value would be displayed.

Two different subscripts are used in each of the three assignment statements at the bottom of the table. The first assignment statement copies the value of x[6] to x[5] (subscripts i+1 and i); the second assignment statement copies the value of x[5] to x[4] (subscripts i-1 and i). The last assignment statement causes a syntax error because there is an expression to the left of the assignment operator.

Using for Loops with Arrays

Frequently, we want to process the elements of an array in sequence, starting with the first—for example, entering data into the array or printing its contents. We can accomplish this *sequential processing of an array* using a `for` loop whose loop control variable, i, is also the array subscript, x[i]. Increasing the value of the loop control variable by 1 causes the next array element to be processed.

Example 9.5   The array cube declared below stores the cubes of the first 10 integers (for example, cube[1] is 1, cube[9] is 729).

```
int cube[10];          // array of cubes
int i;                 // loop control variable
```

The for statement

```
for (i = 0; i < 10; i++)
   cube[i] = i * i * i;
```

initializes this array as shown in Fig. 9.5.

[0]	[1]	[2]	[3]	[4]	[5]	[6]	[7]	[8]	[9]
0	1	8	27	64	125	216	343	512	729

Figure 9.5 Array cube   ∎

Example 9.6   In Fig. 9.6, the statements

```
const int max_items = 8;
float x[max_items];                      //array of data
```

allocate storage for an array x with subscripts 0 through 7. The program uses three for loops to process the array. The loop-control variable i, with i in the range ($0 \leq i \leq 7$) is also the array subscript in each loop. The first for loop,

```
for (i = 0; i < max_items; i++)
   cin >> x[i];
```

reads one data value into each array element (the first item is stored in x[0], the second item in x[1], and so on). The cin line is repeated for each value of i from 0 to 7; each repetition causes a new data value to be read and stored in x[i]. The subscript i determines the array element to receive the next data value. The data shown in the first line of the sample execution of Fig. 9.6 cause the array to be initialized as illustrated in Fig. 9.1.

The second `for` loop

```
sum = 0.0;               // initialize sum
for (i = 0; i < max_items; i++)
   sum += x[i];          // add each element to sum
```

accumulates the sum of all eight elements of array x in the variable sum. Each time the for loop is repeated, the next element of array x is added to sum. The execution of this program fragment is traced in Table 9.3 for the first three repetitions of the loop.

Figure 9.6   Table of differences

```
// FILE: ShowDiff.cpp
// COMPUTES THE AVERAGE VALUE OF AN ARRAY OF DATA AND PRINTS
//     THE DIFFERENCE BETWEEN EACH VALUE AND THE AVERAGE

#include <iostream.h>
#include <iomanip.h>

void main()
{
   // Local data ...
   const int max_items = 8;

   float x[max_items];        // array of data
   int i;                     // loop control variable
   float average;             // average value of data
   float sum;                 // sum of the data

   // Enter the data.
   cout << "Enter " << max_items << " numbers: ";
   for (i = 0; i < max_items; i++)
      cin >> x[i];

   // Compute the average value.
   sum = 0.0;                      // initialize sum
   for (i = 0; i < max_items; i++)
      sum += x[i];                 // add each element to sum
   average = sum / max_items;   // get average value

   // Set i/o flags and precision for output to ensure 1 decimal
   //    place for output.
   cout << setiosflags (ios::fixed | ios::showpoint)
        << setprecision (1);
   cout << "The average value is " << average << endl
        << endl;
```

(Continued)

Figure 9.6   (Continued)

```
    // Display the difference between each item and the average.
    cout << "Table of differences between x[i] and the average."
         << endl;
    cout << setw (4) << "i" << setw (8) << "x[i]"
         << setw (14) << "difference" << endl;
    for (i = 0; i < max_items; i++)
       cout << setw (4) << i << setw (8) << x[i]
            << setw (14) << x[i] - average << endl;
    return;
}
```

——————— Program Output ———————

```
Enter 8 numbers: 16.0  12.0  6.0  8.0  2.5  12.0  14.0  -54.5
The average value is 2.0

Table of differences between x[i] and the average.
    i    x[i]     difference
    0    16.0        14.0
    1    12.0        10.0
    2     6.0         4.0
    3     8.0         6.0
    4     2.5         0.5
    5    12.0        10.0
    6    14.0        12.0
    7   -54.5       -56.5
```

Table 9.3   Partial Trace of Second `for` Loop in Fig. 9.6

STATEMENT PART	i	x[i]	sum	EFFECT
sum = 0.0;			0.0	Initializes sum
for (i = 0; i < max_items; i++)	0	16.0		Initializes i to 0
sum += x[i];			16.0	Add x[0] to sum
increment and test i	1	12.0		1 < 8 is true
sum += x[i];			28.0	Add x[1] to sum
increment and test i	2	6.0		2 < 8 is true
sum += x[i];			34.0	Add x[2] to sum

The last `for` loop,

```
for (i = 0; i < max_items; i++)
   cout << setw (4) << i << setw (8) << x[i]
        << setw (14) << x[i] - average << endl;
```

displays a table showing each array element, x[i], and the difference between that element and the average value, x[i] - average.   ∎

As shown in the first `for` loop in Fig. 9.6, data must be read into an array one element at a time. In most instances, you will also want to display one array element at time, as shown in the last `for` loop in the figure. The reading and display of character strings is an exception (see Section 9.6).

EXERCISES FOR SECTION 9.2

Self-Check
1. If an array is declared to have 10 elements, must the program use all 10 of them?
2. The sequence of statements below changes the initial contents of array x displayed by the program in Fig. 9.6. Describe what each statement does to the array and show the final contents of array x after all statements execute.

```
i = 3;
x[i] = x[i] + 10.0;
x[i-1] = x[2*i-1];
x[i+1] = x[2*i] + x[2*i+1];
for (i = 4; i < 7; i++)
    x[i] = x[i+1];
for (i = 2; i >= 0; i--)
    x[i+1] = x[i];
```

Programming
1. Write program statements that will do the following to array x shown in Fig. 9.1 (see also the program in Fig. 9.6):

   a. Replace the third element (subscript 2) with 7.0.
   b. Copy the element in the fifth location (subscript 4) into the first one.
   c. Subtract the first element from the fourth and store the result in the fifth one.
   d. Increase the sixth element by 2.
   e. Find the sum of the first five elements.
   f. Multiply each of the first six elements by 2 and place each product in the corresponding element of a new array named `answer_array` (of size `max_size`).
   g. Display all even-numbered elements on one line.

9.3 ——— ARRAYS AS ARGUMENTS

The C++ operators (for example, <, ==, >, +, –) can be used to manipulate only one array element at a time. Consequently, an array name in an expression will generally be followed by its subscript. One exception to this rule involves the use of arrays as function arguments. Not only can we pass individual array elements to a function (using a subscript to indicate which element to pass), but we can also pass an entire array. In fact, if several elements of an array are being manipulated by a function, it is generally better to pass the entire array of data instead of individual array elements. In the following examples, we illustrate both of these argument passing features. In the first example, we show how to pass individual elements of an array to a function; in the next two, we pass entire arrays to a function.

Example 9.7   The function **exchange** shown in Fig. 9.7 may be used to switch the contents of its two floating-point arguments. The arguments **a1** and **a2** are used for both input and output and are therefore passed by reference.

This function may be used to exchange the contents of any two floating-point variables, such as **x** and **y**, with the statement

```
exchange (x, y);
```

When the function has completed the execution specified by the call, the original contents of the floating-point variables **x** and **y** will have been switched.

Figure 9.7   Function to exchange the contents of two floating-point memory locations

```
void exchange
   (float& a1, float& a2)
{
// Local data ...
   float temp;

   temp = a1;
   a1 = a2;
   a2 = temp;
   return
}   // end exchange
```

This function may also be used to exchange the contents of any pair of elements of a floating-point array. For example, the function call

```
exchange (s[3], s[5]);
```

would cause elements 4 and 6 of the floating-point array **s** to be exchanged, as shown in Fig. 9.8 (assuming, of course, that **s** has at least six elements).

s[0]	s[1]	s[2]	s[3]	s[4]	s[5]	s[6]	s[7]
16.0	12.0	28.0	26.0	2.5	12.0	14.0	−54.5

s[0]	s[1]	s[2]	s[3]	s[4]	s[5]	s[6]	s[7]
16.0	12.0	28.0	12.0	2.5	26.0	14.0	−54.5

Figure 9.8   Array **s** before (top) and after (bottom) exchange of **s[3]** and **s[5]**

C++ treats this call to **exchange** in the same way as the call involving **x** and **y**. In both cases, the contents of two floating-point memory locations (**x** and **y** in the first case, s[3] and s[5] in the second) are exchanged. The mechanics are the same, whether none, one, or both of the memory cells involved in the exchange are array elements. Of course, the subscripts in the specification of the array elements do not have to be constants, as shown in the following call to exchange, which exchanges two adjacent elements of the array s:

```
exchange (s[k], s[k+1]);
```

If k is equal to 0, this call to exchange would modify array s as shown in Fig. 9.9.

s[0]	s[1]	s[2]	s[3]	s[4]	s[5]	s[6]	s[7]
12.0	16.0	28.0	12.0	2.5	26.0	14.0	-54.5

Figure 9.9 Array s after exchange of s[k] and s[k+1], for k = 0 ∎

The next two examples illustrate the use of arrays as function arguments. In point of fact, the arrays themselves are not transmitted between the calling and the called functions. Rather, the address of the first element of the array is passed. Three floating-point arrays, x, y, and z, each of size 5, will be used in both illustrations:

```
const int max_size = 5;        // size of arrays
float x[max_size], y[max_size], z[max_size];
```

Example 9.8   In this example, we illustrate how to write and call a function, add_array, that can be used to add together, element by element, the contents of any two floating-point arrays of the same single dimension and store the result in the corresponding element of a third floating-point array of the same size. If x, y, and z (declared previously) are three such arrays, then the call

```
add_array (max_size, x, y, z);
```

would cause the addition of corresponding elements in arrays x and y with the result stored in the corresponding element of array z. This problem description may be written more compactly as follows:

   For each value of i between 0 and max_size-1,
       x[i] + y[i] is stored in z[i].

In fact, this statement of the problem provides the main idea in the implementation of the function shown in Fig. 9.10.

The argument correspondence for arrays established by the function call statement

```
add_array (max_size, x, y, z);
```

is shown in Fig. 9.11.

Figure 9.10   Function `add_array`

```
// FILE: AddArr.cpp
// STORES THE SUM OF a[i] AND b[i] IN c[i]

void add_array
  (int size,                    // IN: the size of the three arrays
   const float a[],             // IN: the first array
   const float b[],             // IN: the second array
   float c[])                   // OUT: result array

// Array elements with subscripts ranging from 0 to size-1
//    are summed element by element.
// Pre:  a[i] and b[i] (0 <= i <= size-1)are defined
// Post: c[i] = a[i] + b[i] (0 <= i <= size-1)
{
   // Local data ...
   int i;                       // loop control variable

   // Add corresponding elements of a and b and store in c.
   for (i = 0; i < size; i++)
      c[i] = a[i] + b[i];
   return;
}  // end add_array
```

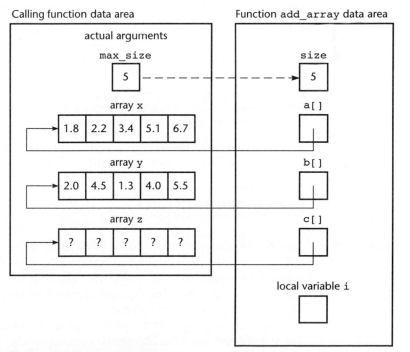

Figure 9.11   Adding two arrays

Because the first formal argument `size` is defined as call-by-value, the contents of the actual argument (`max_size = 5`) are stored in the local memory location set aside for this argument. Because arrays are always passed by reference in C++, arrays a, b, and c in the function data area are represented by the addresses of the original arrays x, y, and z used in the call. Thus the values of the elements of x and y used in the addition are taken directly from the arrays x and y in the calling function, and the function results are stored directly in array z in the calling function. After execution of the function, `z[0]` will contain the sum of `x[0]` and `y[0]`, or 3.8; `z[1]` will contain 6.7; and so on. Arrays x and y will be unchanged. In fact, the use of the reserved word `const` in front of the formal arguments a and b ensures that the contents of the corresponding actual (x and y) arguments cannot be changed by the function.   ■

These and other points about transmitting entire arrays as arguments in function calls are summarized in the following display.

Arrays as Function Arguments

In C++, arrays are passed by reference. Thus a formal array argument in a function (such as `c[]` in Fig. 9.10) represents the address of the first element of the actual array argument (z in Example 9.8).

Corresponding to each formal array argument, a local memory location is set up in the data area for the called function. When the function is called, the address of the first element of the corresponding actual array argument is placed in this location. All references to the formal array argument are, therefore, actually references to the corresponding actual array argument in the calling program.

When passing arrays as function arguments, it is important to remember the following:

1. A formal array argument in a function is not itself an array but rather is a name that represents an actual array argument. Therefore, in the function definition or its prototype, we need only inform the compiler (using the empty brackets `[]`) that the actual argument will be an array.
2. Formal array arguments that are not to be altered by a function should be specified using the reserved word `const` as illustrated in the function `add_array` for formal arguments a and b. When this specification is used, any attempt by the function to alter the contents of the designated array will cause the compiler to generate an error message.

Example 9.9   Function `same_array` in Fig. 9.12 determines whether two arrays are identical. Two arrays are considered identical if their corresponding pairs of elements are equal, that is, if the first element of one is the same as the first element of the other, the second element of one is the same as the second element of the other, and so forth.

We can determine that the arrays are not identical by finding a single pair of corresponding unequal elements. Consequently, the `while` loop in Fig. 9.12

may be executed anywhere from one time (first elements unequal) to `max_size - 1` times. Loop exit occurs when a pair of unequal elements is found or just before the last pair is tested.

After loop exit, the statement

```
return (a[i] == b[i]); // define result
```

defines the function result. If loop exit occurred because the pair of elements with subscript i are unequal, the function result will be 0 (false). If loop exit occurred because the last pair of elements is reached, the function result will be nonzero (true) if this pair is equal; otherwise, the function result will be 0 (false). We say that `same_array` performs a *logical role*, returning a value (nonzero or 0) that can be used directly as a condition in an `if` or `while` statement.

Shown next is an example of how you might use function `same_array`. The `if` statement

```
if (same_array (max_size, x, y))
    cout << "The arrays x and y are equal." << endl;
else
    cout << "The arrays x and y are NOT equal." << endl;
```

can be used to print out the results of the comparison of the arrays x and y.

Figure 9.12 Function `same_array`

```
// FILE: SameArra.cpp
// COMPARES TWO FLOAT ARRAYS FOR EQUALITY BY COMPARING
//      CORRESPONDING ELEMENTS

int same_array
  (int size,                    // IN: size of the arrays
   const float a[],             // IN: float arrays to be compared
   const float b[])

// Pre:  a[i] and b[i] (0 <= i <= size-1) are assigned
//       values.
// Post: Returns 1 (true) if a[i] == b[i] for all i in range
//       0 through size - 1; otherwise, returns 0 (false).
{
   // Local data ...
   int i;                  // loop control variable and array subscript

   i = 0;
   while ((i < size-1) && (a[i] == b[i]))
      i++;
   return (a[i] == b[i]);       // define result
} // end same_array
```

Finding the Minimum or Maximum Value in an Array

One common programming problem involves the determination of the minimum or maximum value stored in an array. In Chapter 3 we wrote a program to find the smallest of three characters. The approach taken to finding the minimum or maximum value in an array is quite similar. The algorithm for finding the maximum value follows.

1. Assume that the first element is the largest so far and save its subscript as "the subscript of the largest element found so far."
2. For each array element
    2.1. If the current element of the array is greater than the largest so far,
            2.1.1. Save the subscript of the current element as "the subscript of the largest element found so far."

The idea is to check each element of the array, in sequence, to determine which is the largest. We begin by assuming that the first element (subscript 0) is larger than the rest. The algorithm proceeds to check all remaining elements to see if any of them are larger than this first element. If such an element is found (say, element `i`), then this element is assumed to be the new largest value.

Function `max_element` in Fig. 9.13 illustrates the implementation of this algorithm for any array of floating-point elements. The function returns the value of the subscript, or index, of the largest element in the array. As shown in the function, the algorithm requires the use of a local integer variable, `max_index`, to keep track of the subscript of the largest element of the array at any point during the execution of the algorithm. Since we are assuming initially that the first element in the array is the largest, the value of `max_index` is initialized to 0. Each time a larger element in the array is found (for example, with subscript `i`), the value of `max_index` is changed (reset to `i`). The execution trace of `max_element` is illustrated in Table 9.4, using the data from array `y` in Fig. 9.11.

Figure 9.13 Function `max_element`

```
// FILE: FloatMax.cpp
// FIND THE LARGEST OF THE VALUES IN A FLOATING POINT ARRAY

int max_element
  (int n,                 // IN: number of elements to be checked
   const float x[])       // IN: array of elements

// Returns the subscript of the largest element in the array.
// Pre:  The first n elements of the array x are defined n >= 1.
// Post: x[max_index] is the largest value in the array.
{
```

(Continued)

Figure 9.13 (Continued)

```
// Local data ...
int max_index;            // index of the largest element found
int i;                    // index of the current element

// Assume the first element is largest and check the rest.
// max_index will contain subscript of largest examined so far.

max_index = 0;

for (i = 1; i < n; i++)
   if (x[i] > x[max_index])
      max_index = i;

// All elements are examined and max_index is
//    the index of the largest element.
return max_index;                // return result
} // end max_element
```

Table 9.4 Trace of `max_element` Function

STATEMENT	i	x[i]	EFFECT
`max_index = 0;`			Initializes `max_index` to 0
			`x[0]` is 2.0
`for (i = 1; i < n; i++)`	1	4.5	Initializes i to 1; 1 < 5 is true
`if (x[i] > x[max_index])`			4.5 > 2.0 is true
`max_index = i;`			`max_index` reset to 1
increment and test i	2	1.3	2 < 5 is true
`if (x[i] > x[max_index])`			1.3 > 4.5 is false
increment and test i	3	4.0	3 < 5 is true
`if (x[i] > x[max_index])`			4.0 > 4.5 is false
increment and test i	4	5.5	4 < 5 is true
`if (x[i] > x[max_index])`			5.5 > 4.5 is true
`max_index = i;`			`max_index` reset to 4
increment and test i	5	?	5 < 5 is false
`return max_index;`			Returns value of 4

It is important to realize that function `max_element` returns the subscript (or index) of the largest value in the array passed to it. It does not return the largest value itself. The following two statements could be used to call `max_element` and use its result to display the largest value in the array `y` shown in Fig. 9.13:

```
k = max_element (5, y);
cout << "The value of the largest element in the array y is "
     << y[k] << endl;
```

Although not quite as easy to read, the single statement below is equivalent; it uses the function reference as the subscript expression.

```
cout << "The value of the largest element in the array y is "
     << y[max_element (5, y)] << endl;
```

EXERCISES FOR SECTION 9.3

Self-Check
1. Give another example (other than those already in the text) of a function to which it is better to pass an entire array of data rather than individual elements.
2. In function `same_array`, what will be the value of `i` when the statement

   ```
   return (a[i] == b[i]);
   ```

   executes if array `a` is equal to array `b`? If the third elements do not match?
3. Describe how to modify function `max_element` to get a new function, `min_element`, that returns the index of the smallest array element.
4. Describe how to modify function `add_array` to obtain a new function, `mult_array`, that does a pair-wise, element-by-element multiply of two floating-point vectors of the same size.
5. Rewrite the `exchange` and `same_array` functions to work with character operands rather than floating-point operands.

Programming
1. Write a function that assigns a value of 1 to element `i` of the output array if element `i` of one input array has the same value as element `i` of the other input array; otherwise, assign a value of 0.
2. Write a function `scalar_mult_array` that multiplies an entire floating-point array `x` (consisting of n elements) by a single floating-point scalar `c`, assigning the result to the floating-point array `y`.

9.4 ____ READING PART OF AN ARRAY

In many applications, we will not know beforehand the exact number of data items we need to store in an array. In fact, the number of items will often change from one run of the program to the next. For example, a general grading program must be written to process classes of different sizes. One way to address this problem is to declare an array that is large enough to accommodate the largest possible lecture section envisioned. In most cases (for all lecture sections of smaller size than this maximum) only part of this array will actually be processed; if at some point we discover that we need to use the program for a lecture section that is larger than this maximum value, the size of the array would have to be changed and the program recompiled.

Example 9.10   The array `scores` can accommodate a lecture section of up to 250 students. Each array element can contain an integer value. Function `read_scores` in Fig. 9.14 reads up to 250 exam scores and prints a warning message whenever the array becomes filled. The actual number of scores read is returned as the value of `section_size`.

Figure 9.14   Function read_scores

```cpp
// FILE: ReadScor.cpp
// READS AN ARRAY OF EXAM SCORES FOR A LECTURE SECTION
//    OF UP TO max_size STUDENTS.

#include <iostream.h>

#include "EnterInt.cpp"

void read_scores
   (int scores[],          // OUT: array to contain all scores read
    int& section_size)     // OUT: number of elements read

// Pre:  None
// Post: The data values are stored in array scores.
//       The number of values read is stored in section_size.
//       (0 <= section_size < max_size).
{
   // Functions used ...
   // READ AN INTEGER WITHIN A GIVEN RANGE (OR A SENTINEL VALUE)
   int enter_int
      (int,        // IN: sentinel value
       int,        // IN: minimum value in specified range of values
       int);       // IN: maximum value in specified range of values

   // Local data ...
   const int sentinel = -1;    // sentinel value
   const int max_size = 250;   // maximum size of the array scores
   const int min_score = 0;    // minimum valid exam score
   const int max_score = 100;  // maximum valid exam score

   int temp_score;             // temporary storage for each score read

   // Read each array element until done.
   cout << "Enter next score after the prompt or enter "
        << sentinel << " to stop." << endl;
```

(Continued)

Figure 9.14 (Continued)

```
    section_size = 0;                 // initial class size
    temp_score = enter_int (sentinel, min_score, max_score);
    while ((temp_score != sentinel) && (section_size < max_size))
    {
        scores[section_size] = temp_score;  // save score just read
        section_size++;
        temp_score = enter_int (sentinel, min_score, max_score);
    }  // end while

    // Sentinel was read or array is filled.
    if (section_size == max_size)
        cout << "Warning: array filled, extra data ignored if any.";
    return;
}  // end read_scores
```

Function `read_scores` is general enough to be reused for reading a collection of integer values falling within a given range into an integer array. The function uses `enter_int` (Fig. 9.15) to ensure that each value read is in the range defined for a valid exam score (0 through 100) or is a sentinel value (−1 in this case). Function `enter_int` continues to prompt the user for an in-range data value or a sentinel value until one or the other is entered. Function `enter_int` has been stored in a separate file and may be reused as often as needed. Once `read_scores` has completed its task, the argument `section_size` can be used to limit the number of array elements that can be accessed in subsequent array processing.

Figure 9.15 Function `enter_int`

```
// File: EnterInt.cpp
// READS AN INTEGER BETWEEN min_value AND max_value OR A SENTINEL
//    VALUE

int enter_int
   (int s,             // IN: sentinel value
    int min_value,     // IN: minimum value in specified range
    int max_value)     // IN: maximum value in specified range
{
// Pre:  min_value and max_value are assigned values.
// Post: Returns the first data value between min_value and
//       max_value. Returns s if min_range > max_range.

    // Local data ...
    int in_range;
    int n;
```

(Continued)

Figure 9.15   (Continued)

```
// Check for nonempty range
if (min_value <= max_value)
   in_range = 0;               // false
else
{
   cout << "Error -- empty range for enter_int" << endl
      << "Program terminated!";
   return s;
}

// Keep reading until a valid number is read
while (!in_range)
{
   cout << "Enter an integer between " << min_value << " and "
      << max_value << " or " << s << endl;
   cin >> n;
   in_range = ((min_value <= n) && (n <= max_value)) ||
      (n == s);
} // end while
return n;
} // end enter_int
```

For example, the following code segment could be used to read a collection of exam scores into the integer array `my_class_scores` and compute the sum and average of these scores. Here, n is assumed to be an integer (the number of scores processed).

```
sum = 0;
read_scores (my_class_scores, n);
for (i = 0; i < n; i++)
   sum += my_class_scores[i];
average = float (sum) / float (n);
```

Only the subarray of `my_class_scores` having subscripts 0, ... , n−1 contains meaningful data; consequently, access to array elements with subscripts larger than n−1 should not be attempted. The variable n should be used to control all other processing on the partially filled array `my_class_scores`.   ∎

Both `enter_int` and `read_scores` can be used to enter restricted-range data into arrays of types other than integer. You should examine both of these functions to see what you would need to change to reuse them, for example, to enter data within a specified range into a floating-point array (see Self-Check Exercise 1 at the end of this section). Note, too, that `read_scores` can be generalized a bit further by passing the valid minimum and maximum values as input arguments, rather than defining them as constants within the function as shown in Fig. 9.14 (see Self-Check Exercise 2).

Self-Check

1. Describe the changes you would have to make to use the functions `read_scores` and `enter_int` for reading floating-point data between 0.0 and 100.0, inclusive. (Be careful to rename `enter_int` accordingly.)
2. The function `read_scores` could be better generalized to accept the minimum and maximum valid values as input arguments, rather than listing them as constants. Describe the changes required in `read_scores` to make this change, and comment (in one or two sentences) on the advantage of the change in terms of the generality of the function.
3. In function `read_scores`, what prevents the user from entering more than `max_size` scores?
4. Rewrite the `while` loop in `read_scores` as a `do-while` loop.
5. Can function `enter_int` still be used even in cases where there is no sentinel value used to control the termination of input? If so, what value(s) would be legitimate as the sentinal value argument?

9.5 _____ SEARCHING AND SORTING ARRAYS

In this section we discuss two additional common problems in processing arrays: searching an array to determine the location of a particular value and sorting an array to rearrange the elements in sequence. For example, we might want to search the array of exam scores read in by function `read_scores` (Fig. 9.14) to determine which student, if any, received a particular score. Or we might wish to rearrange (sort) the scores in either decreasing or increasing order. This would be helpful, for example, if we wanted to display the list in order by score.

Example 9.11   *Array Search.*   We can search an array for a particular element (called the *target* or the *key*) by examining each array element starting with the first (subscript 0) and testing to see whether it matches the target. If a match occurs, we say we have found the target and we can return its subscript as a result of the search. Sometimes we may also want to return a type `int` flag, to indicate whether or not the target was found. The arguments for a function to carry out this search are shown next.

DATA REQUIREMENTS FOR A SEARCH FUNCTION

Input Arguments

items (int[])   — array to be searched
size (int)   — number of items to be examined
target (int)   — item to be found

Output Arguments

(none)

Returns

Subscript of the first element of the array containing the target (−1 is returned if no element contains the target)

Local Variables

next (int)   — subscript of the next item to be tested
not_found (int)   — initialized to true (target has not been
                            found); may be reset to false (if target is
                            found)

We use a linear search algorithm to search the input array for the target value. The idea is to begin with the first element of the array and sequentially examine each element until the target is found or all array elements have been searched.

1. Start with the first array element.
2. Set not_found to 1 (true) (assume the target has not yet been found).
3. While target is not found and there are more elements
    3.1. If the current element matches the target
        3.1.1. Set not_found to 0 (false) (will cause the loop to exit at the next iteration attempt).
   else
        3.1.2. Try the next element.
    3.2. If the target was not found
        3.2.1. Return −1.
   else
        3.2.2. Return subscript of the first occurrence of target.

The while loop in step 3 executes until it finds the target in the array or until it has tested all array elements without success. Step 3.1 compares the current array element (designated by the subscript next) to the target and sets not_found to 0 (false) if they match. If they do not match, the subscript next is increased by 1. Upon loop exit, the if statement defines the function result as −1 if the target was not found or as the value assigned to next when the match occurred. The search function is shown in Fig. 9.16.

Figure 9.16   The function lin_search

```
// FILE: LnSearch.cpp
// SEARCHES AN INTEGER ARRAY FOR A GIVEN ELEMENT (THE TARGET)
```

(Continued)

Figure 9.16   (Continued)

```
int lin_search
  (int target,              // IN: the target being sought
   int size,                // IN: the size of the array
   const int items[])       // IN: the array being searched

// Array elements ranging from 0 to size - 1 are searched for
//    an element equal to target.
// Pre:  The target and array are defined.
// Post: Returns the subscript of target if found;
//       otherwise, returns -1.
{
   // Local data ...
   int next;                // index of the current score
   int not_found;           // program flag -- true if target
                            // has not been found in elements
                            // so far

   next = 0;
   not_found = 1;
   while (not_found && (next < size))
   // Target was not found in subarray a[0] through a[next-1]
   //    and next is less than size.
      if (items[next] == target)
         not_found = 0;
      else
         next++;
   // Target was found or all elements were tested
   //    without success.
   if (not_found)
      return -1;
   else
      return next;
}   // end lin_search
```

The program status flag `not_found` is used to control repetition and to communicate the results of the search loop to the `if` statement that follows the loop. `not_found` is set to 1 (true) before entering the search loop; it is reset to 0 (false) as soon as an element is tested that matches the target. The only way that `not_found` can remain true throughout the entire search is if no array element matches the target.

Note that each time through the `while` loop, the following statement (called a *loop invariant*) must remain true.

```
// Target was not found in subarray a[0] through a[next-1]
//    and next is less than size.
```

This means that the target has not yet been found in any of the elements `a[0]` through `a[next - 1]` and that `next` is less than `size`. Because `next < size` also must be true, `items[size-1]` is the last array element that can be compared to the target.

In the sketch of the array `items` shown in Fig. 9.17, the shaded elements at the left are the ones that have already been tested and the element with the subscript `next` is the one being tested in the current loop iteration. If `items[next]` does not match the target, the collection of items already examined (shaded portion of the array) will grow by one element and the value of `next` will increase by 1. The invariant is true before the first iteration (`next` is 0) because no array element precedes the element with subscript 0. If the current element matches the target, loop exit will occur without changing `next`, so the invariant will still be true. If `next` becomes `size`, all array elements will have been tested without success and loop exit will occur.

Figure 9.17 Array `items`

Example 9.12   *Sorting an Array in Ascending Order.* In Section 6.3 we discussed a simple sort operation involving three numbers. We performed the sort by examining pairs of numbers and exchanging them if they were out of order. In this section, we discuss a fairly intuitive but not very efficient sorting algorithm called a *selection sort*. To perform a selection sort of an array of n elements (with subscripts ranging from 0 to $n - 1$), we locate the smallest element in the array and then exchange this element with the first element (subscript 0). This places the smallest element at the front of the array (at location 0). Then we locate the smallest element in the remainder of the array (the subarray with subscripts 1 through $n - 1$) and exchange it with the first element of this subarray (subscript 1—actually the second element of the original array). Next, we locate the smallest element in the subarray with subscripts 2 through $n - 1$ and exchange it with the element at subscript 2. This process continues until all that remains to be ordered is the subarray consisting of the last two elements (designated by subscripts $n - 2$ and $n - 1$). Once the smallest of these two elements is placed in position $n - 2$, the sort is complete.

Figure 9.18 illustrates a trace of the steps in the selection sort algorithm. The original array is shown in the left-most column. Each subsequent column shows the array after the next smallest element is moved to its final position in the array. The shaded subarray represents the portion of the array that is sorted after each exchange has been completed. Exactly $n - 1$ exchanges will be required to sort an array with n elements.

The development of the algorithm is designed to take advantage of C++ code components developed in earlier sections of this chapter. We have already written a function (`exchange`; see Fig. 9.7) to perform the exchange of any pair of floating-point data items, and we have indicated how this function might be modified to work for data of other types as well (see Self-Check

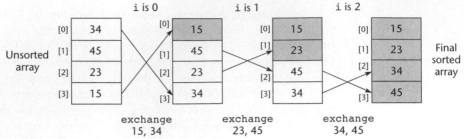

Figure 9.18   Trace of selection sort

Exercise 5 at the end of this section). In addition, in Fig 9.13 we provided a function (`max_element`) that returned the subscript of the largest element in a floating-point array. With a few modifications, we can adapt `max_element` for our sorting problem:

1. change `max_element` to work on an integer array rather than a floating-point array;
2. change the function resulting from modification 1 to find the smallest element in an integer array (see Self-Check Exercise 3, Section 9.3);
3. change the function resulting from modification 2 so that the new function `find_min` will work on any specified subarray including the entire array (having subscripts 0 to $n - 1$).

The new function `find_min` will have the following prototype:

```
// FINDS THE SUBSCRIPT OF THE SMALLEST VALUE IN A SUBARRAY
int find_min
    (int,      // IN: index of first subarray element to be checked
     int,      // IN: index of last subarray element to be checked
     int []);  // IN: the array of elements to be checked
```

With our new functions `exchange` and `find_min`, we can now easily describe the data requirements for our sorting problem:

DATA REQUIREMENTS FOR A SORT FUNCTION

> ### Input Arguments
>
> items (int[])   — array to be sorted
> n (int)   — number of items to be sorted
>
> ### Output Arguments
>
> items (int[])   — original array sorted in ascending order
>
> ### Local Variables
>
> min_sub (int)   — subscript of each smallest item located by
>   find_min

The algorithm can also be easily described:

1. Beginning with the first item in the array (subscript 0) and repeating in steps of 1 through to the n−2 element:
   1.1. Set i equal to the subscript of the first item in the subarray to be processed in the next steps.
   1.2. Find the subscript (min_sub) of the smallest item in the subarray with subscripts ranging from i to n−1;
   1.3. Exchange the smallest item found in step 1.2 with item i (exchange items[min_sub] with items[i]). (This puts the smallest item in the remaining subarray in the first element of that subarray.)

The selection sort function is shown in Fig. 9.19. The rewrite of find_min is left as a programming exercise at the end of this section (Exercise 4).

Figure 9.19   Function sel_sort

```
// FILE: SelSort.cpp
// SORTS AN ARRAY (ASCENDING ORDER) USING SELECTION SORT ALGORITHM
//     USES exchange AND find_min

void sel_sort
   (int items[],       // INOUT: array to be sorted
    int n)             // IN: number of items to be sorted (n >= 0)

{
   // Functions used ...
   // FINDS THE SUBSCRIPT OF THE SMALLEST VALUE IN A SUBARRAY
   int find_min
      (int,            // IN: index of first subarray element to be
                       //     checked
       int,            // IN: index of last subarray element to be
                       //     checked
       int []);        // IN: the array of elements to be checked

   // EXCHANGES TWO INTEGER VALUES
   void exchange
      (int&,           // INOUT: first item
       int&);          // INOUT: second item

   // Local data ...
   int min_sub;        // subscript of each smallest item located by
                       //     find_min
   int i;              // loop index

   for (i = 0; i <= n-2; i++)
   {
```

(Continued)

Figure 9.19   (Continued)

```
// The elements in items[0] through items[i-1] are in their
//    proper place and i <= n-2, for i > 0.
    min_sub = find_min (i, n-1, items);
    exchange (items[min_sub], items[i]);
} // end for
return;
} // end sel_sort
```

In the function in Fig. 9.19, the loop invariant

```
// The elements in items[0] through items [i-1] are in their proper
//    place and i <= n-2.
```

summarizes the progress of the selection sort. The meaning of this invariant is illustrated in Fig. 9.20. Here, the subarray whose elements are in their proper place after each exchange is shaded at the left. The remaining elements, possibly not yet all in place, are known to be larger than all of the sorted elements (larger than `items[i]` through `items[n-1]`). During each iteration, or *pass,* of the `for` loop, the sorted subarray (the shaded portion of the array at the left in Fig. 9.20) grows by one element and `i` is incremented accordingly. When `i` is equal to `n-1`, the first `n-2` elements will be in their proper place; this ensures that `items[n-1]` is also in its proper place.

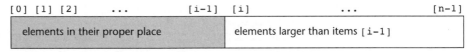

Figure 9.20   Array `items`

As shown in Fig. 9.19, given the two functions `find_min` and `exchange` as the foundation for the solution to the sort problem, the implementation of the problem solution reduces to a `for` loop (with a loop control variable, running from 0 to `n-2`) containing nothing more than calls to these two functions:

```
for (i = 0; i <= n-2; i++)
{
    min_sub = find_min (i, n-1, items);
    exchange (items[min_sub], items[i]);
} // end for
```

Example 9.12 is a good illustration of the importance of component reuse in problem-solving and program engineering. Our goal is always to decompose a complicated problem into simpler subproblems so that as many of these subproblems as possible are solvable using existing and tested components. Occasionally, perhaps, some minimal modification to these components may be needed to tailor them to the current problem. But this is preferable to designing, implementing, and testing a new function from scratch.

EXERCISES FOR SECTION 9.5

Self-Check

1. For the linear search function in Fig. 9.16, what happens if:

    a. the last element of the array matches the target?
    b. several elements of the array match the target?

2. Trace the execution of the selection sort on the following list:

    10   55   34   56   76   5

    Show the array after each exchange occurs. How many comparisons are required?
3. How could you modify the selection sort algorithm to arrange the data items in the array in descending order (largest first)?
4. Modify the selection sort algorithm so that the exchange step is skipped when i and min_sub are equal.
5. Modify the exchange function, Fig. 9.7, to work for integer data.

Programming

1. Write a function to count the number of items in an integer array having a value greater than 0.
2. Another method of performing the selection sort is to place the largest value in position n-1, the next largest in n-2, and so on. Write this version.
3. A technique for implementing an array search without introducing a status flag is to use a while loop that increments next as long as both of the following statements are true:

    a. the target does not match the current element; and
    b. next is less than size-1.

    After loop exit, the element at position next can be tested again to determine the function result. If the element matches the target, the result is next; otherwise, the result is −1. Rewrite the function body for the linear search to reflect this algorithm change.
4. Write the function find_min using the following prototype:

```
// FINDS THE SUBSCRIPT OF THE SMALLEST VALUE IN A SUBARRAY
int find_min
    (int,      // IN: index of first subarray element to be checked
     int,      // IN: index of last subarray element to be checked
     int []);  // IN: the array of elements to be checked
```

9.6 ——— CHARACTER STRINGS

Until now, our work with character data has been limited to the use of variables of type char that hold a single character value. In this section we discuss the manipulation of a new data structure, the *character string*, which may be used to represent a sequence of characters considered as a single data item. In C++, strings of characters are stored in arrays of type char, one character per array element.

We have already seen numerous examples of character strings, particularly in many of our input and output instructions. The strings

```
"The average value is"
"Enter an integer between"
```

and

```
".\n\a\a"
```

(from the Hello Program in Chapter 2) are but a few examples of such strings.

Character strings are distinguished textually from individual characters through the use of double quotes " " (versus the single quote ' ', used to enclose a single character). But strings and type char data also differ in terms of their internal storage. The character constant 'a' is stored as a single 8-bit byte of information, as shown on the left in Fig. 9.21. On the other hand, the length-one character string "a" is stored in a two-element character array, as shown on the right side of the figure.

The character 'a'   The string "a"

| a | | a | \0 |
                              [0] [1]

Figure 9.21   Differences between character constants and strings

All character strings are stored in arrays as pictured in Fig. 9.21. They are terminated by the special character '\0', sometimes called the *null character*, that is used in C++ to mark the end of a character string. The length of the string includes all characters up to but not including the terminating character. Thus the actual length of a string is always one less than the number of characters required to store the string, because the terminator character must always be included.

Example 9.13   a) The character string "Hello world!" in the cout line

```
cout << "Hello world!" << endl;
```

is stored as shown at the top of Fig. 9.22. A total of 13 characters are required to store the string, but its actual length is 12.

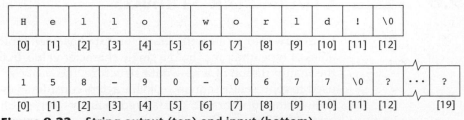

Figure 9.22   String output (top) and input (bottom)

b) Given the character array `my_ssno` declared as

`char my_ssno[20];`

and the typed input

`158-90-0677`

the statement

`cin >> my_ssno;`

reads the typed string and stores it as shown at the bottom of Fig. 9.22.

c) Character strings may also be used to initialize character arrays at their point of declaration. For example, the statement

`char my_ssno[20] = "158-90-0677";`

has the same effect as the `cin` instruction just illustrated. On the other hand, the statement

`char my_ssno[] = "158-90-0677";`

causes an allocation of space that is large enough to accommodate the string plus the termination character (only 12 characters in this case).   ■

Input and Output of Strings

cout with Strings Character strings may be used with stream output just as any other fundamental data type. All characters in the designated string (and more, if the terminator character is not present) will be displayed.

If the `setw` manipulator is used prior to the string to be displayed (for example, `setw(7)`), the string will appear right-justified in a field of the specified length. To force left justification, the `setiosflags` manipulator with the argument `ios::left` must be used. If the length specifier is present but not large enough to accommodate the string being printed, the field will be expanded to fit the string precisely.

cin with Strings With string input, `cin` behaves much the same as it does with numeric data. That is, `cin` skips leading blanks as it looks for an input value, and the first white-space character (blank, newline, tab, etc.) encountered while scanning an input value terminates the input operation for the string. Although this behavior is consistent with what we might expect in C++, it is easy enough to forget the full implication and get seemingly strange results.

When the input operation for a string is complete, the termination character, `'\0'`, is placed in the next available element of the character array given as the corresponding `cin` argument. The string array must be large enough for this termination character, or some other valuable information in your program may be destroyed.

Some examples of string input and output are shown next.

Example 9.14   *Illustrations of cout and cin*

a) Assume that my_name is a character string of length 24 containing the name

Asher Adam Smasher

beginning in element [0] and followed by '\0'. Then

- The output instruction

   cout << endl << my_name;

   would cause the string

   Asher ▯ Adam ▯ Smasher

   to be printed in the left-most 18 positions of a new line (the symbol ▯ is used to represent a blank).
- The instruction

   cout << endl << setw (18) << my_name;

   would produce the same result as above.
- The instruction

   cout << endl << setw (24) << my_name;

   would cause the contents of my_name to be printed right-adjusted in a 24-character field (with 6 preceding blanks):

   ▯ ▯ ▯ ▯ ▯ ▯ Asher ▯ Adam ▯ Smasher

- The instruction

   cout << endl << setiosflags (ios::left) << setw(24)
        << my_name;

   would cause the contents of my_name to be printed left-adjusted (with blank padding on the right) in a 24-character field:

   Asher ▯ Adam ▯ Smasher ▯▯▯▯▯▯

b) If the character string

Asher Adam Smasher

were typed at the keyboard for entry into `my_name`, then the input instruction

```
cin >> my_name;
```

would result in only the first five characters (the substring `Asher`) to be read and placed in the array `my_name` (followed by the character `'\0'`). The same input would result no matter how many blanks preceded the name entered at the keyboard. The first white space (in this case, the blank following the first name `Asher`) would terminate the input of this string.

c) If the characters

```
Donna30
```

were typed at the keyboard for entry to the array `my_name` and integer variable `age`, then the instruction

```
cin >> my_name >> age;
```

would result in the entire string `Donna30` being entered into the array `my_name` (followed by `'\0'`); nothing would be entered into the variable `age`. Remember, any white space at the beginning of the input string would be skipped. The newline character (assumed when the return key is pressed at the end of the string entry) following the string does not terminate processing. The processing of any input following the string `Donna30` would continue. If any numeric data value followed the string `Donna30`, that value would be stored in `age`. If the input following `Donna30` were not numeric, then the `cin` statement would terminate and the value of `age` would be unpredictable.

d) The C++ statements

```
char department[5];
char days[6];
int course_number;
int time;

...
cin >> department >> course_number >> days >> time;
```

would produce the results shown in Fig. 9.23 for both of the following data entry samples (again, the symbol □ represents a blank):

- sample 1: CIS □ 223 □ MWF □ 1130
- sample 2: CIS
    223
    MWF
    1130

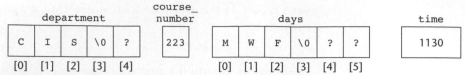

Figure 9.23   Result of data entry from Example 9.14.   ∎

Assignment of strings

Although we consider character strings as single data entities, no fundamental operations are defined for strings. C++, however, does provide an extensive collection of functions in the `string.h` library, which we can use to perform these operations. This library is discussed in more detail in Chapter 13. Here we discuss the functions for assignment and comparison and one additional function for determining the length of a string. We begin with the string assignment, or *copy*, operation.

The function `strcpy` (string copy) has two character array arguments, a destination argument

`char dest[]`

and a source argument

`const char src[]`

This function

`strcpy (dest, src);`

copies the string `src` into the string `dest`. No check is made to determine whether or not `dest` has enough space to accommodate `src`. All characters up to and including the `'\0'` from `src` are copied. The formal description of the second array argument (the source argument) is preceded by `const` to ensure that the contents of the array cannot be changed. Function `strcpy` also returns a value, but we will defer discussion of this return value until Chapter 13.

Example 9.15   The variables `first_name` and `last_name` are declared to hold strings of length 10 or less:

`char first_name[11], last_name[11];`

The statement

`strcpy (first_name, "A.C. Jones");`

stores the string value `"A.C. Jones"` in the string variable `first_name` as shown in Fig. 9.24.

[0]	[1]	[2]	[3]	[4]	[5]	[6]	[7]	[8]	[9]	[10]
A	.	C	.		J	o	n	e	s	\0

Figure 9.24 Array `first_name`

If `first_name` is not a string variable, this statement causes a syntax error. Note that the second argument may be a string variable or a string constant (enclosed in `"  "`). Because `first_name` and `last_name` are of the same size, the statement

```
strcpy (last_name, first_name);
```

copies the string value stored in `first_name` to `last_name`.

It is important to remember that `strcpy` continues copying until the character `'\0'` is encountered. If the string to be copied (`src`) is shorter than the destination string, the remaining characters in the destination string will remain unchanged. The statement

```
strcpy (first_name, "Jones");
```

will change the value of `first_name` to that shown in Fig. 9.25. On the other hand, if the source string is longer than the destination string, storage locations beyond those allocated to the destination string will be overwritten and their contents destroyed. Thus the statement

```
strcpy (first_name, "A.C. Johnson");
```

will change the value of `first_name` to that shown in Fig. 9.26 and will place the characters `'n'` and `'\0'` into locations immediately following the space allocated for `first_name`. This could produce surprising results, which might not become evident until later in the execution of your program. Generally, such errors are hard to detect, because no check is made on the space available in the destination.

[0]	[1]	[2]	[3]	[4]	[5]	[6]	[7]	[8]	[9]	[10]
J	o	n	e	s	\0	o	n	e	s	\0

Figure 9.25 Array `first_name`

[0]	[1]	[2]	[3]	[4]	[5]	[6]	[7]	[8]	[9]	[10]	?	?
A	.	C	.		J	o	h	n	s	o	n	\0

Figure 9.26 Array `first_name`   ■

By now it should be clear that `strcpy` must be used with care. You must ensure that any string to be stored in or copied to a string variable is no longer than the space allocated to that variable.

Another function, `strncpy`, allows the programmer explicitly to limit the number of characters copied. This function has three arguments, destination and source arguments as described for `strcpy`, and a third argument `n` (an integer), which specifies the maximum number of characters that can be copied.

Function `strncpy` copies the first n characters of `src` into `dest`. If a `'\0'` character is encountered in `src` before n characters are copied, then sufficient `'\0'` characters are placed into the destination array to fill the first n elements of the array. As with `strcpy`, we defer discussion of the value returned by `strncpy` to Chapter 13.

Example 9.16   Execution of the statement

```
strncpy (first_name, "Jones", 11);
```

will change the contents of `first_name` as shown in Fig. 9.27. Execution of

```
strncpy (first_name, "A.C. Johnson", 11);
```

will change the contents of `first_name` to that shown in Fig. 9.28. No extra characters are copied. However, the resulting `first_name` is not a valid string value because there is no terminating `'\0'`.

One way to protect against further damage from this situation is always to assign the value `'\0'` to the $(n-1)$th element of the actual destination argument, as in

```
first_name [n-1]  =  '\0';
```

[0]	[1]	[2]	[3]	[4]	[5]	[6]	[7]	[8]	[9]	[10]
J	o	n	e	s	\0	\0	\0	\0	\0	\0

Figure 9.27   Array `first_name`

[0]	[1]	[2]	[3]	[4]	[5]	[6]	[7]	[8]	[9]	[10]
A	.	C	.		J	o	h	n	s	o

Figure 9.28   Array `first_name`

Comparison of Strings

The function `strcmp` (string compare) has two array arguments:

```
const char s1[], const char s2[]
```

The function

```
strcmp (s1, s2);
```

compares the strings s1 and s2 and returns a value less than 0 if s1 < s2 lexicographically (based on the ANSI values of the characters), a value greater than 0 if s1 > s2, and a value of 0 if s1 == s2. The function makes pairwise comparisons of the character elements of s1 and s2, beginning with s1[0] and s2[0]. It stops either when it reaches the end of both strings and finds them equal or when it reaches a pair of elements s1[k] and s2[k] such that s1[k] is not equal to s2[k]. In all three possible cases, the value returned is the difference between the last two elements compared.

It is important to note that if one string (for example, s1) is a substring of the other (s2), s1 will always be less than s2.

Example 9.17   Assume str1 and str2 are two string variables of size 20. Table 9.5 shows the results of strcmp as applied to several different values of these two variables. The last line of Table 9.5 shows the curious result that "3" is greater than "1239". This is due to the fact that the condition result is based solely on the relationship between the first pair of characters '3' and '1' ('3' > '1'). Similarly, "39" > "3897692," but "390" < "39025" because "390" is a substring of "39025".

The function strncmp has three arguments of the form

```
const char s1[], const char s2[], int n
```

This function works in similar fashion to strcmp. It returns a value of less than 0 if s1 < s2, greater than 0 if s1 > s2, and 0 if s1 == s2. It makes at most n pairwise comparisons of s1 and s2, beginning with s1[0] and s2[0]. It stops when s1[k] < s2[k] (returns < 0), s1[k] > s2[k] (returns > 0), or when all n comparisons have been completed and the strings are found to be equal (returns 0).

Table 9.5   Some String Comparison Results (using strcmp)

str1	str2	RETURN VALUE	REASON
"AAAA"	"ABCD"	< 0	'A' < 'B'
"B123"	"A089"	> 0	'B' > 'A'
"127"	"409"	< 0	'1' < '4'
"12AX!"	"12AX!"	= 0	equal strings
"ABC"	"ABCDE"	< 0	str1 a substring of str2
"3"	"1239"	> 0	'3' > '1'

■

Example 9.18   Table 9.6 shows some results of the use of strncmp; here, n is assumed to be 3 in all cases.

Table 9.6   Some String Comparisons (using `strncmp`)

str1	str2	RETURN VALUE	REASON
"AAA"	"ZZZ"	< 0	'A' < 'Z'
"AZZ"	"ZZZ"	< 0	'A' < 'Z'
"AB"	"ABCDE"	< 0	"AB" is a substring of "ABCDE" and has length < n
"ABC"	"ABCDE"	= 0	Strings are identical in the first 3 characters.
"905"	"90562"	= 0	Strings are identical in the first 3 characters.
"xy"	"xy"	= 0	End of identical strings reached.

The Length of a String

Much of the discussion of the assignment and comparison of strings has involved references to "the length of a string." Fortunately, the `string.h` library has a simple function, `strlen`, for determining the length of a string. Function `strlen` has one array argument of the form

```
const char s[]
```

and it returns the length of this string argument (an integer representing the number of characters up to but not including '\0').

Example 9.19   If `name` is a string declared using

```
char name[] = "Cal Ripken Jr.";
```

then the function call

```
strlen (name)
```

returns the value 14.

EXERCISES FOR SECTION 9.6

Self-Check
1. Draw a figure similar to the ones in Fig. 9.22 to illustrate the internal view of the string `"Judith A. O'Shea"` stored in the array `her_name` of size 20.
2. Given the array `first_name[] = "Joe DeBlasi"`, describe by drawing a picture the effects of the following statements:

   a. `strcpy (first_name, "Pat");`
   b. `strncpy (first_name, "Pat McCarren", 6);`

3. When `cin` is scanning a string, what happens if there are more characters (with no white space) than will fit in a specified string variable?
4. Provide a precise, carefully worded explanation of the results illustrated in each of the seven parts of Example 9.14 [four in part a and three more in parts b, c, and d).
5. Write out an algorithm for the function `strcmp`.

Programming   1. Write a program to read a sentence consisting of a sequence of words of 12 or fewer characters each and print each word on a separate line.

9.7 _____ THE struct DATA TYPE

In the preceding sections, we discussed the array, a data structure that is fundamental to programming and included in almost every high-level programming language. We showed how the array could be used for storing information of the same type as a collection or aggregate of related data having the same name. We now turn our attention to another important and common data structure. This structure, which is used for storing information of different types as an aggregate, is called a `struct` in C++.

The individual components of a `struct` are called *members*. Each member of a `struct` can contain data of a different type from the other members. For example, we can use a `struct` to store a variety of information about a person, such as name, marital status, age, and date of birth. We reference each of these data items through its *member name*.

Declaring a struct Type and Variables of That Type

Example 9.20   The staff of our small software firm is growing rapidly. To keep the records more accessible and organized, we decided to store relevant data, such as the following descriptive information, in an employee *database,* a collection of information about all of the firm's employees. An example of the kind of information we might choose to store is given next.

ID: 1234
Name: Noel Goddard
Gender: Female
Number of Dependents: 0
Hourly Rate: 6.00
Total Wages: 240.00

In C++, we can declare a `struct` named `employee` to store this information. There must be six *members* in the `struct`, one for each data item to be stored. We must specify the name of each member and the type of information to be stored in the member. We choose the names in the same way we choose all other identifiers: The names describe the nature of the information represented. The content of each member determines the appropriate data type. For example, the employee's name should be stored as a string of characters and the age as an integer. A sample description of the `employee` structure is shown next.

```
const int string_length = 20;
struct employee
{
    int ID;
    char name[string_length];
    char gender;
    int num_depend;
    float rate, tot_wages;
};
```

It is important to realize that this sequence of C++ statements defines a new data type named `employee`, a *structured type* consisting of members, each of which has a type associated with it. There is no memory associated with this type. However, once it has been defined, we may declare *structure variables* of this type. These variable declarations cause the allocation of storage space in the form defined by the `struct`. For example, the `struct` variables `organist` and `janitor` are declared next.

```
employee organist, janitor;
```

The variables `organist` and `janitor` both have the structure specified in the declaration of the type `employee`. Thus, the memory allocated for these variables consists of storage space for six distinct values. The variable `organist` (of type `employee`) is shown next, assuming that values shown earlier are stored in memory.

```
id              1234
name            Noel Goddard\0
gender          F
num_depend      0
rate            6.00
tot_wages       240.00
```

The `struct` declaration is described in the next display

C++
SYNTAX

struct Type Declaration

This is a restricted form and does not show the full generality of the construct.

Form: struct *struct-type*

        {

            type$_1$ id-list$_1$;

$$type_2 \; id\text{-}list_2;$$
$$\cdot$$
$$\cdot$$
$$\cdot$$
$$type_n \; id\text{-}list_n;$$

```
};
```

Example:
```
struct complex
{
    float real_part, imaginary_part;
};
```

Interpretation: The identifier *struct-type* is the name of the structure being described. Each *id-list$_i$* is a list of one or more member names of the same type separated by commas, and each *id-list$_i$* is separated from the next *id-list* of a possibly different type by a semicolon. The data type of each member in *id-list$_i$* is specified by *type$_i$*.

Note: *type$_i$* can be any fundamental or user-defined data type, including a structured type such as an array or `struct`. If *type$_i$* is a user-defined data type, it must be defined before the `struct` is defined. The name of the `struct` itself is defined as soon as `struct` is reached. Thus, a `struct` may contain elements of the type specified by the `struct` name. ∎

Manipulating Individual Members of a struct

We can reference a `struct` member using the *member access operator,* a period. If `s` is a `struct` variable and `m` is a member of that `struct`, then `s.m` is a member `m` of the `struct` `s`.

Example 9.21   Figure 9.29 shows how data can be stored in a structure variable. A sequence of assignment statements is used to assign appropriate data to each member of the structure variable `organist`.

Figure 9.29   struct **variable** organist

```
organist.ID = 1234;
strcpy (organist.name, "Noel Goddard");
organist.gender = 'F';
organist.num_depend = 0;
organist.rate = 6.00;
organist.tot_wages += organist.rate * 40.0;
```

Once stored in a `struct`, information may be manipulated in the same way as other data in memory. For example, the last assignment in Fig. 9.29

computes the organist's new total wages by adding this week's wages to the previous total wages. The computed result is saved in the `struct` member `organist.tot_wages`.

The statements

```
cout << "The organist is ";
switch (organist.gender)
{
    case 'F': case 'f':
        cout << "Ms. ";
        break;
    case 'M': case 'm':
        cout << "Mr. ";
        break;
}
cout << organist.name << endl;
```

display the organist's name after an appropriate title (`"Ms."` or `"Mr."`); the output line follows:

```
The organist is Ms. Noel Goddard
```
■

EXERCISES FOR SECTION 9.7

Self-Check
1. Each part in an inventory is represented by its part number, a descriptive name, the quantity on hand, and the price. Define a `struct part`.
2. A catalog listing for a textbook consists of the author's name, the title, the publisher, and the year of publication. Declare a `struct catalog_entry` and a variable `book` and write assignment statements that store the relevant data for this textbook in `book`.

9.8 ___ STRUCTS AS OPERANDS AND ARGUMENTS

Because arithmetic and logical operations can be performed only on individual data elements (as opposed to entire collections), `struct` type variables cannot be used as the operands of arithmetic and relational operators. Arithmetic and relational operators must be used with the individual members of a `struct`, as shown in the previous section. This is also true for the input (>>) and output (<<) operators. However, we may assign entire structs (to other structs of the same type) and we can pass structs as actual arguments to functions as long as the corresponding formal argument is of the same type.

struct Assignment

We can assign all of the members of one struct variable to another struct variable of the same type. If organist and janitor are both struct variables of type employee, the statement

```
organist = janitor;  // Copy janitor to organist
```

assigns all members of janitor to the corresponding struct organist. The structures involved in the assignment must be of the same type.

STRUCTS as Arguments

A struct can be passed as an argument to a function, provided the actual argument is the same type as its corresponding formal argument. The use of structs as arguments can shorten argument lists considerably, because a struct variable can be passed instead of its individual members.

Example 9.22   In a grading program, the summary statistics for a class examination might consist of the average score, the highest and lowest scores, and the standard deviation. In previous problems we would have stored these data in separate variables; now, however, it makes sense to group them together as a struct.

```
struct exam_stats
{
    int low, high;
    float average, standard_dev;
}

exam_stats exam;
```

If we are writing a function to manipulate just one or two members of a structure, we might wish to pass those members individually, as we would any other simple data element. However, for a function that manipulates most or all of the members of a struct, it is preferable to pass the entire struct, as illustrated in the function print_stat, shown in Fig. 9.30. This function has a single call-by-value argument of type exam_stat; it displays all four members of an actual argument of this type, one member at a time.

Figure 9.30   Function print_stat

```
// FILE: PrintSta.cpp
// PRINTS THE EXAM STATISTICS
```

(Continued)

Figure 9.30   (Continued)

```
void print_stat
  (exam_stat exam)    // IN: the structure variable to be displayed

// Pre:  The members of the struct variable exam are
//       assigned values.
// Post: Each member of exam is displayed.
{
    cout << "High score: " << exam.high << endl;
    cout << "Low score: " << exam.low << endl;
    cout << "Average: " << exam.average << endl;
    cout << "Standard deviation: " << exam.standard_dev << endl;
    return;
}  // end print_stat
```

■

Entire structures may also be passed as call-by-reference arguments, as illustrated in the next example.

Example 9.23   Before performing a potentially dangerous or costly experiment in the laboratory, we often use a computer program to simulate the experiment. In computer simulations, we may need to keep track of the time of day as the experiment progresses. Normally, the time of day is updated after a certain period has elapsed. The `struct` type `hms_time` is declared as follows.

```
struct hms_time
{
    int hour, minute, second;
};
```

Function `change_time` in Fig. 9.31 updates the time of day, `time_of_day` (type `hms_time`), after a time interval, `elapsed_time`, which is expressed in seconds. Each statement that uses the `%` operator updates a particular member of the `struct` represented by `time_of_day`. The `%` operator ensures that each updated value is within the required range; the `/` operator converts multiples of 60 seconds to minutes and multiples of 60 minutes to hours. The results of the computations are returned to the calling function through the reference argument `time_of_day`.

Figure 9.31   Function `change_time`

```
// FILE: ChngTime.cpp
// UPDATES THE TIME OF DAY, time_of_day, ASSUMING A 24-HOUR
//    CLOCK AND AN ELAPSED TIME OF elapsed_time IN SECONDS
```

(Continued)

Figure 9.31   (Continued)

```
void change_time
  (int elapsed_time,              // IN: increment value
   hms_time& time_of_day)         // INOUT: value to be incremented

// Pre:  elapsed_time and struct time_of_day are assigned
//       values.
// Post: time_of_day is incremented by elapsed_time.
{
   // Local data ...
   int new_hour, new_min, new_sec;

   new_sec = time_of_day.second + elapsed_time;
   time_of_day.second = new_sec % 60;
   new_min = time_of_day.minute + new_sec / 60;
   time_of_day.minute = new_min % 60;
   new_hour = time_of_day.hour + new_min / 60;
   time_of_day.hour = new_hour % 24;
   return;
}  // end change_time
```

■

Reading a struct

Function `read_employee` in Fig. 9.32 could be used to read data into the first five members of a `struct` variable of type `employee`. Only one argument is needed, not five, because we are passing a `struct` variable to `read_employee`. The function call

```
read_employee (organist);
```

causes the data read to be stored in `struct` variable `organist`.

Figure 9.32   Function `read_employee`

```
// FILE: ReadEmp.cpp
// READS ONE EMPLOYEE RECORD INTO one_organist

void read_employee
  (employee& one_organist)    // OUT: The destination for the data
                              //      read
// Pre:  None
// Post: Data are read into struct one_organist
{
   cout << "ID> ";
   cin >> one_organist.id;
   cout << "Name> ";
```

(Continued)

Figure 9.32 (Continued)

```
        cin.get (one_organist.name, string_length);
        cout << "Sex (F or M)> ";
        cin >> one_organist.gender;
        cout << "Number of dependents> ";
        cin >> one_organist.num_depend;
        cout << "Hourly rate> ";
        cin >> one_organist.rate;
        return;
}   // end read_employee
```

EXERCISES FOR SECTION 9.8

Self-Check

1. Consider the `struct employee` given in Example 9.20.

   a. Write a function `print_employee` to print all the members of a structure variable of type `employee`.
   b. Write a function `assign_employee` that assigns all members of one variable of type `employee` to another;
   c. Write a code segment illustrating how you would call `print_employee` and `assign_employee` (include all necessary declarations);
   d. Describe in English what happens when the following assignment is executed:

   ```
   organist.num_depend += 2;
   ```

2. If all members of variable now (type `hms_time`) are initially 0, how is now changed by the execution of the following statements?

   ```
   a. change_time (3600, now);
   b. change_time (7125, now);
   ```

Programming

1. Write a function that initializes all fields of variables of type `hms_time` to 0.
2. Write a function to read in the data for a variable of type `catalog_entry`. (See Exercise 2 at the end of Section 9.7.)
3. Write a function that reads in the coordinates of a point on the x-y plane where point is defined by

   ```
   struct point
   {
       float x,y;
   };
   ```

   The function should return the values read through a single argument of type `point`.

9.9 ___ HIERARCHICAL STRUCTS

To solve any programming problem we must select data structures that enable us to represent efficiently a variety of information. The selection of data structures is an important part of the problem-solving process. The data structures we use can profoundly affect the efficiency and the simplicity of a program.

The data structuring facilities in C++ are powerful and general. They allow us to declare a `struct` with members that are other structs or arrays, or to declare arrays with structured elements that are themselves arrays or structures. We call a `struct` with one or more members that are `structs` a *hierarchical structure.*

We began our study of structs by introducing the `employee struct`. In this section, we modify that `struct` by adding new members for storage of the employee's address, starting date, and date of birth. The `struct new_employee` is declared in Fig. 9.33, along with two additional structs, `address` and `date`.

Figure 9.33 **Declaration of a hierarchical structure**

```
const int string_length = 21;      // Length of all strings
                                   //     except zip code
const int zip_length = 6;          // Length of zip codes

enum month {January, February, March, April, May, June,
            July, August, September, October, November,
            December};

struct employee
{
    int id;
    char name[string_length];
    char gender;
    int num_depend;
    float rate, tot_wages;
};

struct address
{
    char street[string_length];
    char city[string_length];
    char state[string_length];
    char zip_code[zip_length];
};

struct date
{
    month this_month;
    int day;
    int year;
};

struct new_employee
```

(Continued)

Figure 9.33   (Continued)

```
{
    employee pay_data;
    address home;
    date start_date, birth_date;
};
```

If `programmer` is a `struct` variable of type `new_employee`, the hierarchical structure of `programmer` can be sketched as shown in Fig. 9.34. This diagram provides a graphic display of the `struct` form.

The diagram in Fig. 9.34 shows that `programmer` is a `struct` with members `pay_data`, `home`, `start_date`, and `birth_date`. Each of these members is itself a `struct`. The members of each of these substructures are indicated under that substructure.

To select a member in this diagram, we must trace a complete path to it starting from the top of the diagram. For example, the member reference

`programmer.start_date`

selects the member `start_date` as a substructure of type `date` of the variable `programmer`. The member reference

`programmer.start_date.year`

selects the member `year` of the substructure `programmer.start_date`. The member reference

`programmer.year`

is incomplete (which member of `year` is to be selected?) and causes a syntax error.

The `struct` assignment statement

`programmer.start_date = day_of_year;`

is valid if `day_of_year` is a `struct` variable of type `date`. This statement copies each member of `day_of_year` into the corresponding member of the substructure `programmer.start_date`.

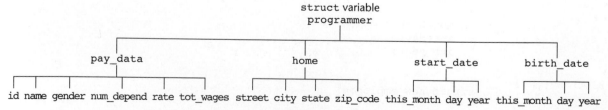

Figure 9.34   `struct` **variable** `programmer` **(type** `new_employee`**)**

Function read_new_emp in Fig. 9.35 can be used to read in a struct of type new_employee. It calls functions read_employee (see Fig. 9.32), read_address, and read_date (see Programming Exercise 1 at the end of this section).

Figure 9.35   Function read_new_emp

```
// FILE: RdNewEmp.cpp
// READS A RECORD INTO STRUCT VARIABLE new_emp

void read_new_emp
   (new_employee& new_emp)       // OUT: The destination for the data
                                 //         read

// Pre:  None.
// Post: Reads data into all members of struct new_emp.
// Uses: Functions read_employee (see Fig. 9.32),
//          read_address, and read_date (see Programming Exercises).
{
   read_employee (new_emp.pay_data);
   read_address (new_emp.home);
   read_date (new_emp.start_date);
   read_date (new_emp.birth_date);
   return;
}  // end read_new_emp
```

EXERCISES FOR SECTION 9.9

Self-Check

1. What must be the type of new_address if the following statement is correct?

   ```
   programmer.home = new_address
   ```

2. Write the member accesses needed to reference each of the following members:

   a. the programmer's salary
   b. the programmer's street address
   c. the programmer's month of birth
   d. the month the programmer started working

Programming

1. Write functions read_address and read_date to read in all address and date information for the new_employee structure shown in Fig. 9.33 and store this information in the proper components of this structure.

9.10 ____ UNIONS (OPTIONAL)

All structs of type new_employee have the same form and structure. This is not always the most efficient use of memory. For example, we might want to include information in our new_employee structure based on the employee's

Figure 9.36   struct type executive

```
enum marital_status {married, divorced, single};

struct executive
{
    employee pay_data;
    address home;
    date start_date, birth_date;
    marital_status ms;
    union
    {
        char spouse_name[string_length];
        date divorce_date;
    };
};
```

marital status. For all married employees, we might want to know the spouse's name. For all divorced employees, we might want to know the date of the divorce. For all single employees, neither of these is required.

Because we presume that the states married, divorced, and single are mutually exclusive, we can share the memory required to store the relevant information. This is accomplished by means of a special type of structure known as the *union*.

In Fig. 9.36, we use the union as a member of a struct to define a type executive. The union itself is *anonymous*. If an anonymous union is included within a struct, the members of the union can be referenced as if they are members of the struct.

We included a member ms to distinguish which of the union members is relevant. This member is known as a *union tag member*. Its value indicates the form of the remainder of the structure. In this example, if the value of the tag member ms is married, we want the member spouse_name treated as a member of the struct. If the value of ms is divorced, we want the member divorce_date treated as a member. If ms has a value single, there is no union member to be included.

The union type declaration is described in the next display.

**C++
SYNTAX**

union Type Declaration

Form: union *union-type*
　　　　　　{
　　　　　　type$_1$ id-list$_1$;
　　　　　　type$_2$ id-list$_2$;
　　　　　　.
　　　　　　.
　　　　　　.
　　　　　　type$_n$ id-list$_n$;
　　　　　　};

Example: `enum logical {true, false};`
```
union hair
{
    logical wears_wig;
    color hair_color;
};
```

Interpretation: The identifier *union-type* is the name of the union being described. Each *id-list$_i$* is a list of one or more member names separated by commas; the data type of each member in *id-list$_i$* is specified by *type$_i$*. Each type/id-list pair is called a *variant* of the union.

Note 1: *type$_i$* can be any fundamental or user-defined data type introduced so far in this book, including a structured type. If *type$_i$* is a user-defined data type, it must be defined before the `union` is defined. All members are defined to begin at the same memory address. The total size occupied by a union is the size required to hold the largest member. All member names must be unique.

Note 2: The identifier *union-type* may be omitted. In this case, the declaration defines an anonymous group. The members of this group must be distinct in name from all other variables in the scope in which the union is declared; they are used directly in that scope without the usual member reference syntax. ∎

Figure 9.37 shows three variants of `struct` variable `boss` (type `executive`), starting with the member `ms`. The other members of the `struct` all have the same form and are not shown. The amount of storage required for each variant depends on how many storage locations are required to store the largest variant on a particular computer. Assuming that `string_length` is equal to 20, the first variant in Fig. 9.37 requires the space to hold the 20 characters of the spouse's name (including the string terminator `'\0'` and should be the largest. All variants will use the same space in memory as required for the 20 characters of the largest variant.

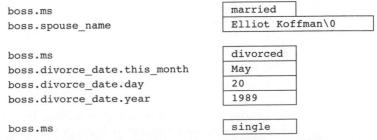

Figure 9.37 Three variants of the `struct` **variable** boss **(type** executive**)**

Example 9.24 If the value of `boss.ms` is `married`, then only the member `boss.spouse_name` can be meaningfully referenced in a program; all other members of the union `ms` within `struct executive` (from Fig. 9.36) are undefined. Assuming the first variant shown in Fig. 9.37 is stored in the variable `boss` (of type `executive`), the C++ code fragment

```
cout << "The spouse's name is " << boss.spouse_name << endl;
```

displays the line

```
The spouse's name is Elliot Koffman.
```

∎

We must ensure that the members of a `union` are referenced in a consistent manner. The compiler and run-time system do not check this. If the value of `boss.ms` is not `married` when the preceding fragment is executed, the information displayed will be meaningless. For that reason a `switch` statement is often used to process a `union`. By using the tag member as the switch selector, we can ensure that only the currently defined variant is manipulated.

Example 9.25 The fragment in Fig. 9.38 displays the data stored in the variant part of the variable `boss`. The value of `boss.ms` determines what information is displayed.

Figure 9.38   Displaying a `struct` containing a `union`

```
// Display of the variant part
switch (boss.ms)
{
   case married:
      cout << "The spouse's name is "
           << boss.spouse_name << endl;
      break;
   case divorced:
      cout << "Divorced on "
           << INT(boss.divorce_date.this_month + 1)
           << "/" << boss.divorce_date.day
           << "/" << boss.divorce_date.year "." << endl;
      break;
   case single: // no action to be taken
      break;
} // end switch
```

We have illustrated one use of the `union` to define a `struct` with both fixed and varying members. We also included a member of the `struct`, called a tag member, to indicate which variant is relevant. This is one use of the `union`. There may be cases in which there are no fixed members and in which the relevant variant is known from other data. In such a case, the `union` may stand alone.

EXERCISES FOR SECTION 9.10

Self-Check
1. Determine how many bytes are needed to store each variant for `struct execu-tive`, assuming two bytes for an `int` or enum type and one byte for a character.
2. Write a statement that displays `boss.spouse_name` if defined or the message `Not Married` otherwise.

Programming
1. Write a function to display a variable of type `struct face` defined as follows:

```
enum color {white, gray, black, brown, blue, hazel};
// Colors of hair and eyes

enum no_yes {no, yes};
struct face
{
   color eyes;
   no_yes bald;
   union
   {
      no_yes wears_wig;
      color hair_color;
   };
};
```

9.11 ⎯⎯ COMMON PROGRAMMING ERRORS

▪ *(Arrays) Use of Non-Integer Subscripts:* Floating-point as well as integral data types are allowed as array subscripts. When characters are used as subscripts, as in `x['A']`, the subscript value is the ASCII value of the character (65 in this case). When floating-point values are used as subscripts, as in `x[3.14159]`, the subscript value (3 in this case) is obtained by truncating the floating-point value. Enumerators may also be used as subscripts; the subscript value for an enumerator is the integer value associated with the enumerator in the enumeration in which it is listed. None of these different subscript types will generate a compiler error, although warnings may be given by some compilers.

▪ *(Arrays) Out-of-Range Subscript References:* Array subscript references that are out-of-range (less than zero, or greater than or equal to the array size), will not generate any error messages. Instead, they will cause access to memory locations outside the range of the array, possibly destroying information necessary to the successful execution of the program or retrieving invalid data. Such errors may be particularly difficult to identify; they may not become readily apparent until the execution of some section of your program that is seemingly unrelated to the point where the problem first occurred. Neither the C++ compiler nor the run-time system detects these errors; it is up to the programmer to build the necessary detection/prevention mechanisms into the programs that are written.

- *(Arrays) Unsubscripted Array References:* Arrays may be used as function arguments and in pointer arithmetic (described in further detail in Chapter 13). Unsubscripted array references in expressions not involving pointers are invalid and will generate an error message. For example, if `x[20]` is an integer array and `y` is an integer, the expression

```
y = y + x;
```

would generate an error message such as "Cannot convert `int*` [the address or pointer specified by `x`] to `int`."

- *(Arrays) Subscripted References to Non-Array Variables:* Subscripted references to non-array variables, such as the reference `b[10]` in

```
a = a + b[10];
```

where `a` and `b` are both simple variables, causes an error message to be generated indicating an "Invalid operation" (often an "Invalid indirection," explained in more detail in Chapter 16).

- *(Strings) String Assignment:* It is often tempting to write an assignment statement such as

```
string1 = string 2;
```

or

```
string1 = "7625 Lawndale Avenue";
```

to assign (copy) one string or another. Such assignments will not always produce an error message, for in some cases, they are perfectly legal. However, they usually will not produce the desired results, either. If both the left and right sides of the assignment operator are pointers, the assignment is legal, but it is a pointer assignment and not a character string copy. Always remember to use the string functions defined in the file `string.h` whenever string manipulations (even assignment) are required in your program.

- *(Arrays) Mixing Types in Passing Arrays to Functions:* When array arguments are passed to functions, differences between actual and formal array argument types will produce error messages. For example, passing an integer array actual argument when a character array is expected will cause the compiler to generate messages such as

"Cannot convert `int*` [an integer pointer or address] to `char*` [a character pointer]"

or

"`Type mismatch in parameter ... in call to ...`".

(In the second of these messages, the first set of dots, ..., represents the parameter position in which the mismatch error occurred; the second set represents the name of the function involved.) Remember that in C++, arrays are passed by address (pointer). Except in special cases, pointer types may not be mixed in C++.

Pointer types may also not be mixed with non-pointer types. Compiler error messages similar to those just described will also be produced when pointer and non-pointer types are mixed. One very typical error involves passing a character actual argument when a string is expected, or vice versa.

Both types of errors just discussed, mixing pointer types or mixing a pointer type with a non-pointer type, are quite common when string functions are being used. You must be careful to check the argument specifications in the prototypes for these functions before using them.

- *(Structs) References to a struct Component with No Prefix:* The dot notation must always be used when referencing a component, comp, of a variable, v, of some structured type. If the dot notation is omitted, the compiler assumes that your intent is to reference a variable that is not part of a structured variable. If comp is not declared outside a structure, a diagnostic such as "undefined symbol comp" will be issued by the compiler. If a variable named comp also happens to be declared in the same function in which the reference occurs, omitting the prefix from a reference to comp will not cause an error but will result in a reference to the wrong data element (the variable rather than the structure component).

- *(Structs) Reference to a struct Component with Incorrect Prefix:* If v is a structured variable with a component named comp and x is a structured variable with no component of that name, then the reference x.comp will also generate an "Undefined symbol 'comp'" message. If the prefix used in a reference to a structured component is the name of a struct (such as coord) rather than the name of a variable of struct type, then a message such as "Improper use of typedef 'coord' might be generated. This is a tip that the name of a user-defined type (coord, in this case) has been used illegally.

- *(Structs) Missing Semicolon Following a struct Declaration:* If the semicolon required at the end of a struct declaration is missing, a variety of error messages might be generated, depending on what follows the declaration. Frequently, another declaration will follow the faulty one. In this case, the following declaration is considered as part of the struct, and a diagnostic such as "Too many types in declaration." will be produced.

CHAPTER REVIEW

In this chapter, we introduced two structured types: the array and the struct. The array is a convenient facility for naming and referencing a collection of like items, and the struct is convenient for organizing a collection of related data items of different types.

We discussed how to declare arrays and structs and how to reference their elements. An individual array element is accessed by placing a subscript in brackets following the array name. Individual members of a `struct` are accessed by placing the name of the member following the name of the `struct`, separating the two by the member access operator (a period).

Two common operations involving arrays were discussed: searching an array and sorting an array. We wrote a function for searching an array and also described the selection sort function.

The `for` statement enables us to reference the elements of an array in sequence. We can use the `for` statement to initialize arrays, to read and write arrays, and to control the manipulation of individual array elements in sequence.

Each individual component of a `struct` must be manipulated separately in an input or output operation or in an arithmetic expression. However, assigning one `struct` variable to another `struct` variable of the same type, and passing a `struct` as an argument to a function, are permitted.

New C++ Constructs   The C++ constructs introduced in this chapter are described in Table 9.7.

Table 9.7   Summary of New C++ Constructs

CONSTRUCT	EFFECT
Array Declaration	
`int cube[10];` `int count[10];`	`cube` and `count` are arrays with 10 type `int` elements.
Array References	
`for (i = 0; i < 10; i++)` `cube[i] = i * i * i;`	Saves `i` cubed in the `i`th element of array `cube`.

`if (cube[5] > 100)`
    `cout << cube[0]`
        `<< cube[1];`
	Compares `cube[5]` to 100.
	Displays the first two cubes.

struct Declaration	

`struct part`
`{`
    `int id;`
    `int quantity;`
    `float price;`
`};`
 	
`part nuts, bolts;`
	A `struct part` is declared with data fields that can store two `int`s and a `float` number. `nuts` and `bolts` are `struct` variables of type `part`.

(Continued)

Table 9.7   (Continued)

CONSTRUCT	EFFECT
struct **References**	
total_cost = nuts.quantity * nuts.price	Multiplies two members of nuts.
cout << bolts.id;	Displays the id field of bolts.
bolts = nuts;	Copies struct nuts to bolts.

✔ QUICK-CHECK EXERCISES

1. What structured data types were discussed in this chapter? What is a structured data type?
2. Which fundamental types cannot be array subscript types? Array element types?
3. Can values of different types be stored in the same array?
4. If an array is declared to have 10 elements, must the program use all 10?
5. When can the assignment operator be used with array elements? with entire arrays? Answer the same questions for the equality operator.
6. The two methods of array access are _____ and _____ .
7. The _____ loop allows us to access the elements of an array in _____ order.
8. What is the primary difference between an array and a struct? Which would you use to store the catalog description of a course? Which would you use to store the names of the students in the course?
9. When can you use the assignment operator with struct operands? When can you use the equality operator?
10. For a_student declared as follows, provide a statement that displays the initials of a_student.

```
struct student
{
    char first[string_length];
    char last[string_length];
    int age, score;
    char grade;
}; // end student

student a_student;
```

11. How many members are there in struct student?
12. If an int uses two bytes of storage, a character one, and string_length is 20, how many bytes of storage are occupied by a_student?
13. Write a function that displays a variable of type student.
14. When would you use unions?

Answers to Quick-Check Exercises

1. Arrays and structs. A structured data type is a named grouping of related values.
2. Floating-point types cannot be used for array subscript types; all types can be element types.
3. no
4. no
5. Both the assignment and equality operators may be used with array elements. Neither the assignment operator nor the equality operator may be used with entire arrays.
6. direct (random) and sequential
7. `for` or `while`, sequential
8. The values stored in an array must all be the same type; the values stored in a `struct` do not have to be the same type. You would use a `struct` for the catalog item and use an array for the list of names.
9. The assignment operator may be used between structs of the same type. The equality operator may not be used to compare structs.
10. `cout << a_student.first[0] << a_student.last[0] << endl;`
11. five
12. 45
13.
```
void write_student
    (student one_stu)    // IN: The data to be written
{
    cout << "Student is " << one_stu.first << " "
        << one_stu.last << endl;
    cout << "Age is " << one_stu.age << endl;
    cout << "Score is " << one_stu.score << endl;
    cout << "Grade is " << one_stu.grade << endl;
}
```
14. When the value of a structure member determines what other information is stored in the structure (for example, married, divorced, or single).

REVIEW QUESTIONS

1. Identify the error in the following code segment. When will the error be detected?

```
void main()
{
    int x[8], i;
    for (i = 0; i < 9; i++)
        x[i] = i;
}
```

2. Declare an array of floating-point elements called `week` that can be referenced by using any day of the week as a subscript. Assume `sunday` is the first subscript.
3. What are the two common ways of selecting array elements for processing?

4. Write a C++ program segment to print out the index of the smallest and the largest numbers in an array x of 20 `ints` with values from 0 to 100. Assume array x already has values assigned to each element.

5. The arguments for a function are two arrays of type `float` and an integer that represents the length of the arrays. The function copies the first array in the argument list to the other array using a loop structure. Write the function.

6. How many exchanges are required to sort the following list of integers, using the selection sort? how many comparisons?

   20 30 40 25 60 80

7. Declare a `struct` called `subscriber` that contains the member's name, `street_address`, `monthly_bill` (how much the subscriber owes), and which paper the subscriber receives (`morning`, `evening`, or `both`).

8. Write a C++ program to enter and then print out the contents of the variable `competition` declared as follows:

```
const int string_length 20;

struct olympic_event
{
    char event[string_length];
    char entrant[string_length];
    char country[string_length];
    int place;
};

olympic_event competition;
```

9. Identify and correct the errors in the following program:

```
void main ()
{
    struct summer_help
    {
        char name[15];
        int emp_id;
        char start_date[15];
        float pay_rate
        int hours_worked;
    }

    summer_help operator;

    strcpy (summer_help.name, "Stoney Viceroy");
    strcpy (summer_help.start_date, "June 1, 1992");
    summer_help.hours_worked = 29.3;
    cout << operator << endl;
}
```

10. Declare the proper data structure to store the following student data:

student_name, GPA, major, and address (consisting of street_address, city, state, zip_code). Use whatever data types are most appropriate for each member.

11. Declare the proper structure for supplies, consisting of the struct types paper, ribbon, and labels. For paper, the information needed is the number of sheets per box and the size. For ribbon, the length (inches), color (yes, no), and kind (carbon or cloth) are needed. For labels, the size and number per box are needed. For each supply, the cost, the number on hand, and the date of the last reorder must also be stored. Use whatever data types are appropriate for each member. (Where a size is required, use two floating-point values representing height and width in inches.)

12. Write a declaration for the structured data type vehicle. If vehicle is a truck, then information (length, width, height) about the bed_size and cab_size is needed. If vehicle is a wagon, then information about whether or not there is a third seat is needed. If the vehicle is a sedan, then the information needed is two_door or four_door. For all vehicles, you need to know the gas mileage rating (gas_mileage) and whether the transmission is manual or automatic. You also need to know if it has air_conditioning, power_steering, or power_brakes. Use whatever data types are appropriate for each member.

PROGRAMMING PROJECTS

1. Write a program for the following problem. You are given a file that contains a collection of scores (type int) for the last exam in your computer course. You are to compute the average of these scores and assign grades to each student according to the following rule:

> If a student's score is within 10 points (above or below) of the average, assign the grade of satisfactory. If a student's score is more than 10 points above average, assign a grade of outstanding. If a student's score is more than 10 points below average, assign a grade of unsatisfactory.

The output from your program should consist of a labeled two-column list that shows each score and its corresponding grade. As part of the solution your program should include functions that correspond to the function prototypes that follow.

```
// READS EXAM SCORES INTO ARRAY SCORES
void read_stu_data
   (ifstream &rss,        // IN: Raw scores data stream
    int scores[],         // OUT: The data read
    int &count,           // OUT: Number of students read
int &too_many);          // OUT: A flag to indicate that more
                         // than max_size scores items are in
                         // input file.


// COMPUTES AVERAGE OF COUNT STUDENT SCORES
float mean (int scores[], int count);

// PRINTS A TABLE SHOWING EACH STUDENT'S SCORE AND GRADE ON A
```

```
// SEPARATE LINE
void print_table (int score[], int count);
// Uses: print_grade

// PRINTS STUDENT GRADE AFTER COMPARING one_score TO AVERAGE
void print_grade (int one_score, float average);
```

2. Redo Programming Project 1 assuming that each line of file `raw_scores` contains a student's ID number (an `int`) and an exam score. Modify function `read_stu_data` to read the ID number and the score from the `i`th data line into array elements `ID[i]` and `scores[i]`, respectively. Modify function `print_table` to display a three-column table with the following headings:

```
ID             Score          Grade
```

3. Write a program to read n data items into two arrays, x and y, of size 20. Store the products of corresponding pairs of elements of x and y in a third array, z, also of size 20. Print a three-column table that displays the arrays x, y, and z. Then compute and print the square root of the sum of the items in z. Make up your own data, with n less than 20.

4. Another approach to sorting an array is to create an index array, where the index is an array whose element values represent array subscripts. An index allows us to access the elements of a second array in sequential order without rearranging the second array's element values. After "sorting," the first element of the index array will contain the subscript of the smallest element, the second element of the index array will contain the subscript of the second smallest element, and so on. For example, if the array `scores` contains the exam scores 60, 90, 50, 100, and 75, then the array `scores_index` should contain the subscripts 2, 0, 4, 1, 3. `scores_index[0]` is 2 because `scores[2]` is the smallest score (50); `scores_index[1]` is 0 because `scores[0]` is the second smallest score (60), and so on. Write a function `index_sort` that creates an index array for its input array arguments.

5. The results of a survey of the households in your township are available for public scrutiny. Each record contains data for one household, including a four-digit integer identification number, the annual income for the household, and the number of household members. Write a program to read the survey results into three arrays and perform the following analyses:

   a. Count the number of households included in the survey and print a three-column table displaying the data. (Assume that no more than 25 households were surveyed.)

   b. Calculate the average household income, and list the identification number and income of each household that exceeds the average.

   c. Determine the percentage of households that have incomes below the poverty level. Compute the poverty level income using the formula

   $$p = \$6500.00 + \$750.00 \times (m - 2)$$

   where m is the number of members of each household. This formula shows that the poverty-level depends on the number of family members, m, and that the poverty level income increases as m gets larger.
   Test your program on the following data.

Identification Number	Annual Income	Household Members
1041	12,180	4
1062	13,240	3
1327	19,800	2
1483	22,458	8
1900	17,000	2
2112	18,125	7
2345	15,623	2
3210	3,200	6
3600	6,500	5
3601	11,970	2
4724	8,900	3
6217	10,000	2
9280	6,200	1

6. Assume that your computer has the very limited capability of being able to read and write only single-integer digits and to add two integers consisting of one decimal digit each. Write a program that can read two integers up to 30 digits each, add these integers together, and display the result. Test your program using pairs of numbers of varying lengths.

   Hints: Store the two numbers in two int arrays of size 30, one digit per array element. If the number is less than 30 digits in length, enter enough leading zeros (to the left of the number) to make the number 30 digits long.

   You will need a loop to add the digits in corresponding array elements. Don't forget to handle the carry digit if there is one!

7. A number expressed in scientific notation is represented by its mantissa (a fraction) and its exponent. Write a function that reads two character strings that represent numbers in C++ scientific notation and stores each number in a struct with two members. Write a function that prints the contents of each struct as a real value. Also write a function that computes the sum, the product, the difference, and the quotient of the two numbers. *Hint:* The string -0.1234E20 represents a number in scientific notation. The fraction -0.1234 is the mantissa, and the number 20 is the exponent.

8. At a grocery store, the food has been categorized and the categories are to be computerized. Write a function to read and store information into a struct that contains a union with appropriate data types.

   The first letter read is M, F, or V (indicating meat, fruit, or vegetable, respectively). The second item read is the name of the food (maximum of 20 letters). The third item is the unit cost, and the fourth item is the unit (O for ounces, P for pounds).

   The last item read is one character that indicates information based on the M, F, or V read earlier. For meat, the valid input values are R for red meat, P for poultry, and F for fish. For fruit, the valid input values are T for tropical and N for nontropical. For vegetables, the valid input values are B for beans, P for potatoes, O for other.

   The function should check that each data item is valid before assigning a value to the struct argument. Also write a function to print the data stored for a food variable.

10 Introduction to Software Engineering

10.1 The Software Challenge

10.2 The Software Life Cycle
CASE STUDY: Telephone Directory
Program

10.3 Procedural Abstraction Revisited

10.4 Data Abstraction and Abstract Data
Types: Program Objects

10.5 Analysis of Algorithm Efficiency: Big-O
Notation

10.6 Software Testing

10.7 Formal Methods of Program Verification

10.8 Professional Ethics and Responsibilities
Chapter Review

Until this point, we have been concerned primarily with writing relatively short programs that solve particular programming problems but that otherwise have little general use. In this chapter, we will begin to consider issues related to writing larger, more complex programs, or *programming-in-the-large*, as it is often called.

The term *software engineering* is used to denote a collection of tools and techniques used by professional programmers to facilitate the design, coding, and maintenance (upkeep) of large-scale programs. Our discussion will focus on some principles of software engineering that have proved useful in programming, especially for programming-in-the-large. We will describe the different phases of a large-scale software project and elaborate on the software engineering method for problem-solving and programming first discussed in Section 2.1. We will discuss how to modularize a large project (so that individual pieces can be implemented by different programmers and at different times) and how to write software modules to simplify their reuse in other projects.

Several other key topics in software engineering will be introduced in this chapter. The first involves the analysis of the efficiency of algorithms that we write. Some of the algorithms presented in Chapter 9 will be used to illustrate how this analysis can be carried out.

We will also consider the question of testing a program and verifying that it works correctly. We will discuss the limitations of program testing and provide a brief introduction to formal methods for proving that a program is correct. Some of the techniques presented in this chapter will be illustrated in the remainder of the text in solving more complicated problems. You should realize, however, that even these problems and their solutions are nowhere near as large or complex as programming systems that consist of hundreds of thousands or even millions of lines of code, as often encountered in practice.

Because this chapter introduces many concepts used by software professionals, the chapter ends with a discussion of professional behavior, ethics, and responsibilities. This chapter also contains important warnings about computer viruses and plagiarism, which apply to student programmers as well as to practicing professionals.

10.1 —— THE SOFTWARE CHALLENGE

Programming in college, especially at the introductory level, is considerably different from the development of the application production systems used in practice. In college, an instructor usually will give you a brief, relatively easy-to-understand problem description, or *specification*. In some cases, this specification is ambiguous or incomplete, and interaction between the instructor and the class is necessary so that the students can pin down the details.

In practice, the impetus for a software project comes from users of an existing software product or potential users of a new software product. The users, or *clients*, may see a need for improving the operation of an existing product or for computerizing a task that is currently performed manually, without the use of computers. This need is communicated to the individual(s) responsible for providing software support in the organization. These people are often called *software systems analysts.*

Because clients are often naive as to the capabilities of a computer, the initial specification for a software product may be incomplete. The specification is clarified through extensive interaction between the users of the software and the systems analysts. Through this interaction, the analyst attempts to determine precisely what the clients want the proposed software to do, and the clients learn what to expect from the software product. This way there are fewer surprises in the end.

Although it may seem like common sense to proceed in this manner, very often a software product does not perform as expected. The reason is usually a communication gap between those responsible for the product's design and implementation and its eventual users. Often, too, clients change their minds over time as the analysts work on this project. Generally, both parties are at fault when the software fails to meet expectations. To avoid this possibility, it is imperative that a complete, written description of the requirements specification for a new software product be generated at the beginning of the project and that both users and designers sign the document. Later modifications to the specifications must also be made in terms of this document and similarly agreed to by the parties involved.

Programming Teams

Another major difference between programming in college and in industry is that a large software project in industry is rarely implemented by a single programmer. Most often, a large project is assigned to a team of programmers. It is important for team members to coordinate beforehand the overall organization of the project.

Each team member is responsible for a set of modules, some of which may be accessed by other team members. Teams generally meet on a regular basis. At some point early in this process, each team member should provide the others with a specification for each module that he or she is implementing. The specification will be similar to the documentation you have provided for each module (function) that you have written and similar to those provided in this text. It will consist of a brief statement of the purpose of the module, its preconditions and postconditions, and its formal argument list. This information is all that a potential user of the module needs to know in order to call it correctly.

Normally one team member will act as "librarian" by assuming responsibility for determining the status of each module in the system. Initially, the library of modules will consist of a stub for each module. As a new module is completed and tested, its updated version will replace the version currently in the library. The librarian will keep track of the date that each new version of a module is inserted in the library and make sure that all programmers are using the latest version of any module.

EXERCISES FOR SECTION 10.1

Self-Check
1. How does the role of the systems analyst differ from that of the librarian during the development of a large software system?
2. Explain how a programming team has the potential to complete a large software project more quickly than a single programmer working independently.

10.2 —— THE SOFTWARE LIFE CYCLE

The steps involved in the initial development and continued operation of a software system comprise the *software life cycle* (SLC), as described below:

1. Requirements specification

   a) Prepare a complete and unambiguous problem statement.

2. Problem analysis

   a) Understand the problem—determine problem output and required input.
   b) Evaluate alternative solutions.
   c) Choose a preferred solution.

3. Program design

   a) Perform a top-down design of the system.
   b) For each module, identify key data elements and subordinate modules, using design tools such as data requirements tables and structure charts.
   c) Design the algorithm for each low-level module, using pseudocode.

4. Program implementation

   a) Code the solution, using the data requirements tables and pseudocode developed for each module.

5. Testing and validation

   a) Test the code, validating that it is correct.

6. Operation, follow-up, and maintenance

   a) Run the completed system.

b) Evaluate its performance.
c) Remove new bugs as they are detected.
d) Make required changes to keep the system up to date.
e) Validate that changes are correct and do not adversely affect the system's operation.

The engineering and scientific method for solving problems specifies that problem analysis should always precede problem solution (synthesis). The first two stages of the SLC (requirements specification and analysis) are the analysis part, and the next two stages (design and implementation) are the synthesis part. The program users (clients) take the lead in developing the requirements specification. The system developers work closely with the program users to understand more thoroughly the problem requirements and to evaluate possible alternative solutions.

This simplified scenario might lead you to believe that the software life cycle is sequential in nature—that step 3, for example, begins once step 2 is complete, and step 4 follows after step 3 has been completed. Please be assured, nothing could be further from the truth! As illustrated in Fig. 10.1, the SLC is a highly circular process, often involving a return to previous steps to make revisions based on new information. For example, during the design phase (step 3), problems may arise that make it necessary to

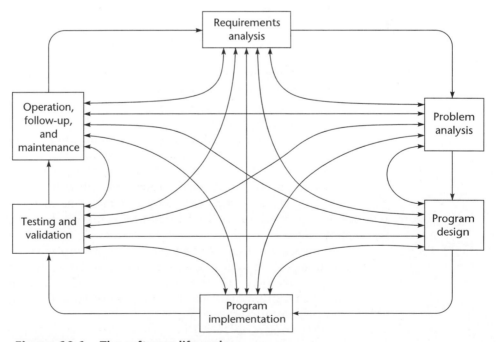

Figure 10.1   The software life cycle

modify the requirements specification. Similarly, during implementation (step 4), it may become necessary to reconsider decisions made in the design phase. Furthermore, as hinted in step 6, systems often change even after they are in use. Regardless of the situation, any changes must be approved by all parties involved in the development process—the systems analysts and the clients.

Once the system is implemented, it must be thoroughly tested before it enters its final stage (operation and maintenance). It is possible to identify necessary system changes in both these stages that require repetition of earlier stages of the SLC. These changes may come about to correct errors identified during testing or to accommodate changes required by external sources (for example, a change in the federal or state tax regulations, or a modification in medical insurance reimbursement policies).

Errors in software itself or in judgment concerning the efficiency or completeness of software can be extremely costly. The $103 million IRS federal income tax form processing system, developed in the early 1980s, cost nearly twice what was projected and was inadequate to the size and complexity of the task. Within five years, another $90 million in enhancements was required. Because of the delays caused by this problem, the IRS was forced to pay another $40 million in interest to taxpayers and slightly over $20 million in overtime wages to its own employees.

The initial launch of the space shuttle *Columbia* was already three years late and cost millions more than had been estimated when it was finally canceled due to problems associated with the synchronization of its five on-board computers.

Estimates vary as to the percentage of time spent in each stage of the software life cycle. For example, a typical system may require a year to proceed through the first four stages, 3 months of testing, then 4 or more years of operation and maintenance. A very large system (over 1,000,000 lines of code) may take 4 to 5 years to develop and test but may subsequently remain in use for another 12 to 15 years. Throughout the entire period, the system will undergo constant change, further enhancement, adaptation, and plenty of correction. Figure 10.2 shows a reasonable estimate of the relative distribution of effort for a typical software project. Although precise, up-to-date figures are difficult to establish, the total cost of producing software for computer manufacturers, software firms, and user organizations in the United States in 1990 has been estimated at over $100 billion.

Keeping these figures and the previous examples in mind, you can see why it is so important to design and document software in such a way that it can be easily maintained. This is especially important because the person who maintains the program may not have been involved in the original program design or implementation.

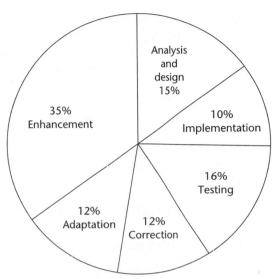

Figure 10.2   Relative distribution of effort in the software life cycle

Prototyping

Before presenting an in-depth discussion of the software life cycle, we should mention that there is an alternative approach to traditional system development called prototyping. In *prototyping*, the systems analyst works closely with the system user to develop a prototype, or model, of the actual system. Initially the prototype will have few working features and will just mimic the input/output interaction of the user with the system. At each stage, the user and analyst decide what changes should be made and what new features should be added, and these changes are incorporated into the prototype. This process continues until a complete prototype is available that performs all of the functions of the final system. The analyst and user can then decide whether to use the prototype as the final system or to use it as the basis of the design for a new system that will have the same look and feel as the prototype but will be more efficient.

Requirements Specification

Although we have illustrated most of the phases of the software life cycle in solving all prior Case Studies, our example problems have been extremely small in scope and uncomplicated. As a result, we have not really had an opportunity to illustrate the requirements specification process or any of the other stages of the SLC in any detail. Each Case Study that we have examined began with a statement of the problem and a brief analysis stage in which we attempted to inject a bit of additional detail and structure into the initial problem statement. In the next Case Study, we provide a bit more insight into and detail of some of the issues and decisions that must be made at each stage of the SLC, beginning with the requirements specification. Although this Case Study proceeds through the stages of the life cycle in a mostly linear fashion, we remind you that we are working in a pristine environment in which our problem statements are relatively constrained. In reality, things rarely work out this way.

CASE STUDY: TELEPHONE DIRECTORY PROGRAM

Problem Statement

Write an interactive telephone directory program that might be used by phone company employees to look up numbers for callers needing information. Your telephone directory will contain a collection of names and telephone numbers. You should be able to insert new entries in the directory, retrieve an entry in the directory, change a directory entry, or delete a directory entry.

Problem Analysis

In practice, the systems analyst works with the software users to clarify system requirements to a highly detailed level. Some of the kinds of issues that may need to be clarified include the extent and format of the client's input to the system, the desired form of any output screens or printed forms, and the need for data validation. Other considerations might include the development of mechanisms for satisfying a user's need to store and selectively process large volumes of information in a *database*. An example of such a database is the student records information at your institution; examples of the kind of selective processing that might be done on this database include sending Dean's List announcements to all students with grade-point averages of 3.0 or more and obtaining and printing counts of the number of majors in each program offering a major at your school.

In fact, you may already have found it necessary to interact somewhat with the "user" (your instructor or lab assistant) of the software you have been asked to develop for class. Each time you talk with your instructor to obtain a clarification of an assignment, you are engaging in this sort of activity. If you are not certain as to what is provided as input, precisely what is required as output, or any other expectations of your client, you must obtain a clarification before proceeding further. In the end, it is important that you and your instructor are clear as to the nature of the required software so that you can begin to focus on the assignment.

For example, assume your instructor has given you the preceding incomplete problem specification for the design of a telephone directory program. Some of the questions that might come to mind and require clarification are the following:

- Is there an initial list of names and numbers to be stored in the directory beforehand, or are all entries inserted at the same time?
- If there is an initial list, is it already stored in a data file, or will it be entered interactively?
- If the file is a text file, what are the formatting conventions (for example, the name starts in position 1 and the phone number starts in position 20)? Are the name and number on the same data line or on separate lines?
- Is the final directory stored in main memory or as a file in secondary memory?
- Is it possible for there to be more than one number associated with a particular name? If so, should the first number be retrieved, the last number, or all numbers?
- Is there a limit on the length of a name? How are the names stored (for example: *last, first,* or *first last*)?
- Are phone numbers stored as numbers or as strings of characters? Do they contain area codes? Are there any special characters in a phone number such as hyphens and parentheses? Should we check for illegal characters in a number or for a number that is too short or too long?
- Should the names be stored in alphabetical order or in the sequence in which they were entered into the directory?
- Do you need a printed list of names and phone numbers for the directory? If so, how should that list be formatted?
- Is it possible to change a person's name as well as the person's phone number?
- What information is needed to retrieve a directory entry?
- When an entry is retrieved, should both the person's name and number be displayed or just the number? What form should this display take?
- What action should be taken if a "new" entry has the same name as a person already in the directory? Should this be flagged as an error?

As you can see, plenty of questions are left unanswered by the initial problem statement. To complete the requirements specification, you should answer these questions and probably many more. Many of the questions deal with details of input data, handling of potential errors in input data, and formats of input data and output lists.

Program Design

Once you have a clear understanding of what is required of your program, the next step is to evaluate different approaches to the program design. As part of this investigation, the systems analyst and users may consider whether they can purchase commercial software packages to satisfy their requirements as an alternative to developing the software in-house from the beginning. They must also determine the impact of the new software product on existing computer systems and what new hardware or software will be needed to develop and run the new system. They determine the feasibility of each approach by estimating its cost and anticipated benefits. The analysis stage culminates with the selection of what appears to be the best design approach.

Although your design choices will be more constrained in your four years of coursework in college, you may eventually become involved in a project for which some major decisions must be made concerning such things as what kind of computer (for example, a personal computer or a large mainframe) is best suited to your problem and how each choice might affect potential solution designs. You may also need to give particular attention to the selection of a programming language to use for the implementation of your software. Some of the factors you should consider in evaluating each design approach include the architectural characteristics of your computer (such as the amount of main memory or external storage), the features of the language you are using, and the time frame and funding for your project. Regardless of these concerns, however, you most certainly will be involved, at every turn, in decisions concerning the structure and organization of internal data, of external files, and of the software itself. Clearly, these have been the concerns of the first half of this text. As we proceed in the second half of the course to examine more complicated problems, we will devote still more attention to these issues. You will see that these decisions are often not trivial; at the same time, they are important to the construction of well-designed software products.

Once you have selected the overall approach to system construction, it is time to develop a high-level design of the system. The top-down approach to design guides us to start at the top level, dividing the original problem into

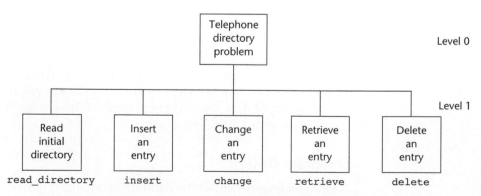

Figure 10.3   **Structure chart for Telephone Directory Problem**

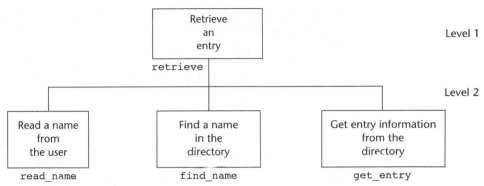

Figure 10.4   **Structure chart for "retrieve an entry"**

subproblems. For each subproblem, we identify a subsystem responsible for the solution of that subproblem. As we have done before, we can use a structure chart to indicate the relationships among the subproblems (and subsystems). One possible structure chart for our telephone directory problem is shown in Fig. 10.3. This figure shows the two top levels of the structure chart, including the original problem and its major subproblems. Each major subproblem should be implemented as a separate subsystem of modules. The modules needed are determined by refining and subdividing the major subproblems into still smaller subproblems. Figure 10.4 shows that to solve the subproblem "Retrieve an entry," we must be able to "Read a name from the user," "Find a name in the directory," and "Get entry information from the directory."

The second part of the design step of the software life cycle is to identify the major data elements and functions for each module. We will use both procedural and data abstraction to accomplish this task, as described next.

EXERCISES FOR SECTION 10.2

Self-Check
1. List the six phases of the software life cycle. Which phase is the longest?
2. Using the refinement of `retrieve` (Fig. 10.4) as an example, draw a structure chart showing a refinement for subproblem `change`.

10.3 —— PROCEDURAL ABSTRACTION REVISITED

Abstraction is a powerful technique that helps programmers (or problem solvers) deal with complex issues in a step-by-step fashion. The dictionary defines *abstraction* as the process of separating the inherent qualities or properties of something from the actual physical object to which they belong. One example of the use of abstraction is representing a program variable (for example, `name` and `tel_number`) by a storage location in memory. We don't have to know anything about the physical structure of memory in order to use variables in programming.

So far you have practiced *procedural abstraction,* a technique guided by the philosophy of separating the concern of *what* is to be achieved by a module from the details of *how* it is to be achieved. In other words, you can specify what you expect a module to do, then use that module specification in the design of a problem solution before you know how to implement it.

As an example of how the process works, we use procedural abstraction (in a manner similar to what we've done many times before) to produce an algorithm fragment for retrieving an entry from the directory.

1. Read the name we are seeking (`read_name`).
2. Locate the name in the directory (`find_name`).
3. If the name is found
    3.1. Retrieve the entry from the directory (`get_entry`).

The above fragment calls three functions first shown in Fig. 10.2. We can fill in the argument lists after the data-flow information is added to the structure chart. We can then essentially complete this program fragment in terms of calls to these functions without yet having mapped out their implementations.

Function Libraries

As you progress through this course, you will write many C++ programs and functions. You should try to keep each new function as general as possible so that you can reuse it in other applications. You will eventually build up a sizable library of your own functions. Reusing tried and tested functions is always much more efficient than starting from scratch; each new function that you write will have to be thoroughly tested and debugged and will require a lot of start-up time in every case. The functions in your personal library already will have been tested, so you will save time if you use them over and over again. Also, don't forget about the wealth of functions in the C++ libraries.

For example, many times we would like to ensure that a given input data value makes sense within the current problem context. That is, we want to verify that it lies within a specific range of values. We might like to read in a character that is an uppercase letter or to read in an integer within some specified range, such as −10 to +11. The function `enter_int` shown in Fig. 10.5 performs the second task. This version of `enter_int` is simpler than the one shown in Chapter 9 (Section 9.4) because it does not take into account the use of a sentinel value. There is no rule stating that function source code must always be used as is, without modification. Although such reuse is often preferred, you will find many situations in which reuse with some modification is still easier than programming from scratch.

We will use both versions of enter_int in programs to be developed later in the text. You could write similar functions, called enter_char and enter_float, for the other fundamental data types of C++. These functions would also be useful additions to a programmer's library.

Figure 10.5   Function enter_int

```cpp
// File: EnterInt.cpp
// READS AN INTEGER BETWEEN min_n AND max_n INTO n

int enter_int
   (int min_n,              // IN: minimum range value for n
    int max_n)              // IN: maximum range value for n

// Pre:     min_n and max_n are assigned values.
// Post:    If min_n <= max_n, returns the first data value read
//          that has a value between min_n and max_n (inclusive).
//          Otherwise, prints a message and exits.
// Returns: First integer read that has a value between min_n and
//          max_n (inclusive).
{
   // Local data ...
   int in_range;
   int n;

   // Check for nonempty range
   if (min_n <= max_n)
      in_range = 0;
   else
   {
      cerr << "*** ERROR: min_n > max_n in enter_int."
           << endl;
      cerr << "Program terminated!" << endl;
      exit(0);
   }

   // Keep reading until a valid number is read
   while (!in_range)
   {
      cout << "Enter a value between " << min_n << " and "
           << max_n << ": ";
      cin >> n;
      in_range = (min_n <= n) && (n <= max_n);
   }  // end while
   return n;
}  // end enter_int
```

A function that returns the uppercase form of an argument that is a lower-case letter would also be useful. Of course, we could write our own (see Fig. 10.6), or we could take advantage of the already written and tested C++ library routine `toupper` (see Appendix C or Table 7.5, Section 7.4).

Figure 10.6   Function `my_toupper`

```
// FILE: MyToUppr.cpp
// CONVERTS LOWERCASE LETTER TO UPPERCASE

char my_toupper
  (char ch)                          // IN: letter to be converted

// Pre:  ch is defined.
// Post: If ch is lowercase letter, returns the corresponding
//       uppercase letter; otherwise returns ch.
{
  // Perform conversion.
  if ((ch >= 'a') && (ch <= 'z'))
     return int (ch) - int ('a') + int ('A');
  else
     return ch;
}  // end my_toupper
```

PROGRAM STYLE

Validating a Library Function's Arguments

Function `enter_int` begins by checking whether its user correctly entered its input arguments, `min_n` and `max_n`. If the arguments define an empty range, an error message is displayed and the function exits, skipping the read operation. You should make sure that you carefully validate input arguments for functions, especially those functions that are candidates for inclusion in a library. Your validation steps should ensure that all input argument values are defined consistently with the preconditions described in the function comments. Because library functions may be reused many times and by many different programmers, this extra effort can pay valuable dividends. ∎

EXERCISES FOR SECTION 10.3

Self-Check

1. List at least three pieces of information that must be known about a library function before it can be called.
2. Why is the validation of function arguments more critical for a library function than for a function that is used in only a single program?

Programming

1. Write function `enter_char`, which returns a data character that lies within a specified range of characters. Your function should display an error message if the specified range is invalid.

2. Redo Programming Exercise 1 for a function that reads a floating-point data value between a specified range of floating-point values.

3. The condition

```
(ch >= 'a') && (ch <= 'z')
```

in function my_toupper is a rather crude and possibly erroneous test for establishing that the character stored in ch is a lowercase letter. For example, the test will work fine for the ASCII character set shown in Appendix A. However, it may return the wrong result for some characters in the EBCDIC character set (also shown in Appendix A). What is the relevant difference between these two character sets that accounts for this phenomenon?

10.4 —— DATA ABSTRACTION AND ABSTRACT DATA TYPES: PROGRAM OBJECTS

In this section, we return to the notion of abstraction in programming. New terminology and ideas related to data abstraction are introduced. Our intent is to provide a brief overview of a different approach to program design, one that focuses first on data rather than algorithms. A few examples are provided in this chapter, but we will begin to put these ideas to work in solving larger problems in Chapter 11.

Abstraction has been one of the key concepts in managing the complexity of computer software. Although the concept, as it relates to building software, has evolved considerably since its earliest inception in the late 1940s and early 1950s, it has always been an important mechanism for helping us think about and design solutions to large, complex problems in terms of less complicated subproblems. In turn, we can apply this concept to each subproblem and try to solve it in terms of still simpler, smaller problems. This process of top-down analysis continues until each subproblem has become small enough that we can successfully work out the lowest-level details of implementation as a single unit.

In fact, this process does not always work in the top-down fashion described. You may have already noticed in using procedural abstraction (writing and using C++ functions) that it is often helpful to be sure you know exactly how to solve certain subproblems before actually working out the higher-level details of the "parent" problem (the one that depends on these subproblem solutions). There is nothing wrong with this! In fact, as we have seen, implementing, testing, and saving smaller problem solutions for later use is a way of establishing a collection of building blocks or tools that can be reused in designing the solutions to more complicated problems.

To this point in the text, our emphasis has been on procedural aspects of problem-solving and on structured programming. Yet even with this focus, we have tried not to lose sight of issues related to data analysis: the identification of information that is relevant to the solution of a problem and the representation of that information in a C++ program. We have illustrated the use of different types of data, such as `int` and `char`, and of two different structures, arrays and structs, for representing information in C++. In addition, we have written functions to perform operations on these data in accordance with the problem specifications we were given.

For several decades, the great majority of programmers have used this *procedure-oriented paradigm* of identifying the types and structures for representing problem data and constructing a program to perform the required operations on these data. The focus of this paradigm has been on the steps to be carried out (the algorithm or procedure) in solving a problem, rather than on the data elements involved in the solution. As this paradigm evolved over time, numerous advances had a profound positive influence on the software development process. Yet as programming systems grew in size and complexity, it became more and more apparent that the procedural paradigm was not adequate to the task.

One of the major flaws in this paradigm that has bothered many computer scientists concerned the scope of definition and visibility of the data used in their programs. Most languages, and the software development approaches that use them, provide little help in controlling the visibility of (access to) data. There has been little methodological incentive or language assistance for programmers to limit data access to only those program components that require such access. This lack of attention to and support for *data access control* is a serious problem in large systems. In the absence of tight access control, program changes to correct or improve one section of code often produce undesirable *side-effects* that cause other, apparently unrelated code sections to fail.

Often seemingly simple, *highly localized* changes ultimately result in changes to large portions of an existing system. To further exacerbate the situation, many of these ripple-effect changes are not recognized immediately and often show up later during testing, or worse, during the production use of a system. In some cases, the entire original design structure of a system may collapse under the weight of a set of changes, making later changes even more difficult to manage.

It is in this connection that the ideas of *information hiding* and *encapsulation* play a major role, providing programmers with a framework within which to view each relevant piece of problem data and the operations on these data as bound together in a single program unit. The process of identifying each problem data item, its properties, and its required operations involves another kind of abstraction, *data abstraction*. Data abstraction enables programmers to isolate all concerns related to a particular problem data element and then to implement a model of this element as a separate program component. It is most desirable to begin this isolation during the analysis phase of software development and carry it through to the design stage, and finally, to implementation.

Through *data abstraction,* we specify the data for a problem and the operations to be performed on these data. We need not be overly concerned with how the data will be represented in memory or how the operations will be implemented. In other words, we can describe *what* information must be stored without being specific as to *how* the information is organized and represented. This is the *logical view* of the data as opposed to its *physical view* (the actual internal representation in memory). Once we understand the logical view and we have an *abstract view* of the operations that we need to have performed, we can use the data and their operations in our programs. However, we (or someone else) will eventually have to implement the data and their operations before we can run any program that uses them.

One simple example of data abstraction is the C++ data type `float`, an abstraction for the set of real numbers (in the mathematical sense). This set includes the integers (such as −10234, 0, and 7098) as well as other numbers, some of which may be represented as fractions (such as $1/4$ or $5/11$) and others of which have no precise fractional representation (such as $\pi = 3.14159$). The computer hardware limits the range of floating-point numbers that can be represented, and not all floating-point numbers within the specified range can be represented (see Section 7.2 on the internal representation of floating-point values). Also, the result of manipulating floating-point numbers is often an approximation to the actual result. However, we can generally use the data type `float` and its C++ operators (+, −, *, /, =, <=, <, and so on), as well as the square root, logarithmic, and trigonometric functions, without being concerned with these details of their implementation. `int` and `char` are other examples of the use of data abstraction in C++.

Collections of data of the same type provide another useful abstraction. The information to be represented consists of the collection itself, a count of the number of items currently in the collection, and perhaps an upper limit or maximum on the number of items allowed in the collection. Given this specification of information to be represented, we must next turn our attention to the operations required on this collection. Clearly, we need to be able to put items into the collection (add an item), remove items from the collection (delete), obtain the value of an item (get an item), and determine the size of the collection. Other operations we might need include sorting the collection, adding all the values in the collection (assuming the elements in the collection are numeric), and displaying the entire collection.

The combined list of the information to be represented and the operations required on that information form an abstract data type (ADT). The diagrams shown in Fig. 10.7 provide a quick-reference illustration for the floating-point and collection abstractions, summarizing the information encapsulated in the abstraction and depicting the operations that may be performed on this infor-

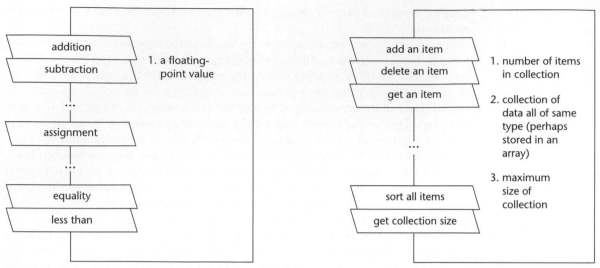

Figure 10.7   Illustrations of the floating-point (left) and collection (right) abstractions

mation. We will use diagrams of this nature throughout the remainder of the text. The operations are shown as *access windows* to the encapsulated information. In fact, only through these windows can information be altered or queried.

Ultimately, an ADT must be implemented in a programming language. In C++, for example, we could choose an array for modeling (or representing) the collection and use integers to represent the number of items and maximum number of items. The operations would each be implemented as functions. The entire set of data structures chosen to model the information, together with the functions, can be *encapsulated* in a single program component called a *class*. The implementation details would be hidden from any other parts of a program that might need to use this class. The concepts of encapsulation, information hiding, abstract data types, and classes are discussed in the following sections.

Encapsulation and Information Hiding

One advantage of data abstraction is that it helps a software designer make implementation decisions in a step-by-step fashion. The designer can postpone making decisions regarding the actual internal representation of data and the implementation of its operations. At the top levels of the design, the designer focuses on how to use data and their operations; at the lower levels, the implementation details are worked out. In this way, the designer can control or reduce the overall complexity of the problem.

If the details of an encapsulated data element's implementation are not known when a higher-level module is implemented, the higher-level module can access the data only through the encapsulated functions. From a software engineering viewpoint, this is an advantage rather than a limitation. It allows the designer to change his or her mind at a later date and possibly to choose a more efficient method of internal representation or implementation. Furthermore, the higher-level module will not have to be rewritten and may not even need to be recompiled when changes are made to the encapsulated component. The process of "hiding" the details of a low-level module's implementation from a higher-level module is called *information hiding*. The programming language implementation mechanism for building information-hiding program components is called an *encapsulation mechanism*.

Abstract Data Types

A primary goal of the remaining chapters of this text is to show you how to write and use abstract data types in programming. As you progress through this course, you will create a large collection of abstract data types in your own program library. Because each such abstract data type will already have been coded, debugged, tested, and maybe even compiled, the use of these ADTs will make it much easier for you to design and implement new applications programs.

Normally, an abstract data type consists of two parts: its definition, or specification, and its implementation. The *specification part* of an ADT describes the problem domain information (such as a collection of data elements of the same type, and its size) to be encapsulated in the ADT and the capabilities of the operations (add, delete, get, etc.) on this information. This is all a potential user of the abstract data type needs to know. The *implementation part* contains the declarations of the data structures needed to store the data for the ADT, as well as the actual implementation of its operations. This collection of details is intended to be hidden from the other program modules that use the abstract data type.

Most languages that support the use of ADTs also provide separate compilation for software components that contain abstract data types. If we compile the abstract data type, then we can link its executable code with other components that need to use it. If we are careful to include a fairly complete and general set of operators in the abstract data type, this component will not have to be recompiled for each new application.

Data Abstraction in C++: Classes and Objects

Not all modern programming languages provide a mechanism for implementing data abstractions defined during the design stage. C++ is one language that does provide such a mechanism, the `class`, however; and this is considered to be a major advantage of the language. In C++, we can use classes to define new data types as encapsulations of data and operations. Then, in much the same way as we declare variables, array elements, and structure members of the fundamental types, we can declare program entities as being of the new type defined by the class. In C++, such entities are called *objects*. The programming paradigm that uses objects as the foundational element of the design of programming systems is called *object-oriented programming*.

In the next chapter, we devote considerable attention to classes, objects, and the object-oriented (o-o) paradigm. In this chapter, and in much of the remaining text, we will focus on this o-o paradigm, developing numerous examples and providing an introduction to a number of important issues related to object-oriented programming in C++. Among other things, we will show how classes can be used to encapsulate information and isolate program details from all but those system components that require them. We will provide some introductory illustrations of the use of classes in designing and implementing new data types to serve as the foundational components of a new system We also will show how these components may be used and reused to serve the needs of a number of different software systems.

Before moving on to this development, however, we need to cover a few more issues of software engineering. These are the subject of the next few sections of this chapter.

EXERCISES FOR SECTION 10.4

Self-Check 1. In a manner similar to what was done in this section for the fundamental type `float`, list the C++ operations and standard functions that should be considered part of the complete specifications for the fundamental data types:

a. `int`   b. `char`

2. What is information hiding and why is it important to a software designer?

10.5 —— ANALYSIS OF ALGORITHM EFFICIENCY: BIG-O NOTATION

It is often important in programming to be able to provide comparative estimates of the efficiency of algorithms for performing a certain task. In this section, we provide a brief introduction to the topic of algorithm efficiency analysis, with a focus on the searching and sorting algorithms introduced in Chapter 9.

There are many algorithms for searching and sorting arrays. Because arrays can have a large number of elements, the time required to process all of the elements of an array can be significant. Therefore, it is important to have some idea of the relative efficiency of the various algorithms for performing these tasks. Unfortunately, it is difficult to get a precise measure of the efficiency of an algorithm or program. For this reason, we normally try to approximate the effect on an algorithm of a change in the number of items, n, that the algorithm processes. In this way, we can see how an algorithm's execution time increases with n, so we can compare two algorithms by examining their growth rates.

Usually, growth rates in execution efficiency are examined in terms of the *largest contributing factor* as the value of n gets large (for example, grows to 1,000 or more). If we determine that the expression

$$2n^2 + n - 5$$

expresses the relationship between the processing time of an algorithm and n, we say that the algorithm is an $O(n^2)$ algorithm, where O is an abbreviation for "the order of magnitude." This notation is known as *big-O notation*. The reason that this is an $O(n^2)$ algorithm rather than an $O(2n^2)$ algorithm or an $O(2n^2+n-5)$ algorithm is that the dominant factor in the relationship is the n^2 term. Efficiency considerations are most relevant for large values of n, because they tend to have the greatest impact on our work for these values. But for large values of n, the largest exponent term has by far the greatest impact on our measurements. For this reason, we tend to ignore the "smaller" terms and constants.

Analysis of a Search Algorithm

To search an array of n elements using the linear search function from Chapter 9, we have to examine all n elements if the target is not present in the array. If the target is in the array, then we have to search only until we find it. However, the target could be anywhere in the array—it is equally as likely to be at the beginning of the array as at the end. So, on average, we have to examine $n/2$ array elements to locate a target value in an array. This means that the linear search is an $O(n)$ process; that is, the growth rate is linear with respect to the number of items being searched. While this might not seem so bad, it is considerably worse, for example, than some other search algorithms that are $O(\log_2 n)$ processes. For example, for a binary search, the worst-case number of examinations, or *probes*, for any given item in a collection of data is $O(\log_2 n)$. For large n, the difference can be significant; for $n = 1,000$, for example, $n/2 = 500$, whereas $\log_2 n$ is approximately equal to 10.

Analysis of a Sort Algorithm

To determine the efficiency of a sorting algorithm, we normally focus on the number of array element comparisons and exchanges that it requires.

Performing a selection sort on an array of n elements requires $n - 1$ comparisons during the first pass, $n - 2$ during the second pass, and so on. Therefore, the total number of comparisons is represented by the series

$$1 + 2 + 3 + \cdots + (n - 2) + (n - 1).$$

The value of this series is expressed in the closed form

$$\frac{n \times (n - 1)}{2} = n^2/2 - n/2$$

The number of comparisons performed in sorting an array of n elements using the selection sort is always the same; however, the number of array element exchanges can vary, depending on the initial ordering of the array elements. During the search for a given smallest element (with subscript `min_sub`) if the smallest element is already in place, we could skip the exchange process. Should this condition never occur, there will be one exchange for each iteration of the main sort loop (*worst-case* situation). If the array happens to be sorted before the sort is called, all its elements will be in the proper place, so there will be zero exchanges (*best-case* situation). Therefore, the number of exchanges for an arbitrary initial ordering is between 0 and $n - 1$, which is O(n).

Because the dominant term in the expression for the number of comparisons shown earlier is $n^2/2$, the selection sort is considered an O(n^2) process and the growth rate is said to be *quadratic* (proportional to the square of the number of elements). What difference does it make whether an algorithm is an O(n) or O(n^2) process? Table 10.1 shows the evaluation of n and n^2 for different values of n. A doubling of n causes n^2 to increase by a factor of 4. Because n^2 increases much more rapidly than n, the performance of an O(n) algorithm is not as adversely affected by an increase in array size as is an O(n^2) algorithm. For large values of n (say, 100 or more), the difference in the performances of an

Table 10.1   Table of Values of n and n^2

n	n^2
2	4
4	16
8	64
16	256
32	1024
64	4096
128	16384
256	65536
512	262144

$O(n)$ and an $O(n^2)$ algorithm is significant (see the last three lines of Table 10.1).

Other factors besides the number of comparisons and exchanges affect an algorithm's performance. For example, one algorithm may take more time preparing for each exchange or comparison than another. Also, one algorithm might exchange subscripts, whereas another algorithm might exchange the array elements themselves. The second process can be more time consuming. Another measure of efficiency is the amount of memory required by an algorithm. Further discussion of these issues goes a bit beyond our purpose in this section. However, they provide a glimpse of the kinds of algorithm and program performance analysis that will be considered in detail in later computer science courses.

EXERCISES FOR SECTION 10.5

Self-Check   1. Determine how many times the cout line is executed in each of the following fragments. Indicate whether the algorithm is $O(n)$ or $O(n^2)$.

```
a. for (i = 0; i < n; i++)
       for (j = 0; j < n; j++)
           cout << i << ' ' << j;
b. for (i = 0; i < n; i++)
       for (j = 1; j <= 2; j++)
           cout << i << ' ' << j;
c. for (i = 0; i < n; i++)
       for (j = n; j > 0; j--)
           cout << i << ' ' << j;
```

Programming   1. Let n be a type integer variable and y_1, y_2, and y_3 be type floating-point. Write a program to compute and print the values of y_1, y_2, and y_3 (below) for n, from 0 to 1,000 inclusive, in increments of 25. Use the function ceil in the math.h library to compute y_3. Do the results surprise you?

$$y_1 = 100n + 10,$$
$$y_2 = 5n^2 + 2,$$
$$y_3 = 1,000 \times \text{ceiling} (\log_2 n).$$

10.6 ___ SOFTWARE TESTING

It does not really matter whether a program is designed carefully and runs efficiently if it does not do what it is supposed to do. One way to gain reasonable assurance that a program does what you want is through testing. However, it is difficult to determine how much testing should be done. Very often errors will appear in a software product after it is delivered, causing great inconvenience. Some notable software errors in operational programs have caused power brownouts, telephone network saturation, and space flight delays. In some situations it is impossible to test completely a software product in advance of its use. Examples are software that controls a missile and software that prevents a nuclear disaster in the event of malfunction of a nuclear power plant.

Preparing a Test Plan Early

It is best to develop a plan for testing early in the design stage of a new system. Some aspects of a test plan include deciding how the software will be tested, when the tests will occur, and who will do the testing. Normally testing is done by the programmer, by other members of the software team who did not code the module being tested, and by users of the software product. Some companies have special testing groups who are expert at finding bugs in other programmers' code. If the test plan is developed early in the design stage, testing can take place concurrently with the design and coding. The earlier an error is detected, the easier and less expensive it will be to correct.

Another advantage of deciding on the test plan early is that it should encourage programmers to prepare for testing as they write their code. A good programmer will practice *defensive programming* and include code that detects unexpected or invalid data values. For example, if a function has the precondition

```
pre: n greater than zero
```

it would be a good idea to place the `if` statement

```
if (n <= 0)
   cout << "Invalid value for argument n -- " << n;
```

at the beginning of the function. This `if` statement will provide a diagnostic message in the event that the argument passed to the function is invalid.

Similarly, if a data value being read from the keyboard is supposed to be between 0 and 40, a defensive programmer would use function `enter_int` shown in Fig. 10.5:

```
cout << "Enter number of hours worked: ";
hours = enter_int (0, 40);
```

The two arguments of `enter_int` define the range of acceptable values for the data element to be read and returned.

Structured Walkthroughs

One important testing technique is called a structured walkthrough. In a *structured walkthrough*, the programmer describes, or "walks through," the logic of a new module as part of a presentation to other members of the software team. The purpose of the walkthrough is for the team members to identify design errors or bugs that may have been overlooked by the programmer because he or she is too close to the problem. The goal is to detect errors in logic before they become part of the code.

Black-Box versus White-Box Testing

There are two basic ways to test a completed module or system: *black-box*, or *specification-based*, testing and *white-box*, or *glass-box*, testing. In black-box testing, we assume that the program tester has no idea of the code inside the module or system. The tester's job is to verify that the module does what its specification says that it does. For a function, this means ensuring that the function's postconditions are satisfied whenever its preconditions are met. For a system or subsystem, this means ensuring that the system does indeed satisfy its original requirements specification. Because the tester cannot look inside the module or system, he or she must prepare sufficient sets of test data to ensure that the system output is correct for all values of valid system input. The tester should especially check the *boundaries* of the system, or particular values for the program variables where the system performance changes. For example, a boundary for a payroll program would be the value of hours worked that triggers overtime pay. Also, the module or system should not crash when presented with invalid input. Black-box testing is most often done by a special testing team or by program users.

In glass-box (or white-box) testing, the tester has full knowledge of the code for the module or system and must ensure that each section of code has been thoroughly tested. For a selection statement (`if` or `switch`), this means checking all possible paths through the selection statement. The tester must determine that the correct path is chosen for all possible values of the selection variable, taking special care at the boundary values where the path changes.

For a repetition statement, the tester must make sure that the loop always performs the correct number of iterations and that the number of iterations is not off by one. Also, the tester should verify that the computations inside the loop are correct at the boundaries—that is, for the initial and final values of the loop control variable. Finally, the tester should make sure that the module or system still meets its specification when a loop executes zero times and that under no circumstances can the loop execute forever.

Integration Testing

In Section 6.8 we discussed the differences between top-down and bottom-up testing of a single system. We also introduced integration testing in conjunction with the Sum and Average and Checking Account Balance Problems. In integration testing, the program tester must determine whether the individual components of the system, which have been separately tested (using either top-down or bottom-up testing, or some combination), can be integrated with other like components. Each phase of integration testing deals with larger units, progressing from individual modules, through subsystems, and ending with the entire system. For example, after two subsystems are completed, integration testing must determine whether the two subsystems can work together. Once the entire system is completed, integration testing must determine whether that system is compatible with other systems in the computing environment in which it will be used.

EXERCISES FOR SECTION 10.6

Self-Check   1. Devise a set of data to test function `enter_int` (Fig. 10.5) using:
   a. white-box testing
   b. black-box testing

10.7 ___ FORMAL METHODS OF PROGRAM VERIFICATION

In the last section, we described some aspects of program and system testing.[1] We stated that testing should begin as early as possible in the design phase and continue through system implementation. Even though testing is an extremely valuable tool for providing evidence that a program is correct and meets its specification, it is difficult to know how much testing is enough. For example, how do we know that we have tried enough different sets of test data or that all possible paths through the program have been executed?

For these reasons, computer scientists have developed a second method of demonstrating the correctness of a program. This method is called *formal* verification. By carefully applying formal rules, we can determine that a program meets its specification just as a mathematician proves a theorem using definitions, axioms, and previously proved theorems. This approach has been shown to work well on small programs, but there is some question as to whether it can be used effectively on very large programs or program systems.

In this section, we confine our attention to two fundamental aspects of program verification, the assertion and the loop invariant. Our discussion will be more intuitive and practical than formal. Our goal is to encourage you to think clearly about the purpose of each C++ code segment or function that you write,

---

[1]This section was adapted from an outline prepared by James C. Pleasant, Department of Computer and Information Sciences, Tennessee State University.

to insert comments concerning this intent where appropriate, and to check to ensure that your algorithms and C++ code are consistent with this intent.

Assertions

An important part of formal verification involves the use of *assertions,* logical statements about the program that are supposed to be true whenever they are encountered during the execution of a program. The C++ library `assert.h` provides support for the use of assertions in the form of *logical predicates:* expressions that can have a value of either true or false. If at any point during the execution of your program a predicate is encountered that has the value of false, a suitable error message is written to the standard error file `stderr` and your program will terminate execution.

We believe it is premature to introduce the formal use of C++ assertions in this text. Instead, we will illustrate how to write each assertion that we use as a program comment describing what is supposed to be true about the program variables at the point at which it appears. We will focus our attention primarily on the special assertions related to program loops.

Example 10.1 The following program fragment contains a sequence of assignment statements, each followed by an assertion:

```
// assert: 5 is a constant
a = 5;      // assert: a is equal to 5
x = a;      // assert: x is equal to 5
y = x + a;  // assert: y is equal to 10
```

The truth of the first assertion, a is equal to 5, follows from executing the first statement with the knowledge that 5 is a constant. The truth of the second assertion, x is equal to 5, follows from executing x is equal to a with the knowledge that a is 5. The truth of the third assertion, y is equal to 10, follows from executing y = x + a with the knowledge that x is 5 and a is 5. In the fragment above, we used assertions as comments to document the change in a program variable after each assignment statement executes.   ■

The task of a person using formal verification is to prove that a program fragment meets its specification. For the fragment above, this means proving that the final assertion, or *postcondition* (y is equal to 10), follows from the initial presumption, or *precondition* (5 is a constant), after the program fragment executes. The assignment rule (described below) is critical to this process. If we know that a is equal to 5 is true, this rule allows us to make the assertion x is equal to 5 after executing the statement x = a.

The Assignment Rule

```
// P(a)
x = a;
// P(x)
```

Explanation: If P(a) (for example, a = 5) is a logical predicate (assertion) about a, the same predicate with x substituted for a will be true after the assignment statement x = a executes.

Loop Invariants

We stated earlier that loops are a common source of program errors. It is often difficult to determine that a loop body executes exactly the right number of times or that loop execution causes the desired change in program variables. A special type of assertion, a *loop invariant*, is used to help establish the correctness of an iterative algorithm. We introduced the loop invariant in Chapter 9. These invariants were written informally as comments using English statements involving program variables. In general, a loop invariant is a logical expression for which the following four points must be shown to be true:

1. The loop invariant must be true initially; that is, it must be true before loop execution begins the first time.
2. The execution of the loop must preserve the loop invariant. That is, if the loop invariant is true prior to the next iteration of the loop, it must still be true after this iteration is complete.
3. The loop must terminate after some finite number of executions.
4. The loop invariant must capture the intent (correctness) of the algorithm. Thus if the invariant is still true when the loop terminates, the algorithm must compute the desired result.

Therefore, the loop invariant defines a relationship among the variables of a loop that remains true as loop execution progresses (hence the name invariant).

As an example of a loop invariant, let's examine the loop below, which accumulates the sum of the integers $1, 2, \ldots, n$ where n is a positive integer and sum and n are integers:

```
// Accumulate the sum of integers 1 through n in sum.
// Assert: n >= 1 (precondition)
sum = 0;
i = 1;
while (i <= n)
{
    sum += i;
    i++;
}  // end while
```

In this example, the invariant should be a logical expression about the loop-control variable i and the accumulating sum. The best way to gain some insight into how to formulate a loop invariant is to trace the progress of the loop through several iterations. Figure 10.8 sketches this loop's progress for the first three iterations. At the end of the third iteration, i is 4 and sum is 6 = 1 + 2 + 3, or the sum of all integers less than 4.

When loop repetition finishes, i will be n+1 and sum will contain the desired result $(1 + 2 + 3 + \cdots + n)$. Therefore, we propose the following as the loop invariant:

```
// Invariant: 1 <= i <= n+1 and sum is equal to the sum of all
//            positive integers less than i.
```

To show that this invariant is correct for the summation loop, we focus on the four points just listed:

- The loop invariant must be true before loop execution begins. Clearly, this is the case, because before loop entry i is 1. Also, the invariant requires that sum be equal to the sum of all positive integers less than i. Because sum is initialized to 0, this is also the case.

- The execution of the loop also must preserve the loop invariant. To prove that this is the case, we need to use the technique of *mathematical induction*. To provide a reasonable demonstration that the invariant is preserved, it is usually sufficient to check the values of all variables affected by the loop during the last iteration (or the next-to-last and last iterations). In this example, when the last iteration begins, i is equal to n and

$$sum = 1 + 2 + \cdots + (i-1)$$

In the $(i+1)$th iteration, i is added to sum. Because i is equal to n at this point, sum is indeed equal to the sum of the integers 1 through n.

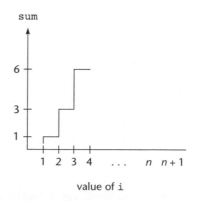

Figure 10.8   Sketch of summation loop for $n = 3$

• Following the addition of i to sum, i is incremented (i now equals n+1), the loop repetition test i<=n fails, and loop execution terminates.

In program verification, the loop invariant is used to prove that the loop meets its specification—that it does what it is supposed to do. For our purposes, we will use the invariant to document what we know about the loop's behavior. We will place the invariant just before the code associated with the loop, as shown Fig. 10.9.

Figure 10.9   The summation loop with invariant

```
// Accumulate the sum of integers 1 through n in sum.
// Assert: n >= 1 (precondition)
// Invariant: 1 <= i <= n+1 and sum is equal to the sum of all
//            positive integers less than i.
sum = 0;
i = 1;
while (i <= n)
{
   sum += i;
   i++;
}   // end while
```

Some computer scientists recommend writing the loop invariant as a preliminary step before coding the loop. Then the invariant can be used as a guide to help determine the correct repetition condition for a loop. This condition, the loop initialization, and the increment of the loop-control variable are the key factors affecting the correct execution of the loop. By hand tracing the execution of a loop with appropriate *boundary cases* of the variables affected by the loop, we can gain a reasonable assurance that the loop behaves as desired. In the summation example, we checked that i and sum had the correct values in the boundary cases involving the first and last iterations of the loop. This typical loop analysis should be performed for all loops you write.

Invariants and the for Statement

Because the loop invariant states what we know to be true about a loop after each iteration, we should be able to write an invariant for a for loop as well as a while loop. Because the loop-control variable in a C++ for loop is incremented just before loop exit and retains its final value, the same preconditions and postconditions and the same loop invariant can be used for both loops:

```
// Accumulate the sum of integers 1 through n in sum.
// Assert: n >= 1 (precondition)
// Invariant: 1 <= i <= n+1 and sum = 1 + 2 + ... i-1.
```

```
sum = 0;
for (i = 1; i <= n; i++)
   sum += i;
```

Invariants and Sentinel-Controlled Loops

Example 10.2   Figure 10.10 shows a sentinel-controlled `while` loop that computes the product of a collection of values. Loop exit occurs after reading in the sentinel value. The loop invariant indicates that the variable `product` is the product of all values read before the current one and that none of these values was the sentinel.

Figure 10.10   Sentinel-controlled loop with invariant

```
cout << "When done, enter: " << sentinel << " to stop.";
// Compute the product of a sequence of data values.
// Assert: sentinel is a constant (precondition).
// Invariant: product is the product of all prior values read
//            into num and no prior value of num was the sentinel.
product = 1;
cout << "Enter the first number: ";
cin >> num;
while (num != sentinel)
{
   product *= num;
   cout << "Enter the next number: ";
   cin >> num;
}  // end while
```

The analysis of this loop with respect to the four points listed earlier requires some explanation. The invariant is true "by default" before loop execution begins because it makes no statement about the value of the product before any values are read in. After the first iteration of the loop, `product` is equal to num × 1, as desired. After each subsequent iteration, `product` is always equal to the product of all values read. Furthermore, because the loop is not repeated once the sentinel has been read, the loop invariant is still preserved.

So far, this seems simple enough. However, two important questions have not yet been considered:

- What if there are no data other than the sentinel value?
- What if there is no sentinel value at the end of the data?

These may seem like silly questions, but they point out two potential errors that can easily occur with the input data to many problems—errors that often are not properly handled by programmers. The first case (no data other than the sentinel value) can be handled in several ways. One way is to state explicitly in the invariant the assumed value of product if there are no data to be processed. The easiest choice for this value of product is 1. This choice yields the following invariant:

```
// Invariant: product is the product of all prior values read
//            into num and no prior value of num was the sentinel.
//            If no values are read in, product is assumed to
//            be 1.
```

If the sentinel value is missing, the program will eventually terminate when an attempt is made to read past the end-of-file. In this case, the value of product may well be correct, but our program will not be able to use it. In cases such as this, it is better to use the C++ end-of-file test to determine when all data have been read. This option is discussed in Programming Exercise 2 at the end of this section.   ∎

Function Preconditions and Postconditions

A function's precondition is a logical statement about its input arguments. The postcondition may be a logical statement about its output arguments (and return value), or it may be a logical statement that describes the change in *program state* caused by the function execution. Any of the following activities represents a change in program state: changing the value of a variable, writing additional program output, reading new input data. It is as important to describe the effect of a function on device input or output and variable or class attributes as it is to indicate the effect on output or input/output arguments.

Example 10.3   The precondition and postcondition for function enter_int (see Fig. 10.5) are repeated next:

```
// READS INTEGER BETWEEN min_n AND max_n INTO n
int enter_int
   (int min_n,    // IN: minimum range value for n
    int max_n)    // IN: maximum range value for n

// Pre:    min_n and max_n are assigned values.
// Post:   If min_n <= max_n, returns the first data value read
//         that has a value between min_n and max_n (inclusive).
//         Otherwise, prints a message and exits.
// Returns: First integer read that has a value between min_n and
//         max_n.

{
   ...
}
```

The precondition tells us that input arguments min_n and max_n are defined before the function begins execution. The postcondition tells us that the function returns the first data value read in that has a value between `min_n` and `max_n` whenever `min_n <= max_n` is true.   ■

EXERCISES FOR SECTION 10.7

Self-Check   1. Write the loop invariant and the assertion following the loop for the `while` loop in function `enter_int` (Fig. 10.5).

2. If the sentinel-controlled loop in Fig. 10.10 were rewritten as a flag-controlled loop, what would the new loop invariant look like? Use zero as the sentinel value, and define the flag `no_zero` as the value of the condition `num != sentinel`. The flag should remain true until a zero value is read.

3. Write the loop invariant for the loop in Fig. 5.14 (temperature conversion).

4. In Example 10.2 (involving the sentinel-controlled loop) we chose 1 for the product value in the case in which no data preceded the sentinel value. Although this was an easy choice, it did not enable us to determine whether the missing data condition occurred. Describe one possible change to the loop in Fig. 10.10 that would enable the program to check for missing data following loop execution.

5. Consider the following version of the loop shown in Fig. 10.10·

```
cout << "When done, enter: " << sentinel << " to stop.";
// Compute the product of a sequence of data values.
// Assert: sentinel is a constant (precondition).
// Invariant: product is the product of all prior values
//            read into num and no prior value of num was
//            the sentinel.
product = 1;
cout << "Enter the first number: ";
while (num != sentinel)
{
    cin >> num;
    product *= num;
    cout << "Enter the next number: ";
}   // end while
```

Does the invariant still hold true for this loop? Carefully explain your answer.

Programming   1. Write a function that returns the count of the number of nonzero digits in an arbitrary integer `number`. Your solution should include a `while` loop for which the following is a valid loop invariant:

```
// Invariant: 0 <= count; number > 0 and number has been
//            divided by 10 count times.
```

The assertion below should be valid following the loop:

```
// Assert: number = 0
```

2. Rewrite the product computation loop shown in Fig. 10.10 to terminate on end-of-file. Be sure to include the appropriate invariant as a comment.

10.8 ___ PROFESSIONAL ETHICS AND RESPONSIBILITIES

Software engineers and computer programmers are professionals and should always act that way. As part of their jobs, computer programmers may be able to access large data banks containing sensitive personnel information, information that is classified "secret" or "top secret," or financial transaction data. Programmers should always behave in a socially responsible manner and not retrieve information that they are not entitled to see. They should not use information to which they are given access for their own personal gain or do anything that would be considered illegal, unethical, or harmful to others.

You may have heard stories about "computer hackers" who have broken into secure data banks by using their own computer to call (by telephone) the computer that controls access to the data bank. Some individuals have sold classified information retrieved in this way to intelligence agencies of other countries. Other hackers try to break into computers to retrieve this information for their own amusement, as a prank, or just to demonstrate that they can. Regardless of the intent, this activity is illegal, and the government will prosecute anyone who does this. Your university now probably addresses this kind of activity in your student handbook. The punishment is probably similar to that for other criminal activity, because that's exactly what it is.

Another illegal activity sometimes practiced by hackers is the insertion of special code, called a *virus*, in a computer's disk memory. A virus will cause sporadic activities to disrupt the operation of the host computer. For example, unusual messages may appear on the screen at certain times. Viruses can also cause the host computer to erase portions of its own disk memory, thereby destroying valuable information and programs. Viruses are spread from one computer to another when data are copied from the infected disk and processed by a different computer. Certainly, these kinds of activity should not be considered harmless pranks; they are illegal and should not be done under any circumstances.

A programmer who changes information in a database containing financial records for his or her own personal gain is guilty of *computer theft* or *computer fraud*. This is a felony that can lead to fines and imprisonment.

Another example of unprofessional behavior is using someone else's programs without permission. Although it is certainly permissible to use modules in libraries that have been developed for reuse by your own company's programmers, you cannot use another programmer's personal programs or programs from another company without getting permission beforehand. Doing this could lead to a lawsuit, and you or your company may have to pay damages.

Another fraudulent practice is submitting another student's code as your own. This, of course, is plagiarism and is no different from copying paragraphs of information from a book or journal article and calling it your own.

Most universities have severe penalties for plagiarism, which may include failing the course and/or dismissal from the university. You should be aware that even if you modify the code slightly or substitute your own comments or different variable names, you are still guilty of plagiarism if you are using another person's ideas and code. To avoid any question of plagiarism, find out beforehand your instructor's rules with respect to working with others on a project. If group efforts are not allowed, make sure that you work independently and submit only your own code.

Many commercial software packages are protected by copyright laws and cannot be copied or duplicated. It is illegal to make additional copies of protected software that you may be using at work in order to use this software at home on your computer or on someone else's computer. Besides the fact that this is against the law, using software copied from another computer increases the possibility that your computer will receive a virus. For all these reasons, you should act ethically and honor any copyright agreements that pertain to a particular software package.

Computer system access privileges or user account codes are also private property. Such privileges are usually granted for a specific purpose. For example, you may be given a computer account for work to be done in a particular course or, perhaps, for work to be done during the time you are a student at your institution. The privilege is to be protected; it should not be loaned to anyone else and should not be used for any purpose for which it was not intended. When you leave the institution, this privilege is normally terminated and any accounts associated with the privilege will be closed.

Computers, computer programs, data, and access (account) codes are like any other property. If they belong to someone else and you are not explicitly given use privileges, then do not use them. If you are granted a usage privilege for a specific purpose, don't abuse the privilege—it can be taken away.

Bear in mind that as students and professionals in computing, we need to be aware of the example we set for others. As a group of individuals who are most dependent on computers and computer software, we must respect both the physical and the intellectual property rights of others. If we set a bad example, others are sure to follow.

CHAPTER REVIEW

Software engineering is an area of study and practice encompassing a broad range of topics. In this chapter we focused on several of these topics, including the software life cycle, algorithm and program efficiency, program testing and verification, and ethics and social responsibility. Special emphasis was placed on the use of abstraction as an important tool in the analysis and design of large, complex programs.

We began our discussion with a description of the phases of the software life cycle:

1. Requirements specification
2. Analysis
3. Design
4. Implementation
5. Testing and validation
6. Operation, follow-up, and maintenance

The concept of data abstraction was introduced. The limitations of procedural abstraction were reviewed, and the advantages of practicing data abstraction in performing systems analysis and design were summarized. The importance of identifying the problem domain information to be represented and manipulated in a program was discussed, and the idea of encapsulating the representations and manipulations for each problem domain entity in a single, encapsulated unit was introduced. The fact that C++ provides a feature (the `class`) for implementing such encapsulations was cited as a major advantage and one of the reasons for using C++ in the beginning course of a computer science curriculum.

Additional issues related to software testing and validation were introduced. We discussed planning for testing, selection of test teams, structured walkthroughs, black-box testing, white-box testing, and integration testing. We also introduced program verification as an alternative to testing and described the use of assertions and loop invariants in this process. In this text, we will use informal versions of these logical statements about programs and loops to aid our understanding of our code and of the demonstration that it does what it is intended to do.

Finally, because we geared the discussion in this chapter to techniques practiced by software professionals, we included a discussion of ethics and professional behavior. We described the special responsibilities that programmers have because of their ability to access sensitive information. We discussed computer viruses and how they are spread. We also described how using another programmer's code or ideas is plagiarism and carries severe penalties in industry as well as in the classroom.

✔ QUICK-CHECK EXERCISES

1. The six phases of the software life cycle are listed below in arbitrary order. Place them in their correct order.

   - testing and validation
   - design

- requirements specification
- operation and maintenance
- implementation
- analysis

2. In which phases are the users of a software product likely to be involved?
3. In which phases are the programmers and analysts likely to be involved?
4. Which phase lasts the longest?
5. _____ testing requires the use of test data that exercise each statement in a module.
6. _____ testing focuses on testing the functional characteristics of a module.
7. Which of these may be false, indicating a programming error?

- loop invariant
- `while` condition
- assertion

8. The use of loop invariants is useful for which of the following?

- loop control
- loop design
- loop verification

9. Write a loop invariant for the code segment

```
product = 1;
counter = 2;
while (counter < 5)
{
    product *= counter;
    counter++;
}
```

Answers to Quick-Check Exercises

1. requirements specification, analysis, design, implementation, testing and validation, operation and maintenance
2. requirements specification, testing and validation, operation and maintenance
3. all phases
4. operation and maintenance
5. white-box
6. black-box
7. `while` condition
8. loop design, loop verification
9. `// Invariant: counter <= 5 and product contains product of all`
   `// integers < counter`

REVIEW QUESTIONS

1. Explain why the principle of information hiding is important to the software designer.

2. Define the terms *procedural abstraction* and *data abstraction*.
3. Which of the following are likely to occur in a programmer's library of functions? Explain your answers.

   a. a function that raises a number to a specified power
   b. a function that writes the user instructions for a particular program
   c. a function that displays the message HI MOM in block letters
   d. a function that displays the block letter M

4. Which of the following statements is incorrect?

   a. Loop invariants are used in loop verification.
   b. Loop invariants are used in loop design.
   c. A loop invariant is always an assertion.
   d. An assertion is always a loop invariant.

5. Briefly describe a test plan for the Telephone Directory Program described in Section 10.2, assuming that integration testing is used.
6. Write a function that computes the average number of characters found on the lines of a text file. Include loop invariants and any other assertions necessary to verify that the function is correct.

PROGRAMMING PROJECTS

1. Write a set of library functions that can be used to determine the following information for an integer input argument:

   a. Is it a multiple of 7, 11, or 13?
   b. Is the sum of the digits odd or even?
   c. What is the square root value?
   d. Is it a prime number?

   Write a driver program that tests your library functions, using the input values 104 3773 13 121 77 3075

2. Each month, a bank customer deposits $50 into a savings account. Assume that the interest rate is fixed (does not change) and is a problem input. The interest is calculated on a quarterly basis. For example, if the account earns 6.5 percent interest annually, it earns one-fourth of 6.5 percent every 3 months. Write a program to compute the total investment, the total amount in the account, and the interest accrued for each of the 120 months of a 10-year period. Assume that the rate is applied to all funds in the account at the end of a quarter, regardless of when the deposits were made.

   Print all values accurate to two decimal places. The table printed by your program when the annual interest rate is 6.5 percent should begin as follows:

MONTH	INVESTMENT	NEW AMOUNT	INTEREST	TOTAL SAVINGS
1	50.00	50.00	0.00	50.00
2	100.00	100.00	0.00	100.00

3	150.00	150.00	2.44	152.44
4	200.00	202.44	0.00	202.44
5	250.00	252.44	0.00	252.44
6	300.00	302.44	4.91	307.35
7	350.00	357.35	0.00	357.35

Carefully design your system in terms of separate functional modules, and use either C++ library functions or your own in writing your program.

3. Redo Programming Project 2, adding columns to allow comparison of interest compounded monthly (one-twelfth of annual rate every month) with continuously compounded interest. The formula for continuously compounded interest is

$$amount = principle \times e^{rate \times time},$$

where *rate* is the annual interest rate and *time* is expressed in years. Carefully design your system in terms of separate functional modules, and use either C++ library functions or your own in writing your program.

4. An employee time card is represented as one long string of characters having the following form:

Positions	Data
1–10	Employee last name
11–20	Employee first name
21	Contains C for city office or S for suburban office
22	Contains U (union) or N (nonunion)
23–26	Employee identification number
27	Blank
28–29	Number of regular hours (a whole number)
30	Blank
31–36	Hourly rate (dollars and cents)
37	Blank
38–39	Number of dependents
40	Blank
41–42	Number of overtime hours (a whole number)

Write a program that processes a collection of these strings stored in a data file and writes the results to an output file.

a. Compute gross pay using the formula

$$gross = regular\ hours \times rate + overtime\ hours \times 1.5 \times rate.$$

b. Compute net pay by subtracting the following deductions:

$federal\ tax = 0.14 \times (gross - 13 \times dependents),$
$social\ security = 0.052 \times gross$
$city\ tax = 4\% \times gross$ if employee works in the city
$union\ dues = 6.75\% \times gross$ for union member

All information read and all values computed in parts a and b should be written to the output file.

Carefully design your system in terms of separate functional modules, and use either C++ library functions or your own in writing your program.

5. Write a menu-driven program that contains options for creating a data file to be processed by the payroll program described in Programming Project 4 (the user should be prompted to enter several time "cards" from the keyboard). Your program should allow the user to display the time cards in the file, add new time cards to the end of the existing file, delete time cards from an existing file based on their ordinal position within the file (e.g., delete the seventh time card), and quit the program.

   Carefully design your system in terms of separate functional modules, and use either C++ library functions or your own in writing your program.

6. For any one of the previous Programming Projects, identify and list all of the problem domain data entities relevant to the problem solution. For each such entity, list the information about the entity needed to solve the problem and provide a list of the operations on this information required in the problem solution.

11

Data Abstraction in C++: The C++ Class

11.1 The C++ Class

11.2 Classes versus Structs

11.3 The Abstract Data Type day

11.4 Automatic Initialization: Class Constructors

11.5 Problem Analysis and Design Using Classes
CASE STUDY: Areas and Perimeters of Different Figures Revisited

11.6 A Complex Number Class (Optional)

11.7 Defining and Using Functions and Classes: Summary of Rules and Restrictions

11.8 Common Programming Errors
Chapter Review

In this chapter, we continue the study of classes and data abstraction outlined in Chapter 10. We show how to use classes to define new data types as encapsulations of data and operations. Then, in much the same way as we declare and manipulate variables, array elements, and structure members of the fundamental types, we can declare program entities as being of the new type defined by a `class`. In C++, such entities are called *objects;* the programming approach (or *paradigm*) that uses objects as the foundational element for software design is called *object-oriented programming.*

Our introduction to object-oriented programming begins in this chapter and continues through Chapters 12, 14, and 16. To begin, the C++ `class` is introduced and illustrated in its simplest form as an implementation mechanism for data abstractions. We show how to define classes creating new user-defined data types and how to declare and manipulate objects of these types. In Section 11.6, we describe a data abstraction defining a complex number data type. The class for implementing this data type is not shown; however, the description of the use of this class is straightforward and illustrates some of the real power and advantages of C++.

11.1 —— THE C++ CLASS

Almost from the very beginning of this text, we have been using a number of abstract data types as the foundational elements in our programming. The types `int`, `float`, `double`, and `char` are examples of data abstractions that are *built into* the C++ language. In Chapter 7, we also saw how to define our own simple data types called enumeration types. All of these abstract data types, the built-in types, and the user-defined enumeration types consist of data items and a collection of operations that can be performed on those items. For example, the type `float` abstraction might consist of 4 bytes (32 bits) of memory. The left-most bit indicates the sign of the number, and the remaining bits are divided into two parts, the characteristic and the mantissa (see Chapter 7). The operations defined on variables of type `float` include addition, multiplication, subtraction, and division. These operations manipulate the sign, characteristic, and mantissa of their operands to produce type `float` results. In point of fact, we rarely need to concern ourselves with the details of either the storage of type `float` values or their manipulation—these details are hidden from the view of most programs that we write. We simply declare variables of this type and use the operations defined on them.

With this in mind, we now turn our attention to the definition of our own *user-defined data types.* This journey will extend through the remainder of this text and will be revisited repeatedly in any subsequent computing science courses that you might take. We will illustrate how to define our own data types as extensions to the C++ language, tailoring them as necessary to the particular problem to be solved, while at the same time making them general enough so that they can be reused repeatedly. The C++ feature that will enable us to do this is the class.

A First Example: The counter Class

Figure 11.1 shows an example of a class for a simple abstract data type, which we have called a counter. The class contains a single integer variable value, which is used as a counter. Four operations on this variable are defined. Three of them, initialize, increment, and decrement, change

Figure 11.1   The abstract data type counter

```
// FILE: CntrADT.h
// COUNTER CLASS DEFINITION AND IMPLEMENTATION

#ifndef CNTRADT_H_              // used to avoid multiple definitions
#define CNTRADT_H_

#include <limits.h>            // contains definition of INT_MAX and INT_MIN

class counter
{
   public:
      // Member Functions...
      // INITIALIZE COUNTER
      void initialize ();

      // INCREMENT COUNTER
      void increment ();

      // DECREMENT COUNTER
      void decrement ();

      // RETURN CURRENT COUNTER VALUE
      int access_value ();

   private:
      // Data Members (Attributes)...
      int value;
}; // NOTE -- a class definition must end with a semicolon
```

public section

private section

definition section

(Continued)

Figure 11.1 (Continued)

```
// INITIALIZE COUNTER
void counter::initialize ()
{
   value = 0;
}  // end initialize




// INCREMENT COUNTER
void counter::increment ()
{
   if (value < INT_MAX)
      value++;
   else
      cerr << "Counter overflow. Increment ignored." << endl;
}  // end increment




// DECREMENT COUNTER
void counter::decrement ()
{
   if (value > INT_MIN)
      value--;
   else
      cerr << "Counter underflow. Decrement ignored." << endl;
}  // end decrement




// RETURN CURRENT COUNTER VALUE
int counter::access_value ()
{
   return value;
}  // end access_value

#endif  // CNTRADT_H_
```

implementation section

the value of the variable. The fourth operation, access_value, is used to retrieve the current value of the variable.

This class consists of two sections of code, a *definition section* and an *implementation section*. The definition section (shown under the screen for class counter) begins with the line that starts with the C++ reserved word class, and consists of everything between the opening brace { (that is, the segments of code beginning with the reserved words public and private) up to and including the semicolon following the closing brace }. The public definition part of a class describes the interface of the class with other program components that use the class. This interface consists of the specification of the variables, types, constants, and function prototypes that a programmer needs to know to use the class successfully. This information is also all the compiler needs to know to correctly compile a program that uses the class.

The class definition section usually also contains a *private section* (beginning with the word `private`) in which the variables, constants, data types, and function prototypes to be hidden from other program components are specified.

The functions specified in a class definition section are referred to as the *member functions* of the class; the variables, constants, and data types are referred to as the *data members* or *storage attributes* of the class (we use these last two terms interchangeably in the text).

The implementation section of the `counter` class (left unscreened in Fig. 11.1) contains the implementation of the class member functions. This information is also hidden from the class users, which do not need to know these details. An important aspect of this section is the use of the *scope resolution operator* `::` as a prefix to the function names in each function header. This operator tells the compiler that the function being defined is a member of the class (`counter` in this case) named just preceding the operator. A class member function can access all of the functions and data members of the class directly as illustrated by the reference to the data member `value` in all four member functions of the `counter` class.

The reserved words `private` and `public` actually have intuitive meanings. Identifiers such as `initialize` and `decrement` (in Fig. 11.1) that are declared in the public section of a class (immediately following the reserved word `public`) may be accessed from outside the class. Those declared in the private section, such as the variable `value`, may be accessed within the class, but not from outside.

The idea of the `class` construct is to enable us to build self-contained program components that may separately be designed, implemented, and tested and then integrated into a larger program system. The C++ class provides a mechanism to *encapsulate*, or build a protective wall around, its data and function members. Only the information provided in the public section of the class is accessible from the outside—everything else is hidden.

This is illustrated in Fig. 11.2 for the `counter` class. As shown in this *class diagram*, the member functions (`initialize`, `increment`, `decrement`, and `access_value`) declared in the public section of the class are accessible outside of the class. No other functions or variables declared inside the class may be accessed from outside.

To help us understand these points, let us look at an example program that uses the `counter` class (see Fig. 11.3). The `#include` line

```
#include "CntrADT.h"
```

is required because we are assuming that the `counter` class has been stored in some file (named `CntrADT.h`) other than the one that contains this program. It is not necessary to store classes in separate files, but it is highly

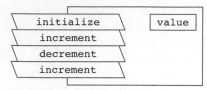

Figure 11.2   Class diagram for the `counter class`

advisable. Doing so enables us to keep each file fairly small and makes it easier for us to locate and reuse classes as the need arises. In fact, in this text, most C++ classes are stored in two separate files, a `.h` file and a `.cpp` file. The `.h`, or *header*, file contains the *header part* of the class, including the `public` and `private` sections, down to and including the semicolon following the right brace. The `.cpp` file normally contains all member function implementations—in our example, `initialize`, `increment`, `decrement`, and `access_value`, as shown in the bottom part of Fig. 11.1. It is important to note that the `.h` and `.cpp` *file extensions* are not standard and may vary from one compiler to another.

All C++ systems with which we are familiar provide a similar mechanism for including in one C++ code file lines of code that are stored in another file. Your instructor can tell you the particular *compiler commands* that can be used with your system to perform this include task.

Figure 11.3   Test program and sample output for `counter` **class**

```
// FILE: CntrTest.cpp
// TEST PROGRAM FOR Counter CLASS

#include <iostream.h>

#include "CntrAdt.h"

void main ()
{
    // Local data ...
    counter c_inc;              // variable of type counter
    counter c_dec;              // a second variable of type counter

    // Initialize counter values.
    c_inc.initialize ();
    c_dec.initialize ();
```

(Continued)

Figure 11.3   (Continued)

```
      // Test increment, decrement and access_value functions.
      for (int i = 0; i < 10; i++)
      {
         c_inc.increment ();
         cout << "c_inc = " << c_inc.access_value () << endl;
      }  // end for

      for (i = 5; i > 0; i--)
      {
         c_dec.decrement ();
         cout << "c_dec = " << c_dec.access_value () << endl;
      }

       // Print results.
      cout << "The final value of c_inc = " << c_inc.access_value ()
           << endl;
      cout << "The final value of c_dec = " << c_dec.access_value ()
           << endl;
      return;
}
```

——————— Program Output ———————

```
c_inc = 1
c_inc = 2
c_inc = 3
c_inc = 4
c_inc = 5
c_inc = 6
c_inc = 7
c_inc = 8
c_inc = 9
c_inc = 10
c_dec = -1
c_dec = -2
c_dec = -3
c_dec = -4
c_dec = -5
The final value of c_inc = 10
The final value of c_dec = -5
```

The first two lines of code inside the main function,

```
counter c_inc;
counter c_dec;
```

declare two new data objects of type counter. These declarations look just like those that we have used previously for the C++ built-in data types, and they have a similar effect. The legal operations on the objects `c_inc` and `c_dec` are defined by the four member functions declared in the public section of the `counter` class. These are the only operations allowed on these counters. The first three of these functions actually *modify* the counter value; the last function, `access_value`, simply *retrieves* the counter value for use in the calling function. This classification of the operations of an abstract data type into those that modify data and those that retrieve a data value is quite typical of all abstract data types. Most of the member functions that you write for a class will fall into one of these two categories.

Examples of the use of the four member functions are illustrated farther down in the main function (Fig. 11.3). The prefixes `c_inc` and `c_dec` specify the objects to which the functions are applied. These prefixes are required in C++; member functions always operate on objects and allow us to use these objects to solve problems. The object to be operated on must be specified in each case, using the dot notation. The sample output from an execution of the program is shown at the bottom of Fig. 11.3.

Some Terminology and Summary of Rules for Use of Classes

In our first example, we used the C++ `class` construct to introduce a new, user-defined data type. Once that type was defined, we created *instances* of that type, using object declarations such as

```
counter c_inc;
```

Here, `counter` is the user-defined type and `c_inc` is the instance that is created. As we pointed out earlier, this declaration is conceptually the same as declarations involving standard data types, such as

```
int value;
```

All of these declarations associate a name with a region of computer memory. We will continue to refer to names associated with the fundamental types and enumeration, array, and `struct` types as variables. Names associated with types defined using the class construct will be referred to as *objects*. Thus `c_inc` and `c_dec` are both objects (of type `counter`) in the test program for the `counter` class; `value`, a variable (of type `int`), is an attribute of the `class`. The member functions of the `class` are `initialize`, `increment`, `decrement`, and `access_value`; these are the functions that any user program component may apply as operations on the objects `c_inc` and `c_dec`. In this example, the member functions for the `counter` class are all publicly accessible. This sometimes is not the case, as classes may have member functions that are private and therefore not directly accessible outside the class.

Similarly, not all class attributes must appear in the private section of a class. However, we will want to have a very good reason for cases in which an attribute is made public and hence not protected from outside reference. It is also not necessary to maintain separate function prototype declarations and definitions. In fact, for functions that have simple implementations, such as those in the `counter` class, this can be more inconvenient than useful. We do it here because it is important at this stage in the learning process to develop and maintain a clear view of what should be kept private and what should be kept public in a class.

A program that uses a class is called a *client* of the class, and the class itself is referred to as the *server*. The client program may declare and manipulate objects of the data type defined by the class. It may do so without knowing the details of the internal representation of the data or the implementation of its operators and without affecting the server program code. Thus, the details of the server are hidden from the client. Among other things, as we proceed through the rest of the text, we will illustrate the benefits of this information hiding capability and its impact in all phases of the software development process.

A summary of the syntax rules for defining a class and its operations is shown in the following two displays.

C++
SYNTAX

Class Construct

This is a restricted form and does not show the full generality of the construct.

Form: `class` *class_name*
        `{`
           `public:`
                list of class attributes (variables, types, constants, and so on) that may be accessed by name from outside the class
                list of prototypes for each member function that may be accessed by name from outside the class

                ...

           `private:`
                list of class attributes (variables, types, constants, and so on) that are intended to be hidden for reference from outside the class
                list of prototypes for each member function intended to be hidden from outside of the class

                ...

```
};
```

... function implementations

Example: class checking_account
```
{
    public:
        // Member functions ...
        // DEPOSIT INTO CHECKING ACCOUNT
        void make_deposit
          (int);            // IN: number of account to
                            //     receive deposit

        // SET SERVICE CHARGE FOR ACCOUNT
        void set_service_charge
          (int,             // IN: number of account to
                            //     be charged
           float);          // IN: amount of service
                            //     charge

    private:
        // Data members ...
        char init_first, init_middle, init_last;
        // initials
        int this_account_number;    // account
                                    //     number
        float balance;              // balance in
                                    //     account
        float service_charge_amount; // amount of
                                    //     service
                                    //     charge
};
```

... function implementations.

Interpretation: The functions, variables, types, and constants that are declared in the class definition are accessible to all class member functions (see next display). However, only those declared as `public` may be accessed by name from outside the class. ∎

C++
SYNTAX

Class Member Function Definition

Form: *type class_name* **: :** *fname*
              (list of formal argument types and names)
              {
                  ...

```
                    function body
                    ...
                }
Example:  // DEPOSIT INTO CHECKING ACCOUNT
          void checking_account::make_deposit
            (int account_number) // IN: number of account
                                 //      to receive deposit
          {
              // Local data ...
              float amount;

              // Make deposit.
              if (account_number == this_account_number)
              {
                 ...
              }
              else
                 cout << "Wrong account number specified."
                      << endl;
              return;
          }
```

Interpretation: The function make_deposit is a member of the class **checking_account**. It is like any other C++ function except that it has access to all class data and function members. To ensure that C++ knows that the functions are associated with a class, the function names must be preceded by the name of the class followed by a pair of colons.

Reminder: Note carefully that all data members (variables, constants, and so on) of a class are directly accessible to the class member functions and do not need to be passed as arguments to these functions.   ■

EXERCISES FOR SECTION 11.1

Self-Check 1. Explain how the *scope resolution operator* :: is used in the counter class shown in Fig. 11.1. Why is this operator needed?
2. Explain why the prefixes c_inc and c_dec are required in references to the functions initialize, increment, decrement, and access_value as shown in Fig. 11.3.

11.2 —— CLASSES VERSUS STRUCTS

Both the **class** and the **struct** define a data type that is a collection of related data elements which may be of different types. Both may also contain function prototype declarations, although we have not illustrated their use with structs, and both provide the capability to specify three levels of access control to the functions and data: public, protected (not discussed in this text), and private. In fact, the only difference between structs and classes is that with structs, the default access is public; with classes, the default is private. We will use structs in this text only when no functions are involved in the structure definition and when all data are to be publicly accessible within the scope of the defining function; otherwise, we will use classes.

11.3 ___ THE ABSTRACT DATA TYPE day

Figure 11.4 shows the class definition for another abstract data type, day, whose values represent the days of the week. An enumeration type and two variables are declared in the private part of this class definition. As we noted earlier (Chapter 7), C++ does not provide a mechanism to read and write enumeration types directly. The class day provides an illustration of how we can define new operations on an enumeration type, in this case, through the member functions read_day and write_day. Function read_day allows the user to read the first two letters of the name of a day. It converts these characters to the correct element of the enumeration type day_enum and stores the result in a_day. write_day displays a character string corresponding to an element of the enumeration type. Remember, an element (such as tuesday) of an enumeration type is just a C++ constant identifier and not a character string (such as "tuesday"). Although we can print character strings, we cannot print C++ identifiers by name, so we must first provide a way to associate a meaningful character string with each such identifier and then display the string.

Figure 11.4   Abstract data type day

```
// FILE: DayADT.h
// SPECIFICATION AND IMPLEMENTATION FOR day

#ifndef DAYADT_H_
#define DAYADT_H_

#include <iostream.h>
#include <ctype.h>

class day
{
```

(Continued)

Figure 11.4 (Continued)

```
public:
   // Member type ...
   enum logical {false, true};

   // Member functions ...
   // INITIALIZES STATE VARIABLE
   void initialize ();

   // BOTH FUNCTIONS RETURN FALSE (0), IF AN ERROR IS DETECTED
   // READS TWO CHARS AND STORES VALUE REPRESENTED
   logical read_day ();

   // DISPLAYS THE VALUE OF A_DAY
   logical write_day ();

private:
   // Data members ...
   enum day_enum {noday = -1, sunday, monday, tuesday,
                  wednesday, thursday, friday, saturday};
   day_enum a_day; // used to store day_enum element indicated
                   //     by letters read
   logical valid;  // indicates if a_day contains a valid value

}; // end class




// INITIALIZES STATE VARIABLE
void day::initialize ()
{
   valid = false;
}  // end initialize




// READS TWO CHARS AND STORES VALUE REPRESENTED
day::logical day::read_day ()

// Pre:  None
// Post: a_day is assigned a value if the two characters read are
//       SU, MO, TU, WE, TH, FR, or SA. In this case a value of
//       true (1) is returned and the status flag valid is set to
//       true (1). Otherwise, a_day is defined to be noday, and
//       the status flag is set to false (0).
{
   // Local data ...
   char daych1;               // input: first letter read in
```

(Continued)

Figure 11.4 (Continued)

```
char daych2;                  // input: second letter read in

// Read in the first two letters of name of day.
cout << "Enter first two letters of the day name: ";
cin >> daych1 >> daych2;
daych1 = toupper (daych1);
daych2 = toupper (daych2);

// Convert to days of the week as represented by day_enum.
valid = true;            // assume legal pair of letters was read
if ((daych1 == 'S') && (daych2 == 'U'))  // multiple
                                         // alternative if
    a_day = sunday;
else if ((daych1 == 'M') && (daych2 == 'O'))
    a_day = monday;
else if ((daych1 == 'T') && (daych2 == 'U'))
    a_day = tuesday;
else if ((daych1 == 'W') && (daych2 == 'E'))
    a_day = wednesday;
else if ((daych1 == 'T') && (daych2 == 'H'))
    a_day = thursday;
else if ((daych1 == 'F') && (daych2 == 'R'))
    a_day = friday;
else if ((daych1 == 'S') && (daych2 == 'A'))
    a_day = saturday;
else
{
    a_day = noday;       // an illegal letter combination was read
    valid = false;
}
return valid;            // return status flag
}  // end read_day


// DISPLAYS THE VALUE OF A_DAY
day::logical day::write_day ()

// Pre:  a_day is defined.
// Post: If a_day is valid (valid is true (1)), displays a
//       string of characters corresponding to the value of a_day.
//       If a_day is not valid (valid is false), returns a value
//       of false (0).
{
    if (valid)
        switch (a_day)
        {
            case sunday:    cout << "Sunday"; break;
            case monday:    cout << "Monday"; break;
```

(Continued)

Figure 11.4 (Continued)

```
         case tuesday:   cout << "Tuesday"; break;
         case wednesday: cout << "Wednesday"; break;
         case thursday:  cout << "Thursday"; break;
         case friday:    cout << "Friday"; break;
         case saturday:  cout << "Saturday"; break;
   }  // end switch
   else
      cerr << "Error in day. Invalid value of day." << endl;
   return valid;
}  // end write_day

#endif  // DAYADT_H_
```

Neither the type day_enum nor the variables a_day and valid are accessible outside of the class, but all may be accessed by the member functions of the class, read_day and write_day. The prototypes for the member functions are declared in the public part of the class definition. Both member functions are therefore accessible from outside the class; they provide the only access to the class attributes. This is illustrated in the class diagram shown in Fig. 11.5. Note that in the definition of functions read_day and write_day, it is necessary to apply the scope resolution operator to type logical so that the compiler knows that this is a reference to the type logical defined in the public section of the class.

The variable valid declared in the private part of the day class plays a unique role in this class. It is used as a *state attribute*. State attributes are used to keep track of the state of an abstract data type from one member function reference to the next. They can be extremely helpful in avoiding the misuse of other data in the abstract data type. For example, in day, valid is defined to be true each time read_day reads a valid pair of characters and records in a_day the corresponding element of the enumerated type; otherwise, valid is false. The value of valid is then checked by write_day, which will not perform a display if valid is false. A caller to write_day can check the value returned at any time to ascertain whether a display was performed as requested.

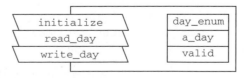

Figure 11.5 Class diagram for day

State attributes are an important part of the data stored in many abstract data types. In C++, however, they may soon be supplanted by the *exception construct.* As of the writing of this text, however, a number of C++ compilers do not support exceptions.

We will provide additional illustrations of the use of state attributes in later chapters of the text.

Using Abstract Type day

The complete abstract data type shown in Fig. 11.4 should be saved as a file on disk. As illustrated in the `counter` example, this file can then be included in any program you write that needs to use `day`. Figure 11.6 shows an example of such a program. The first thing this program must do is ensure that the initialization of the object `today` is correctly carried out. The program then calls `read_day`; if `read_day` executes successfully, it calls `write_day`.

It is quite inconvenient always to remember to initialize explicitly class variables such as `today`, and forgetting to do so will cause errors later in the execution of your program. In the next section, we will see how this explicit initialization step can be avoided through the use of an automatic initialization feature for classes.

Figure 11.6   Testing the abstract data type `day`

```
// FILE: DayTest.cpp
// TEST PROGRAM FOR day CLASS

#include <iostream.h>

#include "DayAdt.h"

void main ()
{
   // Local data ...
   day today;                 // input: day being read
   int good_day;              // a flag, to indicate if a valid day
                              //    was read

   today.initialize ();    // required explicit class attribute
                           //    initialization
   cout << "What day is today? " << endl;
   good_day = today.read_day ();
   if (!good_day)
```

(Continued)

Figure 11.6   (Continued)

```
        cerr << "Error, valid day not entered." << endl;
    else
    {
        cout << "Today is ";
        today.write_day ();
        cout << endl;
    }
    return;
}
```

───────── Program Output ─────────

```
What day is today?
Enter first two letters of the day name> SU
Today is Sunday
```

EXERCISES FOR SECTION 11.3

Self-Check
1. Describe the contents of the definition and implementation sections of an abstract data type.
2. Draw a structure chart for Program DayTest showing the dataflow information among program functions.

Programming
1. Write an abstract data type month containing the declaration for an enumeration type month and functions write_month and month_equivalent. Function month_equivalent has an integer argument that can range in value from 1 to 12 and returns an appropriate enumeration constant as its value.
2. Write a client program that tests your month.
3. Provide an additional member function for day, specifically, a function to access (and return) the value of an object of type day.

11.4 ── AUTOMATIC INITIALIZATION: CLASS CONSTRUCTORS

In both the counter and day abstract data type examples, we provided an initialization member function (named initialize). We showed that any program requiring the use of these abstract data types must contain an explicit call to these initialization methods to ensure that all class data are initialized as required by the other member functions in the class. Perhaps it has already occurred to you that this explicit initialization is easy to forget—that it would be nice if it could be done automatically, without an explicit reference to an initialization method. It turns out that it is indeed possible to provide for automatic class data initialization through the use of the C++ *class constructor*.

The C++ constructor provides guaranteed initialization of the data contained within an object declared to be of a given class. The declaration of the object activates the initialization specified in the constructor. This is illustrated in Fig. 11.7 for the `counter` example shown earlier.

Figure 11.7   **Using a constructor in `counter`; code required within the `counter` class (modified from Fig. 11.1)**

```
...
class counter
{
    public:
        // Member functions ...
        // COUNTER CLASS CONSTRUCTOR
        counter ();

        // INCREMENT COUNTER
        void increment ();

        // DECREMENT COUNTER
        void decrement ();

        // RETURN CURRENT COUNTER VALUE
        int access_value ();

    private:
        // Data members ...
        int value;
}; // NOTE — a class definition must end with a semicolon



// CLASS CONSTRUCTOR
counter::counter ()
{
    value = 0;
}
...
```

As the figure shows, a class constructor has the same name as the class and contains the same initialization code as function `initialize` in the original version of `counter` (see Fig. 11.1). However, a constructor cannot specify a return type or explicitly return a value. The unique feature of a constructor is that it is automatically executed each time an object of type `counter` is created. Thus the declarations

```
counter c_inc;  // variable of type counter
counter c_dec:  // a second variable of type counter
```

used in the `counter` test program (Fig. 11.3) not only cause the allocation of memory for the class variable `value`, they also now cause the `counter` constructor to be executed, resulting in the initialization of `value` to 0. This automatic initialization of class variables is just one of a number of things that can be done with the class constructor. We will revisit this C++ feature later in the text and illustrate other ways in which it may be used to our advantage.

EXERCISES FOR SECTION 11.4

Self-Check   1. Write the constructor for the class `day` and explain what happens when the object `today` is created using the declaration

```
day today;      // input: day being read
```

11.5 —— PROBLEM ANALYSIS AND DESIGN USING CLASSES

The following problem illustrates how to design and implement a program using classes. We show how problem analysis leads to the definition of new data types (in this case, similar data types for different geometric shapes) and how the design and implementation of the program can be constructed in terms of these data types and the operations defined on them. In a very real sense, our three user-defined data types become part of the total collection of types (and associated operators) that can be used to solve our problem. As you will see, most of the main function will be written as a sequence of calls to methods defined in our new classes.

This is typical of what happens if we are careful in the definition of the data types required to solve a problem.

CASE STUDY: AREAS AND PERIMETERS OF DIFFERENT FIGURES REVISITED

Problem Statement

Write a program for determining the area (in square inches) and perimeter (in inches) of a variety of geometric figures. Treat each figure as a different object with its own unique attributes.

Problem Analysis

Our goal is to reduce the complexity of the solution to this problem by first identifying the objects (circle, square, rectangle) we want to manipulate and then designing new data types to model each of these objects. Each of the types will be implemented as a class. The details of the attributes and operations pertaining to each shape will be hidden in its class, and will not be directly accessible to any other program components. Once the classes have been defined, the main function will be written to manipulate objects of the new types, using the member functions defined for each type. Thus the new types will be used to extend the base of abstractions normally available in writing the C++ program required to solve the problem. In addition to the fundamental types, such as int and char, and the structured types array and struct, we will now have additional user-defined types, circle_shape, rectangle_shape, and square_shape, for use in designing our program.

The classes used to define these types will be similar to each other with respect to their class data and function members. The data members include the area and perimeter of each shape and the information required to compute these values—the radius for a circle, the base and height for a rectangle, and the side for a square. Four member functions are required for each shape, one to read and store the given attributes, one each to compute the area and the perimeter of the shape, and a fourth to display the attributes of the shape. For the main function, we simply need a place to store a character to be entered by the user to indicate which kind of figure is to be processed. Once this "figure character" has been read by the main function, it is used to determine which shape is to be processed, and the member functions for this shape are called for all of the computational work that is required. The determination of the shape to be processed and the calls to the appropriate member functions will be embedded in a switch statement written as part of a separate function.

DATA REQUIREMENTS FOR FUNCTION main

Data Types

circle_shape
rectangle_shape
square_shape

Problem Input

fig_shape (char)   — user indication as to shape of figure to
                                             be processed (c or C for a circle, r or R
                                             for a rectangle, or s or S for a square)

the relevant characteristics
of the figure selected

Problem Output

the area of the figure being processed
the perimeter of the figure being processed

We will return to a discussion of issues related to the design of the main function after we have discussed the design and implementation of the classes.

Design of the Circle Class

The area and perimeter computations for the circle require but one data item, the radius of the circle. Thus the radius, area, and perimeter are the only attributes of this class. None of the four member functions (read and store the value of the radius, compute the area, compute the perimeter, and display the attributes of the circle) has any arguments or returns a value.

Attributes for Circle Class

radius (float)	— radius of the circle in inches
area (float)	— area of the circle in square inches
perimeter (float)	— perimeter of the circle in inches

Member Functions for Circle Class

get_known_attributes	— reads and stores the radius
compute_area	— computes the area of the circle: $area = \pi \times radius^2$
compute_perimeter	— computes the perimeter of the circle: $perimeter = 2.0 \times \pi \times radius$
display_attributes	— displays circle attributes

Implementation of the Circle Class

The definition of the new circle data type is shown in Fig. 11.8.

Figure 11.8 The `circle` class

```
// FILE: CirShape.h
// DEFINITION AND IMPLEMENTATION FOR A CIRCLE SHAPE USING INCHES

#ifndef CIRSHAPE_H_
#define CIRSHAPE_H_

// Named constant used ...
const float pi = 3.14159;
```

(Continued)

Figure 11.8 (Continued)

```
class circle_shape
{
    public:
        // Member functions ...
        // GETS KNOWN ATTRIBUTES FROM USER
        void get_known_attributes ();

        // COMPUTES AREA IN SQUARE INCHES
        void compute_area ();

        // COMPUTES PERIMETER IN INCHES
        void compute_perimeter ();

        // DISPLAYS ATTRIBUTES
        void display_attributes ();

    private:
        // Data members ...
        float radius;          // circle radius in inches
        float area;            // circle area in square inches
        float perimeter;       // circle perimeter in inches
}; // end class



// GETS KNOWN ATTRIBUTES FROM USER
void circle_shape::get_known_attributes ()
{
    cout << "Enter radius in inches: ";
    cin >> radius;
}   // end get_known_attributes



// COMPUTES AREA IN SQUARE INCHES
void circle_shape::compute_area ()
{
    area = pi * radius * radius;
}   // end compute_area



// COMPUTES PERIMETER IN INCHES
void circle_shape::compute_perimeter ()
{
    perimeter = 2.0 * pi * radius;
}   // end compute_perimeter
```

(Continued)

Figure 11.8   (Continued)

```
// DISPLAYS ATTRIBUTES
void circle_shape::display_attributes ()
{
   cout << "The circle radius is " << radius << " inches."
        << endl;
   cout << "The circle area is " << area << " square inches."
        << endl;
   cout << "The circle perimeter is " << perimeter << " inches."
        << endl;
}  // end display_attributes

#endif // CIRSHAPE_H_
```

The line

```
const float pi = 3.14159;
```

is used to associate the name `pi` with the constant 3.14159. It would have been preferable to place this statement in the private section of the class definition to ensure that the constant `pi` could not be accessed outside the scope of the class. This is not permitted, however, because initialization of class attributes is possible only inside a class constructor. The current placement of the `const` declaration in `CirShape.h` provides us with the desired access to the identifier `pi` but also makes `pi` accessible within the scope of any file in which `CirShape.h` is included (using `#include`).

Design of the Rectangle Class

The area and perimeter computations for the rectangle require two data items—the base and height of the rectangle. These, and the area and perimeter of the rectangle, constitute the attributes of the class. The four functions needed have the same general purposes and names as those for the circle class.

Attributes for Rectangle Class

base (float)	— base of the rectangle in inches
height (float)	— height of the rectangle in inches
area (float)	— area of the rectangle in square inches
perimeter (float)	— perimeter of the rectangle in inches

Methods for Rectangle Class

get_known_attributes	— reads and stores the base and the height
compute_area	— computes the area of the rectangle: $area = base \times height$

compute_perimeter	— computes the perimeter of the rectangle: $perimeter = 2 \times (base + height)$
display_attributes	— displays rectangle attributes

Implementation of the Rectangle Class

The definition of the new rectangle data type is shown in Fig. 11.9.

Figure 11.9   The `rectangle` class

```
// FILE: RecShape.h
// DEFINITION AND IMPLEMENTATION FOR A RECTANGLE SHAPE
// USING INCHES

#ifndef RECSHAPE_H_            // used to avoid multiple definitions
#define RECSHAPE_H_

class rectangle_shape
{
   public:
      // Member functions ...
      // GETS KNOWN ATTRIBUTES FROM USER
      void get_known_attributes ();

      // COMPUTES AREA IN SQUARE INCHES
      void compute_area ();

      // COMPUTES PERIMETER IN INCHES
      void compute_perimeter ();

      // DISPLAYS ATTRIBUTES
      void display_attributes ();

   private:
      // Data members ...
      float base;              // rectangle base in inches
      float height;            // rectangle height in inches
      float area;              // rectangle area in square inches
      float perimeter;         // rectangle perimeter in inches
};


// GETS KNOWN ATTRIBUTES FROM USER
void rectangle_shape::get_known_attributes ()
{
   cout << "Enter base in inches: ";
   cin >> base;
   cout << "Enter height in inches: ";
   cin >> height;
```

(Continued)

Figure 11.9 (Continued)

```
}  // end get_known_attributes


// COMPUTES AREA IN SQUARE INCHES
void rectangle_shape::compute_area ()
{
   area = base * height;
}  // end compute_area


// COMPUTES PERIMETER IN INCHES
void rectangle_shape::compute_perimeter ()
{
   perimeter = 2.0 * (base + height);
}  // end compute_perimeter


// DISPLAYS ATTRIBUTES
void rectangle_shape::display_attributes ()
{
   cout << "The rectangle base is " << base << " inches." << endl;
   cout << "The rectangle height is " << height << " inches."
        << endl;
   cout << "The rectangle area is " << area << " square inches."
        << endl;
   cout << "The rectangle perimeter is " << perimeter
        << " inches." << endl;
}  // end display_attributes

#endif  // RECSHAPE_H_
```

Design of the Square Class

The design of the square class follows along the same lines as the design of the
rectangle class and is left as an exercise (see Self-Check Exercise 1 at the end of
this section). The implementation is left as an exercise (Programming Exercise 1
at the end of this section), with the C++ code to be saved in file `SqrShape.h`.

Design of Main Function and the Lower-Level Function process_figure

Now that the required data types have been defined, we can complete the
design and implementation of the problem solution. In the past we would
have constructed an algorithm as follows:

1. Determine the type of figure.

2. Read in the figure characteristics.
3. Compute the area of the figure.
4. Compute the perimeter of the figure.
5. Display the attributes of the figure.

However, because of the separation of information and processing for each shape in separate classes, we have chosen a different decomposition, as shown next.

ALGORITHM FOR MAIN FUNCTION

1. Read in the type of the figure to be processed.
2. Process the figure (`process_figure`).

ALGORITHM FOR process_figure

1. Determine the shape of figure to be processed and then based on this result:
     1.1. Read in the known figure characteristic(s) (`get_known_attributes`).
     1.2. Compute the area of the figure (`compute_area`).
     1.3. Compute the perimeter of the figure (`compute_perimeter`).
     1.4. Display all figure characteristics (`display_attributes`).
     1.5. Display error message.

   A structure chart for this decomposition is shown in Fig. 11.10. The level-two functions are all members of the classes indicated in parentheses under the function names. Assuming these classes have been written and tested separately, all that remains is to write and test the main function and `process_figure`.

Implementation of Main Function and process_figure

The main function and `process_figure` are shown in Fig. 11.11.

Commentary

The two functions shown in Fig. 11.11 and the classes shown in Figs. 11.8 and 11.9 are quite simple and short. In fact, function `process_figure` and the classes are even a bit boring and repetitious. They are all similar, each having four identically named functions performing a similar set of tasks. Even the attributes have a certain degree of commonality, because they are the attributes required to compute the area and perimeter of each figure. The shape classes help us solve this particular problem, but they would probably not be useful for solving any other problem involving shapes.

   A quick examination of `process_figure` makes our code look even more suspect; each of the alternatives of the `switch` are the same except for the prefix of the function calls. It is tempting, and in fact quite reasonable, to ask if

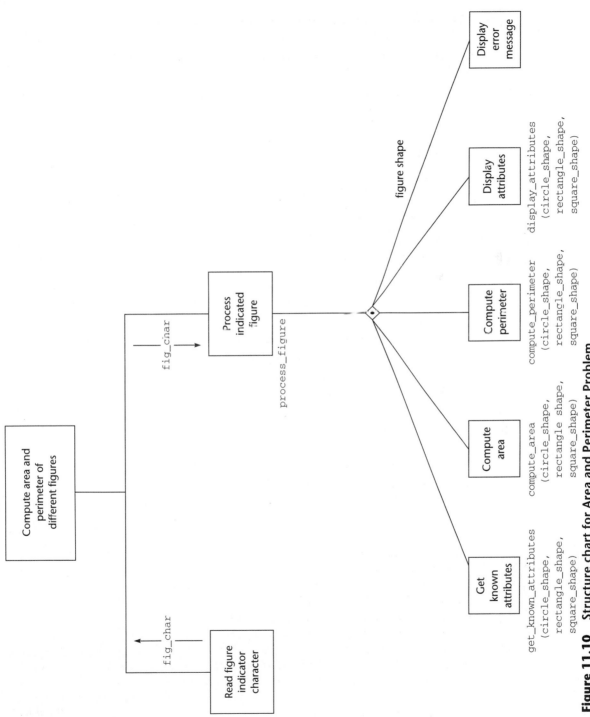

Figure 11.10 Structure chart for Area and Perimeter Problem

Figure 11.11   The Area and Perimeter Program with classes

```
// FILE: FiguresC.cpp
// FINDS PERIMETERS AND AREAS OF VARIOUS KINDS OF FIGURES
//      USES CLASSES

#include <iostream.h>

#include "CirShape.h"
#include "RecShape.h"
#include "SqrShape.h"

void main ()
{
   // Functions used ...
   // PROCESS ONE FIGURE
   void process_figure
     (char);               // IN: indicates figure to be processed

   // Local data ...
   char fig_shape;         // input: indicates type of figure to be
                           //        processed

   // Determine kind of object to be processed and process it.
   cout << "Enter the kind of object to be processed." << endl;
   cout << "C (Circle), R (Rectangle), or S (Square):";
   cin >> fig_shape;
   process_figure (fig_shape);
   cout << "End of program execution." << endl;
   return;
}



// PROCESS ONE FIGURE
void process_figure
  (char fig_shape)          // IN: indicates figure to be processed

// Calls methods for fig_shape to carry out processing.
// Pre:  fig_shape must be defined
// Post: all processing for fig_shape is complete
{
   // Local data ...
   // Objects of new data types
   circle_shape circle;
   rectangle_shape rectangle;
   square_shape square;

   // Process indicated figure.
   switch (fig_shape)
   {
```

(Continued)

Figure 11.11   (Continued)

```
      case 'c' : case 'C':
         circle.get_known_attributes ();
         circle.compute_area ();
         circle.compute_perimeter ();
         circle.display_attributes ();
         break;
      case 'r' : case 'R':
         rectangle.get_known_attributes ();
         rectangle.compute_area ();
         rectangle.compute_perimeter ();
         rectangle.display_attributes ();
         break;
      case 's' : case 'S':
         square.get_known_attributes ();
         square.compute_area ();
         square.compute_perimeter ();
         square.display_attributes ();
         break;
      default:
         cerr << "Incorrect character entered. Re-run program."
              << endl;
   } // end switch
   return;
} // end process_figure
```

there are ways to reduce, if not eliminate, the repetition in this function and take advantage of the similarities among the three classes and define a more general abstract data type for shapes that could be used to solve this problem and reused elsewhere. Happily, the answer to both questions is yes; C++ provides mechanisms (inheritance and virtual functions) for resolving both coding inefficiencies.

To take advantage of the inheritance and virtual function mechanisms of C++, we must first be able to *generalize* what we know about more obvious data abstractions (such as `circle_shape`, `rectangle_shape`, and `square_shape`) and to form higher-level abstractions (such as a geometric shape) exhibiting the common attributes and methods of the lower-level ones. The advantage of this abstraction process lies in first defining a class to model (represent) the higher-level abstraction (such as any geometric shape) and then *deriving* the lower-level classes from this *parent class*. In the derivation, the common elements of the parent class (such as the attributes `area` and `perimeter` and the four functions common to all three shapes) are *inherited* by the lower-level, or *derived, classes*. These lower-level abstractions are then *specialized* by adding new attributes or methods or even by replacing or deleting parent attributes. In this way, new classes are formed with much less effort than if they had been programmed totally separately, without any identification of their commonalities. These classes, such as for a circle, rectangle, or square shape, are *special cases* of the parent. The C++ mechanisms for using inheritance and virtual functions are shown in Appendix E, where the Area and Perimeter example is redone in order to illustrate the advantages of and relationship between these two concepts.

Despite the flaws just cited in our solution to the Area and Perimeter Problem, several important benefits are illustrated by this design, specifically, those related to the separation of concerns, information hiding, and the reduction in the overall complexity of the solution. An important goal of the object-oriented paradigm involves a careful analysis and separation of concerns related to the different entities of a problem domain. We have achieved this separation in our analysis, design, and implementation, encapsulating and hiding the details of each such entity—circle, rectangle, and square—in a separate class.

The use of classes in this solution to the Area and Perimeter Problem also enabled us to build program models of the figures specified in the problem statement and then solve the problem in terms of these models. The ability to model problem domain entities by defining new, abstract data types representing the salient features of these entities is a powerful programming tool, one that we will take advantage of in the remaining chapters of the text. At the same time that we build these different types, we will work to understand the commonalities among these types so as to take advantage of the idea of inheritance to avoid the kind of repetitious code just illustrated.

EXERCISES FOR SECTION 11.5

Self-Check
1. Following the same pattern as shown for the rectangle class, provide the design information for the square class.
2. For each of the four functions in the `circle_shape`, `rectangle_shape`, and `square_shape` classes, list at least one common attribute and one distinguishing attribute.

Programming
1. Implement the square class, with the code assumed to be saved in file `SqrShape.h`.

11.6 —— A COMPLEX NUMBER CLASS (OPTIONAL)

We have now examined two examples and a case study of the use of the C++ class for defining new data types in C++. A language that provides an extension capability such as the class is called an *extensible language*. The C++ extensibility we have just illustrated allows us to define new abstract data types, such as `day` and `counter`, which behave in the same way as fundamental types, such as `char`, `int`, `float`, and `double`. Another example of a user-defined type, one that may be more familiar to those of you with a mathematical orientation, is the arithmetic type *complex*. Although the description of the class that defines this type is beyond the scope of the text, the description of how to use the class is well within our grasp. As long as your instructor has made the complex class available on your computer system, you may use any of the material illustrated next simply by placing the statement

```
#include "Complex.h"
```

at the beginning of your program file.

In the following examples and discussions, we provide detailed illustrations of how complex numbers can be created and manipulated in C++. Several more advanced features of the use of classes are illustrated, including the overloading (redefinition) of existing arithmetic operators, such as +, −, and *, so that they can be used with complex data in much the same way as with integer and floating-point data.

Example 11.1   The *complex number*

$$3.2 - 7.8i$$

has a *real part* of 3.2 and an *imaginary part* of −7.8; the symbol i is defined by the mathematical rule $i^2 = -1$. The declarations

```
complex x, y, z;
```

can be used to declare three objects of type `complex`, each consisting of two floating-point values—the real part and the imaginary part.

New, initialized complex objects may be created using the `complex` class constructor, as in

```
complex w (3.2, -7.8);
```

which creates the C++ representation of the complex number shown earlier. In general, a complex constant is represented in C++ by two floating-point constants as arguments to the constructor `complex`. If double-precision values are used in this fashion, they will be converted to their corresponding single-precision values. The assignment statement

```
w = complex (3.2, -7.8);
```

creates the C++ representation of the complex number $3.2 - 7.8i$ and stores the result in w. We will have more to say about the `complex` constructor and the assignment statement in later sections.   ∎

For any type `complex` object, we can obtain the value of the real part from the class using the complex class member function `re`. The member function `im` can be used to obtain the imaginary part of the complex number. For the previous example, `3.2` would be returned by the function call `w.re ()`; `-7.8` is returned by the call `w.im ()`.

Complex variables and arrays are declared just like other variables and arrays, as shown in the next example.

Example 11.2   The declaration

```
complex seq[10], z;
```

instructs the compiler to allocate storage for an array (`seq`) with 10 objects of type `complex` and for a single complex object (`z`). Each array element provides storage for two values representing the real and imaginary parts of a complex number. In our implementation of the class `complex`, the real and imaginary parts of a complex number are single precision.   ∎

In addition to the member functions `re` and `im` just described, we have defined a number of other operations on complex numbers. In the next few sections, we will examine these operations. We will see some, such as `conj` (complex conjugate function) and `cabs` (the absolute value function), that are defined and used as functions in much the same way as we have done since Chapter 3. We will see others, such as the arithmetic, assignment, and equality operators, that are used in much the same way as for `int` and `float` type variables.

This may seem surprising to you at first, but it illustrates yet another extremely convenient feature of the C++ class definition—the ability to redefine, or *overload*, existing operators so that they can be used in client programs in a natural way to operate on user-defined data. We present some examples of this overloading feature next.

Complex Arithmetic and Assignment

The rules governing complex arithmetic are consistent with those of mathematics, as described in Table 11.1. Since it is most natural for us to be able to write these operations as we have for `int` and `float` data, the class definition

Table 11.1   Rules of Complex Arithmetic (Assume $x = a + bi$ and $y = c + di$ Are Complex Numbers)

OPERATOR	EXAMPLE	RESULT
addition $(x + y)$	$(a, bi) + (c, di)$	$(a + c) + (b + d)i$
subtraction $(x - y)$	$(a, bi) - (c, di)$	$(a - c) + (b - d)i$
multiplication $(x \times y)$	$(a, bi) (c, di)$	$(ac - bd) + (ad - bc)i$
division (x / y)	$(a, bi) / (c, di)$	$[(ac - bd) / d)] + [(bc - ad)/d]i$

in `Complex.h` provides a definition of the *operator functions* (operators, for short) +, −, *, and / involving the use of complex data objects. The compiler will decide which operator to use (for example, from among integer, floating point, and complex addition) based on the operands involved. If either or both operands are complex, then a complex operator will be used by the compiler. An integer or floating-point operand used with a complex operand will be converted automatically to a complex number with an imaginary part of zero before the operation is performed.

To understand what is at work here, it may help to recall that we already have been using overloaded operators for +, −, *, and /. We have used these operators with both floating-point and integer operands and left it to the compiler to decide whether floating-point or integer arithmetic was indicated. The situation with complex numbers is no different—when these four operators are used with one (or two) complex operands, complex arithmetic is performed and a complex result is produced.

Similarly, our new `complex` data type also defines the assignment operator overloaded for complex data. The assignment of a complex value to a complex variable is allowed, as shown next for `z`, `z1`, and `z3`, all of type `complex`:

```
z = (z1 + z3) / z3;
```

Mixed-mode assignments are also allowed, and the following rules apply. When a complex number is stored in an `int` or `float` variable, its imaginary part is lost. When an `int` or `float` number is stored in a complex object, the imaginary part of the complex number will be 0.0 and the real part of the complex number will be the number assigned (converted to `float`, if necessary). Thus the assignment

```
z = 3;
```

results in the assignment of the complex number $3.0 + 0.0i$ to `z` (assuming `z` is of type `complex`). Once again, the decision as to which assignment operation is indicated (integer, floating-point, or complex) is made by the compiler using the knowledge of the types of the data appearing on the left-hand and the right-hand sides of the assignment operator =.

Relational and Equality Operators

The relational operators are not quite so simple because mathematically, no *ordering relation* is defined for complex numbers. Thus, although we can define and apply the C++ equality operators == and != to complex data, the relational operators cannot be applied to complex quantities. Rather, we must apply these operators separately to the real and imaginary parts of a complex object, as shown next.

Example 11.3 If z is complex, then the following is not a valid expression:

```
z <= complex (2.3, 1.0)
```

Instead, we must compare the real and imaginary parts separately:

```
(z.re () <= 2.3) && (z.im () <= 1.0)
```

On the other hand, the logical expressions

```
z == complex (2.3, 1.0)
```

and

```
z != complex (2.3, 1.0)
```

are perfectly legal in C++ (and meaningful mathematically).   ■

The Complex Constructors

There are actually three different versions of the complex constructor: One takes no arguments and simply creates a complex number for which both the real and imaginary parts are zero:

```
complex z;
```

Another takes a single floating-point value and creates a complex number with this floating-point value used as the real part and zero as the imaginary part. The statement

```
complex z (a);
```

creates the complex number $a + 0i$ and stores it in the complex object z. The third constructor takes two floating-point arguments, a and b, and creates the complex number $a + bi$. The assignment

```
complex z (a, b);
```

stores the complex number $a + bi$ in the complex object z.

Conjugate and Absolute Value Functions

In addition to the operators already defined and the two functions re and im, the file Complex.h contains two other functions: conj, a function for computing the conjugate of a complex number, and cabs, a function for computing the modulus or absolute value of a complex number. These functions are described next.

The *conjugate* of a complex number

$$z = a + bi$$

is the complex number

$zbar = a - bi.$

The complex conjugate is an important mathematical concept because it is used to compute the absolute value of a complex number. Many applications require computing the absolute value of a complex number z, which is defined to be the distance of z from the origin:

$$\sqrt{a^2 + b^2} = \sqrt{(a + bi)(a - bi)} = \sqrt{z \times zbar}$$

The function `z.conj ()` returns the complex conjugate of z; `z.cabs ()` returns a floating-point result—the absolute value of z.

Input and Output of Complex Numbers

Our class also provides definitions for the overloaded input (`>>`) and output (`<<`) operators for complex numbers. When a complex value is displayed using the output operator, the real and imaginary parts are displayed as two floating-point variables enclosed in parentheses and separated by a comma, as in

`(2.31, 4.5)`

For input, the numbers may be enclosed in parentheses and separated by a comma

`(2.31, 4.5)`

or they may be merely separated by white space

`2.31 4.5`

In any case, two floating-point values are expected in the input stream.

The Complex Class: A Summary

The operators and member functions and the storage attributes for our user-defined `complex` data type are summarized in Fig. 11.12. The operators and member functions are listed separately to serve as a reminder of the differences in how they are used in a client program.

Nothing prevents us from writing functions `cadd`, `csub`, `cmult`, `cdiv`, `cassign`, `ceq`, and `cneq` for use in performing the basic complex arithmetic, assignment, and equality operations. Thus, for example, a call to the complex function

`cadd (x, y)`

could be used in a client program to perform the addition of the complex objects `x` and `y`; a call to the integer function

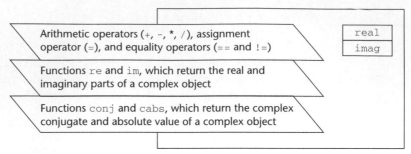

Figure 11.12   A complex number class

```
cneq (x, y)
```

could be used to compare x and y for inequality. However, we believe that the definition of these computations in their operator form provides a far more convenient and concise reference in a client program. Note that a double-precision complex class could easily be defined by changing the definition of the attributes real and imag (the two components of an imaginary number) to be of type double and by changing the return values for any type float operators or functions to be type double.

EXERCISES FOR SECTION 11.6

Self-Check   1. (On complex numbers)

    a. Compute the value $x \times y$ for $x = 3 + 4i$ and $y = 2 - 7i$.
    b. What is the conjugate of the complex number $x = 3 + 4i$?
    c. What is the absolute value of $x = 3 + 4i$?

2. For the complex number class, we defined two functions, re and im, which can be used to obtain the real and imaginary parts, respectively, of a complex object. However, we have not introduced any functions for modifying either the real or the imaginary parts of a complex number (without affecting the other part). We chose not to introduce such functions because these modifications can already be achieved using the complex constructor together with the re and im functions. For example, to change only the real part of a complex variable z, we can use an assignment statement of the form

```
z = complex (a1, z.im ());
```

where a1 is the new value to be assigned to the real part of z. Similarly, to change only the imaginary part of z we can write the statement

```
z = complex (z.re (), b2);
```

where b2 is the new value to be assigned to the imaginary part of z.

    Let z be the complex number $3 + 9i$. Write the two statements required first to change the value of z to $3 - 16i$ and then to change this value to $47 - 16i$. (Provide the actual arguments a1, a2, b1, and b2 for the forms just shown.)

3. Using functions rather than operators, as illustrated in the summary section on the complex class, write a C++ expression to compute z = w + xy where z, w, x, and y are all type `complex` objects. Which is easier to read and write—the version that uses the operator forms or the one using function form?

4. Using functions rather than operators, as illustrated in the summary section on the complex class, write an `if` statement that sets the complex object x to (0,0) if x and y are equal but sets y to (0,0) otherwise. Which is easier to read and write—the version that uses the operator forms or the one using function forms?

5. A rational number is defined as any number that can be represented as the ratio of two integer numbers. Thus the numbers 1/3, 22/7, 15/16, and −5/1 are all considered rational numbers. (In comparison, the number square root of 2 is irrational. It cannot be represented as the ratio of two integer values.) Suppose you are given a class called `rational_number`, similar to the `complex` class, in which a rational number is represented by an *ordered pair* of integers—for example 2/5 = (2, 5).

   a. Write the declaration for a `rational_number` object x.
   b. Write the declaration for a `rational_number` object y = 2/5.
   c. Write the ordered pair representing the sum of rational numbers $x = a/b$ and $y = c/d$; write the ordered pair representing the product of rational numbers $x = a/b$ and $y = c/d$.

   For parts d and e, you may assume the rational numbers $x = a/b$ and $y = c/d$ are simplified (reduced to lowest terms). (The rational number 3/6 reduced to lowest terms is 1/2; 12/16 reduced to lowest terms is 3/4.)

   d. Write the C++ non-member, logical function `rat_eq` to compare two rational numbers x and y for equality and return 0 (false, not equal) or 1 (true, equal).
   e. Write a C++ non-member, logical function `rat_eq` to determine if the rational number x is less than the rational number y and return 0 (false, x is not less than y) or 1 (true, x is less than y). (Unlike the complex numbers, an ordering relation is defined on the rational numbers.)
   f. Write a C++ `rational_number` function to simplify (reduce to lowest terms) a `rational_number` x.

11.7 ___ DEFINING AND USING FUNCTIONS AND CLASSES: SUMMARY OF RULES AND RESTRICTIONS

As you may have realized by now, C++ provides a wealth of program components (functions and classes) that all programmers can use in designing and building their own programs. C++ also provides mechanisms for programmers to build their own program component libraries. Your instructor or lab manager can tell you more about how to build and refer to such user-defined libraries on your operating system and for your version of the C++ language system. Our purpose here is to describe the reuse mechanism as it relates to your C++ programs. We will not go into those issues related to the particular computer system or C++ version you are using.

We can reuse the components in C++ or user-provided libraries by including the library header files in our programs:

```
#include <string.h>
#include "Complex.h"
```

Once this has been done, however, we must be careful to follow the rules and restrictions for using functions (and argument consistency) and for defining and using classes. Failure to use the correct syntax or to follow the other rules that apply can cause significant headaches, especially when you are starting out. The following is an annotated list of the rules and restrictions described in this chapter for using library functions and for defining and using classes. In the annotations for each item in the list, we have attempted to provide some reminders concerning many of the points made earlier in the chapter.

■ *Using Library Components—Functions:* When using a component from a library, you must know the name of the library in which the component is found and you must have a description of the component interface. Functions and classes that are stored in separate files must be either included in your program or separately compiled and linked with your program at execution time. The commands used in either case may vary according to the computer system you are using. Your instructor can give you the commands for your system.

For any functions you wish to use, you must know what the function does (but not necessarily how); what value (if any) it returns; and the number, order, and type of the function's arguments. When you write a call to a function, take care to ensure that there is a one-to-one correspondence and agreement in type between the actual arguments and the formal arguments. Also, be sure that all preconditions for a function's arguments (as listed at the beginning of the function) are satisfied before the function call executes. Calls to member functions of an abstract data type must be prefixed by the name of the object being manipulated by the function, followed by a period, for example,

```
today.read_day ();   or   z.im ();
```

You should be consistent in writing the definitions of any classes you may need. Normally, only the prototypes of the member functions required by the user in manipulating the data of an abstract data type should appear in the public section of the definition. Rarely, if at all, will you need to make public a class attribute (variable, constant, or type) declaration—these belong in the private section of your class. Additional functions, not required by the user but perhaps called by the class methods, may also appear in the private section of a class. Be sure to add the semicolon required after the right brace at the end of a class definition and after each function prototype included in the class definition.

■ *Defining a Class* (see the C++ Syntax Display entitled Class Construct, Section 11.1): The definition of a class should always follow the same form. The class should have a header such as

```
class checking_account
```

and it should have a public section (normally containing the prototypes of those functions that any client program may need to use). Most classes will also have a private section (normally containing the class attributes—variables, types, and constants). Some function prototypes may also appear in the private section, but these will be accessible only within the class and not to any client. Remember that all prototypes must end with a semicolon.

■ *Defining Member Functions of a Class* (see the C++ Syntax Display entitled Class Member Function Definition, Section 11.1): The definitions of the member functions of a class are usually placed in a separate file having the same name as the class header file but with the extension `.cpp` rather than `.h`. This file is compiled separately from the client program and linked with the program after compilation. Whether or not a member function implementation appears in a separate file, the implementation header must include the class name and scope resolution operator preceding the function name, as in

```
day::logical day::read_day ();   or   counter::increment ();
```

This identifies the function as a member of the class and allows it to reference the class and other function members. Functions not preceded in this fashion by a class name will not be considered members of a class by the compiler and will not be allowed to reference class attributes. Types, too, must also be preceded by the scope resolution prefix (as in `day::logical`). Remember that function prototypes appearing in a class definition must be terminated with a semicolon, but a function header is part of the function definition and does not end with a semicolon.

■ *Using Classes* (see the discussion on referencing class operations in Section 11.1): When using classes you must always remember to do the following:

a) include the `.h` file for the class in the program that uses it;
b) be sure to declare all objects of the class that will be used in the program (these declarations should be local to the program components that have a need to know about the object and hidden from those that do not have this need);
c) (for nonoperator, member functions of a class) be sure to prefix the name of the function with the name of the object to which it is to be applied, as in `c_inc.counter ();`

d) (for operator, member functions of a class) be sure that at least one of the operands of each *operand–operator–operand triple* (such as a + b or x / y) is of the proper type.

Remember that member function names and operators appearing in classes may be overloaded—that is, applied to a variety of types of data. The compiler needs help in determining which operator or function you mean to use. For operators, the compiler uses its knowledge about the operator type to make this decision. Thus if both a and b are of type complex, the compiler will apply the complex addition operator as defined in the class complex whenever the expression a + b appears. If either a or b is type complex and the other is an integer, the compiler will convert the integer operand to type complex and generate instructions to perform complex addition. On the other hand, if both a and b are integers, the compiler will not use complex addition for a + b but instead will generate an integer addition operation.

11.8 ___ COMMON PROGRAMMING ERRORS

In Section 11.7, we provided a number of reminders concerning the rules and restrictions to be followed in using functions and classes. In this section, we describe a number of the different error messages you may see when errors occur in your C++ programs. All of the examples used for illustration involve the counter class described in Section 11.1.

▪ *Function Argument and Return Value Errors* (also see the Common Programming Error sections of Chapters 3 and 6): Return value or argument mismatches involving class member functions may cause the compiler not to recognize the function as a member of the class. For example, if the prototype for the function access_value (defined in the counter class) specifies a return value of int but the function definition specifies a return value of float, the message

```
"'counter::access_value ()' is not a member function of 'counter'"
```

will be produced when the compiler attempts to compile the function definition. Even though the name of the function is the same, the return value inconsistency causes the compiler to treat the defined function as different from the prototype. Having the same name is not sufficient—return values and arguments are also used to distinguish among functions.

▪ *Failure to Define a Function as a Member of a Class:* This error can be caused in several ways:

1. failure to prefix the function definition by the name of its class and the scope operator (two colons);

2. failure to spell the function name correctly; or

3. complete omission of the function definition from the class.

In any case, the result is the same—a compiler error message indicating that the referenced function

```
"is not a member"
```

of the indicated class. Thus, if `c_inc` is an object of type `counter` (see Section 11.1) and the C++ statement

```
c_inc.print ();
```

appears in a client program, the message

```
"'print' is not a member of 'counter'"
```

will be displayed.

■ *Prefixing a Class Member Function Call:* Any reference (using the dot notation) to a class member function must be prefixed by the name of an object to be manipulated. For example, for function `increment` defined in class `counter`, the function call

```
c_obj.increment ();
```

is legal only if `c_obj` is declared as an object of type `counter`. If `c_obj` has a different type, the message

```
"Structure required on left side of ."
```

appears; if the identifier is not defined at all, an

```
"undefined symbol"
```

error will occur.

■ *Referencing a Private Attribute of a Class:* Identifiers declared as private attributes or functions in a class cannot be referenced from outside the class. Any such reference attempt will produce an

```
"undefined symbol"
```

error. Even if the correct prefix for such a reference is used—for example, `c_dec.counter::value`—an error message will appear:

```
"'counter::value' is not accessible".
```

This message simply says that the identifier `value` declared in the class `counter` cannot be accessed from outside the class.

■ *Failure to Include a Required Header File:* Numerous messages will be generated by this programming error. Because the header file most likely contains the definitions for a number of the identifiers used in your program, perhaps the most common of these errors will be the

```
"undefined symbol"
```

error.

■ *Missing Semicolon Following a Class Definition:* Failure to place a semicolon at the end of a class definition (after the right brace) will cause a number of errors when the definition is included in and compiled with another file. The semicolon is required to terminate the class definition and separate it from the function implementations (if these are included in the same file as the definition). Error messages that might appear as a result of this syntax error include

```
"Declaration right brace won't stop declaration",
"Declaration occurs outside of class"
```

and,

```
"class_name may not be defined",
```

where `class_name` is the name of the class in which the missing semicolon was detected.

■ *Semicolons in a Function Header and Prototypes:* A missing semicolon at the end of a function prototype may cause a

```
"Statement missing ;"
```

or

```
"Declaration terminated incorrectly"
```

diagnostic (a prototype is a declaration and must be terminated with a semicolon). However, the accidental inclusion of a semicolon separating a function header from its definition will cause numerous compiler errors following the header.

CHAPTER REVIEW

In this chapter we focused attention on the implementation and use of the C++ `class` in programming. A limited form of the syntax for defining a new data abstraction using a class was presented. In addition, we showed how to declare data objects of this new type and reference the operations defined on these objects.

In the Case Study concerning figure shapes, we demonstrated some of the advantages of the use of the class in the software development process. This was a comparatively simple example, and yet it was useful in illustrating the ideas of separation of concerns, information hiding, and the use of classes in defining new building blocks (the new abstract data types for the circle, rectangle, and square shapes) for a software system.

Section 11.6, on the `complex` class, was optional reading. It was included to illustrate the idea of component reuse and to demonstrate that in order to use the operations in a class one need know only what the operations and member functions of a class are, what they do, and how to reference them. You need not know anything about how these operations work or how the attribute information of the class is stored.

The ideas of operator functions and function overloading were also illustrated in Section 11.6. The convenience of the overloaded operator functions permitted a most natural way of specifying commonly used operations, as if the new data type had been a part of the definition of the C++ language rather than a programmed extension.

✔ QUICK-CHECK EXERCISES

1. Why is an object prefix name required before the function name when referencing a member function of a class?
2. How does the C++ compiler know which + operation (`int`, `float`, `double`, etc.) to use when it evaluates an operator–operand–operator triple?
3. A class defines a _____ .
4. A _____ declaration is needed to declare an object of a class type.
5. The declared items in the _____ part of a class may not be directly accessed outside the class. Those in the _____ part are accessible outside the class.
6. Write a type declaration for an array of 12 objects of type `counter`; write an expression to increment the sixth element of your array.
7. True or false? Arrays and structs may not be used in the declarations of class attributes.
8. _____ variables are used to keep track of the state of an abstract data type from one reference to the next.
9. True or false? There is a limit to the number of different shape classes that could be defined in our figure shape example.

Answers to Quick-Check Exercises

1. The prefix is required to specify the object to which the member function is applied.
2. The correct operation is chosen solely on the basis of the type of the operands used in the triple.
3. new abstract data type
4. type
5. private; public

6. ```
counter my_counts[12];

my_counts[5].increment ();
```

7. false—they may be used
8. state
9. false

# REVIEW QUESTIONS

1. Explain why each of the notions of information hiding, separation of concerns, and language extension is important to the software designer.
2. Write a C++ class definition for an abstract data type describing a bookstore inventory consisting of the attributes and methods given. The attributes are as follows:

   - a collection of eight books each having the following characteristics:
     book title (character string of maximum length 32)
     book author (character string of maximum length 20)
     book price (floating-point number having two decimal places)
     count of books on hand (integer)

   The member functions are:

   - a constructor that is used to initialize all eight elements of the array (to any values you want)
   - a function that displays in a readable tabular form the contents of the entire book collection
   - a modify function that, once called, prompts the user first for a book number (1 through 8) and then for a code (T, A, P, or C) indicating which attribute (title, author, price, or count) of the indicated book is to be changed; finally, the function should provide a prompt for the new value of the attribute being altered.

   Reasonable tests for valid input should be performed in the modify function. Write the declaration for an object named `inventory` of the type described by this class.
3. Redo Review Question 2 assuming that

   - your attributes are simply the title, author, price, and count of one book;
   - that your constructor is replaced by an explicit initialization function that initializes the contents of the book objects in your inventory;
   - that your display function displays the information for a single book in your inventory;
   - that your modify function no longer needs the number of the book to be changed (why not?) and begins by prompting for the attribute to be changed.

   (*Hint:* You will need to declare an array of objects, size 8, of your book type.) Write a call to your modify function to change an attribute of one book.
4. Which of the following statements is incorrect?

   a. All class attributes must appear in the private part of a class.
   b. All class member functions must appear in the public part of a class.
```

c. The attributes of a class are allocated memory each time a member function of the class is called; this memory is deallocated when the called function returns control to its caller.

d. Classes may be used in C++ to model problem domain entities.

PROGRAMMING PROJECTS

Problems 2–6 are very similar to problems 1–5 in Chapter 10. These problems, however, require the use of the C++ class feature for complete program implementation.

1. Write a C++ class that defines an abstract data type month consisting of type month_type and member functions for reading and writing the months (jan, feb, mar, apr, may, jun, jul, aug, sep, oct, nov, dec). Write the implementation of all functions as well, and provide a client program to show that all of the functions in your class behave as expected. What you produce from this small problem should parallel the day example in the text. Use a state attribute as shown in the day example.

2. Define a class my_int that has as its single attribute an integer variable and that contains member functions for determining the following information for an object of type my_int:

   a. Is it a multiple of 7, 11, or 13?
   b. Is the sum of the digits odd or even?
   c. What is the square root value?
   d. Is it a prime number?
   e. Is it a perfect number—a number for which the sum of its factors is equal to the number itself (for example, 1 + 2 + 4 + 7 + 14 = 28, so 28 is a perfect number)?
      Write a client program that tests your methods, using the input values 104, 3773, 13, 121, 77, 3075.

3. Each month, a bank customer deposits $50 into a savings account. Assume that the interest rate is fixed (does not change) and is a problem input. The interest is calculated on a quarterly basis. For example, if the account earns 6.5 percent interest annually, it earns one-fourth of 6.5 percent every three months. Write a program to compute the total investment, the total amount in the account, and the interest accrued for each of the 120 months of a 10-year period. Assume that the rate is applied to all funds in the account at the end of a quarter, regardless of when the deposits were made.

   Print all values accurate to two decimal places. The table printed by your program when the annual interest rate is 6.5 percent should begin as follows:

MONTH	INVESTMENT	NEW AMOUNT	INTEREST	TOTAL SAVINGS
1	50.00	50.00	0.00	0.00
2	100.00	100.00	0.00	100.00
3	150.00	150.00	2.44	152.44
4	200.00	202.44	0.00	202.44

5	250.00	252.44	0.00	252.44
6	300.00	302.44	4.91	307.35
7	350.00	357.35	0.00	357.35

Design a class to model the customer bank account, including the attributes for each account and at least five methods needed to initialize, update, and display the information in each account.

4. Redo Programming Project 3, adding columns to allow comparison of interest compounded monthly (one-twelfth of annual rate every month) with interest compounded continuously. The formula for continuously compounded interest is

$$amount = principle \times e^{\,rate \times time}$$

where *rate* is the annual interest rate and *time* is expressed in years.

5. An employee time card is represented as one long string of characters. Write a program that processes a collection of these strings stored in a data file and writes the results to an output file.

a. Compute gross pay using the formula

$$gross = regular\ hours \times rate + overtime\ hours \times 1.5 \times rate$$

b. Compute net pay by subtracting the following deductions:

$federal\ tax = 0.14 \times (gross - 13 \times dependents)$,
$social\ security = 0.052 \times gross$,
$city\ tax = 4\% \times gross$ if employee works in the city,
$union\ dues = 6.75\% \times gross$ for union member.

The data string for each employee has the form

Positions	Data
1–10	Employee last name
11–20	Employee first name
21	Contains C for city office or S for suburban office
22	Contains U (union) or N (nonunion)
23–26	Employee identification number
27	Blank
28–29	Number of regular hours (a whole number)
30	Blank
31–36	Hourly rate (dollars and cents)
37	Blank
38–39	Number of dependents
40	Blank
41–42	Number of overtime hours (a whole number)

Declare the attributes of the class and define and implement five class methods.

6. Write a menu-driven program that contains options for creating a data file to be processed by the payroll program described in Programming Project 5 (the user should be prompted to enter several time "cards" from the keyboard), displaying the time cards in the file on a printer, adding new time cards to the end of an existing file, deleting time cards from an existing file based on their ordinal position within the file (e.g., deleting the seventh time card), and quitting the program.

To add or delete lines from a text file requires copying the original data file to a *scratch,* or temporary, file and then back to the original file. During the copy process, time cards to be deleted are simply not copied to the scratch file. New time cards are added to the end of the file after all the time cards from the original file have been copied to the scratch file. Use classes as you see fit to model the additional abstract data types.

7. Your university runs many hundreds of courses each semester and needs to keep track of a wealth of information on each one. Among other things, for each course, we need to know:

   - the university course identification number;
   - the department course id and section number (for multiple sections of the same course);
   - the number of credits for the course;
   - the days and times the course meets;
   - the room in which the course meets (building id and room number);
   - the maximum course enrollment;
   - the campus on which the course is held;
   - the course instructor;
   - the number of students currently enrolled and the student id of each such student;
   - the course status: open (for additional enrollment), closed, or canceled.

   We must be able to change the value of each of these 10 data items and, upon request, print all of this information. Initially, the values of the first 7 items are known—the last 3 are not. Design and implement an abstract data type that can be used to model this university course entity. List the attributes that you expect to model and how, and list any assumptions that you have made about these attributes. Choose whatever 12 methods defined on objects of this type that you wish to implement as part of the class, and illustrate calls to several of these methods.

8. Write a C++ class definition for an abstract data type **money** that allows you to do basic arithmetic operations (addition, subtraction, multiplication, and division) on floating-point numbers having exactly two digits to the right of the decimal point. You need not write the implementations for the operations, but be sure to include the prototypes for all member functions that would be needed in this class, including any that might be private to the class.

12 Software Engineering: Building Abstract Data Types

12.1 The Indexed Collection as an Abstract Data Type

12.2 Class Extensions: An Introduction to Inheritance
    CASE STUDY: Home Budget Problem

12.3 Extending Reuse: An Introduction to Templates

12.4 Using Old Components to Solve New Problems
    CASE STUDY: Cryptogram Generator Problem

12.5 Common Programming Errors
    Chapter Review

In Chapter 10, we introduced a number of ideas fundamental to building good software—data abstraction, information hiding, encapsulation, component reuse, and objects of user-defined data types. In this chapter, we continue to study these ideas, putting them to work in building programs. In the process, new ways of thinking about software development will be illustrated.

Our focus will be on the use of the C++ `class` in building new data types to model problem space objects and information. Whether we are modeling the exam and homework performance of a collection of students, the properties of geometric shapes, or a simple counter, the most difficult challenge is to decide what information needs to be represented and what operations are required on this information. In this chapter, we provide two case studies illustrating how such decisions are made. Each case study begins with an expanded problem analysis in which the relevant objects and information are identified from the problem statement. We complete each case study with the implementation of a program to solve the given problem. In the implementation, classes are used to build new data types. We will see how these new types, combined with the standard types (`float`, `int`, etc.) and structures (arrays and structs) already provided as part of the C++ language, can be used to define an expanded base of objects that can be manipulated in solving a problem.

This approach to constructing programs is more "bottom up" than "top down" in nature. The top-down approach practiced in earlier chapters will still prove useful in presenting a view of the structural relationship among the components of your programs. This approach also may help in designing algorithms for solving the lower level subproblems of a given problem. However, the solution to more complex problems will require increasing reliance on a more bottom-up approach. This process begins with an analysis of relevant problem space objects. Models of these objects (new abstract data types) are constructed and then implemented as C++ classes containing the necessary data members as well as the operations on these data that are required to solve the problem. Finally, a program is constructed in terms of these operations as well as the operations defined on the simple and structured C++ data types, such as integers, floats, arrays, and so on.

The concepts of parameterized classes and inheritance will be discussed and illustrated as additional tools for building new data types and for relating the common features of these types, while separating their distinguishing features. New approaches to building data abstractions and reusing software components will be introduced in solving new problems.

We begin our work in this chapter by building some simple, rather familiar data types from existing C++ types and structures. Our initial focus will be on a powerful data structure used in writing computer programs, the indexed collection of data.

12.1 ___ THE INDEXED COLLECTION AS AN ABSTRACT DATA TYPE

The storage, manipulation, and retrieval of collections of data are central to the solution of many problems. Yet it is often useful to be able to separate the processing of the elements of the collection from the rest of the work done by the program. If multiple data collections are required, the processing of each should be separated from the others as well as from the other processing duties of the rest of the program. This separation has a number of advantages:

- it helps hide the lower-level details of processing the elements of a collection from the rest of the program, especially the higher-level components that use the collection;
- it helps protect the data stored in the collection by restricting access to these data;
- it provides the basis for extending our earlier ideas on component reuse into a new domain in which the capabilities of an existing, more general component may be easily expanded and/or specialized to form a new component unique to a particular problem;
- it simplifies the testing of a program because the processing of each collection used by the program may be tested separately; and
- it simplifies program maintenance, minimizing the possibility that change in one component of a program will impact others.

In C++, we achieve this separation using the `class` construct to define a new data type called an *indexed collection.* The array data structure introduced in Chapter 9 is a form of an indexed collection. With the C++ array, we have a mechanism (the array declaration) for designating an area of memory having a single name in which to store data elements of the same type. For storage or retrieval of data in an array, we reference specific array elements, using an index (enclosed in brackets [ ]).

However, the array mechanism by itself provides no structured way for achieving the separation of storage, manipulation, and retrieval of its elements. It therefore provides none of the advantages just described for an indexed collection. We will use arrays in our implementation of the indexed collection class. Access to the elements of the class will be similar to array element access—an index will be associated with each element of the collection. This index will be used each time access to that element is required in a program. The array, all of the operations that we need to perform on the array, and any additional data associated with the array will be encapsulated in an indexed collection `class`, thereby providing the desired separation of all array process from the processing tasks of the rest of the program.

An added advantage to the use of the indexed collection concerns the handling of access exceptions, principally subscript range errors. As we indicated in Chapter 9, C++ provides no subscript range checking at compile time or during execution. Out-of-range subscripts result in access to memory locations outside the scope of the referenced array. This access, in turn, usually causes computational errors which show up later during program execution and are often difficult to find.

In all of the indexed collections shown in this chapter, we provide subscript range checking. Out-of-range errors will generate a diagnostic and result in program termination.

Once we have completed defining a class containing the fundamental operations on an indexed collection of data, we will extend it by introducing additional operations as required to solve a particular problem.

General Collections of Data: Attributes and Methods

Every collection of data that we manipulate can be characterized by the collection itself, its data count (the number of data items stored in the collection), and by four operations:

- allocate—brings the collection into existence (among other things, this operation allocates whatever memory is required for storing data in the collection);
- store—places a data item in an element of the collection;
- retrieve—returns a data item from an element of the collection; and
- get_count—returns the number of data items currently stored in the collection.

In some cases, the size of a data collection (total number of elements in which data can be stored) is fixed throughout the life of a program; in others, the size varies as the program executes. It is important to understand the distinction between the maximum potential size of a data collection and the count of the actual number of data items stored in the collection. In some cases, the count may equal the size. Usually, however, the count will be less than the size; in no case can the count of the number of data items stored in a collection exceed the maximum size of the collection.

Indexed Collections: Data and Function Members

An indexed collection of data can be viewed as a *specialized case* of the general collection of data of the same type. The next display contains a summary of the properties of an indexed collection. These properties are expressed in terms of more detailed (and more specialized) descriptions of the data and function members defined for the general collection just described. Following this display, we illustrate one possible implementation of the indexed collection data type using the C++ class.

The Indexed Collection as an Abstract Data Type

Attributes (Data Members)

An indexed collection is a collection of elements of the same data type. The elements of an indexed collection are accessed through an index, an expression of integral value between 0 and `size-1`. Associated with an indexed collection is its `size`, an integral value greater than or equal to 1, which always contains the number of collection elements that may be used to store data.

Member Functions

Three basic operations can be performed on elements of an indexed collection. (The allocation of the collection is discussed later.) The `get_count` function always returns the number of data items currently stored in the collection. The `store` and `retrieve` functions both use an index to specify the particular element of the collection involved in the operation. `store` copies a value into the element of the collection specified by the index. `retrieve` returns the data item that is currently stored in the element indicated by the index. For both the `store` and `retrieve` operations, the value of the index must be between 0 and `size-1`; otherwise, an error will occur. If a meaningful data item has not been stored in the cell referred to by a retrieve operation, the program may produce incorrect results.

We can implement the floating-point indexed collection abstract data type using the class definition shown in Fig. 12.1. The array `collection` is used to store all data. This particular class definition is presented with the assumption that the elements of the collection are all floating point, but we could have just as easily assumed any other data type. We will have more to say about this later in the chapter.

Figure 12.1   Abstract data type for a floating-point indexed collection

```
// FILE: FloatXC1.h
// FLOATING POINT INDEXED COLLECTION CLASS (VERSION 1)
//    DEFINITION AND IMPLEMENTATION

#ifndef FLOATXC1_H_
#define FLOATXC1_H_

#include <stdlib.h>
#include <iostream.h>
```

(Continued)

Figure 12.1 (Continued)

```
class float_index_coll_v1
{
    public:
        // Member functions...
        // CONSTRUCTOR FOR COLLECTION
        float_index_coll_v1
            (int sz = max_size);   // IN: number of elements in array

        // DESTRUCTOR FOR COLLECTION
        ~float_index_coll_v1();

        // STORE AN ITEM IN DESIGNATED COLLECTION ELEMENT
        void store
            (int,                  // IN: index of store
             float);               // IN: value to be stored

        // RETRIEVE AN ITEM FROM DESIGNATED COLLECTION ELEMENT
        float retrieve
            (int);                 // IN: index of retrieval

        // RETURN NUMBER OF ELEMENTS STORED IN COLLECTION
        int get_count ();

    private:
        // Data members ...
        float *collection;         // pointer to collection of
                                   //     floating point objects
        int size;                  // size of the array
        int count;                 // number of elements stored in
                                   //     collection
        enum {max_size = 25};      // default maximum collection size
};


// CONSTRUCTOR FOR COLLECTION
float_index_coll_v1::float_index_coll_v1
    (int sz)                      // IN: number of elements in collection
{
    size = sz;                    // save the size of array
    count = 0;                    // collection empty at start
    collection = new float [size];
    // Construct array of size specified by user (or by default).
    if (collection == 0)
    {
        cerr << endl;
        cerr << "*** ERROR: In float_index_coll_v1, allocator "
            << "failed" << endl;
        cerr << "    to execute correctly.  Execution terminated."
            << endl;
```

(Continued)

Figure 12.1   (Continued)

```
      exit (EXIT_FAILURE);  // terminates program execution
   }
}  // end constructor


// DESTRUCTOR FOR COLLECTION
float_index_coll_v1::~float_index_coll_v1 ()
{
   delete [] collection;
}  // end destructor


// STORE AN ITEM IN DESIGNATED COLLECTION ELEMENT
void float_index_coll_v1::store
   (int index,                    // IN: index of store in collection
    float value)                  // IN: value to be stored

// Pre:  Index must be greater than or equal to zero
//       and less than size.
// Post: Legal floating point value is stored at
//       collection[index].
{
   if ((index < 0) || (index > size-1))
   {
      cerr << endl;
      cerr << "*** ERROR: In float_index_coll_v1::store: index"
           << endl;
      cerr << "    is out of range.  Execution terminated."
           << endl;
      exit (EXIT_FAILURE);
   }
   else
      count++;
   collection[index] = value;
}  // end store


// RETRIEVE AN ITEM FROM DESIGNATED COLLECTION ELEMENT
float float_index_coll_v1::retrieve
   (int index)       // IN: index of retrieval

// Pre:  Index must be greater than or equal to zero
//       and less than size.
// Post: Returns contents of cell indicated by index.
{
   if ((index < 0) || (index > size-1))
   {
      cerr << endl;
```

(Continued)

Figure 12.1   (Continued)

```
        cerr << "*** Error: In float_index_coll_v1::retrieve: index"
             << endl;
        cerr << "    is out of range.  Execution terminated."
             << endl;
        exit (EXIT_FAILURE);
    }
    return collection[index];
}  // end retrieve



// RETURN THE NUMBER OF ELEMENTS STORED IN COLLECTION
int float_index_coll_v1::get_count ()
{
    return count;
}  // end get_count

#endif  // FLOATXC1_H_
```

The constructor header

```
float_index_coll_v1::float_index_coll_v1
  (int sz = max_size)
```

shown in Fig. 12.1 illustrates the use of the C++ *default value argument* mechanism. The single argument (`sz`) for the class constructor (`float_index_coll_v1`) takes on a *default value* (25 in this case) should the constructor be referenced without an argument. If an object of type `float_index_coll_v1` is declared, for example, as

```
float_index_coll_v1 weekly_salaries (100);
```

the number of the elements in the collection would be 100. If an object is declared as

```
float_index_coll_v1 weekly_salaries;
```

the number of elements would be determined by the default value (25 in this case). Default arguments may be used in the formal argument lists of any C++ function. The default value specification is normally placed in the function prototype so that it is always visible wherever the function is used. Our primary use of this feature will be with class constructors, as illustrated in Fig. 12.1.

The line

```
enum {max_size = 25};
```

is used to associate the name `max_size` with the constant 25. Among other things, this constant is used as the default value for the size argument `sz` in the class constructor. Because initialization of class attributes is possible only inside a constructor, a `const` declaration would have been illegal here.

Pointers and Variable Dimension Arrays: An Introduction

In Fig. 12.1, the declaration

```
float *collection;
```

is used to specify the declaration of a *pointer variable* (`collection`) whose type is a *pointer type* (`float *`). A pointer variable, like any other variable, can be used to store data. The data stored must be of type pointer; that is, it must be a memory address. The pointer variable can only point to data of the specified type, `float` in this case. As is the case with all other declarations of this form, no meaningful value has been stored in `collection` as a result of this declaration. We have simply reserved a memory location for a pointer; we have not yet stored anything in this location.

The private section of the definition of the class `float_index_coll_v1` tells us that the class has four attributes (data members):

- a pointer (`collection`) to a floating-point data item;
- an integer (`size`) representing the maximum number of elements that can be stored in `collection`;
- an integer (`count`) representing the actual number of elements stored in `collection` at any given time; and
- an integer (`max_size = 25`) representing the default value maximum size for `collection`.

These attributes are illustrated in the left side diagram in Fig. 12.2.

The statement

```
collection = new float[size];
```

in the constructor in Fig. 12.1 uses the C++ operator `new` to allocate an array of floating-point variables and places the address of the first of these variables in the pointer variable `collection`. The result of the execution of this statement is illustrated in Fig. 12.2 (right). Note that `collection` is essentially not meaningfully defined until the operator `new` is executed in the constructor. At this point, the memory (an array) that will hold the collection of data is allocated, and a meaningful pointer value is inserted into `collection`. In addition, `count` is set to 0, and `size` becomes defined, `size = 100`. (In Fig. 12.2, we are assuming that `s2 = 100`.) Once the number of memory cells indicated by the constructor argument `size` has been allocated, we can access the elements of the new array, using subscripts in the range 0 to `size-1`, as illustrated in Fig. 12.2.

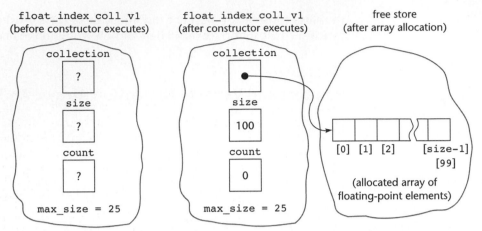

Figure 12.2   Effect of execution of `float_index_coll_v1` **constructor**

The array allocated using the operator new is the same as if it had been declared using the statement

```
float collection[size];
```

(assuming that `size` is a constant). The use of the new operator and the pointer variable frees us from having to specify the maximum size of an array when we are writing a program. Instead, we can allow this size to be determined during the execution of the program and then pass it as an argument to the array constructor at the point at which this determination is made. When the space required for the storage of data is allocated in this manner during execution, we say the storage is *dynamically allocated*. When storage space is fixed by a data declaration as just shown, we say that it is *statically allocated*.

The Memory Model: The Heap or Free Store

Every executing program has a pool of memory, called a *heap* or *free store,* that can be used for the dynamic allocation of memory. Because this pool is finite, it is important to pay some attention to the management of its contents. Whenever you need to allocate a new block of memory from the heap for use in your program, you use the new operator in the manner just shown. This results in the return of the address of the first memory location in the block allocated. In turn, this address should be assigned to a pointer variable declared in your program. The block of memory allocated is accessed using this variable (see Fig. 12.2, right).

Should the amount of memory remaining in the heap not be sufficient to meet the needs of a new request, a zero value (the null pointer) is returned. It is important always to verify that a request for the allocation of a new block of memory has been successful (see Fig. 12.1, in the constructor code)—in other words, the request should not return a zero pointer value.

Destructors

When dynamically allocated memory is no longer needed by a program, it should be deallocated using a `delete` operation. The `delete` will return this memory to the heap for subsequent reallocation. In some C++ environments, consistent failure to return unneeded memory to the heap can quickly exhaust this store and bring your program to a halt. You should be as attentive to the deallocation of unneeded memory as you are to its initial allocation.

Frequently, a class data attribute takes the form of a pointer to dynamically allocated memory (see Fig. 12.1). In such cases, it is good to become accustomed to deallocating memory when it is no longer needed. We therefore need a mechanism for deallocating memory dynamically allocated to an object when that object is destroyed. We could write a function to do this deallocation, but we would need to explicitly call the function when deallocation is required. (Recall that a C++ object exists within the scope in which it has been declared and that it is normally destroyed when the function or block, bracketed by braces, in which it is declared terminates execution. Review Chapter 6 for more discussion.)

C++ provides a class feature called a *destructor* that is automatically called when a class object is destroyed. A destructor has the same name as its class but is preceded by a tilde, ~. It neither specifies a return value nor returns any arguments. The destructor prototype

```
~float_index_coll_v1();        // DESTRUCTOR FOR COLLECTION
```

should be inserted into the class `float_index_coll_v1`, preferably beneath the constructor for this class. The definition of the destructor is as follows:

```
// DESTRUCTOR FOR COLLECTION
float_index_coll_v1::~float_index_coll_v1()
{
    delete [] collection;
}
```

The pointer declaration and the `new` and `delete` operators are summarized in the following C++ Syntax Displays.

C++
SYNTAX

Pointer Type Declaration

Form: *type *variable;*

Example: `float *p;`

Interpretation: This declaration associates a memory location with the pointer variable. Only memory location addresses (pointers) to data of the specified *type* may be assigned to the *variable*. ∎

New Operator

Form: new *type*

Examples: pfloat = new float;
        collection = new float [size];

Interpretation: Storage for an unnamed data element of the specified *type* is allocated from a pool of storage called the *heap,* and a pointer to this data element is returned. The amount of storage allocated is determined by the type specified. If sufficient storage is not available, the new operator returns 0 (the *null pointer*).   ▪

The Delete Operator

Form: delete *variable;*

Example: delete pfloat;   // deletes a single element
        delete [] collection;   // deletes an array of
                    //   elements

Interpretation: The memory cells pointed to by *variable* (which was set from the invocation of the new operator) are returned to the heap. These cells can be reallocated when the new operator is next invoked. (*Note:* Some compilers do not work properly when brackets are used as shown in this text.)   ▪

We will have more to say about pointers and dynamic allocation in Chapter 16. Until then, our use of pointers and the dynamic creation of storage will be limited to the use shown in Fig. 12.1—the dynamic creation of arrays in constructors. In some of the problems we will solve, the ability to allow the size of an array to be specified dynamically (during execution) provides an added measure of flexibility and can help us make more efficient use of storage space. The use of this dynamic array creation feature is illustrated in the following Case Study.

12.2 ___ CLASS EXTENSIONS: AN INTRODUCTION TO INHERITANCE

CASE STUDY: HOME BUDGET PROBLEM

In this Case Study, we illustrate how easily classes can be reused with little, if any, alteration. We begin with the floating-point indexed collection class (float_index_coll_v1). A new class (float_index_coll_v2) can be created from the original through the use of inheritance and extension. The new class inherits all of the data and function members from the original and is then extended through the addition of two other function members. The resulting new class is used as the foundational building block for the solution to our problem.

Problem Statement

Your parents would like you to write a program that keeps track of their monthly expenses in each of several categories. The program is to keep track of these expenses by reading expense amounts one at a time and adding the amount to the appropriate category total. After all monthly expenses have been processed, the program is to print the total expenditure by category and the sum of all expenses. For each expense, the input data consist of the category number (as specified in a menu) and an expense amount for that category for the month in question.

Problem Analysis

Your parents have selected the following seven expense categories:

- entertainment
- food
- clothing
- rent
- tuition
- insurance
- miscellaneous

Therefore, seven separate totals, one for each category, must be accumulated. Upon completion of the processing of the expenses, these totals must be summed to form a grand total of all expenses for the month. Of course, each of the accumulators must be initialized to zero if this is to work properly.

We can use an object of type `float_index_coll_v1` for storing and manipulating the seven floating-point accumulators required. The operations that we need to perform on these accumulators are already defined, except for an initialization operation, which sets each element of the object (each accumulator) to zero at the start. In C++, this initialization is typically carried out as part of the constructor. We will modify the original indexed collection constructor to call a separate member function `init` to perform the needed initialization. `init` is used here as a private member function and is therefore callable only within the indexed collection class and not outside.

With the constructor modified to perform initialization, we define a new data type, `float_index_coll_v2,` consisting of the operations of the original `float_index_coll_v1` data type plus this initialization operation. In addition, we include a new function, `get_size`, similar to `get_count` but returning the size of a collection defined by this data type rather than the count of the number of data elements currently stored in the collection. The size of a collection is an important attribute and is often required by many components in a program. As we proceed through the design and implementation of the program to solve this problem, you will see that the ability to retrieve this value, even though it never changes, is a huge convenience.

Thus the class used to define the new data type is identical to the original class `float_index_coll_v1`, except for the constructor changes and the addition of the functions `init` and `get_size` (their prototypes and definitions) and the change in the name of the class. The prototypes for the new functions are:

```
// GET THE SIZE OF THE COLLECTION
int get_size ();

// INITIALIZES STORAGE ELEMENTS TO SPECIFIED VALUE
// (Private Member Function)
void init
    (float);        // IN: value to be used in initialization
```

The revised class definition section and new function definitions are given in Fig. 12.3.

Figure 12.3   First class extension from `float_index_coll_v1`

```
// FILE: FloatXC0.h
// FLOATING POINT INDEXED COLLECTION CLASS
//     (Version 2 -- with initialization and get_size functions)
//     DEFINITION AND IMPLEMENTATION

#ifndef FLOATXC0_H_
#define FLOATXC0_H_

#include <stdlib.h>
#include <iostream.h>

class float_index_coll_v2
{
   public:
      // Member functions ...
      // CONSTRUCTOR FOR COLLECTION
      float_index_coll_v2
        (int sz = max_size,     // IN: number of elements in array
         float value = 0.0);    // IN: initialization value

      // DESTRUCTOR FOR COLLECTION
      ~float_index_coll_v2 ();

      // STORE AN ITEM IN DESIGNATED COLLECTION ELEMENT
      void store
        (int,                   // IN: index of store
         float);                // IN: value to be stored
```

(Continued)

Figure 12.3   (Continued)

```
            // RETRIEVE AN ITEM FROM DESIGNATED COLLECTION ELEMENT
            float retrieve
               (int);                // IN: index of retrieval

            // RETURN NUMBER OF ELEMENTS STORED IN COLLECTION
            int get_count ();

            // RETURN MAXIMUM NUMBER OF ELEMENTS
            int get_size ();

         private:
            // Data members ...
            float* collection;  // pointer to collection of floating
                                //     point objects
            int size;           // size of the array
            int count;          // number of elements stored in
                                //     collection
            enum {max_size = 25};

            // Private member functions ...
            // INITIALIZES STORAGE ELEMENTS TO SPECIFIED VALUE
            void init
               (float);            // IN: value to be used in initialization
      };


      // CONSTRUCTOR FOR COLLECTION
      float_index_coll_v2::float_index_coll_v2
         (int sz,                // IN: number of elements in collection
          float value)           // IN: initialization value
      {
         size = sz;              // save the size of array
         count = 0;              // collection empty at start
         collection = new float [size];
         // Construct array of size specified by user (or by default).
         if (collection == 0)
         {
            cerr << endl;
            cerr << "*** ERROR: In float_index_coll_v1: allocator "
                 << "failed" << endl;
            cerr << "    to execute correctly.  Execution terminated."
                 << endl;
            exit (EXIT_FAILURE);
         }
         init (value);
      } // end constructor

      ...
```

(Continued)

Figure 12.3   (Continued)

```
// RETURN MAXIMUM NUMBER OF ELEMENTS
int float_index_coll_v2::get_size ()
{
   return size;
} // end get_size


// Private member function
// INITIALIZES STORAGE ELEMENTS TO SPECIFIED VALUE
void float_index_coll_v2::init
   (float value)                        // value to be in initialization

// Pre:  All collection elements undefined
// Post: All collection elements set to value
{
   // Perform initialization.
   for (int i = 0; i < size; i++)
      collection[i] = value;
} // end init

#endif  // FLOATXC0_H_
```

The specification of the data for the Home Budget Problem is now considerably simplified because we can use an object of the modified indexed collection data type to store the expense accumulators for each category. Given this data type (implemented as a class), we can complete the data descriptions as follows.

DATA REQUIREMENTS FOR MAIN FUNCTION

> *Problem Input*
>
> Category and expense amount for each transaction
>
> *Problem Output*
>
> expenses (float_index_coll_v2)   — the seven expense totals
> grand_total (float)   — total of all expenses across cate-
>   gories
> transaction_count (integer)   — number of expense transactions

Program Design

After the collection is allocated and initialized via the constructor function, the program must read each expense category and expense amount and update (via arithmetic addition) the expense accumulator for the specified category. When done with all expense transactions, the program must print a table showing each category and its accumulated total. In addition, the grand total of all expenses for the month and a count of the number of expenses must be printed. The count was not required in the problem statement, but it is so easy to provide and so potentially useful that we should not need to be asked to provide it—it should be provided automatically in all programs that we write.

The relationships among the four steps just outlined are shown in the structure chart in Fig 12.4. As illustrated in the chart, the program carries out its task by calling three functions. The constructor member function is included in the chart as a reminder that initialization is required and is processed in this function. We will adopt the convention of using a heavier outline around boxes that represent steps implemented as operations defined in a class.

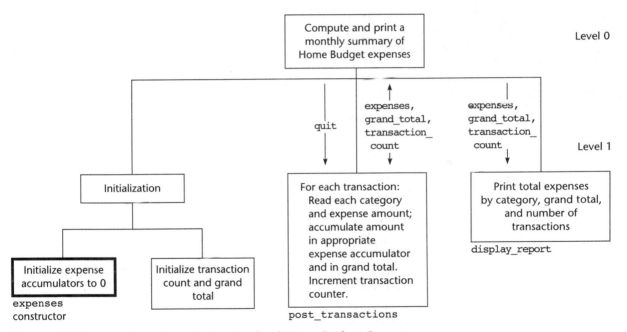

Figure 12.4   **Structure chart for top levels of Home Budget Program**

The algorithm summarizing the sequencing of these steps is shown next.

INITIAL ALGORITHM FOR MAIN FUNCTION

1. Initialize transactions count, grand total, and all expense totals (for each category) to zero.
2. For each expense transaction, read a category and an expense, add the expense to the appropriate category total, increase the count of transactions, and update grand total of expenses (`post_transactions`).

3. Print report, including accumulated expenses for each category, the grand total of expenses, and the number of transactions for the month (`display_report`).

The main function for the Home Budget Case Study is shown in Fig. 12.5. The allocation and initialization of the collection that is to be used to store the accumulated totals for each category is carried out by the class constructor for `float_index_coll_v2`. The execution of this constructor is caused by the presence of the declaration

```
float_index_coll_v2 expenses (max_items, zero);
```

in `main`. In this case, `max_items` is 7; zero = 0.0.

Figure 12.5   **Main program for the Home Budget Problem**

```
// FILE: HomeBudg.cpp
// A SUMMARY OF HOUSEHOLD EXPENSES BY BUDGET CATEGORY

#include <iostream.h>
#include <stdio.h>

#include "FloatXC2.h"
#include "HmBdFncs.cpp"

void main ()
{
   // Local data ...
   const int quit = 0;
   const int max_cat = 7;
   const float zero = 0.0;
   float_index_coll_v2            // expense accumulators for
      expenses(max_cat, zero);    //    all categories
   float grand_total;             // grand total of expenses
   int transaction_count;         // number of transactions

   // Functions used ...
   // READS CATEGORY AND EXPENSE, UPDATES PROPER TOTAL
   void post_transactions
      (float_index_coll_v2 &,     // INOUT: expense totals by category
       int &,                     // INOUT: number of transactions
       float &,                   // INOUT: total of all expenses
       int);                      // IN: quit value

   // PRINTS THE EXPENSES IN EACH CATEGORY
   void display_report
      (float_index_coll_v2,       // IN: expense totals by category
```

(Continued)

Figure 12.5 (Continued)

```
      float,                    // IN: total of all expenditures
      int);                     // IN: number of transactions

   transaction_count = 0;
   grand_total = 0;
   post_transactions (expenses, transaction_count, grand_total,
      quit);
   display_report (expenses, grand_total, transaction_count);
   return;
}
```

We can now move on to the tasks of designing and implementing the two functions, post_transactions and display_report.

Problem Analysis for post_transactions

The function post_transactions is responsible for processing all expense transactions. The function interacts with the program user by first asking for the input of an expense category choice (1 through 7, or 0 for quit). If a valid category choice is given, the user is asked to enter an amount for this transaction. This amount is then added to the expense total for the given category as well as to the grand total, and the count of the number of transactions is incremented. This process is repeated as long as a 0 (quit) category choice is not entered.

DATA REQUIREMENTS FOR post_transactions

Input Arguments

quit (int)	— the sentinel value
expenses (float_index_coll_v2)	— the seven expense totals
grand_total (float)	— grand total of expenses
transaction_count (int)	— number of expense transactions

Output Arguments

expenses (float_index_coll_v2)	— the seven expense totals
grand_total (float)	— grand total of expenses
transaction_count (int)	— number of expense transactions

Local data

choice (int)	— category choice for current transaction (1–7 or 0 to quit)
amount (float)	— amount of current transaction

DESIGN FOR post_transactions

The structure chart shown in Fig. 12.6 illustrates the relationship among the three functions and other steps required for the processing of each transaction.

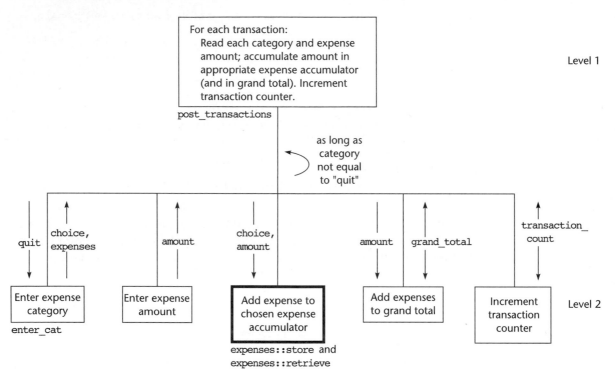

Figure 12.6   **Structure chart for** `post_transactions`

The algorithm for the steps just outlined is shown next.

ALGORITHM FOR post_transactions

1. Get first choice from user (`enter_cat`)
2. As long as choice is not quit
    2.1. Read expense for indicated category.
    2.2. Add expense to the appropriate category total
          (`expenses.retrieve`, `expense.store`).
    2.3. Accumulate expense in grand total.
    2.4. Increment transaction count.
    2.5. Get next choice from user (`enter_cat`)

IMPLEMENTATION OF post_transactions

A `for` loop is used to implement `post_transactions` (see Fig. 12.7). The functions `expenses.retrieve` and `expenses.store` are part of the set of operations defined for the type `float_index_coll_v2`. They are both used in the function call line

```
expenses.store(choice - 1,
               expenses.retrieve(choice - 1) + amount);
```

This line carries out the task of retrieving the current contents of the selected element of `expenses`, adding the current transaction amount to this value, and then storing the result back in `expenses`.

Function `enter_cat` is new. It serves as a user interface for the entry of the expense category choice (1 to 7, or 0 to quit). The function displays a menu of choices, asks the user for a choice, and then checks the validity of the choice. The user is repeatedly prompted for a choice until a valid selection is made. A `do-while` loop is used to implement this function. The code is relatively straightforward and is shown along with the code for function `post_trans-actions` (Fig. 12.7).

Figure 12.7 Code for `post_transactions`, `display_report`, and `enter_cat`

```
// FILE: HmBdFncs.cpp
// A SUMMARY OF HOUSEHOLD EXPENSES BY BUDGET CATEGORY

#include <iostream.h>

// READS A CATEGORY AND EXPENSE, UPDATES PROPER TOTAL
void post_transactions
   (float_index_coll_v2 &expenses,    // INOUT: expense totals by
                                      //        category
    int &transaction_count,           // INOUT: number of transac-
                                      //        tions
    float &grand_total,               // INOUT: total of all expenses
    int quit)                         // IN: quit value

// Pre:  Each element of expense object is initialized to 0.0.
// Post: Each element of expense object is the sum of expense
//       amounts for category.
{
   // Local data ...
   int choice;
   float amount;
```

(Continued)

Figure 12.7   (Continued)

```
   // Functions used ...
   int enter_cat (float_index_coll_v2 &, int);

   for (choice = enter_cat (expenses, quit); choice != quit;
        choice = enter_cat (expenses, quit))
   {
      cout << "Enter the expense amount $";
      cin >> amount;
      expenses.store (choice - 1,
                      expenses.retrieve(choice - 1) + amount);
      grand_total += amount;
      transaction_count++;
   }  // end while
   return;
}  // end post_transactions


// READS THE BUDGET CATEGORY AS AN INTEGER VALUE
int enter_cat (float_index_coll_v2 &expenses, int quit)

// Pre : None
// Post: Choice is an integer greater than or equal to 0.
{
  // Local data ...
  int choice;

  do
  {
     cout << endl;
     cout << "0 - Quit program"  << endl
          << "1 - Entertainment" << endl
          << "2 - Food" << endl
          << "3 - Clothing" << endl
          << "4 - Rent" << endl
          << "5 - Tuition" << endl
          << "6 - Insurance" << endl
          << "7 - Miscellaneous" << endl
          << "Enter the category number> ";
     cin >> choice;
  } while ((choice < quit) || (choice > expenses.get_size()));
  return (choice);
} // end enter_cat


// PRINTS THE EXPENSES IN EACH BUDGET CATEGORY
void display_report
  (float_index_coll_v2 expenses, // IN: expense totals by category
   float grand_total,            // IN: total of all expenses
   int transaction_count)        // IN: number of transactions
```

(Continued)

Figure 12.7 (Continued)

```
// Pre:  Each element of expense object is defined.
// Post: Displays each category.
{
   cout << "  CATEGORY          EXPENSES" << endl << endl;
   for (int next_cat = 0; next_cat < expenses.get_size ();
      next_cat++)
   {
      // Set precision for 2 decimal places.
      cout.precision (2);
      cout.setf (ios::showpoint | ios::fixed);

      // Retrieve expenses and print
      cout << "$ " << expenses.retrieve(next_cat);
      switch (next_cat)
      {
         case 0 : cout << "  Entertainment    " << endl;
                  break;
         case 1 : cout << "  Food             " << endl;
                  break;
         case 2 : cout << "  Clothing         " << endl;
                  break;
         case 3 : cout << "  Rent             " << endl;
                  break;
         case 4 : cout << "  Tuition          " << endl;
                  break;
         case 5 : cout << "  Insurance        " << endl;
                  break;
         case 6 : cout << "  Miscellaneous    " << endl;
      }; // end switch
   }  // end for next_cat

   cout << endl << endl;
   cout << "Grand total of all expenses is: $ "<< grand_total
      << endl << endl;
   cout << "There were " << transaction_count
      << " transactions during program run." << endl;
   return;
}  // display_report
```

Problem Analysis for display_report

Function `display_report` displays a table of the total expenses for each category. Then it displays the grand total of expenses taken over all categories and the count of the total number of transactions. The `expenses` object, the `grand_total`, and `transaction_count`, as computed before the call of `display_report`, are all passed as input arguments to this function. The code is also shown in Fig. 12.7. A `for` loop is used to display the contents of expenses, one element at a time. The function `expenses.retrieve` is used to obtain the element to be displayed in each loop repetition. In order to provide a readable label for each element, a `switch` statement is used inside the `for` loop to print the correct label. In the next chapter, we will see how to store these labels in an array of strings, thereby eliminating the need for the `switch` and enabling us to write a much simpler function.

Program Testing

A sample run of the Home Budget Program is shown in Fig. 12.8. For the sake of brevity, we have displayed the list of categories just once. As indicated in this run, it is not necessary for the data to be in order by category. You should verify that all budget categories without purchases remain zero. Also, verify that out-of-range category values do not cause the program to terminate prematurely.

Figure 12.8   Sample run of Home Budget Program

```
1 - Entertainment
2 - Food
3 - Clothing
4 - Rent
5 - Tuition
6 - Insurance
7 - Miscellaneous
0 - Quit program

Enter the category number> 3
Enter the expense amount $25.00

Enter the category number> 7
Enter the expense amount $25.00

Enter the category number> 3
Enter the expense amount $15.00

Enter the category number> 1
Enter the expense amount $675.00

Enter the category number> 0

    CATEGORY        EXPENSES
    Entertainment    675.00
    Food               0.00
    Clothing          40.00
```

(Continued)

Figure 12.8   (Continued)

Rent	0.00
Tuition	0.00
Insurance	0.00
Miscellaneous	25.00

```
Grand total of all expenses is: $740.00
There were 7 transactions during program run.
```

Commentary

As we can see from the solution to the Home Budget Problem, the object `expenses` is the key data element in the program. It is important to note that access to the attributes of the object is controlled exclusively through the use of the four member functions `get_size`, `store`, `retrieve`, and the constructor. Functions `main`, `post_transactions`, and `display_report` use these functions to carry out their respective tasks. The details of the functions are specified and encapsulated in the `float_index_coll_v2` class and are of no concern to the program developer or implementor (except, of course, for the interface information provided by function prototypes). Note, too, that the argument lists for the member functions are very short, if they exist at all. This is because most of the information relevant to these functions is encapsulated within the same module as the function definitions—namely, the class `float_index_coll_v2`. These class attributes are automatically accessible to the member functions in the class and must not be included as function arguments.

Thus, the class `float_index_coll_v2` provides an extended base of types which we can use in developing the solution to the Home Budget Problem. Of course, all of the operations that we might use on integer, character, and floating-point data are also a part of this base. We often take these for granted, however, because these data types are a standard part of our implementation language. If we are on a reasonable track in designing a piece of software, it is quite natural to expect that many of the lower-level functions in our structure charts will be operations such as `store` and `retrieve` on user-defined data types.

The type `float_index_coll_v2` is not the last extension of the indexed collection data type abstraction that we will see in this text. As new problems arise, we may need to build further extensions to this class to help solve problems. If we had great foresight, it is conceivable that we could have anticipated each of these extensions from the start and built one general class to handle all of these needs. In fact, the more experienced we become as programmers, the more easily we are able to do this. However, in practice, no matter how experienced and thorough we are, new needs are always arising. So the development sequence we will follow for our new class, although somewhat contrived based on our current level of expertise, is nonetheless quite in keeping with what you will find in everyday practice.

Later, you will also come to understand that it is by no means good practice to throw everything but the kitchen sink into a class at the very start. Incremental development of classes, starting with a *base class* and then tailoring this class to the specific needs of a given problem is actually good practice. The idea in each case, however, is to use the base class as the basic building block for everything else that is done. In the object-oriented terminology introduced in Chapter 10, we would say that each extension of an existing class *inherits* the properties of its predecessor and then *specializes* on the base class by adding new properties to the original list. The original class is sometimes called the parent class; each class that specializes on the parent class is called a *derived class*.

C++ defines an *inheritance* mechanism that makes it relatively easy to define derived classes from a given parent. Inheritance is an important concept in program design and implementation. However, learning to use the C++ inheritance mechanism is a bit complicated and not directly relevant to some of the other introductory ideas required in a first course in computing. We therefore have chosen not to present this mechanism in this text. (A brief introduction is provided in Appendix E.) In the meanwhile, as a compromise, we use the concept of inheritance to achieve our goals. By the time you are formally introduced to this mechanism, you will have developed a good sense of why it is important and how it is used. Among other things, this approach will enable us to continue to build on the ideas of information hiding and separation of concerns described when the indexed collection abstract data type was first introduced.

EXERCISES FOR SECTION 12.2

Self-Check
1. What happens if the user of the Budget Program enters the category 9 by mistake?
2. (See also Programming Exercise 1 in this section.) Let `counters` be a class that is similar to `expenses` except that each element is used to keep track of the number of transactions posted to each category rather than the accumulated value of these transactions. The functions and attributes in this new class should be much like those for the `expenses` class except that integers will be used rather than floating-point data.

   a. Write a declaration for the object `counts` of type `counters`;
   b. Write the correct call to the `init` function in the `counters` class constructor.
   c. Write the correct statement for incrementing the proper storage cell in the `counters` class given the budget category for the current transaction.

3. Redesign the Home Budget Program so that the computation of `grand_total` is performed in a separate function. Show the changes you would need in the algorithm, structure chart, and code for the main function, and write the code for the new function. (Instead of accumulating in `grand_total` the value of each transaction

as it is processed, compute this total in a separate function called after all transactions have been processed.)

4. Draw a structure chart for the display_report function.

Programming

1. Write the class counters described in Self-Check Exercise 2 in this section.

2. It can be argued that the variable grand_total used in the Home Budget Problem to store the total value of all expenses (taken over all categories) should have been another attribute in the class float_index_coll_v2 rather than a local variable in the main function. Were this to have been done, the class would have needed yet an additional member function, get_total, to compute this total and return the value to the calling module (perhaps just for display purposes). Write this member function, indicate how it would be called from the main function, and describe the changes that would have to be made to the class float_index_coll_v2 to complete this design modification.

12.3 —— EXTENDING REUSE: AN INTRODUCTION TO TEMPLATES

In Chapter 9, we implemented functions for adding and comparing corresponding pairs of elements in floating-point arrays. We also wrote a function to find the largest element in a floating-point array. Other similar functions also could have been written, such as for multiplying two floating-point arrays or for multiplying a single floating-point value (called a *scalar*) by each element of an array (see the Programming Exercises at the end of Section 9.3). In Section 12.1 we implemented an abstract data type (the class float_index_coll_v1) representing an indexed collection of floating-point data items. We then used an extension of this class (float_index_coll_v2) to implement the Home Budget Problem, illustrating the idea of inheritance by adding new functions to the original class.

By now it may have occurred to you that our floating-point indexed collection and its extension, as well as the functions just described, could have just as easily been written to work for integer data. In fact, as part of the Self-Check Exercises (see Exercise 2, Section 12.2), we suggested that you implement an integer indexed collection abstract data type, int_index_coll_v2, similar to float_index_coll_v2 in all ways except the base type of the collection would be integer instead of floating-point.

To carry this point a bit further, if you examine the functions exchange and same_array (Section 9.3), you will see how they easily could have been written for integer data, character data, or data of enumeration types.

C++ provides a template feature that enables us to specify functions and classes in terms of *parameterized types*. For the purposes of this discussion, we may view these parameters as type place-holders used to represent actual types as needed when we develop our programs. Aside from these parameterized types, the rest of the code in a template remains otherwise unchanged as the template is reused.

The mechanics of writing class and function templates and matching parameterized types in C++ can be quite complicated. However, the concept of templates is a powerful and important one; we will therefore provide a brief introduction here, keeping our discussion as straightforward as possible.

Consider, for example, the *class template* shown in Fig. 12.9. This class definition is similar to the floating-point indexed collection class originally shown in Fig. 12.1 but with the symbol T used as a place-holder for a C++ data type. The only other major difference is that the implementation of each member function is included as part of the class definition. We will follow this convention for template classes primarily because the C++ implementation of template class member functions defined outside the body of a class is somewhat cumbersome. Thus, when specifying a class template definition, we will not use function prototypes but rather the full function definition for each function required in the template.

Figure 12.9   Template definition for indexed collection abstract data type

```
// FILE: TmplXC1.h
// TEMPLATE: DEFINITION AND IMPLEMENTATION OF CLASS TEMPLATE
//     FOR AN INDEXED COLLECTION

#ifndef TMPLXC1_H_
#define TMPLXC1_H_

#include <stdlib.h>
#include <iostream.h>

template <class T>
class index_coll_v1
{
   public:
      // Member functions ...
      // CONSTRUCTOR FOR COLLECTION
      index_coll_v1
        (int sz = max_size)       // IN: number of elements in
                                  //     collection
      {
         size = sz;               // save size of array
         count = 0;               // collection empty at start
         collection = new T [size];
         // Construct array of size specified by user (or by
         //     default).
         if (collection == 0)
         {
```

(Continued)

Figure 12.9   (Continued)

```
          cerr << endl;
          cerr << "*** ERROR: In index_coll_v1: allocator failed"
               << endl;
          cerr << "     to execute correctly."
               << " Execution terminated." << endl;
          exit (EXIT_FAILURE);
      }  // end if
}  // end constructor


// DESTRUCTOR FOR COLLECTION
~index_coll_v1()
{
    delete [] collection;
}


// STORE AN ITEM IN DESIGNATED COLLECTION ELEMENT
void store
   (int index,                  // IN: index of store in
                                //     collection
    T value)                    // IN: value to be stored

// Pre:  Index must be greater than or equal to zero
//       and less than size ;
// Post: Legal value is stored at collection[index].
{
    if ((index < 0) || (index > size - 1))
    {
       cerr << endl;
       cerr << "*** ERROR: In index_coll_v1::store: index"
            << endl;
       cerr << "     is out of range. Execution terminated."
            << endl;
       exit (EXIT_FAILURE);
    }
    else
       count++;
    collection[index] = value;
}  // end store


// RETRIEVE AN ITEM FROM DESIGNATED COLLECTION ELEMENT
T retrieve
   (int index)                  // IN: index of retrieval

// Pre:  Index must be greater than or equal to zero
//       and less than size;
```

(Continued)

Figure 12.9   (Continued)

```
          // Post: Returns contents of cell indicated by index
          {
             if ((index < 0) || (index > size - 1))
             {
                cerr << endl;
                cerr << "*** ERROR: In index_coll_v1::retrieve: index"
                     << endl;
                cerr << "     is out of range. Execution terminated."
                     << endl;
                exit (EXIT_FAILURE);
             }  // end if
             return collection[index];
          }  // end retrieve


          // RETURN THE NUMBER OF ELEMENTS STORED IN COLLECTION
          int get_count ()
          {
             return count;
          }  // end get_count


      private:
          // Data members ...
          T *collection;    // pointer to collection of type T objects
          int size;         // size of the array
          int count;        // number of elements stored in collection
          enum {max_size = 25};
   };

#endif  // TMPLXC1_H_
```

We can use template `index_coll_v1` to create indexed collection objects containing elements of a variety of different types. For example, we can obtain integer and character indexed collections using the *type declarations*

```
typedef index_coll_v1<int> int_index_coll_v1;
int_index_coll_v1 ages (family_size);

typedef index_coll_v1<char> char_index_coll_v1;
char_index_coll_v1 counts (26);
```

where `family_size` and 26 are the arguments passed to the constructors for `int_index_coll_v1` and `char_index_coll_v1`, respectively. We can add functions `init` and `get_size` (see Fig. 12.3) to `index_coll_v1` and obtain a new template, `index_coll_v2`. From this template, the floating-point indexed collection for the expenses in the Home Budget Problem can be obtained by writing the declarations

```
typedef index_coll_v2<float> float_index_coll_v2;
float_index_coll_v2 expenses (max_cat, zero);
```

We can also create indexed collections of structures, such as `employee` defined in Section 9.7:

```
typedef index_coll_v1<employee> employee_index_coll_v1;
employee_index_coll_v1 personnel (nmbr_empl);
```

Note that in each of these examples, two steps are necessary. First, the new data type (`float_index_coll_v2` or `employee_index_coll_v1`) is defined from the template using a `typedef` statement. Then a declaration is required to create objects of the new type. Once one indexed collection type, such as `float_index_coll_v2`, has been defined and tested, it is easier to develop and test the others rather than recreate them from scratch.

The general forms for our simpler version of class templates and for the type and object declarations that use them are presented in the following C++ Syntax Displays. Of course, when defining a new type in this manner, we must be careful not to include accidentally any operations that are not meaningful (or are not syntactically correct). For example, if one type contained methods involving arithmetic operations on type `int` data, we should avoid reusing that class on type `char` or type `employee` data. Nonetheless, as long as we are careful to ensure that all defined data members and member functions of a C++ type make sense, the use of templates can provide a powerful new tool in the reuse of C++ code components.

**C++
SYNTAX**

Template Classes: Introductory Version

This is a restricted form and does not show the full generality of the construct.

Form:
```
template <class T>
class class_name
{
    public:
        list of class variables, types, constants, etc. (if any) that
            may be accessed by name from outside the class
        complete definition of each function that may be accessed
            by name from outside the class
    ...
```

```
      private:
            list of class variables, types, constants, etc., that are intended
                to be hidden from reference from outside the class
            complete definition of each function (if any) to be hidden
                from outside the class
            ...
      };
```

Example: Figure 12.9 shows how the template class is used.

Interpretation: The template class prefix

```
template <class T>
```

specifies that a template is being declared using a *parameter* T. Once T has been introduced in the prefix, it can be used as we would use any type in writing C++ instructions.

Template classes can be used to specify a *template* or form for a group of related classes. A specific class in this group is created through the use of a type definition statement (see the next C++ Syntax Display).   ▪

C++
SYNTAX

Type and Object Definitions Using Template Classes: Introductory Version

This is a restricted form and does not show the full generality of the construct.

Form: typedef *class-template-name<type> new-type-name;*
             new-type-name an-object;

Example: typedef index_coll_v1<int> int_index_coll_v1;
            int_index_coll_v1 my_data;

Interpretation: The prefix typedef indicates that a synonym or new type name is being defined (in this case, the new type name is int_index_coll_v1). *Type* may be any defined data type. *new-type-name* is the name of a new data type that is created when the type specified between the symbols <> replaces its corresponding parameter T in the template class.

The new type created from a class template can be used to declare new data objects, as in

```
int_index_coll_v1 my_data;
```

which declares an object my_data of type int_index_coll_v1.   ▪

Example 12.1   *Templates with Multiple Parameters.*   Template classes may have more than one parameter. For templates with multiple parameters, the parameters in the definition, as well as those in a declaration using the template, must be separated by commas. An actual class template parameter may be a type name, a constant or constant expression, or a function name. Integers can be particularly useful as template argument, for example, for specifying the size of a collection of information of some type T, as shown next.

```
template <class T, int sz>
class container
{
    T x[sz];
    ...
};
```

Given this two-parameter template, we can create objects that consist of arrays of elements of type T and size sz, such as

```
typedef container<double, 50> measurements_container;
measurements_container measurements;

typedef container<complex, 20> coordinates_container;
coordinates_container coordinates;

typedef container<employee, 15> employees_container;
employees_container employees;
```

Note that any user-defined data type, including structs and classes, can be used as actual parameters in creating a new data type from a template.

The choice of the identifier `container` in this example is not accidental. The `typedef` lines in these statements define three related data types—classes that may be used to store and manipulate collections of data of some type. Such classes are often called *container classes,* or simply *containers.* The classes `int_index_v1` and `measurements_container` are examples of such containers. The advantage of containers is that the implementor of the class template that defines a container need not be concerned with the type of the elements or the size of the container. The entire class container (a template) can be implemented in terms of the type and size parameters. The user or client can then define a container specific to his or her needs by providing the type of the elements and the size of the container. This enables the template designer and user to separate completely the implementation details of each other's work.   ■

EXERCISES FOR SECTION 12.3

Programming 1. Write the complete definition for the template class `index_coll_v2` (similar to `float_index_coll_v2`). (This is a non-trivial exercise; you may need help.)

12.4 —— USING OLD COMPONENTS TO SOLVE NEW PROBLEMS

In this section we present an Example and a Case Study illustrating many of the ideas discussed in Chapters 10 and 11 and so far in this chapter. We use (and reuse) existing classes to define a new class (and, therefore, a new data type). We then use this type together with the fundamental and structured types already studied to build programs to solve new problems. In the process, we provide illustrations of the concepts of data abstraction, encapsulation, and information hiding, as well as other concepts of software engineering. Some different points of view related to the practice of reuse are illustrated, and the idea of building software by combining minimally dependent components is emphasized.

As indicated at the beginning of this chapter, our initial focus in the solution of a problem now will be very much oriented toward data more so than algorithms. Specifically, we will work to illustrate the process of developing C++ models of the entities (such as an employee, a car, a shape, or a point in a three-dimensional plane) described in a problem definition. This process is often referred to as the *abstraction of the essential properties of problem domain data*. Once we have determined precisely which properties of these data are relevant to the problem we are trying to solve, we build a class (a new abstract data type) to represent those properties and then complete our program in terms of operations on objects of these new types.

Both problems illustrated in this section involve a form of reuse of the template class `index_coll_v2`, but each takes a somewhat different approach as to how best to reuse this component. After the two programs have been designed and implemented, we discuss the advantages and disadvantages of these two approaches.

Example 12.2   In this example, we write a short program to keep track of the frequencies of occurrence of uppercase and lowercase letters in a line of text. The text itself is read in one character at a time as long as an end-of-file is not encountered. All nonletter characters in the text are ignored; only the letters are counted.

From this problem description, we see that a collection of counters is required for tracking the number of occurrences of the 26 uppercase letters and another collection for tracking the 26 lowercase letters in the alphabet. For the uppercase letters, this tracking of counts can be done using an indexed collection of 26 integer counters (one for each letter), each of which should be initialized to zero. The association between these counters and the uppercase letters is illustrated in Table 12.1. For our purposes, then, the template class `index_coll_v2` is tailor-made. A similar argument can be made with respect to the lowercase letters.

Table 12.1   Letter Count Problem: Tracking the Frequency of Occurrence of Uppercase Letters in a String

UPPERCASE COUNTER	ASSOCIATED LETTER	CONTENTS OF THIS COUNTER
First	'A'	Frequency of occurrence of letter 'A'
Second	'B'	Frequency of occurrence of letter 'B'
...	...	...
Twenty-sixth	'Z'	Frequency of occurrence of letter 'Z'

It seems reasonable, therefore, to build the solution to this problem around two objects, `upper_count` and `lower_count`, declared as follows:

```
typedef index_coll_v2<int> counter_coll;
counter_coll upper_count (26); // default initial value 0.0 used
counter_coll lower_count (26); // default initial value 0.0 used
```

Both of these objects are considered to be a collection of counters, and both consist of 26 counters for storing the frequencies of occurrence of the uppercase (or lowercase) letters.

Given these two objects (of the user-defined data type `counter_coll`), the problem to be solved may be stated as follows:

> Given an uppercase letter in our text string, how do we determine which counter to increment? A similar problem must be resolved for a given lowercase letter.

As you pursue your study of computer science and programming, you will see that this is one example of a common problem, that of *mapping* one kind of program information (in this case, an uppercase or lowercase letter) into an index value used to select a particular element of a collection. In this example, the letter must be mapped to an integer in the range 0 to 25, inclusive. This value can then be used to select the counter to be incremented.

To perform this mapping for our problem, we define two arrays of characters, `uppercase_letters` and `lowercase_letters`:

```
const char uppercase_letters [] = "ABCDEFGHIJKLMNOPQRSTUVWXYZ";
const char lowercase_letters [] = "abcdefghijklmnopqrstuvwxyz";
```

These arrays are initialized to values given as character string constants, each of which happens to contain 26 characters. (The size of each array is dictated by the number of characters in the string plus one for the character that marks the end of the string; see Section 9.1. Strings are discussed in detail in Chapter 13.)

Using these arrays, each letter in the input string can be mapped to the index of its corresponding counter by reusing the function `lin_search` developed in Chapter 9 (Section 9.5). We could simply edit the source code for this function by changing the type of the `target` and `items[]` arguments from `int` to `char`. But a better approach for our purposes is to rewrite `lin_search` as a function template with parameter `T`. The first eight lines of this template are shown next. The rest of the function remains as shown in Section 9.5.

```
// FILE: LinSchTm.cpp
// SEARCHES AN ARRAY OF ELEMENTS OF TYPE T FOR A GIVEN ELEMENT

template <class T>
int lin_search
  (T target,            // IN: the target being sought
   int size,            // IN: the size of the array¹
   const T items [])     // IN: the array being searched²
...
```

The general form of a function template and its use are described in the following two C++ Syntax Displays.

C++ SYNTAX

Template Function Definition

This is a restricted form and does not show the full generality of the construct.

Form: `template <class T>`
        (The remaining portion of a template function definition consists of a typical function definition with the parameter `T` used as needed in place of a specific, previously defined type.)

Example: `template <class T>`
        `void sel_sort`
          `(T [],`   `// IN: the array to be sorted`
           `int size)` `// IN: the size of the array`
        `{`

---

[1]Some compilers may require a second argument of the form `const int size` if a constant is to be used as the second actual argument.
[2]Some compilers may require a third argument of the form `const T *items`.

```
       ⌠  // function body is same as sel_sort
... ⎨  // in Section 9.5, but array elements
       ⌡  // are of type T, not int.
}
```

Interpretation: Template functions can be used to define a form for an entire group of related functions. The prototype for a specific function in this group is generated when the template function name is used with matching types in a function call. The type of each actual argument in the call must match its corresponding formal argument. Actual arguments corresponding to each occurrence of `T` in the formal argument list must be of the same type. In the linear search example, the types of the first and third actual arguments in a call to `lin_search` must be the same (for example, both of type `char` or both of type `float`. This type replaces the place-holder type specifier `T` in the template and the prototype is created (see the next Syntax Display for discussion and example). The third argument must be an array. The second argument must always be a constant expression of type `int`.   ■

Calling Template Functions: Generating a Prototype

This is a restricted form and does not show the full generality of the construct.

Form: There is no special syntax for calling a template function; the name of the template is used exactly as the name of a function.

Example: `index = lin_search (this_letter, 26,`
                            `uppercase_letters);`

where `this_letter` is type `char` and `uppercase_letters` is an array of type `char`.

Interpretation: There can be exactly one definition of a function template of a given name in a program. There can be many function calls, however, each of which causes the automatic generation of a prototype for a specific function in the group defined by the template. For example, the call just shown would cause the automatic generation of the prototype

```
int lin_search
   (char,            // IN: the target being sought
    int,             // IN: the size of the array
    const char []);  // IN: the array being searched
```

Assuming `this_key` is an integer and `all_ages` is an array of integers, the call

```
index = lin_search (this_key, 26, all_ages);
```

would generate the prototype

```
int lin_search
   (int,              // IN: the target being sought
    int,              // IN: the size of the array
    const int []);    // IN: the array being searched
```

which is consistent with the original version of the function definition written in Section 9.5. ∎

Now that we have resolved the issues of storing and accessing our counter information, we can move on to a few relatively simple procedural issues. The algorithm for our program reads as follows:

1. Prompt user to enter a line of characters.
2. Read first character in line.
3. As long as not end-of-line
      3.1. If character is uppercase
            3.1.1. Increment selected uppercase counter for the current character.
        else if character is lowercase
            3.1.2. Increment selected lowercase counter for the current character.
      3.2 Read next character in line.
4. Print nonzero uppercase letter counts in a two-column table.
5. Print nonzero lowercase letter counts in a two-column table.

The code for this problem is shown in Fig. 12.10. The implementation of the template `index_coll_v2` was an exercise in Section 12.3.

Figure 12.10   Counting letters in a line

```
// FILE: LtrCount.cpp
// FINDS AND PRINTS THE NUMBER OF OCCURRENCES OF LETTERS IN A LINE
//    LETTERS WITH ZERO COUNTS ARE NOT DISPLAYED

#include <iostream.h>
#include <iomanip.h>

#include "TmplXC2.h"       // for class template int_array_v2
#include "LinSchTm.cpp"    // linear search function template

typedef index_coll_v2<char> counter_coll;

void main ()
{
   // Local data ...
   const int max_coll = 26;
```

(Continued)

Figure 12.10   (Continued)

```
const char line_terminator = '#';
const char uppercase_letters [] = "ABCDEFGHIJKLMNOPQRSTUVWXYZ";
const char lowercase_letters [] = "abcdefghijklmnopqrstuvwxyz";

counter_coll upper_count (max_coll, 0); // uppercase counts
counter_coll lower_count (max_coll, 0); // lowercase counts
char ch;            // contains next character read
int subs;           // subscript of location of letter in array

// Functions used ...
// PRINTS COUNTS OF LETTERS THAT ARE IN THE LINE
void display_counts
   (const char [],       // IN: characters
    counter_coll,        // IN: counter collection to be displayed
    const int);          // IN: size of the collection

// Count the letters in a line.
cout << "Please, enter a line of characters, terminate with #"
     << endl;
for (cin.get (ch); ch != line_terminator; cin.get (ch))
{
    if ((subs=lin_search (ch, max_coll, uppercase_letters)) >= 0)
       upper_count.store (subs, upper_count.retrieve(subs) + 1);
    else
       if ((subs=lin_search (ch,max_coll,lowercase_letters)) >= 0)
          lower_count.store (subs,lower_count.retrieve(subs)+1);
}  // end while

display_counts (uppercase_letters, upper_count, max_coll);
display_counts (lowercase_letters, lower_count, max_coll);
}


// PRINT COUNTS OF LETTERS THAT ARE IN THE LINE
void display_counts
  (const char letters [],      // IN: characters
   counter_coll upper_or_lower, // IN: counter collection to be
                                //      displayed
   const int size)             // IN: size of collection
{
   // Local data ...
   char this_letter;
   int this_count;    // contains count for current letter
   int subs;          // subscript of location of letter in array

   cout << endl;
   cout <<  "      Letter      Occurrences" << endl;
   for (int i = 0; i < size; i++)
   {
```

(Continued)

Figure 12.10   (Continued)

```
            this_letter = letters[i];
            subs = lin_search (this_letter, size, letters);
            this_count = upper_or_lower.retrieve (subs);
            if (this_count > 0)
               cout << setw (10) << this_letter << setw (10)
                    << this_count << endl;
      } // end for
   } // end display_counts
```

──────── Program Output ────────

```
Please enter a line of characters, terminate with #.
This is it!!#

      Letter          Occurrences
        T                 1

      Letter          Occurrences
        h                 1
        i                 3
        s                 2
        t                 1
```

In examining this code, it is important to remember that `lin_search` returns the array index of the target item or –1 if the target is not found. In our case, for a given target letter, this returned value is the index required to locate the counter collection element to be incremented. For example, for the letter `'G'`, `lin_search` would return a value of 6. The count of the number of occurrences of the letter `'G'` in the input string is stored in element 6 of the counter collection `upper_count`. Thus, the value returned by `lin_search` is the index value needed for the `retrieve` and `store` operations to increment this count.

All that remains to finish the Letter Count Program is to write the `display_counts` function and complete the code for the linear search function template.

The function `display_counts` (Fig. 12.10) is written to display the number of occurrences of each letter appearing in the line of text entered by the user; letters not read (and therefore still having zero counts) would not be displayed. The completion of the linear search function template is an exercise at the end of this section (Programming Exercise 4).

As we mentioned earlier, the need to convert program data into valid indexes for accessing indexed collections is fairly common in programming. In the previous program, the conversion was necessitated by the fact that the data in question were character data (uppercase and lowercase letters) with ASCII values outside the range 0 to 25 (see Appendix A). Thus the letters themselves cannot be used directly to access the correct frequency counter. We have the same problem in the following Case Study.

CASE STUDY: CRYPTOGRAM GENERATOR PROBLEM

Problem Statement

Your local intelligence agency needs a program to encode messages. One approach is to use a program that generates *cryptograms,* coded messages formed by substituting a code character for each letter of an original message. The substitution is performed uniformly throughout the original message; for instance, every A is replaced by an S, every B is replaced by a P, and so forth. Lowercase letters are converted to uppercase before being replaced. All punctuation (including spaces between words) and digits remain unchanged.

Problem Analysis

The program must examine each character in the message to be encrypted. If the character is an uppercase or lowercase letter, we replace it with its code symbol (also a letter); otherwise, we leave the character alone. The key issue in this problem concerns finding an efficient way to determine the encryption code symbol corresponding to each letter found in the initial message. To do this, we need to define the association between these initial message letters and their code symbols. We would like this association to provide *direct access* to the encryption symbol corresponding to each message letter so that repeated, costly searches can be avoided.

One approach to gaining such direct access to each encryption symbol involves the use of a code table consisting of 26 elements, one for each uppercase letter. We associate these elements, in order, with the letters 'A', 'B', ..., 'Z' and then store the code symbol for these letters in the corresponding element, as illustrated in Table 12.2.

Table 12.2 Using a Code Table for Message Encryption

CODE TABLE ELEMENT	INITIAL MESSAGE LETTER ASSOCIATED	CONTENTS OF THIS CODE TABLE ELEMENT
First	'A'	Code symbol for letter 'A'
Second	'B'	Code symbol for letter 'B'
...	...	...
Twenty-sixth	'Z'	Code symbol for letter 'Z'

Perhaps this is beginning to take on a familiar look, because our code table can be represented as an indexed collection of character data. For a given letter in the initial message, finding its encryption code symbol amounts to converting the letter to the C++ index collection range (0 to 25, in this case) and returning the letter stored in that position of the collection. (Lowercase letters are first replaced by uppercase letters prior to conversion.) Thus direct access to the code symbol is achieved through a simple computation determining the index to the table entry containing the correct symbol.

There are enough similarities between this problem and our previous examples in this chapter that we could have stored the code symbols in an object of type `letter_collection`, defined as

```
typedef index_coll_v2<char> letter_collection;
```

However, we have chosen not to do this for several reasons. First, a number of changes to this class would have been required to adapt it as a class useful for our program:

- The initialization process is considerably different from simply setting all elements of our collection to the same value. In this problem, initialization of the code table requires the program user to enter the code symbols at the keyboard. These symbols must be read one at a time and stored in sequence in the table, beginning with the first table element and ending with the last.
- Once this initialization is complete, there is no need for storing additional or changed information in the table. Thus not only is the initialization going to be different but also there will be no need at all for the member function `store`. (There is still a need for a retrieval function, although we will call it by a different name.)

Second, defining a new abstract data type unique to the cryptogram problem will enable us to illustrate several important points about program design. These and other issues are discussed at the end of this section.

We therefore define a new class, `code_table`, to represent the abstract data type of the cryptogram code translation table. This type requires a single attribute, an array (`code_array`) of fixed size (27 character type elements, including space for the null character), which we can use first to store the translation code symbols corresponding to the letters `'A'`, `'B'`, ..., `'Z'` and then to retrieve the correct code symbol for each letter in a message to be encrypted. The first element of `code_array` (corresponding to the letter `'A'`) will contain the code symbol for `'A'`; the second element (corresponding to `'B'`) will contain the code symbol for `'B'`; and so on.

Using `code_array` as a *look-up table*, we will be able to access the code symbol for a given uppercase letter by first converting the letter to the legal index value (once again, 0 though 25) and then using this value to access the proper element of the collection. Two member functions will be included in the class: `read_code`, which is used to read in and store a cryptogram code translation table, and `encrypt`, which is used to encrypt a letter in a message (by returning the code that corresponds to the given letter). The conversion of the uppercase letter to an index is part of `encrypt`.

This discussion concerning the new `code_table` class is summarized in the class information summary shown next. We will continue to use a summary of this sort to map out the pertinent information about all new classes that we introduce from this point on in the text.

CLASS INFORMATION SUMMARY FOR code_table

> *Attributes*
>
> code_array (character array)   — contains code for each letter
>   (size 27)
>
> *Member Functions (public)*
>
> read_code   — reads user-specified string of codes
>   (no arguments)
> encrypt   — returns a code corresponding to
>   *arguments:*   input letter
>   1. letter to be encrypted   — input, type `char`
>
> *Member functions (private)*
>
> get_index   — converts a letter to the index of the
>   element of code_array containing its
>   *arguments:*   code symbol
>   1. letter to be converted   — input, type `char`

> *Exceptions*
>
> 1. Invalid character (not a letter) passed to encrypt. (This exception is not handled in this solution.)

As this summary shows, we first list all attributes to be declared in the class (usually in the private section); then we list all of the public member functions along with a description of the arguments of each (if any). These functions must be accessible to the client program if the class is to serve its purpose. Finally, we list each of the important *exceptions* that should be taken care of by the class. These exceptions are events that could cause a serious failure in our software. For each such exception, the relevant member functions should be indicated and the required corrective action (if any) specified. For example, if an error is detected in the code string (by `read_code`), the string should be retyped because there is little reason to continue execution if the code string is not entered correctly. On the other hand, if an error is detected in the message to be encoded, it might be sufficient to print a diagnostic message to this effect, skip the illegal symbol in the message, and continue executing.

Normally, the decisions concerning corrective action in cases of errors will be specified by the customer who gives you a problem description. Your instructor (as the customer in this case) might have a different idea as to proper corrective action for the exceptions just described, and you may be asked to incorporate these corrective actions into the functions in the class `code_table` (see Programming Exercise 2 at the end of this section).

Once the required class summaries have been prepared for a problem, we should expect to have enough information about the interface between the class and its client program so that we can complete work on the design and implementation of this program. In this case, however, to keep together the development information for each component of our problem solution, we complete the development for the `code_table` class before returning to the development of the main function. We begin by providing the data requirements and design information for the two public member functions associated with the class.

DATA REQUIREMENTS FOR read_code

Input Arguments

(none)

Output Arguments

(none)

Local Variables

next_letter (char)   — loop control variable and value used to access correct element of code translation table

ALGORITHM FOR read_code

1. Display the alphabet `'A'` through `'Z'` as an aid to the user in reading the code symbols once they have been read in by the program.
2. Read the code symbols as one string into the code array.

DATA REQUIREMENTS FOR encrypt

Input Arguments

in_letter (char)   — letter to be encrypted

Output Arguments

(none)

Local Constants

uppercase_letters (char)   — initialized to the 26 uppercase letters

Local Variables

index (integer)   — index of current message letter in the
                                     uppercase letters array

ALGORITHM FOR encrypt

1. If the character to be encrypted is a letter
    1.1. Get the index of the letter in the uppercase letters array.
    1.2. Return the element of the code translation table selected by the
          index.

Implementation of the Class code_table

The C++ code for the class `code_table` is shown in Fig. 12.11. The
`read_code` function asks the user to enter an uppercase letter code for each
letter of the alphabet, `'A'` through `'Z'`. For a given letter in the original message, the function `encrypt` performs the retrieval of the code symbol. The
function converts any lowercase letters in the original message to uppercase
before performing the retrieval. If the character being processed is not a letter,
it is returned unaltered (but no diagnostic message is printed).

Figure 12.11   `code_table` **class implementation**

```
// FILE: CrypCode.h
// CRYPTOGRAM GENERATOR

#ifndef CRYPCODE_H_             // used to avoid multiple definitions
#define CRYPCODE_H_

#include <ctype.h>

class code_table
{
   public:
      // Member functions ...
      // READS IN THE CODE SYMBOL FOR EACH LETTER
      void read_code ();
      // RETURNS CODE SYMBOL FOR GIVEN CHARACTER
      char encrypt
        (char);                    // IN: character to encode

   private:
      // Data members ...
      enum {max = 26};
      char code_array[max+1];      // code array
}; // end class
```

(Continued)

Figure 12.11 (Continued)

```
// READS IN THE CODE SYMBOL FOR EACH LETTER
void code_table::read_code ()

// Pre:  None
// Post: 26 data values are read into array code_array.
{
   // Local data ...
   char next_letter;

   cout << "First let's specify the code." << endl;
   cout << "Enter a code symbol under each letter listed below."
        << endl;
   cout << "ABCDEFGHIJKLMNOPQRSTUVWXYZ" << endl;
   cin.get (code_array, max + 1);    // get 26 characters, store
                                     //      in code_array
   cout << endl;
   return;
}  // end read_code


// RETURNS CODE SYMBOL FOR A GIVEN LETTER
char code_table::encrypt
   (char in_letter)                  // IN: letter to be encrypted

// Pre:  Code_array and in_letter are defined.
// Post: Returns code corresponding to in_letter.
{
   // Local data ...
   int index;

   if (isalpha (in_letter) != 0)
   {
      in_letter = toupper (in_letter);
      index = int (in_letter) - int ('A');
      return (code_array[index]);
   }
   else
      return (in_letter);
}  // end encrypt

#endif // CRYPCODE_H_
```

Analysis for Main Function

The data requirements for the main function are shown next.

DATA REQUIREMENTS

Problem Constant

sentinel = '#' (char)   — sentinel value for encryption loop

Problem Input

next_char (char)   — next character in original message that is
                                     to be encoded

Problem Output

Each character of the cryptogram

Local Variables

code (code_table)   — contains the code symbols for each letter
code_letter (char)   — code symbol corresponding to next_char

Program Design

The structure chart for the Cryptogram Generator Problem is shown in Fig.
12.12; the algorithm follows the chart. The program begins by initializing the
code table and asking the user to type in the message to be encoded. It then

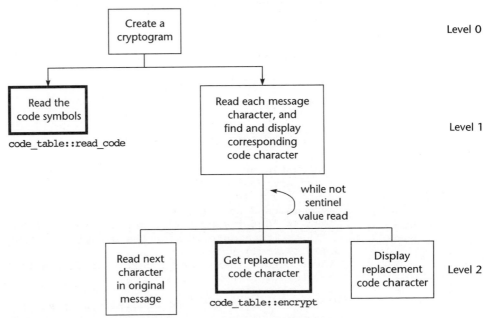

Figure 12.12 **Structure chart for Cryptogram Generator**

steps through this message, one character at a time, and retrieves and prints the encryption code for each letter. This continues until a sentinel character (#) is encountered, at which point the program terminates execution. The implementation of the main function is shown in Fig. 12.13. We can see that once the `code_table` class has been implemented, the main function can be easily written using the operations defined in this class.

INITIAL ALGORITHM

1. Initialize the code table (`code_table::read_code`)
2. Read each message character, determine the code replacement character, and display the code replacement character.

STEP 2 REFINEMENT

    2.1. Display prompt.
    2.2. Process one character at a time as long as it is not the sentinel:
        2.2.1. Read the next character.
        2.2.2. Determine the corresponding code character (`code_table::encrypt`).
        2.2.3. Display the code character.

Figure 12.13   **Cryptogram Generator and sample output**// FILE: CryptoGr.cpp

```
// CRYPTOGRAM GENERATOR

#include <iostream.h>

#include "CrypCode.h"

void main ()
{
  // Local data ...
  const char sentinel = '#';

  code_table my_code;           // class code_table
  char next_char;               // next character read in

  my_code.read_code ();
  cout << "Enter your entire message on one line; "
       << "terminate it with the symbol " << sentinel << endl;
  cout << endl;
  for (cin.get (next_char); next_char != sentinel;
       cin.get (next_char))
  {
    char code_letter = my_code.encrypt (next_char);
```

(Continued)

Figure 12.13   (Continued)

```
    cout << code_letter;
  }

  cout << endl;
  return;
}
```

─────── Program Output ───────

```
First let's specify the code.
Enter a code symbol under each letter listed below.
ABCDEFGHIJKLMNOPQRSTUVWXYZ
BCDEFGHIJKLMNOPQRSTUVWXYZA

Enter your entire message on one line;
terminate it with the symbol #

This is the 9%&! Place.#
UIJT JT UIF 9%&! QMBDF.#
```

Program Testing

In the sample run shown in Fig. 12.13, the code symbol for each letter is entered directly beneath that letter and read by function `read_code`. The sample run ends with two output lines: The first contains the message; the second contains its cryptogram. For one simple test, try using each letter as its own code symbol. In this case, both lines should be the same.

Commentary: Information Hiding—Generality versus Flexibility

The Cryptogram Problem solution illustrates a point of view regarding reuse that is somewhat different from what we have seen so far. Rather than directly reusing the code from the more general abstract data type `index_coll_v2`, we have chosen to use this abstract data type as a guide for designing a new class. In this new class, both the initialization (`read_code`) and retrieval (`encrypt`) member functions were largely recoded (and their names were changed). In addition, as pointed out earlier, the `store` function was eliminated because it was not needed.

In the Letter Count Problem, on the other hand, we were able to reuse the `index_coll_v2` class without modification. This has obvious advantages but also has an important disadvantage; that is, it prevents us from tailoring the class to the particular problem it is designed to serve.

Both approaches have merits. In some cases, it is useful to view existing software components as reusable in their most general form, with little or no modification. On the other hand, when substantial changes may be required to begin with, it may be more helpful to view an existing component as an adaptable or flexible sample for building a new component. The sample provides a guide as to the attributes and member functions that we need to consider in our new class, but it is then modified in any way needed to be most useful in our new application.

The choice of which approach to take in designing a problem solution should be made on the basis of the number and nature of the alterations needed to make an existing class (or class template) useful in a new application. Whichever choice you make, the existing component can help speed the development process.

Translating Problem Domain Index Sets to C++ Array Indexes

One of the issues addressed in both the Letter Count and the Cryptogram Problems involved the need to provide a mechanism for direct access to particular elements of the collection objects used in our solutions. In both cases, a letter was the most obvious problem domain data item for defining the element of the underlying object representation to be accessed. But this need not always be the case.

Many computer programming applications involve the use of indexed collections. In many of these applications, including those we have just examined, the program data used to control access to individual array elements are in some range other than 0 to `size-1` (as required by C++). In fact, in some cases, it would be convenient to be able to use enumerators, characters, or different ranges of integers (including, perhaps, negative numbers) as indexes, rather than just a set of integers beginning with the value 0.

As we showed in Chapter 9, C++ allows the use of enumerators (or, in fact, any expression having an integral result) as an array subscript. But C++ also requires all subscript values to be within the range 0 to `size-1` (for some integral value of size). When other index sets would be more natural or convenient, we are forced to convert these would-be subscripts to the proper range (starting at 0) before accessing the array in question. Examples of such conversions are illustrated in Table 12.3. In the third column of this table, `subs` represents the actual subscript value (between 0 and `size-1`) required to access the array; the variable to the right of the assignment operator represents the desired subscript set based on a typical description of the problem (as indicated in column 2).

Table 12.3   Data Conversions for Direct Access to Array Elements

DESIRED APPLICATION	INDEX SET	CONVERSION
A simulation program to count the frequency of each possible roll (`roll_value`) of a pair of dice.	Integer: range 2 to 12.	`subs = roll_value - 2` (range 0 to 10)
A conversion table for degrees Fahrenheit to Celsius with conversion values required to range from −25 degrees F to 125 degrees F.	Integer: range −25 to +125.	To look up a given temperature in degrees F and obtain the corresponding temperature in degrees C. `subs = degF + 25` `degC = convert(subs)` (range 0, ..., 150)
Keeping track of the number of occurrences of each uppercase letter in this text (as in Letter Count Problem).	Character: range `'A'` to `'Z'`.	Define subs via a search (such as `lin_search`) to find index of the desired letter (range 0, ..., 25)
The number of Temple University faculty teaching on each of the seven days of the week.	Enumeration: enum day {sun, mon, ..., sat} this_day;.	The enumerators shown here may be used as subscripts as long as the array in question contains at least seven elements.

The examples in Table 12.3 illustrate two approaches to handling these conversions. In the Letter Count Problem, the conversion was handled in the main function and was invisible to the reused indexed collection class. In the Cryptogram Problem, the conversion was carried out in member function `encrypt` in the `code_table` class, out of view of the main function. We believe there are valid arguments to support either approach. For example, it can be argued that the need for the conversion is inherent in the use of an indexed collection—some mechanism, either a direct access or a search (or in some cases both), is required to locate a particular collection element. The mechanism(s) should, by this argument, be hidden in the data abstraction itself.

On the other hand, it can also be argued that the nature of the mechanism is very much dependent on the problem application. To hide the mechanism (a simple computation in our examples thus far) in the class that implements the data abstraction is not natural, because the class should be as independent as possible of the application.

Clearly, if you reuse a general class such as `index_coll_v1` (which is highly application-independent), you should specify the conversion function outside the scope of, and therefore hidden from, this class. On the other hand, if you develop your own classes, highly specific to a particular problem, you will likely wish to specify the conversion function in the class itself, completely hidden from the client program. Either way, you should be aware of two things:

- there is indeed a decision to be made;
- whichever decision you make, the conversion to be performed should be implemented in a separate function so that the computation involved is hidden from the user (and so that changes may be made more easily).

Some Guidelines in Selecting Approaches to Class Implementation

The previous discussion on the development of classes may have taken you, perhaps for the first time, into a realm of unexpected indecision and confusion. This is a fine predicament, you may say; programming is not supposed to be this way. Well, for better or worse, the design and implementation of program systems are replete with such uncertainty. Part of our goal in this text is to make you aware of this fact. The rest, of course, is to lay the groundwork to help you resolve such conflicts (which are often far more complex than those we have visited thus far). As a start, we suggest the following guidelines, which may be helpful.

Guidelines for Designing Class Components

1. Begin now to build your own library of the most general components you know how to build. Examples of such components are the templates `index_coll_v1` and `index_coll_v2` and all of their derivatives for other data types. In addition, start now to become familiar with the components available in the libraries provided with the C++ language system you are using.
2. For each new problem that you solve, learn to create, from these general components, more specialized components for use in the given problem.
3. If possible, especially for complicated problems, stage the transition from the general to the specific by creating one or more layers of modules in between.
4. When creating a template, first design and thoroughly test a specific instance of the template, and then replace the specific types (or sizes, etc.) of this instance with the desired parameters. For example, before designing the class `index_coll_v1`, it would be best to build an instance such as `float_index_coll_v1`, thoroughly test this instance, and then use it to build the template by replacing the occurrences of `float` with the parameter `T`.

As we begin to solve larger, more complicated problems in later chapters, we will provide illustrations as to how this process might work. In later courses, as you become more adept at abstraction and the use of objects, you will gain additional insights into how to define components even more general than the array classes illustrated in this chapter. Thus, for example, you may create classes for storing data without regard to the type of the data, to the structure of the storage attribute, or to the access mechanism to be used. From these highly abstract classes, you will then learn how to work toward more specific versions of the classes that you need, finally reaching a class specific enough to your particular application to provide you with the information hiding and flexibility for change that you deem appropriate. This will not happen overnight; much trial and error and practice with a variety of problems will be required.

EXERCISES FOR SECTION 12.4

Self-Check

1. Provide array descriptions similar to those in Table 12.3 for the following applications.

   a. The floor-space area associated with each room in your house (living room, dining room, kitchen, etc.).
   b. The number of students in each grade of an elementary school.
   c. The legal special characters in C++, such as ".", "+", "*", ",", "{", "]", etc., as shown in Appendix D.

2. Prepare a structure chart and data requirements table for the Letter Counts Program shown in Fig. 12.10.
3. In the Letter Count Program, what happens if the character to be processed is neither an uppercase nor a lowercase letter?

Programming

1. Make changes to the Cryptogram Program to encode the blank character and the punctuation symbols , ; : , ?, !, and ..
2. Change functions `encrypt` and `read_code` in the Cryptogram Generator Problem class `code_table` to detect and take appropriate corrective action if a character other than an uppercase or lowercase letter is entered by the user either in the original message to be encrypted (main function) or in the encryption code letters (`code_table::read_code`). Take the corrective action indicated in this section, or redefine the corrective action as indicated by your instructor.
3. Modify the Letter Count Problem so that the letter counts are displayed at the end in descending order rather than in order by letter. Use a modified version of the Sort Program written in Chapter 9 (Section 9.5).
4. Complete the linear search function template, using the linear search function shown in Section 9.5 as needed.

12.5 —— COMMON PROGRAMMING ERRORS

• *Initialization of Attributes and const versus enum in Classes:* Beware of the use of the `const` declaration when declaring the attributes of a class. Initialization of class data members can be done only in a class constructor. In some situations you might want to define a constant to be globally accessible to one or more member functions of a class. This was the case, for example, in Fig. 12.1, where we wanted to name the default value for the size parameter of the constructor for the `index_coll_v1` class. The `const` declaration

```
const int max_count = 25;
```

would have been illegal inside the scope of the class definition (except in the class constructor). As discussed in Chapter 11, one solution to this problem is to place the `const` declaration near the top of the `.h` file, before the start of the class definition.

Another technique that allows us to define the desired identifier/constant association is to use the `enum` construct as shown next:

```
enum {max_count = 25};
```

Either approach will work, but `enum` may be used only if the constant is an integral value.

▪ *The new and delete Operators:* Remember that the `new` operator returns a pointer to an element of the type specified in the operation. This returned value must be stored in a pointer variable of the proper type, as in

```
collection = new float[size];
```

where collection must be a pointer variable of type `float`. Note, too, that the above statement, although similar in form, is quite a bit different from the statement

```
collection = new float(size);
```

The first statement defines `collection` as a pointer to a collection of `size` floating-point variables that are not necessarily initialized to any meaningful value. On the other hand, the second statement defines `collection` to point to a floating-point variable with an initial value of `size`.

All uses of `new` should be accompanied by a test for the null (0 value) pointer indicating that the requested memory allocation failed. At the very least, an error message should be displayed when such an event occurs because the likelihood of successful subsequent program execution is small.

The `delete` operator should be used only on a pointer variable containing the address of memory that is allocated from the free store using the `new` operator. A successful `delete` operation results in the return of the deleted memory to the free store. An attempt to apply `delete` to a pointer variable that is not pointing to dynamically allocated memory is undefined and can lead to unexpected behavior.

- *Constructors and Destructors:* Similar problems can be caused through seemingly minor syntax errors when constructors are referenced. For example,

```
const int family_size = 10;
...
int_index_coll_v1 ages (family_size);
```

results in the allocation of a single object of type `int_index_coll_v1`. The object would contain 10 elements of type integer (presumably, one for each member of a family). On the other hand, given the `counter` class defined in Chapter 11, the declaration

```
counter freq[10];
```

would cause the allocation of an array of 10 objects each of type `counter`. The declaration

```
counter freq(10);
```

would cause an error because the `counter` class has no constructor associated with it.

Remember, if you dynamically allocate memory in a constructor for a class object, you should deallocate the memory in a destructor when the object is destroyed (when it goes out of scope). The destructor is called automatically by the C++ system when the object is destroyed.

- *Index Expression Out of Bounds:* Because our indexed collections all use arrays to store data, they are susceptible to the same `"index expression out of bounds"` run-time error discussed in Chapter 9 (on common programming errors related to the use of arrays). This error occurs when the index value is outside the allowable range for the collection (array) being processed. Index out of bounds errors are discussed in more detail in Chapter 9. Remember, the indexed collection classes provide a run-time test for index out of bounds and provide an error message when this exception occurs. C++ provides no such test or message.

You should also double-check the subscript values at the loop boundaries. If these values are in range, it is likely that all other subscript references in the loop will be in range as well.

- *Template Definition and Use—Parameter Matching:* We have introduced only the simplest forms of definitions of classes and of class and function templates. We urge you to adhere scrupulously to these forms in your program coding. If necessary, especially in the early going, have someone else with more experience check what you have done. Classes and templates introduce a whole new vocabulary of terms into the world of programming. It may take a while for you to become familiar with these terms. As a result, you may encounter class and template compiler diagnostics that are difficult to understand. The best way to avoid these errors is to get some help in reviewing that your class does what it is supposed to do and that the syntax is correct.

Both template classes and functions have strict rules as to what constitutes a legal parameter and a legal parameter match. You should be sure, for example, that actual argument arrays in a function template reference are matched with formal argument arrays in the template definition, that pointers match pointers, that constants match constants, that floating-point actual arguments match floating-point formal arguments, and so on. For example, in the linear search function, failure to include the `const` specifier before the type `int` in the second argument of the template definition will result in an error when the constant 26 is used in referencing the function. Template classes allow only types, constants or constant expressions, and functions as parameters. Any other form of parameter is illegal.

CHAPTER REVIEW

In the first part of this chapter we emphasized the idea of building reusable data abstractions using the C++ class, the idea of inheritance, and the C++ template feature. We began with a discussion of a high-level data abstraction referred to as a collection of data of the same type. We then introduced a somewhat more specific version of this type, an indexed collection of data of the same type. The benefits of such abstractions and their C++ class implementations were discussed in terms of such software engineering issues as component reuse, information hiding, separation of concerns, and program testing and maintenance.

The construction of such abstract data types using the class constructor and the `new` operator was introduced, and the concept of the dynamic allocation of arrays was presented. The idea of building new abstract data types from existing ones was discussed at length, and several approaches were presented. The first involved extension/modification of existing class code and the definition of new classes on the basis of these changes.

The second tool for component reuse, the C++ template, was introduced in a somewhat limited form. The idea of defining classes and functions in terms of placeholder types was discussed and the C++ mechanism for specifying such a "parameterized" construct was illustrated. We then showed how new and different data types could be created from the same template class using a special declaration in which the type placeholder (and perhaps other placeholders as well) were replaced with actual "values." Two case studies and several examples illustrating these ideas were presented. The notion of a function template was also described and illustrated in an example.

New C++ Constructs

A number of new C++ constructs appeared in this chapter. Pointer variables and the new and `delete` operators were introduced. We illustrated how to use these constructs to define dynamic arrays—arrays whose size is determined at execution time. We then used dynamic arrays to implement indexed collection classes. In this chapter, dynamic memory allocation was confined to the constructors in these classes; deallocation was handled in the class destructors. Each of these constructs is summarized in Table 12.4.

Table 12.4 Constructs for Dynamic Memory Allocation

EXAMPLE	EFFECT
Pointer Variable	
`float *p;`	Declares p as a variable in which only pointers to data elements of type `float` may be stored.
new Operator	
`p = new int;` `p = new float[50];`	The first example causes the allocation of a memory location to store a single integer value and stores a pointer to this location in p. The second example causes the allocation of 50 memory locations for floating-point data and stores the pointer to the first of these locations in p. The allocated memory is taken from the heap.
delete Operator	
`delete p;` `delete [] p;`	Causes the deallocation of the memory locations previously allocated using the new operator.

A destructor should be included in any class in which the constructor contains dynamic memory allocation using the new operator. The destructor, specified with the same name as the class name preceded by a tilde, ~, uses the C++ delete operator to deallocate the memory allocated by the constructor. Destructors are automatically executed by the C++ run-time system when an object of a user-defined type goes out of scope.

In the remainder of the chapter, we focused on issues related to the design and implementation of C++ class and function templates. (Displays for both forms of templates are provided in Section 12.3.) We showed how these parameterized constructs could be used to produce entire families of classes (or functions) via substitution for the parameters specified in the template definition. For classes, we specify the desired substitution using a type definition statement such as

```
typedef container<int, 50> integer_container;
typedef index_coll_v2<float> float_index_coll_v2;
```

The class template parameters are enclosed in the symbols <>. The name that precedes these symbols is the name of a class template. The name that follows is that of a new data type defined by the type definition statement. Once this type is defined, we can declare objects of this type in much the same way as we declare objects of any of the C++ types, such as `float`, `int`, or any of the user-defined types involving, for example, the use of structs or enumerators:

```
integer_container frequency_distribution;
float_index_coll_v2 monthly_sales_total (12, 0.0);
```

The second of these declarations specifies the allocation of memory for a single object of type `float_index_coll_v2`. The parameter (12) specifies the size of the object; this object is large enough to contain 12 floating-point data elements.

Templates are an important C++ feature for writing reusable program components.

✔ QUICK-CHECK EXERCISES

1. Describe one advantage of using a language that allows for the definition of new, user-defined data types.
2. Why can't character data be used directly to access the indexed collections illustrated in this chapter?
3. Can values of different types be stored in the same indexed collection? Why or why not?
4. List four concepts fundamental to building good software that are supported by the C++ class feature.
5. A class is used to encapsulate the _____(insert several words)_____of a user-defined data type.
6. List at least three advantages that accrue from using the C++ class to define a new data type such as the indexed collection.
7. The `new` operator causes memory to be allocated from the _____ for use by your program. The _____ operator is used to return this memory to the place from which it was taken.
8. The _____ feature of C++ enables the programmer to specify _____ and _____ in terms of parameterized types.
9. Describe how the `lin_search` function was used in the Letter Count Program.
10. Discuss a major advantage of designing our own class for `code_table` (see the Cryptogram Generator Problem) over reusing an existing class.

Answers to Quick-Check Exercises

1. User-defined data types can be used to expand the domain of objects that we can manipulate in solving a problem.
2. The main problem is that their integral (ASCII) values are not in the correct range of integer values for our collections.

3. No. Arrays are used as the basic storage structure for collection elements.
4. abstraction, encapsulation, information hiding, and component reuse
5. details of data representation and manipulation
6. ▪ It hides lower-level details of processing the elements of a collection from the rest of the program;
   ▪ It helps maintain the integrity of the data stored in the collection by restricting access to these data;
   ▪ It provides the basis for extending our earlier ideas on component reuse;
   ▪ It simplifies program testing.
   ▪ It simplifies program maintenance, minimizing the possibility that change in one component of a program will impact others.
7. free store; `delete`
8. template; classes, functions
9. It was used to look up a letter in an array (string) of letters and determine the index (string position) of the letter in the array. This index was then used directly to select the element of the counter collection to be incremented.
10. We were able to hand tailor our new class precisely to the needs of the problem, hiding all of those operations and only those needed to solve the problem. We did not need to remove, add, or change any operations to accommodate the new problem. We were even able to use meaningful names for these functions.

REVIEW QUESTIONS

1. a. What would happen if we attempted to use an uppercase letter (its ASCII value) directly to designate the element of the uppercase counter collection to be incremented when the letter appeared in our text?
   b. When would the error be detected?

2. In Chapter 9 we introduced the array data structure. In this chapter we wrote several programs that essentially used arrays in solving a problem. However, array declarations virtually disappeared from these programs. How did this come about?

3. Write a function `get_index` as a member function of the class `float_index_coll_v2`. `get_index` should search its indexed collection for a floating-point input argument and return the index (position) of the argument if it is found and –1 if it is not found. Illustrate a call to `get_index` from outside the class `float_index_coll_v2`. `get_index` is virtually identical to the function `lin_search` (see Chapter 9), but it has one argument instead of three. Why?

4. Write a template function `compute` that takes two arguments a and b of type `T` and a third argument op of type `char` and computes the value of

   `a op b`

   You may assume that if op is not one of the characters +, –, *, or /, no operation is performed—a diagnostic message is printed instead, and any result value may be returned. Write a short driver program to test this function. For all calls involving character type arguments, what would you expect to be returned by each of the operators '+', '–', '*', '/' ? Explain your answer in each case.

5. (continuation of Question 4) How does the compiler know which version of the template function is required (so that the correct version of the arithmetic operations is used with the specified operands)?

6. Write a function `copy` for the class `index_coll_v1` that takes an argument of type `index_coll_v1` and one of type `int` (indicating the number of elements stored in the first argument) and copies the elements from this collection into the collection specified in the call. (Thus, if `x` and `y` are both of type `index_coll_v1<int>`, the call

```
x.copy(y, get_count(y));
```

causes the contents of `y` to be copied to `x`.) Be careful to copy as many elements of the argument collection as possible, but without overflowing the collection `x`. Check for errors and output meaningful diagnostic messages should an error occur.

7. Convert the sort function `sel_sort` written in Chapter 9 to a template function in which the parameter `T` is used to specify the base type of the elements of the array to be sorted. The functions `find_min` and `exchange`, written as part of `sel_sort`, should be similarly converted to templates.

8. Use any of the class components (or parts thereof) defined in this chapter and build a class that could be used to store your monthly earnings and the total of these earnings for the year.

9. Use the template `index_coll_v1` defined in this chapter to build a class that could be used to store course grades (as letters) for all of the courses you have taken thus far in your college career. Write an additional function called `compute_gpa` that computes your overall GPA given this collection of grades.

   a. First write `compute_gpa` as a function that is part of the main program and that uses the `retrieve` method of the class to retrieve each grade from the class as it computes the GPA.

   b. Then write `compute_gpa` as a member function of the class that returns a floating-point GPA accurate to two decimal places.

   In either case, use whatever grade weight and GPA computation rule is used at your school.

PROGRAMMING PROJECTS

For all problems in this section, use indexed collections for storing and manipulating each collection of data required. Either build your own indexed collection classes or use derivatives of the classes and class templates defined in this chapter. Some additional hints are given as needed.

1. Write a program to read n data items into two floating-point indexed collections X and Y of size 20. Store the product of corresponding elements of X and Y in a third collection, Z1, and the sum in a fourth collection, Z2, also of size 20. Print a four-column table displaying the collections X, Y, Z1, and Z2. Then compute and print the square root of the sum of the items in Z1 *only*. Make up your own data, with n less

than 20. As indicated, X, Y, Z1, and Z2 should be modeled (represented) as floating-point collections. Each collection should have defined in it two functions, add and mul, one each for the addition and multiplication operations. These functions should take two operands, both of the same object type—floating-point indexed collections. To perform the multiplication indicated by the mathematical expression $Z = X * Y$, you need to write the C++ function reference

```
z.mul(x, y);
```

2. (Optional) Present a discussion concerning a class of vectors, where a vector may be considered an array of floating-point elements of some size given by size. n might be the number of valid entries in the vector; the vector need not always be filled. Pattern your discussion after the one in Section 11.6 on the complex data type. Be sure to find out about vectors and the meaningful mathematical operations defined on them before designing your class. (Your instructor may give you a brief lecture on this or direct you to a math book for additional reading.) Where convenient, you should feel free to assume that some of these operators (if not all) are implemented as function operators (but you need not carry out the implementation).

3. Assume for the moment that your computer has the very limited capability of being able to read and print only single decimal digits at a time, and to add two integers consisting of one decimal digit each. Write a program to read in two integers of up to 10 digits each, add these numbers, and print the result. Test your program on the following numbers:

```
X = 1487625
Y =   12783

X = 60705202
Y = 30760832

X = 1234567890
Y = 9876543210
```

Hints: Store the numbers X and Y in two integer indexed collections X, Y of size 10, one decimal digit per element. If the number is less than 10 digits in length, enter enough leading zeros (in the first few elements of the corresponding collection) to make the number 10 digits long:

	Collection X											Collection Y									
[0]	[1]	[2]	[3]	[4]	[5]	[6]	[7]	[8]	[9]		[0]	[1]	[2]	[3]	[4]	[5]	[6]	[7]	[8]	[9]
0	0	0	1	4	8	7	6	2	5		0	0	0	0	0	1	2	7	8	3

You will need a loop to add the digits in corresponding collection elements, starting with the element with index 9. Don't forget to handle the carry if there is one! Use an integer variable carry (value 0 or 1) to indicate whether or not the sum of the last pair of digits added is greater than 9.

4. Write a program for the following problem. You are given a collection of scores for the last exam in your computer course. You are to compute the average of these scores and then assign grades to each student according to the following rule: If a student's score is within 10 points (above or below) of the average, assign the stu-

dent a grade of Satisfactory. If the score is more than 10 points higher than the average, assign the student a grade of Outstanding. If the score is more than 10 points below the average, assign the student a grade of Unsatisfactory. The output from your program should consist of a labeled three-column list containing the initials, exam score, and grade of each student.

Define a `struct` named `student` to store all the information about each student—the student's three initials, the exam score, and the grade. Then define a new type that is at least based on the type `index_coll_v1<student>`. All operations associated with this collection of students should be hidden in this new type. If you can use the `index_coll_v1` template to your advantage, do so. Otherwise, pattern your class after this one, using whatever ideas are relevant.

5. It can be shown that a number is prime if there is no smaller prime number that divides it. Consequently, in order to determine whether n is prime, it is sufficient to check only the prime numbers less than n as possible divisors. Use this information to write a program that stores the first 100 prime numbers in an integer indexed collection. Have your program print the collection after it is done.

6. The results of a survey of the households in your township have been made available. Each record contains data for one household, including a four-digit integer identification number, the annual income for the household, and the number of members in the household. Write a program to read the survey results into three collections and perform the following analyses:

   a. Count the number of households included in the survey and print a three-column table displaying the data read in. (You may assume that no more than 25 households were surveyed.)

   b. Calculate the average household income, and list the identification number and income of each household that exceeds the average.

   c. Determine the percentage of households having incomes below the poverty level. The poverty level income may be computed using the formula

   $$p = \$6500.00 + \$750.00(m - 2),$$

   where m is the number of members of each household. This formula shows that the poverty level depends on the number of family members, m, and that the poverty level increases as m gets larger.

   For this program, you may want to define a `struct` to contain the relevant data items for each household. Then define an indexed collection of data of that `struct` type for storing the information about all the households.

   Test your program on the following data:

Identification Number	Annual Income	Household Members
1041	$12,180	4
1062	$13,240	3
1327	$19,800	2
1483	$22,458	8
1900	$17,000	2
2112	$18,125	7
2345	$15,623	2

3210	$3,200	6
3600	$6,500	5
3601	$11,970	2
4725	$8,900	3
6217	$10,000	2
9280	$6,200	1

7. Write a template class for an ordered indexed collection of data that is initialized by reading from a data file and that automatically sorts these initial data in ascending order as soon as the read is complete. Thus the sort is part of the initialization process, but the `sort` function should not be callable by any client. Your `store` operation should be written as an insert function that is required to maintain the order of the data (it will need to find the proper position for the insert, push all the data beyond this point back one element in the collection, and then insert the new element into the open position in the collection). If the collection is full when an insert is requested, print an error message and ignore the insert. The only other required operation is a search that looks up a data item and returns its index (or −1 if the item is not found). Your instructor may ask you to write a special kind of search called a *binary search*, which is particularly effective for ordered data.

13

The String Data Type

13.1   String Functions in the string.h Library

13.2   An Illustration of Character String
        Processing
        CASE STUDY: Printing a Form Letter

13.3   Variable-Length Strings (Optional)

13.4   Common Programming Errors
        Chapter Review

In Chapter 9 we introduced the character string (an array of characters terminated by the null character, '\0') and some of the functions provided in the
standard library `string.h`. In this chapter we describe more of the functions
provided in `string.h`. We then show how these functions can be used to
build simple text-processing applications. Finally, we demonstrate the power
of C++ to define a string data type (class) of variable length, which is more
flexible than the standard character string type.

13.1 ___ STRING FUNCTIONS IN THE string.h LIBRARY

Recall from Chapter 9 that there are no operators, such as '+', defined in C++
for use with the character strings. Not even the assignment operator, =, may
be used to assign (copy) one string to another in an executable statement. In
fact, unless you build your own string data type (as shown at the end of this
chapter), you will need to rely on the string functions in the C++ library
`string.h` to perform operations on strings. Table 13.1 presents a summary
description of the most commonly used functions in `string.h`. The use of
these functions is illustrated in the examples that follow. If you examine the
function definitions in the `string.h` library, you will see that the formal
arguments `src` and `trg` are of type `char *`, and `csrc` and `ctrg` are of type
`const char *`. Recall from Chapter 12 that the notation *type* `*` indicates a
"pointer to *type*." In C++, when an array name is used as the actual argument
in a function call, a pointer to (address of) the first element of that array is
passed to the called function. Pointer notation (using the asterisk) is therefore
consistent with the C++ array argument passing mechanism.

In this text, when defining functions that take arrays as arguments, we so far
have used the notation *type*[ ] or *type variable*[ ] rather than the notation *type* `*`
or *type* `*name`. The first two notations better express the intent of the programmer to manipulate an array. However, because the `string.h` functions and
many other C++ references use the *type* `*` notation, it is important to be familiar with this notation as well. Whichever notation you use, it is important to
understand that C++ uses a pointer to the first element of the array when
passing an actual argument array to a function. Therefore, when working with
character strings, we need to be sure to pass a character array (a string) or a
pointer to a place within a string as the actual argument corresponding to
each of the formal arguments `src`, `trg`, `csrc`, and `ctrg`. We must also
remember that although string constants such as `"Dara G. Friedman"` can
be used in correspondence to `const char *` formal arguments (`csrc` and
`ctrg`), these string constants cannot be used with `char *` arguments.

Table 13.1 Commonly Used Functions in the `string.h` Library*

FUNCTION	DESCRIPTION
`char *strcpy (trg, csrc)`	Copy string `csrc` to string `trg` including `'\0'`; return a pointer to (address of) `trg`.
`char *strncpy (trg, csrc, n)`	Copy at most n characters of string `csrc` to string `trg`; pad `trg` with `'\0'` if `csrc` has fewer than n characters; return a pointer to (address of) `trg`.
`char *strcat (trg, csrc)`	Concatenate string `csrc` with its null character to the end of string `trg`; return a pointer to (address of) `trg`.
`char *strncat (trg, csrc, n)`	Concatenate at most n characters of string `csrc` to string `trg`; terminate `trg` with `'\0'`; return a pointer to (address of) `trg`.
`int strcmp (ctrg, csrc)`	Compare string `ctrg` to `csrc`; return an integer < 0 if `ctrg` $<$ `csrc`, 0 if `ctrg` $==$ `csrc`, and an integer > 0 if `ctrg` $>$ `csrc`.
`int strncmp (ctrg, csrc, n)`	Compare at most n characters of string `ctrg` to `csrc`; return an integer < 0 if `ctrg` $<$ `csrc`, 0 if `ctrg` $==$ `csrc`, and an integer > 0 if `ctrg` $>$ `csrc`.
`char *strchr (ctrg, c)`	Return a pointer to (address of) the first occurrence of `c` in string `ctrg`; return NULL if `c` is not present in `ctrg`.
`char *strrchr (ctrg, c)`	Return a pointer to (address of) the last occurrence of `c` in string `ctrg`; return NULL if `c` is not present in `ctrg`.
`char *strpbrk (ctrg, csrc)`	Return a pointer to first occurrence of any character in `csrc` that is also in the string `ctrg`; return NULL if no characters in `csrc` are present in `ctrg`.
`char *strstr (ctrg, csrc)`	Return a pointer to first occurrence of the string `csrc` that is found in `ctrg`; return NULL if the string `csrc` is not present in `ctrg`.
`size_t strlen (csrc)`	Return the length of `csrc` (not including `'\0'`). The type `size_t` is a special integer type used in C++ to define the size of objects. For our purposes, it may be treated as an `int`.

*In this table, the arguments `trg` (target) and `src` (source) are strings (arrays of characters), arguments `ctrg` and `csrc` are constant character arrays—that is, they cannot be altered by the described function. `c` is a character; n is an integer.

Some subtle differences between *type*[ ] and *type* * go beyond the scope of this text. One of these differences is that the notation *type* [ ] cannot be used to designate the return type of a function. Therefore, the return of an array using a `return` statement is accomplished by returning the pointer to (address of) the first element of the array. These points and others are illustrated in the following examples.

Example 13.1   The function `strixstr` shown in Fig. 13.1 returns the index of the first occurrence of the string `csrc` in the string `ctrg`. The value –1 is returned if `csrc` does not appear anywhere in `ctrg`.

Figure 13.1   Function to return index of a substring in another string

```
// FILE: StrIndex.cpp
// RETURNS THE INDEX OF THE FIRST OCCURRENCE OF THE STRING csrc IN
//    THE STRING ctrg. RETURNS -1 IF csrc IS NOT PRESENT IN ctrg

int strixstr
   (const char ctrg [],    // IN: (target) string to be searched
    const char csrc [])    // IN: (source) string to be matched in
                           //     ctrg

// Pre:  ctrg and csrc must be defined.
// Post: i is index in target of first character of source string
//       if source is found.
// Returns: index in target of first occurrence of source string
//          or -1 if source not present in target.
{
   // Local data ...
   int i, j, k;

   // Search target string until it matches the source
   //    string or the end of the target string is encountered.
   for (i = 0; ctrg[i] != '\0'; i++)
   {
      for (j = i, k = 0;
           csrc[k] != '\0' && ctrg[j] == csrc[k];
           j++, k++);
         if (k > 0 && csrc[k] == '\0')
            return i;
   }  // end for

   return -1;
}
```

Figure 13.2 illustrates the argument passing mechanism used when `strixstr` is called with character array `name` of size 50 as the first argument and a character array `subs` of size 4 as the second argument.

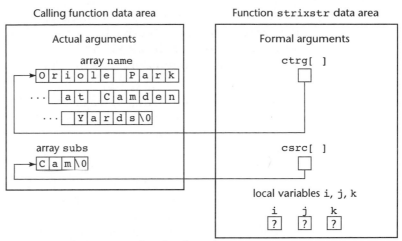

Figure 13.2 Argument passing for function strixstr   ■

As shown, pointers to the first character of the array arguments are passed to the function strixstr, and all references to the names csrc and ctrg are in fact references to the actual arguments in the memory area of the calling module. For this particular example, assuming that the entire string stored in name is "Oriole Park at Camden Yards", a value of 15 would be returned for the required index.

Example 13.2   Assuming index is an integer variable and name and subs are character arrays as defined in Example 13.1, then the function call

```
index = strixstr (name, subs);
```

returns the index value 15, which is stored in index.

We can accomplish the very same task as performed by strixstr using the string.h function strstr. This function behaves in a similar manner to strixstr, but it returns a pointer to the first occurrence of the target string rather than the index, as returned by strixstr. Thus the function call

```
strptr = strstr (name, subs);
```

returns a pointer to the character 'C', the first letter of the substring "Camden" in the string name. The value of the difference

```
index = strptr - name;
```

is 15. Thus, the statements

```
strptr = strstr (name, subs);
index = strptr - name;
```

together provide the same information as provided by the function `strixstr`. The benefit of using these two statements is that we do not have to write a new function ourselves. We simply reuse an existing function in the `string.h` library to produce the same result. ∎

Example 13.3   Let `from` and `to` be strings (arrays of characters) of 35 and 45 elements, respectively; and assume that `from` contains the string `"Most students will graduate!"` Then the function reference

```
strncpy (to, from, 18);
```

copies the 18-character string `"Most students will"` from the array `from` to the first 18 elements of the array `to`. A pointer to `to` is returned. We make no use of this return value in the above statement. The remaining 27 elements of `to` are left undisturbed by this copy. Because the 18 characters copied do not contain the character `'\0'`, this character does not appear in the first 18 characters of the array `to`. Function `strncpy` copies at most n characters (if not stopped sooner by the `'\0'` character). In any case, the `'\0'` is not copied or inserted into the `to` string. ∎

Example 13.4   We need to write a C++ code segment to convert any name of the form

```
Lisa W. Ernst
```

to the last-name-first form

```
Ernst, Lisa W.
```

Let `fnf_name` and `lnf_name` be the two character arrays (size 20) to be used for this exercise, and let `period_ptr` be of type `char *`. Assume that the array `fnf_name` contains the first-name-first information properly terminated by `'\0'`. We can accomplish the required task using the following sequence of C++ `string.h` function calls:

```
period_ptr = strchr (fnf_name, '.');
// copy last name
strcpy (lnf_name, period_ptr + 2);
strncat (lnf_name, ", ", 2);   // concatenate comma, blank and '\0'
strncat (lnf_name, fnf_name, period_ptr - fnf_name + 1);
```

We begin by establishing the pointer to the period following the middle initial. Adding 2 to this pointer provides the position in `fnf_name` of the first character of the last name. The `strcpy` function then copies all the characters, beginning with the character referenced by the second argument, `'E'` in this case, up to and including the `'\0'`.

Next, we concatenate the two characters `", "` to the current end of `lnf_name`, obtaining the partially completed string `"Ernst, \0"`. Note that `strncat` always terminates the newly created string with '\0'. The *pointer expression*

```
period_ptr - fnf_name + 1
```

is an example of an integer computation involving the manipulation of pointers. This particular expression is used to determine the number of characters in the first part (first name and middle initial) of the name. Once we have obtained this value, we can concatenate the characters in the first part of the name to the current end of `lnf_name`, obtaining the completed string `"Ernst, Lisa W."`

∎

The above example provides a simple illustration of the use of pointers and pointer expressions in C++ code. Such pointer manipulation is an important feature of C++ and a powerful programming tool in certain applications areas. However, it must be exercised carefully. As shown in the following display, only a limited number of pointer operations are allowed in C++.

∎

Pointer Arithmetic

Pointer variables contain addresses of computer memory cells. C++ allows some arithmetic operations to be performed on these addresses, but the set of operations is highly restricted so as to ensure the consistency of the results. Thus only a limited number of pointer operations are legal:

- assignment of pointers of the same type (for example, `char *` or `float *`);
- adding and subtracting a pointer and an integer;
- subtracting or comparing two pointers to members of the same array;
- assigning a pointer variable a value of 0 (the NULL pointer);
- comparison of a pointer to 0.

All other pointer arithmetic is illegal. For example, it is not legal to add two pointers or to divide or multiply them. It is also not legal to assign a pointer of one type to a pointer of another without a type cast.

The subtraction of pointers to objects in the same array always yields an integer value (for example, the length of a string). Thus computations such as

```
period_ptr - fnf_name + 1
```

can be used to determine the number of characters to be processed by appropriate C++ string functions. The subtraction of pointers that are not pointers to objects in the same array is not detected as an error by the compiler. The results, however, are not meaningful.

When the addition and subtraction of a pointer and an integer are involved, as in the expressions

```
period_ptr + 2
```

or

```
p++
```

automatic *scaling* is performed to provide the desired result. The effect of the scaling is to ensure that if the pointer involved in the operation points to a data item of a particular type, the newly computed pointer will also point to a data item of that type. The scaling done is determined by the declaration of the pointer. For a pointer to an integer or floating-point item of 4 bytes, the integer involved is scaled by 4. When single-byte characters are involved (as was the case in our example), the integer is scaled by 1.

Were this scaling not performed, the utility of pointer arithmetic would be greatly diminished. For example, in the previous example, we expect the sum

```
period_ptr + 2
```

to determine a pointer to an element of type char (in the array lnf_name). Similarly, we would want to be sure that if p pointed to a 4-byte integer, the pointer value p + 2 would also point to a 4-byte integer, specifically, the integer two elements beyond the one pointed to by p.

Note: The use of an array name by itself in an expression represents a pointer value and is subject to all of the limitations and conditions discussed in this box.

Example 13.5   *Referencing Individual Characters in a String.*   In C++ we can manipulate individual characters of a string just as we manipulate individual elements of any other array. For example, if her_name contains the string "A.C. Looper", the statements

```
her_name[0] = 'P';
her_name[5] = 'C';
```

change the value of her_name to the string "P.C. Cooper". If next_char is type char, the statement

```
next_char = her_name[1];
```

stores a period in next_char.

The following condition is true if i contains the value 1 or the value 3:

```
if (her_name[i] == '.')
   cout << "Period at position " << i << endl;
```

The statement

```
cout << "The character at position " << i << " in her_name is "
     << her_name[i] << endl;
```

prints the character at position i in the string her_name. The statement

```
cin >> her_name[i];
```

reads a character into the ith element of the string.

Individual string characters may also be passed as arguments to functions in the same way that other array elements are passed. Thus if `exchange` is a function to exchange the contents of two character variables, the statement

```
exchange (her_name[0], her_name[2]);
```

would change the value of `her_name` to `"C.P. Cooper"`.   ∎

Remember that when passing individual elements of a string (as opposed to an entire string or a substring) to a function, the same conventions apply as for simple (nonstructured) variables. (This is true for any array, not just type `char` arrays.)

Reading Characters into a String

As we have already seen in numerous examples, reading strings in C++ can be complicated. The iostream input operator (>>), on which we have relied heavily until now, skips over white space (blanks, tabs, newlines, etc.) as it looks for input values and stops scanning a value as soon as it finds the first white space following the input value. This works fine if we know the format of our input and can be sure that the appearance of white space will not interfere with the desired processing of our input.

For example, if we want to read data of the form

```
6 Jun 1946
```

and we know that one or more blanks will appear between the day and the month and between the month and the year, the statement

```
cin >> day >> month_name >> year;
```

will perform the input as desired (with `day` and `year` as `int` variables and `month_name` as a string).

To read input whose format is not fixed (or not known), it is often best to read a line at a time and then try to locate and process each of the pieces of data we need. In the following example, we illustrate one way this might be done.

Example 13.6 The function `read_date` shown in Fig. 13.3 is designed to read and store current date information entered on a single line in either the form

```
6 Jun 1946
```

or the form

```
6/6/46
```

Figure 13.3　Function to read the date

```
// FILE: "ReadDate.cpp"
// READ THE DATE IN EITHER MM/DD/YY FORMAT OR DD MMM YY FORMAT

#include <iostream.h>
#include <string.h>
#include <stddef.h>
#include <stdlib.h>

// READ DATE IN EITHER MM/DD/YY FORMAT OR DD MMM YY FORMAT
int read_date
  (int &month,                  // OUT: month number
   int &day,                    // OUT: day number
   int &year,                   // OUT: year number
   char *month_name)            // OUT: month name

// Pre : The user has been prompted to provide input via cin.
// Post: If the date is in mm/dd/yy format, month, day, and
//       year are set to the values read and 1 is returned.
//       If the date is in dd mmm yy format, day, month_name,
//       and year are set to the values read and 2 is returned.
//       If the format is invalid, -1 is returned.
{
    // Functions used ...
    // getline              member of istream class in iostream.h
    // strpbrk              from string.h
    // strcpy               from string.h
    // atoi                 from stdlib.h

    // Local data ...
    const int max_line = 80;    // The maximum size of an input line
    char line[max_line];        // Space to hold the input line
    char *first_separator;      // Pointer to the first separator
    char *second_separator;     // Pointer to the second separator

    cin.getline (line, max_line); // read an input line
    first_separator = strpbrk (line,"/ "); // find first '/' or ' '
    if (first_separator == NULL)
        return -1;              // invalid date format
    second_separator = strpbrk (first_separator + 1, "/ ");
    if (second_separator == NULL)
        return -1;              // invalid date format

    if ((*first_separator == '/') && (*second_separator == '/'))
    {
        *first_separator = '\0';
        *second_separator = '\0';
        month = atoi (line);
        day = atoi (first_separator + 1);
```

(Continued)

Figure 13.3   (Continued)

```
        year = atoi (second_separator + 1);
        return 1;
    }
    else if ((*first_separator == ' ') &&
             (*second_separator == ' '))
    {
        *first_separator = '\0';
        *second_separator = '\0';
        day = atoi (line);
        year = atoi (second_separator + 1);
        strcpy (month_name, first_separator + 1);
        return 2;
    }
    else
        return -1;
}   // end read_date
```

We have used the iostream function `getline` to read a line of characters. This function reads a line of characters into the first character string argument (`line` in this case). The read continues until one of the following occurs:

- an end-of-file is encountered;
- `max_line` – 1 characters has been read; or
- a special character is encountered.

The maximum number of characters to be read (`max_line` in this case) is specified as the second argument of `getline`, and the special character is specified as the third argument. If no third argument is given, the default third argument (the newline character) is used. The newline character is read, but the null character, not newline is placed at the end of the string. If `max_line` – 1 characters are read before the newline is encountered, reading stops, and the null character is placed at the end of the string just read. An illustration of how `getline` might work is provided in Example 13.7.

Once a full line is read, the function `strpbrk` is used to find the first occurrence in the line of any member of the string `"/ "`. We save this location in `first_separator`. If none is found, then the date format is invalid. Otherwise, we call `strpbrk` again to find the second occurrence, which is stored in `second_separator`. Again, if none is found, the date format is invalid. The state of the program data after the separators have been found is shown in Fig. 13.4.

If both separators are `'/'`, then the date format is *mm/dd/yy*. If both separators are a blank, then the date format is *dd mmm yy*. We then replace the separators with the `'\0'` character.

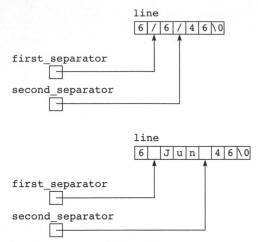

Figure 13.4   Results after separators found

The expression *first_separator used in read_date references the contents of the location pointed to by the address in first_separator as shown in Figs. 13.4 and 13.5. The unary operator * is called the *indirection operator*; its effect may be viewed as causing the pointer contained in its operand (first_separator in this case) to be *traversed* so that the actual memory location accessed is the one "pointed to" by the contents of first_separator and not first_separator itself.

In the expression

```
*first_separator == '/'
```

the indirection operator references an element of the array line (containing a '/' or ' '). The assignment

```
*first_separator = '\0';
```

does not alter the pointer in first_separator, but rather stores '\0' in the location (an element of line) pointed to by first_separator. The state of the program data (after the separators have been replaced) is now as shown in Fig. 13.5. line now represents a string that contains the month (in the *mm/dd/yy* format) or the day (in the *dd mmm yy* format). Starting at first_separator + 1 is a string that contains the day (*mm/dd/yy* format) or the month name (*dd mmm yy* format), and starting at second_separator + 1 is a string that contains the year. The standard function atoi (which is in the library stdlib.h) is used to convert the strings that contain integers into integer values.

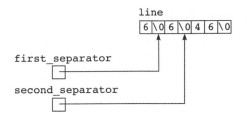

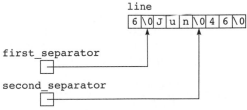

Figure 13.5   Results after separators are replaced by '\0'   ∎

Example 13.7   *An Illustration of* getline.   Figure 13.6 provides an illustration of how the iostream library function getline might work. We have written our own function get_line to read a line of characters of maximum length given by max_line - 1. If the newline character is encountered before max_line - 1 characters have been read, reading stops, and the null character replaces the newline, marking the end of the string just read. If max_line - 1 characters are read, reading stops, and the null character is placed in position s[max_line - 1]. Our function get_line returns the number of characters read. If the end-of-file is encountered, we assume no characters were read. In this case, the read is considered to have failed, and a value of −1 is returned.

Figure 13.6   Function get_line

```
// FILE: GetLine.cpp
// READS A LINE OF CHARACTERS FROM DESIGNATED FILE

#include <iostream.h>

int get_line
  (istream& ins,      // IN: input stream
   char s[],          // OUT: string to receive characters read
   int max_len,       // IN: maximum length (minus 1) of line read
   char nwln = '\n')  // IN: special character terminating the read
```

(Continued)

Figure 13.6   (Continued)

```
// Pre:      Input file must be open and max_len must be less than
//           the size of the actual argument corresponding to string.
// Post:     One line of characters read up to and including newline.
//           File positioned just beyond newline.
// Returns: Line length or -1 if end-of-file encountered.
{
    // Local data ...
    char c;              // contains each character as read
    int i;               // loop control variable

    // Read a line, one character at a time.
    for (ins.get (c), i = 0;
         !ins.eof () && c != nwln  && i < max_len - 1;
         ins.get (c), i++)
    {
        s[i] = c;
    }

    s[i] = '\0';              // append null character to end of string
    if (ins.eof ())
        return -1;
    else
        return i;
}   // end get_line
```

■

EXERCISES FOR SECTION 13.1

Self-Check

1. For the character array name[10], write the following C++ code:

   a. an expression that represents the value of the pointer to the first element of the array;
   b. an expression to determine the pointer to the third element of the array;
   c. an expression to add 1 to the third element of the array and store the result back in the third element;

2. Assuming that p and q are pointers to objects of the same type, which of the following operations are legal? Which are illegal? Justify your answers and describe the result for those operations that are legal.

a. p + q	b. p + 2
c. p - q	d. p * 2
e. p++	f. p += 5

Programming

1. Write a function that finds the working length of a string that is padded with blanks. The blank padding should not be included in the working length.
2. Write the C++ code to copy the characters in the arrays a[5] and b[5] into the character array c[10] in such a way that the characters in b immediately follow those in a. Do this first without the use of the C++ library functions; then rewrite the code, using any of these functions that are needed.

3. Write a function that stores the reverse of an input string argument in its output argument (for example, if the input string is `"happy     "`, the output string should be `"     yppah"`.) The actual length of the string being reversed (excluding blank padding) should also be an input argument.
4. Write a program that uses the function in Programming Exercise 3 to determine whether or not a string is a palindrome. (A palindrome is a string that reads the same way from left to right as it does from right to left; for instance, "level" is a palindrome.)

13.2 —— AN ILLUSTRATION OF CHARACTER STRING PROCESSING

The functions in the `string.h` library can be used as building blocks to improve our ability to manipulate textual data. This is illustrated in the following Case Study.

CASE STUDY: PRINTING A FORM LETTER

Suppose that during the spring semester you begin thinking about a summer job. One thing you might like to do is write a program that prints form letters so that you can do a mass mailing of original-looking letters inquiring about summer job opportunities. Except for the first line, the body of your letter will always be the same; the address and salutation will change depending on the addressee. We will assume that you already have special stationery with your name, address, and telephone number so that no return-address information need be printed on the letter. We will also assume that each copy of the letter that you write will easily fit on a single page.

Problem Statement

We would like a program that can help in generating job application letters. For each letter that is required, the program will read information from two input files, an addressee file (`address_data`) and a letter file (`letter_body`). File `address_data` is to contain the name, address, salutation form, and employer name for an employee (often the Personnel Director) located at an organization to which you will apply. For any given use of this program, this file should contain one or more such listings organized as individual records, each terminated by the string "###" as shown in Fig. 13.7. The salutation form and place of employment each are one line long and are separated from a recipient's name and address by a blank line.

Figure 13.7 File `address_data`

```
Mr. Joseph S. DeBlasi      ⎫
Executive Director          ⎪
ACM                         ⎬   name and address for first record      ⎫
1515 Broadway               ⎪                                          ⎪
New York, NY 10036          ⎭                                          ⎬  first record
                                                                       ⎪
Mr. DeBlasi                 }   salutation for first record            ⎪
ACM                         }   organization name for first record     ⎭
###
Ms. Ann-Marie Kelly         ⎫
Dir. of Conf. and Tutorials ⎪
IEEE Computer Society       ⎬   name and address for second record
1730 Massachusetts Ave, NW  ⎪                                          ⎫
Washington, DC 20036        ⎭                                          ⎬  second record
                                                                       ⎪
Ms. Kelly                   }   salutation for second record           ⎪
IEEE-CS                     }   organization name for second record    ⎭
###
Ms. Donna M. Skalski
President
Skalski Enterprises Unlimited
One Penn Center
Philadelphia, PA 19104

Ms. Skalski
Skalski Enterprises Unlimited
###
Dr. Adele Goldberg
President
ParcPlace Systems
Palo Alto, CA 93905

Dr. Goldberg
ParcPlace Systems
###
```

The `letter_body` file contains a single copy of the letter to be sent to each employer listed on `address_data`. Each letter to be mailed will be created by merging the name, address, salutation, and place of employment information for a particular employer with the letter body. Thus the `letter_body` file will have to be reread for each record in the `address_data` file. As each letter is created from these two files, it is to be sent to an output file for subsequent printing.

Problem Analysis

Each letter consists of a heading, salutation, body, and closing. To individualize a letter, we want to create a special heading, salutation, and first line from the information on the address file. We will call this part of the letter the preamble.

The body and closing of the letter always will be the same. You can use any text editor to create the letter body and closing and to save it as the text file `letter_body`. The heading, salutation, and employer information for each employer must also be stored in a text file (`address_data`).

As the preamble of each letter is created, it will be written to the output file (`letter`). Then we can write the rest of the letter by copying the body from file `letter_body` to file `letter`. An example of a finished preamble, as created from the first record of `address_data`, is shown in Fig. 13.8.

Figure 13.8   Preamble of a job search letter

```
July 27, 1993

Mr. Joseph S. DeBlasi
Executive Director
ACM
1515 Broadway
New York, NY 10036

Dear Mr. DeBlasi:

I am interested in applying for a job at ACM. ....
```

DATA REQUIREMENTS

Global Types

status_type (enum {end_of_file, error, success})

Problem Input

address_data (ifstream)	— name, address, salutation, and employer name for each organization to be contacted
letter_body (ifstream)	— body and closing of the letter

Problem Output

letter (ofstream)	— file of complete letters
letter_count (int)	— number of letters written

Local Data

status (status_type)	— indicates when the end of the address_data file is encountered or if an error occurs in address data file

Design of the Main Function

The input files and the output file must first be prepared for use in the program. This is accomplished using the `open` function to connect input and output files to the corresponding streams to be used in the program. Once this is complete, the program must repeat the process of creating and writing each letter until the `address_data` file is exhausted (end-of-file reached). For each repetition, the program calls functions `write_preamble` and `write_body` to carry out the tasks of creating and writing the preamble of the letter and copying the letter body. After each letter is written, the `letter_body` file must be reset back to the beginning for reuse in the creation of the next letter.

The program terminates (displaying the number of letters processed and a termination message) when the end of the `address_data` file is encountered. No effort is made to ensure the correctness of the information in the `address_data` file. Should this file end prematurely, the last letter to be written may be incomplete. Should there be other errors in the input data, other processing errors are possible. To maintain a focus on string processing in a fairly simplified environment, the correctness of our input files is assumed. The structure chart for the main function is shown in Fig. 13.9. The sequencing of the steps in this chart is shown in the algorithm below.

ALGORITHM FOR MAIN FUNCTION

1. Prepare the files address_data, letter_body, and letter for use.
2. Initialize letter_count.
3. While end-of-file not encountered, repeat:
    3.1. Write the letter preamble: get the current date from the user, extract the name, title, address, salutation form, and employer information from file address_data. Write these data, along with the opening sentence, to file letter. If the end of the address_data file is encountered in the middle of processing (status == error), terminate execution with an error message (`write_preamble`).
    3.2. Write the letter body: copy the body of the letter from file letter_body to file letter (`write_body`).
    3.3. Reset letter_body.
    3.4. Increment letter_count.
4. Display the number of letters created and a termination message.

Implementation of the Main Function

The main function for the Form Letter Problem is shown in Fig. 13.10. The functions `seekg` and `clear` are found in `iostream.h`. They are required to ensure that the stream buffer pointer for stream `ifs2` (connected to the letter body file) is reset back to the beginning, ready to be reread to produce the next letter.

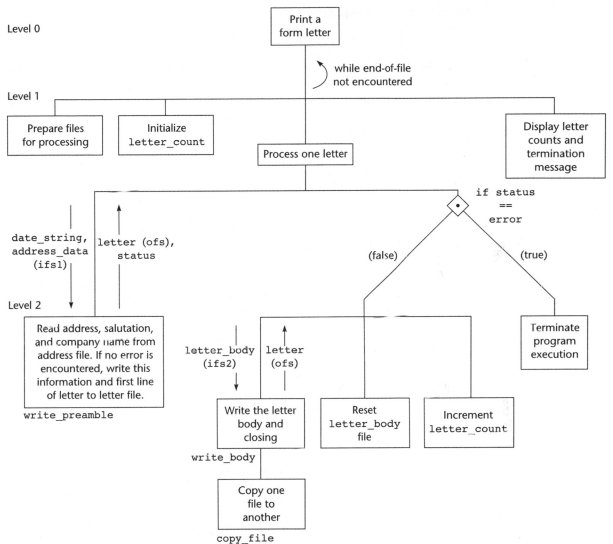

Figure 13.9   Structure chart for Form Letter Program

Figure 13.10   Form Letter Program

```
// FILE: FormLttr.cpp
// WRITES A JOB APPLICATION LETTER TO A FILE FOR SUBSEQUENT PRINTING
//    Letter written in two steps:
//       1. First, a preamble (date, name, address, salutation,
//          etc.) is written.
```

(Continued)

Figure 13.10 (Continued)

```
//          2. Then, the body of the letter is written.

#include <fstream.h>
#include <iomanip.h>
#include <stddef.h>
#include <stdlib.h>

// Global data type ...
enum status_type {end_of_file, error, success};

// ASSOCIATE PROGRAM IDENTIFIERS WITH EXTERNAL FILE NAMES
#define in_file_1 "address.dat"
#define in_file_2 "ltr_body.dat"
#define out_file "letter.dat"


void main ()
{
   // Functions used ...
   // CREATES AND WRITES LETTER PREAMBLE
   status_type write_preamble
     (char[],                    // IN: date of letters
      ifstream&,                 // IN: address_data file stream
      ofstream&);                // OUT: letter file stream

   // WRITE BODY OF LETTER
   int write_body
     (ifstream&,                 // IN: letter_body file stream
      ofstream&);                // OUT: letter file stream

   // Local data ...
   status_type status;      // indicates if eof is reached on input
                            //     file
   int letter_count;        // number of letters processed
   char date_string[20];    // the date of the letters

   ifstream ifs1;           // input stream to address_data file
   ifstream ifs2;           // input stream to letter_body file
   ofstream ofs;            // ouput stream to letter file

   // Open input and output files.  Terminate execution on any
   // error.
   ifs1.open (in_file_1);
   if (ifs1.fail ())
   {
      cerr << "*** ERROR: Cannot open " << in_file_1
           << "    for input. Execution terminated." << endl;
      exit (EXIT_FAILURE);
   }
```

(Continued)

Figure 13.10   (Continued)

```
ifs2.open (in_file_2);
if (ifs2.fail ())
{
    cerr << "*** ERROR: Cannot open " << in_file_2
         << "    for input. Execution terminated." << endl;
    ifs1.close ();
    exit (EXIT_FAILURE);
}

ofs.open (out_file);
if (ofs.fail ())
{
    cerr << "*** ERROR: Cannot open " << out_file
         << "    for output. Execution terminated." << endl;
    ifs1.close ();
    ifs2.close ();
    exit (EXIT_FAILURE);
}

// Process one letter: create and write letter preamble and
//     letter body.
// Get date.
cout << "BEGIN EXECUTION OF FORM LETTER PROGRAM." << endl;
cout << "Enter today's date in desired form for printing: ";
cin.getline (date_string, 20);
letter_count = 1;

for (status = write_preamble (date_string, ifs1, ofs);
     status != end_of_file;
     status = write_preamble (date_string, ifs1, ofs))
{
    if (status == error)
    {
        cerr << "*** ERROR: Premature End of Address File."
             << endl;
        cerr << "    Terminate execution." << endl;
        exit (EXIT_FAILURE);
    }

    write_body (ifs2, ofs);
    ofs << "\n\f\n";          // advance to next page
    cout << "Letter number " << letter_count << " is finished"
         << endl;
    ifs2.seekg (0, ios::beg); // reset to beginning of stream
    ifs2.clear (0);           // clear eof flag
    letter_count++;
}   // end for

cout << "End of file reached in file " << in_file_1 << "."
     << endl << endl;
```

(Continued)

Figure 13.10   (Continued)

```
        ifs1.close ();
        ifs2.close ();
        ofs.close ();
        cout << "Number of letters processed is " << letter_count
             << endl;
        cout << "Program execution complete." << endl;
    }
```

Analysis of Function write_preamble

Only when we reach the point of designing and coding the functions
`write_preamble` and `write_body` are we faced with considerations as to
the processing of the lines of information in the files `address_data` and
`letter_body`. One approach would have been to develop a string abstract
data type based on the notion of an indexed collection of characters. Because
the C++ libraries `string.h` and `iostream.h` already provide most of the
functions we need for this and many other problems involving string manipulation, and because we want to illustrate further the use of these functions,
we have chosen not to pursue this path. In the development that follows,
therefore, we will manipulate strings as described in the previous section, as
character arrays of fixed length.

For each address record stored in the address file, function `write_pream-`
`ble` (see Fig. 13.11) reads the strings needed to create and write out the heading, salutation, and first line of the body of the letter. As this information is
extracted, the appropriate lines of preamble information are written to file
`letter` in the form shown in Fig. 13.8. The function displays a message
when the creation of a letter begins. The function `getline` is used to read
each line from file `address_data`. If the end of file of `address_data` is
detected when attempting to read the first line (a person's name) of the next
address record, `write_preamble` returns with status set to `end_of_file`. If
the end of this file is encountered at any point during the processing of the
preamble, the function returns immediately with the status flag set to `error`.

The input streams connected to the `address_data` file and the `letter` file
are passed to this function, by reference. The date is also passed to this function. The function requires a local string variable for reading the address,
salutation, and employer information from the address file. As information for
the next line of preamble output is acquired, the new line is written. The
function terminates once the entire preamble (including the first line of the letter body) has been written. The data requirements are summarized next.

DATA REQUIREMENTS FOR write_preamble

> ### Input Arguments
>
> date_string (char[])   — the date to be printed on the letters

ifs (ifstream)	— name, title, address, salutation, and employer name for each organization to be contacted

Output Arguments

ofs (ofstream)	— file of complete letters

Local Data

string (char [])	— contains each input line as read
max_line (const int)	— maximum line length for preamble

Design of write_preamble

The algorithm consists of a simple sequence of file read and write operations (using `getline` and stream I/O output). The first line read from file `address_data` is processed as the addressee name and is used to display an informative message indicating that the creation of the next letter has begun. The current date and this name are then written to file `letter`. A for loop is used to read in the remaining lines of the address and write them to `letter`. Then the salutation and employer name information is processed, and the rest of the preamble is written to `letter`. If the end of the `address_data` file is encountered anywhere except when the name is being read, it is considered a data input error. In such cases, `write_preamble` returns immediately with `status` equal to `error`.

Implementation of write_preamble

The code for function `write_preamble` is shown in Fig. 13.11.

Figure 13.11   Function `write_preamble`

```cpp
// FILE: WritePre.cpp
// CREATES AND WRITES A LETTER PREAMBLE

#include <iostream.h>
#include <fstream.h>
#include <string.h>

// Global data type ...
enum status_type {end_of_file, error, success};

// CREATES AND WRITES LETTER PREAMBLE
status_type write_preamble
  (char date_string[],  // IN: the date of the letters
   ifstream& ifs,       // IN: address_data file stream
   ofstream& ofs)       // OUT: letter file stream
```

(Continued)

Figure 13.11   (Continued)

```
// Pre:      Input and output streams must be open.
// Post:     Letter preamble written to output stream.
// Returns: Status indicator. Zero if end-of-file; 1 if error;
//           2 if success.
{
   // Local data ...
   const int max_line = 40;    // maximum line length allowed for
                               //    preamble
   char string[max_line];      // contains current string being
                               //    processed

   // Get name.
   ifs.getline (string, max_line);
   if (ifs.eof ())
      return end_of_file;

   // Print name and date.
   cout << "Letter begun for " << string << endl;
   ofs << date_string << endl << endl;
   ofs << string << endl;

   // Get and print address.
   for (ifs.getline (string, max_line);
        strlen (string) > 1;
        ifs.getline (string, maxline))
   {
      if (ifs.eof ())
         return error;        // error in input file
      ofs << string << endl;
   }

   // Get and print salutation.
   ifs.getline (string, max_line);
   if (ifs.eof ())
      return error;           // error in input file

   ofs << endl;
   ofs << "Dear " << string << ":" << endl;

   // Get and print first line of letter body.
   ifs.getline (string, max_line);
   if (ifs.eof ())
      return error;           // error in input file
   ofs << endl;
   ofs << "I am interested in applying for a position at "
       << string << '.' << endl;

   // Get line "###".
   ifs.getline (string, max_line);
   if (ifs.eof ())
      return end_of_file;     // end of address file
```

(Continued)

Figure 13.11   (Continued)

```
    return success;          // everything is ok
}  // end write_preamble
```

Analysis of Function write_body

The data requirements for function `write_body` are given next.

DATA REQUIREMENTS FOR write_body

> *Input Arguments*
>
> letter_body (ifstream)   — body of the letter to be written
>
> *Output Arguments*
>
> letter (ofstream)   — file of complete letters
>
> *Local Data*
>
> line_count (int)   — count of number of lines processed
>
> *Return*
>
> number of lines processed

Design of write_body

Function `write_body` copies the body of the letter (not shown) from the input file to the output file. The input/output streams connected to the `letter_body` and `letter` files must be passed to this function.

Implementation for write_body

The code for function `write_body` is shown in Fig. 13.12. The basic algorithm for this function involves a straight line-by-line copy from file `letter_body` to file `letter`. To accomplish this task, we reuse the function `copy_file` written in Chapter 8. Once again, the details of the actual copy operation are separated and hidden from `write_body`, which is therefore reduced to a very simple function.

Figure 13.12   Function `write_body`

```
// FILE: WriteBdy.cpp
// COPIES THE BODY OF THE LETTER TO THE LETTER FILE

#include <iostream.h>
#include <fstream.h>
```

(Continued)

Figure 13.12   (Continued)

```
// WRITE BODY OF LETTER
int write_body
  (ifstream& ifs,              // IN: letter_body file stream
   ofstream& ofs)              // OUT: letter file stream

// Pre:  File streams must be defined.
// Post: Output file stream is a copy of the input file stream.
// Returns: Number of lines copied.
{
   // Functions used...
   // COPY ONE FILE TO ANOTHER
   int copy_file
     (ifstream&,              // IN: address of input stream to be copied
      ofstream&);             // OUT: address of output target stream

   // Local data ...
   int line_count;            // number of lines processed

   // Copy letter body.
   line_count = copy_file (ifs, ofs);

   return line_count;
}  // end write_body
```

Program Testing

This Case Study provides an example of the development of multiple layers of code. This approach is useful in the development of readable and understandable code. It can also help speed up the entire development process, from design to testing, through the reuse, especially at lower levels, of previously developed and tested components.

Data and procedural abstraction are powerful tools for building layered systems of reusable components. In this Case Study, for example, the entire discussion of the main algorithm and its structure chart was carried through using terms (nouns and verbs) familiar to the problem domain (creating a collection of form letters with different preambles and the same body). There was no mention of the lower-level, reusable components (getline and copy_file) until we moved into the design of the level-two components write_preamble and write_body. The details of get-line and copy_file were pushed down even further, to level three, and were hidden from the upper-level components. At this level, the tasks to be carried out by these components were sufficiently specialized that simple, previously defined functions could be reused to solve them. We went down still another level (level four), separating `copy_line` from `copy_file` (see Chapter 8). By now, of course, you should be developing quite an extensive arsenal of reusable components of your own.

When testing a layered system such as the one just developed, it is usually helpful to test the lower modules first to make sure that they are sufficiently reliable to warrant use as part of the foundation of your system. Of course, if these lower-level modules are time-tested within your current programming environment, you may simply want to reuse them and not worry quite so much about the testing.

For example, the C++ library components (`istream, ostream`) have already been tested by the compiler manufacturer, whereas `copy_file` and `copy_line` were tested as part of our work in Chapter 8. When reusing program components, it is always important to read the interface documentation to be sure that you understand all of the restrictions and limitations that may have been imposed. Blind or careless reuse of a software component may cause as many problems as having to reconstruct the component from the ground up.

When writing your own functions, be sure to identify and test for any reasonable, potential exceptions, especially input data errors. In testing `copy_line`, for example, see what happens when the data lines being copied are longer than the length of the receiving string or when the data line is exactly the same length as the string variable. In running the Form Letter Program, see what happens when the `address_data` or `letter_body` file is empty or when information is missing from some of the records in the `address_data` file.

Commentary—Linking Separately Compiled Components

In the completely solved problems in previous chapters, all `#include` directives necessary to compile the entire program were specified in the code provided in the text. The complete C++ code required to compile and later execute the program was then included in a single file and processed as a single unit. The Form Letter Program is the first one that did not contain `#include` directives for all of the required program components. Instead, we assumed that the components `write_preamble, write_body,` and `copy_file` would be separately compiled and *linked together* when we were ready to execute the program.

To ensure that separately compiled components are properly linked with the main function, it is necessary to construct a special file, often called a *project file*, indicating where these files can be found. Your instructor or lab assistant can tell you how this is done for the system you are using. Once you understand how this process works on your system, you can follow it for the main function and the components `write_preamble,` write_body, and copy_file required for the Form Letter Program. In this case, the locations of the following four files would have to be specified in the project file:

FormLttr.cpp
WritePre.cpp
WriteBdy.cpp
CopyFile.cpp

EXERCISES FOR SECTION 13.2

Self-Check
1. We used the I/O stream output operator to write to a specified file a string that had been read by function getline. Why couldn't we have used the input operator (>>) instead of getline to read an entire line of characters in one call (without a loop)?
2. Suppose you were asked to write an abstract data type for an indexed collection of characters. List the attributes and member functions you would include in this class and describe how you would build this class. Can you make use of any of the integer or floating-point indexed collection classes used earlier? If so, describe how.

Programming
1. Write a function put_line that can be used to write a line of text to some file after it has been read by getline (or get_line) from some other file. Write a driver program to test getline and put_line. Could you have used the output operator (<<) to test your program in place of the call to put_line and achieved the same results?
2. Write a driver program to test the copy_file function. Be sure to test this function for an empty file.
3. In the Form Letter Case Study, the steps required to process one letter are rather complicated and perhaps should have been written as a separate function, process_one_letter. Write the function process_one_letter and rewrite the body of the main function using a call to this function inside the for loop. Which version of main do you prefer? Why?

13.3 ___ VARIABLE-LENGTH STRINGS (OPTIONAL)

Many computer applications are concerned with the manipulation of character strings or textual data rather than numerical data. For example, a word processor was used in writing this text; computerized typesetters are used extensively in the publishing of books and newspapers; "personalized" junk mail is computer generated (not all uses of computers improve the human condition); and computers are used to analyze great works of literature. A C++ program is just a stream of characters created using an editor or word processor. These characters form a sequence of words and symbols that must be interpreted by a compiler as it performs its translation.

If you have ever used a word processor, you are familiar with the kinds of operations it can perform on strings. For example, we frequently want to insert one or more characters into an existing string, delete a portion of a string (called a *substring*), overwrite or replace one substring of a string with another, search for a target substring, or join two strings to form a longer string.

Fixed-Length and Variable-Length Strings

Up to this point, we have worked with C++ strings represented as an array of characters, the last of which is the special character '\0' (or the null character). In our string declarations, we specify some predefined amount of space of size n to be allocated for such a character array. This space can be used to store a string containing between 0 and n-1 characters, but no more. The size of the array, and hence the maximum length of any string that can be stored in the array, is fixed at n.

C++ provides a large library of functions that can be used to manipulate strings of fixed length. These include functions in the C++ string.h library for the internal manipulation of strings and additional functions in the iostream.h library that can be used for string input and output. One of the string.h functions, strlen, may be used to determine the actual length of a string stored in a character array. Other functions, some with cryptic names, are used to perform string comparisons, string concatenation, substring matching, and insertion.

Considerable care must be taken when using these functions. Among other things, you must always guard against attempts to overwrite existing string data or to place string data into character arrays that are not large enough to accommodate the data. Although these functions can be used in various combinations to build other functions that perform the substring manipulations often found in word processors, the process is often tedious and error-prone and is always subject to the fixed-length limitation.

The C++ class provides the capability to define a new abstract data type for a variable-length string. This new abstract data type, which we have named var_string, can be used to define and manipulate objects (strings) that have no practical limitations on size; that is, they are truly varying in length. The class definition of the variable-length type provides operations that are easier to use and more consistent with the string manipulations found in most word processors. Many of these operations can be used in the same form as those already found in C++ for the fundamental types such as int and float. A textual description of the specification of some of these functions follows. After this description, we provide a number of examples showing how these functions can be used. These examples illustrate the relative ease with which some of the more useful string operations defined in this class can be expressed. The actual class definitions for var_string and for an associated substring class named sub_string are beyond the scope of this text.

SPECIFICA-TION FOR THE CLASS var_string

```
Declaration:
    An object of type var_string may be declared with an optional
    initialization with a C++ string constant. For example:
        var_string s1 = "This is a string";

    An object of type var_string may be declared with an initial-
    ization of a sub_string (described below).

Forming a sub_string:
    If s is a var_string, then s (p,l) is a sub_string of s
    beginning at the pth character (where 0 is the first
    character) and extending for a length l. If p is outside the
    range of the string, then the result is the null string. If
    p+l extends beyond the end of the var_string, then the result
    is the substring of the var_string from p to the end of the
    var_string.

Assignment:
    If s1 is a var_string variable, and s2 a var_string (or
    sub_string) expression, then
        s1 = s2;
    assigns the value of s2 to s1. The length of s1 is made equal
    to that of s2. Assignment to a sub_string is also permitted;
    e.g.,
        s1 (p, 4) = s2;
    The length of the sub_string determines how many characters
    from s2 are copied. If s2 contains fewer than 4 characters,
    null characters are filled to the length 4 in s1 (p,4). This
    destroys the structure and should be avoided.

Accessing an individual character:
    If s is a var_string and i an int expression within the
    range of the var_string, then
        s[i]
    represents the ith character. Note that s[i] may appear on
    either side of the assignment operator (=). If i is not in
    the range of the var_string, the program aborts.

Length of a var_string:
    If s is a variable of type var_string, then
        s.length ()
    returns the length of s.
Comparison:
    The following comparison operators are available between two
```

```
       var_strings (or sub_strings):
          == equality
          != inequality
          >  greater than
          >= greater than or equal
          <  less than
          <= less than or equal
       Note that if s1.length () > s2.length (), and
       s1 (0, s2.length ()) == s2, then s1 > s2.

Concatenation:
    A var_string (s1) and a var_string (or sub_string) (s2)
    expression may be concatenated together to form a new
    var_string as follows:
       s1 + s2
    A var_string (s1) may be extended by appending a var_string
    (or sub_string) expression as follows:
       s1 += s2;

Position:
    If a var_string (or sub_string) expression (s2) is a
    sub_string of a var_string s1, then
       s1.pos (s2)
    returns the position (where the first character is 0) within
    s1 where s2 first occurs. If s2 does not occur within s1,
    then -1 is returned.

Input/Output:
    The stream input (>>) and output (<<) operators are
    available for var_string variables. Output is also available
    for sub_string expressions.
```

Internal Representation of Data Type var_string

The classes var_string and sub_string contain the following two attributes:

```
int len;
char *the_string;
```

len contains the length of the string, and the_string points to the array of characters that contains the string. For the class var_string, this array of characters follows the C++ convention that the last character is '\0'. Thus, there actually are len+1 characters in the string. The member functions (operators) of var_string allocate space for the_string from dynamic storage as required. If len is changed, new space is allocated, and the old copy is returned to dynamic storage. For a sub_string, the_string points to a character within another `var_string`. `len` characters are presumed to belong to the `sub_string`. The operators are illustrated next.

Construction, Assignment, and Input/Output Operators

The contents of a `var_string` may be defined using the input operator (>>) when it is declared (constructed) or when a value is assigned to it. For example, if the data line

```
xyz\n
```

is typed when

```
cin >> sample_str;
```

executes, then `sample_str` will be defined as shown in Fig. 13.13. (The character '\n' is used to indicate when the RETURN key is typed.)

Similarly, the contents of `sample_str` may be defined when a `var_string` object is declared, as in

```
var_string sample_str ("xyz");
```

or via assignment, as in

```
sample_str = "xyz";
```

Either statement will result in `sample_str` having the contents illustrated in Fig. 13.13.

The output operator (<<) can be used to display an object of type `var_string`. The number of characters displayed depends on the length of the string. For example, the statements

```
cout << sample_str;
cout << "*" << endl;
```

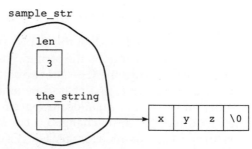

Figure 13.13   Storing data in `var_string` `sample_str`

display the output line

```
xyz*
```

Example 13.8   Assume that `name` is of type `var_string`. The statement

```
cin >> name;
```

reads characters from the keyboard and stores them in `name`. If the characters

```
Jane \n
```

are typed at the keyboard, the string `"Jane "` is stored in `name` and the length of `name` is 5. Remember that when the overloaded input operator, `>>`, is used to read data into an object of type `var_string`, an entire line is read. That is, leading white space is skipped and then the rest of the line, including all blanks, is read; reading does not stop at a blank. This behavior is different from the standard version of the `>>` operator when reading fixed-length strings. ∎

Example 13.9   For the `var_string` name described above, the statements

```
var_string name ("abcde");
cout << "Length of ";
cout << name;
cout << " is " << name.length () << endl;
```

store `"abcde"` in `name` (length is 5) and display the output line

```
Length of abcde is 5
```

The statement

```
name = "Leonardo";
```

stores `"Leonardo"` (length 8) in `name`. ∎

Indexing

Individual characters can be either examined or modified by indexing an object of type `var_string` as if it were an array.

Example 13.10   When the statements

```
ch = expression[0];
if (ch == '+')
    expression[0] = '-';
```

are executed, the `if` statement tests whether the string `expression` begins with a plus sign; if so, the plus sign in position 0 is replaced by a minus sign. If the contents of `expression` are `"+4*Y"`, the value of `ch` is `'+'` and the new contents of `expression` are `"-4*Y"`; the length of `expression` is unchanged (value is 4).   ∎

Substrings

It is often necessary to manipulate segments, or *substrings*, of a character string. For example, we might want to examine the three components (month, day, year) of the string `"Jun 25, 1992"`. Substrings can be used to do this, as shown next.

Example 13.11   Assume that a date string (stored in `var_string  date`) always has the form `"MMM☐DD,☐YYYY"`, where the characters represented by `MMM` are the month name, `DD` the day of the month, `YYYY` the year, and ☐ a blank. Assume `date`, `month_str`, `day`, and `year` are `var_strings`. Then the statement

```
month_str = date (0,3);
```

places in `month_str` the substring of `date` starting at position 0 and consisting of the first three characters. The statement

```
day = date (4,2);
```

places in `day` the two characters that represent the day of the month (positions 4 and 5). Finally, the statement

```
year = date (8,4);
```

places the four characters that represent the year (positions 8 through 11) in `year`. If the contents of `date` are `"Jun  10,  1992"`, the contents of the `var_strings` `month_str`, `day`, and `year` become `"Jun"`, `"10"`, and `"1992"`, respectively.   ∎

Example 13.12   Function `print_words` in Fig. 13.14 displays each word found in its argument `sentence` on a separate line. It assumes that there is always a single blank character between words. The variable `first` always points to the start of the current word and is initialized to 0.

Figure 13.14   Function `print_words`

```
// FILE: PrintWds.cpp
// DISPLAYS EACH WORD OF A SENTENCE ON A SEPARATE LINE

#include <iostream.h>
```

(Continued)

Figure 13.14   (Continued)

```
#include "VarStrng.h"  // variable length string class

// DISPLAYS EACH WORD OF A SENTENCE ON A SEPARATE LINE
void print_words (var_string sentence)

// Pre:  String sentence is defined.
// Post: Each word in sentence is displayed on a separate line.
// Uses: VarStrng.h
{
   // Local data ...
   const char word_separator = ' ';

   var_string word;      // each word
   int first;            // first character in each word
   int next;             // position of next character

   // Display each word of sentence on a separate line.
   first = 0;
   for (next = 1; next < sentence.length (); next++)
   {
      if (sentence[next] == word_separator)
      {
         word = sentence (first, next - first);
         cout << word << endl;
         first = next + 1;
      } // end if
   } // end for

   // Display the last word.
   word = sentence (first, sentence.length () - first + 1);
   cout << word << endl;
} // end print_words
```

During each execution of the **for** loop, the expression

```
sentence[next] == word_separator
```

tests whether the next character is the symbol ' '. If so, the substring occupying the positions `first` through `next-1` in `sentence` is copied to `word` and is displayed on the next line by the statements

```
word = sentence (first, next-first);
cout << word << endl;
```

The values of `first` and `next` are shown in Fig. 13.15 just before the fourth word of a string stored in `sentence` is displayed. The value of `next - first` is 5, so the five-letter word `"short"` is displayed.

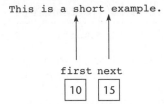

Figure 13.15 Results of execution of function `print_words`

After each word is printed, `first` is reset to `next + 1`, the position of the first character in the next word. After loop exit, the statement

```
word = sentence (first,(sentence.length ()-first + 1)
```

stores the last word of `sentence` in `word`. For the sentence in Fig. 13.15, the value of `first` is 16 and the value of the second parameter is 8 (23 − 16+1), so the last word displayed is the seven-letter word `example`, which begins at position 16, plus the period. ■

Concatenating Strings

You can use the + operator to combine two or more variable length strings to form a new variable length string.

Example 13.13 The following statements join, or concatenate, strings. The `var_string` result is stored in `name`.

```
name = title + last;
name = title + first + last;
```

In Fig. 13.16, the statement

```
name = title + last;
```

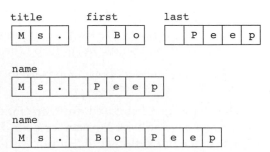

Figure 13.16 String concatenation

stores the string value "Ms. Peep" in name. The statement

```
name = title + first + last;
```

stores the string "Ms. Bo Peep" in name.   ▪

String Search

When processing string data, we often need to locate a particular substring. For example, we might want to know if the string "and " appears in a sentence and, if so, where? If target is a var_string of length 4 with contents "and ", the statement

```
pos_and = sentence.pos (target);
```

assigns to pos_and the starting position of the first occurrence of "and " in var_string sentence. If the string "Birds and bees fly all day." is stored in sentence, the value assigned to pos_and is 6. If "and " is not in sentence, the pos function returns –1.

EXERCISES FOR SECTION 13.3

1. Describe two main differences between fixed-length C++ strings and the variable-length strings defined by the var_string class.
2. Let s1 and s2 be defined as character arrays (of type char[ ]). Describe an algorithm for determining the indexes of the beginning and the ending of s2 in s1. You may refer to C++ string.h functions wherever needed in your algorithm. If s2 is not a substring of s1, set both the beginning and ending values to –1.
3. Let s1 and s2 be defined as character arrays (of type char[ ]). Describe an algorithm for inserting the string contained in s2 into s1 beginning at index i in s1. Be sure to take care of the situation in which the combined lengths of the strings stored in s1 and s2 exceed the size of the array s1.
4. Redo Self-Check Exercise 2 for s1 and s2 declared as variable-length strings.
5. Redo Self-Check Exercise 3 for s1 and s2 declared as variable-length strings.
6. Let s1 and s2 be defined as character arrays (of type char[ ]) containing strings to be concatenated using the function strcat. Describe how you would detect and take care of the case in which the combined lengths of the strings stored in s1 and s2 exceed the size of the array s1.

Programming

1. Write the C++ code sequences for your algorithms in Self-Check Exercises 2 and 4.
2. Write the C++ code sequences for your algorithms in Self-Check Exercises 3 and 5.

13.4 ____ COMMON PROGRAMMING ERRORS

A number of errors occur quite frequently when working with character strings and character string functions. A few of these are described next.

■ *Argument Matching Errors:* These errors are perhaps even more common when you are calling a function in the library `string.h`. The main causes of these errors are

a) omitting an actual argument in a call;
b) listing actual arguments in the wrong order, such as reversing the source and target strings in `strcpy`;
c) failing to ensure that the type and structure of an actual argument is consistent with that of the corresponding formal argument;
d) failing to include the `#include <string.h>` line in your program.

Some of these errors will normally be detected by your compiler, and appropriate diagnostics will be displayed. The most common of these diagnostics should be similar, if not identical, to the message

`"type mismatch in argument"`.

To prevent or to correct this error, it is important that you carefully check each formal argument and its corresponding actual argument for consistency. It is also important to read the specification of each formal argument carefully, be sure you understand what the specification says, and then check to be sure that the corresponding actual argument is consistent with the specification.

For example, consider the function

`int strncpy (trg, csrc, n)`

(see Table 13.1). The second formal argument (corresponding to `csrc`) for this function is of type `const char *`. That is, its corresponding actual argument must be a pointer to an array of characters (a string). The use of the modifier `const` means that the actual argument string corresponding to `csrc` cannot be modified by the function. The first formal argument, corresponding to `trg`, is of type `char *`, again, a pointer to a character array. Because the `const` modifier is not used with this argument, its corresponding actual argument can be modified by the function. The third formal argument is of type `size_t`, an integer. Given this list of arguments, a character string such as `"Shelley Rose"` is perfectly legal when used as a second actual argument of the `strncpy` function, but not when used as the first actual argument. Such use of a string constant also will cause a `"type mismatch"` error. A single character, such as `'T'` (using single quotes), would not be legal in either case; nor would a variable of type `char`. Use of these actual arguments also would result in a `"type mismatch"` error. However, a single character string, such as `"T"` (using double quotes), would be permitted for the second actual argument. Note that if `strcpy` or `strncpy` is called with the first two arguments accidentally reversed, no type mismatch will occur and no error will be generated. But valuable data will be lost when the copy is done.

▪ *Misuse of the Return Values from a String Function:* These errors often accompany the use of `string.h` functions. The most frequent abuses occur with functions that return a pointer value (using the `return` statement) and those that return an integer (using `return`). For example, consider the function

```
strchr (ctrg, c)
```

listed in Table 13.1. This function takes a `const char *` first argument and a `char` second argument and returns a pointer (type `char *`) to the first occurrence of the character `c` in the string pointed to by `ctrg`. There is often a temptation to use this pointer directly as an index to the `ctrg` array. Please don't! Remember that a pointer is an address and not an index. (However, the pointer may be used to determine the correct index, as shown in Example 13.2.)

When an integer is returned by a function, as is the case with the function `strncmp`, there is often a temptation to use the returned value directly in a condition without an explicit equality test, as in

```
if (strncmp (str1, str2, 20))
   // statement;
```

This is perfectly legal. Because the function returns a value of zero if the first 20 characters of `str1` and `str2` are identical and nonzero otherwise, it is conceivable that this condition will behave as expected. It is more likely, however, that it will not. For example, if the intent is to execute the statement under the condition when the first 20 characters of `str1` and `str2` are the same, then the condition just shown will have the opposite effect from what is intended. However, the condition

```
strncmp (str1, str2, 20) == 0
```

will result in the desired behavior.

▪ *Index Expression Out of Bounds:* The most common error when using arrays of any type is an index expression out of bounds. We have discussed this error several times before; it occurs when a subscript value is outside the allowable range for the array being processed. This error is not detected by the run-time system in C++ and can be difficult to detect and debug. For some reason, perhaps because of the way in which we use strings or because of the ease with which `string.h` functions may be misused, the index out of bounds error often occurs when string manipulation is involved.

▪ *Returning Pointers to "Nowhere":* If you write your own function to return a pointer to a string, be careful to ensure that the memory allocated to the string is not local to your function. If it is, then when the function return occurs, your pointer will be returned but the string that it points to will be deallocated when the return is executed, leaving you with a pointer that points to memory that your program no longer controls. A better solution is always to ensure that space is allocated in the calling function for storing the function result. A pointer to this space should then be passed as an actual argument to the function. The function

```
strcpy (trg, csrc)
```

is written in this fashion. The actual argument `trg` is a pointer to a character array that must be allocated in a calling function's memory space prior to any call to `strcpy`. Characters are copied into this space from string `csrc`; upon return from `strcpy`, the copied string still exists with the pointer to it still in the variable `trg`.

▪ *Copying by Assignment:* If variables such as `my_name` and `last_name` are declared to be of type `char *` and are allocated space dynamically using the `new` operator, then assignments statements such as

```
my_name = "fluffie"; or my_name = his_name;
```

will compile and execute correctly. However, these statements do not copy a string from one place in memory to another. They simply change the value of the pointer in `my_name` to point to the string designated on the right. Thus, there is still only one copy of the string on the right, not two as might have been intended. Unless you intend to perform pointer assignment, this kind of operation should be avoided in string manipulation.

CHAPTER REVIEW

In this chapter, we focused our attention on another abstract data type, the string. We examined the C++ representation of strings as arrays of characters ended by the null character `'\0'` and described how to declare and initialize strings. We illustrated how to use a number of the C++ library functions (from `string.h`) as the basic operators on fixed-length strings. With these functions, we were able to manipulate textual information, copying, replacing, deleting, concatenating, and comparing strings and extracting substrings. Because these `string.h` library functions are already defined and learning to use them is an important aspect of the study of C++, we focused primarily on the use of these functions.

We did so at the expense of a different approach in which we might have introduced a new abstract data type with perhaps a different, albeit more convenient, set of operators for text manipulation. In the last section, we presented such an abstraction, but with one limitation (on the maximum string length) removed. The variable-length string presents an abstraction that is far more interesting, easier to use, and more powerful. We discussed the advantages of this abstraction, and we described the attributes and operators for one possible implementation of this abstraction.

New C++
Constructs
The string functions introduced in this chapter are summarized in Table 13.1 (see Section 13.1). Examples of the use of some of these functions as well as C++ statements for declaring and manipulating strings are provided in Table 13.2.

Table 13.2   **Declaring and Using Strings**

CONSTRUCT	EFFECT
Declarations	
`char str[100];`	Causes allocation of space containing up to 99 characters plus the null character, which marks the end of the string.
`char musical_letters[] = "ABCDEFG";`	Causes allocation of space containing 7 characters plus the null character and initializes this space to the uppercase letters shown.
`char *names[5];`	Causes allocation of a space containing 5 pointers to a character data item.

`const char my_arg[];`
or
`const char *my_arg;`
`char names[12][20];`
	Specification of a string (character array) formal argument. Either specification will work.
	Allocates space for an array of 12 strings, each containing up to 19 characters plus the null character.

Using String Functions	
`size_t strlen (cstr)`	Returns the number of characters in the string `cstr` (type `const char *`) up to but not including the null character. `size_t` is a special type that may be treated as an integer for our purposes.
`char *strcpy (trg, csrc)`	Copies all characters in `csrc` (`const char *`) up to and including the null character into `trg` (`char *`). If `trg` is not sufficiently large to accommodate the copied characters, other memory space will be overwritten, causing unpredictable results. This function returns a pointer to the string `trg`.
`char *strncat (trg, csrc, 10)`	Concatenates the first 10 characters of the string `csrc` (`const char *`) to the back of the string `trg` (`char *`). If the length of `csrc` is less than 10, then all characters in `csrc` are copied, up to but not including the null character. The null character is always appended to the end of the newly formed string in `trg`, so `trg` must be large enough to accommodate 11 characters (the maximum of 10 copied characters plus the null character appended at the

(Continued)

Table 13.2   (Continued)

CONSTRUCT	EFFECT
	end). This function also returns a pointer to the string trg.
char *strchr (ctrg, c)	Returns a pointer to the first occurrence in ctrg (const char *) of the character c or the null pointer if c is not present in ctrg.
char *strstr (ctrg, csrc)	Returns a pointer to the first occurrence in ctrg of the string csrc or the null pointer if csrc is not present in ctrg. Both arguments are of type const char *.

✔ QUICK-CHECK EXERCISES

1. Explain the purpose, the input argument types, and the return value type for each of the following functions. Also indicate the library to which the function belongs.

   | islower | strncat | abs | isalpha | atoi |
   | strstr | sin | random | strlen | pow |

2. Turn to Appendix A, which contains descriptions of three character sets. Which of the following expressions might yield different results depending on the character set used on your computer?

   a. char (my_age)   b. 'A' < 'Z'   c. 'A' <= ch && ch <= 'Z'
   d. 'a' < 'A'   e. int (first_initial)
   f. int('A') - int('B')

3. Which of the two C++ declarations

   a. char str1[50];   b. char str2[];

   could be used to represent a locally declared array in a function? Which could represent a formal argument?

4. You have written a program that produces incorrect results on your second set of test data despite the fact that it runs fine on the first set of test data. In particular, the sequence of statements

   ```
   char s2[10], s1[10];

   ...

   cout << s1 << endl;
   cin >> s2;
   cout << s1 << endl;
   ```

   prints the string "Shelley" on one line but a different string on the next line. What could be wrong?

5. What is the minimum size for the variable `str` if it is to hold the names of any one of the baseball teams in the American League East: Baltimore, Boston, Cleveland, Detroit, Milwaukee, New York, Toronto?

6. What is the value of the string in the 40-character array `president` after execution of the following code segment?

```
strcpy (president, "Clinton ");
strncat (president, "belittles", 2);
strncat (president, "and", 1);
strcat (president, strstr (where, "ts Bush"));
```

where the string `"insults Bush"` is stored in the 20-character array `where`.

7. The action of joining two strings, one following the other, is called _____ .

8. Let `s1` be a string that has room for a maximum of 25 characters. Write a statement that assigns to `s1` the tail of the string value `s2` starting with the fourth character, `s2[3]`.

9. Write a C++ code segment that reads an entire line of data and prints the upper-case letters in the line.

10. What is the value of the expression `isdigit(9)`?

Answers to Quick-Check Exercises

1.

FUNCTION NAME AND PURPOSE	INPUT ARGUMENT TYPE	RETURN VALUE TYPE	LIBRARY
`islower` checks whether its argument is the character code corresponding to a lowercase letter of the alphabet	`int`	`int`	`ctype.h`
`strncat` concatenates either all k characters or the first n characters (whichever is smaller) of its second argument to the end of its first argument	`char *` `const char *` `size_t`	`char *`	`string.h`
`abs` determines the absolute value of its argument	`int`	`int`	`math.h`
`isalpha` determines if its argument is the character code for a letter of the alphabet	`int`	`int`	`ctype.h`
`atoi` determines the integer value of a string of digit characters such as `"307406"`	`const char *`	`int`	`stdlib.h`

(Continued)

FUNCTION NAME AND PURPOSE	INPUT ARGUMENT TYPE	RETURN VALUE TYPE	LIBRARY
`strstr` returns a pointer to the first occurrence of the second argument string found in the first argument string or null if the second string is not a substring of the first	`const char *` `const char *`	`char *`	`string.h`
`sin` computes the sine of its argument in radians	`double`	`double`	`math.h`
`random` determines a pseudo-random integer in the range 0 to n, where n is the argument	`int`	non-negative integer	`stdlib.h`
`strlen` determines the length of its string argument (not including the null character)	`const char *`	`size_t`	`string.h`
`pow` determines the value of the first argument raised to the power of the second	`double` `double`	`double`	`math.h`

2. Results differ for a, c, and e.
3. local variable: `str1`, formal argument: `str2`
4. The input operation may be reading a string that is too long to fit into `s2`, and the extra characters may be overwriting the space allocated to `s1`.
5. The longest strings, `"Baltimore"`, `"Cleveland"`, and `"Milwaukee"` each contain 9 characters, so an array of at least 10 characters in length will be required.
6. `"Clinton beats Bush"`
7. concatenation
8. `strncpy(s1, &s2[3], 24);`

9.
```
cin.getline (line, 80);
for (int i = 0; i < strlen (line); i++)
   if (isupper (line[i]))
       cout << line[i];
```

10. 0 (false); however, `isdigit ('9')` would be true.

REVIEW QUESTIONS

Answer Review Questions 1 through 4 in terms of the following declarations:

```
char name1[6], name2[12], name4[20];
char week_day[] = "wednesday";
char rest_day[10] = "sunday";
```

1. What is the size of the array `week_day` as defined by the declaration in the second line?
2. What is the value returned by the call `strlen (rest_day)`?
3. If `name1` contains the string `"Donna"` and `name2` contains the string `" has the key"`, then what is contained in `name4` after execution of the following statements?

```
strcpy (name4, name1);
strcat (name4, name2);
```

4. If `name1` and `name2` are defined as in Review Question 3, then what is contained in `name4` after execution of the following statements?

```
strncpy (name4, name1, 3);
strcat (name4, name2 + 9);
```

5. Let `my_line` be a character array (string) of size 30. Draw a picture of this array with the string literal `"Hi, I'm Patty Carroll."` stored left-adjusted in the array.
6. Write a function `right_blank_pad` that will take any character array (such as `my_line` in Review Question 5) containing a string of some length `len` between 0 and the size of `my_line` and fill the remainder of `my_line` with blanks. *Note:* If the size of the array and the length of the string are the same, this function should exit immediately. Otherwise, the function will add blanks to the right end of the string (first overwriting the null character) until it reaches the last element of `my_line`, where the null character will be stored.
7. Let `my_name` be a string of length 16 containing the name `"Larry Garrett"`. What will the following statements do?

```
a. cout << setw (8) << my_name << endl;
b. cin >> (my_name + 6);        // assume the name "Snyder"
                                // is entered.
c. cout << "My name is " << setw (24) << my_name << endl;
```

8. Use the function `strchr` to determine if the character in `ch` (type `char`) is a vowel. Then write a function to determine if a character in `ch` is a consonant.
9. Use simple pointer arithmetic and some of the `string.h` functions to write a short segment of C++ statements to take a student name (stored last-name-first in the string `name` of size 30, with a comma and one blank separating the last and first names, as in `Bankowski, Hellene`) and copy the name into another string of size 30, with the first name first, followed by a blank and then the last name (as in `Hellene Bankowski`).

PROGRAMMING PROJECTS

1. Write and test a function `hydroxide`, which returns 1 (true) if its string argument ends in the substring `"OH"`. Test your function on the following data:

```
"KOH"     "H2O2"     "NaCl"     "NaOH"     "COH8O4"     "MgOH"
```

2. Write a program to form the plurals of English nouns according to the following rules:

- if the noun ends in `"y"`, remove the `"y"` and add `"ies"`;
- if the noun ends in `"s"`, `"ch"`, or `"sh"`, add `"es"`;
- otherwise, just add `"s"`.

Print each noun and its plural. Test your program on the following data:

`"chair"   "dairy"   "boss"   "circus"   "fly"   "dog"   "church"`
`"clue"   "dish"`

3. Write a program that takes a line of English words and reverses their order. For example, the input line

`this was a close election`

would print as

`election close a was this`

There may be any number of blanks between the words in the input line, and there should be at least one blank between each word in the output line.

4. Write a program that reads a paragraph of English text, and displays this text with each of the three letter words replaced by `"***"`.

5. Assume for the moment that your computer has the very limited capability of being able to read and print only single characters at a time and to add together two integers consisting of one decimal digit each. Write a program to read in two integers represented by strings of up to 10 characters each, add these strings together, and print the result. Test your program on the following strings:

```
s1: "1487625"
s2: "12783"

s1: "60705202"
s2: "30760832"

s1: "1234567890"
s2: "9876543210"
```

6. The results of a true–false exam given to a computer science class have been coded for input to a program. The information available for each student consists of a student identification number and the student's answers to 10 true–false questions. The available data are as follows:

STUDENT IDENTIFICATION	ANSWER STRING
0080	FTTFTFTTFT
0340	FTFTFTTTFF
0341	FTTFTTTTTT
0401	TTFFTFFTTT
0462	TTFTTTFFTF
0463	TTTTTTTTTT
0464	FTFFTFFTFT

STUDENT IDENTIFICATION	ANSWER STRING
0512	TFTFTFTFTF
0618	TTTFFTTFTF
0619	FFFFFFFFFF
0687	TFTTFTTFTF
0700	FTFFTTFFFT
0712	FTFTFTFTFT
0837	TFTFTTFTFT

Write a program that first reads in the answer string representing the 10 correct answers (use FTFFTFFTFT as data). Next, for each student, read the student's data and compute and store the number of correct answers for each student in one array, and store the student ID number in the corresponding element of another array. Determine the best score, best. Then print a three-column table displaying the ID number, score, and grade for each student. The grade should be determined as follows: If the score is equal to best or best−1, give an A; if it is best−2 or best−3, give a C. Otherwise, give an F.

7. Assume a set of sentences is to be processed. Each sentence consists of a sequence of words separated by one or more blank spaces. Write a program that will read these sentences and count the number of words with 1 letter, 2 letters, and so on, up to 10 letters.

8. Write an interactive program that plays the game of Hangman. Read the word to be guessed into string word. The player must guess the letters belonging to word. The program should terminate when either all letters have been guessed correctly (player wins) or a specified number of incorrect guesses have been made (computer wins). *Hint:* Use a string solution to keep track of the solution at any point during the execution of the program. Initialize solution to a string of symbols '*'. Each time a letter in word is guessed, replace the corresponding '*' in solution with that letter.

9. Write a program that stores lists of names (last name first) and ages in parallel arrays and sorts the names into alphabetical order, keeping the ages associated with the correct names. A sample output follows.

Original List		*Alphabetized List*	
Von Stade, Frederica	26	Allen, Thomas	34
Allen, Thomas	34	Figaro, I. M.	99
Ramey, Samuel	29	Moll, Kurt	38
Moll, Kurt	38	Popp, Lucia	15
Te Kanawa, Kiri	19	Ramey, Samuel	29
Popp, Lucia	15	Te Kanawa, Kiri	19
Figaro, I. M.	99	Von Stade, Frederica	26

Wherever possible, reuse classes and other code from previous chapters. Who are all these people, anyway?

14 Arrays with Structured Elements

14.1 Arrays of Arrays: Multidimensional Arrays

14.2 Creating Arrays of Arrays

14.3 Arrays of Structs

14.4 Arrays of Class Elements

14.5 Abstraction and Generalization: Triangle and Polygon Classes

14.6 Modeling the Triangle: Illustrating Alternative Approaches

14.7 Design and Use of Abstract Data Types
CASE STUDY: Assigning Final Grades for a Semester

14.8 Common Programming Errors
Chapter Review

Until now, we have been using individual arrays and structs to store related data items. Sometimes, however, it is useful to be able to think about a collection of related arrays or related structs. We might, for instance, have defined an array or a struct whose elements hold the height and weight of a person. If we had a group of people, perhaps all students in the same physical education class, whose heights and weights were of interest to us, we might want to consider these collected heights and weights as a single entity and perhaps eventually think about modeling this collection as a new C++ data type. In this chapter, we shall investigate various ways of doing this.

14.1 ___ ARRAYS OF ARRAYS: MULTIDIMENSIONAL ARRAYS

Suppose that we wish to write a program to perform computations involving the attributes of triangles. We can assume that we are given the coordinates of the three vertices of a triangle and asked to determine its area and perimeter and the length of its sides. Recall that we can specify the location of a point in the xy-plane by specifying an x position (x-coordinate) and a y position (y-coordinate) for the point. These x- and y-coordinates form an *ordered pair* of values that serve to locate the point. When one sees the ordered pair (x, y) one can interpret it as a point in the xy-plane that is x units to the right of the origin and y units up.

To specify the vertices of a triangle, we can use three pairs of coordinates—an (x, y) pair for each of the three vertices. This represents six numbers. If we wished to define a class to model a triangle, we would need to decide how to store these six numbers as attributes of the class. The first of several possible alternatives, shown in Fig. 14.1, is simple enough, but there are some shortcomings to this approach. First, it does not really emphasize the structural relationships among these six numbers. Because of this, we may find that the member functions we must write to manipulate these attributes may be more

Figure 14.1   A possible representation of a triangle

```
class triangle
{
   ...
   private:
      // Data members ...
      double x1, y1;   // first vertex
      double x2, y2;   // second vertex
      double x3, y3;   // third vertex
      ...
}; // end class triangle
```

cumbersome than necessary. For instance, one member we will surely want is a function to print the vertices, as shown in Fig. 14.2.

Figure 14.2   Print function for the `triangle` **class in Fig. 14.1**

```
void print()
{
    cout << "(" << x1 << ", " << y1 << ")" << endl;
    cout << "(" << x2 << ", " << y2 << ")" << endl;
    cout << "(" << x3 << ", " << y3 << ")" << endl;
    return;
} // end print
```

The fact that we need three nearly identical lines in this function suggests that perhaps there is a better way of representing our data that might lead to an improvement in our print function. The problem is that we are printing three identical things, each representing one vertex. Each of these vertices consists of two identical components, an x and a y coordinate. It therefore seems reasonable to consider representing each coordinate pair as an array of two type `double` elements. Thus, as a second attempt at modeling a triangle, we might write the code shown in Fig. 14.3. This is better in the sense that it enables us to implement the `print` function using a `for` loop (see Self-Check Exercise 1). However, the notion of an (x, y) coordinate pair is hidden; now the x-coordinate of the first vertex is found at `v1[0]` and the y-coordinate at `v1[1]`. Furthermore, we still have not taken into account the fact that the three vertices in fact belong to a single entity—the triangle. What we really want is a way of making a three-element array, each element of which is a vertex. That is to say, we want to make an array of arrays. The C++ language provides a way to do just this.

Figure 14.3   Triangle representation using arrays

```
class triangle
{
    ...
    private:
        // Data members ...
        double v1[2]; // first vertex
        double v2[2]; // second vertex
        double v3[2]; // third vertex
            ...
}; // end class triangle
```

The declaration

```
double vertex[3][2];
```

instructs the compiler to create an array of three elements, each of which is an array of two type `double` elements. The number in the second pair of brackets

[] selects whether we want an *x*-coordinate [0] or a *y*-coordinate [1]. The number in the first pair of brackets chooses which vertex we want. Thus

```
a = vertex[1][0];
```

assigns to the variable a the *x*-coordinate of the second vertex, and

```
b = vertex[2][1];
```

stores the *y*-coordinate of the third vertex in b. Now our print function can be written as shown in Fig. 14.4.

Figure 14.4 `Print` **function for** `triangle` **class shown in Fig. 14.3 (using an array of arrays)**

```
void print()
{
   for (int vert = 0; vert < 3; vert++)
   {
      cout << "The coordinates of vertex " << vert << " are"
           << endl;
      cout << "(" << vertex[vert][0] << ", "
                  << vertex[vert][1] << ")." << endl;
   }
} // end print
```

Structures such as this, arrays of arrays, are called two-dimensional arrays. Arrays of two (and even more) dimensions are quite important in many programming languages. Unfortunately, they also tend to add confusion to many programs. C++ offers alternatives to the use of multidimensional arrays. These alternatives are almost always preferred. We examine some of them next.

EXERCISES FOR SECTION 14.1

Self-Check
1. Rewrite the print function (Fig. 14.2) given the vertex declarations shown in Fig. 14.3.
2. Rewrite the code examples shown in Figs. 14.1 through 14.4 for a pentagon (a polygon of five sides).

14.2 ___ CREATING ARRAYS OF ARRAYS

One of the simplest ways of improving the clarity of our triangle class is to use the `typedef` statement to create a new way of declaring a two-dimensional array. If we write

```
typedef double point[2];
```

then the word "point" henceforth can be used to refer to "an array of two type double elements," with point[0] representing the x-coordinate and point [1] representing the y-coordinate. Now we can write a third version of the triangle class, as shown in Fig. 14.5. This makes explicit the fact that we have an array of three points. In the event that we need to know what a point is, we can look back at the typedef. Most of the time we can simply treat each point as an entity and not worry about its definition. When we make reference to vertex[0] or vertex[1], we are really referring to a point. Because point is defined as a two-element array (using a typedef), vertex[0] and vertex[2] both refer to two-element arrays. We can access the elements of these arrays using a subscript, just as we would access an element of any other array. Thus vertex[2][0] refers to the x-coordinate of the third vertex, and vertex[2][1] refers to the y-coordinate of this third vertex.

Figure 14.5   Triangle **class with vertices of type** point

```
class triangle
{
    ...
    private:
        // Data members ...
        point vertex[3];
        ...

}; // end class triangle
```

As another example, suppose we had a building with rooms of various areas (in square feet). If the building had three floors with seven rooms per floor, we might choose to represent it as shown in Fig. 14.6. To indicate that the fifth room on the second floor is 88.3 square feet, we could write:

```
building[1][4] = 88.3;
```

Figure 14.6   **First representation of a building with three floors (seven rooms per floor)**

```
typedef double floor[7]; // area (sq. ft.) of 7 rooms on a floor
floor building[3];        // the building has 3 floors
```

If we wanted to create a function that would print the areas of all the rooms on a specified floor, we might write a function such as the one shown in Fig. 14.7. To print the areas of the rooms in the entire building, we can write

```
for (int i = 0; i < 3; i++)
{
    cout << "Room sizes for floor " << i+1
        << print_floor (building[i]) << endl;
} // end floor
```

Figure 14.7   Print function for first representation of `building`

```
void print_floor
  (floor this_floor)
{
    for (int room = 0; room < 7; room++)
    {
        cout << "Room number " << room + 1 << " is "
            << this_floor[room] << " square feet." << endl;
    } // end for
} // end print_floor
```

Notice that we pass `building[i]`, a one-dimensional array, to function `print_floor`. This specifies that we want to pass the *i*th floor as a whole, where the *i*th floor is something of type `floor`, for example, an array of seven doubles. However, we can ignore that detail and just concentrate on the fact that `print_floor` requires a floor to work with, and each element of `building` is of type `floor`. We therefore are viewing a building through two layers of abstraction:

- layer 1: a building is a size-three array of elements called floors;
- layer 2: a floor is a size-seven array of elements called rooms.

The areas of the rooms in the building form the third layer of abstraction, the bottom layer for this example. The *base elements* for this layer are all of type `double`. This view of problem domain entities (such as a building or a triangle) as a layered structure of simpler abstractions is an important concept in program design.

EXERCISES FOR SECTION 14.2

Self-Check   1. Describe in English the layered view of a triangle modeled in Fig. 14.5.
2. What benefits can be derived from the development of layered models of problem domain entities? (*Hint:* What benefits were demonstrated in earlier chapters from the top-down layered decomposition of a program in terms of simpler and simpler components?)

Programming   1. Rewrite the code segments in Figs. 14.6 and 14.7 for a building of 11 floors, each containing 12 classrooms with a total number of 132 seats. The base element data for each classroom is its area, as illustrated in this section.
2. Write the declarations needed to store information about a building of seven floors, each containing 13 classrooms, each of which contains some variable number of

seats. The base element data for each classroom now consist of the area of each room and the number of seats in the room.

14.3 ——— ARRAYS OF STRUCTS

Several problems are often associated with the use of arrays of arrays in modeling more complicated data structures. First, use of arrays requires that all elements of the array be of the same data type—be it type `int`, type `float`, or some user-defined type such as an enumeration type. This was not a problem in the examples we examined in the previous section because the base elements we were modeling were all of the same data type (`double`).

A second problem in using arrays of arrays is that it is easy to lose sight of the problem domain attributes being modeled by this structure. To illustrate this point, we return to the triangle example. Recall that in printing the vertices of a triangle (Fig. 14.4), we used a loop to step through the vertices:

```
for (int vert = 0; vert < 3; vert++) ...
```

However, the coordinates to be printed were chosen with constants 0 or 1, as in

```
cout << "(" << vertex[0][vert] << ", "
        << vertex[1][vert] << ")" << endl;
```

Unfortunately, it is no longer clear at this point what the 0 and the 1 represent. The fact that `vertex[0]` represents the *x*-coordinate of a point and that `vertex[1]` represents the *y*-coordinate is no longer as visible or obvious as it could be. We need to investigate whether we can model complicated data structures in better ways that address the issue of clarity and provide more flexibility with regard to data types of base elements.

One alternative to declaring each vertex as an array is to treat it as a `struct` instead, as shown in Fig. 14.8.

Figure 14.8   Modeling a vertex as a `struct`

```
class triangle
{
   public:
      // Member functions ...
      void print();
      ...
   private:
      // Data members ...
```

(Continued)

Figure 14.8 (Continued)

```
struct point
{                       // This defines a struct point consisting
    double x, y;   //    of two coordinates, x and y. (It does
};                      //    not create a variable of type point.)
point vertex[3]; // This creates an array of three points.
...
```

```
}; // end class triangle
```

Now we have an array of three things, each of which is a structure consisting of two type `double` data elements. The name of the first structure in the array is `vertex[0]`. To choose a member of this first structure, we write the structure's name (`vertex[0]`), followed by a dot (`.`) and then the name of the structure member we want to reference (see Chapter 9 for a refresher on the use of dot notation). Thus, for instance, if we want to set the first vertex to be the point (10.3, 5.9), we can write the assignments

```
vertex[0].x = 10.3;
vertex[0].y = 5.9;
```

Our print function now can be written as shown in Fig. 14.9.

Figure 14.9   The `print` function with vertices as structs

```
void print()
{
    for (int vert = 0; vert < 3; vert++)
    {
        cout << "(" << vertex[vert].x << ", "
            << vertex[vert].y << ")" << endl;
    }
}   // end print
```

An array of structs is often viewed as a better choice for storing data than an array of arrays. There are several reasons for this. Most important, many programmers believe that it is easier to make your intentions clear to those who read your program (and to yourself too) if you use arrays of structs. Also, it is usually easier to expand your data structure if you start with a `struct` rather than an array. For instance, consider again the array we designed to represent a building. It might become necessary, later on, to add information about the number of men's and ladies' rooms there are on each floor. Using the `build-ing` structure we initially started with, there is no easy way to accomplish this. For one thing, the base type of this new information is type `int`, whereas the base type of the other information we were storing about the building was type `double`.

However, we might instead have started out by defining the class `edifice` as:

```
class edifice
{
    ...
    private:
        // Data members ...
        struct floor
        {
            double rooms[7];
        }; // A floor is now a struct containing an array.
    floor building[3]; // A building is an array of 3 structs of
                       //      type floor

    ...

}  // end edifice
```

Now, to print the contents of the fifth room of the second floor from within this class, we can write:

```
cout << "Room 5 of floor 2 contains "
     << building[1].rooms[4] << " sq ft." << endl;
```

The `[1]` follows `building` and thus chooses the second element (a floor) of the array named `building`. The notation `.rooms` follows `building[1]` and specifies that we want the `rooms` member of the `struct`. Finally, the `[4]` tells us that we want the fifth element of the `rooms` array.

Now, to add a count of men's and ladies' rooms, we need merely modify our `floor` struct as shown in Fig. 14.10. If we want to create a print member function, it might appear as shown in Fig. 14.11. The use of the `struct` in this example enables us to combine different data types into the same base element of an array. Equally important, however, is that the C++ instructions shown in Fig. 14.11 are more readable and more directly traceable to the problem domain terminology used to describe the object (a building, in this case) being modeled.

Figure 14.10   Modeling a building as an array of structs

```
class edifice
{
    ...
    private:
        // Data members ...
        struct floor
        {
            double rooms[7];
```

(Continued)

Figure 14.10   (Continued)

```
        int mencount;
        int ladiescount;
    };
    floor building[3];
...

} // end edifice
```

Figure 14.11   Printing information contained in an array of structs

```
void print()
{
    for (int i = 0; i < 3; i++)
    {
        cout << "On floor " << i + 1 << " there are "
            << building[i].mencount << " mens rooms." << endl;
        cout << "On floor " << i + 1 << " there are "
            << building[i].ladiescount << " ladies rooms." << endl;
        for (int j = 0; j < 7; j++)
        {
            cout << "Room " << j + 1 << " is "
                << building[i].rooms[j] << " square feet." << endl;
        } // end inner for
    } // end outer for
} // end print
```

EXERCISES FOR SECTION 14.3

Self-Check   1. Describe in English the layered view of a building similar to the one described in Fig. 14.6 but using structs to represent the pertinent information to be stored for each room.

Programming   1. Rewrite the C++ instructions in Figs. 14.10 and 14.11 for a building having the same structure as the one shown in these figures. Add the number of chairs in each room to the information to be stored and printed.

14.4 ——— ARRAYS OF CLASS ELEMENTS

As shown in Fig. 14.12, we can use a class in much the same way as we used a struct (Fig. 14.8) to model a vertex. (We added the member function print to our point class for illustration purposes. It could have just as easily been included in the struct shown in Fig. 14.8.) Given this new data type, our triangle class definition can be written as shown in Fig. 14.13. The implementation of the print function is given in Fig. 14.14. The triangle

Figure 14.12   Using a `class` to model a vertex

```
class point
{
   public:
      // Member functions ...
      // PRINT THE X-Y VALUES OF A POINT
      void print();
      ...
   private:
      // Data members ...
      double x;  // x-coordinate of the point
      double y;  // y-coordinate
      ...

}; // end class point
```

Figure 14.13   Using a `point` class in modeling a triangle

```
class triangle
{
   public:
      // Member functions ...
      // PRINT THE X-Y VALUES FOR EACH VERTEX OF A TRIANGLE
      void print();
      ...
   private:
      // Data members ...
      point vertex[3]; // each vertex is an object of type point
      ...

}; // end class triangle
```

Figure 14.14   Definition of class `triangle` member function `print`

```
void print()
{
   for (int vert = 0; vert < 3; vert++)
   {
      vertex[vert].print();  // uses class point function print
   }
} // end print
```

class function `print` calls the `point` class function `print`; the two print functions are not the same despite the fact that they have the same name.

In this case, we once again have an array of three things, but now each of the things is a member of the class `point`.

14.5 ___ ABSTRACTION AND GENERALIZATION: TRIANGLE AND POLYGON CLASSES

One measure of the utility of a data representation is the ease with which it can be expanded or generalized. For instance, in the case of the building floors, we saw that the original implementation as a two-dimensional array turned out to be a dead end when we wanted to add detail, such as the number of men's and ladies' rooms on each the floor. On the other hand, the implementation that began as a `struct` containing an array was quite easy to augment. In this section, we examine the various representations we have proposed for triangles and see how easy they are to generalize.

One can think of a triangle as a special case of the more general idea of a polygon. For our purposes, a polygon is a collection of n vertices, where n is greater than or equal to 3. When n is 3, we have a triangle; when n is 4, we have a quadrilateral; when n is 5, we have a pentagon; and so on. Attempting this generalization using the first scheme for defining our triangle (Fig. 14.1) holds little promise in terms of ease of generalization. Expanding to include four vertices would require the following code:

```
class quadrilateral
{
    ...
    private:
        // Data members ...
        double x1, y1;
        double x2, y2;
        double x3, y3;
        double x4, y4;
        ...

}; // end class quadrilateral
```

This is still manageable, but imagine what a class for a 20-sided figure would look like. Furthermore, using this technique, there is no way to write a class `polygon` that could hold data for a figure with an arbitrary number of vertices, where the actual number of vertices is decided at execution time.

Other schemes that we have already illustrated are more manageable. For example, using the class `point` defined in Fig. 14.12, we can define a new type `polygon` (as in Fig. 14.15) in such a way that the number of vertices can be determined at execution time. The use of this new class is illustrated in the next section.

Figure 14.15 Modeling a polygon having n vertices (with `point` defined as a class)

```
class polygon
{
   public:
      // Member functions ...
      // CONSTRUCTOR
      polygon
        (int size)                // IN: number of vertices
      {
         n = size;
         vertex = new point[n];
      }


      // DESTRUCTOR
      ~polygon()
      {
         delete [] vertex;
      }

      ...
   private:
      // Data members ...
      int n;                // number of vertices
      point *vertex;    // a pointer to an array of class points
   ...

}; // end class polygon
```

14.6 ____ MODELING THE TRIANGLE: ILLUSTRATING ALTERNATIVE APPROACHES

We conclude our discussion of alternative modeling approaches with five versions of a `triangle` class along with a main function that uses them. The same main function works for all five class definitions because the public information for each class is the same. This illustrates the benefits of practicing a combination of top-down and bottom-up programming. As the requirements of a system are analyzed, the problem space entities (such as a triangle) that need to be modeled are identified and classes describing the essential attributes of and operations on these entities can be designed. The required client software then can be written in terms of the manipulation of objects of the types defined by these classes. The details of implementation of these operations are hidden from the client software and may be changed with minimal or no effect on the client (function main in this case). In addition, the separation of the representations of points and triangles allows us to work through a succession of changes to the triangle class without requiring any changes to the point class.

The main function is shown in Fig. 14.16. The definitions of the five classes are shown in Figs. 14.17 through 14.23. The first four classes are based on the succession of discussions on triangle modeling presented in Sections 14.1 through 14.4. The fifth class is developed from a polygon class template. Full class implementations are illustrated for all but the second and third classes. These implementations are left as exercises (Programming Exercises 2 and 3 at the end of this section).

Figure 14.16   Main function for triangle modeling comparison

```
// FILE: TrngMain.cpp
// MAIN PROGRAM FOR TRIANGLE MODELING COMPARISON
//     TESTS VARIOUS CLASS REPRESENTATIONS OF A TRIANGLE --
//     COMPUTES SIDE LENGTHS, AREAS, AND PERIMETERS OF TRIANGLES

#include <iostream.h>

#include "TriangV1.h"          // <== Insert Correct Header Version.

void main ()
{
    // Local data ...
    const float delta = 0.01;
    triangle data[100];        // 100 triangles
    int num_triangles;
    double sum_area, sum_perimeter;
    double side1, side2, side3;

    // Enter triangle data. A zero area triangle stops the input.
    cout << "About to start triangle program." << endl << endl;
    num_triangles = 0;
    cout << "Data for first triangle:" << endl;

    for (data[num_triangles].read ();
         data[num_triangles].area () > delta;
         data[num_triangles].read ())
    {
        num_triangles++;
        cout << endl << endl;
        cout << "Data for next triangle (enter all 0s to quit): "
            << endl;
    }  // end for

    if (num_triangles == 0)
    {
        cout << "Number of triangles is 0. Execution terminated."
            << endl;
```

(Continued)

Figure 14.16   (Continued)

```
        exit(0);
    }
    else
        cout << "The number of triangles is " << num_triangles
             << endl;

    // Compute side lengths, areas, and perimeters of each
    //     triangle.
    // Compute average area and average perimeter for all
    //     triangles.
    sum_area = 0.0;
    sum_perimeter = 0.0;
    for (int i = 0; i < num_triangles; i++)
    {
        cout << "For triangle " << (i + 1) << " the vertices are: "
             << endl;
        data[i].print ();
        data[i].sides (side1, side2, side3);
        cout << endl;
        cout << "Length of sides = " << side1 << "    "
             << side2 << "    " << side3 << endl;
        cout << "Area = " << data[i].area () << endl;
        cout << "Perimeter = " << data[i].perimeter ();
        sum_area += data[i].area ();
        sum_perimeter += data[i].perimeter ();
    }  // end for

    cout << endl;
    cout << "The average area is " << sum_area / num_triangles
         << endl;
    cout << "The average perimeter is "
         << sum_perimeter / num_triangles << endl;
    return;
}
```

As illustrated in Fig. 14.16, the class `triangle` is expected to contain five public methods: `read`, `print`, `sides`, `perimeter`, and `area`. The prototypes for these member functions must be contained in each version of the triangle class (provided in `.h` files); the implementations of the methods are provided in the corresponding `.cpp` files.

Triangle Class with Vertices as Pairs of Type double Variables

In the first version of the triangle class (Fig. 14.17), each vertex is represented as a pair of type `double` variables. This is not a particularly bad choice of models for a triangle. Rather, its weaknesses become more glaring as we con-

Figure 14.17 Triangle class with vertices represented as three pairs
of type double variables

```
// FILE: TriangV1.h
// MODELS TRIANGLE VERTICES AS THREE PAIRS OF TYPE DOUBLE
//      VARIABLES

class triangle
{
   public:
      // Member functions ...
      // PROMPTS USER FOR AND READS IN VERTICES
      void read ();

      // PRINTS THE THREE VERTICES
      void print ();

      // COMPUTES THE LENGTHS OF THREE SIDES
      void sides
         (double &,              // OUT: the three sides ...
          double &,
          double &);

      // COMPUTES PERIMETER
      double perimeter ();

      // COMPUTES AREA
      double area ();

   private:
      // Data members ...
      double x1, y1;
      double x2, y2;
      double x3, y3;

}; // end class triangle definition



// FILE: TriangV1.cpp
// MEMBER FUNCTIONS FOR VERSION 1 OF TRIANGLE MODELING CLASS

#include <iostream.h>
#include <math.h>

#include "triangv1.h"

// PROMPTS USER FOR AND READS IN VERTICES
void triangle::read ()
{
```

(Continued)

Figure 14.17   (Continued)

```
      cout << "Enter first vertex (x y): ";
      cin >> x1 >> y1;
      cout << "Enter second vertex (x y): ";
      cin >> x2 >> y2;
      cout << "Enter third vertex (x y): ";
      cin >> x3 >> y3;
}  // end read


// PRINTS THE THREE VERTICES
void triangle::print ()
{
      cout << "The first vertex is (" << x1 << ", " << y1 << ")"
           << endl;
      cout << "The second vertex is (" << x2 << ", " << y2 << ")"
           << endl;
      cout << "The third vertex is (" << x3 << ", " << y3 << ")"
           << endl;
}  // end print


// COMPUTES THE LENGTHS OF THEIR SIDES
void triangle::sides
   (double &s1,               // OUT: the lengths of the three sides
    double &s2,
    double &s3)
{
      s1 = sqrt((x2 - x1) * (x2 - x1) + (y2 - y1) * (y2 - y1));
      s2 = sqrt((x3 - x2) * (x3 - x2) + (y3 - y2) * (y3 - y2));
      s3 = sqrt((x1 - x3) * (x1 - x3) + (y1 - y3) * (y1 - y3));
}  // end sides


// COMPUTES THE PERIMETER
double triangle::perimeter ()
{
      // Local data ...
      double s1, s2, s3;

      // Compute the perimeter.
      sides (s1, s2, s3);
      return s1 + s2 + s3;
}  // end perimeter


// COMPUTES THE AREA
double triangle::area ()
```

(Continued)

Figure 14.17   (Continued)

```
{
    // Local data ...
    double area = 0.0;

    // Compute the area.
    area += (y1 + y2) * (x2 - x1) / 2.0;
    area += (y2 + y3) * (x3 - x2) / 2.0;
    area += (y3 + y1) * (x1 - x3) / 2.0;
    if (area < 0.0)
        area = -area;
    return area;

}   // end area
```

sider expansion to polygons with more than three sides, even as few as four or five. In addition, as suggested in Section 14.1, the description of the data members (without comments) provides no hint as to the problem-domain relationships among the variables x1, y1, ..., x3, y3. Finally, an examination of the member functions read, print, and sides would reveal considerable redundancy in the executable instructions of these functions.

Triangle Class with Vertices as an Array of Arrays

The second version of the triangle class, shown in Fig. 14.18, uses an array of arrays to store the vertex information. The private section of the definition

Figure 14.18   Triangle class definition with vertices represented as an array of arrays

```
// FILE: TriangV2.h
// MODELS TRIANGLE VERTICES AS AN ARRAY OF ARRAYS (2-DIM ARRAY)

class triangle
{
    public:
        // Member functions ...
        // PROMPTS USER FOR AND READS IN VERTICES
        void read ();

        // PRINTS THE THREE VERTICES
        void print ();

        // COMPUTES LENGTHS OF THREE SIDES
        void sides
```

(Continued)

Figure 14.18 (Continued)

```
        (double &,            // OUT: the three sides ...
         double &,
         double &);

    // COMPUTES AND RETURNS PERIMETER
    double perimeter ();

    // COMPUTES AND RETURNS AREA
    double area ();

private:
    // Data members ...
    typedef double point[2];
    point vertex[3];

}; // end class triangle definition
```

now more clearly shows the vertices as an array of points, but a point is treated as an array, with no explicit reference to the relationship between the array elements and the *xy*-coordinates of each vertex (see Fig. 14.18). Loops could now be used for reading and printing the vertex data, but the executable instructions would show no evidence of *xy*-coordinate data. The implementation section of this class is left as an exercise (see Programming Exercise 2 at the end of this section).

Triangle Class with Vertices as an Array of structs

The third version of the triangle class, shown in Fig. 14.19, uses an array of structs to store the vertex information. The executable instructions should now show explicit reference to the *xy*-coordinates of each point. This version can be more easily generalized to polygons with more than three sides, and additional attribute data about each triangle can be more easily inserted into the `struct` than into the array of arrays. The implementation section of this class is left as an exercise (see Programming Exercise 3 at the end of this section).

Figure 14.19 `Triangle` class definition with vertices represented as an array of structs

```
// FILE: TriangV3.h
// MODELS TRIANGLE VERTICES AS THREE STRUCTS OF TYPE POINT

class triangle
{
```

(Continued)

Figure 14.19 (Continued)

```
public:
   // Member functions ...
   // PROMPTS USER FOR AND READS IN VERTICES
   void read ();

   // PRINTS THE THREE VERTICES
   void print ();

   // COMPUTES LENGTHS OF THREE SIDES
   void sides
      (double &,            // OUT: the three sides ...
       double &,
       double &);

   // COMPUTES AND RETURNS PERIMETER
   double perimeter ();

   // COMPUTES AND RETURNS AREA
   double area ();

private:
    // Data members ...
   struct point
   {
      double x;
      double y;
   };
   struct point vertex[3];

}; // end class triangle definition
```

Triangle Class with Vertices as an Array of Objects of Type point

The fourth version of the triangle class (Fig. 14.20) uses an array of objects of type point to store the vertex information. The attributes of a point are now encapsulated with operations to read, print, and retrieve information about its xy-coordinates. The implementation of the point class (attributes and methods) is now completely separate from that of the triangle class. Thus, objects of type point and triangle are protected from misuse by each other and by other program system components. In addition, we have greater protection against potential side effects as modifications are made to either of these classes. The definition and implementation of the point class are shown in Fig. 14.21.

Figure 14.20   `Triangle` **class with vertices represented as an array of objects of type** `point`

```
// FILE: TriangV4.h
// MODELS TRIANGLE VERTICES AS THREE POINTS

#include "Point.h"

class triangle
{
   public:
      // Member functions ...
      // PROMPTS USER FOR AND READS IN VERTICES
      void read ();

      // PRINTS THE THREE VERTICES
      void print ();

      // COMPUTES LENGTHS OF THREE SIDES
      void sides
         (double &,          // IN: the three sides ...
          double &,
          double &);

      // COMPUTES AND RETURNS PERIMETER
      double perimeter ();

      // COMPUTES AND RETURNS AREA
      double area ();

   private:
      // Data members ...
      point vertex[3];

}; // end class triangle definition


// FILE: TriangV4.cpp
// MEMBER FUNCTIONS FOR VERSION 4 OF TRIANGLE MODELING CLASS

#include <iostream.h>
#include <math.h>

#include "TriangV4.h"

// PROMPTS USER FOR AND READS IN VERTICES
void triangle::read ()
{
   for (int vert = 0; vert < 3; vert++)
   {
```

(Continued)

Figure 14.20   (Continued)

```
         cout << "Enter vertex number " << (vert + 1) << " (x y): ";
         vertex[vert].read ();
      }
} // end read


// PRINTS THE THREE VERTICES
void triangle::print ()
{
   for (int vert = 0; vert < 3; vert++)
   {
      vertex[vert].print ();
   }
} // end print


// COMPUTES THE LENGTHS OF THE SIDES
void triangle::sides
   (double &s1,            // OUT: the lengths of the three sides ...
    double &s2,
    double &s3)
{
   // Local data ...
   double x1, x2, x3, y1, y2, y3;

   // Compute lengths of sides.
   x1 = vertex[0].x ();
   x2 = vertex[1].x ();
   x3 = vertex[2].x ();
   y1 = vertex[0].y ();
   y2 = vertex[1].y ();
   y3 = vertex[2].y ();

   s1 = sqrt((x2 - x1) * (x2 - x1) + (y2 - y1) * (y2 - y1));
   s2 = sqrt((x3 - x2) * (x3 - x2) + (y3 - y2) * (y3 - y2));
   s3 = sqrt((x1 - x3) * (x1 - x3) + (y1 - y3) * (y1 - y3));
} // end sides


// COMPUTES THE PERIMETER
double triangle::perimeter ()
{
   // Local data ...
   double s1, s2, s3;

   // Computes the perimeter.
   sides (s1, s2, s3);
   return s1 + s2 + s3;
} // end perimeter
```

(Continued)

Figure 14.20   (Continued)

```
// COMPUTES THE AREA
double triangle::area ()
{
   // Local data ...
   double area = 0.0;

   // Computes the area.
   for (int vert = 1; vert < 3; vert++)
   {
      area += (vertex[vert].y () + vertex[vert-1].y ()) *
              (vertex[vert].x () - vertex[vert-1].x ()) / 2.0;
   }
   area += (vertex[0].y () + vertex[2].y ()) *
           (vertex[0].x () - vertex[2].x ()) / 2.0;
   if (area < 0.0)
      area = - area;
   return area;
}  // end area
```

Figure 14.21   Point class definition and function implementations

```
// FILE: Point.h
// DEFINITION OF POINT ADT

class point
{
   public:
      // Member functions ...
      void read ();       // READS THE COORDINATES OF A POINT
      void print ();      // PRINTS THE COORDINATES OF A POINT
      double x ();        // RETURNS THE X-COORDINATE OF A POINT
      double y ();        // RETURNS THE Y-COORDINATE OF A POINT

   private:
      // Data members ...
      double xval, yval;

}; // end class point definition


// FILE: Point.cpp
// IMPLEMENTATION OF MEMBER FUNCTIONS FOR POINT ADT

#include <iostream.h>

#include "Point.h"
```

(Continued)

Figure 14.21   (Continued)

```
// READS THE COORDINATES OF A POINT
void point::read ()
{
    cin >> xval >> yval;
} // end read


// PRINTS THE COORDINATES OF A POINT
void point::print ()
{
    cout << "(" << xval << ", " << yval << ")" << endl;
} // end print


// RETURNS THE X-COORDINATE OF A POINT
double point::x ()
{
    return xval;
} // end x
```

(Continued)

```
// RETURNS THE Y-COORDINATE OF A POINT
double point::y ()
{
    return yval;
} // end y
```

Using a Polygon Class Template to Model a Triangle

Figures 14.22 and 14.23 illustrate the definition and use of a polygon template class in developing a model for the triangle. The template (Fig. 14.22) is defined with a single integer parameter, n, representing the number of vertices (and sides) of the polygon. The constructor creates the polygon representation in the form of n vertices (each of type point). Six methods are defined. The functionality of the member functions is the same as that of the corresponding functions in the fourth example of the triangle model (see Fig. 14.20). The principal difference between this and the fourth example lies in the approach to the implementation of these functions.

Figure 14.22   The polygon class template

```
// FILE: Polygon.h
// DEFINITION OF POLYGON TEMPLATE CLASS

#include <math.h>
```

(Continued)

Figure 14.22 (Continued)

```cpp
#include "Point.h"

template <int n>
class polygon
{
   public:
      // Member functions ...
      // CONSTRUCTOR
      polygon ()
      {
         vertex = new point[n];
      };

      // DESTRUCTOR
      ~polygon ()
      {
         delete [] vertex;
      };

      // PROMPTS USER FOR AND READS IN VERTICES
      void read ();

      // PRINTS THE VERTICES
      void print ();

      // GETS X-COORDINATE OF VERTEX GIVEN BY XVAL
      double x (int);

      // GETS Y-COORDINATE OF VERTEX GIVEN BY YVAL
      double y (int);

      // COMPUTES AND RETURNS PERIMETER
      double perimeter ();

      // COMPUTES AND RETURNS AREA
      double area ();

   private:
      // Data members ...
      point *vertex;

      // Private member functions ...
      double distance(double x1, double y1, double x2, double y2)
      {
         return sqrt((x1 - x2) * (x1 - x2) + (y1 - y2) * (y1 - y2));
      }

}; // end template class polygon definition
```

(Continued)

Figure 14.22 (Continued)

```cpp
// FILE: Polygon.cpp
// IMPLEMENTATION OF MEMBER FUNCTIONS FOR CLASS POLYGON

#include <iostream.h>
#include <math.h>

#include "polygon.h"

// PROMPTS USER FOR AND READS IN VERTICES
template <int n>
void polygon<n>::read ()
{
   for (int vert = 0; vert < n; vert++)
   {
      cout << "Enter coordinates for vertex number" << (vert + 1)
           << ": ";
      vertex[vert].read ();
   }
}  // end read


// PRINTS THE VERTICES
template <int n>
void polygon<n>::print ()
{
   for (int vert = 0; vert < n; vert++)
   {
      cout << "Vertex number " << (vert + 1);
      vertex[vert].print ();
   }
}  // end print


// GETS X-COORDINATE OF VERTEX GIVEN BY XVAL
template <int n>
double polygon<n>::x(int xval)
{
   return vertex[xval].x ();
}  // end double x


// GETS Y-COORDINATE OF VERTEX GIVEN BY YVAL
template <int n>
double polygon<n>::y (int yval)
{
   return vertex[yval].y ();
}  // end double y


// COMPUTES AND RETURNS PERIMETER
template <int n>
```

(Continued)

Figure 14.22   (Continued)

```
double polygon<n>::perimeter ()
{
   double sum = 0.0;

   for (int i = 1; i < n; i++)
   {
      sum += distance (x(i), y(i), x(i - 1), y(i - 1));
   }
   sum += distance (x(0), y(0), x(n - 1), y(n - 1));
   return sum;
}  // end perimeter


// COMPUTES AND RETURNS AREA
template <int n>
double polygon<n>::area()
{
   double sum = 0.0;

   for (int i = 1; i < n; i++)
   {  // uses polygon functions x and y, rather than the point
      //    function
      sum += (y (i) + y (i - 1)) * (x (i) - x (i - 1)) / 2.0;
   }
   sum += (y (0) + y (n - 1)) * (x (0) - x (n - 1)) / 2.0;
   if (sum < 0.0)
      sum = -sum;
   return sum;
}  // end area
```

Figure 14.23 shows the implementations of the member functions, each specific to a polygon of three sides (a triangle). Except for `sides`, the functionality of each member function is "inherited" directly from the polygon template shown in Fig. 14.22. That is, the executable portion of each of the other four member functions in Fig. 14.23 contains a single function call of the form

```
data.fn;
```

where `fn` is the function being called and `data`, declared in the line

```
polygon<3> data;
```

is a 3-element instance of the array of points (vertices) defined in the template.

The member function `sides` shown in Fig. 14.23 was developed a bit differently. In the interest of making our code for `sides` more readable and more efficient, we made the decision to assign the x- and y-coordinate values of each vertex to a local variable. This made the code longer but completely eliminated

Figure 14.23   Implementations of member functions for polygon class

```
// FILE: TriangV5.h
// MODELS TRIANGLE AS A POLYGON OF 3 SIDES
//      "INHERITS" FEATURES OF POLYGON CLASS EXCEPT FOR THE
//          FUNCTION SIDES, WHICH REPLACES THE GENERIC "SIDES"
//          FUNCTION FOR POLYGON

#include "Polygon.cpp"

class triangle
{
   public:
      // Member functions ...
      // PROMPTS USER FOR AND READS IN VERTICES
      void read ();

      // PRINTS THE VERTICES
      void print ();

      // COMPUTES LENGTHS OF THREE SIDES
      void sides
        (double &,                  // OUT: the three sides ...
         double &,
         double &);

      // COMPUTES AND RETURNS PERIMETER
      double perimeter ();

      // COMPUTES AND RETURNS AREA
      double area ();

   private:
      // Data members ...
      polygon<3> data;

}; // end class triangle definition


// FILE: TriangV5.cpp
// MEMBER FUNCTIONS FOR VERSION 5 OF TRIANGLE MODELING CLASS
//      "INHERITS" (USES) CORRESPONDING FUNCTIONS FROM POLYGON
//          CLASS EXCEPT FOR FUNCTION SIDES, WHICH IS SPECIALIZED FOR
//          A TRIANGLE

#include <math.h>

#include "TriangV5.h"

// PROMPTS USER FOR AND READS IN VERTICES
```

(Continued)

Figure 14.23   (Continued)

```
void triangle::read ()
{
   data.read ();
}  // end read


// PRINTS THE VERTICES
void triangle::print ()
{
   data.print ();
}  // end print


// COMPUTES LENGTHS OF SIDES (SPECIALIZED FOR A TRIANGLE)
void triangle::sides
   (double &s1,                  // OUT: the lengths of the three sides
    double &s2,
    double &s3)
{
   // Local data ...
   double x1, x2, x3, y1, y2, y3;

   // Compute lengths of sides.
   x1 = data.x (0);
   x2 = data.x (1);
   x3 = data.x (2);
   y1 = data.y (0);
   y2 = data.y (1);
   y3 = data.y (2);

   s1 = sqrt((x2 - x1) * (x2 - x1) + (y2 - y1) * (y2 - y1));
   s2 = sqrt((x3 - x2) * (x3 - x2) + (y3 - y2) * (y3 - y2));
   s3 = sqrt((x1 - x3) * (x1 - x3) + (y1 - y3) * (y1 - y3));
}  // end sides


// COMPUTES THE PERIMETER
double triangle::perimeter ()
{
   return data.perimeter ();
}  // end perimeter


// COMPUTES THE AREA
double triangle::area ()
{
   return data.area ();
}  // end area
```

both array and `struct` references from the assignment statements involving `s1`, `s2`, and `s3`. However, it also made it difficult to write a general version of the `sides` method—one that we could specialize to suit the needs for any value of the template parameter n. Had we chosen one-dimensional local arrays (perhaps named `x` and `y`) for storing the vertices, or had we decided not to use local storage at all, a generalized version for `sides` would have been more easily obtained (see Programming Exercise 1 at the end of this section).

We have used the term "inherit" here in a very loose sense to describe how the attributes and member functions of a *general data abstraction* (such as the polygon) can be used to obtain a more *specialized model* of that abstraction (such as a triangle, a polygon of three sides). The idea and the advantages of such specialization are important now; the formal C++ mechanism for specifying inheritance is introduced in Appendix E. Concerning the advantages of this notion of inheritance, note that specialized models of any other polygon can be obtained just as easily from the polygon template. If the instructions for one of these derivations are properly tested, it is reasonable to assume that the entire process (implementation, testing, and debugging) associated with safely reusing this template to build other polygons will be easier.

Building an Executable File for Execution

A number of program components must be combined in order to run any one of the five versions of the triangle abstract data type specified in this section. These include the following files:

`TrngMain.cpp`	the main function;
`TriangVi.cpp`	the implementations of the methods for version i of the `triangle` data type;
`Point.cpp`	the implementations of the methods for the point ADT (used only to test the fourth and fifth versions).

The C++ code we have provided does not combine the separate components of the triangle modeling examples; you must do this using whatever program component linker or project management system is available in your programming environment. If the proper components are not combined, you will not be able to execute the version of the triangle example you have selected.

EXERCISES FOR SECTION 14.6

Self-Check

1. Write the C++ code defining a class for a pentagon (a polygon of five sides) having the attributes and member functions that parallel those for the triangle class shown in Fig. 14.23. Provide both the header file (`.h`) and methods implementations (`.cpp`) for your pentagon.

2. What would happen in the main function for the triangle examples if the first triangle entered during a given execution had coordinates (3, 3), (4, 4), (5, 5) and the `if` statement used to test the number of triangles had been missing?

Programming

1. Write a generalizable version of the polygon member function `sides` either using no local variables to simplify the computation, or by compromising and using a one-dimensional array rather than simple variables as the local variables.
2. Write the implementation of the member functions corresponding to the `triangle` class definition shown in Fig. 14.18 (vertices represented as an array of arrays). Your function definitions should be stored in file `TriangV2.cpp`.
3. Write the implementation of the member functions corresponding to the `triangle` class definition shown in Fig. 14.19 (vertices represented as an array of structs). Your function definitions should be stored in file `TriangV3.cpp`.

14.7 ___ DESIGN AND USE OF ABSTRACT DATA TYPES

By this time, you have learned quite a lot about C++ programming. Your knowledge of arrays, structs, and classes will enable you to write programs for solving fairly complex problems. In this section, we develop a general program that might be used by your course instructor in determining final grades for your course section. In solving this problem, we will focus once again on the use of data abstraction. We first identify the relevant data structures to be modeled and describe the attributes of and required operations on these structures. We then build models of these data in the form of classes defining new data types. Our problem solution then will be defined in terms of objects of these new data types.

CASE STUDY: ASSIGNING FINAL GRADES FOR A SEMESTER

Problem Statement

Your computer science professor wants a program that will assist her in assigning final grades for your work in her course. She wants to be able to provide the total number of points given to each student for all work done in the course over the entire semester. The program should read and display each student's name and total points, compute and display all total points statistics (for example, the lowest point total, highest total, average total, median total, and standard deviation), and assign and display letter grades based on the class average and standard deviation.

Problem Analysis

Your professor currently stores the information for her classes in a gradebook. Each gradebook page lists the students on the left and has a column on the right for indicating the total points and the corresponding letter grades. The total points statistics appear at the bottom of the page. A sample entry for one course is shown in Fig. 14.24. The student names and point totals are provided as input data; the letter grades, the number of students, and the total points statistics are all undefined initially.

Figure 14.24   Sample gradebook entry

```
Course Instructor: Carolyn Adams
Spring, 1993
CS 584
Formal Languages and Automata

Number of students      23


Name                Points/Grade
Don Chrupcala       580      ?
Don Baglio          570      ?
Ellen Harmon        560      ?
     .
     .
     .

Lowest Score                 ?
Highest Score                ?
Median Score                 ?
Average Score                ?
Standard Deviation           ?
```

Figure 14.25 shows a sample run of the grading program. The program begins by requesting identification information about the number of students in the course, course instructor, current semester, and course number and title. It then reads the names and scores of three students and computes and displays point total summary statistics. Once these statistics have been computed, grades are assigned and the final student records are displayed.

Figure 14.25   Sample run of Grading Program

——————   Program Output   ——————

```
Your grading program has begun executing ...
Enter number of students to be processed.
```

(Continued)

Figure 14.25 (Continued)

Enter a value between 1 and 1000: 3

Please enter your name: Carolyn Adams
Enter semester and year as a string (max length 12): Spring, 1993
Enter course id as a string (max length 8): CS 584
Enter course title (max length 30): Formal Languages and Automata

Enter the data as requested for each student.
Exactly 3 students can be processed..

Name: Don Chrupcala
Score: 580

Name: Don Baglio
Score: 570

Name: Ellen Harmon
Score: 560

****
Summary of statistics for:
cis 584 - Formal Languages and Automata
Spring, 1993

The Highest Point Total = 580
The Lowest Point Total = 560
The Median Point Total = 570
The Average = 570.00
The Standard Deviation = 10.00
The count of students is 3

The student names, point totals, and grades follow:
Ellen Harmon   560   D
Don Baglio   570   C
Don Chrupcala   580   A

DATA REQUIREMENTS

Problem Input

number of students taking the course
name of each student taking the course
point total for each student taking the course
course identification information
   instructor name
   semester and year
   course ID
   course title

Problem Output

each student's name, point total, and letter grade
course statistics, including low and high point totals, median, average,
    and standard deviation
course identification information (as described for problem input)

DATA REFINEMENTS

Now that we have identified the information relevant to the problem, we need
to decide how to model this information in a meaningful way. Most gradebooks
are essentially a repository of information that identifies a course, the students
in the course, their scores, and their grades for the semester. We begin by
defining an abstraction for such a gradebook, which we call `grade_book`.
Our gradebook ADT will contain information (shown in the data requirements
table) about the course, all student records for the course for the entire semester,
and a summary of pertinent statistics about the class performance.

The student information is, of course, the most important. We will use
another abstract data type, `student`, to represent the information (name, point
total, and grade) required about each student. Given this abstraction, we can
picture the gradebook ADT as shown in the *data structure chart* in Fig. 14.26.

Data structure charts are analogous to the procedural structure charts that
we have been using since Chapter 3. Rather than describe the hierarchical
view of program decomposition, however, data structure charts show the
hierarchical decomposition of a data object. We have found such charts to be
extremely helpful in building a model of complicated data objects.

As shown in Fig. 14.26, our gradebook ADT consists of three components of
information: identification information about the course, statistical summary

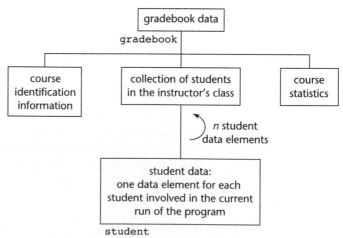

Figure 14.26   Data structure chart for the gradebook ADT

information, and a collection of student records, where the number of students is defined at the beginning of the program (entered by the user). We have already specified in the initial data requirements table and the previous discussion what information is to be associated with each course and student and with the course statistics, so we will not refine these data elements any further in the diagram. Given these decisions, we can complete a refined version of the original data requirements table for the gradebook ADT. The details of the design and implementation of the student ADT follows the implementation of the gradebook ADT.

REVISED DATA REQUIREMENTS (WITH C++ REPRESENTATIONS)

Problem Input

nmbr_students (int)	— number of students taking course
all_students (collection of elements of type student)	— name and point total for each student taking the course
course identification information	
instr_name (char[31])	— instructor name
semester (char[13])	— course semester and year
course_id (char[9])	— course ID number
course_title (char[31])	— course title

Problem Output

all_students (collection of elements of type student)	— name, point total, and grade for each student taking the course
course statistics	
low_total (int)	— low point total
high_total (int)	— high point total
median (int)	— median of all the point totals
average (double)	— average of all the point totals
stddev (double)	— standard deviation
course identification information (as described for problem input)	

Local Data

min (const int)	— minimum number of students that can be processed
max (const int)	— maximum number of students that can be processed

Abstract Data Types

gradebook	— consists of statistical information, course ID information, and a collection of records of information about each student
student	— consists of a record of information about one student—name, point total, and grade

The C++ realization of this model for a gradebook is shown in Fig. 14.27. Also illustrated in this figure is the list of operations required on the data included in this abstraction.

Figure 14.27   Definition for the gradebook ADT

```
// FILE: GrdBkADT.h
// SPECIFICATION FOR GRADEBOOK ADT

#ifndef GRADBKADT_H_
#define GRADBKADT_H_

#include "StdntADT.h"

class gradebook
{
   public:
      // Member functions ...
      // CONSTRUCTOR
      gradebook
         (int);            // IN: number of students in course

      // DESTRUCTOR
      ~gradebook ();

      // ENTER COURSE IDENTIFICATION INFORMATION
      void define_course_id ();

      // READS STUDENT NAMES AND EXAM POINT TOTALS
      void read_students ();

      // DISPLAYS STUDENT NAMES, POINT TOTALS, AND GRADES
      void display_students ();

      // ASSIGNS A LETTER GRADE TO EACH STUDENT
      void assign_grades ();

      // COMPUTES POINT TOTALS STATISTICS
      void compute_stats ();
```

(Continued)

Figure 14.27 (Continued)

```
        // DISPLAYS POINT TOTALS STATISTICS
        void display_stats ();

    private:
        // Data members ...
        // Student information
        student *all_students; // collection of student
                               //     records

        // Course identification information
        char instr_name[31];   // course instructor's name
        char semester[13];     // course semester and year
        char course_id[9];     // course id
        char course_title[31]; // course title

        // Statistical data
        int nmbr_students;     // number of students
        int low_total;         // lowest point total
        int high_total;        // highest point total
        int median;            // median of point totals
        float average;         // average of point totals
        float stddev;          // standard deviation

        // Private member functions ...
        // FINDS THE LOWEST POINT TOTAL
        int find_low ();

        // FINDS THE HIGHEST POINT TOTAL
        int find_high ();

        // COMPUTES THE MEDIAN POINT TOTAL
        int compute_median ();

        // COMPUTES THE AVERAGE OF THE POINT TOTALS
        float compute_average ();

        // COMPUTES THE STANDARD DEVIATION
        float compute_stddev ();

        // EXCHANGES TWO STUDENT RECORDS
        void exchange
           (student &,       // INOUT: the first student record
            student &);      // INOUT: the second student record

        // SORTS THE RECORDS IN ASCENDING ORDER BY POINT TOTAL
        void sort_students ();

}; // end class gradebook

#endif  // GRDBKADT_H_
```

The declaration

```
student *all_students;
```

in the gradebook ADT declares `all_students` as a pointer variable to an element of type `student`. In addition, the number of students in our professor's course is used as an argument to the gradebook ADT constructor, specifying the number of storage elements required to store the data for these students. The constructor for the gradebook ADT used this argument and the new operator to allocate the required storage and place the pointer to this storage area in `all_students`. The student information required for the gradebook is therefore implemented as a specialized instance of an indexed collection (of base type `student`).

To complete the definition of the data requirements for the grading problem, we still must provide a definition for a class `student` that models the required information for one student. The definition for this class is shown in Fig. 14.28. As already discussed, we are tracking only the name, point total, and final grade for each student. Clearly, other information could have been added (see, for example, Self-Check Exercise 1 at the end of this section). Given the information represented in our class, the required methods are easy to establish. These are also shown in Fig. 14.28.

Figure 14.28　Definition for the student ADT

```
// FILE: StdntADT.h
// SPECIFICATION FOR STUDENT ADT

class student
{
   public:
      // Member functions ...
      // READS DATA FOR ONE STUDENT (NAME AND POINTS)
      void read_data ();

      // DISPLAYS DATA FOR ONE STUDENT (NAME, POINTS, AND GRADE)
      void write_data ();

      // RETRIEVES A STUDENT'S NAME
      char *retrieve_name ();

      // RETRIEVES A STUDENT'S POINT TOTAL
      int retrieve_points ();

      // STORES A STUDENT'S LETTER GRADE
      void store_grade
         (char);                   // IN: letter grade
```

(Continued)

Figure 14.28   (Continued)

```
private:
    // Data members ...
    char name[31];          // student name
    int points;             // student point total
    char grade;             // student grade
};
```

Program Design

The main function for our student grading program uses the gradebook ADT as its principal data structure. The main function algorithm is shown next.

ALGORITHM (FOR MAIN FUNCTION)

1. Print beginning messages.
2. Prompt user for and read in the number of students to be processed (enter_int).
3. Prompt the user for and read in the course identification information (gradebook::define_course_id).
4. Read the student data (gradebook::read_students).
5. Compute summary statistics for point totals (gradebook::compute_stats).
6. Print the summary statistics (gradebook::display_stats).
7. Assign letter grades to each student (gradebook::assign_grades).
8. Print each student's final record (gradebook::display_students).

Implementation of Main Function

The main function is shown in Fig. 14.29. As the algorithm indicates, except for steps 1 and 2, the main function body consists solely of calls to the member functions of the gradebook ADT.

Figure 14.29   Main function for the Student Grading Program

```
// FILE: GrdeBook.cpp
// COMPUTES AND DISPLAYS POINT TOTAL STATISTICS FOR STUDENTS
//     IN A COURSE
// ASSIGNS LETTER GRADES TO EACH STUDENT, AND DISPLAYS EACH
//     STUDENT'S RECORD

#include <iostream.h>

#include "GrdBkADT.h"
#include "EnterInt.cpp"
```

(Continued)

Figure 14.29 (Continued)

```
void main ()
{

    // Local data...
    const int min = 1;           // minimum number of students
    const int max = 1000;        // maximum number of students

    int nmbr_students;           // number of students

    // Functions used ...
    // READS INTEGER IN RANGE GIVEN BY ARGUMENTS
    int enter_int
      (int,                      // minimum range for n
       int);                     // maximum range for n

    // Get number of students and create gradebook.
    cout << "Your grading program has begun executing ..." << endl;
    cout << "Enter number of students to be processed." << endl;
    nmbr_students = enter_int (min, max);

    gradebook grade_book(nmbr_students); // create gradebook

    // Process all student data.
    grade_book.define_course_id ();
    grade_book.read_students ();
    grade_book.compute_stats ();
    grade_book.display_stats ();
    grade_book.assign_grades ();
    grade_book.display_students ();
}
```

Implementation of the Member Functions in the Gradebook ADT

The next step is to implement the operators described in the definition section for gradebook. The member function prototypes were given in Fig 14.27; there are six functions, a constructor, and a destructor for this class. The member function definitions are shown in Fig. 14.30. The constructor has a single argument, n, which is used to specify the number of students to be processed. The constructor uses this value to define nmbr_students and to allocate the correct amount of memory in the free store for the required information for each student. Functions read_students and display_students use member functions read_data and write_data, respectively (as defined in student), to read in the initial list of student names and point totals. The statements

```
all_students[i].read_data ();
all_students[i].write_data ();
```

indicate that the specified operation (read_data or write_data) is to be performed on the ith student in the collection all_students.

The remaining functions are self-explanatory. The expression

all_students[i].retrieve_points ()

is used to retrieve the point total for the ith student in all_students.

Figure 14.30   Gradebook ADT member functions for the Student Grading Program

```
// FILE: GrdBkADT.cpp
// GRADEBOOK CLASS IMPLEMENTATION
// IMPLEMENTATION OF GRADEBOOK MEMBER FUNCTIONS

#ifndef GRDBKADT_CPP_
#define GRDBKADT_CPP_

#include <iomanip.h>
#include <string.h>
#include <math.h>

#include "GrdBkADT.h"

// CONSTRUCTOR
// ALLOCATES MEMORY FOR STUDENT DATA. INITIALIZES nmbr_students
gradebook::gradebook
  (int n)                          // IN: number of students
{
   nmbr_students = n;
   all_students = new student[nmbr_students];
}  // end constructor


// DESTRUCTOR
gradebook::~gradebook ()
{
   delete [] all_students;
}  // end destructor


// ENTER COURSE IDENTIFICATION INFORMATION
void gradebook::define_course_id ()

// Pre:  None.
// Post: Course id information is defined.
{
   cout << endl;
   cout << "Please enter your name: ";
   cin >> ws;                                    // skip over whitespace
```

(Continued)

Figure 14.30   (Continued)

```
      cin.getline (instr_name, 31);
      cout << "Enter semester and year as a string (max length 14): ";
      cin.getline (semester, 13);
      cout << "Enter course id as a string (max length 8): ";
      cin.getline (course_id, 9);
      cout << "Enter course title (max length 30):";
      cin.getline (course_title, 31);
      cout << endl << endl;
}   // end define_course_id


// READS STUDENT NAMES AND POINT TOTALS
void gradebook::read_students ()

// Pre:  None.
// Post: Student names and point totals are stored.
{
      cout << "Enter the data requested for each student." << endl;
      cout << "Exactly" << setw (3) << nmbr_students
           << " students can be processed." << endl << endl;
      // Enter student records.
      for (int i = 0; i < nmbr_students; i++)
         all_students[i].read_data ();
}   // end read


// DISPLAYS STUDENTS' NAMES, POINT TOTALS, AND GRADES
void gradebook::display_students ()

// Pre:  The student names and point totals are defined.
// Post: All student records are displayed.
{
      // Display complete student record.
      cout << "The count of students is " << nmbr_students << endl
           << endl;
      cout << "The student names, points, and grades follow: "
           << endl;
      for (int i = 0; i < nmbr_students; i++)
         all_students[i].write_data ();
}   // end display_students


// ASSIGNS A LETTER GRADE TO EACH STUDENT
void gradebook::assign_grades ()

// Pre:  All point totals, average and standard deviation are
//       defined.
// Post: The grade for each student is defined.
```

(Continued)

Figure 14.30   (Continued)

```
{
   for (int i = 0; i < nmbr_students; i++)
   {
      if (all_students[i].retrieve_points () >= average + 1.0 *
         stddev) all_students[i].store_grade ('A');
      else if(all_students[i].retrieve_points () >= average + 0.5
         * stddev) all_students[i].store_grade ('B');
      else if(all_students[i].retrieve_points () >= average - 0.5
         * stddev) all_students[i].store_grade ('C');
      else if(all_students[i].retrieve_points () >= average - 1.0
         * stddev) all_students[i].store_grade ('D');
      else
         all_students[i].store_grade ('F');
   } // end for
} // end assign_grades


// FINDS THE LOWEST POINT TOTAL
int gradebook::find_low ()

// Pre: Point totals are defined.
// Post: Lowest point total defined.
// Returns: The lowest point total.
{
   // Local data ...
   int lowest;

   lowest = all_students[0].retrieve_points ();
   for (int i = 1; i < nmbr_students; i++)
      if (all_students[i].retrieve_points () < lowest)
   lowest = all_students[i].retrieve_points ();
   return lowest;
} // end find_low


// FINDS THE HIGHEST POINT TOTAL
int gradebook::find_high ()

// Pre: Point totals are defined.
// Post: Highest point total defined.
// Returns: The highest point total.
{
   // Local data ...
   int highest;

   highest = all_students[0].retrieve_points ();
   for (int i = 1; i < nmbr_students; i++)
      if (all_students[i].retrieve_points () > highest)
         highest = all_students[i].retrieve_points ();
```

(Continued)

Figure 14.30 (Continued)

```
    return highest;
}  // end find_high


// COMPUTES THE AVERAGE OF THE POINT TOTALS
float gradebook::compute_average ()

// Pre:  Point totals are defined.
// Post: Average point total defined.
// Returns: The average point total.
{
   // Local data ...
   float sum;

   // Compute average.
   sum = 0.0;
   for (int i = 0; i < nmbr_students; i++)
      sum += all_students[i].retrieve_points ();

   return sum / float (nmbr_students);
}  // end compute_average


// COMPUTES THE STANDARD DEVIATION
float gradebook::compute_stddev ()

// Pre:     Point totals and average are defined.
// Post:    The standard deviation is defined or is set to zero.
// Returns: The standard deviation if defined;
//          otherwise, returns zero.
{
   // Local data ...
   float sumsq;
   float temp;

   // Compute standard deviation.
   sumsq = 0.0;
   for (int i = 0; i < nmbr_students; i++)
   {
      temp = all_students[i].retrieve_points () - average;
      sumsq += temp * temp;
   }  // end for

   if (nmbr_students > 1)
      sumsq = sqrt (sumsq / float (nmbr_students - 1));
   else
      sumsq;
```

(Continued)

Figure 14.30   (Continued)

```
      return sumsq;
}   // end compute_stddev


// COMPUTES THE MEDIAN POINT TOTAL
int gradebook::compute_median ()

// Pre:     Point totals are defined.
// Post:    Median is defined.
// Returns: The middle point total if there is an odd number
//          of totals; otherwise, returns the average of the
//          middle two point totals.
{
   // Local data ...
   int middle, median;

   // Compute median.
   middle = nmbr_students / 2;
   sort_students ();
   if ((nmbr_students % 2) == 1)
      median = all_students[middle].retrieve_points ();
   else
      median = (all_students[middle-1].retrieve_points () +
               all_students[middle].retrieve_points ()) / 2;
   return median;
}   // end compute_median


// EXCHANGES TWO STUDENT RECORDS
void gradebook::exchange
   (student &s1,          // INOUT: the first student record
    student &s2)          // INOUT: the second student record

// Pre:  None.
// Post: The two records are switched.
{
   // Local data ...
   student temp;

   temp = s1;
   s1 = s2;
   s2 = temp;
   return;
}   // end exchange

// SORTS THE RECORDS IN ASCENDING ORDER BY POINT TOTAL
void gradebook::sort_students ()
```

(Continued)

Figure 14.30   (Continued)

```
// Pre:  Student records are defined.
// Post: Student records sorted in increasing order by point total.
{
   for (int pass = 0; pass < nmbr_students - 1; pass++)
   {
      for (int i = 0; i < nmbr_students - 1; i++)
         if (all_students[i].retrieve_points () >
               all_students[i+1].retrieve_points ())
            exchange (all_students[i], all_students[i+1]);
   }  // end for
   return;
}  // end sort_students


// COMPUTES THE POINT TOTALS STATISTICS
void gradebook::compute_stats ()

// Pre:  Student records are defined.
// Post: Point total statistics are computed and stored.
{
   average = compute_average ();
   low_total = find_low ();
   high_total = find_high ();
   median = compute_median ();
   stddev = compute_stddev ();
   return;
}  // end compute_stats


// DISPLAYS POINT TOTALS STATISTICS
void gradebook::display_stats ()

// Pre:  Student records are defined.
// Post: All statistics are displayed.
{
   cout << endl << endl;
   cout << "*****************************" << endl;
   cout << "Summary of statistics for:" << endl;
   cout << course_id << " - " << course_title << endl;
   cout << semester << endl << endl;
   cout << setiosflags (ios::showpoint | ios::fixed);
   cout << "The Highest Point Total = " << high_total << endl;
   cout << "The Lowest Point Total = " << low_total << endl;
   cout << "The Median Point Total = " << median << endl;
   cout << "The Average = " << setprecision (2) << average
        << endl;
   cout << "The Standard Deviation = " << stddev << endl;
   return;
}  // end display_statistics
#endif //GRDBKADT_CPP_
```

Implementation of the Member Functions in the Student ADT

All that remains to complete the program system for the Grading Problem is the implementation of the member functions for the student ADT. This requires that we implement functions `read_data` and `write_data` (just described); the `retrieve` functions for the student name and point total; and a `store` function for the grade. (Store methods are not required for a student's name and point total because they are entered by `read_data`.) The implementations of all five of these functions are shown in Fig. 14.31.

Figure 14.31   Student ADT member functions for Student Grading Program

```cpp
// FILE: StdntADT.cpp
// IMPLEMENTATION OF ATTRIBUTES AND MEMBER FUNCTIONS FOR
//    ONE STUDENT

#ifndef STDNTADT_CPP_
#define STDNTADT_CPP_

#include <iostream.h>
#include <string.h>

#include "StdntADT.h"

// READS DATA FOR ONE STUDENT (NAME AND POINTS)
void student::read_data ()
// Pre:  None.
// Post: The data are stored.
{
   cout << "Name: ";
   cin >> ws;                        // skip over whitespace
   cin.getline (name, 31);
   if (strlen (name) != 1)
   {
      cout << "Points: ";
      cin >> points;
      cout << endl << endl;
   }  // end if
}  // end read


// DISPLAYS DATA FOR ONE STUDENT (NAME, POINTS, AND GRADE)
void student::write_data ()

// Pre:  The student record is defined.
// Post: The student record is displayed on the same line.
{
```

(Continued)

Figure 14.31 (Continued)

```
    cout << name << "    " << points << grade << endl;
} // end write


// RETRIEVES A STUDENT'S NAME
char *student::retrieve_name ()

// Pre:  The student name is defined.
// Post: None.
// Returns: The student name.
{
   return name;
} // end retrieve_name


// RETRIEVES A STUDENT'S POINT TOTAL
int student::retrieve_points ()

// Pre:  The student point total is defined.
// Post: None.
// Returns: The student point total.
{
   return points;
} // end retrieve_points


// STORES A STUDENT'S LETTER GRADE
void student::store_grade
  (char student_grade)     // IN: the letter grade

// Pre:  None.
// Post: The student grade is defined.
{
   grade = student_grade;
} // end store_grade

#endif // STDNTADT_CPP_
```

Program Testing

A sample run of the Grading Program was shown in Fig. 14.25. The program has been presented in several stages in which different components have been described. These components are each stored in separate files and should be tested separately before the main function is finally tested. The gradebook and student ADTs must be tested to ensure that their member functions execute correctly (see Programming Exercises 1 and 2 at the end of this section). If `enter_int` had not already been tested, it would have been important to do so early in the testing process. Not much of the program will execute correctly if this function is not working properly.

Once this work has been completed, we are ready for the integration testing of the entire grading program system. At this point, a full set of carefully selected test data should be generated, including data to exercise all of the error checking in the system. All possible combinations of program input that you can identify should be tested.

Commentary: Linking and Executing Grading Program Components

The following files must be combined in order to link and execute the grading program:

`GrdeBook.cpp`	function `main` and its subordinates;
`GrdBkADT.cpp`	the implementations of the methods for the gradebook `ADT` (included in `main`);
`StdntADT.cpp`	the implementations of the methods for the student `ADT` (included in `main`).

In addition, file `EnterInt.cpp` (see Section 10.3) must be included. Again, note that the code we have provided does not combine these separate components; you must do this using your locally available project management system (see similar discussions of combining program components for execution in Chapters 6, 8, and 11).

EXERCISES FOR SECTION 14.7

Self-Check
1. For the data in Fig. 14.24, what value is displayed by each of the following statements? Indicate which statements are not valid.

   a. `cout << "The number of students is " << nmbr_students << "."`
   `   << endl;`

   In what components of the gradebook program is this legal? In which ones is it illegal?

   b. `cout << "The number of students is "`
   `        << gradebook::nmbr_students << "." << endl;`

   In what components is this legal? In which ones is it illegal?

   c. `cout << score << grade << name << endl;`

   d. `cout << "The standard deviation is " << stddev << "."`
   `        << endl;`

   (from within `GrdBkADT.cpp`)

e. cout << "The standard deviation is "\
        << all_students[i].stddev << "." << endl;

f. cout << "The student's name is "
        << all_students[3].name << "." << endl;

g. cout << "The student's name is "
        << all_students[3].retrieve_name << "." << endl;

h. cout << "The average is " << statistics.average << "."
        << endl;

2. How would you change the `sort_students` function in the gradebook ADT to sort the student data collection in descending order by total points (largest point total first)? What changes would be needed to sort the collection of students by student name instead of by score?

3. Because we are ordering the student data collection on the total points field, we propose changing function `exchange` to exchange only the point total fields. Describe the effect of this proposal.

4. Using the function `compute_stddev` shown in Fig. 14.30, write out a mathematical formula for computing the standard deviation of a collection of data items named x. Use summation notation, for example,

$$\sum_{i=1}^{n} x = x_1 + x_2 + x_3 + \cdots + x_n .$$

Programming   1. Write a short driver program to test each of the methods in the student ADT.
2. Write a driver program to test each of the methods in the gradebook ADT.

14.8 ___ COMMON PROGRAMMING ERRORS

■ *Subscript Errors in Multidimensional Array References:* When using multidimensional arrays, make sure the subscript for each dimension is within the specified range for that subscript. Out-of-range subscripts will not be detected during execution and therefore will not directly produce any meaningful run-time diagnostics such as "`subscript out-of-range.`" Instead, your program will reference locations that are not within the range of memory allocated to the indicated array. These references are likely to cause erroneous execution results or produce an execution-time error that could be difficult to diagnose. Similar problems can arise if your subscript references do not match the order of the dimensions you specified when declaring a multidimensional array.

■ *Nested for Loops and Multidimensional Arrays:* If you use nested `for` loops to process array elements, make sure that the loop-control variables used as array subscripts are incorporated into the array references in the correct order. The order of the loop-control variables determines the sequence in which the array elements are processed.

- *Processing Arrays of Structs or Classes:* When processing arrays of structs or classes, remember that the array name and the subscript must be part of the struct or class component selector. For example,

```
all_students[i].retrieve_points ();
```

retrieves the points component of the ith student of `all_students`. The reference

```
vertex[k].x
```

might be used to access field x of the kth vertex of a polygon. Note that

```
vertex.x[k]
```

is illegal in this case and will cause a compiler error message to be generated.

CHAPTER REVIEW

We began this chapter with illustrations of a number of ways to model complicated data structures in C++. Arrays of arrays, arrays of structs, arrays of class elements, and indexed collections of class elements were used to model tables of information, buildings, and so on. A number of comparisons were provided to illustrate the benefits of using arrays of structs (rather than arrays of arrays), or arrays of indexed collections of class elements (rather than arrays of structs). It was shown how program clarity can be improved using arrays of struct or class elements and how the use of classes to encapsulate data abstractions (mostly indexed collections of objects of user-defined classes) improved the quality of the programs that were developed.

The Case Study illustrated the development of models of problem-domain entities using arrays, structs, and classes in various combinations. Our goal was to show that the design and implementation of new abstract data types to model key program objects was as important (if not more so) as top-down procedural design. These new types, combined with C++ types and structures, are the fundamental building blocks of our programs. In the end, the programs themselves were extremely short, consisting of little more than sequences of calls to the member functions encapsulated in the new data type definitions. The member functions defined within the data types were also quite short and uncomplicated, usually taking less than half a page and often written with little, if any, nesting of control structures.

New C++
Constructs

The C++ constructs introduced in this chapter are described in Table 14.1.

Table 14.1   Summary of New C++ Constructs

CONSTRUCT	EFFECT
Declaring Multidimensional Arrays	
`double vertex[2][3];`	Declares a 2×3 array (2 rows, 3 columns) with type `double` base elements.
`typedef double point[2];` `point vertex[3];`	Declares a 3-element array of vertices, each of which consists of a 2-element array `point`.
Referencing Arrays	

`(vertex[vert])[1]`
        or
`vertex[vert][1]`
	References the data element in row `vert+1`, column 2.

`for (int r = 0; r < 3; r++)`
`{`
`    for (int c = 0; c < 3; c++)`
`        cout << ttt[r][c];`
`    cout << endl;`
`}`
	Prints an entire tic-tac-toe board one row at a time with proper spacing but no division markers such as | and –. The column subscript increases the fastest. This results in the display of all the elements of a given row before the row subscript is increased.

Declaring Arrays of Structs and Classes	

`struct point_st`
`{`
`    double x;`
`    double y;`
`};`
	A `struct` consisting of two type `double` elements.

`point_st vertex[3];`	A 3-element array having base elements of type `point_st`.

`class point_cl`
`{`
`    public:`
`        void print();`
`    private:`
`        double x;`
`        double y;`
`}; // end class point`
	A `class` consisting of two type `double` elements.

`point_cl vertex[3];`	A 3-element array having base elements of type `point_cl`.

(Continued)

Table 14.1   Summary of New C++ Constructs

CONSTRUCT	EFFECT
Referencing Arrays of Structs and Classes	
`vertex[i].x`	References the **x**- and **y**-coordinates of
`vertex[i].y`	the **i**th element of the array `vertex` (`vertex[i]` is assumed to be a `struct` of two fields, **x** and **y**).
`vertex[i].retrieve_x();`	Retrieves the **x**-coordinate value for the **i**th vertex object.

✔ QUICK-CHECK EXERCISES

1. In C++, how many subscripts can an array have?
2. What control structure can be used to process sequentially all the elements in a multidimensional array?
3. Write a program segment to display the sum of the values in each column of a 5×3 array `table` with base type `float` elements. How many column sums will be displayed? How many elements are included in each sum?
4. Write the type declaration of an array that stores the batting averages by position (`catcher`, `pitcher`, `first_base`, etc.) for each of 14 baseball teams in each of two leagues (`american` and `national`).
5. Using the declarations from Quick-Check Exercise 4 as needed, write the type declaration for a data structure that stores a player's name, salary, position, batting average, fielding percentage, number of hits, runs, runs batted in, and errors.
6. Write the type declaration for a data structure that stores the information in Quick-Check Exercise 5 for a team of 25 players.
7. If the elements of the array `team` have the structure described in Quick-Check Exercise 6, write a program segment that displays the first two structure members for the first five players.

Answers to Quick-Check Exercises

1. There is no specific limit; however, the size of the array is limited by the memory space available, and multidimensional arrays can require considerable memory.
2. nested `for` loops
3.
```
for (int c = 0; c < 3; c++)
  {
     column_sum = 0.0;
     for (int r = 0; r < 5; r++)
       column_sum += table[r][c];
```

```
        cout << "Sum for column " << c << " is " << column_sum
            << "." << endl;
}   // end for c
```

three column sums; five elements added per column

4. The base type of this array is the fundamental type `float`. We also need the following enumeration types:

```
enum positions {pitcher, catcher, first_base, second_base,
                third_base, short_stop, left_field,
                center_field, right_field};
enum league = {american, national};
```

The required declaration could be written as

```
float averages[right_field + 1][national + 1][14];
```

5. The data elements are of different types:

```
struct player
{
    char name[20];
    float salary;
    positions place;
    float batting_ave, field_pct;
    int hits, runs, rbis, errors;
}   // end player
```

6. `player team[25];`

7.
```
for (int i = 0; i < 5; i++)
    cout << team[i].name << "    " << team[i].salary << endl;
```

REVIEW QUESTIONS

1. Write the declarations for an indexed collection of data that can be used to store each title of the `top40` hits for one week of the year given that the `title_length` will be 20 characters.
2. Write the declaration for an indexed collection that can be used to store the hours that an employee works each day of the week.
3. Write the declarations for the array `cpu_array` that will hold 20 records of type `cpu`. The structure `cpu` has the following fields: `id_number` (11 characters in length), `make` (5 characters), `location` (15 characters), and `ports` (integer).
   Use the following declarations for Review Questions 4 through 8:

```
const int nmbr_employees = 20;

struct employee
{
```

```
        int id;
        float rate;
        float hours;
    }  // end employee

    employee all_employees[nmbr_employees];
```

4. Write the function `total_gross` that will return the total gross pay given the data stored in the array `all_employees`.

5. Explain what is wrong with the following fragment and fix it.

```
i = 1;
while (i <= nmbr_employees)
{
    cout << "The number of hours is " << hours << endl;
    i++;
}  // end while
```

6. Write a C++ program fragment that displays the ID number of each employee who works between 10.0 and 20.0 hours per week.

7. Write a C++ program fragment that displays the ID number of the employee who works the most hours.

PROGRAMMING PROJECTS

1. Write a program that generates the Morse code for a sentence that ends with a period and contains no other characters except letters and blanks. After reading the Morse code into an array of strings, your program should read each word of the sentence and display its Morse code equivalent on a separate line. The Morse code is as follows:

```
A .-    B -...   C -.-.  D -..   E .    F ..-.  G --.  H ....  I ..    J .---
K -.-   L .-..   M --    N -.    O ---  P .--.  Q --.- R .-.   S ...   T -
U ..-   V ...-   W .--   X -..-  Y -.-- Z --..
```

In designing the solution to this problem, you should make use of program components from any previous chapters, especially Chapters 8, 11, and 12. In particular, each letter and its Morse code equivalent should be stored in an index collection of structs, and an appropriate set of methods should be defined for this data abstraction. You should also consider taking advantage of the string-related input and output functions defined in Chapters 8 and 11.

2. Develop a C++ class to model the mathematical notion of a matrix. At a minimum, your class should include methods for addition, subtraction, and multiplication of two matrices, plus at least three other matrix operations that you know about. (If you don't know much about matrices, find a mathematics book that can help.) Before performing the required data manipulation, each method you write should validate its input arguments. In particular, the dimensions of the matrices involved in an operation must be compatible for that operation.

3. The voting district in which you live is partitioned into five precincts. Write a program that reads the election results from each of these precincts and tabulates the total vote in your district for all of the candidates running for election.

The program should begin by asking the user to enter the number of candidates, nmbr_candidates, running for office. It should then read the election returns for each precinct for each candidate, compute the total vote for each candidate, and print the input and the results in the tabular form shown at the end of this problem description.

For each candidate, the program should also compute and display the percentage of the total vote. If there is one candidate whose percentage is better than 50%, print out a message declaring that candidate to be the winner of the election. If there is no such candidate, print out a message indicating the names of the top two vote-getters and indicate that a run-off election will be required.

The voting data should be stored in an index collection of structured elements, each of which contains the name of a candidate, the number of votes in each precinct for that candidate, and the vote total. The index collection should be patterned after version 3 of the index collection data type, as defined in this chapter. The relevant information about each candidate should be modeled by a class containing the definitions of the necessary attributes and methods required for one candidate. The overall data model will be similar to the one used in the Case Study in this chapter.

Test your program for the data shown below and also when candidate C receives only 108 votes in precinct 4.

PRECINCT	CANDIDATE A	CANDIDATE B	CANDIDATE C	CANDIDATE D	TOTAL VOTE
1	192	48	206	37	483
2	147	90	312	21	570
3	186	12	121	38	357
4	114	21	408	39	582
5	267	13	382	29	691
TOTALS	906	184	1429	164	2683

4. Modify Programming Project 3 to make it an interactive, menu-driven program. Menu options should include the following:

- initializing the vote table (prompt the user for the number of candidates, their names, and the number of votes in each precinct);
- displaying the candidates' names and votes received (raw count and percentage of votes cast);
- displaying the winner's name (or names of the top two vote-getters in the case of a run-off); and
- exiting the program.

5. The HighRisk Software Company has employed us to develop a general sales analysis program that they can market to a number of different companies. The program will be used to enter monthly sales figures for a specified range of years and

display these values and some simple statistical measures as requested by the user. The user is to be given a menu from which to choose one of the following options:

OPTIONS	DESCRIPTION
0	Display help information—displays more detailed information about the other options available.
1	Display sales data—displays sales data for the entire range of years using two tables, one covering Jan–Jun and the other covering Jul–Dec.
2	Compute annual sales totals—computes the sum of the monthly sales for each year in the specified range.
3	Display annual sales totals—displays the sum of the monthly sales for each year in the specified range.
4	Display largest monthly sales amount—finds and displays the largest monthly sales amount for a specified year.
5	Graph monthly sales data—provides a histogram for the twelve months of sales for a specified year.
6	Exit—exits from the program.

The program is to run interactively and should begin by asking the user to enter the range of years involved. Next it should prompt the user for the sales data for each of the specified years. From this point on, the program should display the options menu, allow the user to make a choice, and carry out the user's selection. This process should continue repeatedly until the user enters option 6.

6. For the Grading Program (Section 14.7), design and implement two additional classes:

   ▪ a class to model the course information required by the problem;
   ▪ a class to model the statistical information.

   Comment on the overall effect on your code of adding these classes.

7. Design and implement a C++ class to model a telephone directory for a company. The directory should contain space for up to 100 names, phone numbers, and room numbers. You should have operators to:

   ▪ create an empty directory (all names blank);
   ▪ read in the telephone directory from a file;
   ▪ retrieve the entry corresponding to a given name;
   ▪ display the telephone directory; and
   ▪ add a new entry to the directory.

   Also design and implement a class with attributes and methods required to model an individual telephone entry.

8. Write a menu-driven program that tests the operators in Programming Project 7.

9. Design and implement a C++ class to model a building (floors 1 to 3, wings A and B, and rooms 1 to 5). Each entry in the array will be a `struct` containing a person's name and phone number. Provide operators to:

   ▪ create an empty building (all names are blank);

- read data into the building;
- display the entire building;
- display a particular floor of the building;
- retrieve the entry for a particular room; and
- store a new entry in a particular room.

To designate a particular room, the program user must enter a floor number, wing letter, and room number as data. Also design and implement a class with attributes and methods required to model a single room in the building.

10. Many supermarkets use computer equipment that allows the checkout clerk to drag an item across a sensor that reads the bar code on the product container. After the computer reads the bar code, the store inventory data base is examined, the item's price and product description are located, counts are reduced, and a receipt is printed. Your task is to write a program that simulates this process.

    Your program will read the inventory information from the data file on disk into an array of records. The data in the inventory file is written one item per line, beginning with a 2-digit product code, followed by a 30-character product description, its price, and the quantity of that item in stock. Your program will copy the revised version of the inventory to a new data file after all purchases are processed.

    Processing customers' orders involves reading a series of product codes representing each person's purchases from a second data file. A zero product code is used to mark the end of each customer's order. As each product code is read, the inventory list is searched to find a matching product code. Once located, the product price and description are printed on the receipt, and the quantity on hand is reduced by 1. At the bottom of the receipt, print the total for the goods purchased by the customer.

11. Write a program that simulates the movement of radioactive particles in a 20×20-foot two-dimensional shield around a reactor. Particles enter the shield at some random position in the shield coordinate space. Once a particle enters the shield, it moves 1 foot per second in one of four directions. The direction for the next second of travel is determined by a random number from 1 to 4 (forward, backward, left, right). A change in direction is interpreted as a collision with another particle, which results in a dissipation of energy. Each particle can have only a limited number of collisions before it dies. A particle exits the shield if its position places it outside the shield coordinate space before K collisions occur. Determine the percentage of particles that exit the shield, where K and the number of particles are input as data items. Also, compute the average number of times a particle's path crosses itself during travel time within the shield. *Hint:* Mark each array position occupied by a particle before it dies or exits the shield.

15

Recursion

15.1 The Nature of Recursion
15.2 Tracing Recursive Functions
15.3 Recursive Mathematical Functions
15.4 Recursive Functions with Array
     Arguments
     CASE STUDY: Recursive Selection Sort
15.5 Problem-Solving with Recursion
     CASE STUDY: Towers of Hanoi Problem
15.6 Picture-Processing with Recursion
     CASE STUDY: Counting Cells in a Blob
15.7 Common Programming Errors
     Chapter Review

A recursive function is one that calls itself. This ability allows a recursive function to be repeated with different argument values. You can use recursion as an alternative to iteration (looping). A recursive solution is generally less efficient in terms of computer time than an iterative one due to the overhead for the extra function calls; however, in many instances the use of recursion enables us to specify a natural, simple solution to a problem that would otherwise be difficult to solve. For this reason, recursion is an important and powerful tool in problem-solving and programming.

15.1 ——— THE NATURE OF RECURSION

Problems that lend themselves to a recursive solution have the following characteristics:

- One or more simple cases of the problem (called *stopping cases*) have a straightforward, nonrecursive solution.
- For the other cases, there is a process (using recursion) for substituting one or more reduced cases of the problem that are closer to a stopping case.
- Eventually the problem can be reduced to stopping cases only, all of which are relatively easy to solve.

The recursive algorithms that we write will generally consist of an `if` statement with the form shown below.

If the stopping case is reached
    Solve the problem.
else
    Reduce the problem using recursion.

Figure 15.1 illustrates this approach. Let's assume that for a particular problem of size n, we can split the problem into two subproblems—a problem of

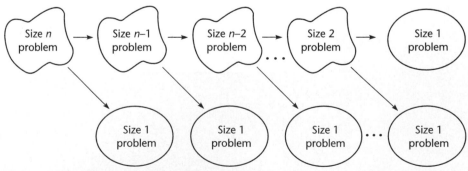

Figure 15.1   **Splitting a problem into smaller problems**

size 1, which we can solve (a stopping case), and a problem of size $n - 1$ that involves recursion. We can split the problem of size $n - 1$ into another problem of size 1 and a problem of size $n - 2$, which we can split further. If we split the problem n times, we will end up with n problems of size 1, each of which can be solved directly.

Example 15.1   As a simple example of this approach, let's consider how we might solve the problem of multiplying 6 by 3, assuming that we know our addition tables but not our multiplication tables. The problem of multiplying 6 by 3 can be split into the two subproblems:

1. Multiply 6 by 2.
2. Add 6 to the result of subproblem 1.

Since we know our addition tables, we can solve subproblem 2 but not subproblem 1. However, subproblem 1 is simpler than the original problem. We can split it into the two problems 1.1 and 1.2 below, leaving us three problems to solve, two of which involve addition.

1.1 Multiply 6 by 1.
1.2 Add 6 to the result of subproblem 1.1.

Even though we don't know our multiplication tables, we are familiar with the simple rule that for any integer m, m × 1 is m. By solving subproblem 1.1 (the answer is 6) and subproblem 1.2, we get the solution to subproblem 1 (the answer is 12). Solving subproblem 2 gives us the final answer (18).

Figure 15.2 shows the implementation of this solution in the form of the recursive function `multiply`. This function returns the product, m × n, of its

Figure 15.2   Recursive function `multiply`

```
// FILE: Multiply.cpp
// RECURSIVE MULTIPLY FUNCTION

// PERFORMS MULTIPLICATION USING THE + OPERATOR
int multiply
   (int m, int n)      // IN: values to be multiplied

// Pre:    m and n are defined and n > 0.
// Post:   Returns m * n.
// Returns: Product of m x n.
{
   // Multiply m and n.
   if (n <= 1)
      return m;                              // stopping step
   else
      return m + multiply (m, n - 1);  // recursive step
}  // end multiply
```

two arguments. The stopping case is reached when n finally equals 1 (the condition n <= 1 is true). In this case, the statement

```
return m;                          // stopping case
```

executes, returning the answer m. If n is greater than 1, the statement

```
return (m + multiply (m, n - 1));   // recursive step
```

executes, splitting the original problem into the two simpler problems:

1. Multiply m by n - 1.
2. Add m to the result of subproblem 1.

The first of these subproblems is solved by calling `multiply` again with n - 1 as its second argument. If the new second argument is greater than 1, there will be additional calls to function `multiply`.   ∎

For now, we will assume that function `multiply` performs as desired. We will see how to trace the execution of a recursive function in the next section.

The next example illustrates how we might solve a more difficult problem by splitting it into smaller problems. We will provide a complete Case Study solution to this problem after you have more experience using recursion.

Example 15.2   The Towers of Hanoi Problem involves moving a specified number of disks that are all of different sizes from one tower to another. Legend has it that the world will come to an end when the problem is solved for 64 disks. In the version of the problem shown in Fig. 15.3, there are 5 disks (numbered 1 through 5) and three towers (lettered A, B, C). The goal is to move the 5 disks from tower A to tower C, subject to the following rules:

- Only one disk may be moved at a time, and this disk must be the top disk on a tower.
- A larger disk can never be placed on top of a smaller disk.

The stopping case of the problem involves moving one disk only (for example, "move disk 1 from tower A to tower C"). A simpler problem than the original would be to move 4 disks subject to the conditions above, or to move 3 disks, and so on. Therefore, we want to split the original 5-disk problem into one or more subproblems involving fewer disks. Let's consider splitting the original problem into the three subproblems shown below:

1. Move 4 disks (numbered 1 through 4) from tower A to tower B.
2. Move disk 5 from tower A to tower C.
3. Move the four disks (1 through 4) from tower B to tower C.

In subproblem 1, we move all disks but the largest to tower B, an auxiliary tower. In subproblem 2, we move the largest disk to the goal tower, tower C.

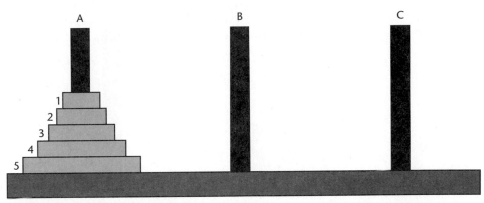

Figure 15.3   Towers of Hanoi

Finally, we move the remaining disks from B to the goal tower, where they will be placed on top of the largest disk.

Perhaps you are concerned that we have not really solved the original problem because we have not indicated how to perform subproblems 1 and 3. If so, please keep reading—the pieces will fit together shortly.

Let's assume that we can simply "follow the directions" indicated in problems 1 and 2 (a stopping case); Fig. 15.4 shows the status of the three towers after the completion of the tasks described in these subproblems. We can now solve the original 5-disk problem by following the directions indicated for subproblem 3. The resulting change to Fig. 15.4 should be fairly obvious.

Unfortunately, we still don't know how to perform subproblems 1 or 3. Both, however, involve 4 disks instead of 5, and so they are in some sense easier than the original problem. We should be able to split them into simpler

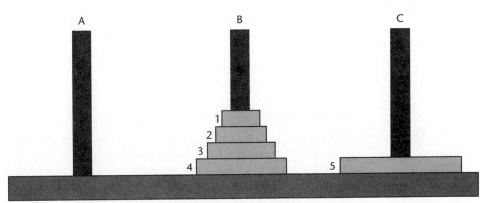

Figure 15.4   Towers of Hanoi after steps 1 and 2

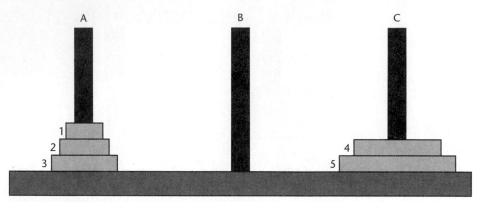

Figure 15.5 Towers of Hanoi after steps 1, 2, 3.1, and 3.2

problems in the same way that we split the original problem. For example, subproblem 3 involves moving 4 disks from tower B to tower C. We split this problem into two 3-disk problems and a 1-disk problem, as follows.

3.1. Move 3 disks from tower B to tower A.
3.2. Move disk 4 from tower B to tower C.
3.3. Move 3 disks from tower A to tower C.

Figure 15.5 shows the status of the towers after the tasks described in subproblems 3.1 and 3.2 have been completed. We now have the 2 largest disks on tower C. Note that tower A was the auxiliary disk for this sequence of moves. Once we complete subproblem 3.3, all 5 disks will be on tower C as required. ■

By repeatedly splitting each *n*-disk problem into two problems involving *n*–1 disks and a 1-disk problem, we will eventually reach all cases of 1 disk, which we know how to solve. We will write a C++ program that solves the Towers of Hanoi Problem later.

EXERCISES FOR SECTION 15.1

Self-Check
1. Draw a picture depicting Fig. 15.4 after step 3 (move 4 disks (1 through 4) from tower B to tower C) has been carried out.
2. Show the subproblems that are generated by the function call `multiply (5, 4)`. Use a diagram similar to Fig. 15.1.
3. Show the subproblems that are generated by attempting to solve the problem "move three disks from tower A to tower C."

15.2 ___ TRACING RECURSIVE FUNCTIONS

Hand tracing the execution of an algorithm provides us with valuable insight as to how that algorithm works. This is particularly true for recursive functions, as shown next.

Tracing a Recursive Function

In the last section, we wrote the recursive function `multiply` (see Fig. 15.2). We can trace the execution of the function call `multiply (6, 3)` by drawing an *activation frame* corresponding to each function call. An activation frame shows the argument values for each call and summarizes its execution.

The three activation frames generated to solve the problem of multiplying 6 by 3 are shown in Fig. 15.6. The part of each activation frame that executes before the next recursive call is shaded; the part that executes after the return from the next call has no shading. The darker the shading of an activation frame, the greater the depth of recursion.

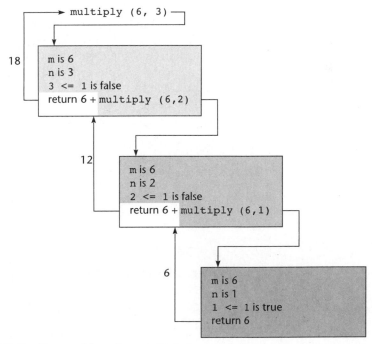

Figure 15.6 Trace of function `multiply`

The value returned from each call is shown alongside each upwardly directed arrow. The return arrow from each function call points to the operator + because the addition is performed just after the return.

When n is 1 in the third and last activation frame (corresponding to the call multiply (6, 1)), the value of m (6) is returned to the second activation frame (corresponding to the call multiply (6, 2)). This returned value is added to m (also 6) and their sum (12) is returned to the first activation frame (corresponding to the call multiply (6, 3)). This returned value is added to m (6) and their sum (18) is returned to the point of the original function call, multiply (6, 3).

Hand tracing the execution of a recursive function can sometimes be cumbersome. We can easily implement a function to provide a trace of itself by inserting display statements at the points of entry to and exit from the function. For example, we could modify the multiply function in Fig. 15.2 to include

```
cout << "Entering multiply with m = " << setw (2) << m
     << " and n = " << setw (2) << n << endl;
```

as the first executable line of the function and

```
cout << "multiply (" << setw (2) << m << ", " << setw (2) << n
     << ") returns " << setw (2) << answer << endl;
return answer;
```

as the last two lines in the function. Here, answer is assumed to be a variable local to multiply that always must be set to the value to be returned regardless of which alternative is selected. Function multiply is currently not written using such a local variable and would have to be further modified to accommodate the trace (see Self-Check Exercise 2 at the end of this section). Once these modifications have been completed, the output from the revised function multiply with actual arguments (8, 3) appears as follows:

```
Entering multiply with m =  8 and n =  3
Entering multiply with m =  8 and n =  2
Entering multiply with m =  8 and n =  1
multiply ( 8,  1) returns  8;
multiply ( 8,  2) returns 16;
multiply ( 8,  3) returns 24;
```

Tracing a Recursive Function with No Return Value

Example 15.3   Recursive function reverse_string in Fig. 15.7 reads in a string of length n and prints it out backward. If the function call

```
reverse_string (5)
```

Figure 15.7   Recursive function `reverse_string`

```
// FILE: RvrsStrg.cpp
// RECURSIVE FUNCTION TO REVERSE THE ORDER OF A CHARACTER STRING

// DISPLAYS A STRING IN REVERSE ORDER
void reverse_string
  (int n)                // IN: length of the string to be processed

// Pre:  n is defined and is greater than or equal to 1.
// Post: Displays n characters in reverse order.
{
   // Local data ...
   char next;            // contains current character being processed

   // Read string and display in reverse order.
   if (n <= 1)
   {                      // stopping step
      cin >> next;
      cout << next;
   }
   else                   // recursive step
   {
      cin >> next;
      reverse_string (n - 1);
      cout << next;
   }
   return;
}  // end reverse_string
```

is executed, the five characters entered at the screen are printed in reverse order. If the characters abcde are entered when this function is called, the characters edcba are displayed on the next line. If the function call

```
reverse_string (3);
```

is executed instead, only three characters are read, and the output cba is displayed.

As with most recursive functions, the body of function reverse_string consists of an if statement that evaluates a *stopping condition,* n <= 1. When the stopping condition is true, the problem has reached a *stopping case:* a data string of length 1. If n <= 1 is true, the input and output lines (cin and cout) are executed. If the stopping condition is false (n greater than 1), the recursive step (following else) is executed. The cin line reads in the next data character. However, before this character can be printed, function reverse_string is called again, with the argument value decreased by 1. When this call occurs, the character just read is saved in the current copy of the local variable `next`. It is not displayed until after the return from the recursive call, when control is returned to the line immediately following the function call (in this case, the `cout` line). For example, the character that is read when n is 3 is not displayed until after the function execution for n equal to 2 has completed.

To help you fully understand this sequence of events, we will trace the execution of the function call

```
reverse_string (3);
```

This trace is shown in Fig. 15.8, assuming the letters `abc` are entered as data. The trace shows three activation frames for function `reverse_string`. Each activation frame begins with a list of the initial values of n and `next` for that frame. The value of n is passed into the function when it is called; the value of `next` is initially undefined.

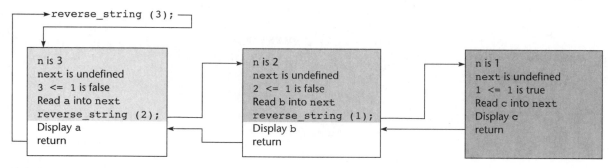

Figure 15.8   Trace of `reverse_string (3);`

The statements that are executed for each frame are shown in Fig. 15.9. Each recursive call to `reverse_string` results in a new activation frame, as indicated by the arrows pointing to the right. The arrows pointing to the left indicate the statement that executes immediately following the return from the recursive call. Tracing the right-directed arrows and then the left-directed arrows gives us the sequence of events listed in Fig. 15.9. To help you understand this list, all the statements for a particular activation frame are indented to the same column.

As shown, there are three calls to function `reverse_string`, each with a different argument value. The function returns always occur in the reverse order of the function calls; that is, we return from the last call first, then we return from the next to last call, and so on. After the return from a particular execution of the function, the character that was read into `next` just prior to that function call is displayed.

Figure 15.9 Sequence of events for trace of `reverse_string (3)`

Call `reverse_string` with n equal to 3.
   Read the first character (a) into `next`.
   Call `reverse_string` with n equal to 2.
      Read the second character (b) into `next`.
      Call `reverse_string` with n equal to 1.
         Read the third character (c) into `next`.
         Display the third character (c).
         Return from third call.
      Display the second character (b).
      Return from second call.
   Display the first character (a).
   Return from original call.

■

Argument and Local Variable Stacks

You may be wondering how C++ keeps track of the values of n and `next` at any given point. The answer is that C++ uses a special data structure, called a *stack*, that is analogous to a stack of dishes or trays. In a cafeteria, clean dishes are placed on top of a stack of dishes. When we need a dish, we normally remove the one most recently placed on the stack. Thus, the top dish is removed, and the next to the last dish put on the stack moves to the top. (The stack data structure is discussed further in Chapter 16.)

Similarly, whenever a new function call occurs, the argument value associated with that call is placed on top of the argument stack. Also, a new memory location that represents the local variable `next` and whose value is initially undefined is placed on top of the stack. Whenever n or `next` is referenced, the value at the top of the corresponding stack is always used. When a function return occurs, the value currently at the top of each stack is removed, and the value just below it moves to the top.

As an example, let's look at the two stacks right after the first call to `reverse_string`.

After First Call to reverse_string

There is one memory location on each stack, as shown below.

```
n    next
|3|    |?|  ←top
```

As we trace the execution of `reverse_string`, we see that the letter a is read into `next` just before the second call to the function.

```
n    next
|3|    |a|  ←top
```

After Second Call to reverse_string

After the second call to reverse_string, the number 2 is placed on top of the stack for n, and the top of the stack for next becomes undefined again, as shown below.

```
n     next
2     ?    ←top
3     a
```

The letter b is read into next just before the third call to reverse_string:

```
n     next
2     b    ←top
3     a
```

After Third Call to reverse_string

Then next becomes undefined again right after the third call:

```
n     next
1     ?    ←top
2     b
3     a
```

During this execution of the function, the letter c is read into next. This value of c is printed immediately because n is 1 (the stopping case):

```
n     next
1     c    ←top
2     b
3     a
```

After First Return

The function return causes the value at the top of each stack to be removed, as shown next:

```
n     next
2     b    ←top
3     a
```

Because control is returned to the cout line that follows the third call to reverse_string, the value of next (b) at the top of the stack is then displayed.

After Second Return

Another return occurs, causing the values currently at the top of the stack to be removed:

```
n     next
3     a    ←top
```

Again, control is returned to the cout line that follows the second call to reverse_string, and the value of next (a) at the top of the stack is displayed.

After Third Return

The third and last return removes the last values from the stack.

```
n    next
|?|   |?|
```

Because these steps are all done automatically by C++, we can write recursive functions without needing to worry about the stacks. We will see how to declare and manipulate our own stacks in Chapter 16.

Implementation of Argument Stacks in C++

For illustrative purposes, we have used separate stacks for n and next in our discussion. The compiler, however, actually maintains a single stack. Each time a call to a function occurs, all its arguments and local variables are pushed onto the stack along with the memory address of the calling statement. This memory address gives the computer the return point after execution of the function. Although multiple copies of a function's arguments may be saved on the stack, only one copy of the function body is in memory.

EXERCISES FOR SECTION 15.2

Self-Check

1. In the reverse_string function (Fig. 15.7), n was passed in as a call-by-value argument. Discuss what happens to the current value of n each time reverse_string recursively calls itself. What happens to the current value of n whenever reverse_string returns to its calling function?
2. Modify function multiply (Fig. 15.2) to print the values of m and n immediately upon entry and to print the value to be returned just prior to exit. You will want to introduce a local variable as a temporary store for the result to be returned.
3. Explain why the six output trace statements shown at the beginning of Section 15.2 for function multiply (see also Self-Check Exercise 2) appeared in the order they did. For example, be sure to explain why the three entry displays ("Entering multiply ...") appeared before any of the exit displays ("multiply ... returns ...") and why the exit displays appeared as they did.
4. Assume the characters *+-/ are entered for the function call statement

   ```
   reverse_string (4);
   ```

   What output line would appear on the screen? Show the contents of the stacks immediately after each function call and return.
5. Trace the execution of multiply (5, 4) and show the stacks after each recursive call.

15.3 ____ RECURSIVE MATHEMATICAL FUNCTIONS

Many mathematical functions are defined recursively. An example is the factorial, *n!*, of a number *n*.

$$0! = 1$$
$$n! = n \times (n-1)!, \text{ for } n > 0$$

Thus 4! is $4 \times 3 \times 2 \times 1$, or 24. It is quite easy to implement this definition as a recursive function in C++.

Example 15.4   Function `fact` in Fig. 15.10 computes the factorial of its argument n. The recursive step

```
return (n * fact (n - 1));
```

implements the second line of the definition above. This means that the result of the current call (argument n) is determined by multiplying the result of the next call (argument n - 1) by n.

Figure 15.10   Recursive factorial function

```
// FILE: RcsvFact.cpp
// RECURSIVE FACTORIAL FUNCTION

// COMPUTES THE FACTORIAL OF N
int fact
   (int n)        // IN: value used in calculation

// Pre:     n is defined and n >= 0.
// Post:    None
// Returns: n!
{
   if (n <= 0)
      return 1;
   else
      return n * fact (n-1);
}   // end fact
```

A trace of a call to `fact`,

```
result = fact (3);
```

is shown in Fig. 15.11. The value returned from the original call, `fact (3)`, is 6, and this value is assigned to the variable `result`. Be careful when using the factorial function; the value computed increases rapidly and could lead to an integer-overflow error (for example, 10! may come out as 24320 on your computer instead of the correct value, 3628800).

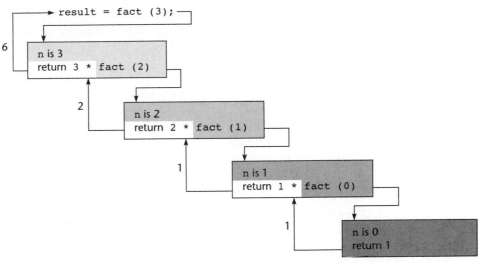

Figure 15.11   Trace of `result = fact (3)`

Although the recursive implementation of function **fact** follows naturally from its definition, this function can be implemented easily using iteration. The iterative version is shown in Fig. 15.12.

Figure 15.12   Iterative factorial function

```
// FILE: IterFact.cpp
// ITERATIVE FACTORIAL FUNCTION

// COMPUTES THE FACTORIAL OF N
int fact
  (int n)        // IN: value used in calculation

// Pre:     n is defined and n >= 0.
// Post:    None
// Returns: n!
{
   // Local data ...
   int i;              // loop control variable
   int factorial;      // resulting value

   factorial = 1;
   for (i = 2; i <= n; i++)
      factorial *= i;
   return factorial;
}  // end fact
```

■

Note that the iterative version contains a loop as its major control structure, whereas the recursive version contains an `if` statement. Also, a local variable, `factorial`, is needed in the iterative version to hold the accumulating product.

Example 15.5   The Fibonacci numbers are a sequence of numbers that have many varied uses. They were originally intended to model the growth of a rabbit colony. We will not go into details of the model here, but you can see that the Fibonacci sequence 1, 1, 2, 3, 5, 8, 13, 21, 34, . . . increases rapidly. The fifteenth number in the sequence is 610, and that's a lot of rabbits!

The Fibonacci sequence is defined using the *recurrence relations* shown below.

- fib_1 is 1
- fib_2 is 1
- fib_n is $fib_{n-2} + fib_{n-1}$, for $n > 2$.

Simply stated, n is the sum of the two preceding numbers. Verify for yourself that the sequence of numbers shown in the above paragraph is correct.

A recursive function that computes the nth Fibonacci number is shown in Fig. 15.13. Although easy to write, the Fibonacci function is not very efficient because each recursive step generates two calls to function Fibonacci.

Figure 15.13   Recursive Fibonacci number function

```
// FILE: Fibonacc.cpp
// RECURSIVE FIBONACCI NUMBER FUNCTION

// COMPUTES THE NTH FIBONACCI NUMBER
int fibonacci
   (int n)                  // IN: value

// Pre:     n is defined and n > 0.
// Post:    None
// Returns: The nth Fibonacci number.
{
   if (n == 1 || n == 2)
      return 1;
   else
      return fibonacci (n - 2) + fibonacci (n - 1);
}  // end fibonacci
```

Example 15.6   Euclid's algorithm for finding the greatest common divisor of two positive integers, GCD (m, n), is defined recursively below. The *greatest common divisor* of two integers is the largest integer that divides them both.

- GCD (m,n) is n if n <= m and n divides m
- GCD (m,n) is GCD (n, m) if m < n
- GCD (m,n) is GCD (n, remainder of m divided by n) otherwise

This algorithm states that the GCD is n if n is the smaller number and n divides m. If m is the smaller number, then the GCD determination should be performed with the arguments transposed. If n does not divide m, the answer is obtained by finding the GCD of n and the remainder of m divided by n. The C++ function GCD is shown in Fig. 15.14.

Figure 15.14 Euclid's algorithm for the greatest common divisor

```cpp
// FILE: FindGCD.cpp
// PROGRAM AND RECURSIVE FUNCTION TO FIND GREATEST COMMON DIVISOR

#include <iostream.h>

void main ()
{
   // Local data ...
   int m, n;        // the two input items

   // Functions used ...
   // RECURSIVE FUNCTION TO FIND GREATEST COMMON DIVISOR
   int gcd
     (int,        // IN: first input item
      int);       // IN: second input item

   cout << endl << "Enter two positive integers separated by a
                   space: ";
   cin >> m >> n;
   cout << endl;
   cout << "Their greatest common divisor is " << gcd (m, n)
        << endl;
   return;
}


// RECURSIVE GCD FUNCTION
// FINDS THE GREATEST COMMON DIVISOR OF TWO INTEGERS
int gcd
  (int m, int n)  // IN: the integer values

// Pre:    m and n are defined and both are > 0.
// Post:   None
// Returns: The greatest common divisor of m and n.
{
   if (n <= m && m % n == 0)
      return n;
   else if (m < n)
      return gcd (n, m);
   else
      return gcd (n, m % n);
} // end gcd
```

(Continued)

Figure 15.14   (Continued)

———— Program Output ————

```
Enter two positive integers separated by a space: 24 84
Their greatest common divisor is 12
```

∎

EXERCISES FOR SECTION 15.3

Self-Check   1. Complete the following recursive function, which calculates the value of a number (base) raised to a power (power). Assume that power is positive.

```
int power_raiser
  (int base,
   int power)
{
   if (power == _____)
      return _____;
   else
      return _____ * _____;
}
```

2. What is the output of the following program? What does function strange compute?

```
// STRANGE PROGRAM
main ()

// Functions used ...
int strange
  (int n);

{
   // Do whatever it is that I do.
   cout << strange (8);
}


// DOES STRANGE THINGS
int strange
  (int n)
{
   if (n == 1)
      return 0;
   else
      return 1 + strange (n / 2);
}  // end strange
```

3. Explain what would happen if the stopping condition for the Fibonacci number function were just (n == 1).

Programming
1. Write a recursive function, `find_sum`, that calculates the sum of successive integers starting at 1 and ending at n (i.e., `find_sum (n)` $= (1 + 2 + \cdots + (n-1) + n)$.
2. Write an iterative version of the Fibonacci function. Compare this version to the recursive version shown in Fig. 15.13. Which is simpler? Which is more efficient?
3. Write an iterative function for the greatest common divisor problem.
4. Write a recursive function to compute the sequence of squares sq_n, of a nonnegative integer n using the following recurrence relations:

$$\left. \begin{array}{l} sq_0 = 0, \\ d_0 = 1, \end{array} \right\} \text{ for } n = 0$$

$$\left. \begin{array}{l} sq_n = sq_{n-1} + d_{n-1}, \\ d_n = d_{n-1} + 2, \end{array} \right\} \text{ for } n > 0$$

Note that d_n always represents the difference between the nth and $n-1$st squares and that for each n, d_n increases by a constant amount, 2.

15.4 ── RECURSIVE FUNCTIONS WITH ARRAY ARGUMENTS

In this section, we examine a familiar problem and implement a recursive function to solve it. The problem involves array processing.

CASE STUDY: RECURSIVE SELECTION SORT

Problem Statement

We discussed the selection sort and implemented an iterative version of this sort function in Section 9.5. Because the selection sort first finds the largest element in an array and places it where it belongs, and then finds and places the next largest element, and so on, it is a good candidate for a recursive solution.

Program Design

The selection sort algorithm follows from the preceding description. The stopping case is an array of length 1, which is sorted by definition. Review Fig. 9.18 to see how the elements of an array are placed in their final positions by a selection sort.

RECURSIVE ALGORITHM FOR SELECTION SORT

1. If n is 1
    1.1. The array is sorted.
    else
    1.2. Place the largest array element in x[n–1].
    1.3. Sort the subarray with subscripts 0, ..., n–2.

Program Implementation

This algorithm is implemented as a recursive function in Fig. 15.15. Function place_largest performs step 1.2 of the algorithm. The recursive function select_sort is simpler to understand than the one shown in Fig. 9.19 because it contains a single if statement instead of nested for loops. However, the recursive solution will execute more slowly because of the extra overhead due to the recursive function calls. If n is 1, function select_sort returns without doing anything. This behavior is correct because a one-element array is always sorted.

Figure 15.15   Functions select_sort and place_largest

```
// FILE: RcsvSort.cpp
// RECURSIVE SELECTION SORT FUNCTION

// SELECTION SORT: SORTS ARRAY OF INTEGERS IN ASCENDING ORDER
void selection_sort
   (int x[],                  // IN: array to be sorted
    int n)                    // IN: number of elements

// Pre:  Array x and size n are defined and n >= 0.
// Post: x[n-1], x[n-2], ... , x[1], x[0] sorted in
//       ascending order.
{
   // Functions used ...
   // FIND AND PLACE LARGEST ELEMENT
   void place_largest
     (int[],                  // IN: subarray to be sorted
      int);                   // IN: number of elements

   if (n > 1)
   {                                // begin recursive step
      place_largest (x, n);
      selection_sort (x, n - 1);
   }  // end recursive step
   return;
}  // end selection_sort



// PLACES LARGEST ELEMENT IN SUBARRAY AT END OF SUBARRAY
void place_largest
   (int x[],                  // IN: subarray to be sorted
    int n)                    // IN: number of elements

// Pre:  x and n must be defined; n >= 0
// Post: Largest element in x[0],..., x[n-1] is placed in x[n-1].
{
   // Local data ...
   int temp;
```

(Continued)

Figure 15.15 (Continued)

```
int j;
int max_index;

max_index = n - 1;
for (j = n - 2; j >= 0; j--)
   if (x[j] > x[max_index])
      max_index = j;

if (max_index != (n - 1))
{
   temp = x[n - 1];
   x[n - 1] = x[max_index];
   x[max_index] = temp;
}
return;
} // end place_largest
```

EXERCISES FOR SECTION 15.4

Self-Check
1. Trace the execution of select_sort on an array that has the integers 5, 8, 10, 1 stored in consecutive elements.
2. What does the following recursive function do? Trace its execution using the data from Self-Check Exercise 1.

```
int mystery
  (int x[],
   int n)
{
   // Local data ...
      int temp;

   // Do whatever I do now.
   if (n == 1)
      return x[0];
   else
   {
      temp = mystery (x, n-1);
      if (x[n-1] > temp)
         return x[n-1];
      else
         return temp;
   } // end outer else
} //end mystery
```

Programming
1. Write a recursive function that reverses the elements in an array x[n]. The recursive step should shift the subarray x[1..n-1] down one element into the subarray x[0..n-2] (for example, x[0] gets x[1], x[1] gets x[2], ..., x[n-2] gets x[n-1]), store the old x[0] in x[n-1], and then reverse the subarray x[0..n-2].
2. Write a recursive function that finds the index of the smallest element in an array.

15.5 ____ PROBLEM-SOLVING WITH RECURSION

CASE STUDY: TOWERS OF HANOI PROBLEM

This Case Study is considerably more complicated than the preceding ones. It leads to a recursive function that solves the Towers of Hanoi Problem we encountered in Section 15.1.

Problem Statement

Solve the Towers of Hanoi Problem for *n* disks, where *n* is the number of disks to be moved from tower A to tower C.

Problem Analysis

The solution to the Towers of Hanoi Problem consists of a printed list of individual disk moves. We need a recursive function that can be used to move any number of disks from one tower to another, using the third tower as an auxiliary.

DATA REQUIREMENTS

> *Problem Input*
>
> | | |
> |---|---|
> | n (int) | — the number of disks to be moved |
> | from_tower (char) | — the *from* tower |
> | to_tower (char) | — the *to* tower |
> | aux_tower (char) | — the *auxiliary* tower |
>
> *Problem Output*
>
> a list of individual disk moves

Program Design

ALGORITHM

1. If n is 1
   1.1. Move disk 1 from the *from* tower to the *to* tower.
   else
   1.2. Move n–1 disks from the *from* tower to the *auxiliary* tower using the *to* tower.
   1.3. Move disk n from the *from* tower to the *to* tower.
   1.4. Move n–1 disks from the *auxiliary* tower to the *to* tower using the *from* tower.

If n is 1, a stopping case is reached. If n is greater than 1, the recursive step (following `else`) splits the original problem into three smaller subproblems, one of which is a stopping case. Each stopping case displays a move instruction. Verify that the recursive step generates the three subproblems (3.1, 3.2, 3.3) listed in Example 15.2 when n is 5, the *from* tower is A, and the *to* tower is C.

Program Implementation

The implementation of this algorithm is shown as function `towers` in Fig. 15.16. Function `towers` has four arguments, `from_tower`, `to_tower`, `aux_tower`, and n. The function call

```
towers ('A', 'C', 'B', 5);
```

solves the problem posed earlier of moving five disks from tower A to tower C, using tower B as an auxiliary.

In Fig. 15.16, the stopping case (move disk 1) is implemented as a `cout` statement. Each recursive step consists of two recursive calls to `towers` with a `cout` line sandwiched between them. The first recursive call solves the problem of moving n-1 disks to the *auxiliary* tower. The `cout` line displays a message to move disk n to the *to* tower. The second recursive call solves the problem of moving the n-1 disks from the *auxiliary* tower to the *to* tower.

Figure 15.16   Recursive function `towers`

```cpp
// FILE: Towers.cpp
// RECURSIVE TOWERS OF HANOI FUNCTION

// RECURSIVE FUNCTION TO MOVE DISKS FROM from_tower TO to_tower
//     USING AUX-TOWER

void towers
  (char from_tower,     // IN: from_tower
   char to_tower,       // IN: to_tower
   char aux_tower,      // IN: aux_tower
   int n)               // IN: number of disks

// Pre:  The from_tower, to_tower, aux_tower, and n are defined.
// Post: The disks are moved from from_tower to to_tower.
{
   if (n == 1)
      cout << "Move disk 1 from tower " << from_tower
           << " to tower " << to_tower << endl;
   else
   {
      towers (from_tower, aux_tower, to_tower, n - 1);
      cout << "Move disk " << n << " from tower " << from_tower
           << " to tower " << to_tower << endl;
```

(Continued)

Figure 15.16   (Continued)

```
        towers (aux_tower, to_tower, from_tower, n - 1);
    }
}  // end towers
```

Program Testing

The function call statement

```
towers ('A', 'C', 'B', 3);
```

solves a simpler three-disk problem: Move 3 disks from tower A to tower C. Its execution is traced in Fig. 15.17; the output generated is shown in

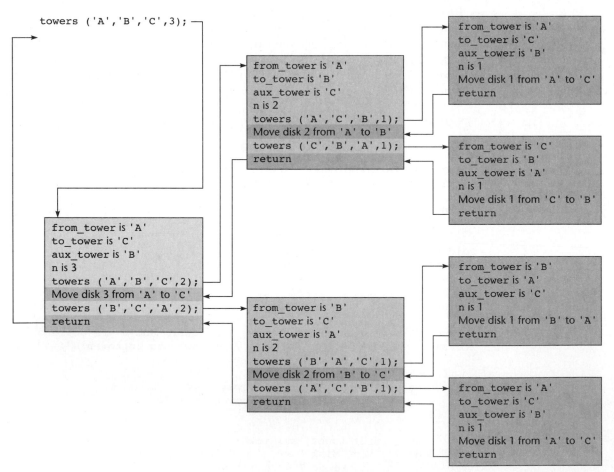

Figure 15.17   Trace of `towers ('A', 'C', 'B', 3);`

Fig. 15.18. Verify for yourself that this list of steps does indeed solve the three-disk problem.

Figure 15.18   Output generated by towers ('A', 'C', 'B', 3);

```
Move disk 1 from tower A to tower C
Move disk 2 from tower A to tower B
Move disk 1 from tower C to tower B
Move disk 3 from tower A to tower C
Move disk 1 from tower B to tower A
Move disk 2 from tower B to tower C
Move disk 1 from tower A to tower C
```

Comparison of Iteration and Recursive Functions for the Towers of Hanoi Problem

It is interesting to consider that function towers in Fig. 15.16 will solve the Towers of Hanoi Problem for any number of disks. The three-disk problem results in a total of 7 calls to function towers and is solved by 7 disk moves. The five-disk problem would result in a total of 31 calls to function towers and is solved in 31 moves. In general, the number of moves required to solve the n-disk problem is $2^n - 1$. Because each function call requires the allocation and initialization of a local data area in memory, the computer time increases exponentially with the problem size. For this reason, be careful about running this program with a value of n that is larger than 10.

The dramatic increase in processing time for larger towers is a function of this problem, not a function of recursion. However, in general, if there are recursive and iterative solutions to the same problem, the recursive solution will require more time and space because of the extra function calls.

Although recursion was not really needed to solve the simpler problems in this section, it was extremely useful in formulating an algorithm for the Towers of Hanoi Problem. For certain problems, recursion leads naturally to solutions that are much easier to read and understand than their iterative counterparts. In these cases, the benefits gained from increased clarity far outweigh the extra cost (in time and memory) of running a recursive program.

EXERCISES FOR SECTION 15.5

Self-Check
1. How many moves are needed to solve the six-disk problem?
2. Write a main function that reads in a data value for n (the number of disks) and calls function towers to move n disks from A to B.

15.6 —— PICTURE-PROCESSING WITH RECURSION

CASE STUDY: COUNTING CELLS IN A BLOB

This Case Study illustrates the power of recursion. The problem is difficult to solve without recursion, but it has a relatively easy recursive solution.

Problem Statement

We have a two-dimensional grid of cells, each of which may be empty or filled. The filled cells that are connected form a blob. (Two cells are said to be connected if they are adjacent to each other horizontally, vertically, or diagonally.) There may be several blobs on the grid. We would like a function (blob_count) that accepts as input the coordinates (x, y) of a particular cell and returns the size of the blob containing the cell.

The sample grid in Fig. 15.19 shows three blobs. If the function arguments represent the x- and y-coordinates of a cell, the result of blob_count(1,2) (the cell marked A) is 5; the result of blob_count(4,1) (the cell marked B) is 2; the result of blob_count(0,4) (marked C) is 0; the result of blob_count(4,4) (marked D) is 4.

Problem Analysis

Function blob_count must test the cell specified by its arguments to see whether it is filled. There are two stopping cases: The cell (x, y) is not on the grid, or the cell (x, y) is empty. In either case, the value returned by blob_count is 0. If the cell is on the grid and filled, then the value returned is 1 plus the size of the blobs containing each of its eight neighbors. To avoid counting a filled cell more than once, we will mark it as empty once we have visited it.

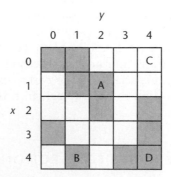

Figure 15.19   Grid with three blobs

DATA REQUIREMENTS

Problem Input

grid (array of elements — the grid
of type state {empty, filled})
x, y (integer) — the x- and y-coordinates of the
point being visited

Problem Output

The number of the cells in the blob containing point (x, y)

Program Design

INITIAL ALGORITHM

1. If cell (x, y) is not in the array
   1.1. Return a count of 0.
   else if cell (x, y) is empty
   1.2. Return a count of 0.
   else
   1.3. Mark cell (x, y) as empty.
   1.4. Add 1 and see whether the blob contains any of the eight neighbors
        of cell (x, y).

Program Implementation

Function `blob_count` is shown in Fig. 15.20. The grid has element values
`filled` or `empty`. The constants `max_x` and `max_y` represent the size of the
x- and y-coordinates, respectively. Function `blob_count` implements the
counting algorithm; function `start_blob` simply makes a copy of the grid
(in the local variable `grid_copy`) and then calls the recursive function
`blob_count`, passing on this copy (actually just a pointer to this new copy) as
well as the other arguments it was passed. `start_blob` eventually returns
the count computed by `blob_count` as its own result. The reason we used
two functions instead of one in the solution of this problem was to protect the
original array (the first actual argument in the call to `start_blob`) from
being modified when filled cells are reset to `empty` by function `blob_count`.
We will come back to this point shortly.

The first formal argument in both functions,

```
state grid[][max_y]
```

is written with its second dimension specified (by `max_y`). (C++ requires
that for a multidimensional array used as formal argument, the size of all
dimensions beyond the first must be specified.) As usual, we have used

Figure 15.20   Recursive function `blob_count` with `start_blob`

```cpp
// FILE: BlobCnt.cpp
// COUNTS THE NUMBER OF FILLED CELLS IN THE BLOB CONTAINING (x, y)

int start_blob
  (const state grid[][max_y],   // IN: blob array
   int x,                       // IN: x-coordinate
   int y)                       // IN: y-coordinate

// Pre:     Array grid and point (x, y) are defined.
// Post:    None.
// Returns: The size of the blob containing the point (x, y).
{
   // Functions used ...
   // PERFORMS COUNTING OPERATION FOR start_blob
   int blob_count
     (state [][max_y],          // INOUT: blob array
      int,                      // IN: x-coordinate
      int);                     // IN: y-coordinate

   // Local data ...
   state grid_copy[max_x][max_y];
   int i,j;                     // indices for initialization loops

   // Count filled cells in all blobs found.
   for (i = 0; i < max_x; i++)
      for (j = 0; j < max_y; j++)
         grid_copy[i][j] = grid[i][j];

   // Call blob_count and return its result.
   return (blob_count(grid_copy, x, y));
}  // end start_blob



// RECURSIVE FUNCTION TO COUNT BLOBS IN A CELL
// PERFORMS COUNTING OPERATION FOR start_blob
int blob_count
  (state grid[][max_y],         // INOUT: blob array
   int x,                       // IN: x-coordinate
   int y)                       // IN: y-coordinate

// Pre:     Array grid and point (x, y) are defined.
// Post:    Resets the status of each cell in the blob to empty.
// Returns: The size of the blob containing point (x, y).
{
   // Local data ...
   int count;
   enum {empty, filled};
```

(Continued)

Figure 15.20 (Continued)

```
// Count cells in one blob.
if (x < 0 || x > max_x - 1 || y < 0 || y > max_y - 1)
   count = 0;
else if (grid[x][y] == empty)
   count = 0;
else
{ // begin recursive step at top left cell relative to (x,y)
   grid[x][y] = empty;
   count = 1 + blob_count(grid, x - 1, y - 1)
           + blob_count(grid, x - 1, y)
           + blob_count(grid, x - 1, y + 1)
           + blob_count(grid, x, y + 1)
           + blob_count(grid, x + 1, y + 1)
           + blob_count(grid, x + 1, y)
           + blob_count(grid, x + 1, y - 1)
           + blob_count(grid, x, y - 1);
}  // end recursive step
return count;
}  // end blob_count
```

the modifier `const` in the specification of this first formal argument in `start_blob` to protect the actual array from accidental modification in this function.

If the cell being visited is off the grid or is empty, a value of zero will be returned immediately. Otherwise, the recursive step executes, causing function `blob_count` to call itself eight times. Each time a different neighbor of the current cell is visited. The cells are visited in a clockwise manner, starting with the neighbor above and to the left. The function result is defined as the sum of all values returned from these recursive calls plus 1 (for the current cell).

Also, the recursive step resets `grid[x, y]` to `empty` before visiting the neighbors of point (x, y). If this were not done first, then cell (x, y) would be counted more than once because it is a neighbor of all its neighbors. A worse problem is that the recursion would not terminate. When each neighbor of the current cell is visited, `blob_count` is called again with the coordinates of the current cell as arguments. If the current cell is `empty`, an immediate return occurs. If the current cell is still `filled`, then the recursive step would be executed erroneously. Eventually the program will run out of time or memory space; lack of memory space is often indicated by a "`stack overflow`" message.

A side effect of the execution of function `blob_count` is that all cells that are part of the blob being processed are reset to `empty`. It was therefore necessary to make a copy of the original grid array before entering the counting function. We chose to do this in the function `start_blob`, so that the user of these functions would not need to be concerned with their internal computations. Thus, in `start_blob`, a copy of the original grid array is made and saved in the local variable `grid_copy`. This local array is passed to `blob_count` and modified in the course of the computations carried out by this function. However, only the copy of the original grid is affected by these changes. The original grid itself is protected from change.

This efficiency could not have been as easily or efficiently achieved if a single function (`blob_count` by itself) had been used. Either we would have altered the copy of the original grid array, or we would have had to make a new copy of this array as the first step in `blob_count`, prior to any recursive call to the function. The second alternative would have been very inefficient.

EXERCISES FOR SECTION 15.6

Self-Check
1. Is the order of the two tests performed in function `blob_count` critical? What happens if we reverse them or combine them into a single condition?
2. Describe the principal inefficiency of using one function, `blob_count,` to solve the cell-counting problem just discussed, assuming that this function would begin execution by copying the initial grid array and then would use this copy throughout execution. Exactly how does this differ from the solution proposed in the text (with the copy of the original grid delegated to a separate function, `start_blob`)?

Programming
1. Write the recursive function `find_min` that finds the smallest value in an integer array x of size n.

15.7 ——— COMMON PROGRAMMING ERRORS

▪ *Stopping Condition for Recursive Functions:* The most common problem with a recursive function involves the specification of the stopping condition. If this condition is not correct, the function may call itself indefinitely or until all available memory is used up. Normally, a `"stack overflow"` run-time error is an indication that a recursive function is not terminating. Make sure that you identify all stopping cases and provide the correct condition for each one. Also be sure that each recursive step leads to a situation that is closer to a stopping case and that repeated recursive calls will eventually lead to stopping cases only.

▪ *Missing Return Statements:* It is critical that every path through a function that returns a value function lead to a return statement. When multiple returns are warranted in a function, it is easy to omit one of these returns. Such an omission will not be detected by the compiler but will result in an incorrect return value whenever the sequence of statements requiring the return is executed.

■ *A Few Optimizations for Recursive Functions:* The recopying of large arrays or other large data structures inside a recursive function can quickly consume large amounts of memory. Such recopying should be done only when data protection is required. Even in this case, if only a single copy is required, a nonrecursive function can be created to make the necessary copy and pass this copy and other arguments to the recursive function (and return any computed result to the caller).

It is also a good idea to introduce a nonrecursive function to handle preliminaries of a recursive function call when error checking is involved. Checking for errors inside a recursive function is extremely inefficient if the error is such that it would be detected only in the first of a sequence of recursive calls.

It is sometimes difficult to observe the result of a recursive function's execution. If each recursive call generates a large number of output lines and there are many recursive calls, the output will scroll down the screen more quickly than it can be read. On most systems, it is possible to stop the scrolling temporarily by pressing a special key or control character sequence (e.g., control-s). If this cannot be done, it is still possible to cause your output to stop temporarily by printing a prompting message such as

```
cout << "Press the space bar to continue.";
```

followed by a keyboard input operation such as

```
cin >> next_char;
```

(where `next_char` is a character data type). Your program will resume execution when you enter a character data item.

CHAPTER REVIEW

This chapter provides several examples of recursive functions. Studying them should give you some appreciation of the power of recursion as a problem-solving and programming tool and provide you with valuable insight regarding its use. It may take you some time to feel comfortable thinking in this new way about programming. However, as you study a wider variety of more complex problems, you will see that in certain cases (such as the Towers of Hanoi Problem) recursion provides a clear, concise, and easy-to-understand solution. In these cases, we are confident that you will view the work in this chapter to have been worth the effort.

Aside from the Towers of Hanoi and Blob Count Problems, the shorter examples and case study illustrate different aspects of the use of recursion. The multiply and factorial functions (Examples 15.1 and 15.4, respectively) provide illustrations of recursive functions involving simple mathematical computations and return the result of these computations. Although there are clearly more direct and efficient algorithms for these computations, the simplicity of the recursive solutions provides a good illustration of the trace of execution of recursive functions that return values.

The reverse string example (Example 15.3) does not involve a return value. It was included to show how local data processed in a recursive function are saved at each point of call and then returned in reverse order to complete processing.

The Fibonacci and Greatest Common Divisor examples (Examples 15.5 and 15.6, respectively) illustrate somewhat more complicated mathematical functions. The Fibonacci function (Fig. 15.13) illustrates the use of recursion in computations involving recurrence relations, where the computation of the nth value in a sequence is specified in terms of values computed earlier in the sequence.

The GCD function (Fig. 15.14) has a slightly more complicated stopping condition and involves conditional recursive calls based on the relationship of its first to the second.

The recursive sort function (Fig. 15.15) illustrates the processing of an array of data, one element at a time. The basic idea behind the algorithm is typical of all of the other recursive algorithms we have examined.

To sort an array of size n in ascending order,

- place the largest element in the array in the nth array cell;
- sort an array of size $n-1$ in ascending order.

When n becomes equal to 1, the sort is complete.

✔ QUICK-CHECK EXERCISES

1. Explain the use of a stack in recursion.
2. Which is generally more efficient, recursion or iteration?
3. Which control statement do you always find in a recursive function?
4. How do you specify a recursive call to a function?
5. Why would a programmer conceptualize a problem solution using recursion and implement it using iteration?
6. In a recursive problem involving n items, why must n be a call-by-value argument?
7. What kind of a programming error could easily cause a "`stack overflow`" message?
8. What can you say about a recursive algorithm that has the following form?

    if (<u>condition</u>)
        Perform recursive step.

Answers to Quick-Check Exercises

1. The stack is used to hold all argument and local variable values and the return point for each execution of a recursive function.
2. Iteration is generally more efficient than recursion.
3. `if` statement
4. By writing a call to the function in the function itself.
5. When its solution is much easier to conceptualize using recursion but its implementation would be too inefficient.
6. If n were a call-by-reference argument, its address would be saved on the stack, not its value, so it would not be possible to retain a different value for each call.
7. Too many recursive calls.
8. Nothing is done when the stopping case is reached.

REVIEW QUESTIONS

1. Explain the nature of a recursive problem.
2. Discuss the efficiency of recursive functions.
3. Differentiate between stopping cases and a terminating condition.
4. Write a recursive function that returns the accumulating sum of the ASCII values corresponding to each character in a character string. For example, if the string value is `"a boy"`, the first value returned would be the ASCII value of a, then the sum of ASCII values for a and the space character, then the sum of the ASCII values for a, space, b, and so on.
5. Write a recursive function that returns the accumulating sum of ASCII values corresponding to each character in a character string (as in Review Question 4). However, this time exclude any space characters from the sum.
6. Convert the following iterative function to a recursive one. The function calculates an approximate value for e, the base of the natural logarithms, by summing the series

$$1 + 1/1! + 1/2! + \cdots + 1/n!$$

until additional terms do not affect the approximation (at least not as far as the computer is concerned).

```
float elog ()
{
    // Local data ...
    float enl, delta, fact;
    int n;

    enl = 1.0;
    n = 1;
    fact = 1.0;
    delta = 1.0;
```

```
    do
    {
        enl += delta;
        n++;
        fact *= n;
        delta = 1.0 / fact;
    }   while (enl != enl + delta);
    return enl;
}   // end elog
```

PROGRAMMING PROJECTS

1. Write a function that reads each row of an array as a string and converts it to a row of grid (see Fig. 15.19). The first character of row 0 corresponds to grid[0][0], the second character to grid[0][1], and so on. Set the element value to empty if the character is blank; otherwise, set it to filled. The number of rows in the array should be read first. Use this function in a program that reads in a cell coordinate pair and prints the number of cells in the blob containing the coordinate pair.

2. The expression for computing $C(n, r)$, the number of combinations of n items taken r at a time is

$$C(n, r) = \frac{n!}{r!(n - r)!}.$$

Write and test a function for computing $C(n, r)$ given that $n!$ is the factorial of n.

3. A palindrome is a word that is spelled exactly the same when the letters are reversed. For example, such words as level, deed, and mom are palindromes. Write a recursive function that returns a value of 1 (true) if a word, passed as an argument, is a palindrome and that returns 0 (false) otherwise.

4. Write a recursive function that returns the value of the following recursive definition:

   $F(X, Y) = X - Y$ if X or $Y < 0$;
   $F(X, Y) = F(X - 1, Y) + F(X, Y - 1)$ otherwise.

5. Write a recursive function that lists all of the two-letter subsets for a given set of letters. For example:

   ['A', 'C', 'E', 'G'] => ['A', 'C'], ['A', 'E'], ['A', 'G'], ['C', 'E'], ['C', 'G'], ['E', 'G']

6. Write a function that accepts an 8-by-8 array of characters that represents a maze. Each position can contain either an 'X' or a blank. Starting at position [0][0], list any path through the maze to get to location [7][7]. Only horizontal and vertical moves are allowed (no diagonal moves). If no path exists, write a message indicating this. Moves can be made only to positions that contain a blank. If an 'X' is encountered in a path, that path is to be considered blocked and another must be chosen. Use recursion.

7. The Eight Queens Problem is a famous chess-related problem that has as its goal the placement of eight queens on a single chess board so that no queen will be able to

attack any other queen. A queen may move any number of squares vertically, horizontally, or along either diagonal on the chess board (an 8-by-8 grid of squares). Write a program that contains a recursive routine to solve the Eight Queens Problem.

Hint: Work across the board, column by column. Begin in column 1 and arbitrarily choose a row in this column for the placement of the first queen. Then move to the next column and attempt to place a second queen safely in one of the rows of that column. Continue this process as long as it is possible to place a queen in the next column (as long as a row can be found for which a placement of a queen is safe). If a dead end is reached (no safe row can be found in a given column), the last-placed queen (in the column to the immediate left of the current one) is removed from the board and repositioned. To do this, the algorithm will need to backtrack to a previous call of the recursive routine, undo the placement of the queen in this column, and attempt to place it in a different row. This process of moving left to right across the board, backtracking as needed, continues until all eight queens have been successfully (safely) placed, one per column. The determination of whether a placement of a queen (in a given row of the current column) is safe is the critical component of this algorithm. Note that a safe placement requires that no previously placed queen is in the same row or in the same diagonal. There are two diagonals to be considered in addition to each row, as shown in Fig. 15.21. You need to find an easy and simple way to verify that a proposed placement of a queen is indeed safe.

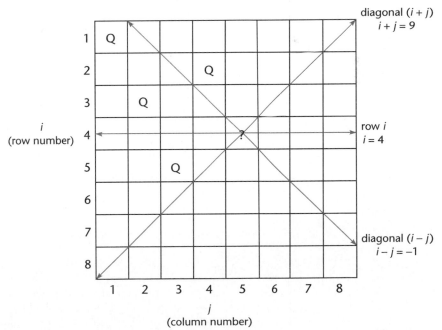

Figure 15.21   Checking row i (column j) and diagonals $(i + j)$ and $(i - j)$ for safety

16

Dynamic Data Structures

16.1 Review of Pointers and the new Operator
16.2 Manipulating the Heap
16.3 Linked Lists
16.4 The Stack as an Abstract Data Type
     CASE STUDY: Evaluating Postfix Expressions
16.5 Implementing a Stack Using an Array
16.6 Linked-List Representation of a Stack
16.7 The Queue Abstract Data Type
16.8 Queue Application
     CASE STUDY: Maintaining a Queue of Passengers
16.9 Implementing a Queue Using an Array
16.10 Linked-List Representation of a Queue
16.11 Common Programming Errors
      Chapter Review

In this chapter, we discuss how C++ can be used to create *dynamic data structures*. Dynamic data structures are data structures that expand and contract as a program executes. A dynamic data structure is a collection of elements (called *nodes*) that are implemented as structs.[1] Unlike an array, which always contains storage for a fixed number of elements, the number of elements stored in a dynamic data structure changes as the program executes.

Dynamic data structures are extremely flexible. For example, it is relatively easy to add new information by creating a new node and inserting it between two existing nodes. It is also relatively easy to delete a node.

In this chapter, we examine several examples of dynamic data structures. These include lists, stacks, and queues. You will learn how to store information in these data structures and how to process that information.

16.1 ___ REVIEW OF POINTERS AND THE new OPERATOR

In Chapter 12 we introduced the pointer data type. We showed how to declare variables (called pointer variables) whose types are pointer types. We also illustrated how to store the memory address of a data element in a pointer variable and, in this way, reference or access the data element through the pointer that points to it.

For example, the declaration

```
float *p;
```

identifies that p is a pointer variable of type "pointer to float." This means that we can store the memory address of a type float variable in p. The statement

```
p = new float;
```

invokes the C++ new operator to create a variable of type float and place the address of this variable in the pointer variable p. Once storage is allocated for the type float value pointed to by p, we can store a value in that memory cell and manipulate it. The exact location of this particular cell is immaterial.

We can represent the value of a pointer variable by an arrow drawn to a memory cell. The diagram at the top of the next page shows that pointer variable p points to a memory cell whose contents are undefined. This is the situation that exists just after p = new float is executed. In the next section, we

---

[1]The C++ reference manual refers to classes, structs, and unions collectively as *classes*. We will use the term "struct" when referring to collections of data and the term "class" when referring to (probably hidden) collections of data and associated functions to manipulate those data.

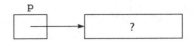

will see how to write C++ instructions to store information in the memory cell pointed to by p.

C++
SYNTAX

Pointer Type Declaration

Form: *type *variable;*

Example: `float *p;`

Interpretation: The value of the pointer variable p is a memory address (pointer). A data element whose address is stored in this variable must be of the specified *type.*   ∎

C++
SYNTAX

new Operator

Form: `new` *type*`;`
            `new` *type*`[`*n*`];`

Example: `new float;`

Interpretation: Storage for a new data element is allocated from a pool of storage known as the *heap,* and a pointer to this element is returned. The amount of storage is determined by the type specified. With the second form shown, n elements of the specified *type* are allocated. If sufficient storage is not available, a zero is returned by the `new` operator.   ∎

Accessing Variables with Pointers

The symbol * (asterisk) is called the *indirection operator.* The assignment statement

`*p = 15.5;`

stores the `float` value `15.5` in memory location `*p` (the location pointed to by p), as shown next.

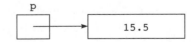

The statements

```
float *p;
p = new float;
*p = 15.5;
cout << "The contents of the memory cell pointed to by p is "
     << *p << endl;
```

produce the result

```
The contents of the memory cell pointed to by p is 15.5
```

A pointer variable can contain only a memory address. If `p` is the pointer variable declared above, the following statements are invalid; you cannot assign a type `int` or a type `float` value to a pointer variable:

```
p = 1000;     // invalid assignment
p = 15.5;     // invalid assignment
```

Structs with Pointer Members

Pointers can be used to construct dynamic data structures. Because we don't know beforehand how many elements (*nodes*) will be in a dynamic data structure, we cannot allocate storage for such a structure in the conventional way, that is, through a variable declaration. Instead, we must allocate storage for each node as needed and then find a way to join that node to the rest of the structure.

We can connect two nodes if we include a pointer member in each node. The declarations

```
struct node
{
    char current[3];
    int volts;
    node *link;
};
node *p, *q, *r;
```

identify the variables p, q, and r to be of type "pointer to **node**." Type **node** is a `struct` with three members: `current`, `volts`, and `link`. The `link` member is also of type "pointer to **node**." We can use this member to point to the "next" node in a dynamic data structure. We illustrate how to connect two nodes in the next section.

Variables p, q, and r are pointer variables and can be used to reference variables of type **node** (denoted by `*p`, `*q`, and `*r`). An address can be stored in a pointer variable through assignment of a pointer variable of the same type or the use of the `new` pointer. The statement

```
p = q;
```

assigns the value of the variable q (a pointer to a `struct` of type **node**) to p (also a pointer to a `struct` of type **node**). The statements

```
p = new node;
q = new node;
```

invoke the new operator to allocate storage for two structs of type node. The memory address of the first of these structs is stored in p, and the memory address of the second of these structs is stored in q. All three members of these two structs are initially undefined.

Accessing struct Members with Pointers

Recall from Chapter 9 that the *member access operator* (.) is used to access a member of a structure. Thus, if n is of type node, then n.volts represents the volts member of the structure node indicated by the variable n.

In C++ the member access operator has a higher precedence than the indirection operator (see Appendix D). Thus *p.volts is interpreted as *(p.volts), which attempts to apply the member access operator to a variable of type "pointer to node," which is illegal, and then to apply the indirection operator to an expression that is not a pointer type, which is also illegal.

The form (*p).volts first applies the indirection operator to the variable p of type "pointer to node," yielding an expression of type node, and then applies the member access operator to this expression, yielding an expression of type int.

Example 16.1   If p is the pointer variable to a structure of type node, the statement

```
(*p).volts = 115;
```

results in the assignment of the value 115, as shown next.

p		current	volts	link
		?	115	?

■

Because accessing members of structures through pointers is a common operation, C++ provides a special notation, as described in the following C++ Syntax Display.

C++
SYNTAX

Structure Member Access Through a Pointer

Form: *p -> m*

Example: p->volts

Interpretation: If p is a pointer to a struct (or class), and if *m* is a member of that struct, then *p->m* accesses the member, *m*, of the struct pointed to by p.   ■

If p and q are declared as pointers to structs of type node, the statements

```
strcpy (p->current,"AC");
p->volts = 115;
strcpy (q->current,"DC");
q->volts = 12;
```

define two members of the nodes pointed to by p and q, as shown in Fig. 16.1. The link members of these nodes are still undefined.

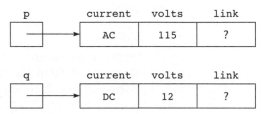

Figure 16.1 Nodes *p and *q

Besides using a new operator to obtain a pointer value, we can also use an assignment statement to store one pointer value in another. The statement

```
r = p;
```

copies the value of pointer variable p into pointer variable r. This means that pointers p and r contain the same memory address and therefore point to the same node, as shown in Fig. 16.2.

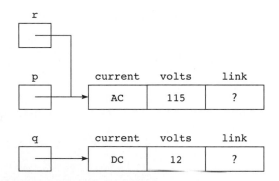

Figure 16.2 Pointers p, q, and r; nodes *p and *q

We can compare two pointer variables using the relational operators == and !=. Assuming that the pointer variables p, q, and r are defined as shown in Fig. 16.2, the following conditions are true.

```
p == r
p != q
r != q
```

The assignment statements

```
p = q;
q = r;
```

have the effect of exchanging the nodes pointed to by p and q, as shown in Fig. 16.3.

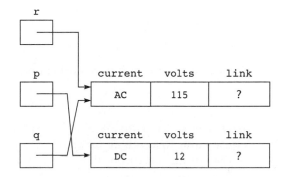

Figure 16.3   Pointers p, q, and r nodes *p and *q

The statement

```
cout << q->current << " " << p->current << endl;
```

displays the `current` members of the structures pointed to by q and p. For the situation depicted in Fig. 16.3, the line

```
AC  DC
```

would be displayed.

The statement

```
q = new node;
```

changes the value of q to the address of a new node, thereby disconnecting q from its previous node. The data members of the new node pointed to by q are initially undefined; however, the statement

```
*q = *r;
```

copies the contents of node *r to node *q. The statement

```
q->volts = 220;
```

sets the `volts` member of the `node` pointed to by q to 220. Figure 16.4 shows the three nodes *p, *q, and *r following the execution of these two assignment statements.

It is important to understand the difference between using p and *p in a program. p is a pointer variable (for example, type "pointer to node") and is

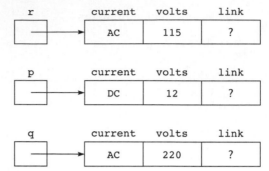

Figure 16.4   Pointers p, q, and r; nodes *p, *q, and *r

used to store the address of a data structure (of type node). p can be assigned a new value through an assignment statement. *p is the name of the struct (node, in this case) pointed to by p and can be manipulated like any other struct (or class) in C++. The member accesses p->current and p->volts can be used to reference data (a string and an int, in this case) stored in the struct pointed to by p.

Connecting Nodes

One purpose of dynamically allocated nodes is to enable us to grow data structures of varying size. We accomplish this by connecting the individual nodes. If you look at the nodes allocated earlier, you will see that their link members are undefined because we have not yet stored any information in them. The assignment statement

```
r->link = p;        // 1
```

copies the address stored in p into the link member of node *r, thereby connecting node *r to node *p. Similarly, the assignment statement

```
p->link = q;        // 2
```

copies the address stored in pointer variable q into the link member of node *p, thereby connecting node *p to node *q. The situation after execution of these two assignment statements is shown in Fig. 16.5. The label next to the arrow denotes the assignment that caused the pointer to be stored.

As shown in the figure, the data structure pointed to by r has now grown to include all three nodes. The first node is referenced by *r. The second node can be referenced by *p or *r->link. Finally, the third node can be referenced by *q, *p->link, or even *r->link->link.

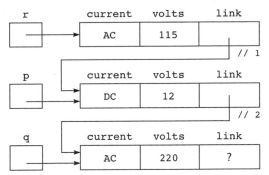

Figure 16.5   Connecting nodes

EXERCISES FOR SECTION 16.1

Self-Check 1. Which of the following statements are valid? Assume that each statement is executed with the computer in the state depicted in Fig. 16.5. What is the state after each valid statement is executed?

a. `strcpy(r->current,"AC");`   b. `*r = *p;`
c. `strcpy(p.current,"HT");`   d. `p = 54;`
e. `r->link->volts = 0;`   f. `p = r;`
g. `strcpy(r->link->link->current, "XY");`
h. `q->volts = r->volts;`

2. The statements

`r = p; p = q; q = r;`

exchange the values of pointer variables p and q (type "pointer to node"). What do the following assignment statements do?

a. `r->current = p->current;`
b. `p->current = q->current;`
c. `q->current = r->current;`

Programming 1. Write a program segment that creates a collection of nodes and stores the musical scale (*do, re, mi, fa, so, la, ti*) in those nodes. Connect the nodes so that *do* is stored in the first node, *re* in the second, and so on.

16.2 —— MANIPULATING THE HEAP

In the last section, you saw that a new variable is created whenever the new operator is executed. You may be wondering where in memory the new variable is stored. As described in Chapter 12, C++ maintains a storage pool of available memory called a heap; memory from this pool is allocated whenever the new operator is invoked.

Effect of the new Operator on the Heap

If **p** is a pointer variable of type "pointer to node" (declared in the last section), the statement

```
p = new node;
```

allocates memory space for the storage of three characters, an int variable, and an address. The contents of the allocated memory is originally undefined (it retains whatever data were last stored), and the memory address of the first location allocated is stored in p. Allocated memory is no longer considered part of the heap. The only way to reference allocated locations is through a pointer variable, such as p (for example, p->current, p->volts, or p->link).

Figure 16.6 shows the pointer variable p and the heap (as a collection of bytes with addresses 1000, 1001, ..., etc.) before and after the execution of p = new node. The diagram at the left shows pointer variable p as undefined before the execution of p = new node. The diagram at the right shows p pointing to the first of nine memory locations allocated for the new variable (assuming that nine memory locations are large enough to accommodate variables of type node). The memory locations still considered part of the heap are shaded.

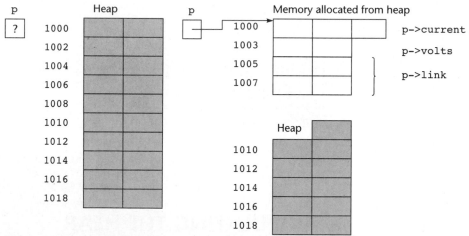

Figure 16.6   Heap before (left) and after (right) execution of p = new node

Returning Cells to the Heap

The operation

```
delete p;
```

returns to the heap the memory pointed to by **p**. The value of the pointer variable becomes undefined, and the data associated with ***p** are no longer accessible. These cells can be reused later when another **new** operator is executed.

C++
SYNTAX

The delete Operator

Form: delete *variable*;
          delete [ ] *array_name*;

Example: delete p;

Interpretation: The memory pointed to by **p** (which was set from the invocation of the **new** operator) is returned to the heap. This memory can be reallocated when the **new** operator is next invoked.   ∎

Often, more than one pointer variable points to the same structure. For this reason, you must be careful when returning storage to the heap. If memory is reallocated after it is returned, or if certain memory locations are returned more than once, errors may result. Such errors are difficult to detect and debug. Make sure that you have no need for a particular structure before you return the storage occupied by it. Also make sure that only pointer variables that were set with values returned by the **new** operator are used as an argument to the **delete** operator.

16.3 —— LINKED LISTS

In this section we introduce an important data structure called a *linked list,* or, simply, *list* and show how to build and manipulate lists in C++.

Abstract Lists

An abstract list is a sequence of nodes in which each node is linked, or connected, to the node following it. An abstract list with three nodes follows:

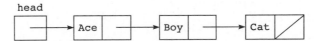

Each node in the list has two members: The first member contains data, and the second member is a pointer (represented by an arrow) to the next list element. A pointer variable (**head**) points to the first element, or *list head.* The last list element always has a diagonal line in its pointer field to indicate the end of the list.

A list is an important data structure because it can be modified easily. For example, a new node containing the string `"Bye"` can be inserted between the strings `"Boy"` and `"Cat"` by changing only one pointer value (the one from `"Boy"`) and setting the pointer member of the new node to point to `"Cat"`. This is true regardless of how many elements are in the list. The following diagram shows the list after the insertion:

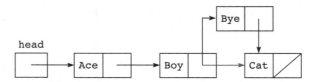

Similarly, it is quite easy to delete a list element. Only one pointer value has to be changed, the pointer that currently points to the element being deleted. The linked list is redrawn, as shown next, after the string `"Boy"` is deleted by changing the pointer from the node `"Ace"`. The node containing the string `"Boy"` is effectively disconnected from the list and can be returned to the heap. The new list consists of the strings `"Ace"`, `"Bye"`, and `"Cat"`.

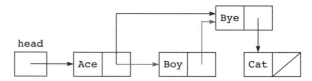

Representing Linked Lists Using Pointers

The preceding abstract list is relatively easy to create in C++ using pointers and dynamic allocation. In Section 16.1, you saw how to connect three nodes with pointer members. Although you didn't know it at the time, the data structure shown in Fig. 16.5 could be considered a list of three nodes with pointer variable `r` as the pointer to its head.

In C++ a pointer value of zero indicates that the pointer does not point to a memory cell. The constant NULL (defined in `<stddef.h>`) is a zero of the correct size (short or long). If `head` is a pointer variable, we can use the assignment statement

`head = NULL;`

to indicate that `head` points to an empty list, a list with zero nodes:

A diagonal line through the box depicts a pointer having a NULL value.

Normally, we assign the value NULL to the pointer member of the last node in a list. After the assignment statement

```
q->link = NULL;
```

is executed, the data structure in Fig. 16.5 would appear as follows:

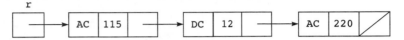

Each node has two data members (current and volts) and one pointer member (link).

We now consider some common list-processing operations and show how to implement them using pointer variables. We assume that the structure of each list node corresponds to the struct list_node, declared as shown next, with pointer variable head pointing to the list head.

```
const int string_size = 4;
struct list_node
{
    char word[string_size];
    list_node *link;
};
list_node *head;
```

Traversing a List

In many list-processing operations, we must process each node in the list in sequence; this is called *traversing a list*. To traverse a list, we must start at the list head and follow the list pointers.

One operation that we often need to perform on any data structure is to display its contents. To display the contents of a list, we traverse the list and display only the values of the data members, not the link members. Function print_list in Fig. 16.7 displays the word member of each node (type list_node) in the existing list whose list head is passed as an argument. If head points to the list

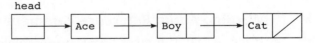

the function call statement

```
print_list (head);
```

displays the lines

```
Ace
Boy
Cat
```

Figure 16.7   Function `print_list`

```
// FILE: PrintLst.cpp
// DISPLAY THE LIST POINTED TO BY HEAD

void print_list
   (list_node *current)      // IN: pointer to list to be printed

// Pre:  current points to a list whose last node has a pointer
//       member of NULL
// Post: The word member of each list node is displayed and the
//       last value of head is NULL
{
   while (current != NULL)
   {
      // Invariant: No prior value of current was NULL.
      cout << current->word << endl;
               current = current->link;
   }
}  // end print_list
```

The `while` condition

`current != NULL`

is common in loops that process lists. If the list to be printed is an empty list, this condition is true initially and the loop body is skipped. If the list is not empty, the loop body executes, and the statement

`current = current->link;`

advances the pointer `current` to the next list element, which is pointed to by the `link` member of the current list element. After the last value in the list is printed, the value NULL is assigned to `current` and the `while` loop exit occurs.

Because `current` is a value argument, a local copy of the pointer is advanced, but the corresponding pointer in the calling program remains unchanged.

PROGRAM STYLE

Warning About Reference Parameters for Pointers

If the formal argument `head` were a reference argument instead of a value argument, function `print_list` would be allowed to change the corresponding actual argument, regardless of our intentions. In `print_list` and many similar functions, the last value assigned to the pointer argument is NULL. If `head` is a reference argument, the corresponding actual argument would be set to NULL, thereby disconnecting it from the list that it pointed to before the function call. ∎

Creating a List

Function `create_list` in Fig. 16.8 creates a linked list by reading in a sequence of length 3 or shorter data strings ending with a sentinel string (`"***"`) and storing each string in a list. If the data lines

```
Ace
Boy
Cat
***
```

are entered, the list shown in the preceding section is created. Notice that the sentinel string is not stored in the list. `list_node`, `head`, and `string_size` are assumed to be defined as shown earlier.

Figure 16.8   Functions `fill_rest` and `create_list`

```cpp
// FILE: CreatLst.cpp

#include "StrucLst.h"    // string size and structure definition

const char sentinel[] = "***";

// CREATE A LINKED LIST OF STRINGS POINTED TO BY HEAD
void create_list
   (list_node *&head)      // OUT: pointer to list that is created

// Pre : None
// Post: head points to the first string entered. head is set
//       to NULL if the sentinel string is the first string.
// Uses: cin.get
{
   // Functions used ...
   // APPEND NEW NODES TO THE END OF A LIST
   void fill_rest
     (list_node *last);          // IN: pointer to list

   // Local data ...
   char first_word[string_size]; // first data word

   // Display instructions to the user.
   cout << "Enter each data string on a line." << endl;
   cout << "Enter " << sentinel << " when done." << endl;

   // Use ws to discard any whitespace.
   cin >> ws;

   // Create and fill the first head with the first word.
   cin.get(first_word, string_size);
   if (strcmp(sentinel, first_word) == 0)
```

(Continued)

Figure 16.8 (Continued)

```
      head = NULL;
   else
   {
      head = new list_node;
      strcpy (head->word, first_word);
      fill_rest (head);
   }
}  // end create_list


// APPEND NEW NODES TO THE END OF A LIST
void fill_rest
   (list_node *last)                    // IN: pointer to list

// Pre : last points to the last node in a list of length n.
// Post: last points to the last node in a list of length >= n.
//       Each data string is stored in a new node in the
//       order in which it was read. The last node contains
//       the data string just before the sentinel.
// Uses: cin.get
{
   // Local data ...
   char next_word[string_size];       // the next data word

   cin >> ws;                          // skip leading white space
   cin.get (next_word, string_size); // read next word
   while (strcmp (sentinel, next_word) != 0)
   {
      // last points to the last node in a list, and
      //    the last string read is stored in node *last,
      //    and no prior data string was the sentinel.
      last->link = new list_node;     // attach a new node to *last
      last = last->link;              // reset last to new end node
      strcpy (last->word, next_word); // store last word read.
      cin >> ws;
      cin.get (next_word, string_size);
   }  // end while
   // The last string read was the sentinel.
   last->link = NULL;                  // mark the end of the list
}  // end fill_list
```

Function `create_list` first displays the user's instructions and then reads the first data word into `first_word`. If `first_word` is the sentinel, `head` is set to NULL to indicate an empty list. If `first_word` is not the sentinel, the statements

```
head = new list_node;
strcpy (head->word, first_word);
```

allocate a new node *head, into which first_word (string "Ace") is copied. The function call statement

```
fill_rest(head);
```

calls function fill_rest to grow the rest of the list. The value of head is passed into fill_rest as the initial value of the argument last. Figure 16.9 shows the partial list right after fill_rest is called.

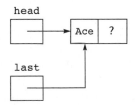

Figure 16.9 List after call to fill_rest

The while loop in fill_rest is repeated until the sentinel is read. Each time the loop is repeated, the statements

```
1. last->link = new list_node;       // Attach a new node to
                                      //     *last
2. last = last->link;                 // Reset last to new
                                      //     end node
   strcpy (last->word, next_word);    // Store last word read
```

attach a new node to the current end of the list, reset last to point to the new end of the list, and then store the data word in node *last. The list after the first execution of the loop body is as shown in Fig. 16.10. Each new pointer value is shown in black, along with the label of the statement that defines it; the previous value of last is shown in gray.

After the loop exit, the statement

```
last->link = NULL;
```

marks the end of the list. If the sentinel string followed "Boy", the link member of the second node in Fig. 16.10 would be set to NULL.

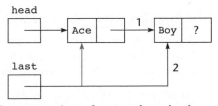

Figure 16.10 List after execution of while **loop body**

Searching a List for a Target

Another common operation involves searching for a target value in a list. A list search is similar to an array search in that we must examine the list elements in the sequence until we find the value we are seeking or we examine all list elements without success. If we reach the list node whose pointer member is NULL, we have examined all list elements without success.

Function search in Fig. 16.11 returns a pointer to the first list node that contains the target value. If the target value is missing, search returns a value of NULL. The while loop exit occurs if all list elements test without success (head == NULL) or the current node contains the target value. In C++, logical expressions are evaluated from left to right (see Section 4.9, on short-circuit evaluation of expressions). Therefore head==NULL will be evaluated before strcmp(head->word,target). This is important because if head is equal to NULL, the expression head->word will access a data value that is undefined. Such errors are difficult to debug.

Figure 16.11   Function search

```
// FILE: SearchLs.cpp

// SEARCH A LIST FOR A SPECIFIED TARGET STRING
list_node* search
    (list_node *head,        // IN: Pointer to list to be searched
     const char target[])    // IN: String to be found

// Pre : head points to a list and target is defined
// Post: Returns a pointer to the first list node that
//       contains target if found. Otherwise, returns NULL
{
    while (head != NULL && strcmp (head->word, target) != 0)
        // no prior list node contains target and
        // no prior value of head was NULL
        head = head->link;
    return head;
}   // end search
```

EXERCISES FOR SECTION 16.3

Self-Check   1. Trace the execution of function search for the list that contains the three strings "Hat", "Boy", and "Cat". Show the value of head after each execution of the while loop. Do this for target strings "Boy", "Cap", and "Dog".

Programming   1. Write a function that finds the length of a list.

2. Write a recursive version of the function search. Your function should implement the following recursive algorithm:

If the list is empty
    Target is missing—return NULL.
else if target is in the list head
    Return a pointer to the list head.
else
    Search the rest of the list.

16.4 ___ THE STACK AS AN ABSTRACT DATA TYPE

In Chapter 15 we introduced the stack as a useful data structure for storing the actual arguments passed in each call to a recursive function. A stack is a convenient mechanism for storing data to be accessed on a last-in-first-out basis; only the top item in a stack can be accessed at any given time. In this section, we illustrate the use of a stack. In the next two sections, we discuss two possible stack implementations: one using an array, and the other using a linked list.

We begin with a description of the information that any user of our stack abstraction would need to know. The stack will be implemented as a *template* class stack<stack_element, max_size>.

Stack<stack_element, max_size> template class specification

```
// Elements:      A stack consists of a collection of elements
//                that are all of the same type, stack_element.
// Structure:     The elements of a stack are ordered according
//                to when they were placed on the stack. Only
//                the element that was last inserted onto the
//                stack can be removed or examined. New elements
//                are inserted at the top of the stack. Space for
//                max_size elements is allocated, default 100.
template <class stack_element, int max_size = 100>
class stack
{
    public:
        // Member functions ...
        // CONSTRUCTOR TO CREATE AN EMPTY STACK
        stack ()
            // Implementation goes here; see Sections 16.5 and 16.6.

        // PUSH AN ELEMENT ONTO THE STACK
        int push
          (stack_element x)      // IN: item to be pushed onto stack
```

```
// Pre : The element x is defined.
// Post: If the stack is not full, the item is pushed onto
//       the stack and 1 is returned. Otherwise, the stack
//       is unchanged and 0 is returned.
// Implementation goes here; see Sections 16.5 and 16.6.

// POP AN ELEMENT OFF THE STACK
int pop
  (stack_element& x)    // OUT: Element popped from stack
  // Pre : none
  // Post: If the stack is not empty, the value at the top
  //       of the stack is removed, its value is placed in
  //       x, and 1 is returned. If the stack is empty, x is
  //       not defined and 0 is returned.
  // Implementation goes here; see Sections 16.5 and 16.6.

// GET TOP ELEMENT FROM STACK WITHOUT POPPING
int get_top
  (stack_element& x) // OUT: Value returned from top of stack
  // Pre : none
  // Post: If the stack is not empty, the value at the top
  //       is copied into x and 1 is returned. If the stack
  //       is empty, x is not defined and 0 is returned. In
  //       either case, the stack is not changed.
  // Implementation goes here; see Sections 16.5 and 16.6.

// TEST TO SEE IF STACK IS EMPTY
int is_empty ()
  // Pre : none
  // Post: Returns 1 if the stack is empty; otherwise,
  //       returns 0.
  // Implementation goes here; see Sections 16.5 and 16.6.

// TEST TO SEE IF STACK IS FULL
int is_full ()
  // Pre : none
  // Post: Returns 1 if the stack is full; otherwise,
  //       returns 0.
  // Implementation goes here; see Sections 16.5 and 16.6.

private:
  // The data members are defined here; see Sections 16.5
  //    and 16.6.
};
```

The template declaration

```
template <class stack_element, int max_size=100>
class stack
```

declares that template class stack takes two parameters, stack_element
(which may be of any type) and max_size (which must be an integer). If the

second template argument (`max_size`) is omitted, the default value of 100 is used. The declaration

```
stack<int> integer_stack;
```

defines a stack of integers of the default size, 100. The declaration

```
stack<char,10> small_character_stack;
```

defines a stack of characters of size 10.

We can illustrate how stacks and their operators work and use them in a client program without worrying about the details of how the stack is represented in memory. Each client program must include a stack template definition (shown later in Figs. 16.21 and 16.24) and then declare stack variables providing the actual type for the template argument `stack_element`, and, optionally, the maximum size. Multiple stacks containing different types can be defined in a given client program. A given stack, however, can hold variables only of a single type.

As with all variables, a stack must be declared before it can be used. The declaration creates an empty stack. For example, the following declares a stack of integers and displays the message `Stack is empty`:

```
stack<int> s;
if (s.is_empty ())
   cout << "Stack is empty." << endl;
```

Example 16.2 A stack s of characters is shown in Fig. 16.12. The stack has four elements; the first element placed on the stack was `'2'`, and the last element placed on the stack was `'*'`. For this stack, the value of `s.is_empty()` is 0. The value of `s.is_full()` is 0 if stack s can store more than four elements; otherwise, the value of `s.is_full()` is 1. The function call

```
s.get_top (x)
```

stores `'*'` in x (type `char`) without changing s. The function call

```
s.pop (x)
```

Figure 16.12 Stack s

removes '*' from s and stores it in x. The new stack s contains three elements, as shown in Fig. 16.13.

```
    | C |
    | + |
    | 2 |
      s
```

Figure 16.13   Stack s after pop operation

The function call

```
s.push ('/')
```

pushes '/' onto the stack; the new stack s, which contains four elements, is shown in Fig. 16.14. The value returned from each operation should be 1.

```
    | / |
    | C |
    | + |
    | 2 |
      s
```

Figure 16.14   Stack s after push operation   ∎

Evaluating Expressions

You may use a calculator that evaluates postfix expressions. A *postfix expression* is an expression in which each operator follows its operands. You can get a pretty good idea of what a postfix expression is by studying the examples in Table 16.1. The grouping marks under each expression should help you to visualize the operands for each operator. The more familiar *infix expression* corresponding to each postfix expression is also shown.

Table 16.1   Examples of Postfix Expressions

POSTFIX EXPRESSION	INFIX EEXPRESSION	VALUE
5 6 *	5 * 6	30
5 6 1 + *	5 * (6 + 1)	35
5 6 * 10 −	(5 * 6) − 10	20
4 5 6 * 3 / +	4 + ((5 * 6) / 3)	14

The advantage of postfix form is that there is no need to group subexpressions in parentheses or to consider operator precedence. The grouping marks in Table 16.1 are only for our convenience and are not required. Next, we write a program that evaluates a postfix expression.

CASE STUDY: EVALUATING POSTFIX EXPRESSIONS

Problem Statement

Simulate the operation of a calculator by reading an expression in postfix form and displaying its result. Each character read will be a blank, a digit character, or one of the operator characters from the set {+, − *, /}.

Problem Analysis

Using a stack of integer values makes it easy to evaluate the expression. Our program will push each integer operand onto the stack. When an operator is read, the top two operands are popped, the operation is performed on its operands, and the result is pushed back onto the stack. The final result should be the only value remaining on the stack when the end of the expression is reached.

DATA REQUIREMENTS

> *Problem Input*
>
> expression (char [ ])   — expression to evaluate
>
> *Problem Output*
>
> result (int)   — expression value
>
> *Local Variables*
>
> op_stack (stack<int>)   — stack of integer operands
> success (int)   — flag indicating result of a stack operation
> next_ch (char)   — next character in expression
> index (int)   — index of character in expression
> new_op (int)   — next integer value in expression
> op1, op2 (int)   — two operands for an operator

Program Design

The structure chart in Fig. 16.15 shows the decomposition of the Postfix Problem program into a main function and two subproblems, get_integer

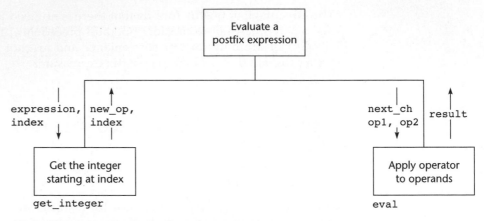

Figure 16.15   Structure chart for program `post_fix`

and `eval`. The data flow between these two functions and `main` is also shown in this figure. The algorithm is shown below.

INITIAL ALGORITHM

1. Create an empty stack of integers.
2. Read an expression as a character string.
3. Set success to 1 (true).
4. While success and not at the end of the expression
    4.1. Get the next character.
    4.2. If the character is a digit
        4.2.1. Determine the value of the integer that starts with this digit (`get_integer`).
        4.2.2. Push the integer onto the stack.
      else if the character is an operator
        4.2.3. Pop the top two operands from the stack.
        4.2.4. Evaluate the operation (`eval`).
        4.2.5. Push the result onto the stack.
5. Display the result.

Member functions of the stack class (the stack class operators) perform algorithm steps 1, 4.2.2, 4.2.3, 4.2.5, and 5. Step 2 is performed by the function `get`, a member of the class `iostream`. Step 4.1 is accomplished by indexing the array of characters that constitute the string. Steps 4.2.1 and 4.2.4 are the only algorithm steps that require refinement. Step 4.2.1 is performed by function `get_integer` and step 4.2.4 by function `eval`.

Table 16.2 shows the evaluation of the third expression in Table 16.1 using this algorithm. The arrow under the expression points to the character being processed; the stack diagram shows the stack after this character is processed.

Table 16.2 Evaluating a Postfix Expression

EXPRESSION	ACTION	STACK
5 6 * 10 – ↑	Push 5	5
5 6 * 10 – 　↑	Push 6	6 5
5 6 * 10 – 　　↑	Pop 6 and 5; evaluate 5*6; push 30	30
5 6 * 10 – 　　　↑	Push 10	10 30
5 6 * 10 – 　　　　↑	Pop 10 and 30; evaluate 30–10; push 20	20
5 6 * 10 – 　　　　　↑	Pop 20; stack is empty; result is 20	

Program Implementation

IMPLEMENTING THE MAIN PROGRAM

The main program is shown in Fig. 16.16. A stack template must be included and a stack of integers (`stack<int>`) must be declared. Each time the stack is manipulated, the flag `success` is set to indicate the success or failure of that operation. If `success` is 0 (false), the program displays an error message and terminates the expression evaluation. If the final value of `success` is 1 (true) and the stack is empty, the result is displayed.

Figure 16.16 Program `PostFix` and sample run

```
// FILE: PostFix.cpp
// DRIVER THAT EVALUATES A POSTFIX EXPRESSION

#include <iostream.h>     // Stream input/output

#include <ctype.h>        // Standard character functions
#include <string.h>       // Standard string operations

#include "ArryStck.h"     // Stack class (array version)
```

(Continued)

Figure 16.16   (Continued)

```
void main()
{
   // Function prototypes ...
   void get_integer
     (char [],          // IN: expression to be evaluated
      int&,             // INOUT: index within expression
      int&);            // OUT: result

   int eval
     (char,             // IN: operator
      int,              // IN: first operand
      int);             // IN: second operand

   // Local data ...
   stack<int> op_stack; // stack of integers
   char expression[80]; // expression to be evaluated
   char next_ch;        // next data character
   int op1, op2,        // operand values from stack
   int new_op,          // new operand for the stack
   int result;          // result of operator evaluation
   int success;         // flag for stack operation

   cout << "Enter your expression" << endl;
   cin >> ws;                   // skip leading white space if any
   cin.get (expression,80);  // read expression (max 79 characters)
   success = 1;
   for (int index = 0; success && expression[index]; index++)
   {
   // op_stack contains all unprocessed operands and results and
   //    there are still characters to be processed.
      next_ch = expression[index];
      if (isdigit (next_ch))
      {  // Digit found; get integer value.
         get_integer (expression, index, new_op);
         success = op_stack.push (new_op);
         if (!success)
            cerr << "*** ERROR: Stack overflow error." << endl;
      }  // end digit
      else if (strchr ("+-*/",next_ch) != NULL)
      {  // operator
         success = op_stack.pop (op2);
         success = op_stack.pop (op1);
         if (!success)
            cerr << "*** ERROR: Invalid expression." << endl;
         else
         {  // Evaluate operator.
            result = eval (next_ch, op1, op2);
            success = op_stack.push (result);
            if (!success)
```

(Continued)

Figure 16.16 (Continued)

```
              cerr << "*** ERROR: Stack overflow." << endl;
          } // end evaluate operator
      } // end operator
  } // end for
  if (success)
      success = op_stack.pop (result);
  if (success && op_stack.is_empty ())
      cout << "Expression value is " << result << endl;
  else
      cerr << "Program execution terminated." << endl;
}
```

——————— Program Output ———————

```
Enter your expression: 5 6 * 10 -
Expression value is 20
```

IMPLEMENTING THE FUNCTIONS

Function get_integer (Fig. 16.17) accumulates the integer value of a string of consecutive digit characters and returns the value through argument new_op. The assignment statement

new_op = 10 * new_op + int (next_ch) - int ('0');

adds the numeric value of the digit character in next_ch to the numeric value being accumulated in new_op. For example, if the current value of new_op is 15 and next_ch is '3', new_op gets the value 153. When get_integer returns to the main program, index points to the last digit of the number just processed.

Figure 16.17 Function get_integer

```
// FILE: PostGInt.cpp

#include <ctype.h>      // for isdigit()

// GET INTEGER FROM AN EXPRESSION
void get_integer
  (char expression[],   // IN: expression
   int& index,          // INOUT: position of beginning of integer
   int& new_op)         // OUT: integer value whose first digit
                        //      is at position index

// Pre : expression and index are defined and the character at
//       index is a digit
```

(Continued)

Figure 16.17   (Continued)

```
// Post: index points to the last digit of the number whose first
//       digit is pointed to by the initial value of index.
//       new_op is the value of that number.
{
   // Local data ...
   char next_ch;             // next data character

   new_op = 0;
   for (next_ch = expression[index]; isdigit (next_ch);
        next_ch = expression[index])
   {
      // Every prior character in next_ch was a digit
      //    and new_op is the numerical value of all digits
      //    processed so far.
      new_op = 10 * new_op + int (next_ch) - int ('0');
      index++;
   }  // end for

   // new_op is the numerical value of the substring processed
   //    and index is just past it.
   index--;                  // point to the last digit
}  // end get_integer
```

Whenever an operator is encountered, the main program pops two operands off the stack and calls function `eval` (Fig. 16.18) to compute the result of applying the operator (passed through `next_ch`) to these two operands (passed through `op1`, `op2`). The `switch` statement in function `eval` selects the appropriate operation and performs it.

Figure 16.18   Function `eval`

```
// FILE: PostEval.cpp

#include <iostream.h>    // Stream input/output

// APPLY OPERATOR TO TWO OPERANDS
int eval
   (char next_ch,      // IN: operator
    int op1,           // IN: first operand
    int op2)           // IN: second operand

// Pre : next_ch is an ooperator and op1 and op2 are defined.
// Post: If next_ch is + returns op1 + op2, and so on.
```

(Continued)

Figure 16.18 (Continued)

```
switch (next_ch)
{
    case '+' : return op1 + op2;
    case '-' : return op1 - op2;
    case '*' : return op1 * op2;
    case '/' : return op1 / op2;
    default  : cerr << "*** ERROR: Error in operator symbol"
                    << endl;
               return 0;
}   // end switch
}   // end eval
```

Program Testing

A full test of the expression evaluation program involves a number of steps to verify that the expression to be evaluated is a valid postfix expression—that is, that the expression satisfies the *rules of formation* for a postfix expression. These rules were informally described at the beginning of this section. In addition to testing the program on valid expressions to ensure that the correct result is computed, it is important to test the program to see what happens when the expression read contains characters other than those expected or when the expression contains legal characters but is still not a valid postfix expression.

EXERCISES FOR SECTION 16.4

Self-Check

1. Assume that the stack s is defined as in Fig. 16.14. Perform the sequence of operations shown below. Show the result of each operation and the new stack if it is changed. Rather than draw the stack each time, use the notation | 2 + c / to represent the stack represented in Fig. 16.14 (we use the bar, " | ", to represent the bottom of the stack).

```
s.push ('$')
s.push ('-')
s.pop (next_ch)
s.top (next_ch)
s.is_empty ()
s.is_full ()
```

2. Trace the evaluation of the last expression in Table 16.1. Show the stack each time it is modified and how the values of new_op and result change as the program executes.

Programming

1. Modify the main program for Postfix Expression Evaluation to handle the exponentiation operator, indicated by the symbol ^. Assume that the first operand is raised to the power indicated by the second operand.

16.5 ___ IMPLEMENTING A STACK USING AN ARRAY

This section discusses how to implement the class `stack` in C++ using an array. A template class `stack`, with the type of an array element and the maximum size of the array as parameters, is illustrated.

Data Members

The private part for the template class `stack` is shown in Fig. 16.19. There are two data members: an integer (`top`), which is the index of the top item of the stack, and an array (`data`), which holds the items. The array `data` is declared to be of size `max_stack`, which has the default value of 100. Storage is not allocated until a variable of type `stack` is declared. The declaration

```
stack<char> s;
```

allocates storage for a stack, `s`, of up to 100 characters. All the storage space is allocated at one time, even though there will not be any items on the stack initially.

Figure 16.19   Private part of class `stack` using an array

```
template <class stack_element, int max_size = 100>
class stack
{

...

    private:
    // Data members ...
        int top;                        // the top of the stack
        stack_element data[max_size];   // the data elements
```

In the diagram that follows, abstract stack `s` (on the left) would be represented in memory as shown on the right. `s.top` is 2, and the stack consists of the subarray `s.data[0]` through `s.data[2]`; the subarray `s.data[3]` through `s.data[99]` is currently undefined.

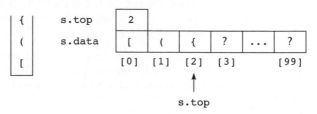

The array element `s.data[s.top]` contains the character value `'{'`, which is the value at the top of the stack.

We can change the capacity of the stack by providing an argument value for `max_size`. Also, we can change the stack elements to another type by providing a different type for the argument `stack_element`. For example, the declaration

```
stack<int, 10> int_stack_10
```

creates a stack, `int_stack_10`, with a maximum capacity of 10 integers.

Example 16.3 Figure 16.20 shows the effect of the statement

```
s.push('(')
```

where the initial stack `s` is shown above. Before push is executed, `s.top` is 2, so `s.data[2]` is the element at the top of the stack. Function push must increment `s.top` to 3 so that the new item (`'('`) will be stored in `s.data[3]`, as shown in the figure.

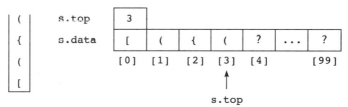

Figure 16.20 Pushing `'('` onto stack `s`   ∎

Stack Operators

The stack operators manipulate the array member data using the integer member `top` as an index to the array. Their implementation is fairly straightforward and can be understood by studying the stack operators shown in the implementation section of the template class `stack`. Figure 16.21 shows the complete include file for the array implementation of a stack template. Recall that the compiler directives

```
#ifndef ARRASTCK_H_

#define ARRASTCK_H_
    .
    .
    .
#endif
```

prevent multiple definitions of the class `stack` if another `include` file should happen to use the same class.

Figure 16.21   Implementation of template class `stack` using an array

```
// FILE: ArryStck.h
// STACK TEMPLATE CLASS USING AN ARRAY

#ifndef ARRYSTCK_H_
#define ARRYSTCK_H_

// Specification of the class stack<stack_element>, max_size>
// Elements:    A stack consists of a collection of elements
//              that are all of the same type, stack_element.
// Structure:   The elements of a stack are ordered according
//              to when they were placed on the stack. Only
//              the element that was last inserted onto the
//              stack can be removed or examined. New elements
//              are inserted at the top of the stack. Space for
//              max_size elements is allocated, default 100.

template <class stack_element, int max_size = 100>
class stack
{
    public:
        // Member functions ...
        // CONSTRUCTOR TO CREATE AN EMPTY STACK
        stack ()
        {
            top = -1;               // A value of -1 indicates empty
        }  // end stack


        // PUSH AN ELEMENT ONTO THE STACK
        int push
          (stack_element x)     // IN: item to be pushed onto stack

        // Pre:  The element x is defined.
        // Post: If the stack is not full, the item is pushed onto
        //       the stack and 1 is returned. Otherwise, the stack
        //       is unchanged and 0 is returned.
        {
            if (top < max_size - 1)     // If there is room
            {
                data[++top] = x;            // increment top and insert
                return 1;                   // indicate success
            }
```

(Continued)

Figure 16.21   (Continued)

```
      else
         return 0;                   // no room, indicate fail
   }  // end push


   // POP AN ELEMENT OFF THE STACK
   int pop
     (stack_element& x)     // OUT: Element popped from stack

   // Pre:  none
   // Post: If the stack is not empty, the value at the top of
   //       the stack is removed, its value is placed in x, and
   //       1 is returned. If the stack is empty, x is not
   //       defined and 0 is returned.
   {
      if (top >= 0)          // if not empty
      {
         x = data[top--];    // remove top element, decrement top
         return 1;           // indicate success
      }
      else
         return 0;           // indicate fail
   }  // end pop


   // GET TOP ELEMENT FROM STACK WITHOUT POPPING
   int get_top
     (stack_element& x) // OUT: Value returned from top of stack

   // Pre:  none
   // Post: If the stack is not empty, the value at the top is
   //       copied into x and 1 is returned. If the stack is
   //       empty, x is not defined and 0 is returned. In either
   //       case, the stack is not changed.
   {
      if (top >= 0)          // if not empty
      {
         x = data[top];      // retrieve top element, do not pop
         return 1;           // indicate success
      }
      else
         return 0;           // indicate fail
   }  // end get_top


   // TEST TO SEE IF STACK IS EMPTY
   int is_empty ()
```

(Continued)

Figure 16.21   (Continued)

```
// Pre:  none
// Post: Returns 1 if the stack is empty; otherwise,
//       returns 0.
{
  return top < 0;
}  // end is_empty


// TEST TO SEE IF STACK IS FULL
int is_full ()

// Pre:  none
// Post: Returns 1 if the stack is full; otherwise,
//       returns 0.
{
  return top >= max_size;
}  // end is_full


  private:
    // Data members ...
    int top;                        // The top of the stack
    stack_element data[max_size];   // The data elements
};

#endif // ARRYSTCK_H_
```

EXERCISES FOR SECTION 16.5

Self-Check   1. Declare a stack of 50 student records, where each record is represented by a `struct` consisting of a student's name, a `var_string` (see Chapter 13); an exam score, an `int`; and a letter grade, a `char`. Can you use the stack operators to manipulate this stack?

Programming   1. Write a member function `depth` that returns the number of elements currently on the stack.

16.6 —— LINKED-LIST REPRESENTATION OF A STACK

In the previous section we showed how to implement a stack using an array for storing the individual elements. Because the number of elements in a stack may vary considerably, it makes good sense to implement this data structure as a dynamically allocated linked list. Think of a stack as a linked list in which all insertions and deletions are performed at the list head. A linked list representation of a stack `s` is shown at the top of Fig. 16.22. The first element of the list, `s.top`, is at the top of the stack. If a new node is pushed onto the stack, it should be inserted in front of the node that is currently at the head of the list. Stack `s` after insertion of the symbol `'*'` is shown at the bottom of the figure.

Stack of three characters

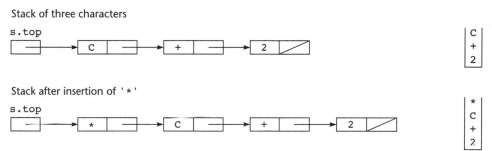

Figure 16.22   Physical stack `s` (left) and abstract stack (right)

Each element of a stack can be stored in a node with the data member (type `stack_element`). By defining a `struct` to hold the data element and a pointer to the next node, the private part of the template class `stack` can be declared as shown in Fig. 16.23.

Figure 16.23   Private part of class `stack` using a linked list

```
template <class stack_element>
class stack
{

   ...

   private:
   // Data members ...
      struct stack_node
      {
         stack_element item;
         stack_node* next;
      };
      stack_node* top; // define the stack as a list,
                       //    initially empty
```

Example 16.4   The declaration

```
stack<char> s;
```

declares s to be an initially empty stack of characters, as shown next.

Assuming that the function push has been written for the linked list implementation of a stack, the statements

```
success = s.push ('+');
success = s.push ('A');
```

should redefine stack s, as shown next.

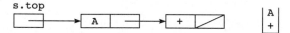

Two new nodes will be allocated to create stack s. Assuming pop has also been modified for the list implementation, the statement

```
success = s.pop (next_ch);
```

should return the character value 'A' to next_ch (type char) and redefine stack s, as shown next.

Stack Operators

Each of the stack operators shown in Fig. 16.21 is rewritten in this section. The complete file, ListStck.h, is shown in Fig. 16.24. Function push calls the new operator to allocate a new stack_node. If the new operator fails to allocate a new stack_node, 0 is returned, indicating that the push operation failed. Otherwise, the data item is placed into the new node, the existing stack is linked to this new node, the new node is made the new head of the list, and 1 is returned, indicating that the push was successful.

Function pop first checks to see if the list is empty. If the list is empty, 0 is returned. Otherwise, the first element is removed and 1 is returned, indicating success. Function is_empty checks to see if the class data member top is NULL. Function is_full always returns 0. No check is made on available heap space.

Figure 16.24   List implementation of a stack

```
// FILE: ListStck.h
// DEFINITION AND IMPLEMENTATION OF A STACK USING A LINKED LIST

#ifndef LISTSTCK_H_
#define LISTSTCK_H_

// Specification of the class stack<stack_element>
// Elements:     A stack consists of a collection of elements
//               that are all of the same type, stack_element.
// Structure:    The elements of a stack are ordered according
//               to when they were placed on the stack. Only
//               the element that was last inserted onto the
//               stack can be removed or examined. New elements
//               are inserted at the top of the stack. The upper
//               limit on the number of items that can be placed
//               on the stack is determined by the amount of free
//               storage on the heap.

#include<stdlib.h>

template <class element_type>
class stack
{
    public:
        // Member functions ...
        // CONSTRUCTOR TO CREATE AN EMPTY STACK
        stack ()
        {
           top = NULL;
        }   // end stack


        // PUSH AN ELEMENT ONTO THE STACK
        int push
          (stack_element x)   // IN: Element to be pushed onto stack

        // Pre:  The element x is defined.
        // Post: If there is space on the heap, the item is pushed
        //       onto the stack and 1 is returned. Otherwise, the
        //       stack is unchanged and 0 is returned.
        {
           // Local data ...
           stack_node* old_top;

           old_top = top;            // save old top
           top = new stack_node;     // allocate a new node at top of
                                     // stack
           if (top == NULL)          // check to see if new was
                                     // successful
```

(Continued)

Figure 16.24   (Continued)

```
    {
      top = old_top;          // if not, restore top
      return 0;               // indicate push failed
    }
    else
    {
      top->next = old_top; // link new node to old stack
      top->item = x;       // store x in new node
      return 1;            // indicate success
    }
}  // end push


// POP AN ELEMENT OFF THE STACK
int pop
  (stack_element& x)    // OUT: Element popped from stack

  // Pre:  none
  // Post: If the stack is not empty, the value at the top
  //       of the stack is removed, its value is placed in
  //       x, and 1 is returned. If the stack is empty, x is
  //       not defined and 0 is returned.
{
    // Local data ...
    stack_node* old_top;
    if (top == NULL)
       return 0;
    else
    {
      x = top->item;          // copy top of stack into x
      old_top = top;          // save old top of stack
      top = old_top->next;    // reset top of stack
      delete old_top;         // return top node to the heap
      return 1;               // indicate success
    }
}  // end pop


// GET TOP ELEMENT FROM STACK WITHOUT POPPING
int get_top
  (stack_element& x)    // OUT: Value returned from stack top
// Pre:  none
// Post: If the stack is not empty, the value at the top is
//       copied into x and 1 is returned. If the stack is
//       empty, x is not defined and 0 is returned. In either
//       case, the stack is not changed.
{
    if (top == NULL)
```

(Continued)

Figure 16.24 (Continued)

```
              return 0;
          else
          {
              x = top->item;
              return 1;
          }
      } // end get_top


      // TEST TO SEE IF STACK IS EMPTY
      int is_empty ()
      // Pre : none
      // Post: Returns 1 if the stack is empty; otherwise,
      //        returns 0.
      {
          return top == NULL;
      } // end is_empty


      // TEST TO SEE IF STACK IS FULL
      int is_full ()
      // Pre : none
      // Post: Returns 0. List stacks are never full. (Does not
      //        check heap availability.)
      {
          return 0;
      } // end is_full


  private:
      // Data members ...
      struct stack_node
      {
          element_type item;
          stack_node* next;
      };
      stack_node* top; // define stack as an initially empty list
};

#endif // LISTSTCK_H_
```

Space Tradeoffs for Stack Implementations

The advantage of using a list to implement a stack is that we can increase the size of the stack when we push on a new element and decrease its size when we pop off an element. In this way, the storage space allocated to the stack expands and contracts as needed. In the array implementation shown earlier, the entire array is allocated at once, whether or not it is all needed.

This saving of memory is not without cost. Each stack element requires an additional pointer member that is used for storage of the address of the next stack element. An array implementation does not require this extra member because the elements of an array are implicitly linked together.

EXERCISES FOR SECTION 16.6

Self-Check   1. Provide an algorithm for a linked list member function `copy_stack` that makes a copy of an existing stack.

Programming   1. Implement `copy_stack` in C++.

16.7 —— THE QUEUE ABSTRACT DATA TYPE

A *queue* is a data abstraction that can be used, for example, to model a line of customers waiting at a checkout counter or a stream of jobs waiting to be printed by a printer in a computer center. A queue differs from a stack in that new elements are inserted at one end (the rear of the queue) and existing elements are removed from the other end (the front of the queue). In this way, the element that has been waiting longest is removed first. In contrast, stack elements are inserted and removed from the same end (the top of the stack). A queue is called a *first-in, first-out* (FIFO) structure; a stack is called a *last-in, first-out* (LIFO) structure.

A queue of three passengers waiting to see an airline ticket agent is shown in Fig. 16.25. The name of the passenger who has been waiting the longest is McMann (pointed to by `front`); the name of the most recent arrival is `Carson`

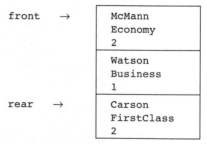

Figure 16.25   A passenger queue

(pointed to by `rear`). Passenger `McMann` will be the first one removed from the queue when an agent becomes available, and pointer `front` will be moved to passenger `Watson`. Any new passengers will follow passenger `Carson` in the queue, and pointer `rear` will be adjusted accordingly.

We can model the queue abstraction using the same approach as used in constructing a model for the stack. We construct a template class `queue<queue_element, max_size>`. The specification for the `class queue` follows; compare it with the earlier specification for the `class stack` given in Section 16.4. Two implementations of the class, one using arrays and the other using linked lists, are discussed in Sections 16.9 and 16.10.

queue<queue_element, max_size> template class specification

```
// Elements:      A queue consists of a collection of elements
//                that are all of the same type, queue_element.
// Structure:     The elements of a queue are ordered according
//                to time of arrival. The element that was first
//                inserted into the queue is the only one that
//                may be removed or examined. Elements are
//                removed from the front of the queue and
//                inserted at the rear of the queue.

template<class queue_element, int max_queue=100>
class queue
{
   public:
       // Member functions:  The following operators are provided
       // CONSTRUCTOR TO CREATE AN EMPTY QUEUE
       queue ()
          // Implementation goes here; see Sections 16.9 and 16.10.

       // INSERT AN ELEMENT INTO THE QUEUE
       int insert
         (const queue_element& x)    // IN: Element to be inserted
          // Pre:  none
          // Post: If the queue is not full, the value x is
          //       inserted at the rear of the queue and 1 is
          //       returned. Otherwise, the queue is not changed
          //       and 0 is returned.
          // Implementation goes here; see Sections 16.9 and
          //    16.10.

       // REMOVE AN ELEMENT FROM THE QUEUE
       int remove
         (queue_element& x)    // OUT: element removed from queue
          // Pre:  none
```

```
                    // Post: If the queue is not empty, the value at the
                    //       front of the queue is removed, its value is
                    //       placed in x, and 1 is returned. If the queue is
                    //       empty, x is not defined and 0 is returned.
                    // Implementation goes here; see Sections 16.9 and 16.10.

              // RETRIEVE COPY OF FIRST ELEMENT WITHOUT REMOVING IT
              int retrieve
                (queue_element& x)    // OUT: the element retrieved
                // Pre:  none
                // Post: If the queue is not empty, the value at the
                //       front is copied into x and 1 is returned. If
                //       the queue is empty, x is not defined and 0 is
                //       returned. In either case, the queue is not
                //       changed.
                // Implementation goes here; see Sections 16.9 and 16.10.

              // TEST TO SEE IF QUEUE IS EMPTY
              int is_empty ()
                // Pre:  none
                // Post: Returns 1 if the queue is empty; otherwise,
                //       returns 0.
                // Implementation goes here; see Sections 16.9 and 16.10.

              // TEST TO SEE IF QUEUE IS FULL
              int is_full ()
                // Pre:  none
                // Post: Returns 1 if the queue is full; otherwise,
                //       returns 0.
                // Implementation goes here; see Sections 16.9 and 16.10.

              // DETERMINE NUMBER OF ITEMS IN QUEUE
              int size_of_queue ()
                // Pre:  none
                // Post: Returns the number of items currently in the
                //       queue.
                // Implementation goes here; see Sections 16.9 and 16.10.

          private:
              // The data numbers are defined here; see Sections 16.9
              //    and 16.10
        };
```

The template header

```
template <class queue_element, int max_size = 100>
class queue
```

indicates that the class queue takes two parameters, queue_element
(which may be of any type) and max_size (which must be an integer). If the

second template parameter (`max_size`) is omitted, the default value of 100 is used. The declaration

```
queue<int> integer_queue;
```

defines a queue of integers of the default size, 100. The declaration

```
queue<char,10> small_character_queue;
```

defines a queue of characters of size 10.

We can illustrate how a queue and its operators work and use them in a client program without worrying about the details of how the queue is represented in memory. We discuss an internal representation for a queue and implement the queue operators in Sections 16.9 and 16.10. Each client program must include the queue template definition (see Figs. 16.35 and 16.37) and then declare queue variables providing the actual type for the template argument `queue_element` and, optionally, the maximum size. Multiple queues containing different types can be defined in a given client program. A given queue, however, can hold variables of only a single type.

EXERCISES FOR SECTION 16.7

Self-Check   1. Draw the queue in Fig. 16.25 after the insertion of first-class passenger `Harris` (three seats reserved) and the removal of one passenger from the queue. Which passenger is removed? How many passengers are left?

16.8 ——— QUEUE APPLICATION

Our queue application is a program that processes a queue of airline passengers.

CASE STUDY: MAINTAINING A QUEUE OF PASSENGERS

Problem Statement

Write a menu-driven program that maintains a queue of passengers waiting to see a ticket agent. The program user should be able to insert a new passenger at the rear of the queue, display the passenger at the front of the queue, and remove the passenger at the front of the queue. Just before it terminates, the program should display the number of passengers left in the queue.

Problem Analysis

We can use the `queue` class and operators `insert`, `retrieve`, and `remove` to process the passenger queue. We can simplify the program by designing a class `passenger` that contains the type declarations for an airline passenger and provides its input/output operators `read_pass` and `write_pass`. The ticket agent queue can then be defined as a `queue` of elements of type `passenger`. We will implement this class later.

DATA REQUIREMENTS

> ### Problem Input
>
> choice (char)   — operation to be performed
>
> ### Problem Output
>
> the number of passengers in the queue
>
> ### Program Variables
>
> pass_queue (queue)   — queue of passengers
> success (int)   — flag for storing the result of a queue oper-
>   ation

Program Design

A structure chart for the program is shown in Fig. 16.26. The initial algorithm is shown on the following page. Step 1 of the algorithm is performed by the

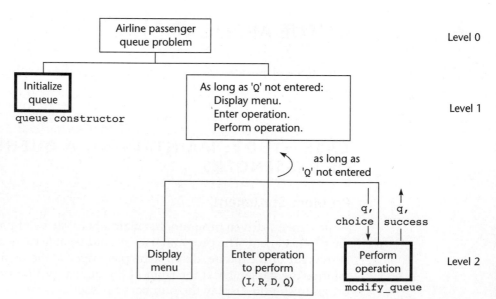

Figure 16.26   **Structure chart for Passenger Queue Problem**

queue constructor. The main program performs steps 2, 2.1, and 2.2. The function modify_queue performs step 2.3, and the queue member function size_of_queue is used to perform step 3.

INITIAL ALGORITHM

1. Initialize the queue.
2. do
    2.1. Display the menu.
    2.2. Read the operation selected.
    2.3. Perform the operation selected (modify_queue).
    while user is not done and queue operations are successful
3. Display the number of passengers left in the queue (size_of_queue, from the queue class).

Program Implementation

IMPLEMENTING THE MAIN PROGRAM

Function main (Fig. 16.27) uses the type declarations for passenger (from the passenger class) and for queue (from the queue class). A queue of passengers is declared using the declaration

queue<passenger> pass_queue;   // passenger queue

This queue is initially empty. In function main, the statement

cout << "Enter I(nsert), R(emove), D(isplay), or Q(uit): ";

displays the menu of choices (step 2.1). After the selection is read into choice, main calls function modify_queue to perform step 2.3. Function modify_queue is discussed next.

Figure 16.27   **Program for Airline Passenger Queue Problem**

```
// FILE: UseQueue.cpp
// MANIPULATES A QUEUE OF AIRLINE PASSENGERS

#include <iostream.h>    // C++ stream I/O

#include "VarStrng.h"    // Variable length string class
#include "Passengr.h"    // Passenger class
#include "ListQue.h"     // Linked list version of the queue class

void main()
{
   // Local data ...
   queue<passenger> pass_queue; // passenger queue
```

(Continued)

Figure 16.27   (Continued)

```
        char choice;                      // operation requested
        int success;                      // program flag

        // Functions used ...
        void modify_queue
          (queue<passenger>&,             // INOUT: queue of passengers
           char,                          // IN: operation to be performed
           int&);                         // OUT: flag indicating success

        // Process all requests until done
        do
        {
           cout << "Enter I(nsert), R(emove), D(isplay), or Q(uit): ";
           cin >> choice;                 // Read first character of choice

           // Process current request
           modify_queue(pass_queue, choice, success);
           cout << endl;
        }
        while ((choice != 'Q') && success);

        // Display passenger count.
        cout << "Number of passengers in queue is " << q.size_of_queue
             << endl;
}   // end use_queue
```

IMPLEMENTING modify_queue

The data requirements table and structure chart for modify_queue are left as an exercise (see Self-Check Exercise 2 at the end of this section). For each operation specified by the user, function modify_queue (Fig. 16.28) calls the queue class member functions required to manipulate the queue and the passenger class member functions needed to read or display a passenger record. The main control structure is a switch statement that determines which operators are called.

Figure 16.28   Function modify_queue

```
// FILE: ModQueue.cpp
// MANIPULATES A QUEUE OF AIRLINE PASSENGERS

#include <iostream.h>        // C++ stream i/o

#include "Passengr.h"        // Passenger class
#include "ListQue.h"         // Linked list version of the queue class
```

(Continued)

Figure 16.28   (Continued)

```
// PERFORMS OPERATION INDICATED BY CHOICE ON QUEUE Q
void modify_queue
   (queue<passenger>&q,      // INOUT: queue of passengers
    char choice,             // IN: operation to be performed
    int& success);           // OUT: flag indicating success

// Pre: q has been created
// Post: q is modified based on choice, and success indicates
//        whether requested operation was performed
{
    // Local data ...
    passenger next_pass;   // new passenger
    passenger first_pass;  // passenger at front of queue

    switch (choice)
    {
        case 'I' :
            cout << "Enter passenger data." << endl;
            next_pass.read_pass ();
            success = q.insert (next_pass);
            if (!success)
                cout << "Queue is full -- no insertion." << endl;
            break; // end insert
        case 'R':
            success = q.remove (first_pass);
            if (success)
            {
                cout << "Passenger removed from queue follows."
                     << endl;
                first_pass.write_pass ();
            }
            else
                cout << "Queue is empty -- no deletion." << endl;
            break; // end remove
        case 'D':
            success = q.retrieve (first_pass);
            if (success)
            {
                cout << "Passenger at head of queue follows." << endl;
                first_pass.write_pass ();
            }
            else
                cout << "Queue is empty -- no passenger." << endl;
            break; // end display
        case 'Q':
            cout << "Leaving passenger queue." << endl;
            break; // end quit
        default:
            cerr << "Incorrect choice -- try again." << endl;
    }  // end switch
}  // end modify_queue
```

Program Testing

You can store the initial passenger list by selecting a sequence of insert operations. In the sample run of the program shown in Fig. 16.29, passenger Brown is inserted first, followed by passengers Watson and Dietz. After passenger Brown is removed from the queue, the new passenger at the front of the queue (Watson) is displayed.

Figure 16.29   Sample run of program use_queue

```
Enter I(nsert), R(emove), D(isplay), or Q(uit): I
Enter passenger data.
Passenger name: Brown
Class (F, B, E, S): E
Number of Seats - Enter an integer between 1 and 30 or 1
2

Enter I(nsert), R(emove), D(isplay), or Q(uit): I
Enter passenger data.
Passenger name: Watson
Class (F, B, E, S): B
Number of Seats - Enter an integer between 1 and 30 or 1
1

Enter I(nsert), R(emove), D(isplay), or Q(uit): I
Enter passenger data.
Passenger name: Dietz
Class (F, B, E, S): E
Number of Seats - Enter an integer between 1 and 30 or 1
3

Enter I(nsert), R(emove), D(isplay), or Q(uit): R
Passenger removed from queue follows.
Name: Brown
Economy
2 Seats

Enter I(nsert), R(emove), D(isplay), or Q(uit): D
Passenger at head of queue follows.
Name: Watson
Business
1 Seat

Enter I(nsert), R(emove), D(isplay), or Q(uit): Q
Leaving passenger queue.
Number of passengers in queue is 2
```

To test the program thoroughly, you should try to display or remove a passenger after the queue is empty. Either attempt should cause the error message "Queue is empty" to be displayed before the program terminates. To check that there is no insertion after the queue is full, you might temporarily redefine the queue capacity by changing the declaration of **pass_queue** to the following:

```
queue<passenger,5> pass_queue;
```

so that the message "Queue is full - no insertion" appears after five passenger insertions take place.

IMPLEMENTING THE CLASS passenger

Figures 16.30 and 16.31 show the definition and implementation for the class **passenger**. Because **name** is a string of variable length (class **var_string**), the include file **varstrng.h** (see Chapter 13) is included by the file **passengr.h**. Member functions **read_pass** and **write_pass** read and write a single passenger's record.

Figure 16.30   Definition section for the passenger class

```
// FILE: Passengr.h
// DEFINITION FOR THE PASSENGER CLASS

// Structure:  An object of type passenger contains the storage
//             space for a collection of items that describe a
//             single airline passenger, such as the
//             passenger's name, flight class, and number
//             of seats reserved.
// Operators:  The following operators are provided.
//    read_pass()  reads one data record
//    write_pass() writes one data record

#include "VarStrng.h"

class passenger
{
   public:
      // Member functions ...
      void read_pass ();
      void write_pass ();

      // Data members ...
      enum flight_class_type
         {first_class, business, economy, stand_by, undesignated};

   private:
      // Data members ...
      var_string name;
      flight_class_type flight_class;
      int num_seats;

      // Private member function ...
      flight_class_type class_convert (char c);
};
```

Figure 16.31   Implementation section for the passenger class

```cpp
// FILE: Passengr.cpp
// STUB DEFINITION OF PASSENGER

#include <iostream.h>

#include "Passengr.h"
#include "EnterInt.h"

// READS ONE PASSENGER RECORD
void passenger::read_pass ()
{
   char class_ch;
   cout << "Passenger name: ";
   cin >> ws >> name;              // skips whitespace characters
   cout << "Class (F, B, E, S): ";
   cin >> class_ch;
   flight_class = class_convert (class_ch);
   cout << "Number of Seats - ";
   num_seats = enter_int (1, 1, 30);
}


// DISPLAYS ONE PASSENGER RECORD
void passenger::write_pass ()
{
   // Local data ...
   static char *flight_class_names[]=
      {
         "First Class",
         "Business",
         "Economy",
         "Stand By",
         "Undesignated"
      };

   cout << "Name: " << name << endl;
   cout << flight_class_names[flight_class] << endl;
   cout << num_seats;
   if (num_seats ==1)
      cout << " Seat" << endl;
   else
      cout << " Seats" << endl;
}  // end write_pass stub


// CONVERTS A CHARACTER TO A CLASS_TYPE (stub)
passenger::flight_class_type passenger::class_convert (char c)
{
   cout << "Stub for class_convert entered; returns economy.";
   return economy;
}  // end class_convert
```

Commentary on Building an Executable File for Execution

Several program components must be combined in order to execute the Passenger Queue program. These include the following files:

UseQueue.cpp — the main program
ModQueue.cpp — the `modify_queue` function
VarString.cpp — the variable string class member function implementations
Passengr.cpp — the `passenger` class member function inplementations
EnterInt.cpp — enter an integer in a given range (Chapter 9)
PassConv.cpp — function `class_convert`

The C++ code we have provided does not combine these separate components; you must do this using whatever component linker or project management system is available in your programming environment.

EXERCISES FOR SECTION 16.8

Self-Check
1. Draw the queue after the completion of the sample run in Fig. 16.29.
2. Write out the data requirements table for function `modify_queue` (see Fig. 16.28). Also draw the structure chart for function `modify_queue`. Clearly indicate all steps in the chart that are performed by member functions in the queue or passenger classes.

Programming
1. Complete function `class_convert` (see Fig. 16.31).

16.9 —— IMPLEMENTING A QUEUE USING AN ARRAY

In this section we illustrate how to implement the template class `queue` in C++ using an array.

Data Members

The private part for the template class `queue` is shown in Fig. 16.32. There are four data members: the integers `front` (the index of the front of the queue), `rear` (the index of the back of the queue), and `num_items` (the count of the number of items in the queue); and an array (`items`) that holds the items.

Figure 16.32 Private part of class `queue`

```
template<class queue_element, int max_queue=100>
class queue
```

(Continued)

Figure 16.32   (Continued)

```
{

...

private:
    // Data members ...
        int front;      // the front of the queue
        int rear;       // the back of the queue
        int num_items;  // the number of items currently in the queue
        queue_element items[max_size];  // the data items
```

The array `items` is declared to be of size `max_size` (default value of 100). Storage is not allocated until a variable of type `queue` is declared. The declaration

```
queue<char> s;
```

declares `s` to be a variable of type `queue<char>` that can store up to 100 characters. If we include the definition of the class `passenger` (from `passengr.h`), the declaration

```
queue<passenger> pass_queue
```

defines a variable `pass_queue` of type `queue<passenger>` that can store up to 100 passengers.

It makes sense to store the first queue item in `items[0]`, the second queue item in `items[1]`, and so on. After a queue is filled with data, `front` has a value of 0 and `rear` points to the last record inserted in the queue (`rear < max_queue`). Figure 16.33 shows a queue, q, that is filled to its capacity (`num_items` is equal to `max_queue`). The queue contains the symbols &, *, +, /, and -, in that order.

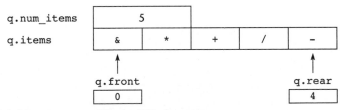

Figure 16.33   A queue filled with characters

Because q is filled to capacity, we cannot insert a new character. We can remove a queue element by decrementing `num_items` and incrementing `front` to 1, thereby removing `q.items[0]` (the symbol &). However, we still cannot insert a new character, because `rear` is at its maximum value. One way to solve this problem is to represent the member array `items` as a circular array. In a *circular array*, the elements *wrap around* so that the first element actually follows the last. If the last item to have been stored in the queue is in `q.items[max_size-1]` the next item would be stored in `q.items[0]`.

Example 16.5   Figure 16.34 shows the effect of inserting a new element in the queue just described. As shown at the top of the figure, three characters are currently in this queue (stored in `q.items[2]` through `q.items[4]`). The question marks in `q.items[0]` and `q.items[1]` indicate that the values that had been stored in these elements have been removed from the queue. The two elements that are currently unused are shown in gray.

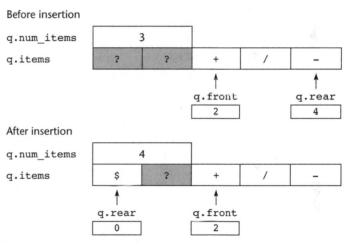

Figure 16.34   A queue as a circular array

The bottom of Fig. 16.34 shows the queue after insertion of a new character (\$). The value of `rear` is reset to 0, and the next element is inserted in `q.items[0]`. This queue element follows the character – in `q.items[4]`. The value of `q.front` is still 2 because the character + at `q.items[2]` has been in the queue the longest. `q.items[1]` is now the only queue element that is unused. The new queue contains the symbols +, /, –, and \$, in that order.

Figure 16.35 shows the include file ArrayQue. The constructor `queue()` is called when variables of type `queue` are declared. This function sets `num_items` and `front` to 0, because array element `items[0]` is considered the front of the empty queue. `rear` is initialized to `max_size-1` because the queue is circular.

Figure 16.35   Template class queue using an array

```
// FILE: ArrayQue.h
// QUEUE TEMPLATE CLASS USING AN ARRAY

#ifndef ARRAYQUE_H_
#define ARRAYQUE_H_

// Specification of the class queue<queue_element, max_size>
// Elements:   A queue consists of a collection of elements
//             that are all of the same type, queue_element.
// Structure:  The elements of a queue are ordered according
//             to time of arrival. The element that was first
//             inserted into the queue is the only one that
//             may be removed or examined. Elements are
//             removed from the front of the queue and
//             inserted at the rear of the queue.

template<class queue_element, int max_size = 100>
class queue
{
   public:
      // Member functions ...
      // CREATE AN EMPTY QUEUE
      queue ()
      {
         num_items = 0;
         front = 0;
         rear = max_size - 1;
      }

      // INSERT AN ELEMENT INTO THE QUEUE
      int insert
        (const queue_element& x)    // IN: Element to be inserted

      // Pre:  none
      // Post: If the queue is not full, the value x is inserted at
      //       the rear of the queue and 1 is returned. Otherwise,
      //       the queue is not changed and 0 is returned.
      {
         if (num_items < max_size)
         {
            num_items++;
            if (++rear >= max_size)
               rear = 0;
            items[rear] = x;
            return 1;
         }
         else
            return 0;
      }  // end insert
```

(Continued)

Figure 16.35   (Continued)

```
        // REMOVE AN ELEMENT FROM THE QUEUE
        int remove
          (queue_element& x)    // OUT: element removed
        // Pre : none
        // Post: If the queue is not empty, the value at the front of
        //       the queue is removed, its value is placed in x, and
        //       1 is returned. If the queue is empty, x is not
        //       defined and 0 is returned.

        ... [Member functions, retrieve, is_empty, is_full,
            size_of_queue and the rest of insert go here.]

    private:
        // Data members ...
        int front;              // the front of the queue
        int rear;               // the back of the queue
        int num_items;          // number of items currently in queue
        queue_element items[max_size];  // the data items
};

#endif // ARRAYQUE_H_
```

In function `insert`, the statement

```
if (++rear >= max_size)
  rear = 0;
```

is used to increment the value of `rear`. When `rear` is less than `max_size`, this statement simply increments its value by 1. But when `rear` is equal to `max_size-1`, this statement sets `rear` to 0, thereby wrapping the last element of the queue around to the first element. Because `queue()` initializes `rear` to `max_size-1`, the first element will be placed in `items[0]`, as desired. Functions `remove`, `retrieve`, `is_full`, `is_empty`, and `size_of_queue` are left as exercises (Programming Exercise 1 at the end of this section). In function `remove`, the element currently stored in `items[front]` must be copied into x before `front` is incremented. In function `retrieve`, the element at `items[front]` must be copied into x, but `front` is not changed.

The number of elements in the queue is changed by functions `insert` and `remove`; therefore, `num_items` must be incremented by 1 in `insert` and decremented by 1 in `remove`. The value of `num_items` is tested in both `is_full` and `is_empty` to determine the status of the queue. Function `size_of_queue` simply returns the value of `num_items`. ∎

EXERCISES FOR SECTION 16.9

Self-Check   1. What are the final values of the `front`, `rear`, and `name` data members of the passengers stored in `items[0]` through `items[3]` after the sample run of `use_queue` in Fig. 16.29?

Programming   1. Write the member functions listed below for class `queue`.

        a. `remove`   b. `retrieve`
        c. `is_full`   d. `is_empty`
        e. `size_of_queue`

16.10 — LINKED-LIST REPRESENTATION OF A QUEUE

We can also implement a queue as a linked list that grows and shrinks as elements are inserted and deleted. We declare class `queue` as follows:

```
template<class queue_element>
class queue
{

...

    private:
        // Data members ...
        struct queue_node
        {
            queue_element item;
            queue_node* next;
        };
        queue_node* front;     // the front of the queue
        queue_node* rear;      // the back of the queue
        int num_items;         // the number of items currently
                               // in the queue
```

The class has three data members: two pointer variables, `front` and `rear`; and an integer, `num_items`. As shown in Fig. 16.36, `front` references the beginning of the list that contains the queue and `rear` references the last element of this list. `num_items` is a count of elements, just as in the array representation.

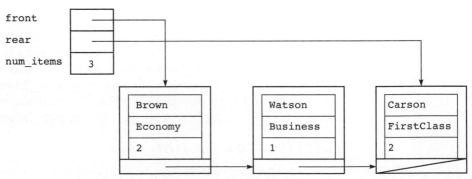

Figure 16.36   Representing a queue as a linked list

In a linked-list representation of a queue, the queue expands and contracts as the queue elements are inserted and removed during program execution. If we store the queue elements in an array, we must allocate storage for the entire queue when the queue is declared.

Queue Operators for Linked-List Representation

The listing for `ListQue.h` is shown in Fig. 16.37.

Figure 16.37   Template class `queue` using a linked list

```
// FILE: ListQue.h
// DEFINITION AND IMPLEMENTATION OF A TEMPLATE CLASS QUEUE
//    USING A LINKED LIST

#ifndef LISTQUE_H_
#define LISTQUE_H_

// Specification of the class queue<queue_element>
// Elements:      A queue consists of a collection of elements
//                that are all of the same type, queue_element.
// Structure:     The elements of a queue are ordered according
//                to time of arrival. The element that was first
//                inserted into the queue is the only one that
//                may be removed or examined. Elements are
//                removed from the front of the queue and
//                inserted at the rear of the queue.

template<class queue_element
class queue
{
    public:
        // Member functions ...
        // CREATE AN EMPTY QUEUE
        queue ()
        {
            num_items = 0;
            front = NULL;
            rear = NULL;
        }

        // INSERT AN ELEMENT INTO THE QUEUE
        int insert
          (const queue_element& x)    // IN: Element to be inserted

        // Pre : none
        // Post: If heap space is available, the value x is inserted
```

(Continued)

Figure 16.37 (Continued)

```
//          at the rear of the queue and 1 is returned.
//          Otherwise, the queue is not changed and 0 is
//          returned.
{
   if (num_items == 0)
   {
      rear = new queue_node;
      if (rear == NULL)        // Check to see that new was
                               //   successful
         return 0;
      else
         front = rear;
   }
   else
   {
      rear->next = new queue_node;
      if (rear->next == NULL)
         return 0;
      else
         rear = rear->next;
   }
   rear->item = x;
   num_items++;
   return 1;
}  // end insert
// REMOVE AN ELEMENT FROM THE QUEUE
int remove
   (queue_element& x)    // OUT: element removed

// Pre : none
// Post: If the queue is not empty, the value at the front of
//       the queue is removed, its value is placed in x, and
//       1 is returned. If the queue is empty, x is not
//       defined and 0 is returned.

... [Member functions retrieve, is_empty, is_full,
     size_of_queue, and the rest of remove go here.]

private:
   // Data members ...
   struct queue_node
   {
      queue_element item;
      queue_node* next;
   };
   queue_node* front;          // the front of the queue
```

(Continued)

Figure 16.37   (Continued)

```
        queue_node* rear;          // the back of the queue
        int num_items;             // number of items currently in the
                                   //   queue
};

#endif    // LISTQUE_H_
```

In operator `insert`, the statements

```
rear = new queue_node;
if (rear == NULL)        // Check to see that new was successful
    return 0;
else
    front = rear;
```

execute when the `queue` is empty. These statements create a new node and set both `rear` and `front` to reference it. If the queue is not empty, the statements

```
rear->next = new queue_node;
if (rear->next == NULL)
    return 0;
else
    rear = rear->next;
```

append a new list node at the end of the queue and then reference `rear` to this new node. By executing both `remove` and `insert`, we shift the element originally at the front of the queue to the rear of the queue. The results of first removing and then reinserting passenger Brown is shown in Fig. 16.38. (The original list is shown in Fig. 16.36.)

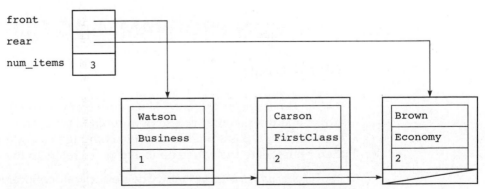

Figure 16.38   Reinserting passenger Brown in the queue

Commentary on Stack and Queue Implementations

Both the stack and the queue class templates (the array and the linked-list versions) were implemented to achieve a high degree of independence from the structure of the base elements of the stack (or queue) structures. The implementations allowed us to use any simple or structured data types, even structs or classes (such as the `passenger` class) as a base type element.

This separation of detail is extremely important in programming. It provides maximum flexibility of design and implementation of program components and improves maintainability, modifiability, and potential for reuse of all program components. We urge you to study the stack and queue implementations carefully to understand how this separation was achieved. Note, for example, how the structure of the data component of each node in a linked stack structure was completely separated from the link component, and how the processing of the data component, such as reading and writing passenger data, was completely separated from the processing of the linked structure itself (see the Passenger Queue Problem implementation, for example).

EXERCISES FOR SECTION 16.10

Self-Check
1. Insert passenger Johnson, Economy class, five seats, in the queue shown in Fig 16.38.

Programming
1. Write the member function `size_of_queue` for the linked-list representation of a queue.
2. Write the member functions `retrieve` and `remove` for the linked-list representation of a queue.
3. Write the member functions `is_empty` and `is_full` for the linked-list representation of a queue.

16.11 —— COMMON PROGRAMMING ERRORS

Syntax Errors

▪ *The Dereferencing Operator:* Make sure that you use the dereferencing operator * and the member access (with pointer) operator –> whenever needed. For example, if **p** is a pointer variable pointing to a node defined as a **struct**, then *p refers to the whole node and p->x refers to the member **x**.

▪ *The new and delete Operators:* The **new** operator allocates storage and returns a pointer. The results should be assigned to a pointer variable having the same type as specified in using the new operator. The delete operator deal-locates storage. It takes a pointer variable as its argument. For example, p = new node is correct, but *p = new node is not; delete p is correct, but delete *p is not.

Run-Time Errors

• There are some typical run-time errors that can occur in writing list traversal code. For example, the while loop

```
while (next != NULL)
   cout << next->word;
   next = next->link;
```

will repeatedly display the word member of the same node because the pointer assignment statement is not included in the loop body, so next is not advanced down the list.

• The while loop

```
while (next->id != 9999)
   next = next->link;
```

may execute "beyond the last list node" if a node with id == 9999 is not found. The statement should be coded as

```
while ((next != NULL) && (next->id != 9999)
   next = next->link;
```

• If a pointer next is a function argument that corresponds to a list head pointer, make sure it is a value argument. Otherwise, the last value assigned to next will be returned as a function result. This may cause you to lose some of the elements originally in the linked list.

• Problems with heap management can also cause run-time errors. If your program gets stuck in an infinite loop while you are creating a dynamic data structure, it is possible for your program to consume all memory cells on the heap. It is important to check the results of new to make sure it is not the NULL pointer. If new returns a NULL pointer, all of the cells on the heap have been allocated.

• Make sure that your program does not attempt to reference a list node after the node is returned to the heap. Such an error is difficult to debug because the program may appear to function correctly under some circumstances. Also, returning a node to the heap twice can cause "strange" results on some systems.

CHAPTER REVIEW

This chapter introduced several dynamic data structures. We discussed the use of pointers to reference and connect elements of a dynamic data structure. The new operator allocates additional elements, or nodes, of a dynamic data structure; the `delete` operator returns memory cells to the storage heap.

We also covered many different aspects of manipulating linked lists. We showed how to build or create a linked list, how to traverse a linked list, and how to insert and delete elements of a linked list.

We introduced stacks and queues and showed how to implement them both as arrays and as linked lists.

New C++ Constructs   The C++ constructs that were introduced in this chapter are described in Table 16.3.

Table 16.3   New C++ Constructs

CONSTRUCT	EFFECT
Pointer Variable Declaration	
```struct node { int info; node *link; }; node *head;```	head is a pointer variable of type pointer to node. node is a struct that contains a member link, which is also of type pointer to node.
new Operator	
`head = new node;`	A new struct of type node is allocated. This struct is pointed to by head and is referenced as *head.
delete Operator	
`delete head;`	The memory space occupied by the struct *head is returned to the storage pool.
Pointer Assignment	
`head = head->link;`	The pointer head is advanced to the next node in the dynamic data structure pointed to by head.

✔ QUICK-CHECK EXERCISES

1. Operator _____ allocates storage space for a data object that is referenced through a _____; operator _____ returns the storage space to the _____.

2. When an element is deleted from a linked list represented using pointers, it is automatically returned to the heap. True or false?

3. All pointers to a node that is returned to the heap are automatically reset to NULL so that they cannot reference the node returned to the heap. True or false?

4. Why do you need to be wary of passing a list as a reference argument to a function?

5. If a linked list contains three elements with values "Him", "Her", and "Its", and h is a pointer to the list head, what is the effect of the following statements? Assume that each node in the list is a struct with data member pronoun, and that link members next. p and q are pointer variables.

```
p = h->next;
strcpy(p->pronoun, "She");
```

6. Answer Quick-Check Exercise 5 for the following segment:

```
p = h->next;
q = p->next;
p->next = q->next;
delete q;
```

7. Answer Quick-Check Exercise 5 for the following segment:

```
q = h;
h = new node;
strcpy(h->pronoun, "His");
h->next = q;
```

8. Write a single statement that will place the value NULL in the last node of the three-element list in Quick-Check Exercise 5.

9. A stack is a _____ data structure; a queue is a _____ data structure.

10. Draw the array representation of the following stack. What is s.items[0]? What is the value of s.top? What is the value of s.items[s.top-1]?

11. Why should the statement s.top = s.top - 1 not appear in a client program that uses the stack class?

12. Write a program segment that removes from the stack the element just below the top of the stack. Use the stack member functions.

13. Write a member function pop_next_top that performs the operation in Quick-Check Exercise 15 (use the array implementation of the stack class).

14. Assume that a circular queue q of capacity 6 contains the five characters +, *, −, &, and #, where + is stored in the front of the queue. In the array representation, what is the value of q.front? What is the value of q.rear? What is the value of q.items[q.rear-1]?

15. Delete the character at the front of the queue in Quick-Check Exercise 17 and insert the characters \ and %. Draw the new queue. What is the value of q.front? What is the value of q.rear? What is the value of q.items[q.rear-1]?

16. Can you have two stacks of float numbers in the same client program? Can you have a stack of integers and a stack of characters in the same client program?

Answers to Quick-Check Exercises

1. new; pointer; delete; heap
2. false; delete must be invoked
3. false
4. The value of the actual argument could be advanced down the list as the function executes, changing the value of the pointer that was originally passed to the function, and part of the list will be lost.
5. "Her", the pronoun member of the second node, is replaced by "She".
6. detaches and then deletes the third list element
7. inserts a new list value "His" at the front of the list
8. h->next->next->next = NULL;
9. last-in, first-out; first-in, first-out

10.

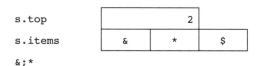

&;*

11. Because the member top is not visible to the client program, this statement will result in an error message. The member top should be part of the private part of the class because the client programs should not be aware of and should not manipulate the internal representation of the data type defined by the class.

12. success = s.pop (x);
    success = s.pop (y);
    success = s.push (x);

13. int pop_next_top
       (stack_element &x)
    {
        if (top > 1)
        {
            x = items[top-1];
            items[top-1] = items[top];
            top--;
            return 1;
        }

```
        else
            return 0;
    }
```

14. q.front is 0; q.rear is 4; &

15. q.front is 1; q.rear is 0; \

16. yes; yes

REVIEW QUESTIONS

1. Differentiate between dynamic and nondynamic data structures.
2. Describe a simple linked list. Indicate how the pointers are used to establish a link between nodes. Also indicate any other variables that would be needed to reference the linked list.
3. Give the missing type declarations and show the effect of each of the following statements. What does each do?

```
p = new node;
strcpy (p->word,"ABC");
p->next = new node;
q = p->next;
strcpy (q->word,"abc");
q.next = NULL;
```

For Questions 4 through 8, you may use the member functions and operations defined for var_string (see Section 13.3). Also, assume the following type declarations:

```
#include "VarStrng.h"      // see Chapter 13
struct list_node
{
    var_string name;
    list_node *next;
};
list_node *the_list;
```

4. Write a program segment that places the names Washington, Roosevelt, and Kennedy in successive elements of the list the_list.
5. Write a program segment to insert the name Eisenhower between Roosevelt and Kennedy.
6. Write a function to delete all nodes with the data value "Smith" from an argument of type list_node* as defined in Review Question 4.

7. Write a function `delete_last` that deletes the last node of `the_list` (defined following Review Question 3).
8. Write a function `copy_list` that creates a new list that is a copy of another list.
9. Show the effect of each of the operations below on `stack<char>` s. Assume that y (type char) contains the character ' & '. What are the final values of x and `success` and the contents of stack s? Assume that s is initially empty.

```
success = s.push ('+');
success = s.pop (x);
success = s.pop (x);
success = s.push ('(');
success = s.push (y);
success = s.pop ('&');
```

10. Assume that stack s is implemented in an array. Answer Review Question 9 by showing the values of the data members `top` and `items` after each operation.
11. Assume that stack s is implemented as a list. Answer Review Question 9 by showing the class members for each step of Question 9.
12. Answer Review Question 9 for a `queue<char>` q. Replace `push` with `insert` and `pop` with `remove`.
13. Assume that queue q is implemented in an array. Show the class members for each step of Review Question 12.
14. Assume that queue q is implemented as a list. Show the class members for each step of Review Question 12.

Review Questions 15 through 18 all relate to the linked-list queue class template (Fig. 16.37). For Questions 15 and 17, you may assume access to this template and its member functions; for Questions 16 and 18, you will be adding a new member function to this template class. For Questions 15 and 17, you may assume that the data components of the nodes being manipulated are all of type `person_data`, where the internal description of this type is not important. Thus, in Questions 15 and 17, the queue being manipulated by your function should be of type `queue<person_data>`.

15. Write a function `move_to_rear` that moves the element currently at the front of a queue to the rear of the queue. The element that was second in line in the queue then will be at the front of the queue. Use the member functions `insert` and `remove` from the queue template shown in Fig. 16.37.
16. Write a new member function `move_to_rear` for the `queue` template (Fig. 16.37). See Review Question 15 for a description of the behavior of this function. (This function will manipulate the private data members of `queue` directly.)
17. Write a function `move_to_front` that moves the element currently at the rear of a queue to the front of the queue. Use member functions `insert` and `remove` from the queue template (Fig. 16.37).
18. Write a new member function `move_to_front` for the queue template (Fig 16.37). See Review Question 17 for a description of the behavior of this function. (This function will manipulate the private data members directly.)

PROGRAMMING PROJECTS

1. Write a client program that uses the queue class to simulate a typical session for a bank teller. queue_element should represent a customer at a bank. Define a class bank_customer that contains the customer's name, transaction type, and amount. Include operators to read and write customers in the class. After every five customers are processed, display the size of the queue and the names of the customers who are waiting.

   As part of your solution, your program should include functions that correspond to the following function prototypes:

```
// SIMULATE ARRIVAL OF A SINGLE CUSTOMER
void arrive
    (queue& waiting_line,       // INOUT
     int& success);            // OUT


// SIMULATE DEPARTURE OF A SINGLE CUSTOMER
void depart
    (queue& waiting_line,       // INOUT
     int& success);            // OUT


// DISPLAY THE SIZE AND CONTENTS OF THE CUSTOMER QUEUE
void show
    (queue& waiting_line);      // IN
```

2. Write a program to monitor the flow of an item into and out of a warehouse. The warehouse will have numerous deliveries and shipments for this item (a widget) during the time covered. A shipment out is billed at a profit of 50 percent over the cost of a widget. Unfortunately, each shipment received may have a different cost associated with it. The accountants for the firm have instituted a last-in, first-out system for filling orders. This means that the newest widgets are the first ones sent out to fill an order. This method of inventory can be represented using a stack. The push operator will insert a shipment received. The pop operator will delete a shipment out.

   Input data should consist of the following:

   - S or O: shipment received or an order to be sent;
   - the quantity received or shipped out;
   - cost: cost per widget (for received shipments only);
   - vendor: a character string that names the company sent to or received from.

   For example, the data fragment below indicates that 100 widgets were received from RCA at $10.50 per widget and 50 were shipped to Boeing:

```
S 100 10.50 RCA
O 50 Boeing
```

   Output for an order will consist of the quantity and the total price for all the widgets in the order. *Hint:* Each widget price is 50 percent higher than its cost. The widgets to fill an order may come from multiple shipments with different costs.

3. Write a program that can be used to compile a simple arithmetic expression without parentheses. For example, the expression

```
A + B * C - D
```

should be compiled as shown below:

OPERATION	OPERAND 1	OPERAND 2	RESULT
*	B	C	Z
+	A	Z	Y
−	Y	D	X

The table shows the order in which the operations are performed (*, +, −) and the operands for each operator. The result column gives the name of an identifier (working backward from Z) chosen to hold each result. Assume the operands are the letters A through F and the operators are +, −, *, and /.

Your program should read each character and process it as follows. If the character is a blank, ignore it. If it is an operand, push it onto the operand stack. If the character is not an operator, display an error message and terminate the program. If it is an operator, compare its precedence with that of the operator on top of the operator stack (* and / have higher precedence than + and −). If the new operator has higher precedence than the one currently on top (or if the operator stack is empty), it should be pushed onto the operator stack.

If the new operator has the same or lower precedence, the operator on the top of the operator stack must be evaluated next. This is done by popping it off the operator stack along with a pair of operands from the operand stack and writing a new line of the output table. The character selected to hold the result should then be pushed onto the operand stack. Next, the new operator should be compared to the new top of the operator stack. Continue to generate output table lines until the top of the operator stack has lower precedence than the new operator or until the stack is empty. At this point, push the new operator onto the top of the operator stack and examine the next character in the data string. When the end of the string is reached, pop any remaining operator along with its operand pair as just described. Remember to push the result character onto the operand stack after each table line is generated.

4. A polynomial can be represented as a linked list, where each node contains the coefficient and the exponent of a term of the polynomial. The polynomial

$$4x^3 + 3x^2 - 5$$

would be represented as the linked list shown in Fig. 16.39.

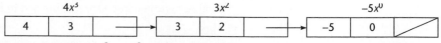

Figure 16.39 $4x^3 + 3x^2 - 5$ as a linked list

Write a class polynomial that has operators for creating a polynomial, reading a polynomial, and adding and subtracting a pair of polynomials. *Hint:* To add or subtract two polynomials, traverse both lists. If a particular exponent value is present in either one, it should also be present in the result polynomial unless its coefficient is zero.

5. Each student in the university takes a different number of courses, so the registrar has decided to use a linked list to store each student's class schedule and an array of structs to represent the whole student body. A portion of this data structure is shown in Fig. 16.40.

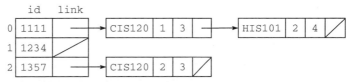

Figure 16.40   Class schedule as an array of structs

These data show that the first student (ID 1111) is taking section 1 of CIS120 for three credits and section 2 of HIS001 for four credits; the second student is not enrolled; and so on. Write a class for this data structure. Provide operators for creating the original array, inserting a student's initial class schedule, adding a course, and dropping a course. Write a menu-driven program that uses the class.

6. The radix sorting algorithm uses an array of queues (numbered 0 through 9) to simulate the operation of a card sorting machine. The algorithm requires that one pass be made for every digit of the numbers being sorted. For example, a list of three-digit numbers would require three passes through the list. During the first pass, the least significant digit (the ones digit) of each number is examined and the number is added to the rear of the queue whose subscript matches the digit. After the numbers have been processed, the elements of each queue, beginning with q[0], are copied one at a time to the end of an eleventh queue prior to beginning the next pass. Then the process is repeated for the next most significant digit (the tens digit) using the order of the numbers in the eleventh queue. The process is repeated again, using the third most significant digit (the hundreds digit). After the final pass, the eleventh queue will contain the numbers in sorted order. Write a program that implements the radix sort using the queue class.

7. A deque might be described as a double-ended queue, that is, a structure in which elements can be inserted or removed from either end. Write a deque class that is similar to the stack and queue classes.

Appendix A Character Sets

The following charts show the character sets: ASCII (American Standard Code for Information Interchange), EBCDIC (Extended Binary-Coded Decimal Interchange Code), and CDC[1] Scientific. Only the printable characters are shown. The ordinal value for each character is shown in decimal. For example, in ASCII, the ordinal value for 'A' is 65 and the ordinal value for 'z' is 122. The blank character is represented using a □.

Left Digit(s) \ Right Digit	ASCII									
	0	1	2	3	4	5	6	7	8	9
3			□	!	"	#	$	%	&	'
4	(	)	*	+	,	−	.	/	0	1
5	2	3	4	5	6	7	8	9	:	;
6	<	=	>	?	@	A	B	C	D	E
7	F	G	H	I	J	K	L	M	N	O
8	P	Q	R	S	T	U	V	W	X	Y
9	Z	[	/	]	^	−	'	a	b	c
10	d	e	f	g	h	i	j	k	l	m
11	n	o	p	q	r	s	t	u	v	w
12	x	y	z	{	|	}	~			

Codes 00–31 and 127 are nonprintable control characters.

[1] CDC is a trademark of Control Data Corporation.

Left Digit(s) \ Right Digit	**EBCDIC**									
	0	1	2	3	4	5	6	7	8	9
6					□					
7					¢	.	<	(	+	|
8	&									
9	!	$	*	)	;	¬	–	/		
10							^	,	%	—
11	>	?								
12			:	#	@	'	=	"		a
13	b	c	d	e	f	g	h	i		
14						j	k	l	m	n
15	o	p	q	r						
16			s	t	u	v	w	x	y	z
17								\	{	}
18	[	]								
19				A	B	C	D	E	F	G
20	H	I								J
21	K	L	M	N	O	P	Q	R		
22							S	T	U	V
23	W	X	Y	Z						
24	0	1	2	3	4	5	6	7	8	9

Codes 00–63 and 250–255 are nonprintable control characters.

Left Digit \ Right Digit	**CDC**									
	0	1	2	3	4	5	6	7	8	9
0	:	A	B	C	D	E	F	G	H	I
1	J	K	L	M	N	O	P	Q	R	S
2	T	U	V	W	X	Y	Z	0	1	2
3	3	4	5	6	7	8	9	+	–	*
4	/	(	)	$	=	□	,	.	≡	[
5	]	%	≠	↱	∨	∧	↑	↓	<	>
6	≤	≥	¬	;						

Appendix B   Reserved Words and Special Characters

The following identifiers are reserved for use as C++ language keywords and may not be used except as intended.

asm	continue	float	new	signed	try
auto	default	for	operator	sizeof	typedef
break	delete	friend	private	static	union
case	do	goto	protected	struct	unsigned
catch	double	if	public	switch	virtual
char	else	inline	register	template	void
class	enum	int	return	this	volatile
const	extern	long	short	throw	while

NOTES

1. Identifiers containing a double underscore (_ _) are reserved for use by C++ implementations and standard libraries and should be avoided by users.
2. The following characters are used for operators or for punctuation in ASCII representations of C++ programs:

```
!    %    ^    &    *    (    )    -    +    =    {    }    |    ~
[    ]    \    :    "    ;    '    <    >    ?    ,    .    /
```

3. The following character combinations are used as operators in C++ :

```
->    ++    --    .*    ->*    <<    >>    <=    >=    ==    !=    &&
||    *=    /=    %=    +=     -=    <<=   >>=   &=    ^=    |=    ::
```

4. The tokens # and ## are used by the C++ preprocessor.

Appendix C Selected C++ Library Facilities

FUNCTION NAME	DESCRIPTION	NUMBER OF ARGUMENTS	TYPE(S) OF ARGUMENTS	RETURN TYPE	HEADER FILE	SECTION NUMBER
abs	integer absolute value	1	int	int	math.h stdlib.h	—
acos	arc cosine	1	double	double	math.h	3.6
asin	arc sine	1	double	double	math.h	3.6
atan	arc tangent	1	double	double	math.h	3.6
atan2	arc tangent	2	double	double	math.h	3.6
atoi	converts character string to an integer	1	char*	int	stdlib.h	13.1
atol	converts character string to a long integer	1	char*	long int	stdlib.h	—
atof	converts character string to a double	1	char*	double	stdlib.h math.h	—
bad	returns nonzero (true) if designated stream is corrupted and recovery is not likely	0	(none)	int	iostream.h	8.5
ceil	smallest integer not less than the argument	1	double or long double	double or long double	math.h	3.6
clear	sets error state of designated stream; argument represents the state to be set	1	int	void	iostream.h	13.2
close	closes file and disassociates it from stream; flushes buffer	0	(none)	returns 0 on error	iostream.h	8.3
cos	cosine	1	double	double	math.h	3.6
cosh	hyperbolic cosine	1	double	double	math.h	—
eof	returns non-zero (true) if end-of-file has been encountered in designated stream	0	(none)	int	iostream.h	8.3
exit	program termination; same as a return statement in function main (closes files, flushes buffers, etc.); 0 argument usually means successful termination; nonzero indicates an error	1	int	void	stdlib.h	12.1

(Continued)

Appendix C   (Continued)

FUNCTION NAME	DESCRIPTION	NUMBER OF ARGUMENTS	TYPE(S) OF ARGUMENTS	RETURN TYPE	HEADER FILE	SECTION NUMBER
exp	exponential function (calculates *e* to the x power, where x is the argument)	1	double	double	math.h	3.6
fabs	double absolute value	1	double	double	math.h	3.6
fail	returns nonzero (true) if an operation on a stream has failed; recovery still possible and stream still usable once fail condition cleared; also true if bad is true	0	(none)	int	iostream.h	8.3
floor	largest integer not greater than the argument	1	double or long double	double or long double	math.h	3.6
get	single character input (extracts single character from stream and stores it in its argument)	1	char	int (zero at eof; else nonzero)	iostream.h	8.3
get	string input (reads from designated stream until n−1 characters are extracted or until delimiter is read or eof encountered; null character is placed at end of string; delimiter not extracted but is left in stream); fails only if no characters extracted	3	char* int n char delim = '\n'	int (zero at eof; else nonzero)	iostream.h	8.3
getline	string input (reads from designated stream until n characters extracted or until delimiter is read or end of file encountered; null character is placed at end of string; delimiter removed from stream but is not stored in string)	3	char* int n char delim = '\n'	int	iostream.h	13.1
isalnum	checks for alphabetic or base-10 digit character	1	char	int	ctype.h	7.4
isalpha	checks for alphabetic character	1	char	int	ctype.h	7.4
iscntrl	checks for control character (ASCII 0–31 and 127)	1	char	int	ctype.h	7.4
isdigit	checks for base-10 digit character ('0', '1', '2', ..., '9')	1	char	int	ctype.h	7.4
islower	checks for lowercase letter ('a', ..., 'z')	1	char	int	ctype.h	7.4

(Continued)

Appendix C   (Continued)

FUNCTION NAME	DESCRIPTION	NUMBER OF ARGUMENTS	TYPE(S) OF ARGUMENTS	RETURN TYPE	HEADER FILE	SECTION NUMBER
`ispunct`	checks for punctuation character (`ispunct` is true if `iscntrl` or `isspace` are true)	1	`char`	`int`	`ctype.h`	7.4
`isspace`	checks for whitespace character (space, tab, carriage return, newline, formfeed, or vertical tab)	1	`char`	`int`	`ctype.h`	7.4
`isupper`	checks for uppercase letter (`'A'`, ..., `'Z'`)	1	`char`	`int`	`ctype.h`	7.4
`log`	natural logarithm (ln)	1	`double`	`double`	`math.h`	3.6
`log10`	base-10 logarithm	1	`double`	`double`	`math.h`	3.6
`open`	opens a file given as first argument and associates it with designated stream	varies	`char*` ...	`void`	`fstream.h`	8.3
`peek`	returns next character in designated stream without extracting it; returns `EOF` if no character present in stream	0	(none)	`int`	`iostream.h`	8.5
`pow`	exponentiation; first argument raised to the power of the second	2	`double`	`double`	`math.h`	3.6
`precision`	sets the number of significant digits to be used when printing floating-point numbers and returns the previous value	1	`int n = 6`	`int`	`iomanip.h`	8.6
`put`	inserts a single character to the designated stream	varies	`char`	`int`	`iostream.h`	8.3
`random`	pseudo-random number generator; returns an integer between 0 and n–1	1	`int n`	`int`	`stdlib.h`	—
`seekg`	moves position of "get" pointer to a file; move is relative either to the beginning, current position, or end of the file	1 or 2	`long` `int`	`int`	`iostream.h`	13.2
`setf`	turns on the format flags and returns the previous flags	1	`long` (bitflags)	`long` (bitflags)	`iomanip.h`	8.6
`setf`	clears the specified bit field and then turns on the format flags; returns previous flags	2	`long` (bitflags) `long` (bitfield)	`long` (bitflags)	`iomanip.h`	8.6
`sin`	sine	1	`double`	`double`	`math.h`	3.6
`sinh`	hyperbolic sine	1	`double`	`double`	`math.h`	—

(Continued)

Appendix C   (Continued)

FUNCTION NAME	DESCRIPTION	NUMBER OF ARGUMENTS	TYPE(S) OF ARGUMENTS	RETURN TYPE	HEADER FILE	SECTION NUMBER
sqrt	square root	1	`double` or `long double`	`double` `long` `double`	`math.h`	3.6
srand	random number generator (RNG) seed function; the RNG is reinitialized (to same start point) if the seed is 1; the RNG can be set to a new starting point if any other seed is used	1	`unsigned int` (the seed)	`void`	`stdlib.h`	—
strcat	string concatenation (appends a copy of the string pointed to by `from` to the end of the string pointed to by `to`	2	`char* to` `const` `char *from`	`char*`	`string.h`	13.1
strcmp	lexical string comparison (returns <0, 0, >0 if `s1` is less than, equal to, or greater than `s2`, respectively)	2	`const` `char* s1` `const` `char* s2`	`int`	`string.h`	9.6
strcpy	string copy (copies the string pointed to by `from` to the string pointed to by `to` up to and including the null character)	2	`char* to` `const` `char* from`	`char*`	`string.h`	9.6
strlen	string length (not counting null character, `'\0'`)	1	`const char*`	`size_t`[a]	`string.h`	9.6
strncat	string concatenation of up to `lim` characters (same as `strcat` except that a maximum of `lim` characters are concatenated; the `to` string is always terminated by `'\0'`)	3	`char* to` `const` `char* from` `size_t`[b] `lim`	`char*`	`string.h`	13.1
strncmp	lexical string comparison of at most `lim` characters (same as `strcmp` except at most `lim` characters are compared)	3	`const` `char* s1` `const char* s2` `size_t`[a] `lim`	`int`	`string.h`	9.6
strncpy	string copy of up to `lim` characters (see `strcpy`) padded by `'\0'` if `'\0'` is found in `from` string before `lim` characters copied	3	`char* to` `const` `char* from` `size_t`[a] `lim`	`char*`	`string.h`	9.6
strchr	search for first occurrence of character in string (returns pointer to first occurrence if found or null pointer otherwise); any character may be used as the source character (to be found)	2	`const char*` `char`	`char*`	`string.h`	13.1

(Continued)

[a]`size_t` is an unsigned integer type.

Appendix C   (Continued)

FUNCTION NAME	DESCRIPTION	NUMBER OF ARGUMENTS	TYPE(S) OF ARGUMENTS	RETURN TYPE	HEADER FILE	SECTION NUMBER
`strrchr`	reverse search for first occurrence of character in string (otherwise, same as `strchr`)	2	`const char*` `char`	`char*`	`string.h`	13.1
`strpbrk`	searches for first occurrence in s of any character in `set`; returns pointer to first character in s matched by a character in `set`	2	`const char* s` `const char* set`	`char*`	`string.h`	13.1
`strstr`	searches for first occurrence in s1 of the substring s2; returns pointer to start of s2 in s1 or null pointer if s2 not found in s1	2	`const char* s1` `const char* s2`	`char*`	`string.h`	—
`system`	calls operating system	1	`const char*`	`int`	`stdlib.h`	—
`tan`	tangent	1	`double` or `long double`	`double` `long double`	`math.h`	3.6
`tanh`	hyperbolic tangent	1	`double` or `long double`	`double` `long double`	`math.h`	—
`time`	returns time measured in seconds since 00:00:00 Greenwich Mean Time, January 1, 1970	1	`long int` (`time_t`)[b]	`long int*` (`time_t*`)	`time.h`	—
`tolower`	converts uppercase letter to lowercase	1	`int`	`int`	`ctype.h`	7.4
`toupper`	converts lowercase letter to uppercase	1	`int`	`int`	`ctype.h`	7.4
`width`	sets the minimum field width to the given size and returns the previous field width (zero means no minimum); the minimum field width is reset to zero after each insertion or extraction	1	`int`	`int`	`iomanip.h`	8.6

[b] `time_t` is a long int type.

Appendix D   Operators

Table D.1 shows the precedence and associativity of those C++ operators discussed in this text. In this table, the horizontal lines partition the list of operators into groups. All operators in one group have equal precedence. Those in the next group down have a lower precedence. The precedence table is followed by Table D.2, which contains a listing of each operator along with its name, the number of operands required, and the first section of the text that explains the operator.

Table D.1   Precedence and Associativity of Operations

PRECEDENCE	OPERATION	ASSOCIATIVITY
highest (evaluated first)	*scope resolution operator:* `::`	left
	member selection operators: `.` `->`	right
	subscripting: `a[..]`	right
	function call: `f(..)`	right
	post increment and decrement: `++` `--`	right
	`sizeof`	right
	logical not: `!`	right
	pre increment and decrement: `++` `--`	right
	unary `+`; unary `-`	right
	address of: `&`	right
	dereference: `*`	right
	`new` `delete` `delete [ ]`	right
	casts (type conversion)	right
	multiplicative binary operators: `*` `/` `%`	left
	additive binary operators: `+` `-`	left
	relational operators: `<` `>` `<=` `>=`	left
	equality operators: `==` `!=`	left
	logical and: `&&`	left
	logical inclusive or: `||`	left
	assignment operators: `=` `+=` `-=` `*=` `/=` `%=`	right
lowest (evaluated last)	*comma:* `,`	left

Table D.2   Where to Find Operators in Text

OPERATOR	NAME	NUMBER OF OPERANDS	WHERE FOUND	
a[..]	subscript	1	9.1	
f(..)	function call	varies	3.3	(also 3.4; 6.3)
.	direct member selection	2	9.7	(also 12.2)
->	indirect member selection	2	16.1	
++	increment	1	5.1	
--	decrement	1	5.1	
!	logical negation	1	2.4	
&	address of	1	6.3	
*	indirection	1	16.1	
	or multiplication	2	2.4	
type name	cast	1	3.5	(also 7.2)
/	division	2	2.4	
%	remainder	2	2.4	
+	unary plus	1	2.4	
	or addition	2	2.4	
–	unary minus	1	2.6	
	or subtraction	2	2.4	
<	less than	2	4.2	(also 7.3)
<=	less than or equal	2	4.2	
>	greater than	2	4.2	
>=	greater than or equal	2	4.2	
==	equality	2	4.2	
!=	inequality	2	4.2	
&&	logical and	2	4.2	
||	logical or	2	4.2	
=	assignment	2	2.4	
+= -= *= /= %=	compound arithmetic assignment	2	5.2	
, (comma)	sequential evaluation	—	13.1	
|	bitwise or operator (I/O flags)	2	4.6	(also 8.6)
::	scope resolution operator	1	11.1	(also 4. 6)
new	dynamically allocates space in free store	varies	12.1	
delete	deallocates dynamically allocated space in free store		12.1	
sizeof	returns size, in bytes, of its operand	1	—	

Appendix E   A Brief Introduction to Inheritance and Polymorphism

In this appendix we introduce *inheritance* and *polymorphism,* which are very powerful features of object oriented languages such as C++. Inheritance allows us to define new classes by extending and adapting existing classes. The new class *inherits* the characteristics of the *parent class,* and may extend or adapt these features to meet the specific needs of an application. Several classes may be *derived* in this way from a common parent. Each such class represents a different *specialized adaptation* of the parent class. Whenever an object of a derived class is declared, the data members associated with the parent class can be used in the derived class and member functions of the parent are applicable in the derived class. This is often described by saying that the derived class and the parent are bound by the *is-a* relationship, as in "A circle is a specialization of a shape."

There are at least a half-dozen forms of inheritance that have been identified by various authors. The first form is one we have informally discussed in this text. It is called *subclassing for specialization.* In this form, we begin with a complete parent class (a working software subcomponent), such as the indexed collection class (`float_index_coll_v1`) introduced in Chapter 12, and develop modified or extended *child classes* (*subclasses*).

For example, the classes `float_index_coll_v2` and `float_index_coll_v3` could have been developed in this fashion using inheritance. In Chapter 12, we developed these two classes by manually (via an editor) copying the attributes and member functions common to all three classes (`float_index_coll_v1`, `float_index_coll_v2`, and `float_index_coll_v3`) and then adding additional attributes (such as the sum of the values of the elements of the collection) and additional functions (such as a function to compute the sum of the elements). It would have been much easier to have derived versions 2 and 3 from version 1 as shown in Fig. E.1 for `float_index_coll_v2`.

Figure E.1   Class `float_index_coll_v2` **derived from** `float_index_coll_v1`

```
// FILE: FloatXC1.h
// FLOATING-POINT INDEXED COLLECTION CLASS (VERSION 1)
```

(Continued)

Figure E.1   (Continued)

```
//    DEFINITION AND IMPLEMENTATION

#ifndef FLOATXC1_H_
#define FLOATXC1_H_

#include <stdlib.h>
#include <iostream.h>

class float_index_coll_v1
{
   public:
      // Member functions...
      // CONSTRUCTOR FOR COLLECTION
      float_index_coll_v1
        (int sz = max_size);// IN: number of elements in array

      // DESTRUCTOR FOR COLLECTION
      ~float_index_coll_v1();

      // STORE AN ITEM IN DESIGNATED COLLECTION ELEMENT
      void store
        (int,               // IN: index of store
         float);            // IN: value to be stored

      // RETRIEVE AN ITEM FROM DESIGNATED COLLECTION ELEMENT
      float retrieve
        (int);              // IN: index of retrieval

      // RETURN NUMBER OF ELEMENTS STORED IN COLLECTION
      int get_count ();

   protected:
      // Data members ...
      float *collection;    // pointer to collection of floating
                            //    point objects
      int size;             // size of the array
      int count;            // number of elements stored in
                            //    collection
      enum {max_size = 25};
};


// CONSTRUCTOR FOR COLLECTION
float_index_coll_v1::float_index_coll_v1
   (int sz)      // IN: number of elements in collection
{
   size = sz;               // save the size of array
   count = 0;               // collection empty at start
```

(Continued)

Figure E.1   (Continued)

```
    collection = new float [size];
    // Construct array of size specified by user (or by default).
    if (collection == 0)
    {
        cerr << endl;
        cerr << "*** ERROR: In float_index_coll_v1: allocator
            << failed" << endl;
        cerr << "    to execute correctly.  Execution terminated."
            << endl;
        exit (EXIT_FAILURE);
    }
}  // end constructor


// DESTRUCTOR FOR COLLECTION
float_index_coll_v1::~float_index_coll_v1 ()
{
    delete [] collection;
}  // end destructor


// STORE AN ITEM IN DESIGNATED COLLECTION ELEMENT
void float_index_coll_v1::store
    (int index,                 // IN: index of store in collection
    float value)               // IN: value to be stored

// Pre:  Index must be greater than or equal to zero
//       and less than size;
// Post: Legal floating-point value is stored at
//       collection[index].
{
    if ((index < 0) || (index > size-1))
    {
        cerr << endl;
        cerr << "*** ERROR: In float_index_coll_v1::store: index"
            << endl;
        cerr << "    is out of range.  Execution terminated."
            << endl;
        exit (EXIT_FAILURE);
    }
    else
        count++;
    collection[index] = value;
    return;
}  // end store


// RETRIEVE AN ITEM FROM DESIGNATED COLLECTION ELEMENT
float float_index_coll_v1::retrieve
    (int index)                 // IN: index of retrieval
```

(Continued)

Figure E.1   (Continued)

```
// Pre:   Index must be greater than or equal to zero
//        and less than size.
// Post: Returns contents of cell indicated by index.
{
   if ((index < 0) || (index > size - 1))
   {
      cerr << endl;
      cerr << "*** ERROR: In float_index_coll_v1::retrieve: index"
           << endl;
      cerr << "    is out of range.  Execution terminated."
           << endl;
      exit (EXIT_FAILURE);
   }
   return collection[index];
}  // end retrieve


// RETURN THE NUMBER OF ELEMENTS STORED IN COLLECTION
int float_index_coll_v1::get_count ()
{
   return count;
}  // end get_count
#endif  // FLOATXC1_H_


// FILE: FloatXC2.h
// FLOATING-POINT INDEXED COLLECTION CLASS
//     (Version 2 -- with initialization method)
//     DEFINITION AND IMPLEMENTATION

#ifndef FLOATXC2_H_
#define FLOATXC2_H_

class float_index_coll_v2 : public float_index_coll_v1
{
   public:
      // Member functions ...
      // Public member functions inherited from base class
      // Store, retrieve, get_count and destructor.

      // CONSTRUCTOR FOR COLLECTION
      float_index_coll_v2
        (int sz = max_size,  // IN: number of elements in array
         float value = 0);   // IN: initialization value

      // RETURN MAXIMUM NUMBER OF ELEMENTS
      int get_size ();

   protected:
      // Data members ...
```

(Continued)

Figure E.1   (Continued)

```
        // Inherited from parent class.

        // Private member functions ...
        // INITIALIZES STORAGE ELEMENTS TO SPECIFIED VALUE
        void init
           (float);              // IN: value to be used in initialization
};


// CONSTRUCTOR FOR COLLECTION
float_index_coll_v2::float_index_coll_v2
   (int sz ,                  // IN: number of elements in collection
    float value)              // IN: initialization value
    :(sz)                     // IN: override default value if needed
{
    size = sz;
    init (value);
}   // end constructor


// INITIALIZES STORAGE ELEMENTS TO SPECIFIED VALUE
void float_index_coll_v2::init
   (float value)              // IN: value to be in initialization

// Pre:  All collection elements undefined.
// Post: All collection elements set to value.
{
    // Perform initialization.
    for (int i = 0; i < size; i++)
       collection[i] = value;
    return;
}   // end init


// RETURN MAXIMUM NUMBER OF ELEMENTS
int float_index_coll_v2::get_size ()
{
    return size;
}   // end get_size
#endif  // FLOATXC2_H_
```

The syntax for defining a derived class is shown in the following display.

C++
SYNTAX

Defining a Derived Class

Form: class *derived : access base*
            { ... };

Example: class circle : public figure
            { ... };

Interpretation: The class *derived* is derived from the class *base*. The access specifier may be `public`, `private`, or `protected`. If it is `public`, then `public` (or `protected`) members of the base class are `public` (or protected) in the derived class. If it is `private` (`protected`), then the `public` and `protected` members of the base class become `private` (or `protected`) members of the derived class. The reserved word `protected` indicates a level of protection between `public` and `private`. Recall that items defined after the reserved word `public` are accessible by any function and that items defined after the reserved word `private` are accessible by member functions of the class in which they are declared. Items defined after the reserved word `protected` are accessible by member functions of both the class in which they are declared and classes derived from this class.

Note: Constructors are not inherited. The base class constructor (in this case, for `float_index_coll_v1`) is executed before the derived class constructor for each declaration of an object of the derived class.   ∎

A second form of inheritance is called *subclassing for specification.* In this form, the parent class provides a specification of some attributes (perhaps) as well as a list of the member functions common to all (or most) of the subclasses. However, no description of the behavior of these functions is provided. The purpose of the parent class in subclassing for specification is to describe *what must be done* but not *how the listed tasks are to be carried out.* In this case, the member functions specified in each subclass *override* the member function specifications in the parent class and provide a description of exactly how the task is to be carried out for the particular subclass in question.

Subclassing for specification is useful in situations where many different subclasses inherit data and function members from a parent and where we would like to have the same function protocol, terminology, and behavior used for the attributes and functions in all of the subclasses. The following Case Study provides an illustration of subclassing for specification.

CASE STUDY: AREAS AND PERIMETERS OF DIFFERENT FIGURES

Problem Statement

In Chapter 11, we wrote a program to determine the area and perimeter for a variety of geometric figures. In this version, we treated each figure as a different object with its own unique attributes. We now abstract the common attributes into a parent class from which the individual shapes can be derived.

Problem Analysis

To solve this problem, we begin by defining a class for each kind of figure. These classes will include member functions (operators) to read the particular characteristics, compute the area and perimeter, and display the results. Figure E.2 shows the three classes `circle`, `square`, and `rectangle`, as they were first illustrated in Section 11.5. You can see that the member functions `read_figure`, `compute_area`, `compute_perim`, and `display_fig` are common to each class. Also the data members `area` and `perimeter` are common to each class. We can therefore define a class `figure` that contains the common elements of the three classes, as shown in Fig. E.3.

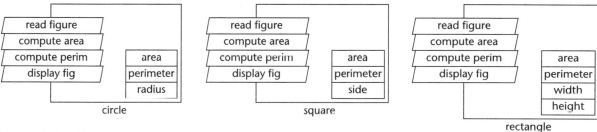

Figure E.2   The classes `circle`, `square`, **and** `rectangle`

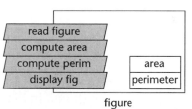

Figure E.3   The class `figure`

Notice that the member functions in Fig. E.3 are shaded. This is to indicate that while the functions are common to all figures, the particular implementation details are specific for each kind of figure. On the other hand, the data members `area` and `perimeter` are common to all figures. Figure E.4 shows the C++ definition of the class `figure`. In this figure, the reserved word `virtual` that precedes the definitions of the member functions indicates that these functions can have different versions for different derived classes. When the virtual function is called, it is the task of the compiler, rather than our program (as was the case in Chapter 11) to determine the appropriate version to be executed.

Figure E.4   C++ definition of the class figure

```
// FILE: Figure.h
// ABSTRACT CLASS FIGURE CONTAINS OPERATORS AND ATTRIBUTES COMMON
//     TO ALL FIGURES
#ifndef _figure_h
#define _figure_h

class figure
{
    // Member functions (common to all figures) ...
    public:
        // READ A FIGURE
        virtual void read_figure ();

        // COMPUTE THE AREA
        virtual void compute_area ();

        // COMPUTE THE PERIMETER
        virtual void compute_perim ();

        // DISPLAY INFORMATION ABOUT THE FIGURE
        virtual void display_fig ();

    // Data members (common to all figures) ...
    private:
        float area;             // The area of the figure
        float perimeter;        // The perimeter of the figure
};
#endif
```

Figure E.5 shows unique elements of the classes `circle`, `square`, and `rectangle`. If you were to overlay each of these on Fig. E.4 you would get the full classes as shown in Fig. E.3. Figures E.6, E.7, and E.8 show the C++ definitions for each of the classes `circle`, `square`, and `rectangle`, as derived from `figure`.

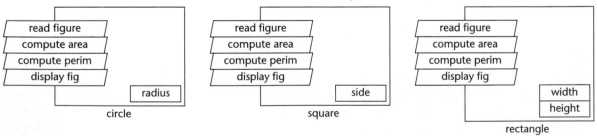

Figure E.5   The classes circle, square, **and** rectangle

Figure E.6   The class `circle`

```
// FILE: Circle.h
#ifndef _circle_h
#define _circle_h

#include "Figure.h"

// THE CLASS CIRCLE
class circle : public figure        // A circle is a figure
{
   // Overriding member functions (unique for circles) ...
   public:
      // READ A CIRCLE
      void read_figure ();

      // COMPUTE THE AREA OF A CIRCLE
      void compute_area ();

      // COMPUTE THE PERIMETER (CIRCUMFERENCE) OF A CIRCLE
      void compute_perim ();

      // DISPLAY CHARACTERISTICS UNIQUE TO A CIRCLE
      void display_fig ();

   // Data members (unique to a circle) ...
   private:
      float radius;                 // The radius
};
#endif
```

Figure E.7   The class `square`

```
// FILE Square.h
#ifndef _square_h
#define _square_h

#include "Figure.h"

// THE CLASS SQUARE
class square : public figure        // A square is a figure
{
   // Overriding member functions (unique for squares) ...
   public:
      // READ A SQUARE
      void read_figure ();
```

(Continued)

Figure E.7   (Continued)

```
        // COMPUTE AREA OF A SQUARE
        void compute_area ();

        // COMPUTE PERIMETER OF A SQUARE
        void compute_perim ();

        // DISPLAY CHARACTERISTICS UNIQUE TO SQUARES
        void display_fig ();

    // Attributes (unique to squares) ...
    private:
        float side;                      // length of side of square
};
#endif
```

Figure E.8   The class `rectangle`

```
// FILE Rectangl.h
#ifndef _rectangl_h
#define _rectangl_h

#include "Figure.h"

// THE CLASS RECTANGLE
class rectangle : public figure  // A rectangle is a figure
{
    // Overriding member functions (unique for rectangles) ...
    public:
        // READ A RECTANGLE
        void read_figure ();

        // COMPUTE THE AREA OF A RECTANGLE
        void compute_area ();

        // COMPUTE THE PERIMETER OF A RECTANGLE
        void compute_perim ();

        // DISPLAY CHARACTERISTICS UNIQUE TO RECTANGLES
        void display_fig ();

    // Data members (unique to rectangles) ...
    private:
        float width;                     // width of rectangle
        float height;                    // height of rectangle
};
#endif
```

Program Design

Given the parent class figure and the derived classes circle, square, and rectangle, we can now design the program for solving the shapes problem. The structure chart is similar to the one shown in Fig. 11.10. The initial algorithm follows.

INITIAL ALGORITHM

1. Determine the type of the figure.
2. Read in the figure characteristics (read_figure).
3. Compute the area of the figure (compute_area).
4. Compute the perimeter of the figure (compute_perimeter).
5. Display the complete data for the figure (display_fig).

Program Implementation

We use the parent class figure and the derived classes circle, square, and rectangle as shown in Figs. E.4, E.6, E.7, and E.8. These classes contain the member functions required to perform steps 2 through 5.

CODING THE MAIN FUNCTION

The main function (Fig. E.9) declares a variable (my_fig) of type pointer to figure. The function get_figure returns a pointer to figure. The main function for loop calls get_figure, which carries out step 1 of the algorithm. Depending upon the input received, the pointer returned by get_ ~·
ure (and stored in my_fig) will point to a particular kind of figure (ci
square, or rectangle). This object, indicated by *my_fig, is passed
function process_figure (Fig. E.9). The member functions of the ~ia>>
figure are called by process_figure to perform steps 2 through 5 of our
initial algorithm. The main function then deletes the object pointed to by
my_fig so that another figure may be defined. The program exits when a zero
pointer is returned from get_figure. Notice that these functions know only
about the class figure and not any of the particular figures derived from it;
there are simply no references to the derived classes here.

Figure E.9   Figures program main function

```
// FILE: Figures.cpp
// MAIN PROGRAM TO ILLUSTRATE THE FIGURES CLASS

#include <stddef.h>

#include "Figure.h"
```

(Continued)

Figure E.9   (Continued)

```
void main()
{
    // Functions called ...
    // GET THE TYPE OF FIGURE
    figure* get_figure ();

    // PROCESS ONE FIGURE
    void process_figure
        (figure&);              // INOUT: The figure to be processed

    // Local data ...
    figure* my_fig;            // a pointer to a figure

    // Process a selected figure until no more figures selected.
    for (my_fig = get_figure(); my_fig != 0; my_fig = get_figure())
    {
        process_figure(*my_fig);
        delete my_fig;         // delete this figure
    }
}

// PROCESS ONE FIGURE
void process_figure
    (figure& fig)              // INOUT: The figure to be processed
{
    fig.read_figure ();        // get characteristics of figure
    fig.compute_area ();       // compute its area
    fig.compute_perim ();      // compute its perimeter
    fig.display_fig ();        // display characteristics
}
```

CODING THE FUNCTIONS

All that remains to be done at this point is to code the function get_figure, and the member functions of the classes figure, circle, square, and rectangle. The function get_figure is shown in Fig. E.10. This function must know about the three kinds of figures and therefore includes the definition files circle.h, square.h, and rectangl.h. It prompts for an input character and calls the new operator to allocate memory for the particular kind of figure specified. If the letter x is input, the function returns a zero pointer to indicate that no figure was specified. If a letter that is not recognized is entered, the function asks for another input.

Figure E.10   Function get_figure

```
// FILE Getfig.cpp
// FUNCTION TO READ THE KIND OF FIGURE AND RETURN A POINTER TO
```

(Continued)

Figure E.10 (Continued)

```
//    AN OBJECT OF THE APPROPRIATE TYPE

#include <iostream.h>
#include <stddef.h>

#include "Circle.h"
#include "Square.h"
#include "Rectangl.h"

figure* get_figure ()
// Pre:  None
// Post: A pointer to the type of figure desired is returned
{
   // Local data ...
   char fig_char;         // A character to indicate the type
                          //   of figure

   for (;;)               // Loop until a valid entry is made
   {
      cout << "Enter the kind of object" << endl;
      cout << "Enter C (Circle), R (Rectangle), or S (Square)"
           << endl;
      cout << "Enter X to exit program" << endl;
      cin >> fig_char;
      switch (fig_char)
      {
         case 'c': case 'C':
            return new circle;
         case 'r': case 'R':
            return new rectangle;
         case 's': case 'S':
            return new square;
         case 'x': case 'X':
            return 0;
      } // end switch
   }
} // end get_figure
```

Figures E.11, E.12, E.13, and E.14 show the implementations of the classes figure, circle, square, and rectangle. With the exception of the function display_fig, the functions in the parent class figure have little work to do. The function figure::display_fig (the function display_fig which is a member of the class figure) displays the perimeter and area of a shape, attributes that are common the all of the kinds of figures. The implementation of the other member functions is straightforward. Notice that each class implementation need know only about itself and not the other classes. Thus figure.cpp needs to include figure.h, circle.cpp needs to include `circle.h`, and so on, but they do not need to include the definitions for the other classes.

Figure E.11   Implementation of the class `figure`

```
// FILE: Figure.cpp
// IMPLEMENTATION OF THE BASE CLASS FIGURE

#include <iostream.h>

#include "Figure.h"


// READ CHARACTERISTICS OF A FIGURE
void figure::read_figure ()
{
    ;                              // The base function does nothing
}


// COMPUTE PERIMETER
void figure::compute_perim ()
{
    perimeter = 0.0;         // The base function sets a constant
}


// COMPUTE AREA
void figure::compute_area ()
{
    area = 0.0;                   // The base function sets a constant
}


// DISPLAY THE COMMON CHARACTERISTICS OF FIGURES
void figure::display_fig ()
{
    cout << "Area is " << area << endl;
    cout << "Perimeter is " << perimeter << endl;
}
```

Figure E.12   Implementation of the class `circle`

```
// FILE: Circle.cpp
// IMPLEMENTATION OF THE CLASS CIRCLE

#include <iostream.h>

#include "Circle.h"
```

(Continued)

Figure E.12   (Continued)

```cpp
const float pi = 3.1415927;


// READ DATA UNIQUE TO A CIRCLE
void circle::read_figure ()
{
   cout << "Enter radius > ";
   cin >> radius;
}


// COMPUTE THE PERIMETER (CIRCUMFERENCE) OF A CIRCLE
void circle::compute_perim ()
{
   perimeter = 2.0 * pi * radius;
}


// COMPUTE THE AREA OF A CIRCLE
void circle::compute_area ()
{
   area = pi * radius * radius;
}


// DISPLAY THE CHARACTERISTICS OF A CIRCLE
void circle::display_fig ()
{
   // Display the type of figure and its radius.
   cout << "Figure Shape is Circle" << endl;
   cout << "Radius is " << radius << endl;
   // Call the base function to display common characteristics.
   figure::display_fig ();
}
```

Figure E.13   Implementation of the class `square`

```cpp
// FILE Square.cpp
// IMPLEMENTATION OF THE CLASS SQUARE

#include <iostream.h>

#include "Square.h"


// READ DATA UNIQUE TO A SQUARE
void square::read_figure ()
```

(Continued)

Figure E.13   (Continued)

```
{
    cout << "Enter side > ";
    cin >> side;
}


// COMPUTE THE PERIMETER OF A SQUARE
void square::compute_perim ()
{
    perimeter = 4.0 * side;
}


// COMPUTE THE AREA OF A SQUARE
void square::compute_area ()
{
    area = side * side;
}

// DISPLAY THE CHARACTERISTICS OF A SQUARE
void square::display_fig ()
{
    // Display the type of figure and its size.
    cout << "Figure shape is Square" << endl;
    cout << "Side is " << side << endl;
    // Call the base function to display common characteristics.
    figure::display_fig ();
}
```

Figure E.14   Implementation of the class `rectangle`

```
// FILE Rectangl.cpp
// IMPLEMENTATION OF THE RECTANGLE CLASS

#include <iostream.h>

#include "Rectangl.h"


// READ DATA UNIQUE TO A RECTANGLE
void rectangle::read_figure()
{
    cout << "Enter width: ";
    cin >> width;
    cout << "Enter height: ";
    cin >> height;
}
```

(Continued)

Figure E.14   (Continued)

```
// COMPUTE THE PERIMETER OF A RECTANGLE
void rectangle::compute_perim ()
{
    perimeter = 2.0 * (width + height);
}


// COMPUTE THE AREA OF A RECTANGLE
void rectangle::compute_area ()
{
    area = width * height;
}


// DISPLAY THE CHARACTERISICS OF A RECTANGLE
void rectangle::display_fig ()
{
    // Display the type of figure and its height and width.
    cout << "Figure shape is Rectangle" << endl;
    cout << "Height is " << height << endl;
    cout << "Width is " << width << endl;
    // Call the base function to display common characteristics.
    figure::display_fig ();
}
```

Commentary

In the figures program in Chapter 11, we used three distinct classes to represent the different kinds of figures. The function process_figure in Fig. 11.11 defined three variables, one for each kind of figure. By means of a switch statement, the member functions for the class corresponding to the kind of figure are called to perform the operations get_known_attributes, compute_area, compute_perimeter, and display_attributes. Extending this program to include additional figures is not conceptually difficult, it is simply a relatively boring, time-consuming, and error-prone exercise.

Compare this with the process_figure function of Fig. E.11. This function contains no switch statement. The switch statement is in the function get_figure, and it simply determines which kind of figure is to be created given the user's input. To extend this new version of the figures program for other kinds of figures is very easy. We merely need to define a new class for our new kind of figure and to modify get_figure to recognize an input that designates it. (As an exercise, you might try to extend the figures program to include the figure class `right_triangle`. Use the following formulas:

$$area = \frac{1}{2}\ base \times height$$

$$hypotenuse = \sqrt{base^2 + height^2}$$

where *base* and *height* are the two sides that form the right triangle and *hypotenuse* is the side opposite the right angle.)

Polymorphism

A function which is only concerned with the common characteristics of a group of objects may operate on different specialized instances without knowing about the specific instance. As illustrated in Fig. E.11, a pointer, such as `my_fig`, to an object of the parent type can point to an object of any of the derived types. Operations, such as `compute_area`, which are common in function to the derived classes, may be accessed through such a pointer, as in `fig.compute_area()`, even though the implementation details of these operations may vary. This is called *polymorphism* (meaning "many forms").

In this example, we have illustrated one form of polymorphism, known as *overriding through the use of a virtual function.* An overridden function name, such as `compute_area`, is polymorphic in the sense that it can be used to refer to many different functions (five, in our example).

The operator + is also polymorphic; it may be *overloaded.* That is, it can be used to specify integer addition, as in

```
19 + 32
```

or floating-point addition, as in

```
6.1 + 8.8
```

To the underlying computer, these are two totally distinct operations. To the programmer, + can be viewed as a single operation that allows the use of different types of arguments. The specific underlying computer operation to be performed is determined by the compiler, based upon the operands involved.

The use of inheritance and polymorphism permits us to define a foundation upon which others can build specialized applications. Commercial software vendors provide such foundation classes for a variety of application domains. Two popular domains are in *graphics user interfaces* and in *data base management.*

Answers

Chapter 1

Section 1.2

1. Contents of memory cell   0: -27.2.
   Contents of memory cell 999: 75.62.

   Memory cell 998 contains the letter x.
   Memory cell 2 contains the fraction 0.005.

Section 1.4

1. `x = a + b + c;`	Add the contents of variables a, b, c. Store the results in variable x.
`x = y / z;`	Divide the contents of variable y by the contents of variable z. Store the results in variable x.
`d = c - b + a;`	Subtract the contents of variable b from the contents of variable c. Add the contents of variable a to this. Store the final result in variable d.
`x = x + 1;`	Add 1 to the contents of variable x. Store the result in variable x.
`kelvin = celsius + 273.15;`	Add 273.15 to the contents of variable celsius. Store the results in variable kelvin.

3. Assembly language has instructions such as ADD X.
   Machine language has instructions that are binary numbers.

Section 1.5

1. The source file contains a program written in a high-level language. The object file is the machine code translation of a source program. The load file contains the object file (of the original program) and any additional object files used by the original program.

   The programmer creates the source file (using an editor), and the compiler creates the object program. The linker creates the load file, which is loaded into memory by the loader.

   The compiler translates the source file into an object file, the linker creates a load file from the object file(s), and the loader brings the load file into memory prior to execution (adjusting addresses according to where in memory the program will be run).

Section 1.6

1. A stand-alone computer system is a single-user system that is not connected in any way to any other computer facilities. In a timeshared system, many users are connected to one central computer. All of these users must share the central facilities, including the CPU, secondary and main memory, and the input/output devices. In a networked system, a number of computers are linked together. Each computer usually has the full capability of a personal computer—its own secondary and main memory, its own CPU, and possibly its own input/output devices (in

addition to a keyboard and a screen). You need to check with your instructor or lab assistant to determine which system your class is using.

Chapter 2

Section 2.1

1. The three steps/stages of the software development method are:
   - Problem analysis
   - Program design
   - Program implementation

3. During the program design stage, the problem is decomposed into smaller, relatively independent subproblems, each of which is considerably easier to solve than the original. A list of steps, called an algorithm, is then developed to solve each subproblem. Once it has been verified that the algorithm solves the problem, the program implementation stage can begin. Here the algorithm is actually implemented as a program. This implementation requires that each step in the algorithm be converted into statements in a particular programming language.

5. An algorithm is an outline of the steps that a program needs to perform. The program consists of instructions telling the computer how to execute these steps. The algorithm is converted into instructions which are dependent on the programming language being used.

Section 2.2

1. The special pair of symbols // denotes a program comment.

3. The #include is a compiler directive. It instructs the compiler to insert the indicated C++ instructions into the program in place of the directive. For example,

```
#include <iostream.h>
```

instructs the compiler to get the file iostream.h and insert its contents in place of the #include line during compilation.

5. It is important to use consistent programming style because consistent style makes your program easier to read, understand, and modify than one that is sloppy and/or inconsistent.

Section 2.3

1. The value of pi (3.14159) should be stored in a constant because this value never changes.

3.
main	valid
const	reserved
y=z	invalid
cin	valid
xyz123	valid
Prog#2	invalid
Bill	valid
123xyz	invalid
ThisIsALongOne	valid
Sue's	invalid
'Maxscores'	invalid
so_is_this_one	valid
start	valid
int	reserved
two-way	invalid
return	reserved
go	valid

Section 2.4

1. data 5.0   7.0
   a = 10.0
   b = 21.0
3. My name is: Doe, Jane
   I live in Ann Arbor, MI, and my ZIP code is 48109

Section 2.5

1. `// This is a comment ? */`

   Legal: No terminating symbol is required when using the `//` symbol. This will not cause an error, however, because `*/` is treated as part of the comment beginning with `//`.

   `/* How about this one /* it seems like a comment */ doesn't it ? */`

   Error: Comments cannot be nested. The compiler will ignore the second `/*` symbol pair. When it reaches the `*/` symbol pair, it will assume that it has reached the end of the comment. This means the `"doesn't it? */ "` portion of the comment will cause an error when the compiler tries to translate it.

3.
```
#include <iostream.h>   // tells the compiler to include this file

void main ( )           // denotes the start of this program
{
    float x, y, z;      // declares three floating-point variables

    y = 15.0;           // assigns the value 15.0 to variable y
    z = y + 3.5;        // adds the value 3.5 to variable y; stores the
                        //   result in z
    x = y + z;          // adds the contents of y and z; stores the
                        //   result in x
    cout >> x, y, z;    // displays the results
    return;
}
```

   Values printed will be 33.5   15.0   18.5.

Section 2.6

1.
15	int
"x"	invalid: must use single quotes
'XYZ'	invalid: only single character permitted
'9'	char
'*'	char
'-5'	invalid: only single character permitted
$	invalid: missing single quotes
'x"	invalid: second quote must be single quote
25.123	float
$4.79	invalid: no $ permitted for float
15.	float
-999	int
.123	float
'x'	char

3. m = (m / n) * n + (m % n)
   m = 45   n = 5
   45 = (45 / 5) * 5 + (45 % 5)
   45 =   9 * 5 + 0

5. a) `i = a % b;`   i is assigned 3
   b) `i = (max_i - 990 / a);`   i is assigned 670
   c) `i = a % y;`   invalid: y must be type int
   d) `i = (990 - max_i) / a;`   i is assigned –3
   e) `i = pi * a;`   i is assigned 9
   f) `x = pi * y;`   x is assigned –3.14159
   g) `x = pi / y;`   x is assigned –3.14159
   h) `i = (max_i - 990) % a;`   i is assigned 1
   i) `x = a % (a / b);`   runtime error: cannot divide by 0
   j) `i = a % 0;`   runtime error: cannot divide by 0
   k) `i = b / 0;`   runtime error: cannot divide by 0
   l) `i = a % (max_i - 990);`   i is assigned 3
   m) `x = a / y;`   x is assigned –3.0
   n) `i = a % (990 - max_i);`   i is assigned –3
   o) `x = a / b;`   x is assigned 0

7. a) `white = color * 2.5 / purple;`   white is assigned 1.0
   b) `green = color / purple;`   green is assigned 0
   c) `orange = color / red;`   orange is assigned 0
   d) `blue = (color + straw) / (crayon + 0.3);`   blue is assigned –3
   e) `lime = red / color + red % color;`   lime is assigned 2
   f) `purple = straw / red * color;`   purple is assigned 0

Section 2.7

1. In interactive programs, the cout line is used to prompt the user to enter input. In a batch program, there is no need for this prompt because the data are obtained from a data file. The cout line is used in a batch file to echo the data. This lets the user know what data values were read.

Chapter 3

Section 3.1

1. Input: hrs_worked, pay_rate
   Output: pay
   Initial Algorithm:

   1. Read hours worked, pay rate
   2. Calculate pay
        2.1. Assign hours worked × pay rate to pay
   3. Display pay

Section 3.2

1.

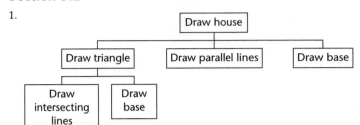

3.

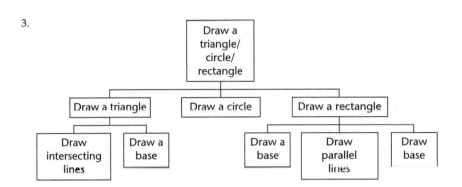

Section 3.3

1. The 5 by 5 letter O prints.
   On the next line, the 5 by 5 letter H prints.
   Three lines are skipped.
   On the next line, the 5 by 5 letter H prints.
   On the next line, the 5 by 5 letter I prints.
   On the next line, the 5 by 5 letter M prints.

Section 3.4

1. The purpose of function arguments is to transmit data back and forth between functions.

Section 3.5

1. a) The top-down design process allows us to focus initially on the overall problem rather than have our attention distracted by details. The details are handled at a lower level, specifically, in a function. By declaring the function prototype we can write the main program as a series of function calls prior to actually writing the functions themselves.
   b) The C++ function prototype provides the type information needed by the compiler to check the consistency of all input arguments and of the returned type for our functions.

3.

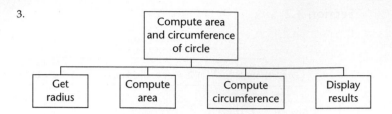

Section 3.6

1. Note: The following function calls assume that all arguments are valid for their respective functions.

   a) `sqrt (u + v * w * w)`
   b) `log10 (pow (x, y))`
   c) `sqrt ((x - y) * (x - y))`
   d) `fabs ((x * y) - (w / z))`

3. a) `disc = square_float (b) - 4.0 * a * c;`   613
      `disc = square_float (b) -(4.0 * a) * c;`   613
   b) `x1 = (-b + sqrt (disc)) / (2.0 * a);`   .04
      `x1 = (-b + sqrt (disc)) / 2.0 * a;`   .36   Results differ because division is done prior to multiplying `2.0` by `a`.

   c) `x2 = (-b - sqrt (disc)) / (2.0 * a);`   8.29
      `x2 =  -b - sqrt (disc)  / (2.0 * a);` −29.13   Results differ because division is done prior to subtracting `sqrt (disc)` from `-b`.

Chapter 4

Section 4.2

1. x = 15, y = 25
`x != y`	True
`x < x`	False
`x > (y - x)`	True
`x == (y + x - y)`	True

3. !(x > y) || (y + 2) >= (x - z)

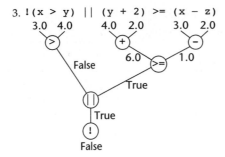

Section 4.3

1. a) Always
   b) OK

Section 4.4

```
1. if (x > y)
   {
       x = x + 10.0;
       cout << "x bigger" << endl;
   }
   else
       cout << "x smaller" << endl;

       cout << "y is " << y << endl;
```

3. Placing brackets around the last two lines in the answer to Question 1 would cause the value of y to be displayed only when y <= x.

Section 4.6

1. a) The value of pi is 3.14159
      The value of radius is   4.5
   b) 4 16
      10100

Section 4.7

1. a) Case 1: Both conditions are true.

ALGORITHM STEP	ch1	ch2	ch3	alpha_first	EFFECT
1. Read three letters	d	j	a	?	Reads the data.
2.1.1. If ch1 precedes ch2					Is 'd' < 'j'? Expression is true.
2.1.2. alpha_first is assigned ch1				d	'd' is first so far.
2.2.1. If ch3 precedes alpha_first					Is 'a' < 'd'? Expression is true.
2.2.2. alpha_first is assigned ch3				a	'a' is first.
3. Display alpha_first					Prints 'a' as the first letter.

b) Case 2: First condition is true; second is false.

ALGORITHM STEP	ch1	ch2	ch3	alpha_first	EFFECT
1. Read three letters.	d	j	q	?	Reads the data.
2.1.1. If ch1 precedes ch2					Is 'd' < 'j'? Expression is true.
2.1.2. alpha_first is assigned ch1				d	'd' is first so far.
2.2.1. If ch3 precedes alpha_first					Is 'q' < 'd'? Expression is false.
2.2.3. alpha_first remains alpha_first					'd' is still first.
3. Display alpha_first					Prints 'd' as the first letter.

c) Case 3: Both conditions are false.

ALGORITHM STEP	ch1	ch2	ch3	alpha_first	EFFECT
1. Read three letters.	j	a	z	?	Reads the data.
2.1.1. If ch1 precedes ch2					Is 'j' < 'a'? Expression is false.
2.1.3. alpha_first is assigned ch2				a	'a' is first so far.
2.2.1. If ch3 precedes alpha_first					Is 'z' < 'a'? Expression is false.
2.2.3. alpha_first remains alpha_first					'a' is first.
3. Display alpha_first					Prints 'a' as the first letter.

3. a)

STATEMENT	tax_bracket	tax	hours	rate	gross	net	EFFECT
	100.00	25.00	?	?	?	?	
cin >> hours;			30.0				Reads hours worked.
cin >> rate;				5.0			Reads rate of pay.
gross = compute_gross (hours, rate);							Calls function to compute gross pay.
return hours; * rate;					150.0		Function returns to calling function with value set to hours × rate.
net = compute_net (gross, tax_bracket, tax);							Calls function to compute net pay.
if (gross > tax_bracket)							150.0 > 100.0: true
return gross - tax;						125.0	Function returns to calling program with function value set to gross − tax

b)

STATEMENT	tax_bracket	tax	hours	rate	gross	net	EFFECT
	100.00	25.00	?	?	?	?	
cin >> hours;			20.0				Reads hours worked.
cin >> rate;				4.0			Reads rate of pay.
gross = compute_gross (hours, rate);							Calls function to compute gross pay.
return hours * rate;					80.0		Function returns to calling function with value set to hours × rate.
net = compute_net (gross, tax_bracket, tax);							Calls function to compute net pay.
if (gross > tax_bracket)							80.0 > 100.0: false
return gross;						80.0	Function returns to calling program with function value set to gross; no taxes due.

Section 4.8

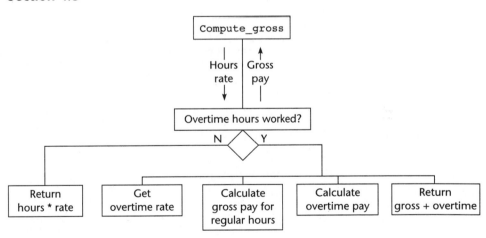

Section 4.9

1.

STATEMENT PART	salary	tax	EFFECT
	13500.00	?	
if (salary < 0.0)			13500.00 < 0.0 is false.
else if (salary < 1500.00)			13500.00 < 1500.00 is false.
else if (salary < 3000.00)			13500.00 < 3000.00 is false.
else if (salary < 5000.00)			13500.00 < 5000.00 is false.
else if (salary < 8000.00)			13500.00 < 8000.00 is false.
else if (salary < 15000.00)			13500.00 < 15000.00 is true.
tax = (salary - 8000.00)			Tax evaluates to 5500.00.
* .25			Tax evaluates to 1375.00.
+ 1425.00			Tax evaluates to 2800.00.

3. x = 6, y = 7

a) `(x > 5) && (y / x <= 10)` evaluates to true.
b) `(x <= 10) || (x / (y - 7) > 3)` evaluates to true.

In this example, because the left-hand side of the expression evaluates to true, it is not necessary to evaluate the right-hand side. Only one side must be true for an OR to evaluate to true. If the right side was evaluated in this example, a runtime error would occur as a result of division by 0.

Section 4.10

1. `red`
3. In Section 4.9, the selection is determined based on a sizable range of values rather than a specific value. With the `switch` statement, selection is based on a single value or a small, easily listable set of values.

Chapter 5

Section 5.1

1. The loop body is repeated three times. Each time, the value of **x** is printed.
   Output: 9
                 81
              6561
3. If the last statement in the loop is omitted, the loop will execute forever because the value of count will never reach 3.

Section 5.2

1.   5
     25
    125
    625

3. The segment should read:

```
count = 0;
sum = 0;
while (count < 5)
{
    cout << "Enter data item: ";
    cin >> item;
    cout << endl;
    sum += item;
    count++;
}

cout << count << " data items were added" << endl;
cout << "their sum is " << sum << endl;
```

Section 5.3

1. The least number of times that the body of a `while` loop may execute is 0. This will occur when the condition tests false the first time.

3. a) Output: 9.45
                5.6
   b) Output: 5.58
                5.58

Section 5.4

1. The last step in the `while` statement must read the new value of `score` so that it can be tested to determine whether the loop body should be repeated. It would be incorrect to have the assignment statement at the end of the loop because that would cause the sentinel value to be added to the sum.

Section 5.5

1. Result: 15.
   Value of `sum` as computed by the formula

$$\text{sum} = \frac{n(n+1)}{2}$$

   is 15. If n were 50, the result would be 1275.
   Using the formula is a much more efficient means of obtaining the result. There are always three calculations required in the formula. Using the loop, there are n calculations.

Section 5.6

1.

STATEMENT	i	j	EFFECT
	?	10	
`for (i = 0;`	0		Initialize i to 0.
`i < 3;`			0 < 5 is true.
`i ++)`			(No action yet.)
`cout << i`			Displays 0.
`<< " "`			Displays space.
`<< j`			Displays 10.
`<< endl;`			Goes to next line.
`j -= 2;`		8	Subtracts 2 from j.
`i++`	1		Adds 1 to i.
`i < 3;`			1 < 3 is true.
`cout << i`			Displays 1.
`<< " "`			Displays space.
`<< j`			Displays 8.
`<< endl;`			Goes to next line.
`j -= 2;`		6	Subtracts 2 from j.
`i++`	2		Adds 1 to i.

STATEMENT	i	j	EFFECT
i < 3;			2 < 3 is true.
cout << i			Displays 2.
<< " "			Displays space.
<< j			Displays 6.
<< endl;			Goes to next line.
j -= 2;		4	Subtracts 2 from j.
i++	3		Adds 1 to i.
i < 3;			3 < 3 is false.

Section 5.8

1. Output: 10
              20
              30
              40
              50
              60
              70
              80
              90
             100

```
for (num = 10; num <= 100; num += 10)
   cout << num << endl;

num = 10;
do
{
   cout << num << endl;
    num += 10;
}
while (num <= 100);
```

3. The do-while loop should be used only in situations where it is certain that the loop should execute at least once. The do-while loop will always execute at least once because the condition test is not performed until the end of the loop.

Section 5.9

1. a) Output: *
                **
               ***
              ****

   b) Output: *****
               *****
               *****

Section 5.10

```
1. count = 0;
   sum = 0;
   cout << "Enter "  << n <<  " integers and press return:" << endl;
   for (int count = 0; count <= n; count++)
   {
      cout << "count " << count << endl;   // debug
      cin >> item;
      sum += item;
      cout << "sum " << sum << endl;        // debug
   } // end for
```

The addition of these debug statements should show that the loop has an "off by 1" error. The prompt is requesting n data items. The loop is expecting n+1 data items. This can be corrected by changing the condition test from <= to <.

Chapter 6

Section 6.2

1. An example of tracing the execution of the following code segments with adj_income set to 34000.00 follows. No constants are listed, as they will not change during the execution.

Trace of code from compute_tax:

STATEMENT	adj_income	tax_amount	EFFECT
	34000.00	?	
if (adj_income < min_valid_amount)			34000.00 < 0.0 is false.
else if (adj_income > cat2_max)			34000.00 > 82150.00 is false.
else if (adj_income > cat1_max)			34000.00 > 34000.00 is false.

else
   tax_amount =
   cat1_rate * adj_income;
		5100.00	tax_amount is assigned 0.15 * 34000.00.

Trace of code from code segment:

STATEMENT	adj_income	tax_amount	EFFECT
	34000.00	?	
if (adj_income < min_valid_amount)			34000.00 < 0.0 is false.
else if (adj_income <= cat1_max)			34000.00 < 34000.00 is true.
tax_amount = cat1_rate * adj_income;		5100.00	tax_amount is assigned 0.15 * 34000.00.

The same results are produced by these two different code segments.

3. a) Preconditions: x, y must be positive (assuming this function is being used to calculate the hypotenuse of a right triangle).
   Postconditions: Computes the hypotenuse of a right triangle. x and y are not changed.
   Return: The square root of the sum of the squares of x and y.
   b) Preconditions: a, b must be defined.
   Postconditions: Function fabs calculates the absolute difference of a and b.

Section 6.3

1.

STATEMENT	change_denom	change_needed	num_units	EFFECT
	5.00	5.56	?	
num_units = int(change_needed / change_denom);			1	Assign num_units the integer value of change_needed / change_denom.
change_needed = change_needed - (num_units * change_denom);		.56		Assign change_needed the decimal portion of the original value of change_needed.

3. a) Assuming data 8.0, 10.0, 6.0 are read into num1, num2, and num3, respectively:

STATEMENT	num1	num2	num3	x	y	temp	EFFECT
	8.0	10.0	6.0	?	?	?	
order (num3, num2);				6.0	10.0		x and y are assigned the values of num3 and num2.
if (x > y) return;							If 6.0 > 10.0 is false: no change.
order (num3, num1);				6.0	8.0		x and y are assigned the values of num3 and num1.
if (x > y) return;							If 6.0 > 8.0 is false: no change.
order (num2, num1);				10.0	8.0		x and y are assigned the values of num2 and num1.
if (x > y) temp = x;						10.0	If 10.0 > 6.0 is true: temp assigned the value of x.

STATEMENT	num1	num2	num3	x	y	temp	EFFECT
x = y; y = temp;				8.0	10.0		x assigned the value of y. y assigned the value of temp.
return;	10.0	8.0					num2 and num1 are now reversed.

Assuming data 10.0, 8.0, 60.0 are read into num1, num2, num3, respectively:

STATEMENT	num1	num2	num3	x	y	temp	EFFECT
	10.0	8.0	60.0	?	?	?	
order (num3, num2)				60.0	8.0		x is assigned 60.0, y is assigned 8.0.

if (x > y)
    temp = x;
    x = y;
    y = temp;
return;
		60.0	8.0	8.0	60.0	60.0	If 60.0 > 8.0 is true:
							temp is assigned 60.0.
							x is assigned 8.0.
							y is assigned 60.0.
							num3 is assigned 8.0 (x)
							num2 is assigned 60.0 (y)
							(the contents of num3
							and num2 are reversed).

order (num3, num1)				8.0	10.0		x is assigned 8.0. y is assigned 10.0.
if (x > y) return;							If 8.0 > 10.0 is false: no change.
order (num2, num1)				60.0	10.0		x is assigned 60.0. y is assigned 10.0.

if (x > y)
    temp = x;
    x = y;
    y = temp;
return;
	60.0	10.0		10.0	60.0	60.0	If 60.0 > 10.0 is true:
							temp is assigned 60.0.
							x is assigned 10.0.
							y is assigned 60.0.
							num2 is assigned 10.0 (x).
							num1 is assigned 60.0 (y)
							(the contents of num2
							and num1 are reversed).

b) As a result of this sequence of calls, the largest value is stored in variable num1, the smallest value is stored in variable num3, and the middle value is stored in variable num2.

5. a) In function order, variables x, y, and temp must all be declared type integer rather than type float. The statements:

```
void order
    (float &x, float &y)

    float temp;
```

become

```
void order
  (int &x, int &y)

int temp;
```

b) In the calling program, the prototype for function order has to be changed. In addition, the variables being used in the function call should also be declared type int. The statements:

```
void order
  (float &,  float &);

float num1, num2, num3;
```

become

```
void order
  (int &, int &);

int num1, num2, num3;
```

Section 6.4

1. Argument correspondence for test (m, -63, y, x, next):

ACTUAL ARGUMENT	FORMAL ARGUMENT	DESCRIPTION
m	a	int, value
-63	b	int, value
y	c	float, reference
x	d	float, reference
next	e	char, reference

Argument correspondence for test (35, m * 10, y, x, next):

ACTUAL ARGUMENT	FORMAL ARGUMENT	DESCRIPTION
35	a	int, value
m * 10	b	int, value
y	c	float, reference
x	d	float, reference
next	e	char, reference

3. Invalid function calls:

   e) must use variable for call by reference
   g) a, b, not declared
   i) must use variable for call by reference
   j) too many arguments

Calls requiring standard conversion:

   a) z becomes int
   d) m becomes float
   j) x becomes int

Section 6.5

```
1. void compute_area (int num_items,  // IN: number of data items
                      float sum,       // IN: sum of data
                      float & ave)     // OUT: average of data

   // Pre:    num_items and sum are defined; num_items must be > 0.0
   // Post:   If num_items is positive, the average (variable ave) is
   //         computed as sum / num_items; otherwise ave is set to 0.0
   // Return: The average (variable ave) if num_items is positive;
   //         otherwise variable ave is set to 0.0

   {
      if (num_items < 1)
      {
         cout << "Invalid value for num_items = " << num_items << endl;
         cout << "Average not computed." << endl;
         ave = 0.0;
         return;
      } // endif
      ave = sum / float (num_items);
      return;
   } // end compute_ave
```

3. Data areas after call but before function execution:

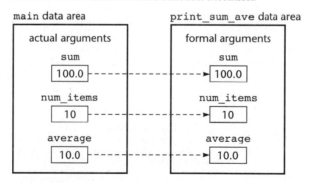

In this example the data areas will contain the same values after `print_sum_ave` executes (but before it returns to main). No values are changed during execution.

5. If `num_items` were 0 or negative:

- In `compute_sum` the `for` loop would attempt to execute. Since `count` would be greater than or equal to `num_items`, control would pass to the statement following the `for` loop. A value of `sum = 0` would be returned.
- In `compute_ave` a runtime error would occur if `num_items` were 0. If `num_items` were negative, `compute_ave` would return with a negative average.
- In `print_sum_ave` if `num_items` were 0, the program would previously have failed due to the runtime error in `compute_ave` caused by an attempt to divide by 0. If `num_items` were negative, `num_items` would be displayed as that negative number, `sum` would be displayed as 0, and `average` would be displayed as a negative number.

7. Initial algorithm:
   1. Read the number of items to be processed.
   2. If the number of items to be processed is negative
       2.1. Print a diagnostic message.
       2.2. Terminate execution.
      else
       2.3. Compute the sum by reading each data item and accumulating it in the sum.
       2.4. Compute the average of the data items.
       2.5. Print the sum and the average.

9. a)

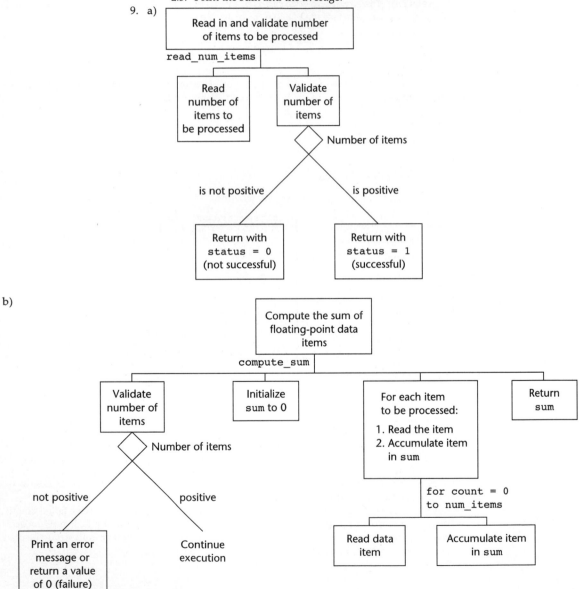

b)

Section 6.6

1. Data Requirements for function `display_record`:

Input: `transaction_code (float)`   — current transaction code of D or C
          `transaction_amount (float)` — current transaction amount
          `current_balance (float)`   — current balance after this transaction
Output: (none)
Local: (none)

Algorithm:
1. Display transaction code.
2. Display transaction amount.
3. Display the balance.
4. If the balance is < 0.
      4.1. Display warning message.

Section 6.8

1. Test data:

```
start_balance  100.00
response       N
start_balance  200.00
response       Γ
start_balance  300.00
response       Y
```

3.
```
// Driver program to test function process_transaction
#include <iostream.h>
#include <iomanip.h>

void main ()
{
// Functions used ...
// PROCESS ALL TRANSACTIONS
   void process_transactions
      (float,           // IN : account balance at start of period
       float&,          // INOUT: current balance at any point
       int&,            // INOUT: number of checks at any point
       int&);           // INOUT: number of deposits at any point

   // Local data ...
   float start_balance;   // input:   balance at start of period
   float current_balance; // output:  balance at end of period
   int num_checks;        // output:  number of checks for the period
   int num_deps;          // output:  number of deposits for the period

   // Output manipulator settings.
   cout << setioflags (ios::fixed | ios::showpoint) << setprecision (2);
   start_balance = 0.0;     // inline for driver; read in function for
                            //    actual program
   process_transactions(start_balance, current_balance,
                        num_checks, num_deps);
```

```
// Display results inline for driver; in function for actual
//    program.
cout << "Starting balance " << start_balance << endl;
cout << "Ending balance " << current_balance << endl;
cout << "Number of checks processed " << num_checks << endl;
cout << "Number of deposits processed " << num_deps << endl;
cout << "End of test" << endl;
return;
}
```

Test data for driver program:

```
transaction_code        C
transaction_amount      100.00

transaction_code        D
transaction_amount      100.00

transaction_code        C
transaction_amount      -5.00

transaction_code        C
transaction_amount      0.00

transaction_code        D
transaction_amount      -5.00

transaction_code        D
transaction_amount      0.00

transaction_code        P
transaction_amount      5.00

transaction_code        Q
```

Chapter 7

Section 7.1

1.
```
const int maxint = 32767;              valid integer
   const int minint = -maxint;           valid integer
   const char last_char = 'z';           valid character

   const int max_size = 50;              valid integer
   const int min_size = max_size - 10;   valid integer
   const int id = 4FD6;                  invalid: integer cannot contain letters

   const int koffman_age = 47;           valid integer
   const int friedman_age = z59;         invalid: integer cannot contain letters

   const float price = $3,335.50;        invalid: float cannot contain $
   const float price = 3335.50;          valid: float
   const float price = "3335.50";        invalid: float cannot contain quotes
```

3. The difference between the #define and the const declaration is that the identifier used in the #define has no storage associated with it. The #define is a compiler directive that tells the compiler to associate a constant with a particular identifier. Using a const declaration involves placing the constant value in a storage location. The contents of this storage location cannot be changed during program execution.

Section 7.2

1. $2^{15} - 1$ (32767)
3. The largest value is 25, when x is 5.0.
   The smallest value is 23, when x is .1.

Section 7.3

CONDITION	COMPLEMENT
1. a) x <= y && x != 15	x > y || x = 15
b) x <= y && x != 15 || z == 7.5	x > y || x == 15 && z != 7.5
c) x != 15 || z == 7.5 && x <= y	x == 15 && z != 7.5 || x > y
d) flag || ! (x != 15.7)	!flag && x != 15.7
e) !flag && x <= 8	flag || x > 8

Section 7.4

1. a) int ('D') - int ('A')
   68 – 65 = 3
   b) char ((int ('M') - int ('A')) + int ('a'))
   77 – 65 + 97
   c) int ('m') - int ('a')
   109 – 97 = 12
   d) int ('5') - int ('0')
   53 – 48 = 5

	TYPE	VALUE	EXPLANATION
3. a) isdigit ('8');	int	Nonzero	'8' is the character representation of a digit.
b) isdigit ('A');	int	0	'A' is not the character representation of a digit.
c) isdigit (7);	int	0	7 is not the character representation of a digit.
d) toupper ('#');	char	'#'	# has no upper- or lowercase.
e) tolower ('Q');	char	'q'	'Q' is uppercase; returns corresponding lowercase.
f) to_digit ('6', i);	int	1, i = 6	'6' is the character representation of a digit; returns the digit equivalent in i.

Section 7.5

1. Integer values 0, 1, 2, 3, 4, 5, 6, and 7 for variable i will provide a meaningful result in expense_category (i).

3. a) `enum logical {true, false};`   valid
   b) `enum letters {A, B, C, D};`   valid
      `enum two_letters {A, B};`   invalid: no identifier may be used more than once in any enumeration within the same scope of definition.
   c) `enum day {sun, mon, tue, wed, thur, fri, sat};`   valid
      `enum week_day {mon, tue, wed, thu, fri};`   invalid: see reason in part b above.
      `enum week_end {sat, sun};`   invalid: see reason in part b above.
   d) `enum traffic_light {red, yellow, green};`   valid
      `int green; invalid:`   see reason in part b above.

Chapter 8

Section 8.1

1. Using `cin` instead of `cin.get` in Example 8.5 would cause the program to wait indefinitely for input because `cin` skips over the newline character.
3. If `cout.put (nwln)` were omitted from the program, the output after the end of the inner loop (`"The number of blanks ..."`) would appear on the same line as the last character output.
5. If there are no data in the input stream, the loops will not execute. If an end-of-file is entered, `line_count` will display as 0 and the program will terminate. If no end-of-file is entered, the program will wait indefinitely for data to be entered.

Section 8.3

1. The `e` is read in the loop in function `copy_line`. It is written to the output file. The `s` is read next and written to the output file. The `.` is read next and written to the output file. The `<nwln>` is read next, causing control to drop out of the loop. `<nwln>` is written to the output file. Control passes back to main. `Line_count` is incremented. Since end-of-file is true, control drops out of the loop. Statistics are displayed on the screen, files are closed, and execution is terminated.
3. Some advantages of using external (permanent) files for program input and output are:

   a) The input data can be reused without being reentered. This is especially helpful while you are debugging your program.
   b) The input data can be examined and edited.
   c) The output information can be printed and examined as often as needed.
   d) The output information can be used as input data for another program.

Section 8.4

1. a) Trailing blanks at the end of the employee name data lines in the input stream for the Payroll Program would be copied to the output file. Trailing blanks at the end of the salary data lines would be skipped over by function `skip_newline`. Therefore, no problems or errors would occur.
   b) The effect of blank lines in the input stream for the Payroll Program would cause various errors, depending upon their location. Blank lines in place of or immediately preceding the employee name data would simply be copied to the output file instead of the employee name. If the blank line were in place of the name, the program would proceed to process

the salary data, but wouldn't have an employee name to associate with those data. If the blank line were immediately preceding the employee name line, the program would attempt to read the salary data from the employee name line; this would cause the salary data to be incorrect. If the blank line were immediately preceding the salary data, the salary data would be read correctly. If the blank line were in place of the salary data, the program would attempt to read the salary data from the next employee data line, causing those data to be incorrect.

Section 8.5

1. a) Function `write_gr_heading` looks for a sentinel value to end the student name. It returns to `process_one_student` with the value of `success` only if this sentinel value is encountered. Upon return, `process_one_student` processes this student's data only if the value of `write_gr_heading` is success; otherwise, it advances to the next student's data.

   Function `course_io` checks to be sure a course id number, grade, and number of credits are included in the data. If not, an error flag is returned to the calling function, `process_one_course`, which in turn passes this information to its calling function, `process_one_student`. `process_one_student` advances to the next student's data without further processing of this student if an error occurs.

   Function `process_one_course` validates the grade and the credits returned from `course_io`. If an error occurs, `process_one_course` returns this information to its calling function, `process_one_student`. `process_one_student` then advances to the next student's data without further processing of this student.

   Note that for all of the above scenarios, no advance to the next student occurs if the flag indicates end-of-file.

   b) The code could check to be sure a student name was actually read prior to the sentinel character in `write_gr_heading`. If no student name exists, `process_one_student` should advance to the next student's data.

3.
```
io_status write_gr_heading
   (ifstream&,                  // IN: student data file stream
    ofstream&,                  // OUT: grade report file stream
    int,                        // IN: semester of report
    int);                       // IN: year of report

io_status process_one_course
   (ifstream&,                  // IN: student data file stream
    ofstream&,                  // OUT: grade report file stream
    int&,                       // INOUT: total credits earned
    int&,                       // INOUT: total credits toward GPA
    int&,                       // INOUT: total points toward GPA
    int&);                      // OUT: course error flag

float compute_average
   (int,                        // IN: total credits toward GPA
    int);                       // IN: total points toward GPA

void write_summary
   (ofstream&,                  // OUT: grade report file stream
    int,                        // IN: total credits earned
    int,                        // IN: total credits toward GPA
```

```
         int,                        // IN: total points toward GPA
         float);                     // IN: student grade point average
                                     //     (GPA)

   io_status advance_record
     (ifstream&);                    // INOUT: student data file stream
```

Chapter 9

Section 9.1

1. x3 is a simple variable. A single value is associated with this single memory location. x[3] is a part of a collection of variables, called an array, all having the same data type. An array is a structured variable. x[3] refers to the fourth element in this array.

3. a) `complex x[1000];`
   b) `float x[saturday + 1];`

Section 9.2

1. No, it is not necessary to use all of the array elements. If the array is initialized at the time of its declaration, any array elements not explicitly initialized through the list will be assigned a value of 0.

Section 9.3

1. When several items in an array of data are to be processed, it is generally better to pass that entire array to a function rather than to call the function with one array element at a time. For example, to print an array of test scores, the entire array of scores, rather than each individual score, could be passed to a function that would then print each score.

3. The function `max_element` can be renamed `min_element` and changed to return the index of the smallest array element. The > should be changed to < in the `if` statement. The variable `max_index` should be changed to `min_index`. This doesn't affect program execution, but it certainly improves readability.

5.
```
void exchange
   (char& a1,       // item to exchange with a2
    char& a2)       // item to exchange with a1

// Pre: a1, a2 are defined.
// Post: contents of a1 are exchanged with the contents of a2.

{
   // Local data ...
   char temp;       // stores (saves) contents of a1 prior to moving
                    //    contents of a2 into a1

   temp = a1;
   a1 = a2;
   a2 = temp;
   return;
}  // end exchange
```

```
int same_array
  (int size,           // IN: size of the arrays
   const char a[ ],     // IN: char array to be compared to array b
   const char b[ ])     // IN: char array to be compared to array a

// Pre:  a[i] and b[i]  (0 <= i <= size-1) are assigned values.
// Post: Returns 1 (true) if a[i] == b[i] for all i in range 0..
//       size-1; otherwise, returns 0 (false).

for (int i = 0;
     i < size - 1&& a[i] == b[i];
     i++);

return a[i] == b[i];

}  // end same_array
```

Section 9.4

1. Enter_int needs to be changed to read and return a floating-point, not integer, value. Its name should be changed to enter_float to avoid confusion (float enter_float). Local data n must be changed from int to float. The user prompt needs to be changed to prompt for a floating-point, not integer, value. All input arguments must be changed from int to float.

   In read_scores, the int array scores must be changed to float. Local data sentinel, min_score, max_score, and temp_score must be changed from int to float. The prototype and call to function enter_int must be changed as described above to refer to enter_float.

3. The while loop prevents the user from entering more than max_size scores.

5. Any value within the valid range could be passed in place of a "real" sentinel value. Since the integer read is first checked to be sure it is within the valid range, no comparison will be made to the "sentinel value" when the data are valid. (OR evaluates to true if either condition is true. The second condition isn't checked as long as the first condition is true.) When the data are invalid, both conditions are false and the loop will continue to prompt for valid data.

Section 9.5

1. a) not_found is set to 0. The array subscript of the item matching target is returned to the calling function.

   b) not_found is set to 0. The array subscript of the *first* item matching target is returned to the calling function.

3. We could use a function find_max to arrange the data items in the array in descending order. We should also change the variable min_sub to max_sub to improve readability.

5.
```
void exchange
  (int& a1,       // item to exchange with a2
   int& a2)       // item to exchange with a1

// Pre:  a1, a2 are defined.
// Post: contents of a1 are exchanged with the contents of a2.

{
// Local data ...
```

```
        int temp;         // stores (saves) contents of a1 prior to moving
                          //    contents of a2 into a1

    temp = a1;
    a1 = a2;
    a2 = temp;
    return;

} // end exchange
```

Section 9.6

1. J u d i t h   A .   O ' S h e a \ 0 ? ? ?
   [0] [1] [2] [3] [4] [5] [6] [7] [8] [9] [10] [11] [12] [13] [14] [15] [16] [17] [18] [19]

3. When cin is scanning a string with more characters than will fit in a specified string variable, the excess characters are ignored. No error messages are generated.

5. Beginning with the first item (subscript 0) in the arrays:
   1. Compare the ith item of array s1 and array s2.
      1.1. If items are the same: increment i.
      1.2. If items are different:
           1.2.1. If item in s1 is less than item in s2: return a value < 0.
           1.2.2. If item in s2 is less than item in s1: return a value > 0.
   2. Return value of 0 (all items matched).

Section 9.7

```
1. const str_len = 20;
   struct part
   {
       int part_num;            // part number
       char descript[ str_len]; // description of part
       int qoh;                 // quantity of part on hand
       float price              // price of part
   };
```

Section 9.8

```
1. a) void print_employee
        (employee one_organist)   // IN: one variable structure
                                  //     employee

      // Pre:  one_organist is defined
      // Post: all members of variable one_organist are printed

      {
         cout << "Employee Id:              " << one_organist.id
              << endl;
         cout << "Employee Name:            " << one_organist.name
              << endl;
         cout << "Employee Gender:          " << one_organist.gender
              << endl;
         cout << "Employee  # of Dependents: "
              << one_organist.num_depend << endl;
```

```
        cout << "Employee Pay Rate:       " << one_organist.rate
            << endl;
        return;
    }  // end print_employee
b) void assign_employee
    (employee emp_1;     // IN: structure variable to be copied from
     employee& emp_2)    // OUT:  structure variable to be copied to

   // Pre:  emp_1 is defined
   // Post: each member of emp_1 and emp_2 contain the same
   //       information

   {
      emp_2 = emp_1;
      return;
   }  // end assign_employee
c) employee this_one, that_one;        // declare 2 variables of
                                       //    structure employee

   print_employee(this_one);           // print_employee prints
                                       //    each member

   assign_employee(this_one, that_one); // copies all members from
                                       //    this_one to that_one
```

d) The num_depend member of organist is incremented by 2.

Section 9.9

1. new_address is type address.

Section 9.10

1. Twenty bytes, the size of the largest variant, are required to store each variant.

Chapter 10

Section 10.1

1. The librarian, normally one of the programmers, assumes the responsibility for determining the status of each module in the system. The librarian must keep track of the date that each new version of a module is inserted in the library. It is also the librarian's job to make sure that all programmers are using the latest version of any module. The systems analyst is responsible for developing the specifications for the software needed by an organization. The analyst must then be sure the software is developed and performs according to these specifications.

Section 10.2

1. The six phases are:

- Requirements specification
- Problem analysis
- Program design
- Program implementation
- Testing and validation
- Operation, follow-up, and maintenance

The longest cycle is generally the operation, follow-up, and maintenance cycle.

Section 10.3

1. Before a library function can be called, the calling function must know the function name, the number and type of arguments, and the return value expected.

Section 10.4

1. a)

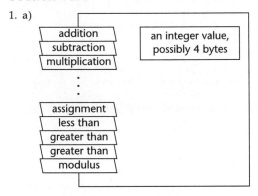

b) The operations and functions for type `char` are the same as for type `int`; however, doing arithmetic on character values without explicit recasting is not recommended.

Section 10.5

1. a) executes n times for each i, or n^2 times; $O(n^2)$.
   b) executes 2 times for each i, or $2n$ times; $O(n)$.
   c) executes n times for each i, or n^2 times; $O(n^2)$.

Section 10.6

1. a) whitebox test data:

min_n	max_n	n
0	100	100
0	100	0
0	100	50
0	100	101
0	100	−1
100	0	
0	0	0

b) blackbox test data:

min_n	max_n	n
0	100	100
0	100	0
0	100	50
0	100	101
0	100	−1
100	0	
0	0	0

The test data are the same for both white- and blackbox testing due to the simplicity of the function. The interactive information essentially describes the workings of this function.

Section 10.7

1. assert: min_n <= max_n
   invariant: n is the first data value read that has a value between min_n and max_n (inclusive)

3. invariant: -20 <= celsius <= 20; fahrenheit = 1.8 * celsius + 32

5. No, the invariant no longer holds true. Since the initial read is not performed prior to testing the loop condition, it is possible for the sentinel value to be processed in the loop body. This would invalidate the invariant.

Chapter 11

Section 11.1

1. The scope resolution operator :: is used as a prefix to the function names of each member function header. This operator tells the compiler that the function being defined is a member of the class named just preceding the operator.

Section 11.3

1. The definition section is usually divided into two sections—public and private. The public section describes the interface of the class with other program components that use the class. This interface consists of the specifications of the variables, types, constants, and function prototypes. The class definition section may also contain a private section in which the variables, constants, data types, and function prototypes to be hidden from other program components are specified.

   The implementation section contains the actual implementation of the class member functions. This information is hidden from the class users, which do not need to know these details.

Section 11.4

```
1. // day class constructor
   day :: day ( )
   {
   valid = false;
   }
```

When the object today is created using the declaration day today;, memory is allocated for class member variable valid. The day constructor is executed at the time today is declared, resulting in the initialization of valid to false.

Section 11.5

1. Attributes for square class (private):

```
side (float)                  — side of the square
area (float)                  — area of the square
perimeter (float)             — perimeter of the square
```

Methods for square class (public):

```
get_known_attributes          — reads and stores the value of the side
compute_area                  — computes the area of the square (area = side²)
compute_perimeter             — computes the perimeter of the square (perimeter =
                                 2 × side)
display_attributes            — displays attributes of the square
```

Section 11.6 (optional)

1. a) $34 - 13i$
   b) $3 - 4i$
   c) 5
3. z = cadd (w, cmult(x, y));
   The use of operators rather than functions provides a more convenient and concise reference that is easier to read and write.

5. a) rational_number x;
   b) rational_number y (2,5);

   c) i. $\dfrac{a \times d + b \times c}{b \times d}$

      ii. $\dfrac{a \times c}{b \times d}$

   d)
```
int rat_eq (rational_number x, y)
   // Pre:  x and y are defined (a, c are numerators; b, d are
   //       denominators).
   // Post: returns 1 (true) when x and y are equal; otherwise,
   //       returns 0 (false).

   {
      if ((a == c) && (b == d))
         return 1;
      else
         return 0;
      // could also be coded as return (a == c) && (b == d);
   } // end rat_eq
```

   e)
```
int rat_lt (rational_number x, y)
   // Pre:  x, y are defined (a, c are numerators; b, d are
   //       denominators).
   // Post: returns 1 (true) when x < y; otherwise, returns 0
   //       (false).
```

```
    {
        int denom;        // common denominator
        int xnum, ynum;  // numerators

        denom = b * d;   // determine common denominator
        xnum = denom / b * a;
        ynum = denom / d * c;

        if (xnum < ynum)
            return 1;
        else
            return 0;
        // could also be coded return (xnum < ynum);
    }  // end rat_lt
```

Chapter 12

Section 12.2

1. The function `enter_cat` continues looping until a valid category, or 0 to quit, is entered.

3.
```
float compute_grand_total
    (float_index_coll_v2 expenses)

// Pre:  collection is defined.
// Post: grand_total is the sum of all expense amounts.

{
    // Local data ...
    float g_tot;

    g_tot = 0.0;
    for (int i = 0; i < get_size (); i++)
        g_tot += expenses.retrieve (i);
    return g_tot;
}  // end calc_grand-total
```

Several changes are required in the main function. Variable `grand_total` is no longer initialized in the main function. `Grand_total` is no longer needed in function `post_transactions`, so it is not passed to this function. Function `compute_grand_total` must be called following the return from `post_transactions`. The main function code appears as follows:

```
transaction_count = 0;
post_transactions (expenses, transaction_count, quit);
grand_total = compute_grand_total (expenses);
display_report (expenses, grand_total, transaction_count);
return;
```

Section 12.3

```
1. #ifndef TMPLXV2_H_
   #define TMPLXV2_H_

   #include <stdlib.h>
   #include <iostream.h>

   template <class T>
   class index_coll_v2
   {
      public:
         // Member functions ....
         // CONSTRUCTOR FOR COLLECTION
         index_coll_v2
            (int sz = max_size  // IN:  number of elements in collection
             T value)           // IN:  initialization value
         {
            size = sz;
            count = 0;
            collection = new T [size];
            // construct array of size specified by user (or by
            //    default).
            if (collection == 0)
            {
               cerr << endl;
               cerr << "*** ERROR:  In index_coll_v1:  allocator "
                    << "failed" << endl;
               cerr << "to execute correctly.  Execution terminated."
                    << endl;
               exit (EXIT_FAILURE);
            }  // end if
         init ( value );
         }  // end constructor

         // DESTRUCTOR FOR COLLECTION
         ~index_coll_v2 ( )
         {
            delete [ ] collection;
         }

         // STORE AN ITEM IN DESIGNATED COLLECTION ELEMENT
         void store
            (int index,         // IN: index of store in collection
             T value)           // IN: value to be stored
         // Pre:  Index must be greater than or equal to zero and less
         //       than size
         // Post: Value of type T is stored at collection[index]
         {
            if ((index < 0)  || (index > size-1))
            {
               cerr << endl;
               cerr << "*** ERROR: In index_coll_v2::store: index"
                    << endl;
```

```
            cerr << " is out of range.  Execution terminated."
                 << endl;
            exit (EXIT_FAILURE);
        }
        count++;
        collection[index] = value;
    }  // end store

    // RETRIEVE AN ITEM FROM DESIGNATED COLLECTION ELEMENT
    T retrieve
      (int index)            // IN: index of retrieval
    // Pre:  Index must be greater than or equal to zero and less
    //       than size
    // Post: Returns contents of cell indicated by index
    {
        if ((index < 0) || (index > size-1))
        {
            cerr << endl;
            cerr << "*** ERROR: In index_coll_v2::retrieve: index"
                 << endl;
            cerr << " is out of range.  Execution terminated."
                 << endl;
            exit (EXIT_FAILURE);
        }  // endif
        return collection[index];
    }  // end retrieve

    // RETURN THE NUMBER OF ELEMENTS STORED IN COLLECTION
    int get_count ()
    {
        return count;
    }  // end get_count

    // RETURN MAXIMUM NUMBER OF ELEMENTS
    int get_size ()
    {
        return size;
    }  // end get_size

private:
    // Data members ...
    T* collection; // pointer to collection of type T objects
    int size;      // size of the array
    int count;     // number of elements stored in collection
    enum {max_size = 25};

    // INITIALIZES STORAGE ELEMENTS TO SPECIFIED VALUE
    void init
      (T value)      // value to be in initialization
```

```
        // Pre:    All collection elements undefined
        // Post:   All collection elements set to value
        {
            // Perform initialization
            for (int i = 0; i < size; i++)
                collection[i] = value;
        }  // end init
};
#endif  // TMPLXV2_H_
```

Section 12.4

1.

APPLICATION	DESIRED INDEX SET	CONVERSION
a) Floor space area associated with each room in your house	enumeration: enum rooms {living_room, dining_room, kitchen, den, bath, bed1, bed2, bed3};	These enumerators can be used as subscripts as long as the array in question has at least eight elements.
b) Number of students in each grade of an elementary school (K through 6).	integer: 0 through 6; here 0 represents K.	No conversion required.
c) The legal special characters such as ., +, *, {, etc.	character: range from first to last special character.	Define subscript via a search to find the index of the desired character. (Range depends on the number of special characters.)

3. If the character to be processed is neither an uppercase nor a lowercase letter, it is ignored (unless, of course, it is the terminator character; in this case, control passes from the for loop to the code following this for loop in the main function). No counters are incremented.

Chapter 13

Section 13.1

1. a) The name of the array can be used to represent a pointer to the first element of the array. See Example 13.4.
   b) `name + 2`
   c) `name[2] += 1`

Section 13.2

1. The input operator >> skips all whitespace. In this situation, the code must read and process the whitespace.

Section 13.3

1. Fixed-length strings have a predefined amount of space of size n allocated. The input operator >> skips all whitespace in a fixed length string.

   Variable-length strings have no practical limitations on size. The input operator >> skips only the leading blanks and processes all other whitespaces in the variable-length strings.

3. Algorithm to insert string s2 into s1 at index i in s1. s1 and s2 are fixed-length strings:

   1.0. Test to see if combining the strings will exceed the maximum size for s1.
       1.1. If maximum size exceeded, print error message and return with function value of −1.
   2.0. Validate index.
       2.1. If index < 0, print error message and return with function value of −1.
       2.2. If index > size of s1, reset index to size of s1.
   3.0. Combine the strings.
       3.1. Determine size of s2—this is the number of characters in s1 that will need to be relocated.
       3.2. Shift the upper part of s1 to the right (including \0) to make room for s2.
       3.3. Insert s2.

5. Algorithm to insert string s2 into s1 at index i in s1. s1 and s2 are variable length strings. There is no need to be concerned with exceeding maximum length as in Self-Check Exercise 3:

   1.0. Validate index.
       1.1. If index < 0, print error message and return with function value of −1.
       1.2. If index > size of s1, reset index to size of s1.
   2.0. Combine the strings.
       2.1. Determine size of s2—this is the number of characters in s1 that will need to be relocated.
       2.2. Shift the upper part of s1 to the right (including \0) to make room for s2.
   3.3. Insert s2.

Chapter 14

Section 14.1

```
1. void print ( )
   {
       for (int vert = 0; vert < 5; vert++)
           cout << "(" << vertex[0] [vert] << ", " << vertex [1] [vert] << ")"
               << endl;
   }  // end print
```

Section 14.2

1. Layer 1: A triangle is a size 3 array of vertices.
   Layer 2: A vertex is a size 2 array of x, y coordinates.

Section 14.3

1. Layer 1: A building is a size 3 array of structures called floors.
   Layer 2: Each floor is a structure consisting of an array of rooms, count of men's rooms, and count of ladies' rooms.
   Layer 3: Rooms is a size 7 array of elements containing the size in square feet of each room.

Section 14.6

```
1. // FILE: pentagon.h
   // MODELS PENTAGON AS A POLYGON OF FIVE SIDES
   // "Inherits" features of polygon class except for the
   // function sides, which replaces the generic "sides" function
   // for polygon

   #include "Polygon.cpp"

   class pentagon
   {
       public:
           // Member functions ...
           // PROMPTS USER FOR AND READS IN VERTICES
           void print ( );

           // COMPUTES LENGTHS OF 5 SIDES
           void sides
             (double &,   ⎞
              double &,   ⎟
              double &,   ⎬  // IN:  the 5 sides...
              double &,   ⎟
              double &);  ⎠

           // COMPUTES AND RETURNS PERIMETER
           double perimeter ( );

           // COMPUTES AND RETURNS AREA
           double area ( );

       private:
           // Data members ...
           polygon<5> data;

   };  // end class pentagon




   // FILE: pentagon.cpp
   // MEMBER FUNCTIONS FOR THE PENTAGON MODELING CLASS
   // "Inherits" (uses) corresponding functions from polygon class
   // except for function sides, which is specialized for a pentagon.

   #include <math.h>

   #include "pentagon.h"

   // PROMPTS USER FOR AND READS IN VERTICES
   void pentagon::read ( )
   {
       data.read ( );
   }
```

```
// PRINTS THE VERTICES
void pentagon::print ( )
{
   data.print ( );
 }

// COMPUTES LENGTHS OF SIDES (SPECIALIZED FOR A PENTAGON)
void pentagon::sides
  (double &s1,
   double &s2,
   double &s3,   // OUT:  the lengths of the 5 sides
   double &s4,
   double &s5)
{
   // Local data ...
   double x1, x2, x3, x4, x5, y1, y2, y3, y4, y5;

   // Compute lengths of sides
   x1 = data.x (0);
   x2 = data.x (1);
   x3 = data.x (2);
   x4 = data.x (3);
   x5 = data.x (4);

   y1 = data.y (0);
   y2 = data.y (1);
   y3 = data.y (2);
   y4 = data.y (3);
   y5 = data.y (4);

   s1 = sqrt ((x2 - x1) * (x2 - x1) + (y2 - y1) * (y2 - y1));
   s2 = sqrt ((x3 - x2) * (x3 - x2) + (y3 - y2) * (y3 - y2));
   s3 = sqrt ((x4 - x3) * (x4 - x3) + (y4 - y3) * (y4 - y3));
   s4 = sqrt ((x5 - x4) * (x5 - x4) + (y5 - y4) * (y5 - y4));
   s5 = sqrt ((x1 - x5) * (x1 - x5) + (y1 - y5) * (y1 - y5));
} // end sides

// COMPUTES THE PERIMETER
double pentagon::perimeter ( )
{
   return data.perimeter ( );
} // end perimeter

// COMPUTES THE AREA
double pentagon::area ( )
{
   return data.area ( );
} // end area
```

Section 14.7

1. a) The value displayed is 3. This statement is valid in the main function because the variable nmbr_students is declared in the main function. nmbr_students is also used to identify a member of the gradebook class. This reference is therefore also legal in any member function of the gradebook class. nmbr_students may not be referenced in the student class.

   b) The value displayed is 3. This statement is redundant in the gradebook class and illegal otherwise since nmbr_students is a private member of the gradebook class.

   c) Invalid—score is not declared as a variable in the main function, the gradebook class, or the student class.

   d) The value displayed is 10.0.

   e) Invalid—stddev is a member of the gradebook class, not a member of all_students.

   f) Invalid—There are only three student objects. all_students[3] is out of range.

   g) Invalid—There are only three student objects. all_students[3] is out of range.

   h) Invalid—Average is a member of the gradebook class, not a member of statistics.

3. In order to exchange only the point-total fields, it would be necessary to make changes to function exchange and class student. These changes would be:

   - A new function, store_points, would need to be included in the student class. Its prototype would appear as:

   ```
   void store_points (int);
   ```

   - Function exchange would need to be rewritten to call functions retrieve_points and store_points as part of the exchange process. The function arguments would remain the same. Local variable temp would be declared as an integer. The code would read:

   ```
   temp = s1.retrieve_points ( );
   s1.store_points (s2.retrieve_points ( ));
   s2.store_points (temp);
   ```

Chapter 15

Section 15.1

1.

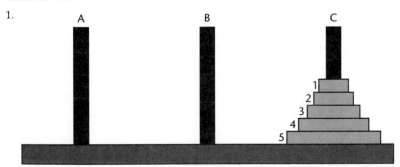

3. 1. Move 2 disks from A to B.
    2. Move 1 disk from A to C.
    3. Move 2 disks from B to C.

Section 15.2

1. The current value of n is placed on the stack each time `reverse_string` recursively calls itself. Upon return to its calling function, whether this is another function or itself, the current value gets popped off the stack. The value of n in the calling function becomes the new current value.

3. The entry displays appear in the order in which the function is recursively called. They appear prior to any exit displays because of the location of the exit displays in the function. Since the exit display is coded to occur after the recursive call to the function, it isn't executed until the stopping step is performed.

5. Trace of `multiply (5, 4)`:

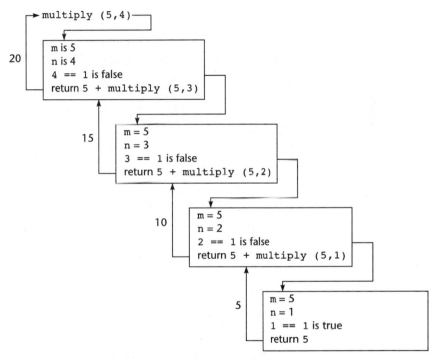

Immediately after each function call, the stacks will appear as:

CALL 1		CALL 2		CALL 3		CALL 4	
m	n	m	n	m	n	m	n
5	4	5	3	5	2	5	1
		5	4	5	3	5	2
				5	4	5	3
						5	4

Section 15.3

1. ```
int power_raiser
   (int base,
    int power)
```
```

```
{
  if (power == 0)
      return 1;
  else
      return base * power_raiser (base, power-1);
}
```

3. If the stopping condition for the fibonacci number function were just (n == 1), the function would call itself indefinitely. This occurs because not testing for (n == 2) allows n to become less than the stopping value of 1, for example, n – 2 = 0. Since the stopping value of 1 is passed over and can never be reached, 2 is continually subtracted from n, and the function continues indefinitely.

Section 15.4

1. Trace of recursive function selection_sort:

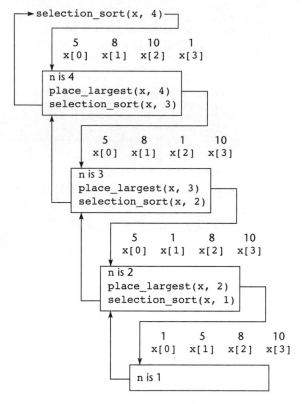

Note that the actual arrangement of values is done each time place_largest is called. No manipulation of array elements takes place at return from selection_sort.

Section 15.5

1. Sixty-three moves are needed to solve the six-disk problem. The number of moves required to solve the n-disk problem is $2n – 1$.

Section 15.6

1. Each time function `blob_count` called itself, another copy of the grid array would be made. This is much less efficient than calling function `start_blob` to make the copy one time prior to calling function `blob_count`.

Chapter 16

Section 16.1

1. a) valid—no change
   b) valid—the contents of the node pointed to by p are copied to the node pointed to by r.
   c) not valid—must use -> notation to access structure members through a pointer.
   d) not valid—cannot assign a type int value to a pointer variable.
   e) valid—p->volts becomes 0.
   f) valid—p now contains the same memory address as r.
   g) valid—q->current becomes "XY".
   h) valid—The contents of r->volts is copied to q->volts; q->volts becomes 115.

Section 16.3

1. Trace of function search for BOY, CAP, DOG:

```
list_node* search
   (list_node *head,                    head points to HAT
    const char target[])                target contains BOY

head != NULL                            true
strcmp (head->word, target) != 0        true
head = head->link                       head points to BOY

head != NULL                            true
strcmp (head->word, target) != 0        false
return head                             head points to BOY

list_node* search
   (list_node *head,                    head points to HAT
    const char target[])                target contains CAP

head != NULL                            true
strcmp (head->word, target) != 0        false
head = head->link                       head points to BOY

head != NULL                            true
strcmp (head->word, target) != 0        false
head = head->link                       head points to CAT

head != NULL                            false
return head                             head points to NULL

list_node* search
   (list_node *head,                    head points to HAT
    const char target[])                target contains DOG
```

```
head != NULL                              true
strcmp (head->word, target) != 0          true
head = head->link                         head points to BOY

head != NULL                              true
strcmp (head->word, target) != 0          true
head = head->link                         head points to CAT

head != NULL                              false
return head                               head points to DOG
```

Section 16.4

1.

STACK	OPERATION	RESULT OF OPERATION	STACK FOLLOWING OPERATION
| 2 + C /	s.push ('$')	$ is placed on top of the stack.	| 2 + c / $
| 2 + C / $	s.push ('-')	– is placed on top of the stack.	| 2 + C / $ -
| 2 + C / $ -	s.pop (next_ch)	– is removed from top of the stack; next_ch contains –.	| 2 + C / $
| 2 + C / $	s.top (next_ch)	Stack remains the same; next_ch contains $.	| 2 + C / $
| 2 + C / $	s.is_empty ( )	Stack remains the same; s.is_empty ( ) returns 0; indicating that the stack is not empty.	| 2 + C / $
| 2 + C / $	s.is_full ( )	Stack remains the same; s.is_full ( ) returns 0, indicating that the stack is not full.	| 2 + C / $

Section 16.5

1.
```
struct student
{
    var_string name;
    int score;
    char grade;
}; // end student

stack<student,50>  student_records_50;
```

Yes, the stack operators push, pop, get_top, is_empty, is_full, and stack can be used on a stack of structures in the same manner as they are used on a stack of integers, characters, or floating-point variables. Each record structure will be manipulated as a whole when the operations are performed.

Section 16.6

1. Algorithm for `copy_stack`:

    1.0. Initialize new stack.
    2.0. While the existing stack isn't empty
        2.1. Get the next item from the existing stack.
        2.2. Allocate space in the new stack.
        2.3. Copy data to new stack.
        2.4. Link to previous item in the new stack.

Section 16.7

1.

ORIGINAL QUEUE	QUEUE AFTER INSERTION OF HARRIS AND REMOVAL OF ONE PASSENGER
McMann Economy 2	Watson Business 1
Watson Business 1	Carson FirstClass 2
Carson FirstClass 2	Harris FirstClass 3

McMann is removed. There are three passengers left.

Section 16.8

1. Watson
Business
1

Dietz
Economy
3

Section 16.9

1. Following the sample run of `use_queue`, the value of `front` is 1, the value of `rear` is 2, and the value of `num_items` is 2. The names contained in the items array are:

name:	Brown	Watson	Dietz	?
	items[0]	items[1]	items[2]	items[3]

Although `Brown` is still contained in `items[0]`, this name is inaccessible due to the values of `front`, `rear`, and `num_items`.

Section 16.10

1.

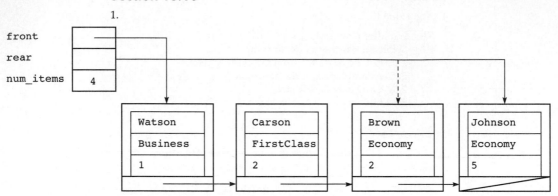

Index

Index

abstract data type (ADT), 513,
515–516
definition (specification), 515
design and use of, 727–744
implementation, 515
queue as, 830-833
stack as, 809-813
abstraction, 12, 56
data, 132, 513
of essential problem domain
characteristics, 618
and generalization, 708–724
levels of, 674–675, 730
procedural, 102–104, 132,
316–318, 507–508
acos (x), 129
activation frame
for local function data and arguments, 761
actual argument, 110
Ada, 14
addition
floating-point, 57
integer, 58–59
operator, 57–59
address, 8–9
aggregates, 434
algorithm, 32
checking correctness of an,
169–173
algorithm efficiency, 516–519
searching, 517
sorting, 517–519
aliases, avoidance of, 317–318
allocation
dynamic, 593–596
static, 593
ampersand,&, 269
ANSI (American National
Standards Institute), 6
Apple Computer, 6
argument
actual, 110
array, 444–451
call-by-reference, 271–274

call-by-value, 271–274
class object as, examples, 809–851
to constructor, 553–555
correspondence, 120–121
default value, 592
formal, 110
input, 108–109
in/out, 262
list correspondence for functions,
283-286
list length, 286
list writing (formal), 273
matching errors, in strings, 686
output, 269–283
passing, 115–117
reference, 269–286
scope of definition, 121
substitution, 121
in template functions, 620–624
to new, 596
type consistency, 121
type conversion, 122
use, 111–124
validation, 263, 510
value, 108-110
arithmetic
floating-point, 57
integer, 58–59
overflow, 339
pointer, 655–657
type, 57–59
underflow, 339
arithmetic expressions
mixed-type, 62
rules for evaluation, 63
arithmetic-logic unit (ALU), 10
arithmetic operators
complete table of, 869–870
initial table of, 46
array
as arguments, 444–451
base elements of, 435–437, 702
const, example, 447–448
constructor and, 593–596
declaration, 434, 437

delete and, 593–596
dimension, 437
dynamic allocation, 593–594
exchanging elements of, 445–446
finding minimum and maximum
values in, 450–452
initialization, 619
manipulation of elements, 435
multidimensional, 698–702
new and, 593–596
operator [], 435–437
and pointers, 593–594
reading part of, 452–456
search, 456–459
sequential procesing of, 441–444
sort, 459–463
subscript, 435–437
unsubscripted references, 488
array elements
selection for processing, 439–443
arrays
of arrays, 698–702
of characters, 463–472
of class elements, 706–708
of structs, 703–706
ASCII character set, 342, 861
asin(x), 129
assembly language, 16–17
<assert.h>, 125
assertions, 522–529
assignment
mixed-type, 64–66
operator (=), 46
operator (+-), 214
to pointer, 792–794
statement, 45
atan (x), 129, 864
Atanasoff, John, 3
atoi ( ), 864
AT&T Bell Laboratories, 5
attaching (connecting) streams and
external files, 383–386
Augusta, Ada, 5
automatic initialization, using constructors, 553

Babbage, Charles, 5
\, backslash, 101
Backus, John, 5
bad ( ), 408
bars, 22
base class, 610
BASIC, 14
batch mode, 71–73
batch processing, 381–382
    versus interactive processing,
        381–382
binary digit, 333
bit, 9, 333
black-box testing, 521
booting a computer, 22
Borland C++, Version 3.1, 24
boundaries (loop), 248
boundary case verification, 526
break statement, 189–190
    proper use of, 191–192
breakpoints, 248–249
Bricklin, Dan, 6
buffer register, 10
byte, 9

C, 5–6
C++
    evolution of, 5–6
    libraries, 124-132
    library header file, 37
    library table, 125
    standardization, 15
call
    argument passing mechanisms,
        271–274
    function, with arguments, 119
    function, without arguments,
        96–107
    function, invalid examples, 285
    to member function, 542–545
    by reference, 271–274
    by value, 271–274
    to virtual function, 871
cancellation error, 339
case, 189–190
case label, 189–190
Case Studies
    Areas and Perimeters of
        Different Figures Revisited,
        555
    Assigning Final Grades for a
        Semester, 727–745

Checking Account Balance
    Problem, 303–315
Computing Interest Dividends,
    177–181
Computing Overtime Pay,
    174–176
Converting Units of
    Measurement, 34–37
Counting Cells in a Blob, 780–784
Cryptogram Generator, 625
Drawing Simple Figures, 93–95
Evaluating Postfix Expressions,
    812–819
Finding Alphabetically First
    Letter, 169–172
Finding the Area and
    Circumference of a Circle,
    89–92
Finding the Value of a Coin
    Collection, 59–62
General Sum and Average
    Problem, 287–301
Home Budget Problem, 596–609
Maintaining a Queue of
    Passengers, 833–840
Preparing a Payroll File, 391–398
Preparing Semester Grade
    Reports, 398–421
Printing a Form Letter, 663–674
Recursive Selection Sort, 773–775
Sorting Three Numbers, 277–282
Telephone Directory, 504–507
Towers of Hanoi, 776–779
cast
    operator, 122, 344
    use for argument type conver-
        sion, 122
CDC character set, 862
ceil(x), 129
central processing unit (CPU), 10
cerr, standard error stream, 388
char
    integer representation, 342–343
    type, 42, 67–70
char_bit, 335
character
    constant, 67
    control (non-printable), 349
    as enumerator value, 356
    \, escape, 68
    functions, 348–353
    functions, table of, 350

internal representation, 342–343
lowercase, 40
printable, 349
reading into a string, 657–661
set, ASCII, 342, 861
set, CDC, 862
set, EBCDIC, 862
special, 40
special pairs, 38
string, 38
string, referencing elements in,
    656–657
string versus a character, 464
uppercase, 40
used with relational operators,
    348–349
variables, 348–353
checking boundary values, 342
cin, 47
    with external streams, 397
    processing newline character,
        372–378
    processing white space, 374–378
    use for reading, 374–382
circle
    area and circumference, 91, 112,
        555–558
    drawing, 93–95
    perimeter, 555–558
class, 514, 539–547
    attributes (data members), 541
    attributes, initialization, 637
    base, 610
    as building blocks, for software,
        610
    complex numbers, 566–572
    constructor, 553–555, 639
    container, 617
    data member declaration, 541–542
    data members (attributes), 541
    defining an ADT, 539
    definition section, 540
    derived, 565
    design of, 636
    destructor, 595–596, 639
    diagram, 541–542
    encapsulation in, 514
    extensions to, 596–600, 609
    header part of, 542
    generalization, 565
    implementation guidelines, 636
    implementation section, 540

indexed collection classes, 587–594 , 597–600
instance (object), 544
interface, 538–542
member, private, 541
member, public, 541
member data, 541
member data access, 577
member function declaration, 545
member function definition, 546–547
member functions, 541
prefix, for member function reference, 544
private section, 540
and problem analysis, 555
public section, 540
and software design, 555
specialization, 565, 610
stack class template, 809–813
storage attributes (*see also* data members), 541
versus struct, 547
template, 615–616
variable length string class, 676–685
clear ( ), 666
client (of a class), 545
clients (people), 499
close ( ), 387
COBOL, 14
cohesive functions, 264–265
collating sequence, 352
collection, general
data and function members, 588
comma operator, 869–870
comments
/* */, 54–56
//, 37, 54–56
in functions, 101
comparisons
involving enumeration types, 358
Compatible Time Sharing System (CTSS), 5
compilation
conditional, 247
separate, 675–676, 726, 745, 840
compiler directive, 37, 43
complement (of a logical expression), 346–347
complex number, 567
absolute value, 570

arithmetic, 567–568
assignment, 567–568
conjugate, 570
equality operators, 569–570
imaginary part, 567
input, 571
output, 571
real part, 567
relational operators, 569–570
complex number class, 566–572
<complex.h>, 566
complexity, managing, 32, 511
component
reuse, 618–624
composition operator
used with manipulators, 167
compound statements, 142–143
computer, 2
cost, 2
electronic, 2
electronic mail, 7
laptop, 6
network, 7
notebook, 6
personal, 2
size, 2
stand-alone, 7
stored-program, 3
supercomputer, 7
computer system environment, 21
Borland C++, Version 3.1, 24
networked, 22
timeshared, 21
computing
history of, 4–6
concatenation, 651, 654–655, 679, 684–685
condition, 144
conditional compilation, 247
conditional loop, 215–218, 237
connecting (attaching) streams and external files, 383–386, 424
constant
character, 67
declaration, 41
enumeration (enumerator), 353–358
expression, 437
floating-point, 57
global, 115
identifier, 43, 330–331
integer, 58

numeric, 335
special, 335–336
used to enhance readability and maintenance, 165
constructor
and array, 593–596
and automatic initialization, 553–555
and class, 553–555
and destructor, 593–596
and heap, 593–596
and new, 593–596
header, 592
container class, 617
control language commands, 22
control statements, 143
if, 151–157
control structures, 142–143
categories of, 142
control unit, 10
controlled access to data, 512
conversion
in argument passing, 119–123, 133–134, 320
arithmetic, 56–58, 343–345
by assignment, 56–58, 343–345
explicit type, 344–345
implicit, 343–344
by integral promotion, 343–344
letters to integers (for grades), 417–418
numeric, 343–344
by return, 119–123, 134–135
sequence of characters to integer on input, 378–381
by type casting, 343–344
value-preserving, 343
copying
files, 383–386
correspondence
argument 120–121
cos(x), 129
cost
computer, 2
software, 502
counter-controlled (or counting) loop, 205, 215–218, 227
cout, 47
with external streams, 397
use for writing, 374–382
Cray-1, 5
creating a linked list, 805

cryptogram generator, 625
<ctype.h>, 125, 349
cursor, 50

data
    abstraction, 512
    access control, 512
    access windows, 514
    analysis, 87
    identification and description, 86
    scope of definition, 512
    visibility, 512
data members, of a class (*see also* storage attributes), 541
data requirements table, 35, 500
data structure chart, 730
data types
    basic (pre-defined, or built-in), 42, 56–57
    integral, 334, 342
    internal representations of, 332–346
    ordinal, 70
    simple (or scalar), 330, 434
    structured, 434–492
    user-defined, 354, 538
data views
    logical, 513
    physical, 513
database, 504
dbl_dig, 336
dbl_epsilon, 336
debug flags, 247
debugger programs (use of), 248–249
debugging, 74, 246–249, 318–320
DEC, 5
    PDP-7, 5
    VAX 11-780, 5
declaration
    array, 437
    class, 545
    constant, 41
    enumerator, 355
    in for statement, 233–234
    function (prototype), 97
    local (to functions), 100
    pointer, 595–596
    statement, 41–44
    template class, 615–616
    template function, 620–622
    type, 616

typedef, 616
    variable, 41
decomposition
    data oriented, 511–515, 586, 618, 727
    functional, 103, 132
decrement operator, 207–208
default statement, 190–192
default value
    argument, 592
#define, 331, 386, 404–405
delete, 595–596, 638
DeMorgan's Theorem (viewed in C++), 347
dereferencing operator, ->, 795–798, 850
derived class, 565
design
    and classes, 636
    process and functions, 260–265
destructor, 595
    and delete, 595
device
    input, 8
    output, 8
    storage, 11–12
diagnostic statement, 246
digit characters, conversion, 378–380
direct access search, 625
directory, 11
    subdirectory, 11
disk, 11
    floppy, 11
    hard, 11
disk directory, 11, 382–383
    subdirectory, 11
disk drive, 11
display
    user instructions, 105–106
distinctions among integral types, 358–359
divide and conquer, 33
division
    integer, 58-59, 336–338
    floating-point, 57
    operator, 57–59, 336
    by zero, 388
do-while statement, 237–240
    difference from while loop, 237
    review, 240–242
    syntax, 237–238

used to control a menu-driven program, 238–239
documentation, 54, 87
dot operator, . , 475–476, 542-544
double, 334
downloading (a file), 22
draw
    circle, 93–95
    intersecting lines, 93–95
    rectangles, 104
    triangle, 93–95
driver program, 263–264
dynamic allocation
    in constructor, 593–596
    using new, 792–793, 799–800
dynamic data structures, 792–852
    connecting nodes, 798–799
    and the delete operator, 800–801
    and the heap, 799–801
    and the new operator, 792–793, 799–800
    and pointers, 792–793

EBCDIC character set, 862
echo print, 73, 382
Eckert, John Presper, 5
editor, 18, 24
electronic computer, 2
else, 154
else if, 184
encapsulation, 512, 514–515
    in a class, 514
end of file (eof), 378, 387
    reading past, 425
#endif, 405
endl, 167
ENIAC, 3, 5
enum, 353–357
enumeration type, 353–362
    comparisons involving, 358
    declarations, 355
    motivation for using, 360–361
    values, reading and writing, 359–360
    variables as loop control variables in for statements, 357–358
enumerator
    default association, 354
    list, 354
    values, 354
equality operators, 144–145

errors
  cancellation, 339
  detection and recovery, 421
  handling on input, 391–420
  link, 77
  logic, 79
  off-by-one, 247–248
  representational, 338
  run-time, 78–79
  syntax, 75–77
escape character, 101
ethics, 530-531
Euclid's algorithm, greatest com-
    mon divisor, 770–772
exchange, 445–446, 459–463
executable file
  building for execution, 675–676,
    726, 745, 840
executable statements, 44–52
EXIT_FAILURE, 386
EXIT_SUCCESS, 386
exp ( ), 129
explicit type conversion, 344–345
expression
  complement, 346–347
  evaluation, 812–819
  logical, 143–151, 346–348
external files
  accessing and using, 382–387
  disk directory, 382–387
  and streams, 381–387

fabs ( ), 129
factorial example, 768–770
fail ( ), 386–387
fibonacci numbers, example, 770
FIFO, first-in-first-out structure, 830
file extensions
  .h, 542
  .cpp, 542
file names, 383
  external, 383
  three letter extensions, 383
files, 11
  copying, 383–386
  external, processing examples,
    663–674
  input, 11
  library header, 37
  load, 18
  object, 18
  output, 11

program, 11, 18
source, 18
and streams, 372–382
fixed, 166–168, 424
flag-controlled loops, 225–227
  general structural pattern, 226
flags, 165-168
  debug, 247
  status, 225
float, 42, 57, 334
<float.h>, 125, 335
floating-point, 42, 57
  implementation dependency, 334
  internal representation, 332–333
  manipulation problems, 339
  variations of, 334
floor ( ), 129
flow of control, 102
flt_dig, 336
flt_epsilon, 336
flt_max, 336
flt_min, 336
for statement
  examples, 233–237
  header, 227
  with input-controlled repetition,
    388–389
  introduction, 227–233
  parameter expressions, 389
  review, 240–242
  same behavior as while loop, 227
  syntax, 235–236
  using enumeration type variable
    as loop control variable in,
    357–358
formal argument, 110
  list, 114
  specification, 110
  use of, 117
formal verification, 522
formatted output, 165–168
FORTRAN, 5
Frankston, Bob, 6
fraud, 530
free store (see also heap), 594–596
<fstream.h>, 386–387
function, 38
  without arguments, 96–107
  body, 100
  call, 96, 98
  character, 348–353
  cohesive, 264–265

declaration, 97
definition, 95–101
  in the design process, 260–265
  documentation, 261–263
  flow of control between, 102
  generalization, 109
  header, 100
  with input arguments, 108–111
  interfaces, 290
  mathematical, 126–131
  members, of a class, 541
  multiple input, 120
  postconditions, 261–263, 528
  preconditions, 261–263, 528
  predefined, 129–131
  as program building blocks,
    124–132
  prototype (declaration), 97, 118
  recursive, 756–784
  recursive mathematical, 767–771
  with return values, 108–111
  return values used for decision
    and loop control, 265–268
  stepwise design, 287 301, 316–318
  syntax rules with argument lists,
    283-286
  transfer of control, 102
  type specification, 100
  used to implement individual
    algorithm steps, 301
  virtual, 565
function keys, 11

generalization
  of classes, 565, 726
  with respect to data abstractions,
    565
get ( ), read a character at a time,
    376–378, 387
get_line ( ), read a line at a time,
    661
global
  constant, 115
  type, example, 402–405
greatest common divisor, 770–772

hackers, 530
hand-trace, 31–33
hardware, 8
header part, of a class, 542
heap (free store), 594–596, 799–801

high level programming languages,
    14–20
    processing of, 17–20
history of computing, 4–6
Hollerith, Herman, 5

IBM, 4
IBM PC, 6
icons, 22
identifier
    constant, 43, 330–331
    local, 104
    user-defined, 41
    valid/invalid, 42
if statement, 151–157
    with compound alternatives,
        155–157
    format of, 153
    multiple-alternative decision
        form, 183–184
    nested and multiple-alternative
        decisions, 182–189
    nested versus a sequence of if
        statements, 183
    nested versus the switch state-
        ment, 192
    one alternative, 154
    two alternatives, 154
#ifndef, 404
<ifstream.h>, 386
#include, 43, 114, 541
increment operator, 207–208
independent modules
    and subproblems, 93
index
    array, 439–440
    bounds checking, 587–588
    expression, 439–440
    out-of-bounds, 587–588, 639, 687
indexed collection, 587–594,
        597–600
    ADT, 587
    data members, 587–594
    function members, 587–594
indirection operator, *, 660, 793
infix expression, 812
information hiding, 103, 512, 514-
        515, 633–634
inheritance, 565
    illustration with polygons and
        triangles, 723
    introduction to, 596–600, 610

initial read, 224
initialization, of class attributes,
        637–638
input arguments, 108–111
input file, 11
input operation, 47
input operator >>, 48–49, 372
input stream
    buffer pointer, 374–383
instance (object) of a class type, 544
instruction register, 10
int, 42, 58–59
int_max, 335
int_min, 335
integer, 42, 58–59
    code, 342
    division, 336–338
    internal representation, 332–334
    long, 334
    short, 334
    variations of, 334
integral promotions, 343–346
integral types
    distinctions among, 358–359
integration testing, 521–522
interactive mode, 71–73
interactive processing, 381–382
    versus batch processing, 381–382
internal representations of data
        types, 332–346
intersecting lines, 93-95
<iomanip.h>, 167, 372
<iostream.h>, 125, 372
isalnum ( ), 350
isalpha ( ), 350
iscntrl ( ), 350
isdigit ( ), 350
isgraph ( ), 350
islower ( ), 350
isprint ( ), 350
ispunct ( ), 350
isspace ( ), 350
isupper ( ), 350

Jobs, Steve, 6

keyboard, 10

laptop computer, 6
largest value, finding, 450–452,
        773–775
layered system, 675

ldbl_dig, 336
left, 424
libraries
    class, 575–576,
    function, 508, 575–576
LIFO, last-in-first-out structure,
        830
<limits.h>, 125, 335
linear search (array), 456–459
linked lists, 801–809
    abstract lists, 801–803
    creation of, 805–807
    empty list, 802
    list head, 801
    representation using pointers,
        802–803
    search, 808–809
    traversal, 803–804
linker, 18
linking program components
    for execution, 675–676, 726, 745,
        840
load file, 18
loader, 18
local
    (controlled) access to data, 512
    declarations, 100, 104
    identifiers, 104
    memory, 22
log ( ), 129
log10 ( ), 129
logical
    complement, 146
    expressions, 143–151, 188,
        346–348
    operators, 144–147
login/logout, 23
long double, 334
long_max, 335
long_min, 335
lookup table, 626
loop
    body, 204
    boundaries, 248
    conditional, 215–218, 237
    counter-controlled (or counting),
        205, 215–218, 227
    design, 218–227
    flag-controlled, 225–227
    generalization, 212
    infinite, 206
    initial read, 224

initialization (determining), 222–223
iteration (or pass), 206
invariants, 458, 524–528
processing, 219
repetition condition, 205, 217
sentinel-controlled, 223–225
structural pattern development, 218
used to accumulate a sum or product, 209–215
used to display a table of values, 220–222
with zero iterations, 220
loop control, 219
critical steps in, 206, 218
using function return values for decision and, 265–268
loop control variable, 206, 234–235
declared and used in for loop header, 243–244
as local variable, 229
using enumeration type variable as (in for statement), 357–358
loops
nested, 242–246
nested with multidimensional arrays, 706, 746–747

machine language, 16–17
Macintosh, 6
main memory, 8
mainframe, 4
managing complexity, 32, 511
manipulator flags, 422–424
partial table of, 423–424
manipulator member functions, 387–388, 422–424
partial table of, 423
manipulators, 165–168
partial table of, 167–168
matching
data in stream to variables in cin, 425
<math.h>, 125
mathematical functions, 126–131
partial table of, 129
mathematical induction, 525
Mauchly, John, 5
maximum value, finding in array, 450–452
member function declaration, 545

member function definition, 546–547
member functions, of a class, 541
private, examples, 627–630
public, examples, 627–630
memory, 8
addresses, 8–9
buffer register, 10
cells, 8
local, 22
main, 8
permanent, 11
secondary, 8
volatile, 11
menu-driven program (controlled by do-while), 238–239
menus, pulldown, 22
microcomputers, 6
Microsoft, 6
minicomputers, 6
minimum value, finding in array, 450–452
mixing types, 343 346
modifying a problem solution, 174
modulus
integer, 58–59, 336–338
operator, 57–59, 336
monitor, 10
mouse, 11
multidimensional arrays, 698–702
multiple declarations of identifiers in a program system, 301
multiple-alternative decision
form, 183–184
to implement a decision table, 186
order of conditions, 185
writing, 184
multiplication
integer, 58–59
floating-point, 57
operator, 57–59

'\n', newline character, 372–378
advancing past, 397
processed by cin, 372–378, 425
nested loops, 242–246
networks, 12, 22–23
new operator, 596, 639, 792–793, 799–800
notebook computer, 6
'\0', null character, 464, 650, 651
null pointer, 802

numeric constant, 335
numeric conversions, 343–346
numeric (integer) code, 342
numeric types
differences between, 332–334
numerical inaccuracies, 338–342

object file, 18
object (instance) of a class type, 544
object-oriented
paradigm, 516
programming, 516, 538
off-by-one errors, 247–248
<ofstream.h>, 386
open ( ), 386–387
operating systems, 14, 18
operator precedence, 147–148
operators (assignment), 46–47, 209–214
operators (unary)
decrement, 207–208
increment, 207–208
use of (prefix and postfix), 208
operators (used in logical expressions)
equality, 144–145
logical, 144–147
relational, 144–145
ordinal types, 70
output
arguments, 269–283
file, 11
formatted, 165–168
operation, 47
operator <<, 48, 50–51, 372

parameter matching
in template classes, 611–612, 639
in template functions, 620–622, 639
parent class, 565
parent component, 97
Pascal, 5
Pascal, Blaise, 5
passing
arguments, 115–116
return values, 115–116
Payroll Problem
introduction to, 92
peek ( ), 418
permanent memory, 11
personal computer, 2

plagiarism, 531
point
    model of, 702–707
pointer
    arithmetic, 655–657
    data type, 792–793
    declaration, 793
    indirection operator, 793
    null, 802
    in representing linked lists,
        802–803
    in structs, 794
    type declaration, 595
    variable, 595
pointers to nowhere, 687–688
polygon
    described by n points, 698–702
    model of, 708–726
post conditions, 261
postfix expression, 812
pow (), 129
precision (), 396
preconditions, 261
predefined functions, 129–131
prefix, for member function
        reference, 544
preparing files for i/o, 424
printer, 11
private, 540
private section of a class, 541
problem
    analysis, 31–33, 86–89
    constant, 35
    input, 33, 35
    output, 33, 35
    refinement, 33, 35
    solution modification, 174
problem analysis using classes, 555
problem domain
    indexes, translation to C++ array
        indexes, 634–636
    information, 618
    mapping into C++, 618
problem solving, 12–13, 86–89
    process, 86–89, 123–124
    strategy, 30–33, 86–89, 143,
        173–181
    using recursion, 756–760
procedural abstraction, 102–104,
        132, 316–318, 507–508
program debugging, 246–249
program design, 31–33, 35, 86–89
program development

from initial documentation, 87
    process, 30–33, 86–89
program file, 11
    creation of, 23
    saving, 24
program implementation, 31–33, 35,
        86
program modification
    localized change, 512
    side-effects, 512
program prompt, 38
program statements, 15
program stubs, 299
program system, 299
    debugging and testing, 318–320
    multiple declarations of identi-
        fiers in, 301
program testing, 30–33, 36, 246–249,
        318–320, 674–675
program verification, 522–529
programming-in-the-large, 498
programming language
    extensibility, 566
    standard, 15
    syntax, 15
    translator, 17
programming languages, 14–18
    Ada, 14
    assembly, 16–17
    BASIC, 14
    C, 14
    C++, 14
    FORTRAN, 14
    high level, 14–20
    machine, 16–17
    Pascal, 14
programming style, 40
programming teams, 499–500
prototype
    with arguments, 118
    without arguments, 97
    generating a function template,
        621
prototyping, 503
pseudo-code, 500
public, 540
public section of a class, 541
punctuators, 38
put (), 376–378, 387

quadratic equations, 130
queue, 765
    as an abstract data type, 830–833

class operations, 831–832
FIFO, first-in-first-out structure,
        830
implementation using an array,
        841–845
implementation using a linked
        list, 845–849

reading
    characters into a string, 657–661
    part of an array, 452–456
    struct members, 479–480
rectangle
    area, 555–559
    draw, 104
    perimeter, 555–559
recurrence relation, 770
recursion, 756–784
    problem decomposition, 756–760
    stopping case, 756
    stopping condition, 763
recursive functions, 756–784
    optimizations for, 785
recursive mathematical functions,
        767–771
redirection (input/output) 72, 73
refinement, of problem steps, 32–33,
        35
registers, 10
    instruction, 10
relational operators, 144–145
    used with characters, 348–349
representational error, 338
requirements specification, 503–504
reserved words
    complete table, 863
    initial table, 42
return, 109
    missing return, compiler-time
        error, 784
return value, 109
    type consistency, 121
reuse
    of predefined functions, 129–131
    of software components, 508–509
    of structural forms or patterns of
        solutions, 174
    using class templates, 611–624
right, 424
Ritchie, John, 5

scale factor, floating-point, 57, 334
scaling, in pointer arithmetic, 656

scientific, 168, 424
scientific notation (floating point), 57
scope of definition
    argument, 121
    of a function, 121
scope resolution operator, ::, 541
search
    an array, 456–459
    direct access, 625
    linear, 456–459, 620
    linked list, 808
secondary memory, 8, 12
seekg ( ), 666
selection sort, 459–463
sentinel-controlled loops, 223–225
    general structural pattern, 225
sentinel value, 223
sequential processing of an array,
    441–444
server (computer), 7
server (use of class as a), 545
setf ( ), 396, 423
setiosflags, 166–167, 423
setprecision, 166–167, 423
setw, 166–167, 423
short-circuit evaluation of logical
    expressions, 188
showpoint, 166–168, 424
shrt_max, 335
shrt_min, 335
simple (or scalar) data types, 330, 434
simple variables, 434
sin ( ), 129
single-step execution, 248
size_t, 864
skipws, 424
smallest value, finding, 450–452,
    773–775
software
    cost, 502
    design using classes, 555
    development method, 30–33
    development stages, 31–34
    engineering, 132, 316–318, 498
    life cycle, 500–501
    systems analysts, 499
    systems approach, 31
    testing, 519–522
solution by analogy, 143
sort
    selection, 459–463
    recursive selection, 773–775
source file, 18

space shuttle Columbia, 502
special constants, 335–336
specialization
    of classes, 565, 610, 726
sqrt ( ), 129
square
    area, 555–561
    perimeter, 555–561
stack, 765
    as an abstract data type, 809–813
    class operations, 809–813
    implementation using an array,
        820–823
    implementation using a linked
        list, 824–829
    LIFO, last-in-first-out structure,
        830
    use with arguments, 765
    use in recursion, 765–766
stack overflow, run-time error,
    783–784
stand-alone computer, 7
standard input device, 48
standard output device, 48
state attribute, of a class, 551
statements, 38
    compound, 142–143
    control, 143
    debugging, 319
    declaration, 38
    diagnostic, 246
    executable, 38, 44–52
status flags, 225
<stdlib.h>, 125, 387
stepwise design with functions,
    287–301, 316–318
stepwise refinement, 33
stopping case, recursion, 756
stopping condition, recursion, 763
storage attributes, of a class (see also
    data members), 541
stored-program computer, 3
strcat ( ), 651
strchr ( ), 651
strcmp ( ), 470–472, 651
strcpy ( ), 468–470, 651
stream and file connection, 383–387
stream names, 383, 386
streams
    and external files, 381–387
    and files, 372–387
    as a sequence of lines, 373
    standard input (cin), 372

standard output (cout), 372
string constant versus character
    constant, 464
string copy by assignment, 688
string functions, 650–655
    partial table of, 651, 864–868
string variable, 650
<string.h>, 125, 650–651
strings
    assignment (copy) of, 468–470
    comparison of, 470–472
    input/output of, 465–468
    length of, 472
    variable length, 676–685
strlen ( ), 651
strncat ( ), 651
strncmp ( ), 470–472, 651
strncpy ( ), 470, 651
Stroustrup, Bjarne, 6
strpbrk ( ), 651
strrchr ( ), 651
strstr ( ), 651
struct
    as arguments, 477–479
    versus class, 547
    data type, 473–476
    hierarchical, 480–483
    member access, 475–476
    member access operator, . ,
        475–476, 795
    member access operator using
        pointers, ->, 795
    member access (using pointers),
        795–798
    as operands, 476–477
    reading, 479–480
    type declaration, 473–476
    and unions, 483–487
    variables, 474
structs
    containing pointers, 794–795
structure charts, 93–95
    adding data flow information to,
        159, 164–165
structure entry guard, 187
structured data types, 434–491
structured programming, 14
structured variables, 434–491
structured walkthroughs, 521
stubs, 299
subproblems, 93
    and independent modules, 93
subscript, array, 435–437

non-integers as, 487
out-of-range references, 487–488
use of, 439–443
subtraction
   integer, 58–59
   floating-point, 57
   operator, 57–59
supercomputer, 6
`switch` selector, 189–190
`switch` statement, 143, 189–194
   versus nested `if` statements, 192
   positioning of the `case` labels, 192
   used for function calls, 192–193
syntax rules, 40
syntactic elements, 40

`tan ()`, 129
template
   class, 611–617
   function, 620–622
   parameter matching, 611–612, 620–622, 639
   with multiple parameters, 616–617
   and reuse, 611
template parameters, 611–617, 620–622, 639
terminal, 10
test plan preparation, 521
testing for a range of values, 148
testing software, 246–249, 519–522
   black-box testing, 521
   bottom-up, 318
   integration testing, 300, 521–522
   test plan preparation, 520
   top-down, 318
   structured walkthroughs, 520
   stub, 318
   white-box testing, 521
theft, 530
`<time.h>`, 125
timeshared computer system, 21, 23
`tolower ()`, 349
top-down
   design, 87
   programming, 506, 511
`toupper ()`, 349
Towers of Hanoi, example, 758–760, 776–779
tracing
   hand-tracing, 31–33
   recursive functions, 761–767

transfer of control, functions, 102
traversing a linked list, 803–804
triangle
   area, 712–724
   as an array of arrays (points), 714–715
   as an array of objects of type point, 716–720
   as an array of pairs of type double (points), 711–714
   as an array of structs (points), 715–716
   described by three points, 698–702
   drawing, 93–95
   length of side, 130
   model of, 708–726
   perimeter, 712–724
   as polygon class with $n = 3$, 720–723
truncation, 344
type casting, 343–346
type consistency
   arguments, 121
   function return values, 121
type declaration
   using `typedef`, 614–616
type specification
   function, 100, 109
`typedef`, 614–616

unary minus, 67
unary operators, 207–208
   use of (prefix and postfix), 208
unions, 483–487
   anonymous, 484
   tag member, 484
   type declaration, 484
   variant, 485
UNIVAC, 5
UNIX, 5
`unsetiosflags`, 423
`unsetf ()`, 423
uploading (a file), 22
user-defined
   data types 354, 434, 538
   identifier, 41

value-preserving conversion, 343
variable, 15, 35, 41
   character, 348–353
   declaration, 41
   simple, 434

subscripted, 435
structured, 434–492
validating the value of, 187
variable length strings, 676–685
   assignment, 678–681
   comparison, 678–679
   concatenating, 684–685
   construction operator, 680–681
   indexing in, 682
   input, 681
   internal representation, 679–680
   length function, 676
   output, 681
   searching in, 685
   substring of, 677, 682–684
verification of programs, 522–529
   assertions, 523
   boundary case verification, 526
   final assertions, 523
   formal verification, 522
   function postconditions, 528
   function preconditions, 528
   initial presumption, 523
   loop invariants, 524–528
   postconditions, 523
   preconditions, 523
`void`, 97
virtual functions, 565
viruses, 530
Visicalc, 6
volatile memory, 11
Von Liebnitz, 5
Von Neumann, John, 3, 5

`while` statement, 204–209
   condition (loop repetition), 205, 217
   difference from `do-while` loop, 237
   formatting, 207
   review, 240–242
   same behavior as `for` statement, 227
   syntax, 206–207
white space
   processed using `cin`, 374–378, 425
white-box testing, 521
`width ()`, 423
windows, 6
Wirth, Niklaus, 5
workstations, 6
Wozniak, Steve, 6